STRATEGIC MANAGEMENT

McGraw-Hill Series in Management

Fred Luthans and Keith Davis, *Consulting Editors*

STRATEGIC MANAGEMENT

Arthur Sharplin

Northeast Louisiana University

McGRAW-HILL BOOK COMPANY

New York St. Louis San Francisco Auckland Bogotá
Hamburg Johannesburg London Madrid Mexico Montreal New Delhi
Panama Paris São Paulo Singapore Sydney Tokyo Toronto

This book was set in Times Roman by Better Graphics.
The editor was John R. Meyer;
the production supervisor was Charles Hess.
The cover was done by Kao & Kao Associates.
R. R. Donnelley & Sons Company was printer and binder.

STRATEGIC MANAGEMENT

2 3 4 5 6 7 8 9 0 DOC DOC 8 9 8 7 6 5

ISBN 0-07-056513-9

Library of Congress Cataloging in Publication Data

Sharplin, Arthur.
    Strategic management.

    (McGraw-Hill series in management)
    Includes bibliographies and index.
    1. Corporate planning. 2. Industrial management.
I. Title. II. Series.
HD3028.S42 1985   658.4'012   84-19453
ISBN 0-07-056513-9

To: Kathy
From: Art

CONTENTS

STRATEGIC FORMULATION

THE CASE METHOD

CASES

PREFACE

Every school which is a member of the American Assembly of Collegiate Schools of Business (AACSB) is expected to offer a senior-level capstone course on the topic of strategic management or "business policy." Most other business schools, whether or not aspiring to accreditation by the AACSB, have such a course.

While Harvard University traces its strategic management course back to 1911, the real impetus for teaching such a course in thousands of business schools across the country came in 1959 with the publication of two landmark studies on business education in America. The Gordon and Howell Report and the Pierson Report, sponsored, respectively, by the Ford Foundation and the Carnegie Foundation, both noted a deficiency in the degree to which business schools taught administration of the total enterprise. The Gordon and Howell Report was specific in recommending a partial solution:

> The capstone of the core curriculum should be a course in "business policy" which will give students an opportunity to pull together what they have learned in the separate business fields and utilize this knowledge in the analysis of complex business problems. The business policy course can offer the student something he . . . will find nowhere else in the curriculum: consideration of business problems which are not prejudged as being marketing problems, finance problems, etc.; emphasis on the development of skill in identifying, analyzing, and solving problems in a situation which is as close as the classroom can ever be to the real business world; opportunity to consider problems which draw on a wide range of substantive areas in business; opportunity to consider the external, nonmarket implications of problems at the same time that internal decisions must be made; situations which enable the student to exercise qualities of judgment and of mind which were not explicitly called for in any prior course. Questions of social responsibility and of personal attitudes can be brought in as a regular aspect of this kind of problem-solving practice. Without the responsibility of having to transmit some specific body of knowledge, the business policy course can concentrate on integrating what already has been acquired and on developing further the student's skill in using that knowledge. The course can range over the entire curriculum and beyond.

Ten years after the Gordon and Howell and Pierson reports, the AACSB included in its standards for accreditation a requirement for the study of "integrating analysis and policy determination at the overall management level.'' In general, this has been interpreted to require a course in strategic management or ''general management'' as a prerequisite to AACSB accreditation. This text is designed for such a course. While the use of the term *strategic management* is clearly emerging as the appropriate one, those who prefer the more traditional title ''business policy'' should not be confused. The topic is the same.

The eight chapters of text are organized around the emerging strategic management process model. Equal emphasis is given to strategy formulation (planning) and strategic implementation (doing). The text material covers strategic management tools including the popular business portfolio matrices and McKinsey and Company's ''seven-S'' framework as well as state-of-the-art approaches like Michael Porter's ''competitive forces model,'' the concept of corporate culture, and the just emerging ideas of stakeholder mapping and analysis. There are numerous graphic displays which serve to reinforce and clarify the text material.

Each text chapter begins with an introductory outline and an exciting casette exemplifying the topic of that chapter. Each chapter ends with a carefully prepared summary, a list of important concepts, comprehensive discussion questions, and an extensive list of references.

The array of case materials is spread across several dimensions: (1) a number of newly written cases and a few classics; (2) small and intermediate-sized companies and a few from the Fortune 500; (3) several long, complex cases and a number of short ones; and (4) mostly profit-seeking businesses but a few nonprofit and public sector organizations. There are ''high-tech'' cases, international ones, and manufacturing, retailing, and natural resource cases. There are many about high-profile companies and high-interest industries.

I was aided and inspired by many friends and colleagues in completing this exciting project. Preeminent among them was Wayne Mondy of Northeast Louisiana University, whose friendship I cherish and without whose encouragement and guidance I would not have had the courage to begin. A special debt of gratitude also goes to Barbara Pace, who operates a word processor the way Van Cliburn operates a piano. My children, now young adults, provided moral support as well as very practical clerical help. Dee Dee transcribed dozens of tapes of dictated material, and both she and Danny helped in many ways at critical points in manuscript preparation.

I would also like to thank my superiors and colleagues at Northeast Louisiana University. David Loudon, my department head, Dean Van C. McGraw, and President Dwight Vines ensured that the necessary physical and human resources were available, and my fellow business school professors, too numerous to list here, helped me to sharpen many of the concepts presented in the text as well as to class-test a number of the cases. Among the more important human resources provided by the University was my research assistant, Linda Eubanks. Linda worked diligently and thoughtfully throughout the project and deserves much of the credit for the quality of the documentation contained in the text. Last of all, I wish to thank my wife, Kathy, to whom this book is dedicated and for whom my love and respect grow deeper each year.

The exceptional staff of McGraw-Hill Book Company also has my gratitude. John Meyer and Laura Warner, particularly, showed outstanding patience and skill in managing the text project. Fred Luthans, the consulting editor, offered valuable advice and vital support. A special note of thanks goes to the following academic reviewers: Peter Goulet, University of Northern Iowa; Lawrence P. Huggins, Manhattan College; Gordon C. Inskeep, Arizona State University; Phillip D. Jones, Xavier University; Lane Kelley, University of Hawaii at Manoa; William M. Lindsay, Northern Kentucky University; Lance H. Masters, California State College—San Bernadino; David C. Murphy, Boston College; C. Dick Roman, University of Alabama, Birmingham; William Ruud, University of Toledo; Chuck Stubbart, University of Massachusetts; Walter H. Warrick, Drake University; and James M. Wilson, Pan American University.

Arthur Sharplin

STRATEGIC MANAGEMENT

STRATEGIC MANAGEMENT
AND ITS ENVIRONMENT

AN OVERVIEW OF
STRATEGIC MANAGEMENT

"Hey, Sylvia. Who's a good teacher for strategic management?" asked Mike Roby.

"I don't know," answered Sylvia, "I haven't had that course yet."

"Do you know much about the class? Is it tough?" asked Mike.

"I don't know much about it," said Sylvia, "but I do hear that it's tough."

Mike said, "It probably is hard. Almost everything in the business school is a prerequisite for the course. I have to take it anyway, to graduate next fall. But I think I'll go and visit Dr. Porter to learn a little more about the course."

"Mind if I tag along?" asked Sylvia, "I'll graduate in May of next year, so I'll have to take it either in the fall or next spring." Mike nodded, and the two began the short walk from Hardee's Restaurant to the business administration building.

Mike Roby and Sylvia Thurman were students at the University of Maryland. Dr. James Porter was Mike's faculty adviser. As they approached Dr. Porter's office, Sylvia and Mike saw him hang up the phone and glance through the half-open office door. "Hi, Mike and Sylvia," he said. "What do you have there, Mike. Looks like a preregistration packet."

"It is," answered Mike, "But before I fill out the schedule I would like to learn something about the strategic management course. What's it all about?"

"Well," answered Dr. Porter, "it's the capstone course. That means it pulls together what you've learned in your other courses, like finance and marketing and management. It helps you see things from an overall organization perspective and to make the transition to the business world."

"Is it a hard course?" asked Sylvia, "If it is, I think I'll wait until the spring to take it."

"Well," Dr. Porter replied, "I suppose it's pretty hard for most students. It's designed to review and integrate what you have learned in four years of business education." Dr. Porter continued to explain to Mike and Sylvia that the strategic management course was usually taught using the case discussion method, with students, individually or in teams, responsible for most of the discussion. He explained that, while some teachers present a number of lectures or mini-lectures during the semester, the course centers primarily upon discussion of actual experiences of operating organizations.

"I heard Dr. Wall say he used the Socratic technique," said Sylvia, "What does that mean?"

"That means getting the students to learn by asking them leading questions," explained Dr. Porter. "This is the way Socrates is said to have taught his students. You might find it disconcerting at first; but if your teacher is good at it, you'll like it."

As carefully as he could, Mike explained to Dr. Porter that he was excited about the strategic management course, but that he wondered if it was possible to substitute some other course for it.

"I'm afraid not," was Dr. Porter's answer. "The AACSB (American Assembly of Collegiate Schools of Business) expects every accredited school to require this capstone course of its students, and most schools have it in their curriculum whether they are AACSB-accredited or not." Dr. Porter explained that the course was an important one and that the dean of the business school allowed no substitutions. Mike told Dr. Porter that he would be back later to have his adviser's card signed.

As Mike and Sylvia walked slowly down the hall, Mike said, "It sounds interesting, doesn't it, Sylvia? I like case discussions. I talk a lot anyway."

"Yeah," replied Sylvia, "it does sound interesting, but I'm glad I don't have to take it until next spring."

If students like Sylvia and Mike are expected to read hundreds of pages and spend seemingly endless hours learning about strategic management, it is perhaps useful to discuss what the term means. William Glueck (1980, p. 6) defined *strategic management* as "that set of decisions and actions which leads to the development of an effective strategy or strategies to help achieve corporate objectives." This suggests that strategic management is mainly planning, albeit high-level planning. James Higgins, (1983, p. 3), of Rollins College, sees strategic management more as a process of doing than of planning to do. He says, "Strategic management is the process of managing the pursuit of organizational mission while managing the relationship of the organization to its environment." Steiner, Miner, and Gray (1982, p. 6) describe strategic management as though it includes both planning and doing. They say the term "is the phrase currently in use to identify top corporate policy/strategy formulation and its implementation in private and public organizations."

Christensen, Berg, and Salter (1980, p. 5), whose landmark strategic management casebook is now in its eighth edition, say, "It has been our experience . . . that precise and exact definitions are neither desirable nor possible." Despite this widely held view, it is useful to attempt to define the terms that we use. Others agree that it is difficult, but important, in the case of *strategic management* (Leontiades, 1982; Shirley, 1982). Therefore, throughout this text, care will be taken to explain what important terms mean. The primary source of information in this regard, however, will not be the various textbooks or articles in the field, but rather *Webster's Third New International Dictionary*.

Let us first consider the words *strategic*, *strategy*, and *management* separately. The root of the word *strategic* is a Greek word relating to the art of generalship or being a general. In the sense used in this text, **strategic** means *"of great or vital importance within an integrated whole"* (*Webster's Third New International Dictionary*). This suggests that strategic matters may extend far down into the company, although they are probably concentrated at the top management level (see Bower, 1982, and Shirley, 1982); that is, the level of the general for military matters, or the "general manager" for nonmilitary matters. A **strategy** is *a plan or course of action which is of vital, pervasive, or continuing importance to the organization as a whole.*

Management is defined as *"the conducting or supervising of something (as a business); esp: the executive function of planning, organizing, directing, controlling, and supervising any industrial or business project or activity with responsibility for results"* (*Webster's Third New International Dictionary*). In light of this and with due consideration for the foregoing definitions by respected authors, **strategic management** will be defined as *the formulation and implementation of plans and the carrying out of activities relating to matters which are of vital, pervasive, or continuing importance to the total organization.* If we define *strategic management* this way, we avoid the debate about the importance of strategy. Any matter which is "of great or vital importance" to the organization as a whole is strategic. Planning or doing (formulation or implementation) relating to such matters is strategic management.

THE LEVELS OF STRATEGIC MANAGEMENT

It has been found to be useful to consider the levels of strategic management in organizations. This is particularly true in light of the growth in recent decades of multi-industry and multinational corporations, especially conglomerate enterprises such as United Technologies, Allied Corporation, and Textron. To facilitate the management of such complex organizations they are usually divided into strategic business units (SBUs). A **strategic business unit** is *any part of a business organization which is treated separately for strategic management purposes.* In general, an SBU engages in a single line of business. Less frequently, several related operations are combined to form as SBU. Many companies set up their SBUs as separate profit centers, sometimes giving them virtual autonomy. Other companies exercise extensive control over their SBUs, enforcing corporate policies and standards down to very low levels in the organization. Figure 1.1 illustrates the organizational levels of a typical multibusiness corporation, with the corresponding levels of strategic management. As will be seen later, the tools, the processes, and the management personalities which find usefulness at the three strategic management levels differ.

Corporate-level strategic management is *the management of activities which define the overall character and mission of the organization, the product/service segments it will enter and leave, and the allocation of resources and management of synergies among its SBUs.* Corporate-level strategic management seeks to answer such questions as the following: What are the purposes of the organization? What image should the organization project? What are the ideals and philosophies the organization desires its members to possess? What is the organization's business or businesses? How can the

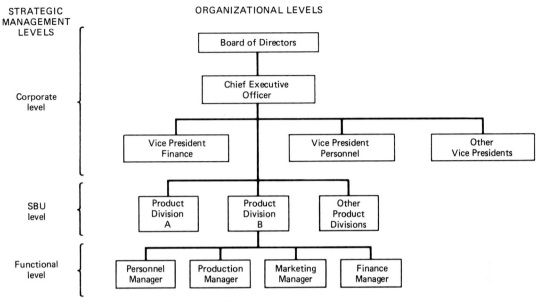

FIGURE 1.1   The levels of strategic management

organization's resources best be used to fulfill corporate purposes? As indicated in Figure 1.1, corporate-level strategic management is primarily the responsibility of the organization's top executives. The primary focus of corporate-level strategic management is upon formulating and implementing strategies to accomplish the organization's mission. *Organizational mission* is *the organization's continuing purpose with regard to certain categories of persons—in short what is to be accomplished for whom.*

SBU-level strategic management is *the management of an SBU's effort to compete effectively in a particular line of business and to contribute to overall organizational purposes.* At the SBU level, strategic questions include the following: What specific products or services does the SBU produce? Who are the SBU's customers or clients? How can the SBU best compete in its particular product/service segments? How can the SBU best conform to the total organization's ideals and philosophies and support organizational purposes? In general, SBU-level strategic management is the responsibility of the second tier of executives, vice presidents or division heads, in large organizations. In single-SBU organizations, senior executives have both corporate- and SBU-level responsibilities.

Within each SBU, practically every important organization is divided into functional subdivisions. Most businesses have separate departments for production (or operations), marketing, finance, and personnel (or human resources management). Military installations have supply, police, and maintenance departments, among others. Churches have preaching, education, and music ministries. Each of these functional subdivisions is typically vital to the success of the respective SBU and, therefore, to the total organization. *Functional-level strategic management* is *the management of relatively narrow areas of activity which are of vital, pervasive, or continuing importance to the total organization.* Strategic management of the finance function involves establishing budgeting, accounting, and investment policies and the allocation of SBU cash flows. In the personnel areas, policies for compensation, hiring and firing, training, and personnel planning are of strategic concern. Strategic management at the functional level does not include the supervision of day-to-day activities but mainly general direction and oversight through setting and enforcing policies.

Although not a "level" per se, the concept of *enterprise strategy* is an important one. Enterprise strategy answers the question: What do we stand for? (Freeman, 1984, p. 90). **Enterprise strategy** *is the organization's plan for establishing the desired relationship with other social institutions and stakeholder groups and maintaining the overall character of the organization.* In this text, enterprise strategy will be treated as an aspect of mission determination. This, in turn, is a function of corporate-level strategic management.

THE ORGANIZATIONAL STRATEGISTS

For most organizations, it is difficult to say exactly who the organizational strategists are. In ancient Greece, perhaps, strategy was determined by the general. For many companies today, strategy clearly emanates from the top. Lee Iacocca, chairman of Chrysler Corporation, Robert Goizueta, president and chief executive officer (CEO) of Coca-Cola, and Frank Borman, president and chairman of Eastern Airlines, seem to call the shots, at least from a strategic management standpoint. Many companies employ in-house **staff strategic management specialists**, *specialists who serve in a staff capacity to assist and advise managers in strategic planning.* Remember that strategic management involves planning and doing, that is, formulation and implementation. Staff strategic management specialists, where employed, are especially involved in the planning, or formulation, phase. At General Electric (GE), the corporate planning staff includes over 100 persons.

Many organizations retain consultants to assist in designing and implementing strategy. Consultants are particularly useful for performing marketing and other research to provide an informational base for strategic decisions. Robinson (1982) believes that consultants can play an effective part in strategic planning, even for small firms. In fact, most small firms cannot afford full-time staff strategic management specialists. So, employing consultants may be the most economical approach to strategic planning.

At least to a limited extent, every manager is an organizational strategist (Polyczynski and Leniski, 1982). Each manager is responsible for activities related to continuing and vital corporate objectives. It should be recognized that what is considered an overwhelming matter by the personnel director—for example, the size of the annual personnel department budget—might be relatively incidental from the standpoint of the total organization. It is not a question of whether a matter is important to any one individual that determines whether it is a strategic matter or not. It is the question of its importance to the organization as a whole and the degree to which it has continuing significance. So **organizational strategists** are generally considered to be those *persons who spend a large portion of their time on matters of vital or far-ranging importance to the organization as a whole.* In general, this includes the top two levels of management, in-house staff specialists in strategic management, and retained consultants in the area.

THE STRATEGIC MANAGEMENT PROCESS

Before penetrating too deeply into the details of strategic management, it is useful to study the overall process. The basic strategic management process model, illustrated in Figure 1.2, will be repeated a number of times throughout the text and will serve to organize and give coherence to the chapters which follow. The model is useful as an

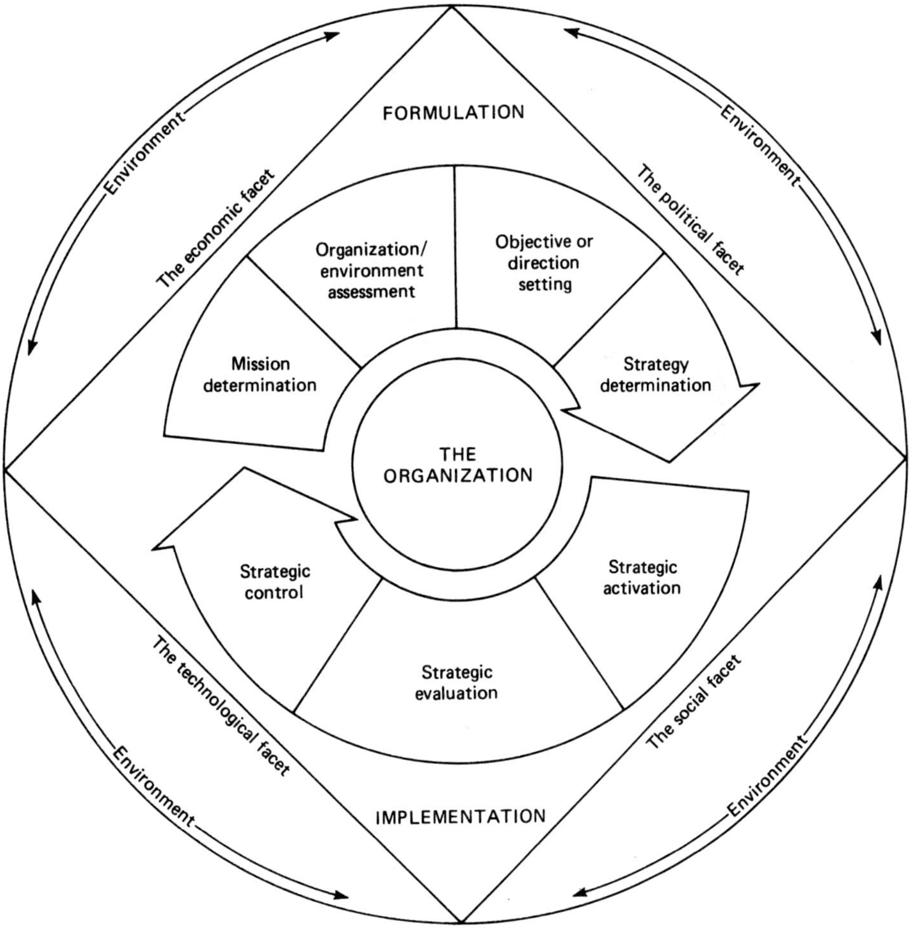

FIGURE 1.2   The basic strategic management process model

expository device. However, no model can accurately represent real-world diversity (Gluck, Kaufman, and Walleck, 1982, pp. 11–12).

Before discussing the model in detail, we will begin with a brief overview. Figure 1.2 illustrates that strategic management is designed to effectively relate the organization to its environment. The environment includes political, social, technological, and economic elements.

Strategic management can be seen as consisting of two phases, each of which involves several steps. The first phase is *strategy formulation*. This involves four steps: (1) determination of the organizational mission, (2) assessment of the organization and its environment, (3) setting of specific objectives or direction, and (4) determination of strategies for accomplishing those objectives. This procedure is often called strategic planning. The second phase, *strategy implementation*, is the process of doing what has been planned. Strategy implementation consists of three steps: (1) activation of strategies, (2) strategic evaluation, and (3) strategic control. All these terms will be discussed in detail later.

In general, the terms *strategy* and *policy* have referred mainly to the formulation of strategy. With increased use of the term *strategic management* the second phase, implementation, has taken on more importance. In fact, many consider implementation the more vital function. In the remainder of this chapter we will explain the strategic management process model shown in Figure 1.2.

Environmental Considerations: The Context of Strategic Management

The outermost part of the model represents the environment in which the strategic management process takes place. The environment can be viewed as consisting of four elements: the social, political, technological, and economic facets. The **social facet of the environment** consists of *the human relationships of the organization and its strategists to individuals, to groups, and to society in general*. This facet involves ethical and moral considerations and the responsibilities strategic managers have to individuals because of their humanity and not because of any legal, economic, or political forces they may bring to bear. While some would have the strategic manager be completely rational, perhaps even self-serving, it is true that every manager, indeed every human, experiences the emotions of friendship, love, pity, admiration, and so forth. These emotions properly influence the behavior of organizational strategists, and therefore of organizations. They are part of the social facet.

The **political facet of the environment** consists of *the laws and regulations applicable to the enterprise and the courts and government officials who interpret and enforce them, along with other groups and institutions in society which wield power*. The increasing burden of laws and regulations is of concern to every manager. A major goal of the Reagan presidency has been to diminish the number of regulations and laws. Still, thousands of government agencies, many with overlapping areas of responsibility—or interests—encumber organizational activity. To the extent that the laws are objectively stated and uniformly enforced, they serve as constraints or limits on the activities of organizational strategists. Inconsistently applied, they impart uncertainty.

In addition to government, there are many other groups and institutions in society which hold power. Organizational strategists both are influenced and seek to influence these groups and institutions. For example, contributions to the Republican or Democratic party might be made to strengthen this power center because corporate strategists agree with the ideologies it supports. Such contributions might also be made to influence the powerful group in question.

Technology is defined as *"the science of the application of knowledge to practical purposes . . . the totality of the means employed by a people to provide itself with the objects of material culture"* (*Webster's Third New International Dictionary*). So the **technological facet of the environment** is *the sum total of machines, materials, and knowledge which go into the production of goods and services.* The technological facet should not be confused with *"**high-tech**,"* which is *the advanced, mostly electronic, technology involved in computers, robotics, space travel, and so forth.* The technological facet includes these elements, of course, but it also includes all kinds of machines and systems for accomplishing practical purposes.

The **economic facet of the environment** consists of *financial markets, sources of capital, product and service markets, demand for goods and services, and opportunities for profits along with changes and trends in the economy.* The economic facet of the organizational environment is considered by many to be the most important. For example, Nobel laureate economist Milton Friedman once said, "The only social responsibility of business is to earn a profit within the rules of the game" (Friedman, 1962). In what has been called the "Capitalist Manifesto," Adam Smith suggested that, if entrepreneurs seek their own best economic interests, society will benefit (Smith, 1776).

Each of these facets of the environment will be discussed in greater detail in Chapter 2. Let us now turn to a brief description of strategy formulation and implementation.

Formulating Strategy

Chapter 3 discusses strategy formulation at the corporate level. Chapter 4 is devoted to SBU- and functional-level strategic planning. Remember, *corporate-level* strategic management relates to decisions about what businesses to enter and the relative allocation of resources and management of synergies among those businesses. The process is similar to that followed by a professional investor who decides which stocks and bonds to buy and the distribution of the total investable funds among individual investments. *Business-* or *division-level* strategic management involves determining how to compete in a given business or product area. It is generally a business-level decision, for example, to determine whether to attempt to maintain market dominance through additional advertising, through production efficiencies, or through research and development (R&D) in a given product area.

In essence, business-level decisions are similar to corporate-level decisions. At the business level, the allocation of resources—money, material, and managerial energies—is among functional departments or areas of activity. At the corporate level, the allocation is among different businesses or product areas.

While the levels of strategic management represent an important dimension, it is useful to consider the process which occurs—or should occur—in developing strategies, whatever the level. The upper curved arrow in Figure 1.2 shows the steps in this process.

The first step is to determine the corporate mission. This should involve answering the question: What are we, in management, attempting to do for whom? Should we maximize profit so that shareholders can receive higher dividends or so that share price will increase? Or should we emphasize stability of earnings so that employees remain secure? We will see that there are many other possibilities. Mission determination involves deciding the overall character of the organization. What are the principles upon which management decisions will be based? Will the corporation be honorable or dishonorable, ruthless or considerate, devious or forthright, in dealing with its various "publics"? The answers to these questions, once arrived at, tend to become embedded in an organizational ethos or philosophical climate which tends to validate the corporate mission in a way that no policy statement can.

Once the mission has been determined, the organization must be assessed for strengths and weaknesses, and the threats and opportunities in the environment must be evaluated. In light of this assessment, specific objectives can be established and strategies developed for accomplishing those objectives. For example, through environmental assessment BIC Corporation discovered during the early 1980s that there was an opportunity to market disposable safety razors. Organizational assessment revealed that BIC had a greater capability for mass-producing small plastic-based items than almost any other American company. The company set sales, production, and profit objectives, designed strategies, and quickly became the world's leading marketer of disposable safety razors.

The formulation of strategy involves information flows both from the organization and from the environment. From the organization comes information about organizational competencies, strengths, and weaknesses. Scanning the environment allows the organizational strategists to identify threats and opportunities as well as constraints. The job of the strategists in the planning phase is to develop strategies which take advantage of the company's strengths and minimize its weaknesses in order to grasp opportunities and avoid threats in the environment.

Implementing Strategy

Strategy implementation consists of three steps: (1) strategy activation, (2) strategic evaluation, and (3) strategic control. This is illustrated in Figure 1.2. Let us look more closely at strategy activation and then at strategic evaluation and control.

Strategy Activation   *Strategy activation* is *initiating activities in accordance with a strategic plan.* This attribute of implementation, "getting things going," is the subject of Chapters 5 and 6. Waterman (1982, p. 69) says, "The proof is in the execution." Activation must be accomplished in the context of organizational structure. Strategies are activated through (1) changing organizational structure, (2) policies and directives, (3) resource commitment, (4) motivation and leadership, and (5) power and politics. Chapter 5 is concerned with the first three of these; and Chapter 6 covers the other two.

Organizational structure is *the set of relationships within the organization which are established or are consistent over time*. All strategies must take account of structure, and it is often necessary to modify structure in order to activate strategies. For example, if a company has a product improvement strategy which requires extensive R&D, it may be useful to establish a R&D department. When that is done, the R&D department head will need to know the reporting relationships involving the new department. From this simple example, it can be seen that structure is a vital aspect of strategy activation.

A *policy* is "*a definite course or method of action selected . . . from among alternatives and in light of given conditions to guide and usually determine present and future behavior*" (*Webster's Third New International Dictionary*). A *directive* is "*a pronouncement urging or banning some action or conduct*" (*Webster's Third New International Dictionary*). Let us consider how strategies may be activated through establishing and enforcing policies and directives. A company which decides upon a strategy of paying according to results will have to actuate that strategy by changing its compensation policies. A piece-rate pay policy for factory workers might be promulgated along with a commission schedule for the sales force. The paymaster may then receive a directive to place the policy into effect.

Motivation, leadership, and power and politics are also critically important in the activation of strategic plans. Organizational strategists must give consideration to the dynamics of organizations: How will people respond to strategic initiatives? What motivates workers to engage in thoughtful and intense activity? How does one motivate managers to pursue corporate goals instead of individual goals—to be cooperative rather than antagonistic? And how can a manager use influence and social relationships to facilitate goal accomplishment and avoid being thwarted by the political tactics of others? In answering these questions, strategists must be familiar with the principles of motivation, leadership, and power and politics.

Strategic Evaluation and Control   The organizational strategist's job does not end when the strategic plan is activated. Strategy must be continuously evaluated—and changed. Not only must the plan normally be restated, but activities must be checked and modified to conform to plans. The organization is dynamic. Decisions which seem right today may seem silly tomorrow.

Strategic evaluation is *obtaining information about strategic plans and performance and comparing the information with standards*. A *standard* is "*any measure by which one judges a thing as authentic, good, or adequate*" (*Webster's Third New International Dictionary*). The standards used in strategic evaluation may be nebulous ones, perhaps existing only in the mind of the chief executive or other strategist. Or, they may be more definite, like a certain percentage of profit or a certain level of sales. In either case, the evaluation phase of strategic management involves information gathering and comparison, resulting in a decision as to whether or not a modification of strategic plans or activities is indicated. Strategic evaluation of plans involves comparing the existing plan with the best plan which can be developed at any point in time. So the best conceivable plan becomes the standard. The degree to which the existing plan varies from that standard, and the cost of that variation compared to the cost of revising the plan, will determine whether corrective action should be taken.

Strategic control is an active concept. *Control* is defined as "application of policies and procedures for directing, regulating, and coordinating production, administration, and other business activities in a way to achieve the objectives of the enterprise" (*Webster's Third New International Dictionary*). In this sense, control does not mean gathering information; it refers to the "application" of policies and procedures. It is, in short, guiding or taking corrective action. If activities have departed too far from the strategic plan, control means taking actions to enforce the plan. If the plan needs modifying, of course, control means doing this. **Strategic control** is *the process of changing the strategic plan in light of changed conditions or additional knowledge and/or taking corrective action to bring activities into conformity with the plan.*

Strategic evaluation and control are necessary for three principal reasons. First, it is never possible to completely specify a strategic plan. Some details are always left out. Second, it is never possible to know exactly what the future holds. When conditions do not turn out as forecasted, plans must be changed. Third, most organizations evidence a perverse tendency to move rapidly from a condition of order to one of disorder. This has been called "organization entropy" and is analogous to the concept of entropy in physics and thermodynamics, which refers to the tendency of any system to degrade or run down. Without some sort of control mechanism, no system, human or mechanical, can operate efficiently for long.

The ability to process large amounts of information in microseconds has made the strategic manager's job easier in one sense, because volumes of vital information can now be obtained on a "real-time" basis. However, this "information revolution" has made the job more challenging because competitors, customers, and other managers also have that capability.

The Dynamic Nature of the Model

The strategic management process has two attributes which are particularly significant. First, it is iterative; that is, as illustrated in Figure 1.2, the process continues over and over in a never-ending cycle. Second, it is nonsequential in actual practice. It is easy to think of formulating, activating, evaluating, and controlling strategy, but more difficult to do it in separate steps. In fact, it does not normally occur in precise order. Some suggest that models usually fail for this very reason (Gluck, Kaufman, and Walleck, 1982, p. 13). Any single manager might at one moment be involved in one or several of the steps in strategic management. It is still useful, if one is cautious, to think of strategic management as a series of steps. In this way, we impart order to what can be an infinitely complex process.

SUMMARY

Recent textbook definitions of strategic management differ in the emphasis they give to planning as opposed to doing. One textbook states that precise definitions are neither desirable nor possible. In this text, important terms are carefully defined, with *Webster's Third New International Dictionary* being the primary source.

Strategic management is concerned with matters of vital, pervasive, or continuing importance to the organization as a whole. Most complex organizations are divided into SBUs for strategic management purposes. There are three levels of strategic management. At the corporate level, decisions relate to the character and mission of the organization, which areas of business to enter or leave, and the allocation of resources and management of synergies among SBUs. At the SBU level, ways of competing in a given business are involved. The functional level involves narrow areas of activity such as personnel, finance, and so forth.

Organizational strategists in general include the top two levels of management, in-house staff specialists in strategic management, and consultants. However, every manager is involved in strategic matters to some degree. Strategic management relates the organization to its environment and can be viewed as consisting of two phases: strategy formulation (planning) and strategy implementation (doing). The environment of strategic management consists of social, political, technological, and economic elements. The strategy formulation phase involves mission determination, organizational and environmental assessment, objective setting, and strategy determination. Strategy implementation consists of strategy activation, strategic evaluation, and strategic control. Recent increased use of the term *strategic management* instead of *strategy* and *policy* signifies an increasing emphasis on implementation by organizational strategists.

The social facet of the environment consists of the human relationships of the organization and its strategists to individuals, to groups, and to society in general. The political facet includes laws and regulations and those who wield power in the environment. The technological facet is the sum total of machines, materials, and knowledge which go into the production of goods and services, and the economic facet consists of financial markets, sources of capital, product and service markets, demands for goods and services, and opportunities for profits, along with changes and trends in the economy.

Strategy is formulated at several levels in the organization, but the process is essentially the same at all levels. The first step is to determine the corporate mission. The second is to search the environment for threats and opportunities and to assess the organization's strengths and weaknesses. Then specific objectives are established. The job of the strategist in the planning phase is to develop strategies which take advantage of the company's strengths and minimize its weaknesses in order to grasp opportunities and avoid threats in the environment.

Strategy implementation consists of three essential steps. First, *strategy activation* is initiating activities in accordance with a strategic plan. Second, *strategic evaluation* is checking the strategic plan and activities to determine if corrective action needs to be taken. Third, *strategic control* involves taking corrective action. Without evaluation and control any organization or other system will fall into disarray over time. The strategic management process is a dynamic one, but it is still useful to think of it as a series of steps if one does so cautiously.

IMPORTANT CONCEPTS

Strategic	Political facet of the environment
Strategy	Technology
Management	Technological facet of the environment
Strategic management	High-tech
Strategic business units (SBUs)	Economic facet of the environment
Corporate-level strategic management	Strategy activation
Organizational mission	Organizational structure
SBU-level strategic management	Policy
Functional-level strategic management	Directive
Enterprise strategy	Strategic evaluation
Staff strategic management specialists	Standard
Organizational strategists	Strategic control
Social facet of the environment	

DISCUSSION QUESTIONS

1 Give at least three definitions of *strategic management*. Include the one preferred in this text and discuss how it differs from the others.
2 Explain the three levels of strategic management and illustrate with the use of an organization chart.
3 Define the term *organizational strategists* and discuss the three categories of persons usually included in this definition.
4 Discuss the two phases of the strategic management process and the steps involved in each phase.
5 Describe the four facets of the environment of strategic management.
6 Explain the difference between SBU-level and corporate-level strategic management.
7 Discuss and give an example of the use of policies and directives to accomplish strategy activation.
8 Why is the knowledge of motivation, leadership, power, and politics important in the strategic activation step of strategic management.
9 Explain how strategic evaluation and control can result in changes in the plan as well as in the activities contemplated by the plan.
10 Define *control*, and give an example of how it might be used in an actual situation.
11 Discuss the extent to which the strategic management process model fails to accurately describe the strategic management process as it exists in the real world.

REFERENCES

Andrews, Kenneth. *The Concept of Corporate Strategy*. Homewood, Ill.: Richard D. Irwin, 1980.

Astley, W. Graham, et al. "Complexity and Cleavage: Dual Explanations of Strategic Decision-Making," *Journal of Management Studies*, 19:4, October 1982, pp. 357–375.

Bower, Joseph L. "Business Policy in the 1980s," *Academy of Management Review*, 7:4, October 1982, pp. 630–638.

Bradley, James W., and Donald H. Korn. "The Changing Role of Acquisitions," *Journal of Business Strategy*, 2:4, Spring 1982, pp. 30–42.

Carrol, Peter J. "The Link between Performance and Strategy," *Journal of Business Strategy*, 2:4, Spring 1982, pp. 3–20.

Chakravarthy, Balaji S. "Adaptation: A Promising Metaphor for Strategic Management," *Academy of Management Review*, 7:1, January 1982, pp. 35–44.

Christensen, C. Roland, Kenneth R. Andrews, et al. *Business Policy: Text and Cases*. Homewood, Ill.: Richard D. Irwin, 1982.

Christensen, C. Roland, Norman A. Berg, and Malcolm S. Salter. *Policy Formulation and Administration*. Homewood, Ill.: Richard D. Irwin, 1980.

Christensen, H. Kurt, and Cynthia A. Montgomery. "Corporate Economic Performance: Diversification Strategy versus Market Structure," *Strategic Management Journal*, 2:4, October/December 1981, pp. 327–343.

"Corporate Culture: The Hard-to-Change Values That Spell Success or Failure," in William F. Glueck and Neil H. Snyder (eds.), *Readings in Business Policy and Strategy from Business Week*. New York: McGraw-Hill, 1982.

Diffenbach, John. "Finding the Right Strategic Combination," *Journal of Business Strategy*, 2:2, Fall 1981, pp. 47–58.

Edmunds, Stahrl W. "The Role of Future Studies in Business Strategic Planning," *Journal of Business Strategy*, 3:2, Fall 1982, pp. 40–46.

Fayol, Henri. *General and Industrial Management*, Constance Storrs (trans.). London: Pitman Publishing, 1949.

Freeman, R. Edward. *Strategic Management: A Stakeholder Approach*. Boston: Pitman Publishing, 1984.

Friedman, Milton. *Capitalism and Freedom*. Chicago: University of Chicago Press, 1962.

Gibbs, Matt, and Toby Kashefi. "A Cause of Business Failures," *Pittsburgh State University Business and Economic Review*, 8:2, November 1982, pp. 3–11.

Ginter, Peter M., and Donald D. White. "A Social Learning Approach to Strategic Management: Toward a Theoretical Foundation," *Academy of Management Review*, 7:2, April 1982, pp. 253–261.

Gluck, Frederick, Stephen Kaufman, and A. Steven Walleck. "The Four Phases of Strategic Management," *Journal of Business Strategy*, 2:3, Winter 1982, pp. 9–21.

Glueck, William F. *Business Policy and Strategic Management*. New York: McGraw-Hill, 1980.

Goodpaster, Kenneth E., and John B. Matthews, Jr. "Can a Corporation Have a Conscience?" *Harvard Business Review*, 60:1, January/February 1982, pp. 132–141.

Gordon, Robert A., and James E. Howell. *Higher Education for Business*. New York: Columbia University Press, 1959.

Grinyer, Peter H., Masoud Yasai-Ardekani, and Shawki Al-Bazzaz, "Strategy, Structure, the Environment, and Financial Performance in 48 United Kingdom Companies," *Academy of Management Journal*, 23:2, June 1982, pp. 193–220.

Harrington, Diana R. "Stock Prices, Beta, and Strategic Planning," *Harvard Business Review*, 6:3, May–June 1983, pp. 157–164.

Harris, Philip R. "The Seven Uses of Synergy," *Journal of Business Strategy*, 2:2, Fall 1981, pp. 59–66.

Higgins, James M. *Organizational Policy and Strategic Management: Text and Cases*. Chicago: Dryden Press, 1983.

Hofer, Charles W. "Toward a Contingency Theory of Business Strategy," *Academy of Management Journal*, 18:4, December 1975, pp. 784–810.

Hosmer, LaRue Tone. "The Importance of Strategic Leadership," *Journal of Business Strategy*, 3:2, Fall 1982, pp. 47–57.

Kiechel, Walter, III. "Wanted: Corporate Leaders," *Fortune*, May 30, 1983, pp. 135, 138, 140.

Lamb, Bob, and Charles Hofer. "A Look at the Strategic Planning Consulting Firms," *Journal of Business Strategy*, 3:2, Fall 1982, pp. 83–86.

Lamb, Robert. "Is the Attack on Strategy Valid?" *Journal of Business Strategy*, 3:4, Spring 1983, pp. 68–69.

Leontiades, Milton. "The Confusing Words of Business Policy," *Academy of Management Review*, 7:1, January 1982, pp. 45–48.

Leontiades, Milton. "A Diagnostic Framework for Planning," *Strategic Management Journal*, 4:1, January/March 1983, pp. 11–26.

MacMillan, Ian C., and M. L. McCaffery. "How Aggressive Innovation Can Help Your Company," *Journal of Business Strategy*, 2:4, Spring 1982, pp. 115–119.

Marayanan, V. K., and Liam Fahey. "The Micro-Politics of Strategy Formulation," *Academy of Management Review*, 7:1, January 1982, pp. 25–34.

Mintzberg, Henry. "Strategy-Making in Three Modes," in Edmund R. Gray (ed.), *Business Policy and Strategy: Selected Readings*. Austin, Texas: Austin Press, 1979.

Mintzberg, Henry, and James A. Waters. "Tracking Strategy in an Entrepreneurial Firm," *Academy of Management Journal*, 25:3, September 1982, pp. 465–499.

Muse, William V. "If All the Business Schools in the Country Were Eliminated . . . Would Anybody Notice?" *Collegiate News & Views*, XXXVI:3, Spring 1983, pp. 1–5.

Nees, Danielle B. "Simulation: A Complementary Method for Research on Strategic Decision-Making Processes," *Strategic Management Journal*, 4:2, April/June 1983, pp. 175–185.

Pierson, Frank C., et al. *The Education of American Businessmen*. New York: McGraw-Hill, 1959.

Polyczynski, James J., and Jason Leniski. "Inviting Front-Line Managers into the Strategic Planning and Decision Making Process," *Appalachian Business Review*, IX:3, 1982, pp. 2–5.

Porter, Michael E. "How Competitive Forces Shape Strategy," in George A. Steiner, John B. Miner, and Edmund R. Gray (eds.), *Management Policy and Strategy*. New York: Macmillan, 1982.

Quinn, James Bryan. "Strategic Change: 'Logical Incrementalism,'" *Management Preview: Strategies for the 80s—A Collection of Reprints from the Sloan Management Review*, 1979, pp. 3–17.

Rappaport, Alfred. "Corporate Performance Standards and Shareholder Value," *Journal of Business Strategy*, 3:4, Spring 1983, pp. 28–38.

Robinson, Richard B., Jr. "The Importance of 'Outsiders' in Small Firm Strategic Planning," *Academy of Management Journal*, 25:1, March 1982, pp. 80–93.

Shirley, Robert C. "Limiting the Scope of Strategy: A Decision Based Approach," *Academy of Management Review*, 7:2, April 1982, pp. 262–268.

Smith, Adam. *The Wealth of Nations*. New York: Modern Library, originally published in 1776.

Steiner, George A. "The Critical Role of Top Management in Long-Range Planning," *Arizona Review*, April 1966, pp. 1–8.

Steiner, George A. "The Critical Role of Top Management in Long-Range Planning," in Edmund R. Gray (ed.), *Business Policy & Strategy: Selected Readings*. Austin, Texas: Austin Press, 1979.

Steiner, George A., John B. Miner, and Edmund R. Gray. *Management Policy and Strategy*. New York: Macmillan, 1982.

Tichy, Noel. "The Essentials of Strategic Change Management," *Journal of Business Strategy*, 3:4, Spring 1983, pp. 55–67.

Trostel, Albert O., and Mary Lippitt Nichols. "Privately-Held and Publicly-Held Companies: A Comparison of Strategic Choices and Management Processes," *Academy of Management Journal*, 25:1, March 1982, pp. 47–62.

Vancil, Richard F. "Strategic Formulation in Complex Organizations," *Management Preview: Strategies for the 80s—A Collection of Reprints from the Sloan Management Review*, 1979, pp. 39–55.

"Wanted: A Manager to Fit Each Strategy," in William F. Glueck and Neil H. Snyder (eds.), *Readings in Business Policy and Strategy from Business Week*. New York: McGraw-Hill, 1982.

Waterman, Robert H., Jr. "The Seven Elements of Strategic Fit," *Journal of Business Strategy*, 2:3, Winter 1982, pp. 69–73.

Wissema, J. G., A. F. Brand, and H. W. Van Der Pol. "The Incorporation of Management Development in Strategic Management," *Strategic Management Journal*, 2:4, October/December 1981, pp. 361–377.

THE ENVIRONMENT OF STRATEGIC MANAGEMENT

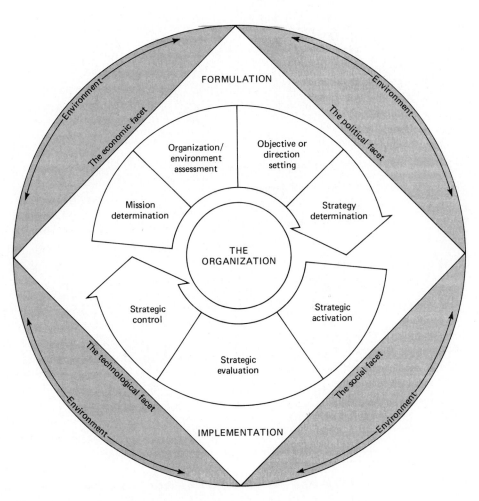

On August 26, 1982, Manville Corporation, formerly Johns-Manville, filed for protection under Chapter 11 of the bankruptcy law. This climaxed an eighty-year history during which Manville had grown to one of America's largest, most prestigious industrial corporations.

The founder of what was to become Manville Corporation, Henry Ward Johns, built a sizable fortune in the late 1800s mining asbestos and inventing new uses for it. But in 1898 he died of "dust pthisis pneumonitis," now called *asbestosis*. By the 1930s, it was clear that the problem of breathing asbestos dust was a serious one. Nearly fifty years later, a Federal Appeals Court concluded, "The unpalatable facts are that in the twenties and thirties the hazards of working with asbestos were recognized." By 1930, however, Manville was the world's largest producer of asbestos and new uses were being found for the product every year. It was eventually used in most automobiles, school buses, hospitals, schools, factories, and commercial facilities. Asbestos filled the bill anywhere a fireproof, permanent fibrous material was needed.

Manville successfully defended lawsuits brought by asbestos victims beginning in the 1920s. In 1934 Manville's chief lawyer wrote, "[It] is only within a comparatively recent time that asbestosis has been recognized by the medical and scientific professions as a disease—in fact [this has been] one of our principal defenses.''

Manville opposed publication of information about asbestos dangers during 1934. A Manville executive wrote in 1934, ''I quite agree that our interests are best served by having asbestosis receive the minimum of publicity.'' He was writing to another asbestos industry executive about a letter from the editor of *Asbestos*, an industry trade journal. The editor had written, ''Always you have requested that for obvious reasons, we publish nothing, and, naturally your wishes have been respected.''

In 1950, Manville's chief physician at the time reported to top management that all but 4 of 708 asbestos workers he had studied had evidence of lung damage. Of the 7 who had the most severe conditions, the physician wrote, ''The fibrosis of this disease is irreversible and permanent . . . it is felt that [they] should not be told of [their] condition so that [they] can live and work in peace and the company can benefit from [their] many years experience.'' Efforts were made during the fifties to clean the air breathed by Manville workers. But the dangers to users and installers of asbestos products were concealed. The physician mentioned above later told of his unsuccessful efforts to have warning labels placed on asbestos products in the early fifties.

Until an extensive study in 1964 resulted in public awareness of the problem, Manville placed no warnings on the thousands of tons of asbestos fiber it distributed worldwide. Even after 1964, the Manville label simply stated, ''Inhalation of asbestos in excessive quantities over long periods of time may be harmful.'' With increasing public attention, however, substitute products began to be found and asbestos use declined precipitously after about 1975.

Asbestos had always been very profitable for Manville. But it became even more profitable as competitors left the industry upon discovering the disaster they had helped to create. In 1976, although asbestos fiber constituted only 12 percent of Manville's sales, it accounted for 51 percent of operating profits. As asbestos use in the United States declined by one-half and as thousands of asbestos victims began filing increasingly successful lawsuits, the Manville management tried to diversify into other products. The firm bought dozens of small companies and eventually purchased the huge Olinkraft Corporation, a paper company in West Monroe, Louisiana. Nothing worked. With an entrenched and elderly management team and with the easy profits from asbestos rapidly disappearing, Manville was unable to keep the net income from collapsing. Inflation-corrected earnings declined steadily from 1978 onward, to a $223 million loss in 1982.

By 1982, potential asbestos liabilities were estimated by Manville to exceed $2 billion, and by others to be many times that. Through legal maneuvering, the company was able to delay payment of practically all the asbestos judgments. The Chapter 11 filing in August 1982 stopped the asbestos lawsuits.

As receivables flowed in and debts no longer had to be paid, the company received over $300 million in extra cash. The bankruptcy filing also secured for

Manville's top managers a few more years of respectability, extensive corporate benefits, and half-million-dollar annual salaries.

Fifteen thousand or more asbestos victims and their families waited for the cumbersome Chapter 11 process to end, although most admitted that their claims were unlikely to be paid anyway. And, each month, hundreds more discovered that they had asbestosis or, worse yet, mesothelioma, the very rapidly growing, always-fatal asbestos cancer.

Manville's unrepentant lawyer/chief executive, J. A. McKinney, who had been with the company for over thirty years, disclaimed responsibility. He wrote, "There has been no cover-up. . . . your corporation has acted honorably." In late 1983, the company began an extensive public relations and lobbying effort aimed at getting the government to protect Manville and help pay for the asbestos injuries. Then Manville filed its proposed reorganization plan with the bankruptcy court. The plan provided for a surviving corporation, Manville II, which would keep the assets of the old company but be immune from asbestos lawsuits.

Organizational strategists are responsible for the strategic management process which molds and directs the organization and relates it to the environment. The story of Manville Corporation illustrates how the four facets of the environment offer opportunities and threats.

Remember that the *social facet* consists of the human relationships of the organization and its strategists to individuals, groups, and society in general. Manville executives disclaim any breach of their social responsibilities. For decades, the corporation was apparently viewed as a closed system, and no responsibility is acknowledged for the impact on those outside the system.

The *political facet* includes the laws and regulations applicable to the enterprise and the courts and government officials who interpret and enforce them, along with other groups and institutions in society which wield power. For decades Manville was able to avoid significant government influence relative to the asbestos question. Later, though, many government agencies became involved. The company's executives have not been unaware of the impact of political forces on their future. Protected by the bankruptcy court from lawsuits, with a $300 million "war chest," and with a lawyer as chief executive, the company was in a truly powerful position in 1983.

The *technological facet* of the environment has been both Manville's salvation and its downfall. Thousands of uses of asbestos, beginning with those discovered by Henry Ward Johns, represented technological advances. Later, when the world sensed that asbestos was dangerous, its use continued because it was so vital to the operation of ships, factories, and so forth. When the perceived danger became great enough, however, substitute products were found—fiberglass and rock wool for insulation, nylon for reinforcement fibers, and metal-foil coatings for heat resistance. As these substitutions occurred, asbestos sales plummeted. So what had begun with technology ended with technology.

For Manville, the *economic facet* of the environment was the dominant concern. Asbestos offered an opportunity to make money. Manville's fortunes worsened when the decline in asbestos sales was aggravated by a general downturn that began in 1979 and lasted through 1982. From the standpoint of Manville executives, the other facets of the environment may have been important largely because of their economic impact.

Let us now look at each facet of the environment in greater detail and in relation to organizations in general, not just Manville Corporation.

THE SOCIAL FACET OF THE ENVIRONMENT

One of the difficulties in considering the relationship between an organization and the society in which it exists is that the problem is largely an ethical one—a question of what is right or wrong. As an aid to answering such questions, a model of ethics is developed below. This will be followed by a discussion of the traditional view of social responsibility as enunciated by Adam Smith and as more recently endorsed by Nobel laureate Milton Friedman. Next, the changing values of American society will be discussed. Then it will be suggested that organizational strategists should take an open-systems view, thinking of the business or nonbusiness organization as part of the broader social system. This will lead to a brief discussion of the social contract which exists between the organization, particularly the business organization, and society.

A Model of Ethics

Ethics is defined as "*the discipline dealing with what is good and bad or right and wrong or with moral duty and obligation*" (*Webster's Third New International Dictionary*). As Hershey and Linda Friedman (1982, especially p. 11) have observed, ethics is "everybody's business." A model of ethics is presented in Figure 2.1. From the figure it can be seen that ethics consist mainly of two relationships, indicated by arrows in the figure. A person or organization is ethical if these relationships are strong.

First, there are a number of sources that one might use to determine what is right or wrong, good or bad, or moral or immoral behavior. These include the Bible, the Koran, and a number of other "holy" books. They also include that "still small voice" which many refer to as conscience. Millions believe that conscience is a gift of

FIGURE 2.1   A model of ethics

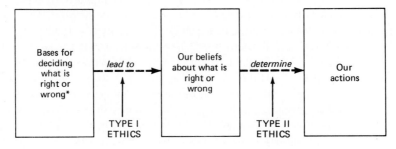

* *Examples:* (1) Bible, Koran, and other "holy" books; (2) conscience; (3) behavior and advice of "significant others"; (4) codes of ethics; (5) laws.

God, or the voice of God. Others see it simply as a developed response based upon internalization of societal mores.

Another source of ethical guidance is the behavior and advice of what psychologists call "significant others"—our parents, friends, role models, and members of our churches, clubs, and associations. For organized professionals, especially, there are often codes of ethics which prescribe behavior. When any type of act is sufficiently hurtful to others, it is often prohibited by law. So enacted laws offer guides to ethical behavior. If a certain behavior is illegal, most would consider it unethical. There are exceptions, of course. For example, through the 1950s, laws in most southern states relegated black persons to an inferior status, the backs of buses, and so forth. Today, many consider it to have been highly moral that Martin Luther King opposed such laws and, in fact, disobeyed them.

Some would say that, if a person believes a certain behavior to be acceptable, then that behavior is ethical for that individual. However, most would agree that persons have a responsibility to avail themselves of the sources of ethical guidance. In short, individuals should care about what is right and wrong and not just be concerned with what is expedient. *The strength of the relationship between what an individual or an organization believes to be moral and correct and what available sources of guidance suggest is morally correct* is **type I ethics**.

Type II ethics is *the strength of the relationship between what one believes and the way one behaves.* Generally, a person is not considered ethical unless possessed of both types of ethics. Simply having strong feelings about what is right and wrong and basing those feelings on the proper sources does not make one ethical. Even "situation ethicists" would agree that to do what one believes is wrong is unethical. For example, if a student knows that it is wrong to look at another's examination answer sheet while taking a test and does so anyway, the student has been unethical, in a type II sense. If a business manager accepts a responsibility to keep the environment clean, yet dumps poisonous waste in a nearby stream, this behavior is unethical also.

It is difficult to think of an organization as having an opinion about what is right or wrong. Ethics, most would agree, is the strength of the two connections mentioned above for individuals within the organization. Still, many organizations, through policy statements, practices over time, and the leadership of one or more morally strong individuals, develop an ethos of concern for moral issues. Many companies have programs of community involvement for their executives. Many cooperate with fund drives such as the United Way. An open-door policy, grievance procedures, executive sensitivity training, and employee benefit programs often stem as much from a desire to do what is right as from a concern for productivity and avoidance of strife. And these tend to be attributes of organizations, not individuals. In fact, Goodpaster and Matthews (1982) argue that a corporation can have a conscience. Organizational strategists have a great influence over the matter because they normally establish policies, develop the company's mission statement, and so forth.

When a corporation behaves as if it had a conscience, it is said to be socially responsible. **Social responsibility** is *the implied, enforced, or felt obligation of managers, acting in their official capacities, to serve or protect the interests of stakeholder groups other than themselves.*

In summary, ethics is often thought of as the degree to which one's behavior conforms to one's ideals. We have extended that definition somewhat by saying that ethics also involves the degree to which one's ideals accord with the various sources of guidance available. This attribute of ethics is an outgrowth of (1) moral seriousness, or a concern for what is right or wrong, and (2) intelligence, which equips one to discern right from wrong.

While one can usually provoke a lively discussion by simply mentioning the phrase *business ethics*, there are certain abiding principles of ethics which most would accept as valid. Table 2.1 lists several of these. The ideas listed come from a number of sources, but they have been generally accepted in civilized societies for many centuries. Ethical behavior results from searching out such principles—and other less abiding, less generally accepted ones—internalizing them as beliefs, and acting in accordance with those beliefs.

Business ethics is *the application of ethical principles to business relationships and activities*. While Table 2.1 may appear to apply mainly to personal ethics rather than business ethics, most unethical business activities violate one or more of the principles shown. For example, embezzlement is theft and violation of a trust, and pollution of the environment may severely hurt others.

The Traditional View of Social Responsibility

In 1776, Adam Smith published *The Wealth of Nations*, which has sometimes been called the "Capitalist Manifesto." In that book he described a system where individuals and businesses pursued their own self-interests and government played a limited role. This became the model for American capitalism. Adam Smith (1776, p. 423) wrote:

> [An individual or business] generally, indeed, neither intends to promote the public interest, nor knows how much he is promoting it. . . . He intends only his own gains, and he is in this, as in many other cases, led by an invisible hand to promote an end which was no part of

TABLE 2.1 ACCEPTED ETHICAL PRINCIPLES

Wrong, Unethical, Immoral	Right, Ethical, Moral
Murder	Giving to the poor or disadvantaged
Rape	Working hard
Lying under oath	Gathering knowledge and wisdom
Theft	Repaying obligations
Incest	Being truthful
Severely hurting someone economically, psychologically, or physically	Caring for offspring
	Caring for forebears
Violating a trust	Considering the long-term outcomes of
Anarchy	behavior
Violating laws	
Sacrificing the future for today	

his intention, nor is it always the worse for society that it was no part of it. By pursuing his own interest he frequently promotes that of the society more effectively than when he really intends to promote it.

This idea—that unfettered capitalism allows the serving of the public interest by individuals and businesses who seek maximization of satisfaction or profit—is the very foundation of the American economic system. Traditionally, companies were not expected to serve social goals, except indirectly. For example, until the mid-1930s it was illegal for an American corporation to make charitable contributions. This law was based upon a precedent set in an 1883 lawsuit in Great Britain, *Hutton v. West Cork Railway Corporation*. The court in that case ruled that the corporation should be concerned only with the equitable distribution of its earnings to its owners. This could not include corporate philanthrophy (Wren, 1979, p. 109). It was not until 1935 that the Federal Revenue Act made provisions for the deductibility of corporate charitable contributions. Under that revision, corporations could deduct only up to 5 percent of their net income for charitable purposes. By 1953, however, the right of businesses to make extensive charitable gifts was clearly established. That year, in *A. P. Smith Manufacturing Company v. Barlow et al.*, the New Jersey Supreme Court concluded that business support of higher education was in society's best interests (Wren, 1979, p. 453).

Nobel laureate economist Milton Friedman (1962, p. 133) called the idea of corporate social responsibility a "fundamentally subversive doctrine." Friedman said, "There is one and only one social responsibility of business—to use its resources and engage in activities designed to increase its profits so long as it stays within the rules of the game, which is to say engages in open and free competition without deception or fraud" (also see Leavitt, 1958).

Friedman's statement is often quoted as an example of a radical view. However, far from being a radical, Friedman simply subscribes to the idea that, in the long run, the public interest is served by individuals and businesses pursuing their own best interests, primarily financial well-being, through participation in a relatively free economy. In fact, Friedman sets a rather high standard, suggesting that businesses should operate within the "rules of the game," practicing neither deception nor fraud. The rules of the game obviously include international, national, and other laws, as well as accepted ethical practices. How many corporations actually are willing to tell the absolute truth in their advertisements and to engage in "open and fair competition," avoiding all kinds of collusion, price fixing, and so forth? The general public would be greatly surprised if STP Corporation were to admit that the lubricating oil additive STP has no real value, as has been shown (Hartley, 1981). Also, few would expect Coca-Cola Company to admit that the "Pepsi challenge" really showed that most Americans preferred the taste of Pepsi to Coke.

Many who oppose Friedman would place upon business managers the burden of devoting corporation resources, including both money and time, to social motives. Yet, much of the corporate philanthrophy in America has derived from fortunes amassed by individuals who blatantly violated the Friedman principles of free enterprise (see

Josephson, 1934, and Tarbell, 1905). This is why many of today's great universities and charitable foundations bear the names of individuals such as Daniel Drew, John D. Rockefeller, J. P. Morgan, Cornelius Vanderbilt, and Andrew Carnegie, whom Matthew Josephson (1934) dubbed "the robber barons."

Despite all this, there is evidence that few subscribe to Friedman's hard-line views. Let us look at how values concerning social responsibility are changing.

Changing Values toward Social Responsibility

The recent trend has been for America's corporate executives to see themselves as either arbiters of the various claims on organizational productivity or as legitimate servants of a variety of constituencies. In a political sense, *constituency* means "a body of citizens or voters that is entitled to elect a representative to a legislative or other public body" (*Webster's Third New International Dictionary*). The intention of political constituents is that they will be represented by the person they elect.

Unlike political constituencies, those of corporate managers may or may not have the power to elect those managers. An **organizational constituency** is *any identifiable group which organizational managers either have or acknowledge a responsibility to represent.* For some executives, the common shareholders make up only one of many constituencies to be served—and not even the primary one. For example, at Lincoln Electric Company, the world's largest producer of arc-welding products, corporate executives see the customers as their primary constituency. Employees are in second place, with stockholders only a distant third. James Lincoln, the company's founder and president until his death in 1965, said, "The last group to be considered is the stockholders, who own stock because they think it will be more profitable than investing money in any other way" (Lincoln, 1961, pp. 38, 122).

Some even suggest that, in pursuing societal goals, organizational strategists in various firms should view strategy from a collectivist perspective (Fombrun and Astley, 1983, pp. 47–54). Others propose a government-business partnership (Fox, 1981, p. 99).

Clearly, every business or other organization has a large number of stakeholders, some of which are recognized as constituents and some of which are not. An **organizational stakeholder** is *an individual or group whose interests are affected by organizational activities.* A number of stakeholders, whose claims on organizational resources may or may not be considered legitimate, are listed in Table 2.1. Figure 2.2 illustrates a few of the stakeholders identified for Crown Metal Products, Inc., a small manufacturer of metal furniture near Boise, Idaho. The stakeholders which the Crown management views as constituencies are identified by asterisks.

Today, many corporate executives see the interests of employees, customers, individuals in society, and so forth, as legitimate and sometimes serve those interests to the acknowledged detriment of the common shareholder. For example, a number of corporate managements have recently placed large amounts of company stock in employee stock ownership trusts for the purpose of avoiding takeover attempts clearly in the interest of common shareholders—although not in the interest of the managers themselves. Other companies make gifts of company resources, often cash, to univer-

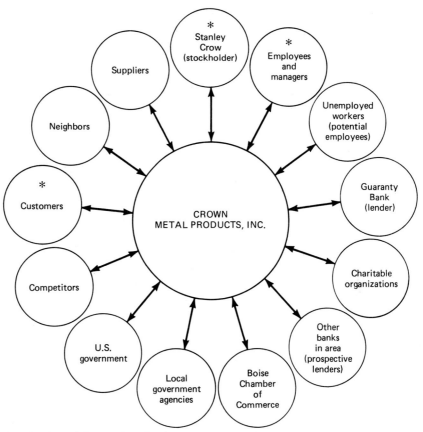

FIGURE 2.2   Stakeholders of Crown Metal Products

sities, churches, clubs, and so forth, knowing that any possible benefit to shareholders is remote and unlikely. Some authorities suggest that members of the public should be placed on the boards of directors of major corporations to protect the interests of nonowner stakeholders (Jones and Goldberg, 1982, pp. 603–605).

Even though no manager can reasonably consider all stakeholder interests at once, some strategists claim to try. Yet, it is clear that optimizing the interest of one constituency results in some suboptimization of the interests of others (Jones and Goldberg, 1982, p. 604). Representing such a diversity of interests requires that the organizational strategist answer questions such as the following: During an economic downturn, should employees be afforded continuous employment even when this is not in the long-term best interest of the owners of the corporation and does not accord with their preferences? Should managers be concerned about whether suppliers receive a reasonable profit on the items purchased from them or should management simply buy the best inputs at the lowest price possible? Many corporate strategists cop out on such questions by simply saying—or assuming—that it is in the long-term best interest of

TABLE 2.2   STAKEHOLDERS (POTENTIAL CONSTITUENTS)

Common shareholders	Competitors
Preferred shareholders	Neighbors
Trade creditors	The immediate community
Holders of unsecured debt securities	The national society
Holders of secured debt securities	The world society
Intermediate (business) customers	Corporate management
Final (consumer) customers	The organizational strategists themselves
Suppliers	The chief executive
Employees	The board of directors
Past employees	Government
Retirees	Special interest groups

the common shareholder to serve the interests of other constituencies. When this is true, there can be no argument: The real constituency being served is the common shareholder, and the purpose of giving customers a better product at a lower price than the market requires, or suppliers a higher price for inputs than the market requires, is simply a means to an end, not an end in itself. The questions involve ethical issues only when the interests of stakeholder groups are in some degree of conflict. *And they always are.*

So what is the conscientious manager to do? There can be no debate about whether corporations should acknowledge and respond to the interests of every stakeholder to the extent that the interests are embodied in law or enforced by market forces. For example, no one would suggest that a company insist on selling its product for a higher price than is available in the marketplace. To do so would result in zero sales. Customers do not have to buy. Also, no company should dump waste at illegal dump sites or fail to pay suppliers for products which are purchased. The debate is ongoing, however, about whether the plural stakeholders should be served as legitimate claimants in their own right rather than simply as a way of serving the primary corporate constituency, the common shareholder (see, for example, Bloom and Greyser, 1981). The judgment of society in general on this question today is "yes." This truly places strategists in a position, within the limits set in the marketplace and by laws and regulations, of apportioning the largess produced by organizational activity among a number of recognized groups. It is a difficult assignment, perhaps a "mission impossible," but many modern executives choose to accept it.

The Organization as an Open System

An **open system** is *an organization or assemblage of things which affects and is affected by outside events.* It probably was never adequate to view an organization as a closed system, and probably no intelligent manager ever did so. However, it is useful to remind ourselves that the organization is a part of a much larger socioeconomic and physical system and to view corporate boundaries as permeable. In the case discussed at the beginning of the chapter, Manville Corporation acknowledged a responsibility to protect employees, although somewhat belatedly. However, the company failed to evaluate the obvious impact on those outside the organization—the users of asbestos.

Even employees do not stay in the organization like a sequestered jury. Sooner or later, usually sooner, they make contacts outside. In fact, most of us are members of dozens of organizations. We become communications channels for them. Most corporate strategists recognize the existence of the **grapevine** or *the informal communications system inside and outside the organization.*

A **closed system** is *an organization or assemblage of things which neither affects nor is affected by outside events.* There are no closed systems, of course. In the long run, Manville's chief physician told the outside world what he had told his superiors twenty-five years earlier. Many companies develop competence in new fields by "pirating" executives from competitors who are already successful in those fields. Former International Business Machines (IBM) executives, for example, populate the management offices of dozens of smaller computer firms.

The open-systems view involves recognizing the relationships between organizations and their environments and evaluating those relationships in an intelligent, not necessarily moral, way. It is not an ethical concept. However, it is clear that the organization has obligations to other elements of society, some of which are not spelled out in law or in any other formal way. This is called the *social contract* and is the topic of the next subsection.

The Social Contract

In a sense, organizations and society enter into a contract. This **social contract** is *the set of written and unwritten rules and assumptions about behavior patterns among the various elements of society.* Like a legal contract, the social contract often involves a *quid pro quo* (something for something) exchange. Byron (1982) even suggests that certain aspects of the social contract are enforceable. One party to the contract behaves a certain way and expects a predictable pattern of behavior from the other. Much of the social contract is imbedded in the customs of society. It is customary to pay employees at the end of a pay period, not at the beginning, for example. Some of the contract provisions result from practices between parties. For example, a relationship of trust may have developed between a manufacturer and the community in which it operates. Because of this, each may inform the other well in advance of any planned action which might cause harm (e.g., the closing of a plant by the company or the imposition of a new dumping regulation by the community).

Thinking of the social contract from the standpoint of the business or nonbusiness organization, organizational strategists should contemplate expected or prescribed relationships with individuals, with government, with other organizations, and with society in general. This is illustrated in Figure 2.3.

Obligations to Individuals It is through joining organizations that individuals find healthy outlets for their energies. From the church, they expect guidance, ministerial services, and fellowship, and they devote time and money to its sustenance.

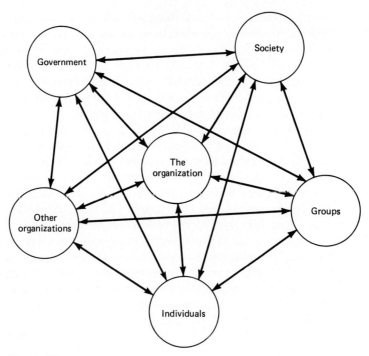

FIGURE 2.3   The social contract

From their employers, they expect a fair day's pay for a fair day's work—and perhaps much more. Many expect to be given time off, usually with pay, to vote, perform jury service, and so forth. Clubs and associations provide opportunities for fellowship and for community service. To the extent that these expectations are acknowledged as responsibilities by the organizations involved, they become part of the social contract.

Obligations to Other Organizations   Organizational strategists must be concerned with relationships involving other organizations of similar kinds—such as competitors—and vastly differing organizations. Commercial businesses are expected to compete with one another on an honorable basis, without subterfuge or reckless unconcern for their mutual rights. Charities such as United Way expect support from businesses, often including the loaning of executives and facilitation of annual fund drives. At the same time, charitable institutions are expected to come "hat in hand," requesting rather than demanding assistance. Customer organizations expect to be treated as "customers." To some degree, most of our society still subscribes to the notion that "the customer is king."

Obligations to Government   Government is a most important party to the social contract. Under the auspices of government, companies have a license to do business. They have written patent rights, trademarks, and so forth. Churches are often incorporated under state laws and given nonprofit status. Many quasi-governmental agencies, such as the Federal Depository Insurance Corporation, Regional Planning Commissions, and Levee Boards, have been given special missions by government. In addition, organizations are expected to recognize the need for order rather than anarchy and to accept some degree of government intervention in organizational affairs. For example, the law no longer gives an Occupational Safety and Health Administration inspector the right to intrude into an organization without permission, but it is usual to accept such intrusion.

Obligations to Society in General   Businesses are expected to creatively abide by laws which are passed for the good of society. That is, as responsible corporate citizens, businesses should follow the spirit as well as the letter of the law. Many companies which created huge hazardous waste dumps throughout the country now defend themselves by saying that the dumps were legal when they were created. In fact, the laws and regulations controlling hazardous waste dumping were designed to protect the public health. The dumping of certain concentrations of certain substances was prohibited. In many cases, such as the notorious Love Canal case involving Hooker Chemical, dangerous substances not yet covered by regulation and dangerous but legal concentrations of other substances were dumped over an extended period of years. As a result public health in those areas has been endangered. It is clear that society now considers this unacceptable.

One writer Byron (1982, p. 190), among many others, feels that protecting the public is simply a matter of "managerial self-interest." If this were true, as Sir Thomas More said (in Bolt, *A Man for All Seasons*), "Common sense would make us good, and greed would make us saintly." It is the clear consensus among Americans today that corporate strategists must protect other stakeholders, even when doing so conflicts with managerial self-interest or with the interests of stockholders. A number of recent studies indicate that many executives agree (Holmes, 1976; Ostlund, 1977; Bowman, 1977).

One writer (Strand, 1983, p. 90) thoughtlessly argues that, "Organizational adaptation to the social environment is not a normative question that is debatable—it is an area of scientific study." The questions of the organization's responsibilities under the social contract and the degree to which strategists should acknowledge them are intensely moral ones. To view this matter as simply an "area of scientific study" is to cop out on the whole question of social responsibility and ethics.

THE POLITICAL FACET OF THE ENVIRONMENT

Corporations today spend hundreds of millions of dollars on political contributions and lobbying. Sometimes these contributions are designed to support principles which corporate executives believe are worthwhile for society. More often, however, they probably are self-serving. This is evidenced by the fact that few political contributions are made anonymously. The political facet of the environment is concerned with the organization's relationships to government officials and to other individuals and groups who hold political power.

Political Action Committees

Recently there has been fear that political contributions, especially those made by political action committees (PACs), are likely to subvert governmental processes by causing elected officials to serve the interests of those groups which make the contributions. *Political action committees* are *tax-favored organizations formed by special interest groups to accept contributions and influence governmental action*. The growth of PACs has afforded an avenue whereby corporations contribute hundreds of millions of dollars to political candidates, much of it obviously aimed at serving the special interests of those corporations. Billions in subsidies and price supports were approved for the dairy industry and even the tobacco industry in 1983 after PACs representing those industries made large contributions to key legislators.

Increasing Government Influence on Business

While the general public is justifiably concerned about the influence of PACs and other private organizations on government, most managers express greater concern for the pervasive involvement of government in business activities. One prominent law school dean, Thomas Erlich of Stanford University, complained that the increasing "legal pollution" in America unduly constrains business ("Complaints about Lawyers," 1978, p. 44). Not only have laws become more numerous, but the propensity of citizens to litigate has become greater. Business and nonbusiness organizations find themselves in a sea of political forces. The organizational strategist must take account—if not advantage—of these forces.

The Cost of Government Intervention

John Dunlop, dean of the faculty of arts and sciences at Harvard and U.S. Secretary of Labor in 1975 and 1976, said, "The past decade has seen a vast expansion in the scope and detail of government regulation of business decisions, beyond those of the New Deal era, beyond regulating the public utility industry, and beyond temporary periods of wage and price controls" (Dunlop et al., 1979, p. 82). Harvard's Ronald Fox (1981, p. 98) estimates that regulation may cost American business as much as $100 billion per year. The great historian Alfred Chandler indicates that the problem is more severe in America than in other countries (Dunlop et al., 1979, p. 88). Crawford Greenwalt, former chairman of the board at DuPont, asks, "Why is it that my American colleagues and I are constantly being taken to court—made to stand trial—for activities that our counterparts in Britain and other parts of Europe are knighted or given peerages or comparable honors for?" (Dunlop et al., 1979, p. 88).

The View from Government

Taking a more balanced view, George Shultz, U.S. Secretary of State in the Reagan administration, acknowledges that "Government seems to be an opponent, not a friend or even a neutral referee" (Dunlop et al., 1979, p. 93). He also suggests that the issue looks different from the government's side. Shultz says that businesses can serve their political interests by doing their homework better and by "looking beyond the very narrow interests of the individual company or industry and offering some connection between what the businessman wants and the broader public interest" (Dunlop et al., 1979, p. 93).

The Recent Trend

Certainly, the business-government interface is often an abrasive one. The very recent trend, however, has been toward lessening regulation and reducing government interference in business and private activities. For example, the airlines industry, the trucking industry, and the banking industry are now largely deregulated. Incidentally, it is noteworthy that deregulated industries themselves tend to be the most vehement opponents of deregulation. It is likely that this opposition arises as much from a fear of rapid and unmanageable change as from a preference for regulation per se (Reich, 1982, p. 74).

THE TECHNOLOGICAL FACET OF THE ENVIRONMENT

Recall that technology includes all the ways that knowledge is applied to the production of goods and services. The pace of technological change has been accelerating at least since the Middle Ages. Only recently has this been widely viewed as a problem. But technology may also offer a solution. In any case, business strategists must be prepared to deal with continuing technological change.

A Technological Problem

In 1969 Alvin Toffler (1970, p. 2) coined the term *future shock* to describe the *"shattering stress and disorientation that we induce in individuals by subjecting them to too much change in too short a time"*. How much greater is the rate of technological change today than that which existed in 1965? Scientists had not yet landed on the moon. Electronic calculators were just beginning to become manageably small. Microwave ovens were only experimental. It is in this environment of ever-accelerating technological progress that the organizational strategist must plan and implement strategies. The strategist has no greater problem or opportunity than that presented by the rapid pace of technological change.

A Technological Solution

If technology presents a problem, though, it also may provide the solution. The current information revolution allows the organizational strategist to accumulate and process data more rapidly than ever before. W. Edwards Deming, for whom the Japanese have named two national productivity prizes, attributes much of his success in helping the Japanese attain eminence as a manufacturing country to the use of "statistical control" in managing organizations.

With today's modern computers, it is possible to obtain strategic information on a real-time basis for the first time in history. Hundreds of Seven-Eleven Stores, for example, are tapped into a main computer in Dallas. They are able to order needed items and have those items immediately programmed for loading in computer-selected order in specially designed trucks. When a truck, following the route defined by the computer, reaches a particular store, the items for that store are readily accessible. Southland Corporation, Seven-Eleven's parent company in Dallas, can immediately call up sales, inventory turnover, and profitability data (and much more) for any store in the system. Southland's strategic managers can discover not only what items sell best in which stores, but what items sell best at which shelf locations in stores. Most major merchandisers now have "point-of-sale" electronic accounting systems. When a customer order is checked out at the "cash register," the inventory is immediately updated. An order for a replacement item is entered if necessary, and the impact on sales, profitability, and other strategic variables immediately calculated. As unsettling as many of the advances are, in the final analysis most of them result in the production of goods and services at a lower cost in terms of both time and materials. If economic endeavor has a single goal, this has to be it.

The Impact of Technological Change on Business

Organizational strategists who ignore technological changes do so at their peril. Manufacturers of mechanical adding machines, large propeller-driven aircraft, or plastic-reinforced automobile safety glass would find almost no market for their products today. The same may be true of old-fashioned double-edged safety razors, bias-belted tires, and black-and-white television sets.

Boris Petrov (1982, p. 70) describes three possible effects of technological change:

- It can change relative competitive cost positions within a given business.
- It can create new markets and new business segments.
- It can collapse or merge previously independent businesses by reducing or eliminating their segment cost barriers.

In any case, when technology advances, all participants in the respective business segment are affected. To survive today, companies must continually innovate. This is not because of some external force which has imposed upon the world a new and fearsome order of things, but because technological improvement is possible. When improvement is possible in a free economy, someone will attempt it. The company or person who does, and succeeds in producing a better product at the same cost or a cheaper version of the same product, will be able to dominate the marketplace. Companies which do not, as Adam Smith envisioned in 1776, will be driven from the economic scene. Even when competitors make the appropriate technological response, as U.S. auto manufacturers are attempting to do (through robotization in an attempt to compete with the Japanese), lost market shares may not be regained (Abernathy, Clark, and Kantrow, 1981, p. 71).

THE ECONOMIC FACET OF THE ENVIRONMENT

Business organizations can be thought of in many ways—as individuals working together, as social systems, as workers and managers and the resources they use, or simply as systems of relationships devoid of content. However, the business organization is above all an economic entity. It has as its goal the production of goods or services. Most would agree that the goods or services should be produced at the lowest possible cost in labor and material. This is true for business and nonbusiness organizations. Even churches have budgets and employ workers at economically determined wages. They must provide services which are compatible with the desires of those upon whom they depend for support. So every organization must consider the economic facet of the environment as a dominant concern.

A Conduit for Social, Political, and Technological Forces

In fact, it is largely through economic forces that the other aspects of the environment—social, political, and technological—have their impact. For example, an advancement in word processing technology might not be of concern to a typewriter manufacturer if it did not affect the sale of typewriters.

Government would have a hard time enforcing environmental and employee safety regulations without a system of fines and provisions for stopping the economic activity of offending businesses. Marlow (1982, p. 165) concludes that the Occupational Safety and Health Administration must "increase the costs of noncompliance that it imposes on firms" if it is to be effective. Greer and Downey (1982, p. 496) conclude that economically based compliance systems are most likely to work for regulators in general.

Does Economic Competition Work?

Since the New Deal days in the depths of the Depression, there has been a continuing socialization of the U.S. economy. Transfer payments have become a larger and larger portion of government budgets, while taxes have expanded as a proportion of the gross national product (GNP). Now it is estimated that 25 percent of total spending in the U.S. economy is done by the government. Yet the free enterprise system continues to function roughly as Adam Smith envisioned it.

I have often said to my students in my classes that if they do not believe that competition works they need only start a food store and charge 3 percent above what others charge, or 3 percent below. After a discussion, most students realize that market forces do not permit such freedom. No major food retailer is able to consistently earn a 3 percent profit on sales. It is an extraordinary business which earns a net profit of 10 percent of sales, and a number of industries average 2 percent or less. It is clear that government regulation, as long as it does not take the form of price controls, does not prevent competition from driving inefficient producers out of business and encouraging efficient producers to become more and more efficient. Government regulations are just one of the many constraints with which organizational strategists have to contend. Within all those constraints—some of them economic, some noneconomic—organizations compete economically.

Worldwide Economic Forces

In a recent *Wall Street Journal* article, Louis E. Lehrman called for the use of a world currency to replace all the national currencies. This may seem somewhat far-fetched, but it is reflective of the fact that the economic facet of the environment is influenced by worldwide forces. The U.S. auto and electronics industries have been severely impacted by foreign competition, mostly Japanese. Recently, when it appeared that the oil producers' and exporters' cartel (OPEC) was about to fall apart, there was fear that this would result in a number of developing countries defaulting on their debts to major U.S. banks, with a consequent increase in U.S. interest rates. The recession which began in 1979 was a worldwide phenomenon, and the recovery which began in 1983 appears to be the same. International travel is more feasible than it has ever been in the past, and more and more companies engage in international business. Every organization is affected by worldwide forces.

Changing but Staying the Same

In short, the economic facet of the environment is a rapidly changing one. But the more it changes, the more it stays the same. Organizational strategists still must compete on an economic basis. As long as prices for goods and services are set in free markets, it will be on the basis of economic variables that the organization sets its goals and measures it performances. Some (Weiss, 1978; Jones and Goldberg, 1982; Stone, 1976) see this utter dependence on market variables as a major flaw in our system of corporate governance. Others, including the author, consider it one of America's greatest strengths.

SUMMARY

The story of Manville Corporation shows the importance of environmental considerations. The company failed because it did not adequately respond to the opportunities and threats which existed in the environment.

The relationship of an organization to the society in which it exists is largely a question of what is right or wrong. Ethics is the discipline dealing with what is good or bad and right or wrong or with moral duty. The degree to which we are ethical or unethical depends upon how well our beliefs conform to the available sources of guidance about right and wrong and how closely our actions conform to our ideals.

Since organizations are made up of groups of individuals, it is useful, though difficult, to think of a corporation as having ethical principles. The traditional view of social responsibility is that businesses should attempt to earn profits, thereby serving social purposes. The recent trend, however, has been for America's corporate executives to see themselves as either arbiters of the various claims on organizational productivity or as legitimate servants of a variety of constituencies.

There is a wide range of stakeholders which corporate strategists could serve. However, optimizing the interests of one results in some suboptimization of interests for others. The interests of certain stakeholders have been embodied in laws. Others, such as customers, can enforce their interests in the marketplace. Of course, both these forces must be obeyed. Beyond this, it has become the attitude of society that corporate stategists should serve the interests of stakeholders in a balanced way.

In addition, the organization should be viewed as an open system whose members are members of numerous other organizations. Organizational activities influence and are influenced by other systems. In fact, organizations enter into a social contract. The organization is bound by the social contract to behave in certain ways toward individuals, government, other organizations, and society in general. The contract spells out society's expectations of the organization, as well as the organization's expectations of society.

The political facet of the environment is concerned with the organization's relationships to government officials and to other individuals and groups who hold political power. Corporations attempt to influence government through political contributions and lobbying. Many feel that government unduly constrains businesses. Certainly the business-government interface is an abrasive one.

Technology includes all the ways knowledge is applied to the production of goods and services. Rapid technological change has produced the problem of future shock, but it also may provide a solution in the form of information processing capability. Strategists ignore technological change to their peril. Survival requires continuing innovation.

The other three facets of the environment have their primary impact on the organization through the economic facet. Business organizations are primarily economic entities which produce goods and services and earn profits. The American economy has become increasingly socialized since the 1930s. This constrains business activities but, as long as prices are not set, it does not prevent the system from working. As long as prices for goods and services are set in free markets, organizations will set their goals and measure their performance on the basis of economic variables.

IMPORTANT CONCEPTS

Ethics

Type I ethics

Type II ethics

Social responsibility

Business ethics

Organizational constituency

Organizational stakeholder

Open system

Grapevine

Closed system

Social contract

Political action committees (PACs)

Future shock

DISCUSSION QUESTIONS

1 Define the four facets of the environment and discuss how each contributed to Manville Corporation's success and eventual failure.
2 Define *ethics* and discuss the sources upon which ethical principles are based.
3 Can a corporation have a conscience? Explain your answer.
4 Explain the traditional view of social responsibility, take a position pro or con, and defend that position.
5 Is every stakeholder a constituent? Why or why not?
6 Define *open system* and describe how a well-known organization you select is affected by events outside that organization.
7 What is the social contract? Explain some of its provisions.
8 Define *political action committee* and discuss why you believe or do not believe PACs should be legal.
9 Explain the term *future shock* and discuss how it has affected your life or explain why it has not.
10 Discuss the three effects of technological change identified by Boris Petrov.
11 If a company wins a market share because of improved technology, what is likely to happen to that market share when competitors catch up technologically? Explain your answer.
12 Discuss how the social, political, and technological facets of the environment can have an impact through the economic facet.
13 How has increasing government regulation affected the workings of competitive forces in the economy?

REFERENCES

Abernathy, William J., Kim B. Clark, and Alan M. Kantrow. "The New Industrial Competition," *Harvard Business Review*, 59:5, September/October 1981, pp. 68–81.

Bloom, Paul N., and Stephen A. Greyser. "The Maturing of Consumerism," *Harvard Business Review*, 59:6, November/December 1981, pp. 130–139.

Bowman, J. S. "Business and the Environment: Corporate Attitudes, Actions in Energy-Rich States," *MSU Business Topics*, 25:1, 1977, pp. 37–49.

Byron, William J. "In Defense of Social Responsibility," *Journal of Economics and Business*, 34:2, 1982, pp. 189–192.

"Complaints about Lawyers," *U.S. News and World Report*, July 21, 1978, p. 44.

Dunlop, John T., et al. "Business and Public Policy," *Harvard Business Review*, November/December 1979, pp. 85–102.

Fombrum, Charles, and W. Graham Astley. "Beyond Corporate Strategy," *Journal of Business Strategy*, 3:4, Spring 1983, pp. 47–54.

Fox, J. Ronald. "Breaking the Regulatory Deadlock," *Harvard Business Review*, 59:5, September/October 1981, pp. 97–105.

Friedman, Hershey H., and Linda W. Friedman. "Ethics: Everybody's Business," *Collegiate News and Views*, XXXV:2, Winter 1981–1982, pp. 11–13.

Friedman, Milton. *Capitalism and Freedom*. Chicago: University of Chicago Press, 1962.

Goodpaster, Kenneth E., and John B. Matthews, Jr. "Can a Corporation Have a Conscience?" *Harvard Business Review*, 60:1, January/February 1982, pp. 132–141.

Greer, Charles R., and H. Kirk Downey. "Industrial Compliance with Social Legislation: Investigations of Decision Rationales," *Academy of Management Review*, 7:3, July 1982, pp. 488–498.

Hartley, Robert F. *Marketing Mistakes*, 2nd ed. Columbus, Ohio: Grid Publishing, 1981.

Holmes S. L. "Executive Perceptions of Corporate Social Responsibility," *Business Horizons*, 19:3, 1976, pp. 34–40.

Jones, Thomas M., and Leonard D. Goldberg. "Governing the Large Corporation: More Arguments for Public Directors," *Academy of Management Review*, 7:4, October 1982, pp. 603–611.

Josephson, Mathew. *The Robber Barons*. New York: Harcourt Brace Jovanovich, 1934.

Leavitt, Theodore. "The Dangers of Social Responsibility," *Harvard Business Review*, 36:5, September/October 1958, pp. 41–50.

Lincoln, James F. *A New Approach to Industrial Economics*. New York: Devin Adair, 1961.

Marlow, Michael L. "The Economics of Enforcement: The Case of OSHA," *Journal of Economics and Business*, 34:2, 1982, pp. 165–171.

Ostlund, L. E. "Attitudes of Managers toward Corporate Social Responsibility," *California Management Review*, 19:4, 1977, pp. 36–49.

Petrov, Boris. "The Advent of the Technology Portfolio," *Journal of Business Strategy*, 3:2, Fall 1982, pp. 70–75.

Reich, Robert B. "Why the U.S. Needs an Industrial Policy," *Harvard Business Review*, 60:1, January/February 1982, pp. 74–81.

Smith, Adam. *The Wealth of Nations*. New York: Modern Library, originally published in 1776.

Stone, C. D. "Public Directors Merit a Try." *Harvard Business Review*, 54:2, March/April 1976, pp. 20–34, 156.

Strand, Rich. "A Systems Paradigm of Organizational Adaptations to the Social Environment," *Academy of Management Review*, 8:1, January 1983, pp. 90–96.

Tarbell, Ida. *History of Standard Oil*. New York: Harper and Row, 1905.

Toffler, Alvin. *Future Shock*. New York: Random House, 1970.

Weiss, E. J. "Governance, Disclosure, and Corporate Legitimacy," in W. R. Dill (ed.), *Running the American Corporation*. Englewood Cliffs, N.J.: Prentice-Hall, 1978, pp. 58–85.

Wren, Daniel. *The Evolution of Management Thought*, 2nd ed. New York: John Wiley, 1979.

STRATEGIC FORMULATION

FORMULATING STRATEGY AT THE CORPORATE LEVEL

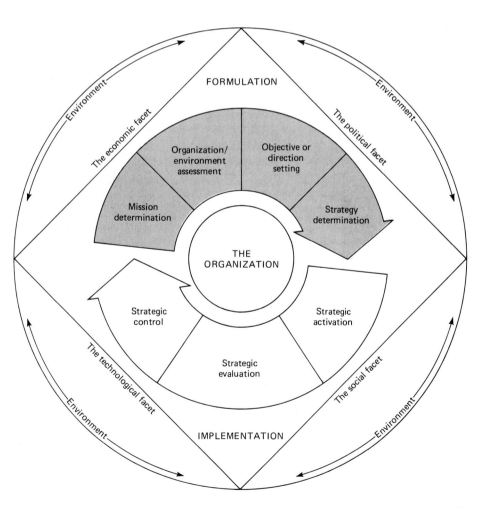

Until 1983 eight-tenths of the 180 million telephones in the United States were operated by the mammoth American Telephone and Telegraph Corporation (AT&T) through its regional subsidiaries such as South Central Bell, Southeastern Bell, and so forth. The other 35.3 million telephones were controlled by about 1500 so-called independent telephone companies. The largest of these independents is General Telephone and Electronics (GTE), with annual telephone revenues exceeding $6 billion. The independents range in size down to tiny home-operated systems in places like Oak Ridge, Louisiana, and Jack's Port, Missouri.

Century Telephone Enterprises, Inc., headquartered in Monroe, Louisiana, is the eighth largest of the independents. In 1968, the Century system included only 14,000 telephones. Today the company operates over 300,000 phones in ten midsouth states plus Idaho, Indiana, West Virginia, and Wisconsin. Century's telephone revenues for 1982 were $92 million. Its growth was accomplished primarily through the acquisition of dozens of small local companies which were included in a corporate network with Century operating as a holding company. Century now owns thirty-five telephone systems in fourteen states, as well as seven construction, service, and supply companies.

During the rapid growth phase of cable television, in 1981–1982, Century moved into that business, eventually forming or buying a total of six cable television companies in six different states. The cable television business is similar to the telephone business in a number of ways. It provides a communication service to individual subscribers through conducting wires or cables. Customers are billed on a monthly basis at standard rates plus special charges for a number of options. The business has some attributes of a natural monopoly. As in the case of telephone service, it may be impractical to have more than one or two cable television companies operating in a given city. Like telephone systems, cable television systems tend to be somewhat regulated.

In 1982 two events occurred which signaled the need for new directions at Century. First, the long-term chief executive, Clark M. Williams, Sr., moved up from his position as president and became chairman of the board. Clark M. Williams, Jr., became president of what had become a rather large "small business."

The second, and more important, event of 1982 was the enforced divestiture by AT&T of its twenty-two regional Bell operating companies, such as South Central Bell, Southeastern Bell, etc. These companies were recombined into seven independent corporations with no legal connections to AT&T or to each other. AT&T will continue to own the "long-lines" network, which facilitates long-distance calling, and will continue to sell and manufacture telephone equipment.

Clark Williams, Jr., feels that the demise of the Bell system will strongly influence the independent telephone industry for a number of years. In 1982, 52 percent of Century's telephone revenues came from long-distance calls utilizing AT&T's facilities. Century's share of long-distance revenues has in the past been determined by regulatory agencies. Now, as part of AT&T's antitrust settlement with the Justice Department, these revenues must be negotiated directly with AT&T or with whomever else furnishes the long-lines services. Clark Williams, Jr., expects those revenues to fall and says, "We must devise new strategies to replace this lost revenue."

Among the new businesses Century is considering entering is "cellular radio," primarily mobile telephone service utilizing centrally located antennae. Century is planning to expand its current $15 million investment in the cable television business.

Century has also considered expanding some of its present diversified divisions. For example, Century Computer-Phone Concepts was established in 1981 to sell computer hardware, software, and services. Century Printing and Publishing is a commercial printing company. Falcon Communications, another Century subsidiary, specializes in the "sale, rehabilitation, and installation of central office equipment by the independent telephone industry." And Century Area Long-Lines, Inc., operates one long-distance cable in Wisconsin and has the capability of expanding to other areas.

No matter which new businesses Century enters or which existing ones are expanded, added funds are likely to be needed. In the recent past more than half of the company's capital expenditures have been financed internally. A 2.2 million share common stock issue provided added equity funds in 1982. Century has bank credit lines of $7 million. In addition, Century has available $10 million in approved funding from the Rural Electrication Administration (REA). REA, a quasi-governmental agency, provides funds for regulated utilities, such as electric and telephone companies. Since the REA funds are the lowest-cost source, Century applied for $39 million of additional REA funds to be used either for expansion or for retirement of present debt.

Clark Williams, Jr., and other organizational strategists at Century are concerned at once with each of the three levels of strategic management. At the *corporate or enterprise* level, they must determine the overall character of the company and decide whether to concentrate on the telephone business, expand certain of their other divisions, or enter entirely new businesses. Century's top managers must also create and manage synergies among businesses (Yavitz and Newman, 1982, p. 17). Perhaps this management of synergies is the greatest challenge Mr. Williams faces. Clearly, it is a "whole new ballgame," but Century may have certain advantages. Century's management believes that the company is large enough to have better access to resources and technology than its smaller competitors, yet small enough to avoid the bureaucratic inflexibilities of its larger competitors, including the previous Bell subsidiaries. Strategic management is in large part a matter of identifying and taking advantage of such strengths.

At the *SBU* level, Century must compete in its present primary business, the provision of telephone services to subscribers. The problem has just grown more complex. Century's main competitor, "Ma Bell," has been broken up into seven independent companies. In addition, Century has undergone several years of rapid growth, absorbing dozens of smaller telephone systems.

At the *functional* level, Century must determine how to finance any capital investment the company chooses to make. Of course, functional-level strategies are also necessary in the areas of personnel, production, and marketing. Century's strategists must be vigilant and active in those areas as well.

Let us turn now to the focus of this chapter, strategic planning at the *corporate* level. We will first describe the process of strategy formulation. Then we will discuss several tools which are available to the corporate-level strategist. In the final section of the chapter, a number of "grand strategies" will be described and their usefulness evaluated.

THE PROCESS OF STRATEGY FORMULATION

First, let us make it clear that strategy formulation is planning. Yet, all plans are not strategies. **Strategies** are *plans concerning matters of pervasive, vital, and/or continuing importance within the organization.* They are usually broad-based and relatively long-range.

Strategic planning can be represented as shown in Figure 3.1. The figure illustrates a simple sequential process, but planning does not often occur that way. In most

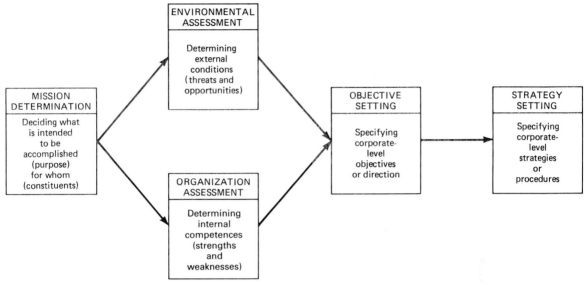

FIGURE 3.1   Formulating strategy

organizations, all the steps are occurring at any one time. Emphasis at Century Telephone may be upon analyzing the environment. However, this does not mean that the organizational strategists, like Clark Williams, Jr., can avoid considering the company's existing objectives and possible changes in them. It is important to remember that the planning process is both nonsequential and iterative. That is, the steps do not always occur in the order shown and the process—or parts of it—is repeated a number of times. Still, it is useful to think of strategy formulation in a systematic way. Let us look at the individual steps as if they follow one after the other.

Mission Determination

Webster's Third New International Dictionary defines *mission* as "a continuing task or responsibility that one is destined or fitted to do or specially called upon to undertake: like work, vocation." In a military sense the term is defined this way: "a major continuing duty assigned to a military service or command as part of its function in the national military establishment." Mission is often thought of as the *raison d'etre*, or reason for existence. In this text, **mission** will be taken to mean *the organization's continuing purposes with regard to certain categories of persons—in short, what is to be accomplished for whom?*

Every organization affects the interests of a diverse array of *stakeholders*. But most managers acknowledge only a limited number of stakeholder groups as *constituents*. The three most commonly recognized constituents are owners, customers, and employees. We will discuss them in order.

Owners as Constituents Most businesses are started by entrepreneurs to make money. Clark Williams, Sr., founder of Century Telephone, went into business for this purpose many years ago. As the sole owner, Williams was the only constituency. And making money (in the long and/or short term) was the central purpose. No one else claimed the right to tell Williams how to run the business. And no one demanded that his business be run for their benefit. Recall that the American free enterprise system is based upon the premise that, in pursuing essentially private interests, businesses, without necessarily meaning to, serve the economic interests of society. So, single-mindedly seeking profit for himself was a responsible thing for Williams to do. He recognized, of course, that he had to provide value to customers. But this was a strategy for earning profits, not an end in itself.

When Williams decided to "take the company public," a new group of stakeholders was created. These were the common shareholders, most of whom purchased stock because they believed it to be a good investment. Economic purists would suggest that common shareholders simply stand in the place of the owner/entrepreneur and have precisely the same claim on the company. However, it is clear that shareholders, at least in most publicly held companies, take little interest in company operations, viewing their stock purchases only as financial investments. Rarely do stockholders attend annual meetings or participate in any significant way in the governance of the corporation. In a way, they do vote—by selling or buying the company's stock. However, they usually base this "vote" entirely upon expected price and dividend performance. So the position of owners as sole constituents is not as clear for publicly owned corporations as for closely held ones.

Yet, the common shareholders are generally considered to be the primary constituency of corporate management. There are others, such as employees, who have a much larger stake in the company's performance, but they are not usually given as much allegiance. To the extent that stockholders desire only financial gain from the business, there are only two things which corporate strategists can do for them: (1) increase the amount of dividends and other payments to owners, and (2) increase the value of each share of company stock.

But the share price should reflect expected dividend patterns. Financial theorists tell us that the decision as to whether to pay out company profits as dividends or to invest them within the company should be based upon whether the stockholder or the company has an investment which will pay the higher after-tax return (considering both personal and corporate taxes). Since dividends are taxable as unearned personal income to stockholders and reinvested retained earnings avoid the personal income tax, many experts believe dividends are seldom justified. In any case, stockholders who prefer dividends are likely to bid up the share prices for companies which pay them. Thus, the share price should reflect the present value of expected dividends, as well as the present value of expected returns from the investment of retained earnings. The reasoning is that the earnings will either be paid out in dividends or reinvested in order to produce more earnings, whichever will produce the higher return for the shareholders. It seems reasonable to assert that corporate strategists, if they represent only the common shareholders' financial interests, should concern themselves mainly with increasing the share price of the company's stock.

The share price represents the present value of all expected cash flows from the company. Theoretically, this includes the value of the company's existing net assets plus all expected future earnings. Even though the company may never be liquidated, the stockholders, in the aggregate, have the right to liquidate it. So, the present value of the company's expected net assets at any future time must be included in the stock price even if no dividends are ever paid.

Even if financial markets are not efficient, maximizing the stock price is a reasonable goal. If the stock market price is lower than the real value of the business, the company's value can be enhanced by purchasing its own shares on the open market. If the stock market overvalues the firm, issuing additional equity securities and paying off debt will increase the firm's value. Some have even suggested that unrestricted insider trading, now generally prohibited, might make the stock market more efficient (Seligman, 1983). Managers, knowing the company's value better than outsiders do, would buy or sell shares when the stock market value varied from what they believed was the actual value.

Customers as Constituents It is common to seem to place the customer first by saying something like, ''Only through serving customers can a company exist and prosper in the long run.'' If ''exist and prosper'' means provide a high return to shareholders in future years, then serving the shareholder is the primary goal and the customer is merely a means to that end. Let us consider the difficulties of serving customers in meaningful ways.

If the customers are the primary constituency, there are only two things the organization strategist can offer: (1) a lower price for a given quality and quantity of good or service, and (2) a higher quality or quantity of good or service for a given price. Simply offering low price and quality or high price and quality is not performing a service to the customer, who undoubtedly has other ways to obtain such *average* value. In this context, **quality** means *the degree of excellence of the entire bundle of goods and services offered the customer*. It can be thought of as the degree to which purchase of the company's products and services improves the customer's quality of life. For example, a company which sells an item with a very low failure rate but has no service organization may be offering lower quality than a company with an excellent service organization but twice the failure rate. A company with a service-oriented sales force which ensures that the customer's product selection matches actual customer needs is offering higher quality than a company which sells an identical product line but to whomever will buy it.

Price, too, should be broadly construed. The term means ''*the cost at which something is obtained*'' (*Webster's Third New International Dictionary*). In some parts of the country, farmers sell fruits and vegetables in the field. The ''price'' is lower than that available in supermarkets. However, to purchase a bag of apples from the supermarket, a homemaker may have to drive a block or two and pay the store cashier perhaps $3.00. On the other hand, the homemaker might drive ten miles, climb an apple tree, and pick the apples, paying a farmer only $1.00 for them. The customer's cost in this case is probably much higher. The *price*, in the sense used here, includes not only the $1.00 paid the apple grower but also the cost of the gasoline and wear and tear on the car, as well as the value of the homemaker's time. It still may be that the homemaker has received a bargain in the farm-fresh apples. The opportunity to enjoy fresh air and sunshine along with the absolute knowledge that the apples are fresh may be worth much more than the added costs. But the price is higher. By making available farm-grown produce, the farmer may in fact be offering higher quality for a higher price.

In general, it is difficult to serve customers as a primary constituency, either through higher quality or quantity or through lower prices. If the price is lower than the market demands, then the product will have to be rationed, thereby becoming of lower average quality to customers. In fact, to those customers who are prevented from obtaining the product it has zero quality. It is possible, of course, to give preference to one customer over another—to give a relative a 50 percent discount, for example. However, it is very difficult to offer much more than the market requires for customers in general. When the owner of Village Hardware in St. Louis decided that every home should have a smoke alarm, he learned this lesson well. He offered smoke alarms at below cost, 50 percent lower than prices elsewhere in St. Louis. Nearly 200 people were at his door the morning the sale began, and he was out of smoke alarms before noon. Many customers were inconvenienced, by either having to wait in line for the product or having to drive a significant distance only to find that they were to receive zero quality, that is, no product at all. Only when goods and services are rationed (or the number of customers limited) can the customers' interest actually be the primary goal of corporate strategists. Even then, the goal must be to serve the interests of some selected group of customers and not those of customers in general.

Employees as Constituents A similar dilemma arises when strategists attempt to represent employees. Strategists can offer employees better pay and benefits for a given level of work demands or lessened work demands for a given level of pay and benefits. As used here, ***pay and benefits*** means *the net monetary value to the employee of everything the organization provides the employee, including wages, working conditions, health care, job security, social relationships, and so forth.* And ***work demands*** refers to *the net monetary value to the employee of everything the organization demands of the employee, mainly the employee's attendance and mental and physical work effort.* High pay and benefits–high work demands (a "Calvinistic" shop) or low pay and benefits–low work demands (a "siesta" shop) is no favor to the workers.

Just as it is possible to serve a certain group of customers with relatively high quality at a relatively low price, it is possible to serve a certain group of employees by giving them greater pay and benefits or placing fewer demands upon them than the market requires. The Lincoln Electric Company, for example, pays its employees an average of about twice the going rate for similar work and offers them lifetime job security as well. However, only about 10 percent of those who apply for Lincoln jobs get them. And there is always a very long list of applicants.

Several years ago, General Motors (GM) built a modern headlamp factory in Monroe, Louisiana. The plant was to employ about 800 local people. Partly to avoid a unionizing attempt, General Motors intended to pay about twice the prevailing wage rates in the Monroe area. Before the factory was completed, there were thousands of applicants. Many attempted to use political influence, relationships with friends, and so forth, to try to get the choice jobs. The workers who were eventually employed did receive higher benefits and wages than the market demanded. But thousands of other prospective employees, who would have done the same work for less pay, were denied that opportunity.

Because of the complexities involved in attempting to serve potential employees in any significant way, many corporate strategists, such as those at Lincoln Electric, identify their present employees as the constituent group. Sometimes management has no choice in the matter. Employees often form unions, and management is forced to bargain with the union over benefits and work demands. In these cases, the union and/ or the company limits access to the jobs involved so that benefits above those demanded in the labor market can be paid to these select few. Unionized workers constitute about one-sixth of the U.S. work force. In general, they receive better benefits and experience lower work demands than the other five-sixths. They are thus subsidized by their nonunion counterparts.

Of course, when a company pays more than the market demands for inputs and sells its outputs in a free market, it is at a relative disadvantage. That is why the U.S. auto industry is not able to compete in world markets without tariffs and import restrictions. Industrywide collective bargaining has resulted in unit wage costs above what free markets would require and well above those of foreign competition. The present "big four" auto makers would not even be able to compete in U.S. markets if nonunion competitors could arise. However, organizational strategists for companies capable of entering the U.S. auto market would expect that the combined forces of government and industrial unionism would prevent a new competitor from remaining nonunion for any period of time.

The Corporate Mission: General Comments   There are a large number of categories of stakeholders. They are all potential constituents of corporate management. The major stakeholder groups were listed in Table 2.2. Corporate strategists may choose to serve any or all stakeholders. Most acknowledge obligations to common shareholders, customers, and employees. What is important is that they think through what is entailed in representing each potential constituent group.

This text is not about strategic management only as it is expressed in annual reports or press releases. (For an interesting discussion of the four "strata" of strategy, from that which is publicized to that which the chief executive comprehends, see Andrews, 1981.) It is about the actual process of strategic management as it is and should be carried out. Therefore, it is appropriate to consider the corporate mission in terms of this question: What does the strategist intend (not just desire) to accomplish for whom? The corporate strategist who subscribes to traditional economic principles will choose (or be forced) to deliver what the market requires and little more. Especially ethical strategists may engage in "open and free competition without deception or fraud" (Friedman, 1962, p. 133). In general, the market will require a "reasonable return" to the common shareholder in the form of present and expected earnings. For customers, the price of the product or service must reflect its quality as customers define quality.

For employees, working conditions in accord with both the spirit and letter of safety and health legislation should be provided. Monetary compensation must be adequate to obtain required labor inputs and above limits set by minimum wage laws. Total benefits should be designed to maintain the optimum relationship between the cost of producing the product or service and the quality of that product or service.

WOTS-Up

Before discussing environmental assessment and organizational assessment (immediately following this section), it is useful to provide a framework for analysis. A common approach is to make assessments in terms of the strengths and weaknesses of the organization and the opportunities and threats it faces in the environment. This is often called *WOTS-Up* analysis.

Strengths and Weaknesses   *Strengths* are *internal competencies possessed by the organization in comparison with its competitors.* Strengths may be based upon the capabilities, contacts, and motivation of the organization's personnel—in other words, what they know, who they know, and how much effort they will put forth. Strengths may also result from the quality of physical facilities, attributes of the organizational structure, or financial resources and structure. If the organization excels in comparison with its competitors in any of these areas, this represents a strength. If the organization is deficient in any way when compared with its competitors, that deficiency is a weakness. *Weaknesses* are *attributes of the organization which tend to decrease its competence in comparison with its competitors.*

At the corporate level, strengths and weaknesses tend to be defined in terms of the company's ability to make valid portfolio decisions (deciding what businesses to enter or leave), resource allocation decisions (determining the types and amounts of support to give to subunits), and decisions concerning the management of synergies among subunits.

Every organization has both strengths and weaknesses. Managers tend to be well aware of the strengths of their organizations, but less knowledgeable about their weaknesses. In a study of fifty managers in six diverse companies, H. H. Stevenson (1976) determined that strengths tended to be clearly recognized and documented with historical data, but few managers were able to describe their weaknesses in an objective way and few relevant data concerning the identified weaknesses were available. Perhaps more is to be gained from a thorough understanding of organizational weaknesses than from attempting to enhance what is already a clear recognition of strengths.

Opportunities and Threats   Just as organizational assessment should reveal the strengths and weaknesses of the organization, environmental assessment is aimed at determining the threats faced by the organization and the opportunities available to it. A *threat* is *a reasonably probable event which, if it were to occur, would produce significant damage to the organization.* An *opportunity*, on the other hand, is *a combination of circumstances, time, and place which, if accompanied by a certain* *course of action on the part of the organization, is likely to produce significant benefits.* Threats are often defined in terms of the organization's competitors, while opportunities are usually thought of in terms of new technologies and new markets. For example, the major manufacturers of personal computers, Apple, Commodore, and Radio Shack, saw IBM's introduction of the PC, Jr. (or Peanut) personal computer in early 1984 as a major *threat.* IBM, already dominant at the upper end of the personal computer market, was apparently about to overwhelm competitors at the lower end. Texas Instruments had already dropped out, and the others were facing a head-to-head battle with ''Big Blue,'' a name not so affectionately given to the world's largest manufacturer of computers.

At about the same time, Coleco, already a major competitor in the video games market, was pursuing an *opportunity* to market a competent integrated computer system at the very low end of the personal computer market. Coleco's Adam personal computer, initially priced at just over $600, included a printer, a disk drive, and other features which had theretofore been extra-cost options on low-priced personal computers. Adam represented new technology for Coleco, and the demand for an integrated low-cost computer was creating a new market.

When companies take advantage of opportunities, as IBM and Coleco tried to do, competitors often feel threatened. Consider how technological innovations can produce opportunities and threats. According to Petrov (1982, p. 71) technology can ''(1) change relative cost positions within a business, (2) create new markets and new business segments, (3) collapse or merge previously independent businesses by reducing or eliminating their segment cost barriers.'' Examples abound: the IBM ball-element typewriter, the Norelco minicassette dictating equipment, certain Hewlett-Packard programmable calculators, and the highly efficient Boeing 767 passenger airplane. Technological innovations include new ways of forming concrete developed by U.S. Industries, Inc., in Ohio; the application of plasma-arc welding to metal pipe manufacturing introduced by Cabot Corporation of Kokomo, Indiana; the use of wedges to make trees fall in the desired direction when they are cut; the use of tarpaulins to keep cotton dry in Texas cotton fields; and the use of smudge pots to protect Florida orange groves from frost bite. All these innovations were threats to competitors when they were introduced. Of course, they represented the grasping of opportunities by the innovators. The great economist Joseph Schumpeter (1883–1950) felt that technological innovation was the driving force behind economic progress (Drucker, 1983, p. 126).

Applying WOTS-Up to Miller Brewing, Nucor Steel, and K-Mart   In the early seventies, Philip Morris Corporation purchased Miller Brewing. Miller had been slowly going downhill for some years, apparently because of management's inability to adjust (a weakness) to the emergence of national beer marketers such as Anheuser-Busch and Schlitz (a threat). Because of its extensive marketing expertise Philip Morris was able to turn Miller around (an opportunity), revolutionizing the beer industry in the process (another opportunity, since the change was to Miller's benefit). As a result of the introduction of Miller Lite and the Miller Pony, market segmentation, and aggressive advertising, Miller expanded its market share severalfold.

In 1969 Nucor Steel Company was only a small producer (a weakness, in this industry) of steel bar joists. But Nucor saw an opportunity to compete with the major integrated steel companies in making certain steel products. Nucor began to process scrap steel into small shapes, such as round bars and angles, in what came to be called "minimills." The minimills could be built at relatively low costs (a strength), because they did not have to process iron ore into steel. They only had to melt steel and roll it into various shapes. In addition, Nucor's labor costs were low (a strength). The company was able to avoid unionization (a threat) by the United Steel Workers, whose members cost more than $26 per hour in 1982. The minimills were located in rural areas where the traditional work ethic was strong (a strength) and where unionism was weak. Nucor had the additional advantage that part of the output from the minimills could be used in the company's joist-making operations (a strength). By 1983 Nucor enjoyed half-billion-dollar annual sales and good profitability, although the integrated steel producers like U.S. Steel and Bethlehem were suffering huge losses. In fact, things are so bad for the integrated producers that U.S. Steel plans to concentrate on other businesses. Steel-related assets are expected to account for only 48 percent of U.S. Steel's assets portfolio by 1990 (Kirkland, 1981, p. 31). So Big Steel responds to the threats foreign and domestic competitors pose, while Nucor exploits opportunities in the same market.

Many opportunities are not so remarkable as those found by Nucor. In evaluating environmental information, strategists should look for ways to expand sales in existing markets, cut costs, open up new markets, develop new uses for existing products, add value to existing products, and so forth. When K-Mart, America's largest discount retailer, looked for ways to bolster profits in 1981, a number of less-than-glamorous opportunities were found. Stores were remodeled, ways were discovered to restock shelves faster, and warehouse labor was cut by half. Point-of-sale terminals were planned to tie K-Mart's 20,000 checkout counters to a central computer in Troy, Michigan. In general, the opportunity K-Mart found by observing other discounters was to cut costs, especially overhead costs, while improving value (Main, 1981). According to M. G. Wellman, K-Mart's planning chief, the opportunity-grasping effort has only just begun.

Now, hopefully with a firmer grasp of what environmental and organizational assessments should assess, let us take a closer look at those processes.

Environmental Assessment

After corporate strategists have contemplated the corporate mission and, hopefully, expressed it in writing, it is important to scan the environment to determine external conditions, threats, and opportunities. Note from Figure 3.1 that concurrently with this process an organizational assessment should be performed. This subsection is devoted to environmental assessment, and organizational assessment is the topic of the next subsection.

Environmental assessment requires two activities: (1) information gathering, and (2) evaluation. As previously pointed out, the job of the strategist is to effectively relate the organization to its environment. Environmental assessment helps to determine the relationship as it exists. The purpose of the environmental assessment by itself is simply to determine external conditions and, more particularly, to identify any threats or opportunities.

Relevant Information Only Of course, in seeking information the corporate strategist should not do so randomly. Only information which is relevant should be obtained. Bower (1982, p. 32) suggests that the corporate manager explore:

- The political, social, and economic structure of the countries (or other political subdivisions) in which the firm operates
  - The individual markets which supply its raw materials and purchase its products
  - The behavior of competitors
  - The technology of the industry and potentially competitive or complementary industries

Like every one else in today's information age, the strategist often suffers from information overload. To avoid this, it is important to impose some structure on the information-gathering process. The extent of information-processing capabilities varies greatly for different companies. GE has a corporate planning staff of over 100 persons and an extensive computer network. In addition to this, unlike most corporations, GE has a board of directors which is actively involved in strategy formulation (Andrews, 1981, p. 175). The typical small entrepreneur has only a clerk or two and perhaps no computer at all. So, the amount and types of data obtained from outside the company must be compatible with the needs and information-processing capability of the organization.

Never Enough Information As a general guide, strategists should always be prepared to make decisions with inadequate information. There will seldom be a time when the strategist cannot think of something that needs to be researched before a decision is made. Yet, it is often true that an approximately correct decision made today is better than a perfect one made a year or two from now. One way strategists can be better prepared for quick decision making is by thinking through various scenarios, especially those the environmental assessment suggests are most likely (Hamilton, 1981, p. 82).

Published Sources The sources of information about matters external to the organization are virtually unlimited. Table 3.1 provides a list of a number of sources. This list is intended only to provide examples. Far more comprehensive compendia of environmental information are referenced at the end of this chapter (Gouldner and Kirks, 1976; DeCarbonnel and Donance, 1973).

Espionage Within the bounds of legality and ethics, corporate strategists should use every means at their disposal to obtain information which will be useful in guiding the organization. This may include industrial espionage, to the extent that *espionage* means secret but legal and morally justified observation. Research to determine why a competitor's customers trade with the competitor falls into this category. Grocers

TABLE 3.1   SOURCES OF ENVIRONMENTAL INFORMATION

1 *Bibliography of Publications of University Bureaus of Business and Economic Research*, University of Colorado
2 *Business Education Index*, McGraw-Hill
3 *Business Periodicals Index*, H. W. Wilson
4 *Census of Manufacturers*, U.S. Government
5 *Census of Wholesale Trade*, U.S. Government
6 *Commercial Atlas and Marketing Guide*, Rand McNally
7 *County and City Data Book*, U.S. Government
8 *Directory of Corporate Affiliations*, National Register Publishing
9 *Encyclopedia of Associations*, Gale Research
10 *Encyclopedia of Business Information Sources*, Gale Research
11 *F & S Index of Corporations and Industries*, Predicasts
12 *Federal Reserve Bulletin*, U.S. Government
13 *Guide to American Directories*, Prentice-Hall
14 *Monthly Catalog of U.S. Government Publications*, U.S. Government
15 *Monthly Checklist of State Publications*, U.S. Government
16 *Moody's Industrial Manual*, Moody's Investor Service
17 *Reference Book of Corporate Managements*, Dun and Bradstreet
18 *Reference Book of Dun and Bradstreet*, Dun and Bradstreet
19 *Standard and Poor's Register of Corporation Directors and Executives*, Standard and Poor's
20 *Statistical Abstract of the United States*, U.S. Government
21 *The New York Times Index*, New York Times Company
22 *Thomas Register of American Manufacturers*, Thomas Publishing

frequently visit competing stores to see what items are on special so that the same items can be promoted by the spying store. Acquisition-minded companies need to know which merger consultant takeover candidates are using.

Fortune magazine (Flax, 1984) recently provided the following list of ways companies "snoop" on competitors, admitting that some of the approaches are "utterly sleazy":

Milking potential recruits
Picking brains at conferences
Conducting phony job interviews
Hiring people away from competitors
Interviewing competitors
Encouraging key customers to talk
Getting customers to put out phony bid requests
Grilling suppliers
Pumping buyers
Studying aerial photographs
Obtaining Freedom of Information Act filings
Taking plant tours
Taking competitors' products apart
Buying competitors' garbage

Employment Practices   Another way of obtaining information about the external environment is through employment practices. For example, regulated businesses frequently hire ex-government officials who have worked for the respective regulatory agencies. This is an effective way of learning about the inner workings of government. As suggested above, many companies hire managers, scientists, and others from among competitors, customers, and suppliers. These individuals bring with them a great deal of important information about their previous employers.

Trade Associations   Another vital source of information about the external environment is trade associations. These range from the National Association of Manufacturers, with many thousands of members and an annual budget in the millions, to small local associations of general contractors, which cooperatively accept bids from subcontractors.

The major trade associations usually collect and summarize extensive data on a number of organizations. The National Welding Supply Association (NWSA), for example, publishes extensive financial data on welding products distributors every year. Reviewing the NWSA report, the strategist for an individual welding supply house is able to compare that company's financial statements and ratios with the average for companies all across the country.

Many associations publish monthly or quarterly journals, such as *Mortgage Banking*, issued by the Mortgage Bankers Association, and *The Builder*, published by the American Association of Home Builders. Reading these kinds of publications helps the corporate strategist to stay abreast of much that relates to strategic management.

Finally, trade associations conduct meetings where specialists make presentations about certain aspects of the business. At these meetings, it is possible to make contact with others in the same business, though not in direct competition. In many cases, managers are eager to tell what has proven successful for them in the past, especially if they are asked for the information in an appreciative way.

Organizational Assessment

The organizational assessment, like the environmental assessment, consists of two phases: information gathering and evaluation. Sources of information within the organization are much clearer and usually more reliable than those outside.

The Return-on-Investment Model   Perhaps the most widely used system of obtaining and assessing internal information is the return-on-investment (ROI) approach. **Return on investment** is defined as *the percentage return earned on assets employed by a business unit*. Depending on the financial theories to which strategists subscribe *return* may mean net profit, net profit plus interest, or any of several other earnings measures. With the ROI approach, financial information is collected from each organization subunit and the ROI computed for that subunit. Then, management is evaluated and resources are allocated in accordance with ROI criteria. This requires that the asset value be strictly calculated along with realistic expense and sales figures.

With the use of the ROI model, it is possible to systematically gather information and objectively evaluate that information for each subunit and for the organization as a whole. This model is built around the following formula:

$$\text{Return on sales} \times \text{asset turnover} = \text{ROI}$$

ROI as a tool of SBU management is discussed in Chapter 4.

Limitations of Purely Financial Data   Few corporate managements would be happy with total reliance upon financial data. Particularly, financial data may not reveal the company's long-term strengths and weaknesses. Many agree that the most vital asset most companies possess is their investment in personnel. While recruiting, training, and developing costs appear as expenses on the income statement, the value of the resulting asset is not shown on the balance sheet. So ROI calculations tend to oppose this most vital kind of investment. It is necessary for the organizational strategist who wishes to do a good job to obtain information about personnel matters. In fact, the strategic management information system should look for strengths and weaknesses in the areas of marketing, production, and personnel, as well as in finance.

The Need for Focus   It is best not to "run off in all directions" in gathering internal information. Corporate strategists should determine their own strengths and weaknesses and the strengths and weaknesses of the organization in comparison with those of other strategists and similar organizations. The purpose of this is not to find out who is best but to find out how to manage better. Bower (1982, p. 33) recommends focusing on the following internal factors: (1) resources, (2) values (of managers), (3) structure, and (4) style. The McKinsey "Seven S" framework, discussed later in this chapter, provides another way to structure the information-gathering process.

Using Organizational and Environmental Information

Resources should be allocated to minimize the impact of weaknesses, avoid threats, and apply strengths to take advantage of opportunities which have been discovered in the environmental assessment. For example, in 1982, BIC strategists determined that the company had great strength in mass production and advertising, having been successful in manufacturing and marketing low-priced ballpoint pens for many years. BIC then began to manufacture and market safety razors of the low-cost disposable variety, and the company found tremendous success in that area.

An organizational strategist might identify a high degree of organization and control ability among its top managers. It may be that opportunity exists in the area of acquiring poorly managed companies. Companies with strength in R&D might acquire others with a need for product development. A company with stable cash-producing divisions might buy another with an exciting new product which requires investment to get it going.

The most important result of an organizational assessment is acquiring a knowledge of the organization's strengths and weaknesses. Like the environmental assessment, it should be a continuous process. Together, the two provide a framework for the setting of objectives.

Objective or Direction Setting

Stating objectives explicitly and directing all activities toward their attainment is certainly not the only approach to strategic management. It may not even be the best approach for some organizations at certain times. However, since Peter Drucker coined the phrase ''management by objectives'' in the 1950s, it has been generally accepted that specific, measurable objectives improve the process of management. This is no less true at the corporate level of strategic management than it is for the miler who wishes to better the existing world record. There are two essential characteristics of effective objectives.

First, objectives should be challenging but attainable. If the miler mentioned above were capable of running near world-record speed but were to set an objective of a five-minute mile, it could be easily achieved. However, the miler would probably not run at maximum speed. On the other hand, if the objective were set at three minutes, no one in the world could come close. Anyone who attempted it would be frustrated. Corporate objectives, too, should offer a reasonable opportunity for accomplishment. The probability of accomplishment should not be zero, to avoid frustration, and it should not be nearly 100 percent, to avoid suboptimum performance.

Second, objectives should be specific, preferably quantifiable, and measurable. An objective to ''maximize profits'' offers little specific guidance. ''To earn $1.2 million in profits or to increase profit by 5 percent over last year's level'' is a specific objective. The more specific objectives are, the more definite can be the strategies designed to accomplish them.

Herbert Simon (1960) has suggested that managers in general do not attempt to optimize or maximize corporate results. He believes that the term ''satisficing'' more correctly describes what managers do. According to Simon's theory, managers typically accept the first satisfactory outcome they are offered. For example, the manager who believes that 10 percent is a reasonable ROI is likely to approve any ROI objective which exceeds 10 percent. If Simon is right, any corporate strategist may be more concerned with establishing direction than with setting specific objectives. As long as this year's sales and profits are above last year's, that may be acceptable because the direction is upward. There are many effective organizations which have never set specific objectives. In fact, there are some that have only a vague understanding of the direction in which they are headed. However, it appears likely that any organization can improve its performance by setting objectives which are challenging but obtainable and specific, preferably quantified.

Strategy Setting

Once objectives are set, or a direction is determined, strategies or plans for accomplishing these objectives should be made. For many organizations, written strategic plans are limited to financial budgets. And some don't even have budgets. However, most authorities consider it worthwhile to reduce strategies to writing. Whether strategies are written or not, it is the function of the organizational strategists to clearly enunciate how the organization intends to accomplish its goals. Before the strategy can be stated, however, it must be determined.

A major focus of corporate-level strategy is upon merger and acquisition, divestiture, and liquidation activity. A **merger** is simply *the combination of two or more business units*. An **acquisition** is *the purchase of one company or subunit by another*. Two companies may combine to form a third company. Or, one company might acquire the common stock of another, the assets and liabilities, or just the assets. The possibilities are endless. **Divestiture** means *ridding the organization of an asset or subunit, usually by selling it*. **Liquidation** means *converting an asset, subunit, or the entire organization to cash*. When a unit is liquidated, the debts of that unit are usually paid and any surplus dispersed.

Remember that the purpose of corporate-level strategy is to determine what businesses to go into and the relative allocation of resources and management of synergies among them. The distinction between corporate-level and business-level strategy is made largely for expository purposes. As noted, before, there is no essential difference between buying a business (a corporate-level strategy) and buying any other asset (usually a business-level strategy). Also, individual assets, whether SBUs or machines, cannot be considered in isolation. Still, it is usual and, we believe, useful to treat corporate-level strategic management separately. Let us now turn to several approaches available for determining corporate-level strategies.

SOME TOOLS OF CORPORATE-LEVEL STRATEGIC MANAGEMENT

Before discussing the tools of corporate-level strategists, it is helpful to review the definition of a SBU. Recall that the SBU is a segment of the overall organization which is distinguished from other segments for strategic management purposes. The SBU usually has an identifiable group of employees, customers, suppliers, and so forth. A SBU is usually considered a separate business. SBUs are often autonomously managed.

The Boston Consulting Group Matrix

During the 1970s there were a number of attempts to rationalize the process of corporate-level strategic management. Recent research shows that half or more of America's largest corporations practice some kind of formal business portfolio planning (Haspeslagh, 1982, p. 63). Most of them use any of a number of two-dimensional matrices. These business portfolio grids were each designed to display various attributes of a diversified corporation's group of businesses (or SBUs) in a concise way. The best known is that developed by the Boston Consulting Group (BCG). The BCG matrix is illustrated in Figure 3.2. Each circle on the BCG matrix represents a different SBU. The area of each circle is proportional to the sales revenue of the respective business.

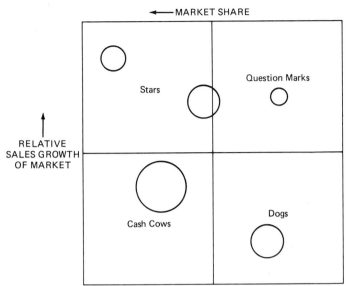

FIGURE 3.2 The BCG matrix

The relative position of a circle along the horizontal axis is determined by the respective SBU's market share as compared to that of the largest rival firm. It is most useful to think of this market share in the relevant market area. For example, Danny's Pizza Company of Phoenix, Arizona, has less than one-hundredth of 1 percent of the fast food business in the United States. Among pizza restaurants, Danny's percentage market share is several times that, perhaps one-fourth of 1 percent. However, among pizza restaurants in Phoenix, the relevant market area, Danny's has a 20 percent market share, more than that of its closest rival. It would thus be plotted near the left side of the BCG matrix.

The vertical axis of the BCG matrix measures market growth rate, not the growth rate in sales of the individual business. A business gaining a market share is growing more rapidly than the market in general. The rate of growth of Danny's Pizza has recently been about 30 percent a year. Still Danny's would fall near the vertical center of the BCG matrix—representing the rate of growth of the pizza business in Phoenix, about 10 percent.

An implicit assumption of the BCG analysis is that a market share in a given business signifies strength and that the market growth rate signifies opportunity. Businesses with high market shares in high-growth-rate industries are given the favorable designation, "Stars." Theoretically, they offer the best profit and growth opportunities for the company. SBUs with low market shares in low-growth industries are called "Dogs," because their market shares suggest competitive weakness and because the slow industry growth rates suggest approaching market saturation.

The major focus of the BCG analysis is upon cash flows. It is theorized that SBUs which hold high market shares in low-growth industries should not be expanding investment rapidly (because there are better investments available). The high market shares, BCG analysts reason, should allow those businesses to earn profits. Research suggests that the profitability of such companies depends mostly on employee productivity, capital utilization, and pricing policies, not added investment (MacMillan, Hambrick, and Day, 1982, pp. 752–754). Since there is no need for added investment in the business, the profits can be used to finance the corporation's other businesses, particularly Stars. So businesses which plot in the lower left-hand quadrant of the BCG matrix are called "Cash Cows."

Usually when a company enters a new business, it at first has a low market share. If the business segment is growing rapidly, like the home computer industry recently has, any new entry faces an uncertain future. So, low-market-share businesses in high-growth industries are called "Question Marks" on the BCG matrix. Typically, they require large amounts of cash for further development into Stars. Sometimes a new business grows so rapidly and is so profitable that, although technically a Question Mark, it can generate the cash flows required for growth.

The corporate-level strategist who subscribes to the BCG approach must ask, "What are the strategic implications for the corporation as a whole? What does BCG analysis say about resource allocation among businesses and about disposition of the various SBUs?" First, BCG proponents argue, the corporation's overall cash flow must be balanced. There should be enough Cash Cows in the business portfolio to fund the cash needs of the Stars and Question Marks offering the greatest promise. Second, the BCG clearly feels that positions on the BCG matrix imply certain strategies. Divestiture or liquidation is recommended for Dogs and perhaps weak Cash Cows. Growth is the right path for Question Marks and Stars and extraction of the investment for Cash Cows. Some researchers feel that resource allocation is an important but often ignored use of the BCG matrix and other business portfolio grids (Gluck, 1981; Haspeslagh, 1982). In other words, BCG analysis, they feel, should not be limited to buy-sell and invest-disinvest decisions but should be used to distribute funds within the corporation.

The BCG approach may be too simplistic. In a free market, economic forces should cause business entities (SBUs) shown on a corporation's BCG matrix to flow to their best use. If a Cash Cow is needed by the parent corporation to fund a particular Question Mark business, the first inclination would be to keep the Cash Cow. However, if other corporations have more severe cash needs or better opportunities to use the cash flow from the Cash Cow (or if they have a higher estimation of what that cash flow is likely to be), the price of the Cash Cow may be bid up in financial markets. If at any point a business unit is of higher value to someone outside the corporation than to the parent company, the business unit should be sold—even though it is a Cash Cow (or a Star, for that matter).

If a certain business is a Question Mark, a strategist might initially recommend growing it into a Star or divesting it. However, if it is a Question Mark in one corporation's portfolio, it is likely to be a Question Mark for other corporations.

Consequently, that SBU will be priced very low in the financial markets. So, even if the parent corporation does not have the funds to grow the Question Mark into a Star, it might be best to simply hold it, especially if the Question Mark business requires little of the corporation's management resources.

Some corporations have a number of Question Mark businesses at any point in time. The decision might be made to invest heavily in those offering the greatest promise, while divesting or holding others. On the other hand, if a corporation has a Star which has superior promise, it might be a reasonable strategy to divest or place on hold all Question Mark businesses so that attention can be concentrated upon the Star. It also might be a good strategy to divest all Cash Cows to obtain immediate funds to take advantage of an exceptional Star.

In summary, it is not the position on the BCG matrix which should impel a certain strategy—divest, grow, and so forth—but market forces. The position on the BCG matrix does say something about the value of a SBU to the parent corporation. If one accepts the BCG analysis as valid—and many do—an individual business unit should be placed in the hands of the corporation to which its value is highest. To some degree, the BCG approach assumes that the corporation is a closed system which must internally fund its cash flows. Clearly, however, if the corporation consists of just one rapidly growing Star or one exceptional Question Mark, it is often possible to obtain the required funds through the sale of equity securities.

So, we are left with a rather simple conclusion. Corporate-level strategists should arrange the purchase of assets (through acquisition and mergers) which are relatively undervalued in the marketplace and should at all times be willing to sell (divest) those assets which are relatively overvalued. Ideally, of course, the value of the asset should not be simply a matter of opinion. It should be the present value of expected cash flows from the asset. As previously pointed out, assets, including whole businesses, should flow to their best uses—that is, to corporations which would pay the highest prices for them because they can use them the most effectively.

The GE Planning Grid

There have been a number of elaborations of the BCG matrix. A very popular one is the GE planning grid. This matrix is illustrated in Figure 3.3. GE strategic thinkers were not willing to accept market share as the sole indicator of competitive strength. In the GE framework, business strength or competitive position is a function of profitability, market growth rate, product or service image, the caliber of management, and so forth. Instead of sales growth rate, GE substituted long-term product-market attractiveness. This is a composite of market size and market growth rate, the profitability of the industry, and a number of social, environmental, and legal considerations. An inconsequential difference between the BCG and GE matrices is that the GE matrix is separated into nine cells rather than just four. Of course, the GE analysts are right, market share is not a totally accurate reflection of business strength, and market growth rate is not a totally accurate representation of industry attractiveness. However, the overall thesis of both approaches is unquestionable. That thesis is as follows:

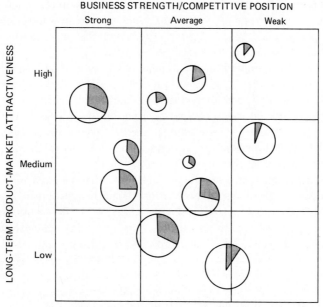

FIGURE 3.3 The GE planning grid

Corporations (or individuals) will benefit economically in the long run if they concentrate attention and resources on those businesses where the company has the greatest strengths and which are the most attractive from an investment standpoint.

The buying and selling of business units (acquisition and divestiture) has been a major focus of corporate-level strategy. But, just as the vacuum cleaner salesperson should assess the buyer's need for the product, the organizational strategist considering the sale of a business must assess the needs of potential buyers. To the extent that one believes that market share is strength and market growth rate is attractiveness, business units should be sold to those corporations for whom the business units plot closest to the upper left-hand corner of the BCG matrix. Within a corporation, resources should be allocated to these businesses.

The Hofer Matrix

Another "advance" beyond the BCG matrix was made by Charles W. Hofer (1975). Hofer substituted "stage of product/market evolution" for market growth rate. The Hofer matrix is shown in Figure 3.4. There has been a great deal of research which indicates that product life-cycle stage is a major determinant of which strategies will be successful. We will discuss this in more detail in the next chapter. It is sufficient to note here that Hofer's analysis reflects the results of this research, a good part of which he conducted. On the Hofer matrix, the sizes of the circles represent the industry

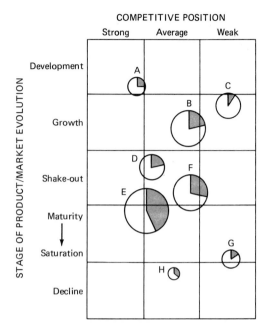

FIGURE 3.4   The Hofer matrix [*Adapted from C. W. Hofer*, Conceptual Constructs for Formulating Corporate and Business Strategies (*Boston: Intercollegiate Case Clearing House #9-378-754, 1977) p. 3.*]

revenue for the market segment, and the darkened wedges represent the SBU's market share within that industry.

Like the BCG and GE strategic theorists, Hofer suggests that positions on his matrix indicate certain strategies. For example, business A would probably be an emerging Star on the BCG matrix and a target for resource allocation. The output of business B would be somewhat further along in the product life cycle, but this SBU has both a smaller market share and a weaker competitive position, making it a poorer candidate for resource allocation. Businesses E and F are average competitors in maturing industries. They are what the BCG matrix would classify as Cash Cows. These should require little additional investment, if any, and should perhaps be used to fund the cash needs of business A. Business G is in a declining industry, and the company has both a small market share (although possibly more than anyone else) and a weak competitive position. Hofer would suggest that business G is likely to soon become a Dog and should, perhaps, be sold or liquidated, either immediately or over a period of a few years.

Spreading Products across the Life Cycle

Corporate strategists who value stability in sales and earnings will tend to diversify among businesses, of course, but they will also tend to promote a balance of products and services across product life-cycle stages. That product life cycles exists is a truism. Certainly, every product must go through the stages of product development, market development, growth, maturity, and decline. Some products get a new lease on life, though. For example, a few years ago, Arm & Hammer baking soda, well into the decline phase of the product life cycle, saw renewed growth in response to a national advertising campaign touting its multiple uses. Still, for most products, the cycle is a rather consistent one, with variation only in the length of the various stages and the amount of sales and profits earned at each stage. Because of this, many companies, especially consumer goods companies such as Proctor & Gamble, try to have a certain number of products or services in each stage of the product life cycle at all times. That way, as one product goes into the decline stage, another is experiencing sales growth and the company has a stable source of profits from those products which are in the mature stage. The astute reader will recognize that this differs little from the analysis suggested by the BCG.

The Profit Impact of Market Strategies Project

Started by GE, but now under the aegis of the nonprofit Strategic Planning Institute, the profit impact of market strategies (PIMs) project is perhaps the most comprehensive study of strategic factors ever conducted. The project is an ongoing one. It has built up a huge array of data from over 1500 product and service businesses, or SBUs, representing 200 corporations. Early results indicated that ROI was most significantly affected by market share, investment intensity, and corporate diversity (see Schoeffler, Buzzell, and Haney, 1974). Investment intensity and market diversity are difficult to operationalize. Market share can usually be objectively determined. But it is difficult to say whether market share determines profitability, as the BCG theorists hypothesized, or whether distinctive competence determines both profitability and market share. Certainly, most companies seek high market shares in those businesses in which they are earning their highest profits. The PIMS data suggest a number of other conclusions which have relevance for the corporate-level strategists.

THE McKINSEY SEVEN S FRAMEWORK AND CORPORATE CULTURE

Originally conceptualized in 1977, but publicized only in the 1980s, the McKinsey seven S framework is a powerful addition to the arsenal of organizational strategists. The seven S's are illustrated in Table 3.2.

Peters and Waterman (1982) call strategy and structure the "hardware" of organization and suggest that the "software," style, systems, staff, skills, and shared values, are often ignored by corporate strategists. Athos and Pascale (1981) call structure, strategy, and systems "the hard S's," and staff, skills, style, and shared values "the soft S's." They argue that "the four 'soft' elements can no longer be regarded as frosting on the corporate cake. They are indispensable parts of any corporate commitment to long time success" (Athos and Pascale, 1981, pp. 83–84). Proponents of the seven S framework believe their research shows that organizations which balance their emphasis on all of the seven are more likely to be successful. As evidenced by the outstanding success of the books *In Search of Excellence* and *The Art of Japanese*

TABLE 3.2   THE McKINSEY SEVEN S's

1 *Structure.* Those attributes of the organization which can be expressed through an organizational chart (span of control, centralization vs. decentralization, etc.)

2 *Strategy.* Actions the organization plans or undertakes in response to or in anticipation of the external environment

3 *Systems.* Procedures and processes regularly followed by an organization

4 *Staff.* The kinds of specialties or professions represented in an organization ("engineering types," "used car salesmen," "MBAs," and "computer jocks")

5 *Skills.* Distinctive attributes and capabilities of the organization and its key people in comparison with its competition

6 *Style.* Patterns of behavior and managerial style of senior managers

7 *Shared values.* Spiritual or philosophical principles and concepts that an organization is able to instill in its members

Management, which use the seven S analysis and which have sold millions of copies, the framework appears to be a powerful expository tool.

The seven S model is useful for three purposes. First, as an expository device, it helps managers and analysts understand the corporate culture in their organizations. Second, as a comparative device, it helps strategists evaluate their organizations along each of the seven dimensions, thereby identifying organizational strengths and weaknesses. Third, as a tool of strategy implementation, the seven S model can help managers change the attributes of the corporate culture which they consider vital to success and to do so in a systematic way.

In terms of the seven S's, **corporate culture** has been defined as "*a system of shared values (what is important) and beliefs (how things work) that interact with a company's people, organizational structures, and control systems to produce behavioral norms (the way we do things around here)*" (Uttal, 1983, p. 66). Arguing eloquently for their model, McKinsey consultants Peters and Waterman (1982, p. 11) say:

In retrospect, what our framework has really done is to remind the world of professional managers that "soft is hard." It has enabled us to say, in effect, "All that stuff you have been dismissing for so long as the intractable, irrational, intuitive, informal organization *can* be managed. Clearly, it has as much or more to do with the way things work (or don't) around your companies as the formal structures and strategies do. Not only are you foolish to ignore it, but here's a way to think about it. Here are some tools for managing it. Here, really, is the way to develop a new skill."

The difficulty of changing corporate culture and the time required to do so should not be underestimated. When Frederick W. Taylor, "the father of scientific management," argued that what was needed in 1898 was a "mental revolution," he expressed the opinion that accomplishing this might take as much as five years (Wren, 1979, p. 156). The time frame for cultural change has changed little since Taylor's day. Under the guidance of such consulting firms as the Management Analysis Center of

Cambridge, Massachusetts, a number of modern U.S. corporations, including Chase Manhattan Bank, AT&T, and First Chicago Corporation, have attempted to extensively change their corporate cultures. The efforts have not been altogether successful. One researcher who analyzed ten cases of attempted cultural change was provoked to say that "it costs a fortune and takes forever" (Uttal, 1983, p. 70). *Fortune* magazine's Bro Uttal (1983, p. 72) says, "Executives who have succeeded in fundamentally transforming a culture put a more precise estimate on how long the process requires: '6 to 15 years'." Still, if culture is a major determinant of corporate success—as it clearly is—strategists will, and should, continue to search for ways to manipulate it. Corporate culture is discussed in much greater detail in Chapter 6.

SEVERAL GRAND STRATEGIES

In the previous section, corporate-level strategies were described in the generic language. Now it is useful to place a label on certain corporate strategies. This is done in reverse of the usual order for two reasons. First, the field of organizational strategy is relevant only in relationship to other fields. Communication with practitioners and academics in those other fields is encumbered by the use of jargon. Second, having described in generic terms much of the nature of the process which is to be labeled, it is now easier to know what is included under each label.

Integration

A commonly used term among organizational strategists is *integration*, "*the unified control of a number of successive or similar economic, esp. industrial processes, formerly carried on independently*" (*Webster's Third New International Dictionary*). So, the combining of companies is integration. Integration also includes a company taking over a portion of the industrial or commercial process previously owned by others. Integration need not involve ownership, only control. So, supply and marketing contracts are forms of integration. *Integration toward the final users of a company's product or service,* as when Goodyear opened its tire outlets, is *forward integration. A company taking control of any of the sources of its inputs, including raw materials, labor, and so forth,* is *backward integration.* Southland Corporation's 1983 purchase of the petroleum refinery which supplies gasoline to the company's Seven-Eleven stores is an example of backward vertical integration. *Buying or taking control of competitors at the same level in the production and marketing process* is *horizontal integration.* For example, when Firestone, already in the auto service business, recently took over J. C. Penney's auto service centers, that was horizontal integration.

Each of these types of integration can be a means of accomplishing different strategic objectives. For example, if the objective is to decrease the cost of inputs, one possibility is to buy out suppliers who earn profits producing the inputs. If the strategic objective is to obtain additional market share, horizontal integration might accomplish this. Backward and forward integration are usually designed to accomplish one or both of two purposes: capturing additional profits or obtaining better control—of the supply channels if backward integration or of the distribution channels if forward integration. Obviously, if a supplier or an intermediate customer is making what are deemed to be exorbitant profits, vertical integration may be justified. If any company can perform the functions of suppliers or intermediate customers more effectively and efficiently than others do, vertical integration is probably justified. If better control of sources of supply or distribution channels is the objective, there may be better strategies available. Vertical integration often involves a company in businesses with which its managers are unfamiliar. To avoid this while obtaining control, some companies make franchise agreements with intermediate customers and long-term supply agreements with suppliers.

While recognizing its possible disadvantages, Harrigan (1983, p. 31) lists the following competitive advantages of integration:

- Improved marketing and technological intelligence
- Superior control of the firm's economic environment
- Product differentiation advantages

Diversification

Another common strategic management term is ***diversification***, "*the act or policy of increasing the variety of products or manufacture (as of a manufacturing concern)*" (*Webster's Third New International Dictionary*). Diversification may be conglomerate, that is, "made up of parts from various sources composed of various kinds" (*Webster's Third New International Dictionary*) or concentric. Concentric means, "having a common center" (*Webster's Third New International Dictionary*). So ***conglomerate diversification*** simply means *going into businesses which are unrelated to the firm's current businesses*, and ***concentric diversification*** means *going into businesses which are related to the firm's current businesses*. (In a technical sense, the term *related diversification* is better than *concentric diversification*, but the latter has found more widespread use.) As a grand strategy, diversification usually has as its purpose the reduction of risk. A company involved in a number of different businesses avoids having "all its eggs in one basket." Ideally, when some of a conglomerate firm's businesses decline, others will be on the increase. Countercyclical businesses are hard to find (The do-it-yourself hand tool market is one of the rare exceptions.) About the best that can be hoped for is a group of SBUs whose valleys and peaks occur at different times in the business cycle. Of course, diversification into related businesses may not appear to serve the risk reduction objective as well as conglomerate diversification. However, concentric diversification tends to be more successful in improving ROI (Bettis, 1981; Bettis and Hall, 1982).

Diversification often occurs as a by-product of bargain hunting by corporate strategists. Even if the preference is for a related merger candidate—or even one in the same business—corporate-level strategists may opt for an SBU in an entirely different business because it is deemed to be greatly underpriced or to have great synergy with the acquiring company. When this happens, the acquiring corporation becomes diversified. Diversification can also be a product of a desire for growth. In this case, diversification is not the strategy. Acquisition is the strategy for accomplishing the growth objective. Diversification is just one (perhaps unwanted) result.

The social benefits of conglomerate diversification are often questioned (see especially Salter and Weinhold, 1982, and Davidson, 1981). When Allied Corporation purchased Bendix in 1982 after a bitter takeover battle, a number of legislators complained that the huge investment Allied made did nothing to improve the productive capability of American industry. However, it is clear that many corporate managements have special competencies in managing large organizations. These managements are able and willing to take the steps necessary to restore failing companies to profitability or to enhance the profitability of others. When a company acquires another, and introduces new production technology, the benefit is clear. But, when improvement is produced by the introduction of better managerial technology, many question it. Concentric diversification or vertical or horizontal integration within a single product or service area is probably the most clearly justified kind of acquisition or expansion activity. Still, conglomerate diversification can often be justified on technological grounds. Even if neither production technology nor managerial technology is improved through the merger, though, it is possible that the acquiring company can improve the public image of the acquired one and thus serve shareholder interests (Allen, Oliver, and Schwallie, p. 17). This is not to condone the tendency of some strategists to seek growth because of their own predispositions or personal financial interests. A number of writers have shown that such self-serving behavior is not uncommon (Davidson, 1981; Salter and Weinhold, 1982).

Retrenchment

Another grand strategy, usually reserved for emergencies is retrenchment. ***Retrenchment*** means "*reduction, curtailment, excision*" (*Webster's Third New International Dictionary*), and few corporate managements are willing to do that. When a retrenchment strategy is followed, the goal is often survival. Actually, retrenchment should be considered as viable an option as growth. Prompt excision of losing businesses has been the hallmark of many successful corporate-level managers. Although growth is often an objective per se, retrenchment seldom is.

SUMMARY

The Century Telephone example illustrates all three levels of strategy formulation. Century must decide what, if any, additional businesses to enter, how to compete in its primary business, and how to support the company's on-going operation through strategies in finance, personnel, production, and marketing. The process of strategy formulation at the corporate level consists of five essential steps.

First, strategists must determine the mission—the organization's continuing purposes with regard to certain groups. Most businesses are started for the purpose of serving owners. Two things the typical stockholder desires are dividends and stock value increase. The stock price should include the present value of expected future dividends and the future liquidation value of the company. Risk, if present, requires higher expected earnings. Strategists might wish to give customers higher quality or a lower price than the market requires. But this typically requires rationing the product. Employees may be offered better benefits or lower work demands than the labor market requires if access to the jobs is restricted.

When a company pays more for inputs than the market requires and sells its outputs in free markets, it is at a relative disadvantage. Economic theory indicates that strategists will deliver to stockholders, customers, and employees what the market requires and little more. This includes a reasonable return to shareholders, a fair price for customers, and benefits to labor as required in the marketplace.

WOTS-up analysis provides a framework for environmental and organizational assessment. Strengths and weaknesses represent areas in which the organization excels in comparison with competitors. Threats are often defined in terms of the organization's competitors, while opportunities are usually thought of in terms of new technologies and new markets. When companies grasp opportunities, competitors often feel threatened. Innovations are opportunities for the innovators but threats to competitors. Miller, Nucor, and K-Mart are examples of companies which took advantage of strengths and overcame weaknesses in order to avoid threats and grasp opportunities.

The second step is environmental assessment. Only relevant information should be obtained. There will never be quite enough information at decision-making time.

The third step in corporate-level strategy formulation is organizational assessment. This is often done through financial models such as the ROI model. Financial data may not reveal long-term strengths and weaknesses or investment in personnel. Only useful information should be sought.

The fourth step in corporate-level strategy formulation is to set specific objectives or direction. Good objectives are challenging but attainable and specific, preferably quantifiable and measurable. Some successful organizations set no objectives and only vaguely understand the direction in which they are heading.

The last step in strategic planning is strategy setting. A major focus of corporate-level strategy is upon merger and acquisition activity. But corporations can change their business profile through internal growth as well.

There are a number of tools which have been found useful in corporate-level strategic management. The BCG matrix allows strategists to display the company's businesses on a single grid based upon relative market shares and the rates of growth in the respective market areas. Businesses with a high market share in a high-growth-rate industry are called Stars. Those with low market shares in low-growth industries are called Dogs. Cash Cows have high market shares in low-growth business segments, and Question Marks have low market shares in high-growth areas. BCG analysis suggests that a corporation's cash flow should be balanced mainly among Stars and Cash Cows. Question Marks should be grown into Stars, and Dogs divested. In fact, market forces determine whether something should be sold or bought. SBUs should flow to those corporations which can make the best use of them. The GE planning grid is a nine-cell matrix which plots business strength for SBUs against long-term product-market attractiveness. Charles Hofer added product or industry life-cycle considerations to the GE and BCG analyses. Like BCG and GE theorists, Hofer feels that positions on his matrix indicate certain strategies. Many companies try to ensure that their product mixes include products which are at various stages of life-cycle development. The PIMS project assembled data from over 1500 SBUs in 200 corporations. The factors which the PIMS data indicate have the greatest strategic relevance are market share, investment intensity, and corporate diversity.

The McKinsey seven S model is a valuable tool for strategists. Emphasis should be balanced among the hard S's and soft S's. The model is useful as an expository and comparative device and as a tool of corporate cultural change. However, it takes a long time to change corporate culture.

There are several grand strategies which corporate-level strategists can follow: forward, backward, or horizontal integration; diversification; and retrenchment.

IMPORTANT CONCEPTS

Strategies	Acquisition
Mission	Divestiture
Quality	Liquidation
Price	Corporate culture
Pay and benefits	Integration
Work demands	Forward integration
Strengths	Backward integration
Weaknesses	Horizontal integration
Threat	Diversification
Opportunity	Conglomerate diversification
Return on investment (ROI)	Concentric diversification
Merger	Retrenchment

DISCUSSION QUESTIONS

1 Explain how Century Telephone strategists might be involved in all three levels of strategic management at once.
2 List the steps in the corporate-level strategy formulation process and explain what is entailed in each step.
3 Do organizational strategists have the same obligations to a large and diverse group of shareholders as they would to an individual who owned the entire company? Explain your answer.
4 Explain how the common share price includes, or does not include, future dividends and liquidation value.
5 Explain the two benefits companies can give to customers in general and the problem which arises when they try to give either.
6 How can compensation and benefits systems for corporate strategists give them an incentive to serve shareholder interests?
7 Discuss several weaknesses in using purely financial data for organizational assessment.
8 Discuss the characteristics of good objectives.
9 Explain what Herbert Simon means by ''satisficing'' and discuss your own view of whether managers do this.

10 Distinguish between a merger and an acquisition and discuss two ways that either might be accomplished.

11 Draw and explain the BCG matrix.

12 How does the GE planning grid differ from the BCG matrix?

13 Describe how a corporation's strategy for a SBU in the upper left-hand corner of the Hofer matrix might differ from the strategy for an SBU in the lower right-hand corner.

14 Define each of the McKinsey seven S's and explain the relative emphasis each should receive.

15 Define "integration" and list the three kinds of integration along with possible purposes of each.

16 Distinguish conglomerate diversification from concentric diversification and explain why you think one or the other might be better in general.

17 Describe circumstances under which you believe a company should engage in a retrenchment strategy.

REFERENCES

Allen, Michael G., Alexander R. Oliver, and Edward H. Schwallie. "The Key to Successful Acquisitions," *Journal of Business Strategy*, 2:2, Fall 1981, pp. 14–24.

Andrews, Kenneth R. "Corporate Strategy as a Vital Function of the Board," *Harvard Business Review*, 59:6, November/December 1981, pp. 174–176, 180–184.

Athos, Anthony G., and Richard T. Pascale. *The Art of Japanese Management: Applications for American Executives*. New York: Simon & Schuster, 1981.

Bettis, Richard A. "Performance Differences in Related and Unrelated Diversified Firms," *Strategic Management Journal*, 2:4, October/December 1981, pp. 379–393.

Bettis, Richard A., and C. K. Prahalad. "The Visible and the Invisible Hand: Resource Allocation in the Industrial Sector," *Strategic Management Journal*, 4:1, January/March 1983, pp. 27–43.

Bower, Joseph L. "Solving the Problems of Business Planning," *Journal of Business Strategy*, 2:3, Winter 1982, pp. 32–44.

Davidson, Kenneth M. "Looking at the Strategic Impact of Mergers," *Journal of Business Strategy*, 2:1, Summer 1981, pp. 13–22.

DeCarbonnel, Francois E., and Roy G. Donance. "Information Sources for Planning Decisions," *California Management Review*, Summer 1973, pp. 42–53.

Drucker, Peter F. "Schumpeter and Keynes," *Forbes*, May 23, 1983, pp. 124–128.

Flax, Steven. "How to Snoop on Your Competition," *Fortune*, May 14, 1984, pp. 28–33.

Friedman, Milton. *Capitalism and Freedom*. Chicago: University of Chicago Press, 1962.

Gluck, Frederick. "The Dilemmas of Resource Allocation," *Journal of Business Strategy*, Fall 1981, pp. 67–71.

Gouldner, C. R., and Laura M. Kirks. "Business Facts: Where to Find Them," *MSU Business Topics*, Summer 1976, pp. 23–76.

Hamilton, H. Ronald. "Scenarios in Corporate Planning," *Journal of Business Strategy*, 2:1, Summer 1981, pp. 82–87.

Harrigan, Kathryn Rudie. "A Framework for Looking at Vertical Integration," *Journal of Business Strategy*, 3:3, Winter 1983, pp. 30–37.

Haspeslagh, Philippe. "Portfolio Planning: Uses and Limits," *Harvard Business Review*, 60:1, January/February 1982, pp. 58–73.

Hofer, Charles W. "Toward a Contingency Theory of Business Strategy," *Academy of Management Journal*, 18:4, December 1975, pp. 784–810.

Kirkland, Richard I., Jr. "Big Steel Recasts Itself," *Fortune*, April 6, 1981, pp. 28–34.

MacMillan, Ian C., Donald C. Hambrick, and Diana L. Day. "The Product Portfolio and Profitability: A PIMS-based Analysis of Industrial-Product Businesses," *Academy of Management Journal*, 25:4, December 1982, pp. 733–755.

Main, Jeremy. "K-Mart's Plan To Be Born Again, Again," *Fortune*, September 21, 1981, pp. 74–76, 80, 84–85.

Peters, Thomas J., and Robert H. Waterman, Jr. *In Search of Excellence*. New York: Harper and Row, 1982.

Petrov, Boris. "The Advent of the Technology Portfolio," *Journal of Business Strategy*, 3:2, Fall 1982, pp. 70–75.

Salter, Malcolm, and Wolf Weinhold. "What Lies Ahead for Merger Activities in the 1980s," *Journal of Business Strategy*, 2:4, Spring 1982, pp. 66–99.

Schoeffler, S., R. D. Buzzell, and D. F. Haney. "Impact of Strategic Planning on Profit Performance," *Harvard Business Review*, March 1974, pp. 137–145.

Seligman, Daniel. "An Economic Defense of Insider Trading." *Fortune*, 108:5, September 5, 1983, pp. 47–48.

Simon, Herbert A. *The New Science of Management Decision*. New York: Harper and Row, 1960.

Stevenson, H. H. "Defining Corporate Strengths and Weaknesses." *Sloan Management Review*, Spring 1976, pp. 51–66.

Uttal, Bro. "The Corporate Culture Vultures," *Fortune*, 108:8, October 17, 1983, pp. 66–72.

Wren, Daniel A. *The Evolution of Management Thought*. New York: John Wiley, 1979.

Yavitz, Boris, and William H. Newman. "What the Corporation Should Provide Its Business Units," *Journal of Business Strategy*. 3:1, Summer 1982, pp. 14–19.

STRATEGY FORMULATION AT THE SBU LEVEL

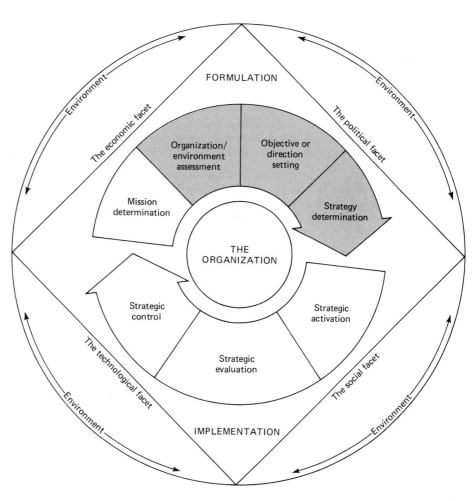

Atari, Inc., was founded in 1972 in California's ''silicon valley.'' By 1974, the company was producing about 10,000 units per year of the Pong electronic table tennis games invented by the founder, Nolan Bushnell. In cooperation with Sears, Roebuck, and Company, Atari introduced a home video version of Pong in 1975. The game sold quickly, 100,000 the first year. But the company was not able to produce and finance the number which could have been sold. Bushnell considered two options: selling stock to the public or selling out to a larger company which could finance the anticipated growth.

In October 1976, Warner Communications, Inc., bought Atari for $28 million. With annual sales of more than $3 billion and a wide array of high-technology businesses, Warner could provide the needed financing as well as research and development capabilities. In 1977, Atari introduced its video computer system (VCS). Buyers of this system could play a number of games simply by changing a cassette. The VCS, however, sold slowly at first.

Shortly after the acquisition, Warner's top management began to intervene in the management of Atari. In 1978, Bushnell, a conceptualizer with a disdain for detail, was replaced by Raymond Kassar, a detail man with a reputation as a business turnaround artist. Kassar made many management changes, set specific sales and marketing goals, and established formal reporting procedures and financial controls. The results were immediate. Though Atari's production capacity was expanded rapidly, demand expanded faster. VCS units could not be produced fast enough during 1979 and 1980. Stockouts were frequent. By 1980, Atari had developed dozens of different game cartridges for the VCS. Space Invader cartridges alone sold over a million units that year. Atari began television advertisements through the year rather than just at Christmas. The growth in sales of home-use video games was paralleled by a growth in demand for coin-operated machines. The company shipped 70,000 of these in 1980. In 1981 Atari's revenues doubled to $1.23 billion.

In May of 1981, the Atari 400 home computer was introduced. It was followed by the Atari 800 less than a year later. The Atari home computers were designed to connect to the VCSs. By September 1982, over 5 million American households owned Atari video games. Atari marketers saw these VCS owners as a huge untapped market for home computers.

As the company grew, it was divided into three divisions: the coin-operated games division, the consumer games division, and the home computer division. The potential market for home video games alone is huge. Less than 1 in 5 of the 83 million television households in the United States have any type of programmable home video game. Outside the United States (disregarding communist countries) the market is three times as large, with only about 2 percent penetration.

By 1982, a host of competitors were selling video game cartridges for their own and for Atari systems. The leading challengers were Coleco's ColecoVision and Mattel's Intellivision, and dozens of other companies marketed video games and/or cartridges. While most of Atari's competitors spent 3 to 4 percent of sales on R&D, Atari spent 8 percent. To reduce costs and increase capacity, Atari moved much of its production offshore in 1982, mostly to Hong Kong and Taiwan. Coming during a U.S. recession, the move created something of a furor. Coleco publicized its own efforts to preserve American jobs by manufacturing only in the United States.

In late 1982, Atari reported significantly reduced sales and earnings prospects. Instead of doubling and tripling, as sales and profits had done for several years, they increased only slightly for 1982. Because of this news, Warner Communications stock fell by 25 percent the day of the announcement, wiping out $1.2 billion in market value.

Atari expects to continue to lead the video games industry. At any time the company has forty to fifty video games in various stages of development. Every few months, Atari markets a new and more advanced home computer. In the coin-operated games area, Atari now sells a number of games developed by other companies. The company is engaging in top secret research in the telecommunications area. One known objective of this effort is to develop a marketable video phone. Still, Warner's stock showed scant signs of recovery in 1983. To make matters worse, just before Christmas Coleco started airing a series of television advertisements comparing Coleco's video game systems with Atari's supposedly inferior ones. As if to rub salt into Atari's wounds, Coleco ended each advertisement with, "Sorry Atari."

The Atari story illustrates four important attributes of SBU-level strategy formulation, or strategic planning. First, every business firm is primarily an economic entity. By meeting an economic demand, Atari was able to earn profits. This allowed the company to survive, make additional investments, and earn more profits. By the time Bushnell outgrew his capacity to finance the company internally, his $500 investment had grown to $28 million in value to Warner Communications. Because of the huge profits available in video games, competitors moved into the field, making it necessary for Atari to continue to innovate in order to survive—and eventually forcing price competition. When price competition forced Atari's earnings prospects downward, financial markets reevaluated Warner Communications stock. Atari strategists attempted to maintain market dominance and restore investor confidence in the parent company through extensive R&D, cost reduction, and aggressive advertising.

Second, the Atari case suggests the necessity for approaching strategy from a marketing standpoint. This requires adoption of what has been called "the marketing concept," implying a complete focus on the customer. Customer desire for recreation made the Pong game a success. Because of customer preferences for the highest quality available at the lowest price, Atari had to improve its games continually in order to survive. The customer identification and confidence which Sears commands allowed Atari to finance and market its first home video system. Throughout Atari's history, customers have rewarded the company with profits which were roughly proportional to the degree to which the company's products satisfied customer desire more than competing products did.

Third, Atari's experience shows the value of a number of special—purpose strategies. At every point in its history, Atari has required a product development strategy. The company grew slowly at first. After merging with Warner, Atari has developed specific growth objectives and strategies for accomplishing them. Strategies for dominant firms differ from those for low-market-share firms. In video games, Atari remains dominant. In home computers, the company is dominated by firms like Texas Instruments, Apple, and Tandy Corporation (Radio Shack). In telecommunications, Atari has no significant market share at all. With the video games industry already showing signs of maturity, Atari must make plans now for the time when the industry becomes a .declining one. Then, special strategies for firms in declining industries will be needed.

Finally, the short history of the video games industry offers a highly compressed example of the impact of industry and product life cycles on business-level strategy. Auto, steel, airline, and other industries have taken many decades to go through the developmental and growth stages to maturity (and in some cases to decline). For the video games industry, signs of maturity were visible within a decade. For individual products, such as the Atari 400 home computer, product life cycles have been shortened to just a year or two.

In Chapter 3, we discussed strategy formulation at the corporate level. Recall that the corporate-level strategist was seen as an investment portfolio manager, deciding upon the overall character and mission of the company, which investments (SBUs) to buy (or develop), and the allocation of resources and management of synergies among them. The steps in the strategy formulation process at the business level are the same as those at the corporate level. This is shown in the illustration at the start of this chapter. The SBU mission is often dictated by corporate-level strategists. Consequently, mission determination is not highlighted in the illustration. In a departure from the approach taken in Chapter 3, the *principles* of strategy formulation rather than the *process* will provide the framework for this chapter.

In this chapter, we discuss the kinds of strategies which help the company to compete in a particular business or in a product or service segment and to contribute to overall organizational success. As we go along, keep in mind that there are many single-SBU organizations. **Single-SBU organizations** are *organizations which either produce only one kind of product or service or treat a multiproduct or service operation as a single unit for strategic purposes.* The SBU will first be viewed as an economic entity. Then a marketing view will be taken. Next a number of special-purpose strategies will be discussed. In the last section of the chapter, the impact of industry and product or service life cycle upon business-level strategy formulation will be described.

THE SBU AS AN ECONOMIC ENTITY

As mentioned earlier, whatever view one takes of the business organization—as a social system, as a collection of resources and the people who manage them, as a tool of society through which human needs are satisfied, or as an abstract system devoid of content—it is primarily an economic entity. In general, funds for investments which promise no return cannot be obtained, employees who receive no pay will not keep working, products and services which produce no profit will not long be produced, and customers who have no money cannot obtain those which are.

Profit is the goal of most businesses. Even most nonprofit organizations can be viewed as economic in nature. In general, the missions of organizations like the Red Cross, Save the Children Foundation, and thousands of others is to collect money and use it efficiently to accomplish worthwhile purposes. In business, profit is often taken to be the appropriate measure of how effectively and efficiently corporate resources are used. In fact, most SBUs are treated as profit centers by their parent corporations.

What Is the Correct Economic Goal?

Corporations pursue various "profitability" goals. Many SBU strategists find that they really have little choice as to the SBU's mission. It is usually established by corporate-level strategists as maximization of profit, ROI, return on equity, or some other economic parameter. In a strict sense, it is the *present value of the managed firm* to the parent corporation which the SBU strategists should try to maximize. But, what is the present value of the firm? Is it the total value of all debt and equity securities?

We will argue that it is only the value of the SBU's common stock or other representation of equity ownership. The obligation to debt security holders is a legally enforceable, fixed obligation and consequently should not be viewed as a goal but as a constraint. Debt obligations must be met before other obligations can be considered. Preferred stock is somewhat like debt in that the dividends typically must be paid before any dividends can be paid on common stock. Preferred stock can be designed to be almost like debt (cumulative preferred with a mandatory sinking fund provision) or almost like equity (noncumulative, participating preferred). However, it is typically more debtlike than equitylike. Therefore, as a general rule, it is the *present value of expected future earnings available to common stock* which should be maximized. If the financial markets are efficient, this should maximize the SBU's contribution to the *current-period common stock price* of the parent corporation.

In general, SBU strategists find maximization of the firm's value a difficult goal to operationalize. Three subordinate purposes, which are easier to apply, are (1) increasing long-term earnings capability, (2) improving current-period profitability, and (3) optimizing cash flow.

Strategies for Improving Long-Term Earning Capacity

The future earning capability of the firm is often enhanced or retarded most significantly by investment decisions involving which assets to buy, divest, improve, or deplete. There are a number of criteria which can be used in making investment choices. The most common approach is ROI. This is roughly how ROI decision making works: When investment or disinvestment opportunities arise, the expected profits which will flow from the investment are estimated. Only those investments which promise a percentage return above some set minimum level are considered. Ideally, all the available investments should be compared, and those which offer the highest return should be made until the SBU runs out of investment funds. If retrenchment is necessary, investments are liquidated in reverse order of ROI until the firm's minimum cash needs are met. Since expected profit depends upon who the expector is, what time of day it is, and a number of less concrete variables, many corporations use current-period accounting ROI rather than expected ROI to allocate resources among divisions.

A theoretical fallacy in ROI investment decision making is that ROI is not profit and that it is profit (technically, the present value of future profit) which usually should be maximized. A profitable company which sells portions of its assets and leases them back will almost always increase ROI, although the profits and future earnings capability may not be affected. And a company which borrows money to buy investment assets which earn a little more than the interest charges on the debt will increase profitability, although ROI will normally decline. To some degree, this fallacy is mitigated by the impact of additional debt on the riskiness of investments. It is generally accepted that debt increases risk to the common shareholder and that common shareholders require (or deserve) a higher level of profitability for their more risky investment. Another problem with ROI as an investment criterion is that both return and investment can be computed in a number of different ways—with greatly varying results.

Despite its shortcomings, ROI is perhaps the most widely used criterion for investment decision making, both at the corporate and business levels. ROI is also very popular for allocating resources among SBUs and for evaluating SBU managers.

Another common approach to investment decision making is to accept only those investment projects which promise less than some maximum payback period. ***Payback period*** is *the time it takes (or is expected to take) for the net cash flows produced by a capital asset to total the cost of the asset.* For example, if a certain machine costs $10,000 and is expected to produce $2000 a year in contribution to net income, ignoring depreciation, the machine has a payback period of five years. Payback period is frequently used as a capital budgeting tool at the business level. Lincoln Electric Company, for example, accepts only those investment projects with payback periods of less than two years. Payback period is seldom used for the allocation of resources among operating divisions or for evaluating managers.

There are a number of more complex approaches to investment decision making, such as internal rate of return (IRR), net present value (NPV), and the capital asset pricing model (CAPM). The ***internal rate of return*** is *the discount rate which equates the present value of the expected net cash flows from an investment asset with the cost of the asset.* A firm which uses this method will compare investment alternatives on the basis of the IRR each provides and will usually establish a minimum acceptable IRR. ROI and IRR are essentially identical concepts. However, ROI is normally computed for a SBU (an aggregation of all kinds of assets) on the basis of ex post data, while IRR usually relates to a single capital asset and is often based on ex ante estimates.

Net present value is *the present value of the expected net cash flows from an investment asset minus the cost of the asset.* Strategists must decide what discount rate to use in the NPV computation. A common approach is to estimate the firm's cost of capital and to use that figure in the NPV computation. This is often the weighted average of (1) the earnings-price ratio for common stock, (2) the dividend-price ratio for preferred stock, and (3) the interest rate on new long-term debt. Some strategists prefer to use the expected cost of funds which will be used to purchase the respective asset as the discount rate for the NPV calculation. Whatever discount factor is used, only those investments providing a positive NPV are acceptable, and alternative investments are preferred according to the NPVs they offer.

The ***capital asset pricing model*** is *a mathematical model which states that the return which capital markets will afford for any asset is the risk-free rate plus a risk premium proportional to the sensitivity of returns on the assets to changes in market returns.* The CAPM attempts to explicitly consider risk and, though its logic is appealing, it has seen limited use in SBU-level decision making. One corporation, Alaska Interstate, Inc., attempted to use the CAPM to evaluate subsidiaries and acquisition candidates. However, in 1982 the company abandoned its diversification effort, along with the CAPM, and returned to more conventional decision-making tools (Harrington, 1983).

Strategies for Improving Profitability

We said earlier that it is expected profit that gives current value to a business. The best indicator of future profitability is present profitability. European and Japanese managers have criticized Americans for sacrificing long-term viability for short-term profits. Some authors have suggested that the problem can be corrected through executive compensation schemes which emphasize the long run (e.g., Stonich, 1981, and Salter,

FIGURE 4.1 Profitability strategies

1973). However, few corporate managers believe that the future is significantly predictable beyond about five or ten years, particularly in light of recent price-level volatility. So, perhaps what appears to be a short-term focus on the part of American managers may simply be a recognition of reality.

The formula for net profit (net profit = revenues − expenses) is well known to every student of finance and to practically every business manager. It is clear from this formula that net profit can be increased only by increasing revenues or by decreasing expenses or by using some combination of both which nets out to the same thing. So, business-level strategies aimed at increasing current profitability should probably either increase revenues or decrease expenses. This is illustrated in Figure 4-1. Among the strategies for increasing revenues are (1) increasing the price for price-inelastic products, (2) decreasing the price for price-elastic products, (3) increasing and/or redirecting promotional efforts, (4) increasing the product quality perceived by potential customers, either through increasing the actual quality or through changing the presentation of the product or service, (5) broadening the product line, and (6) expanding into new territories.

Strategies for reducing expenses include (1) motivational schemes for improving the productivity of labor, (2) improving existing technology through machine repair, rearrangement, and so forth, (3) adopting new technology through machine replacement, redesign, and so forth, (4) redesign of products and services to require fewer or less costly inputs, (5) substituting labor-intensive processes for capital-intensive ones where labor costs per unit are lower than capital costs per unit, and (6) substituting capital-intensive processes for labor-intensive ones where the reverse is true.

Strategies for Producing Cash

Often a business-level strategic manager adopts increased cash flow as a goal. Sometimes, it is a matter of survival. Whatever the basic cause of business failures, they are almost always manifested through what are called cash-flow problems. A business which loses money continuously (an *earnings* problem) will eventually be unable to pay its bills (a *cash-flow* problem).

Even when an SBU is profitable, it may have to serve as a Cash Cow for other SBUs. Maximization of profitability at the corporate level may require withdrawing funds from certain SBUs and investing them in those with a higher earning capability. When this occurs, business-level strategists must shift from a focus on maximizing profitability and concentrate on maximizing cash flow from the business. There are a number of common strategies for doing this. Several are shown in Figure 4-2.

First, a debt avoidance or delay strategy might be followed. This can range from paying obligations a few days later than usual to filing for protection under Chapter 11 of the Bankruptcy Code, sometimes entirely avoiding all outstanding debts. Paying obligations late can product large quantities of cash. For example, in 1981 Manville Corporation had over $300 million in accounts payable. Paying the accounts just two weeks later than the usual thirty days would have increased Manville's cash on hand by $150 million. Of course, when Manville filed for Chapter 11 reorganization in August 1982, the company avoided paying all these accounts plus many other debts; and the result was huge cash balances on hand during 1983. A smaller company with only, say, $1 million in annual sales, and $60,000 in accounts payable can increase its cash balances by $30,000 by just paying its accounts payable fifteen days late, assuming it previously paid on a thirty-day basis.

Second, a company can increase cash balances through a capital asset depletion policy. In order for most fixed assets to continue to produce income, some reinvestment is required in the form of repairs and maintenance, replacement of machines and

FIGURE 4.2   Ways of producing cash

parts which wear out, and so forth. A company which requires cash in the short term can forgo these expenditures for a time. If this occurs, of course, the ability of the company to earn profits will slowly decline. In essence, this is a form of disinvestment. Just as investment requires cash, disinvestment produces cash. One reason the U.S. steel industry is in such dire financial straits is that operating cash has been obtained for several decades by allowing the steel mills to run down and become antiquated.

Third, cash can be obtained through current-asset management. This too is a form of disinvestment. A company which is in a bind for cash might fail to replenish inventories as they are sold. When the cash need is critical enough, some companies even sell inventories at below cost. Of course, every company should manage its inventories to increase profitability, as discussed in the previous section. But here we are discussing obtaining cash, possibly to the detriment of profitability. Another current asset which can be milked for cash is accounts receivable. The credit terms can be shortened, and discounts for early payment given. Customers can be "Dunned" even though this might hurt future sales.

Fourth, any strategy that increases the value of a liability or equity, all else being equal, produces cash. This includes borrowing or issuing more equity securities. If this is done with due regard for the interests of corporate stakeholders, it can be a reasonable and responsible strategy. In fact, rapidly growing companies almost always tend to be cash-hungry. However, when the purpose is simply to obtain cash and avoid more difficult strategic decisions, most would not consider this practice socially responsible.

THE SBU FROM A MARKETING STANDPOINT

In the previous section, we discussed strategic management from an economic perspective. Now our vantage point will be a marketing one. Just as it is true that the corporation is, above everything, an economic entity, it is true that, to be economically effective, an organization must satisfy needs and/or wants in the marketplace. Several decades ago the term *the marketing concept* was coined to designate *the proposition that all of a company's efforts, whether in the area of finance, production, personnel, or sales, should be focused upon the customer.* Rather than being a new view of marketing, however, this is just a different way of looking at the job of strategic management. When the marketing concept is adopted, marketing is not seen simply as one of several functional areas (the others being production, finance, and personnel) which make up the job of management. The marketing concept signifies a market-focused approach to managing the total organization.

The strategist who subscribes to this view begins with such questions as: What *needs* is the organization seeking to fill? What are the characteristics of customers with these needs? The answers to these questions lead to adoption of basic marketing strategies like "define a market niche" and "position the firm in the marketplace." From these basics of strategy come derived strategies which can be summarized under "the four P's of marketing." In actuality they could as well be called "the four P's of strategic management," for they provide a powerful way of relating the organization to its environment. By the way, Kenichie Ohmae would add a "T" for timing to the four

P's (Ohmae, 1982). Timing is, of course, a vital consideration. With this prelude, let's consider the four P's—product, price, promotion, and place—as they relate to strategic management at the business or division level. It is emphasized that it is not *marketing* as a functional area which is being discussed, but *strategic management from a marketing perspective.*

Product

Webster's Third New International Dictionary defines a *product* as "something produced by physical labor or intellectual effort: the result of work or thought." As used in this book, **product** means *the total bundle of goods and services available to the customer*. For most purposes it is unnecessary to distinguish between *goods* and *services*. They are both results of physical labor and/or intellectual activity, and both have value to customers and cost something to produce. In fact, many companies have come to view a physical product more in terms of the services it provides than in terms of its physical nature. For example, oil companies should see themselves as providers of energy, auto companies should offer transportation, and television manufacturers should produce entertainment. So the product should be described from the standpoint of what it will do for the purchaser and how effectively and efficiently it can be produced (Buaron, 1981, p. 10). The obvious objective is to produce the maximum perceived value for the customer at the lowest cost in terms of resource inputs. The connection between the product aspect of marketing and the production strategy is a well-recognized one (Stobaugh and Telesio, 1983). It is perceived value which determines what the customer will pay for a product or how aggressively the customer will seek the product at a given price. This requires an understanding of customer needs as well as efficient and effective production capabilities.

There are essentially two approaches to increasing the value provided to the customer: (1) develop new products, and (2) improve the quality of existing ones. New products may be created through R&D. Atari, in the story at the beginning of this chapter, has chosen to spend a relatively huge amount on R&D for this very purpose. Simply spending money on R&D, however, is not enough. It is as important to discover new needs and to exploit them as it is to make new products to meet known needs. Market research, either formal or casual, rigorous or intuitive, can help determine where the product development opportunities are. Research must be focused upon a need or a potential need in the marketplace. Remember, however, that the marketing research and the subsequent R&D should be designed to improve the degree to which the product meets customer needs and desires.

The second way to improve value is to improve the quality of existing products. There are a number of strategies for doing this. Quality control standards can be imposed or improved. W. Edwards Demming, for whom two of Japan's national productivity prizes are named, credits most of his success to what he calls "statistical control" of the production process. Another approach is automation or robotization. Machines are much more consistent in producing goods and services than are humans. Much of Japan's success in the auto and steel industries is credited to reliance on machines. Through the use of computers, banks, retailers, and many other businesses have decreased the number of errors they make in serving customers, improving the speed of service as well as accuracy. Incidentally, an American company, Hewlett-Packard, won the Demming quality control prize in 1982.

Another way to improve quality is to engage employees in quality control efforts. Employees can help both in terms of idea generation and quality-conscious performance. The first strategy is exemplified by the use of quality control circles, or quality circles, made famous in Japan and adopted by many U.S. companies. *Quality circles* are *groups of workers, usually consisting of eight to ten persons each, who meet together regularly for the purpose of discovering and recommending or implementing ways to improve the production process, in terms of either efficiency or quality.* Lomas and Nettleton, America's largest mortgage banking firm, recently began involving employees in quality circles. They have found the widest use, however, in manufacturing concerns.

Suggestion systems also encourage workers to come up with ways of improving quality. A few companies have included quality considerations as a part of their compensation programs. For example, at Lincoln Electric Company, workers are required to pay for warranty costs traceable to their output. In addition, high marks for quality increase workers' year-end bonuses. Because of Lincoln's extensive statistical control system, warranty costs *are* traceable to the output of the worker who caused them. At Ford Motor Company, the theme, "Quality is job one," was adopted for the purpose of both promoting the quality of Ford products in the marketplace and developing enthusiasm for quality among Ford employees. Ford's current emphasis on quality was a reaction to a disastrous decline in the popularity of American cars, which many feel could have been avoided by earlier adoption of the marketing concept.

If one accepts traditional economic theory, there is no doubt that price is the primary marketing weapon of the business unit strategist—and one which is too often overlooked. As far as economists have been able to determine, there is no such thing as a "*Giffen good*," *a product for which an increase in price produces an increase in quantity demanded* (Glahe and Lee, 1981, p. 151; Maurice, Phillips, and Ferguson, 1982, p. 144; McCloskey, 1982, p. 75; Stigler, 1966, p. 24).

There are few tools, perhaps none, other than price, which have such a clearly predictable direction of impact. However, focusing entirely on price would clearly be a mistake. It is price for a given perceived quality of product or service which encourages the purchaser to buy, not price alone. This is not to ignore the fact that price often transmits information about product quality. Most people believe that, at least to some extent, "you get what you pay for." Price should complement the desired product image. When L'eggs pantyhose were sold in different test markets at varying prices, it was found that, when the pantyhose were priced too low, many customers thought they were of inferior quality. This kind of effect, though, usually lasts for only a brief period. Once the customer has tried the product or service, price becomes less important as a source of information. It should also be remembered that proper promotion can overcome any negative information transmitted by price. This is why price competition among pantyhose manufacturers has been fierce for a number of years now. It also is why Atari must compete on a price basis with Mattel's Intellevision and Coleco's Colecovision electronic games, although Atari had a clear price and quality image advantage at first.

So, the direction of the impact of price on the quantity of a given product or service sold is clear. By decreasing price, volume can normally be increased. However, any significant change in price could severely affect the product image and subsequently decrease the market share. However, the effect on profitability is not always so clear. If a company prices its product below cost, sales may very well increase markedly, but profits will evaporate. The reverse is also true—and this is frequently overlooked. If a company increases its prices, unit sales may very well decline while profits increase, particularly if the business has a high percentage of variable costs as compared to fixed costs.

The setting of price for an individual customer or even for an individual product may not be a strategic matter. However, the company's overall approach to pricing its products and services is strategic. There are essentially four approaches to pricing policy, one based upon the cost of producing the product or service, and the other three based upon the market.

First, cost-based pricing is useful when the production costs for various competitors are similar, or at least proportional. In the construction industry most competitors simply calculate what their cost is expected to be for a given job and add a certain percentage to that figure. Many retailers have a certain percentage markup which they apply to the products they sell. For most who practice cost-based pricing, it is really done for simplicity. Such pricing is indirectly based on market forces, with the markup varying from product line to product line depending on what the market will bear. At least one company, Lincoln Electric Company, claims to "at all times, price on the basis of cost and keep downward pressure on costs." In doing this, Lincoln Electric claims to serve its primary constituency, the customers. Lincoln Electric is a rare exception to the general rule, however. For most companies, cost-based pricing is just a convenient way of responding to market forces.

Second, an approach to pricing commonly followed during the early stages of product life cycle is "skim pricing." **Skim pricing** is *pricing a product or service high while the selling firm has an availability or quality advantage over competitors for the purpose of earning monopolistic-type profits in the short run.* Skimming is really useful as a pricing policy when there is no close substitute for the product in question or when barriers to entry prevent competitors from producing substitutes. For example, when Xerox patented the dry process copier in the 1950s and when IBM patented the Selectric typewriter in the 1960s, it was possible for each company to reap huge profits for an extended period through skim pricing. As each new evolution in home computers is introduced by Apple or IBM or one of the other computer makers, the introducing company can use skim pricing for a brief period until competitors catch up.

As competitors enter the market, however, it becomes necessary to follow the third approach to pricing, a competitive pricing strategy. In general, it is true that innovators are able to profit from skim pricing but that imitators must price more competitively. Innovators, in the sense used here, are companies which concentrate attention upon bringing out new or improved products or services earlier than competitors can. Imitators are companies which look for new or improved products or services in the marketplace and attempt to market similar products or services at a profit. There is a middle ground between imitation and innovation, and the Japanese have found it. In the early 1980s, they copied (imitated) and improved upon (innovated) a number of American developments, with outstanding success. **Competitive pricing** is *pricing at or slightly below the competitor's prices for a given quality of product*. Competitive pricing should be accompanied by attempts to differentiate the company's product or services, either through promotion or through product design and development. After IBM's patent on the Selectric typewriter ran out, a number of competitors introduced ball-element typewriters. IBM, already very experienced in the technology involved, introduced several improvements, such as an automatic erasing feature, and actually lowered the price at which the typewriter sold.

The fourth approach to pricing is often called **penetration pricing**, *pricing the product or service at well below the existing market price, perhaps even below cost, for the purpose of gaining market share*. It was through penetration pricing from 1972 to 1977 that Texas Instruments came to dominate the hand-held calculator market (Buaron, 1981, pp. 8–9). Strategists know that market share tends to be "sticky downward." Once a company attains a large market share, it often takes years for that market share to decline significantly, even if the price-quality relationship is about the same as that of competitors. Though the technology of Texas Instrument's calculators is no longer remarkable, the company remains the sales leader in the U.S. market for hand-held calculators.

Another good reason for penetration pricing is to elevate sales so that economies of scale can be obtained. For years BIC has used penetration pricing for all its products. BIC's strengths are in the areas of mass production and marketing of low-priced products. Long dominant in the ballpoint pen business, BIC introduced a disposable razor in 1982 at what some considered a ridiculously low price. In fact, the whole razor cost less than a single competitive razor blade. Through this pricing strategy, however, coupled with an efficient mass production system, BIC appears to be headed toward domination of the disposable razor market.

Penetration pricing also has relevance to the experience curve. The **experience curve** is *a graphical representation of the proposition that, for certain industries, the cost of producing a certain quality of product or service declines in a predictable way with the total cumulative volume the company has produced*. Penetration pricing can allow a company to get further out on the experience curve, thereby decreasing its costs and allowing profits to be made. For products and services to which the experience curve applies, pricing below cost for a period of time may be justified as an investment which will return profits in the long run. There is a certain risk involved in this tactic. Any major improvement in the basic product may diminish experience curve advantages. The experience curve is discussed in greater detail later in this chapter.

Promotion

The third P relates to the company's **promotion strategy**. This is *the plan for informing and convincing the customer*. The usual objective of promotion is to improve the price/quality trade-off from the company's standpoint or to increase the sales volume. Of course, it is conceivable that a company which views the customers as a major constituency might wish to advise them about the product just to increase its usefulness. However, the only way to keep this from being reflected in increased sales or prices is to limit the information to certain customers and to keep others from finding out about the additional usefulness. Otherwise, the product or service will have to be rationed.

Promotion can be accomplished in one of three main ways: through advertising, through personal selling, or through word of mouth. For years Church and Dwight Company's Arm & Hammer baking soda was marketed essentially without advertising. Its sales were relatively stable. The low price, quality, and product identification had driven most competitors from the market. A few years ago an aggressive advertising campaign was begun, which touted the multiple uses of Arm & Hammer baking soda (antacid, cleaner, deodorant, tooth powder). What had been a solid but relatively unprofitable performer became a high flyer.

In some cases, promotion results in an increase in the perceived value of a product relative to its real value to the customer. The oil additive STP is commonly agreed to have no significant value in terms of increasing engine life or improving performance (Hartley, 1981, pp. 193–205). However, when Andy Granatelli began hawking the product on television, sales skyrocketed. Few customers have the expertise to determine whether oil additives actually improve performance or engine life. Consequently, it was possible through promotional efforts to convince them that STP did, and to keep them convinced. The STP example flies in the face of conventional marketing wisdom, which suggests that promotion cannot create a successful product but can only increase market acceptance.

In no other aspect of the strategic manager's job are ethical considerations more paramount than in promotion activities. The strategists must determine to what degree promotional efforts are designed to inform the customer about the real attributes of the product or service and to what degree they are designed simply to convince the customer to buy—or even to convince the customer that the product or service has attributes it does not possess.

The choice between concentrating on advertising, personal selling, or word of mouth is not usually a clear one. Many companies use a combination of all three. Of course, if word of mouth is the choice, the primary strategy might be to build a better product or offer a better service at a lower price. Often a kind of mystique develops concerning a certain product, making word of mouth a most effective strategy. This has been true at times for Coors beer, L. L. Bean sporting goods, Gravely garden tractors, and a wide range of other products. Through personal selling and advertising, however, it is often possible to improve the customer image for a given quality of product or service. Further, while selling and advertising are artistic-type endeavors, they are not mystical.

The organizational strategist must typically decide not only what type of promotion strategy to follow, but also the amount of money the company is willing to spend on promotion. Often a policy is established through which a certain percentage of company sales is spent on advertising. The typical pattern in the respective industry may be used as a guide. Other companies base their advertising expenditures upon a desire to accomplish certain sales objectives. Whatever the approach, the design of a promotional strategy, including both expenditure and method, is a vitally important function of SBU strategists.

Place

In discussing this functional aspect of marketing, a number of modern marketing texts substitute *physical distribution* for *place*. Whatever term is used, what is referred to are any and all efforts the company undertakes to give its product or service what economists call "place utility." **Place utility** is *the usefulness a product or service has because it is available at a certain place.*

From a strategic management standpoint, *place* refers not only to where the product or service is to be distributed, but also how. This includes identification of the appropriate distribution channel as well as the means of compensating and controlling the channel members. Among the choices are (1) distributing through the company's own sales outlets, (2) selling through franchised outlets, (3) using the services of manufacturers' agents to market the product through specialized or nonspecialized wholesalers and/or retailers, (4) using the company's own sales force to distribute the product directly to end users or through specialized or nonspecialized wholesalers and/or retailers, (5) distributing through mail or parcel delivery services on the basis of orders from catalogs or coupon ads placed in the mass media.

Distribution should be viewed as part of the production process. The method of distribution—the outlet where the product is sold—should complement the quality, dependability, and value of the product itself. As stated earlier, products are best defined in terms of the services they provide. Distribution is as vital to the creation of value for the customer as is manufacture. Thus, distribution strategy becomes just an extension of production strategy, both being directed at profitably filling needs in the marketplace.

SALES GROWTH AND SPECIAL-PURPOSE STRATEGIES

Given a certain product or products, the sales growth an individual company or SBU experiences is a direct result of four factors: (1) growth of end markets for the firm's products or products incorporating them as components, (2) additional uses for the company's output, either as final or intermediate goods, (3) price increases without decreases in the quantity demanded (requiring discovery of the elusive Giffen good), and (4) increases in the firm's market share (McLagan and Buffa, 1982, p. 49). Obviously, a company can also grow by adding products. Growth strategies, to be effective, must affect one or more of these variables.

The Growth, Stabilization, or Retrenchment Decision

Most people, and Americans especially, believe that growth is not only desirable, but essential. "Grow or die" is an accepted axiom. When a company actively pursues growth, as most do, this is called a *growth strategy*. Only when businesses are forced

into it do they commonly plan to allow sales to stabilize. Most organizational strategists view declining sales as a sign of failure. Even when strategists admit to following
a retrenchment (cutting-back) strategy, it is usually only seen as a necessity during an
unhappy interlude, after which growth will resume.

To the extent that company management is the constituency being served, sales
growth is always desirable as long as the company remains profitable. Larger company
size usually carries with it both prestige and higher executive salaries. So, growth
becomes an objective, and profitability a constraint. However, if the objective is to
maximize return for stockholders or for a corporate parent, this concentration upon
growth may not be entirely appropriate. If growth is achieved at the expense of future
profitability, it may be to the detriment of all concerned. For example, a company may
choose to cut product costs by reducing quality and then compete in the marketplace on
the basis of price. This may increase sales and profits until the change in product
quality becomes apparent to customers. In the long run, sales may decline and the
company's reputation for quality could be permanently hurt.

Like decisions about other objectives, those relating to whether and to what extent
to seek sales growth should be based on sound business reasoning, not on an emotional
aversion to retrenchment. There are cases where companies have followed the most
extreme retrenchment policy, liquidation with distribution of the proceeds to stockholders, with excellent results. If a company's liquidation value is above the market
value of its securities, liquidation may be a reasonable alternative.

The decision of whether or not to seek sales growth cannot simply be based upon
whether the relevant market is growing. A recent *Forbes* magazine article (Baldwin,
1983) describes how three companies with small market shares in low-growth industries—Dogs, according to BCG devotees—bucked market trends with excellent results.

The most important criterion for the growth, stabilization, or retrenchment decision
is probably the company's degree of distinctive competence in the product or service
area. IBM was not a major competitor in the typewriter market until the company
invented and patented the ball-element, or Selectric, typewriter. IBM chose to grow
rapidly in this area and quickly became dominant at the upper end of the office
typewriter market, even though the market was growing only moderately. At the same
time, Olivetti, a marketer of premium office typewriters, was forced to accept a
retrenchment strategy. This ultimately resulted in Olivetti being combined with Under-
wood, a company which concentrated upon moderately priced typewriters. IBM's
patent ran out in the late 1970s, and other manufacturers were then able to market ball-
element typewriters. But by that time the entire office typewriter industry was beginning to decline because of the availability of word processors, and most typewriter
manufacturers were forced to retrench. Thus, this one small industry segment illustrates both how an individual company's growth strategy can be somewhat independent
of industry trends at various points in time and how that of competitors in the aggregate
cannot.

The *urgency* with which growth should be sought is largely dependent upon the
degree and stability of a company's distinctive competences. A ***distinctive competence***
is *any advantage a company has over its competitors because it can do something they*

cannot or because it can do something better than they can. Distinctive competences can be based upon technical or managerial expertise, legal rights, ownership or control of financial, material, or human resources, or a wide range of other advantages. When IBM patented its ball-element typewriter, the company knew that for seventeen years it would have a significant advantage over its competitors. By the time the seventeen years (the life of a patent) was up, IBM was far out on the experience curve. Although IBM's distinctive competence based on the patent right had run out, the company still had another kind of distinctive competence based on manufacturing experience. The company was thus able to produce its Selectric typewriter with both higher quality and lower costs than any competitor. Because the advantage was relatively permanent, IBM chose to price the typewriter at the upper end of the market (skim pricing), knowing that the company would be able to gain market share for a number of years.

On the other hand, when Coleco developed its Adam computer system in 1983, the decision was made to price it at only $600, even though it was thought to be a year ahead of anything else on the market. Accepting the idea that market share is sticky downward, companies like Coleco have to reap the benefits of innovation rather quickly in terms of sales growth. After obtaining a high market share, and lowered production costs (as a result of experience curve effects), profits can be made while competitors catch up on the technology. In Coleco's case, the strategy did not work well because the company's apparent competitive edge evaporated with highly publicized problems involving the early demonstration units of Adam, severe production foul-ups which limited availability for the 1983 Christmas season, and the introduction of IBM's PC, Jr.

In summary, the growth decision is a relatively complex one. It is based largely upon (1) a company's strengths and weaknesses compared to those of competitors in the particular product or service field, and (2) the permanancy of those strengths and weaknesses.

SBU strategists often must follow the lead of corporate-level strategists who attempt to manage the larger entity made up of a number of SBUs. Even though a particular business unit might have desirable growth prospects and substantial distinctive competencies compared to its competitors, it may not represent a good investment relative to other SBUs in the corporation. When this is true, corporate-level strategists may decide to extract investment funds from the SBU and allocate them to other, even more outstanding, businesses. On the other hand, if corporate-level strategists manage a number of SBUs all of which have low earnings prospects, a particular SBU may be encouraged to grow because it is the most competent SBU within the organization, although not strong relative to its competitors.

This suggests that corporate-level strategists might sometimes take a "closed-systems view" of the organization. They may not consider the whole universe of investment opportunities, but just those within the corporation. These strategists may be committed to growth from within and internal financing only. Sometimes this is due to the personal preferences of strategists. At other times, it may be favored for tax reasons. The closed-systems view is not totally unreasonable. To some extent, taxes and other costs close the boundaries of corporations. Dividends are taxed. New stock issues result in significant transaction costs. Corporate acquisitions and divestitures distract management from business-level competitive efforts and involve investment of time and money. The corporation remains an open system, but in some respects the openness is far from perfect.

Let us turn now to consideration of the usefulness of various special-purpose strategies, assuming that the company or SBU has decided upon a particular growth objective. The three possibilities we will consider are growth, stabilization, and retrenchment.

Strategies for Growth

Assuming that the SBU strategists have decided that it is desirable to grow, there are a number of ways that this can be accomplished. In this section we will discuss a rather wide range of strategies for growth. Some of them are designed to accomplish growth, and some to simply facilitate it. First, though, let us briefly consider how sales growth can be financed.

Financing Growth   Whenever a company grows, it is necessary to finance the asset increases which both facilitate and result from that growth. When sales increase, investment in accounts receivable typically increases. Additional productive capacity involves not only fixed assets but also raw materials, work-in-process, and finished goods inventories. In general, the asset increases can be financed through internal or external sources. If the business can increase earnings quickly, by either decreasing costs or increasing revenues, this will provide a net increase in cash flows. The cash flows which are available can be more completely retained by eliminating or reducing dividends or by decreasing the company's cost of capital through renegotiating borrowing arrangements, and so forth.

Usually, however, when growth is rapid, funds must be obtained from outside. When Atari grew too fast for internal financing, Bushnell arranged for Warner Communications to buy it. The $28 million purchase price was not a source of funds for Atari. It went to the previous stockholders, primarily Bushnell, in exchange for their stock. However, Warner Communications was able to provide investment resources as well as to enhance the borrowing capacity of Atari. Another common approach to obtaining additional capital to sustain growth is through an additional (or initial) issue of debt or equity securities. When a closely held company first offers stock for sale to the general public, this is called "going public." This was an alternative Bushnell considered before he decided to sell out to Warner Communications.

Facilitating Growth through Cost Reduction   An obvious strategy for growth is to produce a product or service at a lower cost than competitors can. This allows controlled growth through price and promotional competition along with expansion of production capacity. Sometimes the best way to obtain a product at a lower cost is to let others produce it. This is why the major U.S. auto companies have recently done more and more *out-purchasing—the buying of component parts which had previously been produced in house*. In many cases, the out-purchasing is done offshore, that is, in

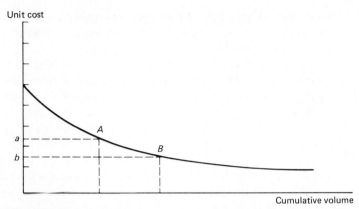

Unit cost

Cumulative volume

FIGURE 4.3   The experience curve

foreign countries. Because of out-purchasing, many, perhaps most, small American cars have Japanese engines. Both Texas Instruments and IBM use microprocessor chips purchased from Intel Corporation.

Another strategy for decreasing costs is simply getting out on the experience curve. Through penetration pricing it may be possible for a company to sell large volumes of a certain product or service. In producing a large volume, the company is often able to reduce its costs for two reasons: First, costs may be less because of economies of scale. *Economies of scale* are *changes in the cost of producing a product or service because of changes in the volume produced during a given time period*. This is a relatively ancient concept. Second, as previously indicated, costs may go down because of *experience curve effects*. This term refers to *the extent to which production costs vary over time with the cumulative volume of product or service produced*. The experience curve is a modern concept, and it is based upon our ability to learn how to do a job better over time. Experience curve theorists suggest that, for every doubling of cumulative volume in certain industries, unit costs decline by 25 percent or so. The hypothesized shape of the experience curve is shown in Figure 4-3. Note that company B has produced about twice as many total units as company A and has about a 25 percent cost advantage. The BCG, who developed the concept of the experience curve, tested the theory on the costs of refrigerators, automobiles, beer, and vacuum cleaners, and it worked for all these products (Kiechel, 1982).

Growth through Promotion   Given the capability of producing increasing volumes of a product or service, it is often possible to grow simply through promotional efforts. Even if no economies of scale exist, if advertising dollars are more than offset by the gross profit on additional sales produced, the advertising may be justified. For many products, such as detergents, powders, motor oils, insect repellants, beers, and a host of others, there are no significant differences in product quality, or even content, among the several top brands. So other aspects of the market mix—price, promotion, and physical distribution—largely determine the volume sold. Soap manufacturers differentiate their products with "blue granules" and so forth. Beer producers show happy people enjoying a "cool one" at the end of a hard day. And cola manufacturers fight for shelf space in stores while engaging in sporadic price competition.

Growth through Product Development   Another strategy related to growth is product development. This may be accomplished through spending on R&D, as most major companies do. Products may also be improved by enlisting the aid of the entire work force. This can be done through suggestion programs, quality circles, and other participative devices. At Lincoln Electric, for example, the advisory board, made up of employees, meets every two weeks to discuss ways of improving company operations, including product modification. Whatever approach is taken, success in product development requires attention from top management (Adamec, 1981, p. 39).

Growth through Integration   Product quality may also be improved through vertical integration. Sales growth normally follows this, or any, quality improvement. In addition, integration results in capturing the value added by suppliers or intermediate customers, which can increase profits. Backward vertical integration (i.e., toward the sources of supply of raw materials) can also improve an SBU's control over the quality and quantity of material inputs. Sears, Roebuck, and Company is noted for having purchased many of its suppliers. This was partly to reduce costs and partly to maintain Sears' reputation for quality. Vertical integration forward, toward the final user of the product, can help the company to control its distribution channels. This can result in more complete satisfaction of customer needs and wants. For example, by owning its retail outlets for Radio Shack computers, Tandy Corporation is able to offer point-of-sale advice and service as well as warranty administration. This is equivalent to an improvement in product quality. Forward vertical integration also directly increases sales, as the markup charged by intermediate customers, such as wholesalers and retailers, is captured.

Growth through the Purchase of Technology   Another way to develop new or improved products is to purchase technology. This can be accomplished through the buying of patent rights or even though the purchase of small companies which have made significant product innovations. For example, Phoenix Computer Graphics in Lafayette, Louisiana, has developed a number of improvements in graphics. A number of major computer manufacturers have held confidential discussions with Phoenix relative to purchase of the company to acquire its technology.

Growth through Attacks on Competitors   Another, often ill-advised, strategy for growth is an attack on competitors. During what was called the "great burger war" in 1982 and 1983, Burger King demeaned the tastiness of McDonald's and Wendy's "fried" hamburgers as compared to Burger King's "flame-broiled" ones. While negative comparison is usually considered to be a losing tactic in advertising, Burger King's market share increased significantly. Perhaps this can be explained. Although there may be some negative reaction to efforts to discredit competitors, it is usually the customer's price-quality perceptions of the various products which determine whose product that customer will buy. Consequently, if a company has only one or two major competitors, as does Burger King, any negative effect may be outweighed by a change in the customer's estimation of relative quality. In addition, the media publicity surrounding the great burger war is estimated to have been equivalent to $20 million in free advertising for Burger King.

Growth through Market Area Expansion Another approach to growth is through market area expansion. When the Adolph Coors Company decided to grow rapidly during the 1970s, it immediately began to expand outside its traditional eleven-state area. Although market shares in the added states never matched those in states bordering Colorado, Coors' home base, sales did increase sharply. Because of high earnings and a very strong balance sheet, Coors was able to finance most of the growth internally, although a public stock offering was made at one point. The company's brewery at Golden, Colorado, was expanded to allow the additional production required. For a time another large brewery was planned for the Shenandoah Valley of Virginia.

Market area expansion is a very common approach to growth. Insurance companies open sales offices in additional states, chain stores open new stores in other areas, and so forth. When markets start to become saturated and growth levels off in the U.S. market, domestic companies often expand to foreign countries. Holiday Inns, McDonald's, IBM, Xerox, and Otis Elevator have offices all over the world. All these companies were dominant in relatively saturated U.S. markets before they expanded internationally.

Growth through Market Intensification Market intensification is another approach to growth. When a good salesperson is given a new territory, the first calls are made on the larger and more profitable customers. As time goes on, smaller and smaller customers are selected until a point of diminishing returns is reached. The same is true of businesses. Many local companies never branch out beyond the city limits of their home cities. Yet, they open additional stores, employ additional salespersons, or engage in advertising through different media and at different times in order to reach additional customers. Major franchisers have standards for traffic flow which must be met before they will allow a new sales outlet at a certain location. As time goes on and markets become more saturated, standards are lowered. For example, for many years Pamida Stores opened new stores only in towns with populations of 7000 to 10,000 in Pamida's selected market area, the upper midwest. Although Pamida stayed in the same territory, it was possible to continue a relatively rapid rate of growth by changing the acceptable population size to 4000 to 12,000. The same pattern has been followed by Sears, K-Mart, Wendy's, and a host of other companies.

In summary, once a company has chosen to pursue relatively rapid growth, there are a number of strategies which can be followed. Some of them are designed to achieve the growth. These include investment in fixed assets, improved product quality, promotional efforts, market area expansion, market intensification, and so forth. Others are designed to increase profitability while growth is occurring, thereby facilitating the growth. These include cost reduction, quality improvement, vertical integration, and cost-of-capital reduction. If the aim of business-level strategists is to serve the interests of stockholders, sales growth should be viewed as a way of capitalizing upon the company's distinctive competences. This way, growth will not result in a reduction in the company's future earnings prospects and a concomitant reduction in share price, the only valid measure of the "wealth of the common shareholder" as it relates to a particular company.

Strategies for Stabilization

The strategies in this section could be precisely the same as those discussed under strategies for growth. As unusual as it may be, it is conceivable that a company would choose zero sales growth along with high prices and high profits instead of a more rapid rate of sales growth obtained through price competition and consequently low profitability. In fact, a well-administered company will recognize the trade-off between growth and profitability. Since market share is sticky downward, gaining a market share at the expense of current profitability may be justified by the prospect of the future profitability the added market share brings. But, if a company believes it will be unable to capitalize on the added market share, it might be better to stabilize sales and increase profits today. From these comments, it can be seen that a leveling off of sales may be—and should be—a conscious policy. Organizational strategists always have a rather wide range within which they can control sales, or any other single parameter. If the company is profitable but has chosen not to expand, the profits can be used either in the payment of dividends or for the retirement of securities, either debt or equity.

Recall that the decision as to whether to grow should be based on the special competences an SBU has relative to its competitors or relative to other SBUs in the corporate portfolio. If the company does not have any special distinctive competences, an obvious objective should be to try to attain such competences. In this connection, all the strategies discussed above for improving profitability, product attractiveness, and so forth, are available. A company can be better than its competitors (i.e., have distinctive competences) in R&D, marketing, production, possession of patent or other rights, ability to influence the government, management expertise, and/or work-force qualifications and motivation. In short, anything which helps a company win out over competitors is a distinctive competence. In addition to trying to build strengths and eliminate weaknesses, SBUs can select from among certain strategies which are especially applicable to periods of stabilization. Two of these are efficiency improvement and risk management.

Efficiency Improvement as a Stabilization Strategy   A particularly useful strategic focus during periods of stable sales is efficiency improvement. Labor costs can often be cut through various motivational strategies. Donnelly Mirrors, Inc., of Holland, Michigan, has a Scanlon-type group incentive plan which has allowed it to remain profitable when its major customers, the major auto companies, suffered declines. Lincoln Electric Company, of Cleveland, Ohio, has an incentive plan which offers individual piece rates along with large year-end bonuses based upon group and individual performance. Many companies motivate employees through participative approaches such as quality circles, suggestion boxes, open-door policies, and so forth. Periods of level sales offer good opportunities to look into and initiate such plans.

Efficiency improvement can also be obtained through fixed-asset management and reduction. If sales are not increasing, any improvement in fixed-asset efficiency can allow the elimination of some of these assets. For example, Cabot Corporation, a major producer of corrosion-resistant pipe, located in Kokomo, Indiana, made major improvements in its plant in Arcadia, Louisiana, during a recent recession. Machines were rearranged, and the work flow redesigned to shorten and speed up the production process. Some machines and materials-handling devices were completely eliminated. Unit product costs have declined significantly. Now that the company has a significant advantage over its competitors, a distinctive competence, it might choose to pursue a growth strategy. On the other hand, Cabot may decide to raise prices during periods of economic resurgence, thereby reaping current profits rather than a growth in sales. It is not intended here to dwell much on the details of process improvement, but merely to suggest that a period of planned sales stability offers a good opportunity for improving efficiency.

Risk Management as a Stabilization Strategy   In addition to efforts to improve current and future profitability through more efficient use of people and machines and efforts to develop distinctive competences through product development, quality improvement, and so forth, the SBU strategists must also consider the riskiness of the company's situation. If stock values are in fact determined in risk-return space, as modern portfolio theory suggests, it is as useful to reduce risk as it is to increase return. During periods of stabilized sales, the strategists have a good opportunity to earn high returns and, since investment needs are diminished, to distribute those returns to stockholders in the form of dividends or repurchase of company stock. But, the strategists can also reduce the riskiness of the company by debt reduction, making long-term supply and marketing contracts, negotiating favorable labor agreements, and establishing solid customer relationships.

In summary, strategies for periods of stable sales don't necessarily differ from those applicable during growth periods. The level of sales growth, within a very broad range, should be the result of conscious strategic decisions made by organizational strategists. However, once a company has chosen a stable sales policy, a good opportunity presents itself to focus inward on process improvement, efficiency measures, and so forth. Finally, stockholders are assumed to prefer decreased risk, given a rate of return on their investment. Consequently, organizational strategists might as well focus on risk reduction as upon profit improvement measures during periods of stable sales.

Strategies for Retrenchment

A dictionary definition of *retrenchment* is "reduction, curtailment, excision, cutting down of expenses," or in the military sense, "a defense work . . . constructed within another to prolong the defense when the enemy has gained the outer work" (*Webster's*

Third New International Dictionary). The term is used by organizational strategists in both senses. **Retrenchment** means *cutting back—reducing sales or production capacity*.

The second dictionary definition above illustrates the attitude most strategists take toward retrenchment. It is a strategy to be followed only after competitors have "gained the outer work" and defeat is imminent. This suggests that retrenchment is to be pursued as a strategy only when the company has been outdone by its competitors or is threatened by market force. It is true that few companies intentionally cut back on sales. Thus, retrenchment is often viewed as a reactive strategy rather than *proactive*.

The focus here is not upon retrenchment as an objective, but upon strategies which tend to be successful in meeting organizational goals during periods of retrenchment. It is doubtful that retrenchment per se is often adopted as a goal. But, the goals of profitability, risk reduction, enhancement of future earnings capability, and so forth, are as relevant during periods of retrenchment as at any other time.

Retrenching Profitably   There are several ways that a company can retrench effectively. First, it is possible to cut back on sales by simply increasing the price. This does not mean that the company has "given up." Sharpco Fabricators, Inc., a manufacturer of land-clearing equipment and heavy equipment repair facility in Monroe, Louisiana, recently retrenched by raising prices. The company had been doing well. Sales and profits had increased every year since the company was founded in 1972. But, the owner/manager, James Sharplin, was becoming more and more burdened by the growing number of customers who had to be serviced, the increasing employee force, and the requirement to continually expand production facilities. Sharpco's primary strength was its good reputation for quality. This resulted, Sharplin felt, from the personal attention he gave every job and every customer. He had no intention of expanding his operation beyond a size which he could personally supervise. With sales at about $1.3 million per year, Sharplin decided to increase prices by an average of 15 percent. This was accomplished by increasing the hourly rates for repair work, the bid prices for contract jobs, and the list prices for land-clearing equipment. Sales declined significantly, profits increased, and Sharpco was able to sustain its excellent reputation for quality.

Even though the recession which began in 1979 intensified in 1982, causing a further reduction in sales, Sharpco still earned record profits that year. Sharplin feels that the retrenchment has been a good strategy. In addition to the improved profit picture, he now has more free time and is able to do a better job of supervision. An additional benefit accrued from the retrenchment: Sharpco's land-clearing equipment sales had recently declined because most of the timberland in northern Louisiana had been cleared and Sharpco's customers were trying to sell their land-clearing equipment, not buy more. Because of the decreased demands of the business, Sharplin was able to spend time improving the repair and parts segment of his business to replace the disappearing sales in the land-clearing equipment area. This suggests that rapid retrenchment might often be a good strategy for business segments which are declining. Then attention can be paid to developing replacement products and markets.

Turnaround Retrenchment is often considered a kind of turnaround strategy. If sales and/or profits have declined because of market forces or internal weaknesses, the organizational strategists may decide upon one of three approaches: (1) increase sales with the expectation of improving profits at some time in the future, (2) increase sales and profits, or (3) increase profits while allowing sales and productive capacity to decline.

If the first approach is taken, sales might be obtained through aggressive price competition, additional marketing expenditures, and so forth. This is particularly useful for companies that have high fixed costs. For such companies, when sales exceed the breakeven point, profits increase rapidly with additional increases. Expending promotional funds or forgoing revenues through price breaks can be viewed as an investment for building company sales to a profitable level over time. This can certainly be overdone, though. Arrow Electronics is a $404 million electronics parts distributor. The company has led its industry in growth over the past ten years. However, CEO John Waddell says that this was accomplished at the expense of most other considerations.'' In 1982, the company lost $1.19 per share. Waddell says, "Our strategy for a decade has been to get position. . . . Now it's time to turn our attention to cashing in on a ten-year investment" (McGough, 1983, p. 82). Hopefully, Waddell has not waited too long.

If sales and profits are to be increased together, it is often best to take a dual approach, paying attention to marketing *and* production. Marketing expenditures might be increased and efforts made to spend marketing funds more efficiently. At the same time, unless sales increase rapidly, it may be necessary to decrease production costs. This can be accomplished through more efficient use of capital and/or labor. This kind of dual focus is probably the most common kind of turnaround strategy, except for extreme cases. When Edward Finkelstein took over as CEO of Macy's, Inc. (parent corporation of Bamburger's department stores, Davison's department stores, and four regional divisions of Macy's stores) in 1980, the company's financial performance had been decidedly mediocre. By boosting sales per square foot and cutting costs, Finkelstein made Macy's one of the most profitable chains in its industry (Chakravarty, 1983). An extensive study by Hambrick and Schecter (1983) showed that, for industrial product business units, successful turnarounds were related to efficiency improvements and market share increases.

Reducing sales and production capacity intentionally is usually reserved for extreme cases. In these situations, turnaround may be accomplished by lopping off poorly performing segments of the business, disposing of related assets, and enhancing the best performing parts of the business. Often a turnaround specialist is employed for such purposes. Sanford Sigoloff was brought into Wickes Corporation to do this. And J. B. Freeman was hired by AM International Corporation. When Manville Corporation decided in 1982 to concentrate upon its forest products SBU, Albert Dunlop was hired to turn that business around. In the classic style of turnaround specialists, Dunlop released hundreds of employees, sold assets, established a new organizational structure, and attempted to increase the profitability of his division. A similar sequence of events occurred at International Harvester under Donald D. Lennox, at Chrysler

Corporation under Lee Iacocca, and at Kentucky Fried Chicken under Richard P. Mayer.

Bankruptcy Reorganization   The federal bankruptcy law allows companies to seek protection from creditors while attempting to reorganize and become profitable again. Prior to 1978, it was assumed that companies would declare bankruptcy only if they were insolvent. However, the 1978 bankruptcy code contains no reference to insolvency as a prerequisite for filing. In order to obtain court protection against creditors, a company need only file a bankruptcy petition with one of the U.S. bankruptcy courts. Unless the petition is deemed by the bankruptcy judge to be in bad faith, creditors are immediately barred from taking action to collect debts, labor agreements and other contracts are voided at the option of the company, and the company comes under the control of the U.S. Bankruptcy Court.

The court's control is usually exercised through the office of the U.S. Trustee, a specialist in bankruptcy matters, in each bankruptcy district. The company has 120 days, a period which can be extended indefinitely by the bankruptcy judge, to prepare a plan of reorganization. Typically, the reorganization plan provides for the repayment of some portion of the debts which were outstanding at the time of the filing and discharge of the rest.

When a company files for protection under Chapter 11, it typically obtains a significant cash windfall as accounts receivable flow in and accounts payable no longer have to be paid. When Manville Corporation filed for bankruptcy on August 26, 1982, the company owed over $300 million in accounts payable and had receivables of about the same amount. Within three months, Manville's cash balance exceeded $200 million.

Under Chapter 11, company managers are free to continue the "ordinary course of business." With the approval of the bankruptcy judge, who consults with various committees made up of creditors' and stockholders' representatives, rather extreme actions can be taken. For example, Sambo's Restaurants sold off most of its divisions and assets while in Chapter 11, yet continued a long downhill slide in profitability. Braniff Airlines, a major international carrier before its bankruptcy filing, emerged from Chapter 11 reorganization with flights to only twenty U.S. cities. A number of companies, including Wilson Foods Corporation and Continental Airlines, canceled labor contracts by filing under Chapter 11, and many more have obtained concessions from labor unions by threatening to file for bankruptcy.

Even in the rare bankruptcy cases where creditors are eventually paid in full, payment is usually made without interest, except to certain secured creditors. Consequently, a company almost always benefits at its creditors' expense after filing for Chapter 11 reorganization, at least in the short run. In addition to the corporations mentioned above, the following U.S. companies, among thousands more, took the Chapter 11 route in the 1982–1984 period: Osborne Computer, Revere Copper and Brass, Bobbie Brooks Clothing, and Baldwin United.

In the early 1980s the business failure rate in the United States was at a post-Depression high. An extensive study by Altman (1983) concludes that the increased failure rate resulted mainly from four factors: (1) low real economic growth, (2) low stock prices, (3) a slow money supply growth, and (4) an increased rate of business formation. However, the benefits available to corporate managers under the 1978 bankruptcy law were surely a factor.

Liquidation The most extreme retrenchment strategy is outright liquidation, either under the provisions of the U.S. Bankruptcy Code or without filing for bankruptcy. In a sense, publicly traded companies are being liquidated continuously through the sale of their stock by the public. When we think of liquidation, however, we normally mean the sale of the company's assets. Since few companies liquidate without being insolvent, proceeds from such sales normally do not cover all creditor claims. Stockholders, common and preferred, usually receive nothing. Chapter 7 of the U.S. Bankruptcy Code envisions what is called a "hammer sale." The assets of the company are simply auctioned off and the proceeds allocated among creditors and other claimants as prescribed by the code.

Liquidation does not have to be the result of bankruptcy. It may logically be chosen as a strategy if corporate strategists believe that the stock market undervalues the company stock. If it is the company's earning power which is undervalued, seeking to be acquired is a reasonable approach. In this way, the whole company is sold as a unit. Sometimes the stockholders receive cash for their shares. At other times they receive a combination of cash and debt or equity securities—or just securities. When Manville Corporation bought Olinkraft in 1978, some Olinkraft stockholders received cash. Others received one Manville Corporation preferred share in exchange for each Olinkraft common share held. Stockholders who received preferred shares were free to sell them on the open market for cash.

If it is the company's assets which are undervalued and not the unique synergy among those assets represented by the company's earning power, it might be desirable to liquidate, sell off the assets, pay the liabilities, and distribute the remainder of the proceeds to the stockholders. This is very rarely done. One reason for this is that the amounts invested in fixed assets (actually a "sunk cost" and, therefore, irrelevant to current decisions) tends to become an "exit barrier" in the minds of organizational strategists (Harrigan, 1981, pp. 306, 322).

Retrenchment to Fund Other SBUs Short of liquidation, many SBUs find it necessary to retrench significantly because corporate-level strategists desire disinvestment in one SBU in order to invest in others. As previously suggested, it may even be best for some single-SBU companies to retrench slowly, allowing equipment and facilities to run down and sales to fall off, but earning high profits in the process. Companies which do this can pay high dividends. This would be particularly appropriate for a business with competence only in a certain market segment which happens to be declining without a significant chance of revitalization. Just as a company can increase its market share by price competition, perhaps at the expense of current profitability, the opposite is also possible. If the company has a high market share, it can earn profits by increasing prices, even though that may cause the market share to erode. A company which correctly anticipates the demise of an industry before its competitors do can slowly price itself out of the business, leaving its competitors to participate in the death throes of the industry. *Plans for competing in dying industries are called **endgame strategies***.

In summary, strategic management decisions are always constrained to some extent. Within whatever constraints there are, organizational strategists should be *proactive*, that is, they should decide what specific strategies should be followed and to what extent growth or retrenchment should take place. Retrenchment is seldom a strategic goal in itself. The question is not how a company retrenches but how a company accomplishes its organizational purposes while retrenching or through retrenchment.

THE PRODUCT LIFE CYCLE AND STRATEGY

Perhaps no variable has been so clearly related to appropriate strategies as product life cycle. A great body of research suggests that strategies which are appropriate for products experiencing a rapidly growing demand are inappropriate for those for which demand is declining. This idea is intuitively appealing as well. It seems reasonable that successful companies in, say, the (growing) home computer industry would have different strategic foci than those in the (declining) mechanical calculator industry. There is some disagreement about exactly which strategies are best during the various stages of industry or product life cycle. But, the concept has enough proven validity to warrant consideration.

What Is Product, Service, or Industry Life Cycle?

Product, service, or industry life cycle is *the process of introduction, growth, maturity, decline, and extinction through which every product or service and every industry must go*. It is illustrated in Figure 4-4. There is no doubt that any product or service which attains any degree of market penetration has to begin at some point in time; that is, it must be introduced. After introduction, the product must go through a period of market development during which sales are promoted and new uses may be found for the product. After the development phase, a period of growth normally occurs during which product sales increase at an increasing rate. At some point, however, sales have to level off, resulting in what is called the maturity phase. Since no product can be expected to have the same relative level of usefulness forever, a decline phase must follow. That the product life cycle exists is a truism. Its application to strategic management is a subject of research and conjecture.

SBU Strategies for Different Life-Cycle Stages

As indicated in the previous main section of this chapter, there is no necessary relationship between industry growth and the growth pattern chosen by a particular competitor. However, as demand for a particular product accelerates, levels off, and

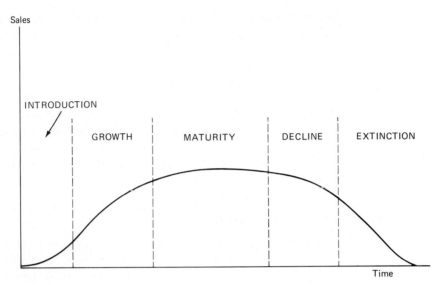

Sales

INTRODUCTION

GROWTH | MATURITY | DECLINE | EXTINCTION

Time

FIGURE 4.4   Product/service/industry life cycle

then declines, organizational strategists must respond. As suggested before, better than even responding is anticipating and developing strategies for the stages of the product life cycle.

Changing the Life-Cycle Curve

Sometimes, it is even possible to change the shape of the life-cycle curve. This was done with Arm & Hammer baking soda, which had undergone a long stable maturity stage and was declining in the 1970s. Through an extensive promotional effort in the early 1980s, the company convinced homemakers of the multiple uses of the product and a new growth phase occurred. As the only significant producer in the baking soda market, Arm & Hammer benefited greatly from the increased sales.

Collectivist Strategies

Few companies can determine the shape of the product life-cycle curve by themselves. Through collectivist strategies, though, whole industries often attempt to promote the industry's product. When cotton was threatened with replacement by rayon and other synthetic fabrics, the U.S. Cotton Council, with $1 a bale revenues from cotton producers, developed various kinds of promotional efforts for cotton. The coolness and naturalness of cotton fiber was promoted, and as a result a number of fashion garment manufacturers began to use more cotton in their products. Similar efforts were made by the Florida Orange Growers Association and many other trade groups. So, when organizational strategists anticipate a product life-cycle development with which they are not especially prepared to compete, they can collectively try to forestall that development. This is especially true of companies which have huge capital investments in declining product areas.

Bucking the Industry Life Cycle

Assuming that the total demand for a certain product or service is essentially beyond the control of an individual SBU, there are a number of other obvious relationships between the appropriate strategy and the life-cycle stage involved. However, the likelihood is that the truly successful SBU will not be experiencing the same growth pattern as the industry. If a particular competitor has an exceptional distinctive competence, especially one which can be expected to last (e.g., IBM and the Selectric typewriter, Xerox and the dry process copier, both patented), growth beyond the industry rate of growth can be anticipated. If the company has little distinctive competence but a large market share, a more desirable strategy might be to pursue relatively slower growth than more competent competitors would (Harrigan, 1980). As previously described, this would allow the company to reap profits as its market share declines.

The Life Cycle and Overcapacity

Companies in declining industries with heavy fixed investments must be prepared for a potential overcapacity condition. This is likely to result in extensive price competition. This occurred in the U.S. auto industry as foreign competitors took a large proportion of what was at the time a declining market. As a result, U.S. auto makers laid off hundreds of thousands of workers and shut down many plants, leaving billions of dollars in machinery and equipment idle.

It is possible to have overcapacity in a rapidly growing industry, like the home computer industry in 1983. Anticipating the rapid growth of that business, dozens of competitors worldwide developed production and marketing capabilities. When Texas Instruments reported a $100 million loss for the second quarter of 1983, industry analysts laid it to overcapacity in the home computer field. (Texas Instruments later dropped out of the home computer business.) Home computer sales had been growing at more than a 100 percent annual rate, with growth in the same range anticipated for a number of years. Because of this overcapacity, and the anticipation of future profit opportunities, price competition in home computers was rampant. Obviously the home computer industry is not a mature industry. A sort of "dynamic maturity" had set in, resulting in both overcapacity and price competition. Just as competitors in mature industries must innovate, differentiate their products, and concentrate on market segmentation, so must home computer manufacturers which expect to succeed.

The problem of overcapacity may be even more severe when it occurs in growing industries. Competitors in mature or declining industries tend to expect overcapacity and take it into account in their planning (Harrigan, 1982, pp. 707–708, 729–730). The effects of dynamic maturity in the home computer industry seem to have taken competitors by surprise. For several days after Texas Instruments first reported its expected loss on home computers, all the major computer stocks declined significantly, Texas Instruments alone losing more than $1 billion in market value.

Responding to Corporate-Level Needs

At the corporate level of strategy many strategists believe that a balanced portfolio of companies confronting various stages of the product or service life cycle is appropriate. Accordingly, a given SBU may be assigned an overall strategic approach to life-cycle-related strategy by corporate strategists. If this is done, as the BCG analysis in Chapter 3 suggests, SBUs in mature or declining industries will tend to be used as Cash Cows to fund growth for SBUs in rapidly growing industries. So life-cycle strategy may not be a business-level strategic decision. To some degree, SBU managers must conform to the needs of the corporation's portfolio of companies and the corporate-level strategists' preferences.

SUMMARY

The Atari story illustrates a number of important attributes of business-level strategy formulation. First, every business firm is primarily an economic entity, earning profits by meeting demands in the marketplace. Second, business-level strategy should be approached from a marketing standpoint, applying the marketing concept to organizational activity. Third, Atari's experience shows the value of a number of special-purpose strategies concerning product development, growth, and decline. Finally, the short history of the video games industry offers a highly compressed example of the impact of industry and product life cycles on business-level strategy.

The SBU is primarily an economic entity. Even most nonprofit organizations collect money and attempt to use it efficiently to accomplish worthwhile purposes. There are a number of profitability goals. But, in a strict sense, it is the present value of the SBU to the parent corporation which strategists should try to maximize. Since this is a difficult concept to operationalize, many SBU strategists concentrate on improving earnings capability, profitability, or cash flow.

Earning capability is most affected by investment decisions, which are often made on the basis of ROI. The ones which earn the highest ROI are funded. If retrenchment is necessary, investments are liquidated in reverse order of ROI.

Another common approach to investment decision making involves the payback period. The payback period is seldom used for resource allocation. More complex approaches to investment decision making include the IRR and NPV methods and the CAPM.

Net profit can be increased only by increasing revenues or decreasing expenses, or by some combination of both which gives the same relative result. There are six common strategies for increasing revenues and five for reducing expenses. When survival is in question, or if corporate-level managers direct it, SBU profitability may take a backseat to cash flow. Other than through earning profits, cash flow may be improved through (1) debt avoidance or delay, (2) capital asset depletion, (3) current-asset management, and (4) borrowing or issuing equity securities.

Adoption of the marketing concept suggests a complete focus on the customer through attention to the four P's of marketing. First, the product, or total bundle of goods and services, should be produced efficiently but with attention to the value it delivers to the purchaser in terms of both quantity and quality. Quality can be improved through statistical quality control efforts, quality circles, and suggestion systems, among other methods.

Second, since there is no such thing as a Giffen good, price is an important strategic weapon which has a clearly predictable direction of impact. The price-quality trade-off determines whether a customer will buy. Prices are infrequently based upon costs. Three market-based pricing strategies are skim pricing, competitive pricing, and penetration pricing.

Third, promotion strategy is the plan for informing and convincing the customer, including advertising, personal selling, and word of mouth.

The fourth P of marketing, place, often called physical distribution, relates to how the product or service is delivered to the end user.

Sales growth for an individual SBU can be a result of four factors: end-market growth, new uses for the SBU's products or services, price increases, and increases in market share. Growth strategies must affect one or more of these variables.

"Grow or die" is an accepted maxim. Growth is almost always beneficial to company management but is less likely to be beneficial to other constituents. Sometimes retrenchment is the best strategy for them.

The decision as to whether to seek sales growth cannot be based simply upon whether the relevant market is growing. It probably should be based upon the company's degree of distinctive competence in the product or service area.

Since market share is sticky downward, it is often desirable to seek rapid growth with the idea of profiting later from market position or experience curves effects. Sometimes the SBU manager has no choice and is directed to grow or retrench by corporate-level strategists. There are a number of strategies which can accomplish or facilitate growth.

First, growth may be financed through internal sources such as retained earnings or asset management or from external sources such as borrowing or equity issues. Second, costs may be reduced and growth facilitated through out-purchasing or the effects of experience and economies of scale. This will allow controlled growth through price and promotional competition. Third, a promotion strategy can increase sales profitably if economies of scale are involved. Fourth, product development or integration may improve product quality and therefore increase sales. Fifth, companies often purchase technology in order to compete better in the marketplace. Finally, promotional attacks on competitors, although often ill-advised, sometimes increase sales.

During periods of stable sales, the same strategies which produce and facilitate growth may be successful. In addition, companies often practice efficiency improvement and risk management when stable sales place a downward pressure on costs.

When companies decide to retrench or are forced to retrench, there are a number of ways to do so profitably. First, sales reductions may result from price increases which increase profitability. Second, new products and services may be developed to replace those which are declining in sales.

If sales and/or profits have declined, organizational strategists may (1) try to increase sales with the expectation of improving profits later, (2) try to increase sales and profits at the same time, or (3) try to increase profits while allowing sales and productive capacity to decline. Price competition alone may accomplish the first result. Marketing efforts, along with concentration upon productive efficiency might be the best way to accomplish the second method. And, shutting down and selling the least productive assets may accomplish the third.

The federal bankruptcy law allows companies to seek protection from creditors while attempting to reorganize and become profitable again. This often results in a major cash windfall. Corporate strategists in such companies are free to continue the ordinary course of business.

The most extreme retrenchment strategy is outright liquidation, either under the bankruptcy law or otherwise. This may be done because the company is in trouble or because it is undervalued by financial markets. Short of liquidation, many SBUs find it necessary to retrench because corporate-level strategists desire disinvestment in one SBU in order to invest in others. Rapid retrenchment may also be part of an endgame strategy.

Perhaps no variable has been so clearly related to appropriate strategies as product life cycle. That the life cycle exists is a truism. There are a number of strategies that are appropriate for different stages of the life cycle.

Some companies have found it possible to even change the shape of the life-cycle curve, individually and collectively. Others have learned to buck the industry life cycle and to grow more rapidly or slower than the industry in a profitable way.

During the maturity stage of the life cycle, overcapacity typically results. This has occurred in the home computer industry, which is now experiencing dynamic maturity. Many companies have learned to maintain a balanced portfolio of companies confronting various stages of product or service life cycles.

IMPORTANT CONCEPTS

Single-SBU organizations
Payback period
Internal rate of return (IRR)
Net present value (NPV)
Capital asset pricing model (CAPM)
The marketing concept
Product
Quality circles
Giffen good
Skim pricing
Competitive pricing

Penetration pricing
Experience curve
Promotion strategy
Place utility
Distinctive competence
Out-purchasing
Economies of scale
Experience curve effects
Retrenchment
Endgame strategies
Product, service, or industry life cycle

DISCUSSION QUESTIONS

1 What is the correct economic goal for a SBU to pursue? Explain your answer.
2 Distinguish among ROI, payback period, IRR, and NPV as tools of investment decision making.
3 Discuss four strategies for increasing revenues and for reducing expenses for a particular SBU.
4 Explain why a SBU might adopt increasing cash flow as a major goal to the detriment of long-term profitability.
5 Discuss four strategies not including increased profitability for a SBU which desires to improve cash flow.
6 Describe two strategies for improving product quality and give an example where one or the other might be preferable.
7 Explain cost-based pricing, skim pricing, and penetration pricing and the rationale for using each.
8 Define the experience curve and the relationship it has to penetration pricing.
9 Discuss how the organizational strategist might choose between a concentration on advertising, personal selling, or word of mouth as a means of promotion.
10 What is the appropriate criterion for deciding upon a growth, stabilization, or retrenchment policy? Explain your answer.
11 Under what circumstances might an SBU strategist be required by corporate-level strategists to extract investment funds, even though the particular SBU has viable growth prospects?
12 Explain how vertical integration might result in improved product quality?
13 Under what circumstances would market area expansion tend to be a better way of increasing sales than would market intensification?
14 Explain why efficiency improvement is an especially useful strategy during periods of stable sales.
15 Describe a situation in which a company has retrenched while increasing profitability.
16 Describe how bankruptcy reorganization works and especially why it usually results in a cash windfall.
17 Under what circumstances might a company choose to liquidate without declaring bankruptcy? Explain your answer.
18 Sketch the product, service, or industry life-cycle curve and label the phases it depicts.
19 Discuss the validity of the comment, ''The truly successful SBU will probably not be experiencing the same growth pattern as the industry.''
20 Discuss the concept of dynamic maturity as it relates to the home computer industry.

REFERENCES

Adamec, Richard J. ''How to Improve Your New Product Success Rate,'' *Management Review*, 70:1, January 1981, pp. 38–42.

Altman, Edward I. ''Why Businesses Fail,'' *Journal of Business Strategy*, 3:4, Spring 1983, pp. 151–21.

Baldwin, William. ''The Market Share Myth,'' *Forbes*, 131:6, March 14, 1983, pp. 109–110, 114–115.

Buaron, Roberto. ''How to Win the Market-Share Game? Try Changing the Rules,'' *Management Review*, 70:1, January 1981, pp. 8–17.

Chakravarty, Subrata N. ''The Per-Square-Foot Approach,'' *Forbes*, 131:3, January 31, 1983, pp. 33–34.

Glahe, Fred R., and Dwight R. Lee. *Microeconomics: Theory and Applications.* New York: Harcourt Brace Jovanovich, 1981.

Hambrick, Donald C., and Steven M. Schecter. "Turnaround Strategies for Mature Industrial-Product Business Units," *Academy of Management Journal*, 26:2, June 1983, pp. 231–248.

Harrigan, Kathryn Rudie. "Strategy Formulation in Declining Industries," *Academy of Management Review*, 5:4, October 1980, pp. 599–604.

Harrigan, Kathryn Rudie. "Deterrents to Divestiture," *Academy of Management Journal*, 24:2, July 1981, pp. 306–323.

Harrigan, Kathryn Rudie. "Exit Decisions in Mature Industries," *Academy of Management Journal*, 25:4, December 1982, pp. 707–732.

Harrington, Diana R. "Stock Prices, Beta, and Strategic Planning," *Harvard Business Review*, 6:3, May–June 1983, pp. 157–164.

Hartley, Robert F. *Marketing Mistakes*, 2d ed. Columbus, Ohio: Grid Publishing, 1981.

Kiechel, Walter, III. "Corporate Strategists under Fire," *Fortune*, December 27, 1982, pp. 34–39.

Maurice, S. Charles, Owen R. Phillips, and C. E. Ferguson. *Economic Analysis: Theory and Application.* Homewood, Ill.: Richard D. Irwin, 1982.

McCloskey, Donald N. *The Applied Theory of Price.* New York: Macmillan, 1982.

McGough, Robert. "Phoenix," *Forbes*, 131:12, June 6, 1983, p. 82.

McLagan, Donald, and Ben Buffa. "How to Grow in a Slow-Growth Decade," *Journal of Business Strategy*, 2:3, Winter 1982, pp. 45–49.

Ohmae, Kenichi. "The Secret of Strategic Vision," *Management Review*, 71:4, April 1982, pp. 9–13.

Rudolph, Barbara. "Minding Its Own Business," *Forbes*, 131:6, March 14, 1983, pp. 55–56.

Salter, Malcolm S. "Tailor Incentive Compensation to Strategy," *Harvard Business Review*, March–April 1973, pp. 94–102.

Stigler, George. *The Theory of Price*, 3d ed. New York: Macmillan, 1966.

Stobaugh, Robert, and Piero Telesio. "Match Manufacturing Policies and Product Strategy," *Harvard Business Review*, 61:2, March/April 1983, pp. 113–120.

Stonich, Paul J. "Using Rewards in Implementing Strategy," *Strategic Management Journal*, 2:4, October–December 1981, pp. 345–352.

STRATEGY
IMPLEMENTATION

CHAPTER 5

STRATEGY ACTIVATION: STRUCTURE, POLICIES, AND RESOURCE COMMITMENT

As Delta Airlines' fiscal year 1983 wore on, a number of the company's long-standing policies were put to the test. First, Delta had not laid off a single employee since 1957. Although the "no-layoff" policy was not contractual—not even written for that matter—the tradition was well established and both managers and workers felt that it would be continued. But with airline travel down sharply as a result of the recession, and extensive price cutting having become the rule rather than the exception, Delta's profits had evaporated. Other airlines had laid off thousands of persons in attempts to cope with reduced revenues, and one, Braniff Airlines, had failed outright. It would have been understandable if Delta had released a few workers under such dire circumstances.

Second, Delta had always tried to keep its fleet of airplanes more modern than those of all its major competitors. During 1983 Delta accepted delivery on a number of new, highly efficient Boeing 767 aircraft. Many of the other airlines canceled orders for new planes and even sold some of their existing planes in order to raise cash and lower their financial breakeven points. Sticking with the policy of maintaining the most modern fleet in the country was difficult enough. A less confident management team would surely have declared a moratorium on new airplane purchases. But Delta brought in over $300 million worth of new airplanes during fiscal year 1983 alone. During that same time the company was involved in the ongoing construction of a $100 million terminal at O'Hare field in Chicago, a $90 million terminal at New York's LaGuardia airport, a $50 million expansion at the Dallas/Fort Worth airport, and a $30 million improvement in Tampa, Florida, as well as a new $50 million computer building in Atlanta.

Third, prior to 1983, Delta had generated 85 percent of its required capital expenditures internally. That year, reduced revenues and losses of $86 million made those funds unavailable. In addition, the company's policy of borrowing money only on an unsecured basis appeared to be in jeopardy, since both Moody's and Standard and Poor's had reduced Delta's bond ratings. Even the percentage of debt in Delta's capital structure was higher than the planned levels established by company management, although still lower than that of any other major airline.

The capital expenditures and the loyalty to past policies were necessary, Delta management thought, to accomplish one of Delta's continuing objectives, remaining the lowest-cost producer of airline services in the country. Except for the pilots, Delta workers had never seen fit to unionize and were acknowledged to be the most devoted and productive in the industry. In fact, to show their loyalty, the employees bought the company a new Boeing 767 airplane in 1983. Over 70 percent of the workers contributed to the fund, which was established by the employees themselves.

Delta's organizational structure probably reflects as well as contributes to the cooperativeness of the employees. While the company has no organization chart—to avoid a highly structured mentality—the structure which exists is very flat and extremely flexible in some respects. A ticket agent at the Cincinnati airport, for example, has only two managers between her and the company president. And, because of a faithful open-door policy, she may even bypass them if she likes.

The company is functionally divisionalized. Senior vice presidents head up seven highly centralized divisions. The personnel division is especially centralized. Every employee is invited to contact the personnel office about any job-related matter. And, important personnel actions—such as firing—require central office approval. Other divisions include technical operations, engineering, quality control, material services, and finance.

By late 1983, the airline industry was slowly recovering and Delta managers were unanimously bullish about the company's future. John Berry, manager of public relations, said: "Delta is looking good. I think we're going to impress you. Give us two more quarters and you will see the triple figures (an annual rate of over $100,000,000) in the black ink again. That's my prediction." Mr. Berry's forecast was a bit too optimistic, but the company was returning to profitability as 1984 began.

Most would agree that in comparison with other airlines Delta has done a good job of strategic planning, or strategy formulation. However, Delta managers give as much credit to faithful implementation of strategic plans as to the quality of the plans themselves. As can be seen from the illustration which opens this chapter, strategy implementation consists of three subactivities. The first is activation. Recall that *strategy activation* has been defined as initiating activities in accordance with a strategic plan. The second step in strategy implementation is to evaluate both the plan and the actions which result from the plan. The third step is to take corrective or guiding action, either modifying the plan or forcing activities to accord with the plan.

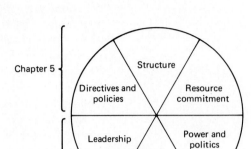

FIGURE 5.1   Elements of strategy activation

Strategy activation is the topic of this chapter and the next. Evaluation and control are reserved for Chapter 7.

In discussing strategy activation we will consider six subactivities: (1) imposition of structure on the organization, (2) issuance of directives and policies, (3) resource commitment, (4) organizational leadership, (5) application of motivational techniques to strategic activities, and (6) use of the principles of power and politics. These are shown in Figure 5.1. The last three of these are discussed in Chapter 6. Let us consider how the first three are exemplified by the Delta Airlines story recounted above.

First, Delta's flat and flexible organizational structure helps the company respond to its rapidly changing environment. Highly centralized management of vital functions and other aspects of structure ensure consistency of practices regarding personnel, quality control, and so forth. Second, Delta's personnel policies undoubtedly account in large measure for the productivity and loyalty of Delta employees. This not only helps the company keep labor costs down but allows management to concern itself with the details of running an airline without the distractions of strikes and worker-related lapses in quality. Good human relations resulting from Delta personnel policies might also account for the fact that Delta has avoided many of the safety problems which have plagued some other airlines. Third, regarding resource commitment, Delta has certainly "put its money where its mouth is," committing hundreds of millions of dollars to investment in the future.

Let us now consider the application of the first three attributes of strategy activation—structure, policies, and resource commitment—to all kinds of organizations. First, we will discuss important questions relating to organizational structure. Then, the use of policies and directives in strategy activation will be described. The last section of the chapter is devoted to resource commitment.

STRATEGY ACTIVATION AND ORGANIZATIONAL STRUCTURE

The term *structure* denotes some degree of physical or conceptual rigidity. When an analogy is made between physical structures and organizational structure, we often think of the organizational chart which spells out who reports to whom and who directs whose activities. A number of writers have recognized that, to be consistent, we must extend the meaning of the term *organizational structure* to include relationships not spelled out in the organizational chart (e.g., Blackburn, 1982; Grinyer and Yasai-Ardekani, 1981). In fact, many companies—Delta Airlines among them—do not have organizational charts. Yet, most would agree that all have a structure. Whereas physical structures tend to be static, representing a constancy of *position* of the component parts relative to one another, organizational structure is dynamic, representing consistent *patterns of behavior*. So we have defined **organizational structure** as *the set of relationships within an organization which are established or consistent over time*.

Organizational structure can be viewed as having three dimensions. The first, **centralization**, is *the degree to which decision-making authority is retained by higher levels in the organization*. The second, **specialization**, is *the extent to which organizational activities are separated into distinct functions*. For example, when an organization has four functional departments concerned, respectively, with personnel, finance, production, and marketing, this suggests a moderate degree of specialization. When the personnel function is divided up among specialists in training, compensation, industrial relations, and record keeping, the organization is even more specialized. The third dimension, **organizational rigidity**, is *the degree to which organizational relationships tend to remain constant over time*. Organizational structure, like physical structure, can be rigid or flexible. As a fixed physical structure becomes more and more flexible, eventually it becomes a blob—and then not a structure at all. In the same way, behavior patterns within organizations range from the completely structured ("This is the procedure and you do exactly what it says and nothing else") to the extremely flexible ("As long as you finish the job on time, I don't care how you go about it").

Only through having some structure, however, does an organization become an organization. And the imposition of structure is a valuable tool through which organizational strategists perform their function of molding and shaping the organization and relating it to its environment. Let us now look at several important questions involving strategy and structure.

Does Structure Follow Strategy?

The debate as to whether structure follows strategy, or vice versa, has continued for decades. The matter was well settled by Alfred Chandler (1962), who concluded that structure follows strategy. The relationship between structure and strategy was also very clear to a number of other writers (Cyert and March, 1963; March and Simon, 1958; Lindblom, 1959). The problem is that many of them "knew" exactly the opposite of what Chandler did. The answer all depends upon one's perspective, perhaps. Burgelman (1983) has suggested that strategy and structure are interactive. A few examples of using structure to implement strategy (structure follows strategy) will help clarify the matter.

Suppose a company decides that its strategy for competition in the marketplace will be an extensive and continuing R&D effort aimed at product improvement and new product development. Part of the implementation of this strategy may be the creation of an entirely new department called the R&D department. Setting up the department would constitute a change in organizational structure. Assume, instead, that the company expects to compete on the basis of product quality but that the quality control manager reports to the production manager, creating a conflict of interests. Implementation of this strategy might result in a change in reporting relationships. To make the quality control manager more independent, that department is often placed directly under the chief operating officer or another senior official. This too, is a change in organizational structure for the purpose of implementing strategy. Grinyer and Yasai-Ardekani (1981) have shown that a good fit of structure to strategy promotes better coping with the environment.

On the other hand, strategy must take into account the structure which exists. That is, to some degree strategy must follow structure. Consider a retail store chain, like WalMart stores, which decides to engage in aggressive price competition as a strategy for market penetration. If the company has a centralized organizational structure with prices determined at company headquarters, it may only be necessary to change the prices and issue new price lists. If the company has a decentralized structure, with pricing authority and responsibility residing in the individual store managers, the strategy for price competition would be quite different. Because of the decentralized structure, it may be necessary to explain the company's decision in detail to store managers, seeking their active cooperation rather than just their acceptance of corporate authority.

Whether strategy follows structure, or vice versa, is entirely optional with the organizational strategists, who can change both structure and strategy. In fact, determination of the appropriate organizational structure and changes is a major part of strategy formulation. Still, most successful organizations, like Delta Airlines in the short story at the beginning of this chapter, develop strategies which take into account the existing structure, allowing that structure to evolve slowly.

A great deal of research money has been spent on the question. As one would expect in such matters, research results conflict. Depending upon the research design and the sample, strategy has been found to be the independent variable or the dependent variable, and strategy and structure have been found to be mutually interdependent. Of course, the latter is the case. The more relevant way of asking the question is to ask whether organizational strategists should be completely constrained by the organizational structure which exists or whether this too should be the subject of strategic decision making. Again, the answer is relatively clear. Through the modification of prescribed organizational relationships—that is, structure—strategists can change *patterns* of behavior in the organization. This is more clearly a strategic matter than controlling *individual instances of behavior*, a function of all leaders and managers.

Is Decentralization or Centralization of Authority the Better Strategy?

The question of whether centralization or decentralization of authority works best is assumed by many to be passé: Decentralization is good, centralization is bad. Centralization is often considered a necessary evil, at best. Certainly, decentralization gives middle- and lower-level managers who are granted authority and held responsible added incentives to do their jobs well. But, even with the added incentives, they may not make important decisions as competently. Managers are presumably promoted to higher positions because they are better at managing than those who are not promoted (this does not always happen, of course). Once in those positions, they also have access to decision-making assistance—information and advice—unavailable at lower levels. Therefore, centralization should place decisions in the hands of persons more capable of making those decisions correctly.

At the same time, while senior managers may be able to make better decisions in most cases, lower-level managers, since there are more of them, are capable of making more decisions and of allocating more time to the decisions they do make. Also, lower-level managers may be more highly specialized and thus can often make more valid decisions in their areas of expertise.

Continuing the argument for decentralization, many suggest that decentralization provides greater flexibility in decision making and is more applicable to dynamic situations. If major decisions have to be referred to headquarters, it is likely that they will be delayed—so the reasoning goes. If each important decision has to be approved by four ascending levels of management, for example, it is likely that rapid response to environmental changes will be impossible. However, again the case is not quite that simple. When Lee Iacocca took the helm at Chrysler, decision making became much more centralized and the performance of Chrysler Corporation, in what was then a dynamic auto industry, improved significantly.

In addition to environmental dynamism, decentralization is considered appropriate for situations where the organization is faced with various organizational elements which differ significantly. Companies with offices in various countries which have greatly different cultures often give managers within those countries the authority to respond to local situations. The same is true of merchandisers who have rural and urban stores or stores in the South and stores in New England. Often, local attitudes and buying habits differ from region to region. Even within a region, competitor behavior may differ from time to time in various small market areas. For example, a gasoline price war recently raged for a brief period on the north side of Houston, Texas, and Texaco station managers there were authorized to match local prices. On the south side of Houston, the gasoline business continued pretty much as usual. Because authority was decentralized, Texaco stations in both areas responded appropriately. So, decentralization of authority not only allows additional flexibility for the whole organization in responding to environmental circumstances, but also gives additional flexibility within the organization.

What types of decisions should be centralized? The principle of specialization of labor provides a good answer. Just as the American economy is based upon resources, including workers, flowing to their best use—that is, doing the jobs for which they are best fitted—managers within an organization should "flow to their best use." When we slice the organization horizontally, it is easy to understand that machine work is better done by machinists using modern machine tools than by secretaries using typewriters. If the volume of machine work increases, we would simply hire more machinists and buy more machines, not allocate machine work to the typing pool.

When the organization is sliced vertically, a similar picture appears. The skills needed by managers at various levels differ (Pavett and Lau, 1983; Leontiades and Tezel, 1981). Individuals who have higher-level management jobs tend to be those who have better analytical and conceptual skills, the skills required in effective managerial decision making. Lower-level managers and workers tend to evidence a higher degree of manipulative and technical skills. Typically, both groups have enhanced their respective skills through practice. So, in general, decisions which require analytical and conceptual skills should be centralized, while those requiring manipulative and technical skills should be decentralized.

If the strategic decision is to centralize authority, there are many ways to facilitate implementation of the decision. One useful approach is to establish rapid and efficient information systems to provide upper level managers with summarized information on a real-time basis. Seven-Eleven Stores has such an advanced information system. Top managers at company headquarters are able to immediately call up information for any one of thousands of stores or for regional and size-based groupings of stores. Computerized warehousing facilities allow store shelf replenishment to be done daily by trucks which are loaded in computer-determined order and travel along computer-designed routes to individual stores. Managers in Dallas are able to analyze the sales of various items in different stores and in various sections of the country, as well as at different shelf locations within the stores. Because of the extremely efficient information systems, Seven-Eleven's lower-level managers do not need to make pricing decisions, determine how much and what kind of products to order, or even determine where to place products within the store. This results in a highly centralized management system, but at the same time a highly efficient one.

Similarly, there are accepted strategies for implementing a decision to decentralize authority. One way to obtain organizational efficiency along with environmental responsiveness in a decentralized organization is through an accountability-and-reward structure. Near the turn of the century, DuPont de Nemours and Company developed what has been called the DuPont system of financial control. Under that system, managers are evaluated and resources are allocated on the basis of the ROI earned by operating divisions. ROI is the major criterion used by many corporations to evaluate management performance. When this approach is taken, division managers tend to act more responsibly because they are being held accountable and are receiving some of the benefit from the division's performance.

To What Degree and on What Basis Should the Organization Be Departmentalized?

Much research has been conducted to determine which is more effective—product, geographic, or functional departmentalization. Certainly, there can be no clear answer. The decision as to how to departmentalize is a strategic one which must be interrelated with many others. Such a decision must take into consideration environmental and technological factors, as well as the competences and preferences of persons within the firm.

Most large organizations involve some degree of departmentation in all of the ways mentioned above, as well as others. Sometimes functional departmentation, especially for staff departments, cuts across geographic or product lines. For example, the chief financial officer at the corporate level may issue directives and receive reports from accounting managers in all the SBUs in the corporation. A quality control director may do the same. Through such practices, it may be possible to highly centralize personnel, accounting, and quality control functions while the production and marketing functions are decentralized.

The primary purposes of departmentation are (1) to break the organization into manageable units, and (2) to facilitate specialization by managers and workers. There are a number of other strategic purposes which can be served through various forms of departmentation. An organization may be split apart with the purpose of encouraging competition among units. Plymouth Tube Corporation, for example, has a number of plants which make identical products. Plants which do the best job of minimizing waste, decreasing raw material and labor costs, and attaining high levels of quality are held up as models throughout the company. In many large conglomerate corporations, diversified departments compete on the basis of ROI or profitability.

Another strategic reason for departmentation or redepartmentation may be to overcome organizational inertia, bureaucratization, or what might be called "calcification" of the organization. Many companies, like individuals, become "set in their ways." Most things are done in certain ways because "that's the way it has always been done around here." Techonological innovations are rare in such organizations. Managers who attempt to make changes are accused of "rocking the boat." As long as the environment is extremely stable and competitors don't innovate, such companies can continue this way for years. This happened in the U.S. auto industry until the environment became dynamic in the late 1970s. When organizational strategists perceive the need to break out of such calcified structures, it is often not feasible to do so a little at a time. Instead, the company may be completely reorganized. This can be viewed as "change for the sake of change," and to some extent, this is the case. But, it has been shown to be beneficial in a number of cases. Miller and Friesen (1982, pp. 867–8 and 890–1) argue that drastic change in such cases is generally better and less costly than gradual or incremental change. Thomas R. Horton, president of the American Management Association, says, "The organizational layered look has brought us the laminated look, with some strengths but many rigidities. Layer-shedding is essential, but it won't be easy" ("In the News," 1982).

POLICIES AND STRATEGY ACTIVATION

We have already said that strategic implementation is the process of doing. Actually, though, many define management as the "process of getting things done through the efforts of other people" (Mondy, DeHay, and Sharplin, 1983, p. 4). As we will see in the next chapter, this involves leadership, power, and a knowledge of human motivation. To keep from continuously having to "reinvent the wheel," it is important for strategists to set out continuing guides to action in the form of organizational policies. A ***policy*** is *a rule, procedure, or other guide to action.* Policies may be oral or written—or they may simply result from past practices. "That is the way we have always done it around here," means the same as, "That is the policy here." Of course, the more detailed and rigid policies are, the less room there is for individual initiative.

On the other hand, policies serve to focus organizational activities on group objectives. Policies help to make the organization more predictable, both in terms of processes and outcomes.

The Hierarchy of Policies

Policies may emanate at any level of the organization and may concern matters great and small. The tendency is for those relating to matters of far-reaching importance to come from top management. Often top management also dictates policies relative to minor matters which affect a number of departments or divisions. Ideally, policies established at lower levels in the organization should be designed to support and implement those issued at higher levels. Policies coming from upper management tend to emphasize company purpose, broad objectives, and business philosophy. They also tend to be more or less permanent. As we move to lower levels in the organization, policies become more explicit, narrower in focus, and shorter in time frame. For example, at Ford Motor Company the corporate policy that "quality is job one" says little about an individual worker's behavior. However, the policy that a particular assembly line worker should install no part with a visible defect prescribes the worker's behavior rigidly.

Our initial reaction is to suggest a simple decision rule: Top management policies should be broad, general, and flexible—lower-level policies should be narrow, explicit, and rigid. The matter is not that simple, however. There is evidence that flexible policies at all levels result in improved initiative and motivation. On the other hand, the experience of the Japanese as described by W. Edwards Deming (Ringle, 1981, pp. 8327–8328) has been that efficiency is enhanced by statistical control from the top to the bottom of the organization. Often there is a trade-off between technical efficiency (enhanced by rigid, detailed procedures) and practical efficiency and effectiveness (which may be improved by minimizing policy directives and emphasizing individual motivation and responsibility).

The really compelling argument against trying to prescribe behavior too rigidly is the usual lack of organizational competence for doing so. Top managers simply cannot be involved in all the details at the lower levels. Seven-Eleven stores, however, have shown that, when the information processing capability exists, top management can be more explicit in its directives. That information-processing and decision-making capability can result from individual competence, as in the case of Lee Iaccoca and Chrysler, or electronic data processing capability, as in the case of Seven-Eleven stores.

Functional Area Policies

We have chosen in this text to examine strategic management from four functional viewpoints: finance, personnel, production, and marketing. Just as corporate-level strategy tends to determine the relative emphasis on various SBUs, business-level strategy tends to relate to resource allocation among functional areas. For example, in a very broad sense, a company may seek a strategic advantage through production efficiencies or through aggressive marketing in the form of promotional expenditures. Within these functional areas, policies prescribe the process of competition. Let us look at each functional area and see what kinds of policies are useful.

In *finance*, a dividend policy may require stable dividends, dividends amounting to a certain percentage of earnings, or no dividends at all. Growth may be financed internally, as in the case of Nucor Steel, or externally, as in the case of most young high-tech firms. Reliance may be largely upon debt or upon equity financing. Finance policies often spell out the company's approach to depreciation, capital budgeting, and so forth.

In the *personnel* area, policies relate to the six functional areas of personnel: (1) planning, recruitment, and selection, (2) training and development, (3) health and safety, (4) employee and labor relations, (5) personnel research, and (6) compensation. For example, personnel planning, recruitment, and selection policies may state the type of new employee required (e.g., honor graduates from Ivy League schools), what will be done to attract them (annual recruiting trips), and who is responsible for recruiting. In the area of compensation, policies may express which workers will receive salaries and which ones will be paid on an hourly basis or by piece rates. Policies usually establish salary ranges and hourly pay ranges for various employee categories. In light of the importance of the personnel resource, no group of organizational policies is more vital to success than those relating to people.

In the area of *production*, which we take to include process-related R&D, policies should answer the following questions: How concerned is the company with quality, and what procedures are followed to control it? What is the production process? Assembly line, as in American automobile factories? Production teams, as in Sweden's Volvo factory? Or process-type production, as in most petrochemical and paper products plants? Does the company produce to order or to inventory? Is production allowed to go up and down with seasonal valleys and peaks or is an attempt made to level production over the year? How aggressively are new technologies incorporated into the production process? To what degree is the process labor-intensive? Capital-intensive? This is just a brief sampling of the policies which could be related to production. As a functional area, production includes everything directly involved in making and distributing the product or providing the service which is the company's merchandise. For banks, this includes processing checks, accepting deposits, and even financial counseling. For grocery stores, it includes purchasing goods, stocking shelves, cleaning the floors, and operating the checkout counters. Probably the most reliable distinctive competence a company can have is the ability to produce a product or service of higher quality at a given cost or at a lower cost for a given quality than its competitors. Effectively administering the production process requires the thoughtful and intelligent generation and implementation of production policies.

Marketing policies relate to product, price, promotion, and place. What are the company's distribution channels to be—through its own retail outlets, like Sears; through franchise stores, like most fast food companies; or through specialty whole-salers, like most producers of drugs and sundries? What is the sales territory and who is the target market? What is pricing policy to be—skimming, penetration, or competitive? Is price to be based on the market, or on costs? What product characteristics are to be highlighted, and how strongly will marketing be allowed to influence product characteristics? Marketing policies formally set the amount which will be spent on advertising and the kind of advertising to be used. As previously discussed, the company which subscribes to the marketing concept will consider marketing the primary focus of the organization.

The question of what level in the organization should make functional area policy is a difficult one. As a general guide, however, it is well to refer to something said previously. Whether the organization is sliced horizontally or vertically—or diagonally for that matter—decisions should be made and functions should be performed by those elements most competent to do them. At the same time, it is clear that policies which affect the general focus of the organization, such as whether to adopt the marketing concept or not, should be established by top management. Those of relatively less importance, especially those applicable for only a short time, should be made by lower-level managers. It is a reasonable assumption that the marketing manager, being a specialist, knows the most about marketing and should be involved at least on a consulting basis in the establishment of marketing policies. The same is true of the production manager for production policies, and so forth.

STRATEGY ACTIVATION THROUGH RESOURCE COMMITMENT

Plans represent expectations and hopes. Policies are guides to behavior. But nothing really happens until resources are committed. The job of the organizational strategist culminates in the effective commitment of physical, financial, and human resources to serve useful purposes. Not until resources are committed do plans become irrevocable. In fact, it is precisely through the commitment of resources that strategists have their major impact. But resource allocation and commitment are difficult. Gluck (1981, p. 67) identifies three dilemmas in resource allocation: (1) deciding what criteria to use, (2) matching resource needs with resource availability, and (3) scheduling resource commitment over time. This suggests the immense complexity of the resource allocation job. Organizational modeling is generally becoming more common as computers become cheaper and more competent. In this final section of the chapter, we will view the organization as a system which takes the input—money, people, and physical assets—and uses them to produce output. This is illustrated in Figure 5.2. First we will discuss how all these resources are substitutable, at least in the long run. Then we will describe how each becomes involved in the strategy activation process.

Resource Substitution

It has been said that the most flexible resource of all is money, because it can be used to purchase the others. Holding money is often seen as a good way to be prepared for change. To an extent, of course, this is true. Once money is used to buy office buildings and factories and to hire workers to whom the organization becomes committed, a good deal of flexibility is lost. Organizations can retain this money-based flexibility either by holding cash balances or by keeping a conservative balance sheet. Delta Airlines, for example, has limited its cash balances but has guarded its borrowing

FIGURE 5.2   The organization as a system

capacity. Because Delta had been so conservatively managed from a financial stand-point it was easy to obtain the funds needed to purchase new airplanes and facilities in 1983.

However, it may have been because of excessive concern for liquidity that Montgomery Ward began its long downward slide in comparison with Sears and Roebuck. As reported in *Fortune*:

> While Sears confidently bet on a new and expanding America, Avery [CEO of Montgomery Ward] developed an *idée fixe* that postwar inflation would end in a crash no less serious than that of 1929. Following this idea, he opened no new stores but rather piled up cash to the ceiling in preparation for an economic debacle that never came. In these years, Ward's balance sheet gave a somewhat misleading picture of its prospects. Net earnings remained respectably high, and were generally higher than those of Sears as a percentage of sales. In 1946, earnings after taxes were $52 million. They rose to $74 million in 1950, and then declined to $35 million in 1954. Meanwhile, however, sales remained static, and in Avery's administration profits and liquidity were maintained at the expense of growth. In 1954, Ward had $327 million in cash and securities, $147 million in receivables, and $216 million in inventory, giving it a total current-asset position of $690 million and net worth of $639 million. It was liquid, all right, but it was also the shell of a once great company. ("Montgomery Ward: Prosperity is Still around the Corner," 1960, p. 140.)

There tends to be a fixed relationship among money, physical assets, and labor. In general, dollar values can be assigned to units of each. Strategists may choose to purchase a large number of advanced machines or robots and become more capital-intensive, or they may choose to use older, less sophisticated machines and hire workers to do what the machines otherwise would do. We should note in passing that management does not have complete freedom in this regard. There are no labor-intensive competitors in the oil-refining industry, for example, and it has not yet been possible to make clothing without hiring a large number of workers.

Entrepreneurial ability or managerial competence, part of the human resource, can be used to expand the resource base. When Steve Wozniak was making the first Apple computer in his garage, he did not have the resources available to manufacture thousands of computers monthly, as the company he founded is now doing. In fact, most of today's great organizations can trace their histories back to times when only very limited resources were available. Because managerial competence was high, or because the ideas and philosophies upon which companies were based were good ones, America's capitalistic economy made resources available to those organizations. Let us turn now to consideration of the individual kinds of resources which must be obtained and allocated in the implementation process.

Committing Money

Most organizations allocate money through formal budgets. There are often expense budgets, capital budgets, raw materials budgets, and sometimes even human resources budgets (discussed in the next subsection).

The budgeting process is normally an annual one. Capital goods purchases are usually planned a number of years in advance, and expenses are planned in detail just for the coming year. Ideally, of course, funds would be allocated to each division or department of the organization based upon which would make the best use of those funds in serving constituencies. Also, the funds should be divided up among capital goods, raw materials, labor, and other expenses on the basis of the same criterion.

To simplify the process, we typically assume that the purpose of the company is to make a profit, as Nobel Laureate economist Milton Friedman said, "within the rules of the game." Few organizations are willing to say that they serve managerial interests as well as the interests of a number of other stakeholders. Yet this is undeniably true. So, in budgeting, the stated purpose is to allocate funds to the uses which will produce the greatest value for the common shareholder, that is, earn the highest profit in the short or long run. ROI is the conventional basis for doing this although, as pointed out in earlier chapters, ROI maximizes neither short-term profits nor long-term earning capability. It does provide a central rationale, however, around which a great deal of variability is allowed for allocating funds within most organizations. Some companies use other profitability-type measures such as return on equity to decide how available monies are to be distributed.

For nonprofit organizations, of course, ROI is not calculable. So other, more nebulous means are used. The typical basis of this year's budget is last year's budget as modified by the political structure within the organization. Most profit-making companies use this approach to some extent as well. Such a seemingly nonrational approach may be used for three reasons, among others: (1) Capital goods are not usually reallocable in the short term and would be useless without other resources which are budgeted annually. (2) It is difficult to measure the impact of various resources upon the degree to which we serve various constituencies. (3) Many managers really do not believe that profitability is a completely valid criterion anyway. Even if we are purely rational about this matter, risk must be considered—and no valid method has been developed to specify the riskiness of various investments. In addition, there are few managers who really want to be tied down to purely rational decision making. So there are political reasons not to impose too high a degree of rationality within the organization.

There is another side to this argument. The efficient use of resources to accomplish worthwhile purposes is vital to the welfare of society, any society. The recession of 1979–1983 pointed up the fact that America had become a less efficient producer of goods and services than many foreign countries, especially Japan. Only through the rationalization of resource allocation and use can companies become more efficient. It is vital that organizational strategists allocate funds to those divisions, organizational levels, tasks, and ways of doing things which will result in the most efficient production of goods and services. It may be necessary for the strategist to view "goods and services" as benefits delivered to any of the organization's diverse constituencies. But the primary output of the organization still has to be the benefits provided its customers for a price, and the primary incentive to do that efficiently in a capitalist economy still must be profit. Accordingly, within the limits imposed by organizational power and politics, the job of the strategist should be to allocate resources to obtain the most efficient production of goods and services possible for the purpose of maximizing earning capability.

American managers have been criticized for seeking short-term profit instead of long-term viability (Seed, 1983, p. 18). There is no necessary societal benefit to be obtained from the viability of any single business organization. In fact, it is through the elimination of inefficient producers that the economy becomes more productive. So, it is not necessarily socially responsible to seek organizational survival at all costs. However, pursuit of short-term profit to the exclusion of long-term profitability results in suboptimal use of resources. It is probably true that organizational strategists in America concentrate on ex post (after the fact, but factual and objective) measures rather than ex ante (before the fact, but predictive and subjective) measures in allocating funds. For example, if ROI is chosen as the appropriate budgeting criterion, estimated total returns for the future are more relevant than the returns that a certain division earned last year. However, the strategist must choose between using last year's earnings, which are known with a reasonable degree of accuracy and which have a great deal of relevance to future earning capability, or future earning capability, which can only be estimated. The choice most companies make is to allocate resources to those divisions which have used their existing resources most efficiently to produce profit.

Committing Human Resources

What about people? Are they resources just like money? Are human beings simply to be used in the ruthless pursuit of gain for the common shareholder? Of course not! Many companies view employees as a separate constituency with a legitimate claim on the largesse (or ''smallesse'') produced by corporate activity. Yet the time and energy of workers are purchased in relatively free markets, like other purchased inputs. These human resources must be rationally applied to the efficient production of goods and services. Unlike money or physical resources, a person does not have a fixed value. Not only do individuals differ, but each individual may put forth much effort or little effort and may be or become skilled or unskilled largely as a matter of individual volition. All this suggests that human resource allocation is a difficult process to rationalize.

Few organizations attempt to control the human resource through an organization-wide objective process. In most companies, hiring is done at relatively low levels in the organization. For example, most supervisors make the final hiring decision for those who work for them. This is true even for companies like Delta Airlines and Lincoln Electric with highly centralized personnel functions. When a manager receives the financial budget, salaries and wages are a part of it. Therefore, the allocation of human resources to divisions and departments is often a function of the allocation of money.

Personnel theorists have developed rather sophisticated ways of determining what the personnel budget should be, but the usual technique can be summarized very briefly. Let us assume that you are to determine the line item ''wages and salaries'' in the financial budget for the GM headlamp plant in Scotia, New York. First, the tasks involved in producing the headlamps are determined through time-and-motion studies and other similar techniques. Second, the tasks are broken down into groups according to the kinds of skills required. Third, tasks requiring similar skills are separated into jobs which can be performed by individual workers. Fourth, the number of workers or positions in each category is determined, based upon the volume of work to be performed, compared to how much one worker can be expected to do. Fifth, wage rates in the Scotia area are evaluated to determine how much it will cost to fill each position. Finally, the total of all the wages and salaries for all the positions becomes the budget item ''wages and salaries.''

In practice, it is not quite so simple. The company must decide whether workers will be transferred from other GM factories, hired in the local area, or a combination of the two. The usual practice is to allocate a cadre of experienced employees from other plants and to hire the remainder of the work force locally. But who is to be moved from another division? Here the matter cannot be based simply on who will do the best job of training the new workers. Worker preference must be taken into consideration. Obviously, if the skill of a certain manager or worker is vital to the new plant, that person must be encouraged to transfer. In some companies, generally not at GM, workers are simply directed to move. The usual approach is to view workers' preferences as a constraint within which management must obtain the most efficient allocation of human resources practicable.

There are those who view the worker as a resource which is bought and sold and used to produce goods and services just like any other resource. When workers are represented by powerful unions and union-imposed work rules and standards specify both the amount and kind of work each worker can do, the worker essentially becomes a commodity. Electricians do only electrical work, with the quantity specified at a level of minimal exertion. Painters paint so many square feet per hour. Assembly lines operate at ''comfortable'' speeds. Under such conditions, management can calculate with a fair degree of accuracy both the numbers and types of workers required to do any job.

This ''standardization of labor inputs'' cannot occur in free labor markets. In free markets, workers who are willing to work faster bargain for higher wages, and inept or lazy workers find demand for their services flagging. But labor markets are not free. Where labor unions have been able to enforce collective bargaining, especially industrywide bargaining, it has been possible to impose upon organizations rules which, in essence, fix the unit labor cost for each unit of product or service produced. When this is done for an industry, as in the case of the auto industry, that unit cost is simply passed along to the ultimate consumer.

Historically, management has been willing to accept such situations, partly because it makes the human resource allocation job easier (since the worker can be treated as a commodity) but largely because management has simply been given no choice in the matter, being threatened with strikes, violence, and government intervention if it fails to "bargain in good faith." It is significant that there was no major economic incentive to avoid standardizing labor input because the cost of doing so could simply be passed along. This is largely why unionism has been strongest in powerful oligopolistic-type industries like the auto, metals, and petroleum industries.

Less than 20 percent of the U.S. work force is unionized; it is certainly not appropriate to treat the other 80 percent as a commodity. Of course, the strategist must ensure that workers are assigned and reassigned with due consideration for their individual needs and preferences. But the most important criterion has to be economic efficiency. Even companies like Delta Airlines, Lincoln Electric, Hewlett-Packard Corporation, and Nucor Steel, which all acknowledge a rather firm long-term commitment to employees, tend to justify that commitment on the basis of economics. Those companies feel that workers who view the company as their lifetime employer will put forth greater effort to make that company successful. This idea, some believe, accounts in large measure for recent Japanese successes. When companies acknowledge a permanent commitment to workers, those workers cannot be simply allocated to maximize short-term profitability. They cannot be treated as a commodity.

Rationality would suggest that employees be administered so as to maximize their long-term value to the organization. This may mean extensive training periods during which workers produce little. If such a long view is taken, however, strategists must ensure that worker commitment to the firm is strong. This can be done by establishing retirement plans, medical programs, stock ownership plans, and so forth. It can also be accomplished in part by developing a corporate ethos of "belongingness." Under such conditions, it is possible that workers will cooperatively pursue organizational interests, partly because those interests are identical with their own and partly because they feel an obligation to serve the corporation which has treated them decently and fairly. Mary Cunningham (1983, p. 88), Seagram's former chief planner, describes this "family" kind of corporate model as "one that stresses the importance of human relationships and places the needs of the individual at least alongside the needs of the institution as a whole."

Committing Physical Assets

Organizational strategists tend to be of two types with regard to their attitude toward investment in physical facilities. There are those, usually technically oriented persons, who see physical assets as a reflection of status for a certain division or for the corporation as a whole. Then, there are those who see investment in facilities as an undesirable, although necessary, freezing of part of the company's funds (Seed, 1983). Strategists of the first type will tend to seek larger and larger investment in machinery and facilities, which will result, of course, in suboptimal allocation of resources.

The second view is the correct one. Money should be spent on plant equipment and facilities only when the expected return from those investments is the highest expected return available to the organization. As pointed out earlier, when management represents management and managers have a preference for impressive and expensive surroundings, unproductive or suboptimally productive buildings and equipment tend to be purchased. In 1970, Richard Goodwin, Johns-Manville's new psychologist/

president decided to spend $192 million, over half the company's net worth, on a new, luxurious world headquarters near Denver, Colorado. Journalists at the time called it a demonstration of "corporate environmental concern." But most would agree that the headquarters never produced a return on the huge investment made in it and, in fact, was a large factor in Johns-Manville's eventual failure. If profitability and efficiency are the goals, there is only one applicable criterion for the allocation of physical resources: Investment should be made in those activities or divisions which offer the highest present value of expected future returns. This is difficult to operationalize and, as stated earlier, strategists typically resort to simpler calculations using ex post financial data.

The business portfolio matrix concept provides a rationale for resource allocation and commitment (Gluck, 1981; Weintraub, 1979). Divisions which have significant strength in growing market areas (Stars) are funded by those which are strong in stable or declining markets (Cash Cows). At the business level, capital goods which are expected to become obsolete in the near future are used to earn profits to fund investment in more modern machines and facilities.

SUMMARY

The Delta Airlines story illustrates three attributes of strategy activation: (1) organizational structure, (2) directives and policies, and (3) resource commitment. Organizational structure is the set of relationships within an organization which are established or consistent over time. It involves three dimensions: centralization, specialization, and organizational rigidity. The debate as to whether structure follows strategy, or vice versa, has continued for decades. Structure can often be a result of strategy (structure follows strategy). But strategy must take into account the organizational structure which exists (strategy follows structure). Organization strategists can change both structure and strategy. In fact, it is through the modification of structure that strategists can expect *patterns* of behavior as opposed to individual *instances* of behavior.

Decentralization is considered by many to be good, per se. Decentralization gives middle- and lower-level managers added incentives to do their jobs well. On the other hand, high-level managers should be able to make better decisions because they are generally better at managing and because they have access to decision-making assistance unavailable at lower levels. Many suggest that decentralization provides greater flexibility in decision making and is better for dynamic situations. However, in some cases, centralization can improve responsiveness.

The principle of specialization of labor suggests that those decisions requiring analytical and conceptual skills—more likely to be possessed by top managers—should be more centralized than decisions requiring manipulative and technical skills.

The implementation of a decision to centralize authority can be facilitated by establishing a rapid and efficient information system. An effective accountability and reward structure can make decentralization more feasible.

The decision as to how to departmentalize is a strategic one which must be interrelated with many others. Most large organizations departmentalize to some degree along product, geographic, and functional lines. The main purposes of departmentation are to break the organization down into manageable units and to facilitate specialization by managers and workers. Another reason for departmentation may be to overcome organizational inertia or bureaucratization.

The term *policy* refers to a rule, procedure, or guide to action. Policies help the organization avoid ''reinventing the wheel.'' They also make the organization more predictable, both in terms of processes and outcomes.

Lower-level policies should be designed to support and implement those issued at higher levels. One is tempted to suggest that top management policies should be broad, general, and flexible and that lower-level ones should be narrow, explicit, and rigid. At every level, though, there is a trade-off between technical efficiency through rigid policies and practical efficiency through individual motivation and responsibility. The really compelling argument against trying to prescribe behavior too rigidly is the usual lack of organizational competence in doing so.

Within the functional areas of finance, personnel, production, and marketing, policies prescribe the process of competition. In finance, policies relate to dividends, sources of financing, depreciation, capital budgeting, and so forth. In personnel, policies relate to the six functional areas of personnel. In production, there are quality control policies, policies which describe the production process, innovation policies, and so forth. In marketing, policies are concerned with product, price, promotion, and place. Policies which affect the general focus of the organization should be established by top management. Those of relatively less importance, especially those applicable for only a short time, should be made by lower-level managers.

Nothing really happens until resources are committed. In fact, it is precisely through the commitment of resources that strategists have their major impact. Some companies have used computer modeling to simplify the task of resource allocation.

Organizational resources, money, people, and physical assets, can be substituted for one another to a great extent. Money is the most flexible of all because it can be used to purchase labor or physical assets. There tends to be a fixed relationship among money, physical assets, and labor. Management competence, though, can be used to expand the resource base.

Money is usually allocated through formal budgets. Budgets are normally compared annually. The usual purpose of budgeting is to allocate money to the uses which will produce the greatest value for the common shareholder. This is often done according to the ROI model.

Most nonprofit organizations, and many companies, do not use ROI but base this year's budget on last year's. This may be justified for certain reasons—some rational, some political. Within the limits imposed by organizational power and politics, however, the job of the strategist should be to allocate resources to obtain efficient production of goods and services and maximum earnings.

American managers have been criticized for seeking short-term profit instead of long-term viability. There is another side to this: Not only is the viability of a single business not of great social value, but future measures of earnings can only be estimated. So resource allocation tends to be based on ex post measures of efficiency.

People are not like other resources. They cannot simply be used in the ruthless pursuit of gain for the common shareholders. They are often treated as a separate constituency. Unlike money or physical resources, a person does not have a fixed value. Few organizations attempt to control the human resource through organization-wide objective processes. Personnel theorists have developed rather sophisticated ways of determining what the personnel budget should be, but that does not end the human resource allocation problem. Personal preferences and needs must be taken into consideration.

There are those who view the worker as a resource which is bought and sold and used to produce goods and services just like any other resource. When the labor input is standardized through union agreements or in other ways, it is possible to treat labor as a commodity. Where unionism is industrywide, management has been willing to accept work rules and restrictions, because this makes the human resource allocation job easier and often because management has had no choice.

It is inappropriate to treat nonunion workers as a commodity. However, even companies which acknowledge a long-term commitment to employees tend to justify that commitment on the basis of economics. Workers should be allocated so as to maximize their long-term value to the organization. This may involve extensive training periods, retirement and medical programs, stock ownership plans, and so forth. The value of the human resource can also be improved by developing a corporate ethos of belongingness.

Physical assets are viewed by some as a reflection of status and by others as an undesirable freezing of part of the company's funds. The second view is correct. Managers who represent themselves may invest large quantities of funds in unproductive assets. However, other constituencies are served by investing in those activities or divisions which offer the highest present value of expected future returns.

The business portfolio matrix concept provides a rationale for resource allocation and commitment. Assets used in growing market areas are funded by cash flows from those which are strong in stable or declining markets.

IMPORTANT CONCEPTS

Organizational structure	Specialization
Centralization	Policy
Organizational rigidity	

DISCUSSION QUESTIONS

1 Discuss how the Delta Airlines story illustrates the use of organizational structure, directives and policies, and resource commitment in strategy activation.
2 List and explain the three dimensions of organizational structure.
3 Does structure follow strategy, or vice versa? Support your position.
4 What are the advantages of centralization? Decentralization?
5 How does having exceptionally competent people at lower levels in the organization facilitate decentralization?
6 Explain the direct relationship between lower-level policies and top management policies.
7 Explain how a centralized organization might be responsive to a dynamic environment.
8 Distinguish between line managers and staff managers and sketch an organizational chart for a line and staff organization.

9 Discuss three reasons why organizations may be departmentalized.

10 Is it true that top management policies should be broad, general, and flexible and that lower-level policies should be narrow, explicit, and rigid? Explain your answer.

11 Discuss the kinds of policies which might exist in finance, personnel, production, and marketing.

12 Explain the relationship of resource commitment to strategy activation.

13 Why is money considered the most flexible resource in the organization? How is it normally allocated?

14 Discuss the statement, "People are not like other resources." Take a position and defend it.

15 Describe the two views of investment in physical assets discussed in the text. Which view do you hold and why?

16 Explain how the BCG matrix might be used in resource allocation.

REFERENCES

Aivazian, Varouj A., and Jeffrey L. Callen. "Uncertain Externalities, Liability Rules, and Resource Allocation: Comment," *American Economic Review*, December 1980, pp. 1058–1059.

Bender, Paul S., William D. Northrup, and Jeremy F. Shapiro. "Practical Modeling for Resource Management," *Harvard Business Review*, 59:2, March/April 1980, pp. 163–173.

Bettis, Richard A., and C. K. Prahalad. "The Visible and Invisible Hand: Resource Allocation in the Industrial Sector," *Strategic Management Journal*, 4:1, January/March 1983, pp. 27–43.

Blackburn, Richard S. "Dimensions of Structure: A Review and Reappraisal," *Academy of Management Review*, 7:1, January 1982, pp. 59–66.

Burgelman, Robert A. "A Model of the Interaction of Strategic Behavior, Corporate Context, and the Concept of Strategy," *Academy of Management Review*, 8:1, January 1983, pp. 61–70.

Chandler, Alfred D. *Strategy and Structure: Chapters in the History of the American Industrial Enterprise*. Cambridge, Mass.: MIT Press, 1962.

Chonko, Lawrence B. "The Relationship of Span of Control to Sales Representatives' Experienced Role Conflict and Role Ambiguity," *Academy of Management Journal*, 25:2, June 1982, pp. 452–456.

Collier, Don. "Strategic Management in Diversified, Decentralized Companies," *Journal of Business Strategy*, 3:1, Summer 1982, pp. 85–89.

Conlon, Edward J., and Gerritt Wolf. "The Moderating Effects of Strategy, Visibility, and Involvement on Allocation Behavior: An Extension of Staw's Escalation Paradigm," *Organizational Behavior and Human Performance*, 26:2, October 1980, pp. 172–192.

Cunningham, Mary E. "Planning for Humanism," *Journal of Business Strategy*, 3:4, Spring 1983, pp. 87–90.

Cyert, R. M., and J. G. March. *A Behavioral Theory of the Firm*. Englewood Cliffs, N.J.: Prentice-Hall, 1963.

Ford, Jeffrey D. "The Occurrence of Structural Hysteresis in Declining Organizations," *Academy of Management Review*, 5:4, October 1980, pp. 589–598.

Gluck, Frederick. "The Dilemmas of Resource Allocation," *Journal of Business Strategy*, 2:2, Fall 1981, pp. 67–71.

Grinyer, Peter H., Masoud Yasai-Ardekani, and Shawki Al-Bazzaz. "Strategy, Structure, the Environment, and Financial Performance in 48 United Kingdom Companies," *Academy of Management Journal*, 23:2, June 1982, pp. 193–220.

Grinyer, P. H., and M. Yasai-Ardekani. "Strategy, Structure, Size, and Bureaucracy," *Academy of Management Journal*, September 1981, pp. 471–486.

Hosmer, LaRue Tone. "The Importance of Strategic Leadership," *Journal of Business Strategy*, 3:2, Fall 1982, pp. 47–57.

"In the News," *Fortune*, February 22, 1982, pp. 7–8, 13, 16.

Jelinek, Mariann, and Michael C. Burnstein. "The Production Administrative Structure: A Paradigm for Strategic Fit," *Academy of Management Review*, 7:2, April 1982, pp. 242–252.

Leontiades, Milton, and Ahmet Tezel. "Some Connections between Corporate-Level Planning and Diversity," *Strategic Management Journal*, 2:4, October/December 1981, pp. 413–418.

Lindblom, Charles E. "The Science of 'Muddling Through'," *Public Administration Review*, Spring 1959, pp. 76–84.

March, J. G., and H. A. Simon. *Organizations*. New York: Wiley, 1958.

Miller, Danny, and Peter H. Friesen. "Structural Change and Performance: Quantum versus Piecemeal-Incremental Approaches," *Academy of Management Journal*, 25:4, December 1982, pp. 867–892.

Mondy, R. Wayne, Jerry M. DeHay, and Arthur Sharplin. *Supervision*. New York: Random House, 1983.

"Montgomery Ward: Prosperity Is Still around the Corner," *Fortune*, November 9, 1960, pp. 138–143.

Pavett, Cynthia M., and Alan W. Lau. "Managerial Work: The Influence of Hierarchical Level and Functional Specialty," *Academy of Management Journal*, 26:1, March 1983, pp. 170–177.

Ringle, William M. "The American Who Remade 'Made in Japan'," *Nation's Business*, February 1981, pp. 8325–8328.

Seed, Allen H., III. "New Approaches to Asset Management," *Journal of Business Strategy*, 3:3, Winter 1983, pp. 16–22.

Weintraub, Victor. "Strategic Planning Approach to Resource Allocation," *SAM Advanced Management Journal*, 44:3, Summer 1979, pp. 47–54.

CHAPTER 6

ACTIVATION OF STRATEGIC ACTIVITIES: CORPORATE CULTURE AND POWER AND POLITICS

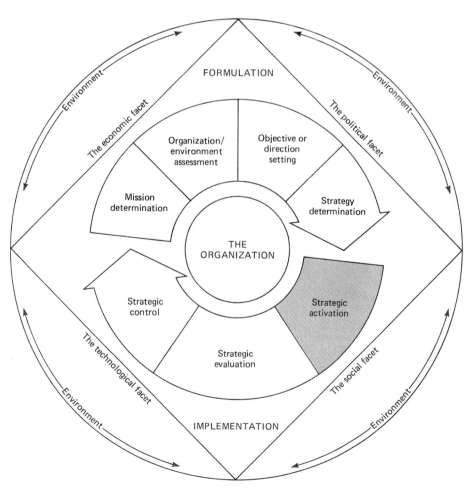

"Years ago we ran an ad that said simply, 'IBM means service.' I have often thought it was our very best ad. It stated clearly just exactly what we stand for. *We want to give the best customer service of any company in the world*." So wrote Thomas J. Watson, Jr., shortly after he succeeded his famous father as chairman of IBM.

This service orientation at IBM is much more than talk. It is their practice to answer every customer complaint within twenty-four hours. The customer orientation is enforced through incentives for keeping customers and disincentives for losing them. For example, if a customer terminates a lease within a year after equipment is installed, the account representative responsible for that customer must give up salary and a bonus to make up for the company's loss. Sales representatives receive fifteen months of basic sales training. Customer satisfaction is formally surveyed once a month, and quarterly employee attitude surveys are largely concerned with how well customers are being served.

There is much more to the IBM tradition than customer service, however. Tom Watson, Jr., touts "respect for the individual as the company's first principle." The senior Watson started an open-door policy in the 1920s and a $1 a year country club for all employees. IBM offers a wide range of other employee benefits—lifetime employment, daycare centers, and recreational facilities. During the Depression, IBM made parts for inventory and stored them to avoid layoffs.

But IBM demands a lot of its people, too. The traditional gray suit and white shirt is a reflection of the senior Watson's demand for "tasteful" dress. Sales representatives operate under a quota system, and quotas are increased each year or sales territories are cut. New employees are closely supervised and graded according to how well they meet frequently modified goals.

Watson, Sr., is famous for having used "almost every kind of fanfare" to create enthusiasm. According to a recent *Wall Street Journal* article:

> Achievement is followed by immediate rewards. Insiders say that the most cherished of these isn't money, it's having your name and quota on the bulletin board with a notation saying, "100%." It's having a party thrown for you at your branch because you have satisfied a prickly customer. It's a steady flow of letters of commendation. (Chace, 1982, p. 18)

And almost everyone is eligible for some kind of award. There is a "Gold Circle" for the top 10 percent of IBM's sales representatives, but 80 percent are eligible for the "One Hundred Percent Club." In fact, sales quotas are engineered so that more than two-thirds of the sales representatives make their quotas.

Contrary to popular opinion, IBM has seldom been the first to market new technology—waiting with its personal computer, for example, until others were well established in that market. The IBM 360 and 370 Mainframes stayed on the market for years after other manufacturers had developed more advanced technology. IBM chose to leave those machines in use as long as they were making money for the company. Still, IBM traditionally has promoted internal competition among new product ideas. R&D managers were encouraged to encroach upon one another's turf and to come up with multiple solutions to the same problem. Then they were given the opportunity to sell their solutions to the sales force through performance "shoot-outs," where demonstrations compared the actual working hardware and software, not just product descriptions.

The authority structure at IBM is a strong one. Every employee receives an annual performance plan involving specific written goals. Meeting or exceeding the plan results in promotions and raises. The *Wall Street Journal* article mentioned above tells of a female IBM veteran who was demoted from her management position because she had a personal relationship with a competitor's employee. Another former IBM manager, who worked at corporate headquarters in Armonk, New York, is quoted as saying, "In my 15 years there I never lost the feeling that I was breaking a rule, but I never knew what the rule was."

In 1982 IBM was featured in the landmark book, *In Search of Excellence*. The corporate culture at IBM was credited by the authors with much of the company's success. The main elements of that culture, as described above, have been reasonably constant for several decades, being outgrowths of the personal philosophies of Thomas J. Watson, Sr., who ascended to the presidency of IBM in 1914. But beginning in the 1980s, corporate culture became a tool of strategy as well as a determinant of strategy. Writing about the "lean, mean new IBM," *Fortune* reports:

> Competitors have felt the ground tremble. Their nemesis from Armonk has revolutionized the way it does business, from grand strategy to the finest tactical detail, and has emerged a tougher opponent than ever before. IBM now speeds products to market faster than in the past, attacks its rivals with unprecedented price cuts and outraces competitors to emerging new businesses. . . . To its old motto "Think," IBM seems to have appended the word "Differently." (Petre, 1983, p. 69)

IBM has begun to market its computers through retailers like Computerland and Sears, reducing its control over customer service. The company has moved into joint ventures with the Japanese, buying 12 percent of Intel Corporation. Since 1981, IBM has started fourteen new companies which can more or less independently seek opportunities in robotics, medical technology, and communications equipment. In a major departure from past strategies, IBM encourages customers to buy rather than lease, further deemphasizing the company's responsibility for its products.

IBM has begun to emphasize price more than in the past. At the high end of its line, the company cut prices on the IBM 3081 supercomputer a month after Amdahl began to market a similar product and quickly sold fifty to Amdahl's biggest customer, AT&T. IBM now gives special prices to customers who sign volume purchase agreements. IBM has priced its PC and PC, Jr. (Peanut) personal computers near the prices competitors charge for similar units.

Finally, the company's people dependency has been changed somewhat by the $10 billion sunk into its plant and equipment since 1977. *Fortune* concludes:

As Opel (IBM's chairman and chief executive) says, "Dominance may be a very transitory thing." By transforming itself rather than clinging to old strategies, IBM has increased its command over the future. When a dominant company's advantage wanes, seemingly perilous, tradition shattering change can be the course of least risk. (Petre, 1983, p. 82)

In Chapter 5, we discussed the relatively hard elements of strategy activation—organizational structure, policies, and resource commitment. In this chapter, we turn to the softer components, which loosely fit under the heading "corporate culture." One definition of *culture* is "the body of customary beliefs, social forms, and material traits constituting a distinct complex of tradition of a racial, religious or social group" (*Webster's Third New International Dictionary*). Just as every country has its own culture, so does each organization, although the cultures of various organizations may be more or less distinct than national cultures and may involve different elements. For example, in the discussion above, even if one were to eliminate mention of IBM, the name of the company would still be clear from the specifics of culture which are presented.

Stanley M. Davis, professor of organizational behavior at Boston University and a recognized expert on corporate culture, emphasizes the elusiveness of the concept: "It's like putting your hand in a cloud," he says ("Corporate Culture . . . ," 1980). In order to distinguish the topic of this chapter from the much broader concept of culture used in the political and social sciences, and to make it a bit less elusive, we will define **corporate culture** as *the system of shared values, beliefs, and habits within an organization which interact with structure and policies to produce behavioral norms*. According to Howard M. Schwartz, vice president of Management Analysis Center, Inc., a leader in corporate culture consulting, "Culture gives people a sense of how to behave and what they ought to be doing" ("Corporate Culture . . . ," 1980, p. 148).

In the early 1980s a spate of best-selling books, a number of which are included among the references listed at the end of this chapter, stressed the importance of corporate culture to organizations and the people in them (Deal and Kennedy, 1981; Ouchi, 1982; Peters and Waterman, 1982). In 1981, Harvard University introduced its first course on corporate culture (Salmans, 1983, p. D3). Writing much earlier, Antony

Jay (1967, p. 231) states, "It has been known for some time that corporations are social institutions with customs and taboos, status groups and pecking orders, and many sociologists and social scientists have studied and written about them as such. But they are also political institutions, autocratic and democratic, peaceful and war-like, liberal and paternalistic." What Jay was writing about, although the term had not then achieved broad usage, was corporate culture, as defined above. In this chapter we will discuss two components of corporate culture: (1) the political environment within the organization, and (2) the leadership and motivational climate. Then we will consider the dilemma the corporate strategist faces in deciding whether to use corporate culture as a tool of strategy or to view it as a constraint.

POLITICS AND POWER

All corporate cultures include a political component. This is particularly true of large companies. In the classic book *Management and Machiavelli*, Jay (1967, p. 10) writes, "The root of the matter is that the great modern corporations are so similar to independent or semi-independent states of the past that they can only be fully understood in terms of political and constitutional history, and management can only be properly studied as a branch of government."

Power and influence may fill a basic human need. The great psychologist Alfred Adler believed that human behavior is explainable in terms of the human need for competence and control over one's environment. To the extent that the environment involves other people, this need is filled only through influencing, manipulating, and controlling them. ***Power*** is *the ability to influence others*. Power is related to politics but is not the same thing. Farrell and Petersen (1982, p. 405) define political behavior in organizations as "those activities which are not required as part of one's organizational role but which influence or attempt to influence the distribution of advantages and disadvantages within the organization." Accordingly, we will define ***organizational politics*** as *the carrying out of activities not prescribed by policies for the purpose of influencing the distribution of advantages and disadvantages within the organization*. Farrell and Petersen specify political behavior as either legitimate or illegitimate, vertical or lateral, and external or internal to the organization. This results in the typology of political behavior shown in Table 6-1. Most Americans tend to subscribe to the negative view of political activity evident in this table. The concepts of power and politics provoke images of domination, manipulation, and so forth. Having noted the "negative face of power," let us adopt a more positive view, however.

Organizational strategists are appropriately concerned with power and politics for two principal reasons. First, knowing about power concepts helps one avoid domination and manipulation by others. At its best, strategic management is active rather than reactive. The strategist, by definition, attempts to influence rather than be influenced. Second, knowing about power concepts helps the strategist in the influence process, clearly a vital part of the job. Sussman and Vecchio (1982, p. 185) have argued that power concepts offer a useful approach to motivating subordinates. Being certain of the best course of action for the organization accomplishes little unless others can be provoked to follow that course. It is also important that strategists be able to influence

TABLE 6-1 A TYPOLOGY OF POLITICAL BEHAVIOR IN ORGANIZATIONS

Legitimate		Illegitimate	
Vertical	**Lateral**	**Vertical**	**Lateral**
Internal			
Direct voice	Coalition forming	Sabotage	Threats
Complain to supervisor	Exchanging favors	Symbolic protests	
Bypassing chain of command	Reprisals	Mutinies	
Obstructionism		Riots	
External			
Lawsuits	Talk with counterpart from another organization	Whistleblowing	Organizational duplicity
	Outside professional activity		Defections

Source: Dan Farrell and James C. Petersen, ''Patterns of Political Behavior in Organizations,'' *The Academy of Management Review*, 7:3, July 1982, p. 407.

superiors—and even persons outside the organization. The SBU manager, for example, who has the best investment opportunity in the corporation may be ineffective unless corporate-level strategists can be influenced to allocate investment funds to his SBU. Strategists like Sanford Sigoloff of Wickes Corporation, Lee Iacocca of Chrysler, and Victor Kiam of Remington Products, Inc., who have sought to turn around dull or failing corporations, must influence creditors to stay their claims, customers to buy the company's products, and investors to provide necessary funds for expansion and renewal of assets. Victor Kiam and Lee Iaccoca accomplished this kind of influence partly through national television advertisements similar to those used by major political candidates. Sanford Sigoloff used news releases and sophisticated presentations before civic and professional groups around the country, as well as addresses to employees and managers.

A caveat is in order. Kanter (1983, pp. 19–20) argues that successful architects of corporate cultural change must tacitly agree to keep their power invisible once others have agreed to yield. She writes, ''Others' participation may be contingent on a feeling that they are involved out of commitment or conviction—not because power is being exercised over them.''

A number of useful power concepts which have helped corporate strategists accomplish their personal and professional missions are discussed below. A careful analysis of the political aspect of an organization's structure is necessary to determine how appropriate each is for use in a given circumstance.

The Bases of Power

In the late 1950s, French and Raven (1959) theorized that any individual's power springs from five sources which they called ''power bases.'' The degree to which managers and others within an organization depend upon each of these power bases is a major aspect of corporate culture. Power is classified as reward power, coercive power, legitimate power, expert power, and referent power. While typologies have been proposed by a number of authors, the French and Raven schema is by far the most satisfying and most widely accepted. In describing the power bases, we will be concerned only with the power level of the strategists, although it is recognized that the power that others have over the organizational strategists is based upon the same principles.

Reward power is *power arising from the perception by others that the strategist can produce positive outcomes for them and that the rewards they receive are contingent upon their conformity with the strategist's desires*. *Coercive power*, on the other hand, is *influence ability based upon the perception that the strategist will mediate negative outcomes for those who do not behave as desired*. The astute reader will recognize that coercive and reward power form the basis of expectancy theory, currently the most prominent theory of human motivation. Thompson and Strickland (1981, pp. 180–181) write, "Motivation is brought about most fundamentally by the organization's reward-punishment structure." In essence, strategists who emphasize reward and coercive power simply assume that others rationally seek their own best interests. Such strategists create and use the perception that they can and will control positive and negative outcomes for others. A great deal of research suggests that reward power is more likely to be effective in motivating subordinates than is coercive power (Sharplin, 1977; Podsakoff, Todor, and Skov, 1982, pp. 810, 819). On the other hand, some respected corporate turnaround specialists are well known for ruling through terror. Albert Dunlap, manager of Manville Corporation's ailing forest products division for a short while in 1982 and later chief executive at Lily-Tulip, Inc., has such a reputation. *Time* quotes acquaintances as saying, "Dunlap is sort of like a General Patton, a 180-day guy who ignores the long view. . . . His people are living in fear of him—absolute fear" (Lily-Tulip . . . , 1984, p. 70).

The third kind of power is *legitimate power*. This is *power based upon the belief that the strategist has a legitimate right to control or influence the behavior of others*. This feeling of legitimacy may arise from a respect for the organizational structure ("He is the boss, so I should do what he says") or from a belief that a certain category of person (males as opposed to females, whites as opposed to blacks, older persons as opposed to younger persons) has a right to be in charge. The assignment of titles of supremacy (department head, chief executive officer, plant manager, and so forth) typically enhances the legitimate power base. The "divine right of kings" perhaps epitomizes this aspect of power. Of course, the right of the executive to direct others is not a birthright. Legitimate power is not based upon the rational serving of self-interest, but on some concept of rightness or "oughtness."

A staff corporate planner might enhance the legitimate power base by seeking the title of director of corporate strategy. A line manager who is a man might have greater legitimate power over females than males, and over persons younger than himself whether they are male or female. Legitimate power may be effective outside the organization as well as inside. The controller who approaches an investment banker about a new stock issue for the corporation may be ascribed greater legitimacy than an equally competent and intelligent personnel director. Legitimate power is based upon belief in principles, not upon self-interest.

Referent power is *influence ability which derives from a liking for or a desire to be like the power holder*. To be comprehensive we must extend this power base to include charisma, personality, and so forth. The strategist who depends upon referent power will tend to emphasize friendships, positive mental attitudes, and other attributes which cause others to emulate or like the strategist. The referent power base is largely derived from emotional attachment to the strategist.

The last and perhaps most dependable kind of power is expert power. *Expert power* is *influence ability based upon the perception by others that the strategist has special competence, knowledge, or expertise regarding whatever matter an influence attempt concerns*. A strategist who is a nationally recognized financial analyst tends to be able to influence subordinates, superiors, and those outside the organization with regard to matters of capital structure and investment of liquid assets. "Red" Adair, the world-renowned oil well firefighter, has a high degree of expert power over most "rough necks" (oil field workers) who know of his reputation. Supreme Court Justice Sandra Day O'Conner, in addition to her immense legitimate power, has great expert power over young attorneys. Expert power may arise from a rational desire to achieve positive outcomes and avoid negative outcomes. However, it is not based upon the strategist's mediation of those outcomes. It may be based upon the belief that, since the strategist is an expert, following the strategist's advice or directives is most likely to result in choosing the proper course of action.

It is the perception of expertness which gives one expert power. But most strategists will find the perception hard to sustain without the actuality. Strategists who wish to develop expert power will emphasize education, research, and experience as ways of maintaining the actuality of expertness. They will emphasize degrees, citations, and testimonials as means of sustaining the impression.

Expert power is based upon expertness regarding that very thing concerning which influence is attempted, not expertness in general. For example, the fact that the author has written three textbooks and a number of articles on management would not cause readers to follow his advice about crepe cookery or drilling oil wells or anything else except management and, perhaps, writing.

When Ian McGregor took over the British Steel Company (BSC) in 1980, it was losing more than $4 million a day. Though he closed a number of plants and eliminated 70,000 jobs, he retained the respect and devotion of BSC's employees. Robert Lubar (1981, p. 88) explained McGregor's success in terms of expert power:

> He was, for one thing, thoroughly familiar with steel technology. The degrees he earned from two Scottish universities were in metallurgy, and it was as a specialist in tank armor on a British procurement mission that he first came to the U.S. in 1940. He convincingly demonstrated his managerial qualifications during his ten years' stewardship at Amax—a decade of successful expansion and growth for the mineral company. As an investment banker, he helped engineer the merger that was the salvation of LTV's Jones & Laughlin steel subsidiary. As deputy chairman of BL Ltd., the beleaguered auto manufacturer, from 1977 to 1980, he was able to observe at first hand the tribulations of a state-owned enterprise.

One of the difficulties organizational strategists face is in attempting to wield power over those who deem themselves to be more expert in their special fields than the strategists. For example, a strategist might recommend or direct a certain personnel strategy with which the personnel director may disagree. Instead of simply accepting the strategy out of respect for the strategist's expertise, the personnel director may oppose it until convinced personally that it is the best course. So a good part of the organizational strategist's time is involved in sales work. This is why many strategists, especially staff planners, concentrate upon the process of strategic management rather than its substance. It is also why many believe that line managers can be more effective when they "come up through the ranks," so that by the time they become organizational strategists their expertise in a number of areas is respected. For this reason, management training programs typically involve rotation among a number of assignments. Organizational strategists who would make maximum use of the expert power base should attempt to develop expertise in a wide range of areas, as well as to be knowledgeable and competent concerning the strategic management process as described in this text.

Machiavellianism

Perhaps no book has had a more profound influence upon thinking about power and politics than Machiavelli's *The Prince* (1908). In that book, the author emphasized the amoral use of coercive influence as a way of sustaining supremacy over others. Machiavelli wrote, "It is much safer to be feared than loved, if one of the two has to be wanting." While many claim that Machiavelli has been misunderstood, ***Machiavellianism*** is appropriately defined as *the ruthless use of power, particularly coercive power, and manipulation to attain one's personal goals*. The exceptional success of recent books such as Michael Korda's *Power: How to Get It, How to Use It* and Robert J. Ringer's *Winning through Intimidation* suggests that Machiavellianism is alive and well.

Anthony Jay (1967, p. 4) argues that Machiavelli had sage advice for even highly ethical managers. According to Jay, "And yet in fact Machiavelli, however marginal his relevance to academic historians, is bursting with urgent advice and acute observations for top management of the great private and public corporations all over the world."

While it is difficult to justify the use of raw power by managers, there is little doubt that coercive power is a potent means of influence. Even the morally serious strategist will do well to recognize its effectiveness and the prevalence of Machiavellianism. It is illogical to oppose Machiavellianism on the basis of effectiveness. There is no doubt that coercion and manipulation often work, particularly if those affected are not forced to admit the real reason for their compliance (Kanter, 1983, pp. 19–20). In the final analysis it must be opposed, if at all, on the same basis as white collar crime and income tax cheating—on moral grounds.

Coalitions

The management pyramid, with each level of managers reporting to a smaller number of more powerful managers until the top division heads and vice presidents report to an all-powerful chief executive, rarely tells the real story. Most organizations are at least partly managed by coalitions which cut across formal organizational lines. A *coalition* is *an alliance of persons within an organization which is not prescribed by the formal organizational structure*. Sometimes the coalition is based upon nepotism, with a junior executive who happens to be related to the boss wielding disproportionate influence. Sometimes a "good ol' boy" network develops, and those who would wield power must "belong to the club." Sometimes there are opposing coalitions, the "young Turks" against the "establishment," for example.

When a new executive takes over any organization, it is not uncommon to replace strategically located managers at various levels in the organization with the new executive's hand-picked followers. Lee Iacocca did this after he took over at Chrysler. Such managers often become a coalition which, at a minimum, keeps the "old guard" in check, providing both information and support to the new executive. Once formed, a dominant coalition is unlikely to admit new members (Pearce and Denisi, 1983, p. 127), so some coalitions tend to be as stable as formal relationships in the organization.

Coalitions may serve very useful functions, particularly if they are based upon philosophical kinship and concerned with promoting the interests of the organization as a whole. Research suggests that political factors are usually more important than personal ones in coalition formation (Pearce and DeNisi, 1983, p. 127). This suggests that many coalitions may not serve organizational interests. Whether they are useful or not, they cannot be avoided. So the organizational strategists must take them into account, providing incentives for the useful ones to support organizational purposes and disincentives for the hurtful ones to exist.

Coalitions may be the major factor in strategy determination and implementation if the chief executive is weak or if especially strong power centers exist within the organization. Cyert and March (1963) feel that objectives and strategies are often determined through a bargaining process whereby "policy side payments" are made for support in certain matters. These payments might involve increases in budgeted funding, promises of support in some future policy matter, friendship, favors, and so forth. Through what Cyert and March call "quasi-resolution of conflict" individuals within the organization form temporary or relatively permanent alliances which yield significant power. Strategists must take these into account as a minimum. Optimally, they should be turned to the organization's benefit.

Particularly astute organizational strategists will use coalitions that exist and form others in order to accomplish organizational goals. Rosabeth Kanter (1983) tells how one strategist formed and used a coalition.

> Putnam was an assistant department manager for product testing in a company that was about to demonstrate a product at a site that attracted a large number of potential buyers. Putnam heard through the grapevine that a decision was imminent about which model to display. The product managers were each lobbying for their own, and the marketing people also had a favorite. Putnam, who was close to the product, thought that the first-choice model had grave defects and so decided to demonstrate to the marketing staff both what the problems with the first one were and the superiority of another model.
>
> Building on a long-term relationship with the people in corporate quality control and a good alliance with his boss, Putnam sought the tools he needed: materials for testing from the materials division, a budget from corporate quality control, and staff from his own units to

carry out the tests. As Putnam put it, this was all done through one-on-one ''horse trading''—showing each manager how much the others were chipping in. Then Putnam met informally with the key marketing staffer to learn what it would take to convince him.

As the test results emerged, Putnam took them to his peers in marketing engineering and quality control so they could feed them to their superiors. The accumulated support persuaded the decision makers to adopt Putnam's choice of a model; it later became a strong money-maker. In sum, Putnam had completely stepped out of his usual role to build a consensus that shaped a major policy decision.

LEADERSHIP AND ACCOMPLISHMENT OF PURPOSE

In preceding sections of this chapter we have discussed power and politics in relation to organizational strategists in general. Remember that to some extent every manager is a strategist. However, our emphasis has been upon the top two levels of management and upon corporate planning. In discussing leadership, our focus will narrow somewhat. The view taken will be that of the top general manager who leads those in the organization toward worthwhile purposes. This manager is variously called the CEO, president, chief operating officer, or chairman of the board. According to Edgar Schein (1983), organizations with homogeneous and successful corporate cultures often owe their cultural development to one entrepreneurial leader, usually the founder. In this section we will discuss the part the strategist plays as architect of leadership climate and as personal leader. First, though, let us briefly consider several leadership theories.

Theories of Leadership

The *trait approach to leadership* is *the view that effective leaders have special traits which ordinary persons do not possess—or possess in a more limited degree.* These might include physical strength and stamina, size, intelligence, integrity, wisdom, and so forth. Certainly, to some extent, we all subscribe to this theory. Legend has it that Benjamin Franklin wrote the traits which he wished to develop on cards and carried a different card with him each day. During the day, he would concentrate on the trait written on the card. There is not much we can do to develop traits such as physical stature and attractiveness (although we can keep our bodies trim), nor even what one might call ''native intelligence.'' But, to some degree, every executive attempts to develop those attributes which will contribute to success as a manager. The trait theories of leadership are given little validity in the management literature. Yet, it is the observable traits of good leaders, past and present, which offer the best guidance for the general manager who wishes to emulate those leaders' success.

A number of researchers such as Calder (1977) have supported the pessimistic proposition that leadership traits cannot be developed—that a person is a good or bad leader because others say so. This is based on what is called attribution theory. The implication is that leadership is simply attributed to leaders by those who are led. As useful as this idea may be for research purposes, it has no relevance at all to strategic management because it posits that a leader cannot become a better leader by working at it, but must wait for others to make the necessary attribution (McElroy, 1982, p. 413).

A number of leadership theories emphasize the "style" of the effective leader. Leaders may be participative, nonparticipative, autocratic, democratic, or laissez-faire. The debate as to which approach is best resulted in the conclusion that no particular style is best in all situations. This gave rise to "contingency" theories of leadership. Robert Tannenbaum and Warren Schmidt, two pioneering contingency theorists, suggested that individual leaders should vary their styles based upon forces in the manager, forces in the subordinates, and forces in the situation. They proposed a "continuum of leadership behaviors," from autocratic (i.e, manager makes decision and announces it) through various levels of participativeness (e.g., manager presents problem, gets suggestions, makes decision) to essentially laissez-faire (manager permits subordinates to function within limits defined by superior).

Extensive studies during the 1950s (notably at Michigan State and Ohio State universities) attempted to relate the manager's degree of emphasis on getting the job done (called "production orientation," "initiating structure," etc.) and concern for people (called "consideration," "behavioral orientation," etc.) to success as a leader. The results were inconclusive except for the rather obvious facts that (1) a manager who has no concern for productivity will hardly lead others to produce, and (2) a manager who has no concern for human relationships will be unable to lead at all. A more important outgrowth of the research of the fifties and sixties was rather universal recognition of the need for leaders to have a dual focus, upon productivity on the one hand and upon human relationships and needs on the other.

In a more prescriptive vein, Robert Blake and Jane S. Mouton developed their "managerial grid" based upon the premise that concern for people and concern for production are not mutually exclusive. Blake and Mouton felt that the best leaders evidenced high concern for both production and people. The Blake and Mouton grid has been used extensively in management development programs aimed at maximizing both concerns.

Fred Fiedler attempted to specify the particular leadership style which would be most appropriate in different situations. The aspects of the situation which Fiedler thought relevant were (1) leader/member relations, (2) task structure, and (3) leader/position power. Fiedler's research seems to indicate that in either highly favorable or highly unfavorable situations autocratic-type leadership seems to be the most successful, and in situations of moderate favorableness to the leader participative approaches tend to work best. A favorable leadership situation is considered to be one in which leader/member relationships are good, tasks are highly structured, and the leader has high position power.

The Strategist as Personal Leader and Architect of Leadership Climate

The importance of personal leadership in achieving organizational purposes is well established. As previously stated, we often think of good leadership in terms of the traits effective leaders possess. The effective leader, most believe, should be active rather than passive, consistent rather than inconsistent, principled as opposed to unprincipled, powerful as opposed to impotent, and communicative instead of taciturn. According to Antony Jay (1967, pp. 71–72), imperial England felt a leader should be "courageous, disciplined, reserved, honest, conformist, incorruptible, ascetic," while effective leaders in modern England should have "imagination, inventiveness, quick-wittedness, toughmindedness, brashness, scientific brilliance, technical expertness, individualism, sociability." Yet few leaders possess all of these positive traits to any remarkable degree.

Peters and Waterman (1982) argue that legendary leaders, like IBM's Thomas Watson, Sr., MacDonald's Ray Kroc, and Henry Ford, are not uniquely charismatic. Rather, say these experts, such architects of culture are "smart enough to know what kind of culture is best for the business, persistent enough to harp on values in word and deed for decades, and dedicated enough to tailor their actions to the value system" (Uttal, 1983, p. 72). Consider the examples of two eminently successful leaders given in Table 6-2.

So we are left without a clear indication of the correct leadership style, or even of what leadership approach works best in any particular situation. Yet many agree upon certain generalizations about what good executive leadership is. First, good personal leadership is *humane*. Organizational goals should never be sought at all costs. The

TABLE 6-2   DESCRIPTIONS OF THE STYLES OF TWO PRESIDENTS

President 1

(Forty-five years old. The company has sales of $225 million, has multiple products, and is divisionally organized.)

Sparks subordinates by questioning mind, youthful energy, ideas, and efforts to stretch them.

Pushes executives to set high standards. Is a tough evaluator and will replace mediocrity.

Decisions are fact-based and are made after discussions with subordinates.

Use of authority is reasonably permissive within limits of achievement goals. Authority is more implied than used.

Seeks change, pushes for it, and is thorough in programming to carry it out.

Is deeply involved in planning, goal setting, and evaluation against targets, with the result that he has a good understanding of each business and has close, frequent contact with each key executive.

President 2

(Fifty-three years old. The company has sales of $325 million, has a single product, and is functionally organized.)

Drives others by the sharpness and toughness of his thinking. Is respected but not held in affection.

Is highly demanding and critical, and imposes his own standards. Becomes emotional over difficult people decisions and will bypass but not fire the mediocre performer.

Makes decisions based heavily on intuition and long experience, which involve relatively little consultation with subordinates and which are held too steadfastly.

Is highly authoritarian, is positive in point of view, and imposes decisions with force.

Although intellectually prepared for change, is fearful of it because of anticipation of mistakes and concern over organizational readiness.

In spite of efforts to delegate, maintains over-the-shoulder control. Holds onto operations, although much thought is given to strategy.

Source: George A. Steiner, John B. Miner, and Edmund R. Gray, *Management Policy and Strategy: Text, Readings, and Cases,* New York: Macmillan, 1982, p. 99.

strategic manager who drives subordinates through fear may be highly successful, both in the long and short term, but few can live in a continuous state of fear without suffering physiological or emotional harm. None of the companies Peters and Waterman (1982) describe in *In Search of Excellence* appear to have oppressive cultures. A really good leader is not just effective in accomplishing organizational goals, but does so with concern for the personal cost to those within and outside the organization.

Next, good executive leadership is *farsighted*. It enhances the future as well as the present. In large measure this is an argument for integrity. Leadership based upon a false belief in the leader's character, ability, or performance is likely to have short-lived success. The leader who seeks a position of supremacy, and all must to some extent, should actually try to be eminent in certain respects. In other words, dependence upon politics and power *only* is less likely to be successful in the long run than development of one's own abilities through education, practice, and thought. This is partly because "you cannot fool all of the people all of the time." In the long run, organizational members are able to evaluate the strategist with a high degree of accuracy. It is possible, but highly risky, to enhance one's ability to lead by misrepresenting one's own capabilities, experiences, or attitudes.

Third, good leadership should be *inspired*. It was the great dream of Martin Luther King which caused southern blacks to follow him, and which extended the effects of his leadership quite beyond his own lifetime. Great leaders serve purposes which extend beyond the here and now. Sometimes the purpose is to face a great challenge, as in the cases of Lee Iaccoca at Chrysler and Sanford Sigoloff at Wickes, both of whose companies were near failure when they took over. In both cases, the challenge was to return the company to profitability. Sometimes the inspiring goal is self-fulfillment through service to others. At Lincoln Electric the main constituency is said to be Lincoln's customers who are promised a "better and better product at a lower and lower price." From the top of the Lincoln organization to the bottom, everyone knows that this is the main purpose. Through a consistency of pronouncement and practice, Ted Willis—and before him James Lincoln—has been able to inspire subordinates to follow in pursuit of this goal.

Until recently the principles of capitalism furnished a sufficient goal, the *raison d'etre*, for many business leaders. The purpose of business, it was argued, was to maximize profit or maximize the present value of the firm or "the wealth of the common shareholder." With the current trend toward serving multiple constituencies, the practice of collectivist strategies, and the modern stakeholder approach to strategic management, this apologetic is no longer adequate. Leaders today must serve more than financial purposes, not because those purposes are less valid than they were, but because followers are less likely to be inspired by them.

Finally, good leadership should be *confident*. It wasn't enough that Martin Luther King "had a dream," he had to have and evidence confidence that concerted action by his followers would help to accomplish that dream. The confidence great leaders have must be displayed. When Lee Iaccoca decided to pay off $1.5 million in government-guaranteed loans to Chrysler in mid-1983, this was a supreme display of confidence in the future of the company. The loans did not have to be repaid until seven months later, and Chrysler had been profitable for only a brief period. By paying off the loans early, Iaccoca showed his subordinates that he expected the progress to continue. In just two years the company had come from the verge of bankruptcy to lead the auto industry in the growth of both sales and profitability. In an attempt to display the same kind of confidence, in early 1983 International Harvester developed a major advertising campaign around the theme, "We're not giving up; we're going on." That company, the nation's largest farm equipment maker and one of the major truck and construction equipment manufacturers, had been in serious financial trouble for months, and a bankruptcy filing was expected at any time. No great turnaround occurred at International Harvester. Perhaps this was because there was no charismatic leader to communicate that the confidence expressed in the slogan was genuine. In the case of Chrysler, Iaccoca was available to the press, active in company affairs, and involved in a nationwide television advertising campaign where he came across as a beaming, optimistic leader of a great company. At International Harvester the company dragged along with the same challenge to survive, perhaps with inspired leadership, but without the confidence that survival was possible.

Fairchild Industries believes in the possibility of inspiring good leadership. Charles Carlos, who retired as executive vice president after a thirty-six year career with Fairchild, was asked to share his experiences with younger managers at the company. A number of other executives were also involved in this effort to perpetuate good leadership. The results appear to have been mixed. *Fortune* magazine (Dreyfus, 1983, p. 104) reports:

> Measuring the effect of Fairchild's experiment is difficult. So much of the wisdom passed on dealt with intangibles: better understanding of the company's self-image, insights about the perspective of the corporate staff, glimpses into the thinking of senior executives, acceptable modes of behavior under pressure. But the participants came away sold on the seminars, in large part because of the sense of continuity they created between generations. Several managers got to know the retirees socially and promised to get together. One invited a retiree to look at a problem he was having. Another decided to replicate the seminars at his division level. "I would really like my people to interact with these guys," says Anthony I. Spuria, president of Fairchild Aircraft. "These guys have made so many mistakes it's beneficial to hear them."

Hopefully, the inspiration to lead effectively will come more from the successes of great leaders than from their failures. However, the critical importance of leadership to productivity and of productivity to societal well-being can hardly be debated.

CORPORATE CULTURE: STRATEGIC TOOL OR STRATEGIC CONSTRAINT?

In Chapter 5, we discussed the perennial debate among management theorists as to whether strategy follows structure, or vice versa. A similar debate has arisen regarding corporate culture: Should it be viewed as a constraint or as a tool? Let us first consider the two opposing views. Then we will try to place the matter in its proper perspective.

The Experts Disagree

Fortune's Bro Uttal (1983, p. 66) argues, "It isn't clear that most corporations can consciously create a new culture for themselves." Two large management consulting firms—Booz, Allen, and Hamilton, and McKinsey and Company—are reluctant to attempt to change corporate culture to accomplish strategic purposes (Uttal, 1983, p. 69). Allan A. Kennedy, coauthor of *Corporate Cultures*, also discourages companies from attempting large-scale cultural change. "It costs a fortune and takes forever," he says (Uttal, 1983, p. 70). Taking the negative view of corporate cultural change one step further, Wilkins and Ouchi (1983, p. 468) say, "We claim that the existence of local organizational cultures that are distinct from more generally shared background cultures occurs relatively infrequently at the level of the whole organization."

The prestigious Management Analysis Center (MAC) of Cambridge, Massachusetts, however, has successfully marketed cultural change. MACs "CEO's change agenda" gives six steps through which the strategist can implement strategy by changing corporate culture (Uttal, 1983, p. 68). Organizational change consultant Edgar Schein (1983) gives advice for managing culture in founder-dominated companies, and a number of recent articles provide the advice of other experts on using culture for strategic purposes (Kanter, 1983; Cleland, 1981; Inzerilli and Rosen, 1983).

A number of major companies, particularly in the fast-moving computer industry, have found cultural change not only feasible but necessary. Russell (1984, p. 67) writes about Apple Computer, "Things have changed since its salad days before IBM entered the market in August 1981 (when IBM became an Apple competitor by introducing its personal computer), a time when Apple was seen as a kind of playground for ambitious and idealistic computer wizards. There are rumblings among some Apple staffers that the company is becoming regimented and is losing its entrepreneurial soul." Just as Apple is noted for a corporate culture which emphasizes blue jeans and tennis shoes, video games outside the executive offices, free thinking, and a flexible organizational structure, IBM traditionally has emphasized white shirts and gray suits and conservative thinking. But IBM is changing too. That company's new strategy, as seen in the story at the beginning of this chapter, appears to be aimed toward becoming more like Apple—while Apple is becoming more like IBM. Other companies which have accomplished broad-scale cultural change include AT&T, Pepsico, Chase Manhattan, and Twentieth Century Fox ("Corporate Culture . . . ," 1980).

A Model of Cultural Change Feasibility

Should culture be a strategy or a constraint? As in the strategy-structure debate, there can be no clear and permanent answer to this question. But it is not simply a "chicken-or-egg" question. Donaldson and Lorsch (1983) argue that all companies must change their cultures or die, though the change may be revolutionary or evolutionary. Allan Kennedy identifies five possible reasons for imposing rapid cultural change (Uttal, 1983, p. 70):

1 If your company has strong values that don't fit a changing environment
2 If the industry is very competitive and moves with lightning speed
3 If your company is mediocre or worse
4 If your company is about to join the ranks of the very largest companies
5 If your company is smaller, but growing rapidly

But even if quick cultural change is justified according to Kennedy's criteria, is it feasible? A possible answer is illustrated in Figure 6-1. ***Cultural homogeneity***, as used in the figure, is *the degree to which values and beliefs are widely and consistently held in an organization, particularly as reflected in patterns of behavior of organization members*. For simplicity, organizational size and complexity are represented together on the vertical axis. But it is recognized that they do not always correlate. The figure is based upon two premises. First, if an organization is large and complex, the imposition of rapid cultural change is likely to be more difficult than if the organization is small and less complex. Second, cultural change is likely to be more difficult in an organization with a high degree of cultural homogeneity than in organizations with more heterogeneous cultures.

In cases where structural change is necessary, or even highly desirable, strategists must find ways to implement it, no matter how great the difficulty. Not to do so may jeopardize organizational survival and stability, which are perhaps more important goals than profitability (Dickson, 1983, p. 101). In the industrial downturn of 1979–1983, many prominent companies found their survival threatened by union-oriented and bureaucratized corporate cultures. This was apparently true for Wilson Foods (the major U.S. pork producer), Braniff, Continental, and Eastern airlines, Chrysler Corporation, and International Harvester, all of which were near failure during 1981–1983. While survival was not thought to be an issue for IBM, clearly cultural change is vitally important to that company as well.

Prior to the recession, all these companies were large and complex and several had a high degree of cultural homogeneity. Yet, all have undergone major cultural change.

FIGURE 6.1   Difficulty of imposing cultural change

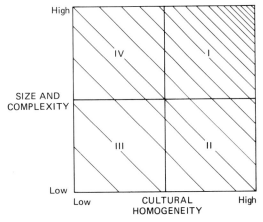

Note: Darker shading suggests greater difficulty in imposing cultural change.

In reference to Figure 6-1, Braniff, a quadrant I company, filed for Chapter 11 reorganization, completely shut down its flight operations, and laid off most of its work force. In the ensuing months, Braniff strategists sold planes and other assets, thereby reducing the size and complexity of the organization and making cultural change easier. At one-third its previous size, the new Braniff moved to quadrant II. At the same time, the insecurity and disorientation caused by wage reductions, layoffs, and cancelations of union contracts virtually destroyed the cultural homogeneity which existed in previous years. By the time in 1983 when Hyatt Corporation bought Braniff from its previous public shareholders, the company clearly fell into quadrant III of Figure 6-1. It was thus easy for Hyatt to begin to impose a very different culture on the Braniff organization.

A somewhat different situation existed at Chrysler Corporation. Buoyed by government loan guarantees, the company was able to remain very large, although thousands of layoffs occurred at all the other auto companies. The work force at Chrysler was represented by the United Auto Workers, and Douglas Frazier, president of the United Auto Workers, served on the Chrysler board. Thus, the heavily union-oriented culture at Chrysler remained somewhat homogeneous. Thus, Chrysler probably fell in quadrant I when Lee Iaccoca took over the reins in 1981. Despite the difficulty in changing corporate culture suggested by Chrysler's quadrant I status, Iaccoca seems to have been able to modify corporate culture significantly at Chrysler. The new culture is more collaborative, more quality-conscious, and more customer-oriented. There is a higher degree of optimism and mutual respect between management and labor. This was possible partly because, though cultural change was immensely difficult, Iaccoca was imbued with great personal power. Having been responsible for the highly successful Mustang and a number of other important innovations at Ford, his expertise in auto manufacture was unquestioned, affording him expert power. Iacocca's personal charisma, as evidenced by the success of his television commercials, suggests a high level of referent power. The fact that he was commissioned by the board of directors to see Chrysler through its dire financial straits, and given a virtually free hand in doing so, gave him a high level of legitimate power. His coercive power and reward power were reflected in his willingness to remove many Chrysler managers and replace them with former Ford executives, and by his ability and willingness to close down plants, forcing layoffs when workers failed to cooperate.

So, as suggested before, the mere fact that a company falls into quadrant I in Figure 6-1 does not mean that cultural change is impossible. It just means that it can be accomplished only over a long period or by organizational strategists of immense power. Corporate culture is clearly a tool of strategic management in most cases. Even in cases where strategists must be constrained by the existing culture, it is possible to change that culture over time.

SUMMARY

This chapter is concerned with the softer components of strategy activation, which loosely fit under the heading "corporate culture." This term refers to the system of shared values, beliefs, and habits within an organization which interact with structure and policies to produce behavioral norms. Attention has recently been focused on corporate culture because of a spate of best-selling books on the subject.

All corporate cultures, particularly those of large companies, include a political component. Power, the ability to influence others, may fill a basic human need. This is related to organizational politics—the carrying out of activities not prescribed by policies for the purpose of influencing the distribution of advantages and disadvantages within the organization. Most Americans tend to have a negative view of political activity. Organizational strategists, though, are appropriately concerned with power and politics to avoid domination and manipulation by others and to help in the influence process, which is a vital part of their jobs. Managers must be concerned with influencing superiors and subordinates within the organization and persons outside the organization as well. Kanter argues that successful architects of corporate cultural change must tacitly agree to keep their power invisible once others have agreed to yield.

Power may be classified according to its source. Reward power and coercive power, based on the perception that the power holder can mediate rewards and penalties, form the basis for the expectancy theory of motivation. Research suggests that reward power is more effective, yet some respected corporate turnaround specialists are well known for ruling through terror. Legitimate power is based upon the belief that the strategist has a legitimate right to influence others. This may be based upon the organizational structure, age, sex, or titles of supremacy. Referent power is influence ability which derives from a liking for or a desire to be like the power holder. To enhance referent power the strategist might emphasize charisma. Expert power is based upon the perception by others that the strategist has special competence, knowledge, or expertise. Expert power might result from making sure that others are aware of one's education and experience.

Machiavellianism is the ruthless use of power, particularly coercive power, and manipulation to attain one's personal goals. The concept has recently received emphasis in popular books and is also useful for the strategist, even one who is highly moral.

Most organizations are at least partly managed by coalitions which cut across formal organizational lines. New executives often replace strategically located managers for the purpose of creating coalitions. Coalitions may serve useful functions, particularly if they are based upon philosophical kinship and concern with promoting the interests of the organization as a whole. They also may be the major factor in strategy determination in an organization with a weak chief executive. A particularly astute organizational strategist will use coalitions that exist and form others in order to accomplish organizational goals.

The organizational strategist plays an important part as an architect of leadership climate and as a personal leader. The trait approach to leadership is the view that effective leaders have special traits which ordinary persons do not possess, or possess in a more limited degree. It is the observable traits of good leaders which offer the best guidance for the general manager who wishes to emulate those leaders' success. Attribution theory suggests that leadership traits cannot be developed. A number of leadership theories emphasize the style of the effective leader: participative, nonparticipative, autocratic, democratic, or laissez-faire. The contingency theories of leadership state that no particular style is best in every situation. The Tannenbaum and Schmidt leadership model, those growing out of the Michigan State and Ohio State studies during the 1950s, Blake and Mouton's managerial grid, and Fred Fiedler's leadership theory offer varying approaches to determining the correct leadership style for a particular situation.

There is some agreement as to what traits good leaders should possess, yet few leaders possess all these positive traits to any remarkable degree. Good leadership should be humane, farsighted, inspired, and confident.

A debate has arisen as to whether corporate culture should be viewed as a strategic constraint or as a tool of the corporate strategist. *Fortune* magazine and a number of researchers argue that corporate cultural change is difficult to accomplish, but the MAC has successfully marketed cultural change. A number of major companies have found cultural change not only feasible but necessary. The question is not simply a "chicken-or-egg" problem. Cultural change is difficult to accomplish in organizations of large size and complexity and in those with a high degree of cultural homogeneity. But even where cultural change is extremely difficult, it can still be accomplished given enough time and a powerful enough strategist.

IMPORTANT CONCEPTS

Corporate culture

Organizational power

Politics

Reward power

Coercive power

Legitimate power

Referent power

Expert power

Machiavellianism

Coalition

Trait approach to leadership

Organizational leadership

Cultural homogeneity

DISCUSSION QUESTIONS

1 Describe the corporate culture at IBM as explicitly as you can and explain how it is changing.
2 Distinguish between power and politics.
3 Discuss two reasons why the organizational strategist should be concerned with power and politics and list the groups and individuals that strategists typically must influence.
4 Define and discuss the five bases of power identified by French and Raven.
5 Explain how the strategist can develop expert power.
6 Define *Machiavellianism* and support or oppose its use in strategic leadership.
7 Define *coalition* and explain how coalitions form and serve useful purposes.
8 Explain how the trait approach to leadership can be useful to the organizational strategist.
9 Explain *leadership style* and discuss how Tannenbaum and Schmidt suggest that the appropriate style should be determined.
10 Explain Fiedler's leadership theory.
11 Explain what is meant by the statement, "Good personal leadership is humane, far-sighted, inspired, and confident."
12 Explain whether corporate culture, in your view, is a strategic tool or a strategic constraint and discuss the validity of the model presented in Figure 6-1.

REFERENCES

Baldwin, William. "This Is the Answer," *Forbes*, July 5, 1982, pp. 50–52.

Calder, B. J. "An Attribution Theory of Leadership," in B. Straw and G. Salancik (eds.), *New Directions in Organizational Behavior*. Chicago: St. Clair Press, 1977, pp. 179–204.

Chace, Susan. "Rules and Discipline, Goals and Praise, Shape IBMer's Taut World," *Wall Street Journal*, April 8, 1982, pp. 1, 18.

Charan, Ram, and Ian MacMillan. "Productivity Improvement: Fads Won't Do It," *Journal of Business Strategy*, 2:3, Winter 1982, pp. 74–77.

Cleland, David I. "The Cultural Ambience of the Matrix Organization," *Management Review*, 70:11, November 1981, pp. 24–39.

"Corporate Culture: The Hard to Change Values that Spell Success or Failure," *Business Week*, October 27, 1980, pp. 148–160.

Cyert, and Jay March, *The Behavioral Theory of the Firm*, Englewood Cliffs, N.J.: Prentice-Hall, 1963.

Deal, Terrence E., and Allan A. Kennedy. *Corporate Culture*, New York: Addison-Wesley, 1981.

Dickson, Douglas. "How Corporate Culture Impacts Financial Decisions," *International Management*, September 1983, pp. 96–102.

Donaldson, Gordon, and Jay Lorsch. *Decision Making at the Top*. New York: Basic Books, 1983.

Dreyfuss, Joel. "Handing Down the Old Hands' Wisdom," *Fortune*, June 13, 1983, pp. 97–98, 100, 104.

Farrell, Dan, and James C. Petersen. "Patterns of Political Behavior in Organizations," *Academy of Management Review*, 7:3, July 1982, pp. 403–412.

Fombrun, Charles. "Environmental Trends Create New Pressures on Human Resources," *Journal of Business Strategy*, 3:1, Summer 1982, pp. 61–69.

Ford, Jeffrey D. "The Occurrence of Structural Hysteresis in Declining Organizations," *Academy of Management Review*, 5:4, October 1980, p. 589–598.

French, John R. P., and Bertram Raven. "The Bases of Social Power," in Dorwin Cartwright (ed.), *Studies in Social Power*. Ann Arbor, Mich.: University of Michigan Press, 1959, pp. 150–167.

Hamermesh, Richard G. (ed.). *Strategic Management*. New York: John Wiley, 1983.

Hosmer, LaRue Tone. "The Importance of Strategic Leadership," *Journal of Business Strategy*, 3:2, Fall 1982, pp. 47–57.

Inzerilli, Giorgio, and Michael Rosen. "Culture and Organizational Change," *Journal of Business Research*, 11:3, September 1983, pp. 281–292.

Jay, Antony. *Management and Machiavelli*. New York: Holt, Rinehart and Winston, 1967.

Kanter, Rosabeth. "Change Masters and the Intricate Architecture of Corporate Culture Change," *Management Review*, 72:10, October 1983, pp. 18–28.

Kanter, Rosabeth. "The Middle Manager as Innovator," in Richard G. Hamermesh (ed.), *Strategic Management*. New York: John Wiley, 1983, pp. 429–430.

Latham, Gary P., and Timothy P. Steele. "The Motivational Effects of Participation versus Goal Setting on Performance," *Academy of Management Journal*, 26:3, September 1983, pp. 406–417.

"Lily-Tulip: Going Public, But Will Its Cure Last?" *Business Week*, February 27, 1984, pp. 69–70.

Lubar, Robert. "An American Leads British Steel Back from the Brink," *Fortune*, September 21, 1981, pp. 88, 92, 97, 100, 105, 108.

Machiavelli, Niccolo. *The Prince*, W. K. Marriott (trans.). London: J. M. Dent, 1908.

Marayanan, V. K., and Liam Fahey. "The Micro-Politics of Strategy Formulation," *Academy of Management Review*, 7:1, January 1982, pp. 25–34.

May, Todd, Jr., et al. "A Japan-like Surge in Labor Productivity," Fortune Forecasts, *Fortune*, May 30, 1983, pp. 41–42.

McElroy, James C. "A Typology of Attribution Leadership Research," *Academy of Management Review*, 7:3, July 1982, pp. 413–417.

Mitchell, Terence R. "Motivation: New Directions for Theory, Research, and Practice," *Academy of Management Review*, 7:1, January 1982, pp. 80–88.

Ouchi, William G. *Theory Z: How American Business Can Meet the Japanese Challenge*, New York: Avon Books, 1982.

Pascale, Richard Tanner, and Anthony G. Athos. *The Art of Japanese Management*, New York: Simon and Schuster, 1981.

Pearce, John A., II, and Angelo S. DeNisi. "Attribution Theory and Strategic Decision Making: An Application to Coalition Formation," *Academy of Management Journal*, 26:1, March 1983, pp. 119–128.

Peters, Thomas J., and Robert H. Waterman, Jr. *In Search of Excellence: Lessons from America's Best Run Companies*. New York: Harper and Row, 1982.

Petre, Peter D. "Meet the Lean, Mean New IBM," *Fortune*, 107:12, June 13, 1983, pp. 69–82.

Podsakoff, Philip M., William D. Todor, and Richard Skov. "Effects of Leader Contingent and Noncontingent Reward and Punishment Behaviors on Subordinate Performance and Satisfaction," *Academy of Management Journal*, 25:4, December 1982, pp. 810–821.

Reilly, Bernard J., and Joseph P. Fuhr, Jr. "Productivity: An Economic and Management Analysis with a Direction towards a New Synthesis," *Academy of Management Review*, 8:1, January 1983, pp. 108–117.

Russell, Sabin. "Steve Job's Mega-Risk," *Venture*, 6:3, March 1984, pp. 66–72.

Salmans, Sandra. "The New Vogue: Company Culture," *New York Times*, January 7, 1983, pp. D1, D3.

Sasaki, Naoto. *Management and Industrial Structure in Japan*. Oxford: Pergamon, 1981.

Schein, Edgar A. "The Role of the Founder in Creating Organizational Culture," *Organizational Dynamics*, 12:1, Summer 1983, pp. 13–28.

Sharplin, Arthur. "Power Base Effectiveness Perceptions in Four Work Organizations," doctoral dissertation, Louisiana State University, 1977.

Sussman, Mario, and Robert P. Vecchio. "A Social Influence Interpretation of Worker Motivation," *Academy of Management Review*, 7:2, April 1982, pp. 177–186.

Tannenbaum, Robert, and Warren H. Schmidt. "How to Choose a Leadership Pattern," *Harvard Business Review*, March–April 1958, pp. 95–101.

Thompson, Arthur A., Jr., and A. J. Strickland, III. *Strategy and Policy: Concepts and Cases*. Plano, Tex.: Business Publications, Inc., 1981.

Uttal, Bro. "The Corporate Culture Vultures," *Fortune*, 108:8, October 17, 1983, pp. 66–72.

Watson, Thomas J., Jr. *A Business and Its Beliefs: The Ideas That Helped to Build IBM*. New York: McGraw-Hill, 1963.

Wilkins, Allan L., and William G. Ouchi. "Efficient Cultures: Exploring the Relationship between Culture and Organizational Performance," *Administrative Science Quarterly*, 28:3, September 1983, pp. 468–481.

STRATEGIC EVALUATION
AND CONTROL

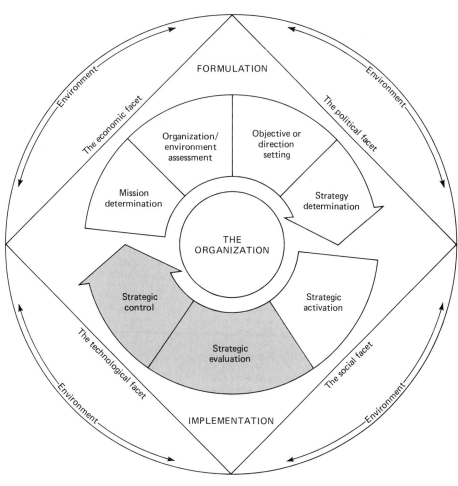

In 1927, young Jodie Thompson recommended that his boss allow him to sell watermelons along with the ice he dispensed at the Houston ice dock where he worked. No one could have imagined the exciting American success story that was just beginning. Soon it was bread and milk in addition to the watermelons, and over the years a wide array of other convenience items. By 1940, 300 Southland convenience stores dotted the area from Texas to Florida.

After he was promoted to a position of responsibility with the Southland Ice Company, Jodie sought a name for the stores, which had become the most profitable part of Southland's business. "Why not let the customers know our working hours by the name we give our stores," Jodie must have thought. The black-and-white Southland Ice Company signs were soon replaced with colorful new ones saying simply, "7-Eleven." Today, there are over 7000 Seven-Eleven stores throughout the world, most of them in the United States.

Three of Jodie Thompson's sons, John, Jere, and Jodie, Jr., are senior officials of Southland Corporation, Seven-Eleven's parent company. The Seven-Eleven stores produce about 85 percent of Southland's income. The other 15 percent comes from a number of smaller operations, such as the dairy products group and the gasoline supply division, which furnish goods and services to Seven-Eleven and also sell to other companies.

Jodie Thompson, Sr., installed gasoline pumps at a few Southland stores in about 1930. The idea flopped then, and the pumps were removed. Thirty years later, his sons took a new look at Dad's idea and decided the time was right. The trend toward self-service gasoline stations was just beginning. Southland installed gasoline pumps at a small percentage of high-traffic stores. The strategy was a marginal success at first, and by 1972, only 200 Seven-Eleven stores sold gasoline. But in the mid-seventies gasoline prices skyrocketed as a result of the Arab oil embargo, and bargain-hungry consumers thronged to Seven-Eleven's self-service gas pumps.

The Thompsons began to relocate a few of the stores from their traditional midblock locations to corners, a proven marketing technique for gasoline stations but not for convenience stores. The corner locations produced extra sales of 50 percent. Of the several thousand stores added since the mid-1970s, almost all sell gasoline and almost all are on corners. The typical Seven-Eleven store makes most of its profit on 3000 grocery and convenience items. The gasoline provides a very small profit margin, but every gasoline customer must come inside to pay, and many make purchases other than gasoline.

Seven-Eleven has been a leader in the distribution and computerization of store operations. Seven-Eleven stores in America are supplied from four automated distribution centers. Specially designed trucks deliver prepriced items along computer-designed routes to individual stores. Careful analysis is made of which items sell best in which stores and at what shelf locations. When trends change, items which no longer sell well are discontinued. Southland continually tests new products in a few strategically located stores. When a product appears to be a rapid seller, it is tried nationwide.

Because of the limited floor space and wide array of merchandise, inventories must be tightly controlled. Using central computers in Dallas, Southland is able to determine what items to stock and, in general, what prices to charge. In addition, it is possible to analyze the operations of each store in the system in terms of profitability, inventory turnover, and so forth. When stores don't measure up to standards, they are often simply closed. When stores look like losers, John Thompson says, ''We would rather close them than take our licks.'' The system of tight control and disciplined management which has characterized Southland Corporation over the years may be a reflection of the personality of the founder, Jodie Thompson, Sr. His only sister wrote, ''The biggest influence on Jodie's life, I believe, was discipline.''

Discipline is just another word for control. Evaluation and control have obviously played a large part in Southland Corporation's success. The computerized system of inventory, pricing, and distribution control ensures that costs are kept low while the customer is well served with a wide array of fresh merchandise. Not only are activities such as restocking continually evaluated and controlled, but management strategies themselves are subject to continuing modification. Jodie Thompson, Sr., reversed the strategic move toward gasoline marketing when sales were not up to standards. The younger Thompsons moved from the test-marketing of gasoline to the installing of pumps at practically every new Seven-Eleven store when environmental changes made self-service gasoline a winner. This led to moving stores to street corners, where gasoline sales would bring in more customers. Because of an efficient mechanism for evaluating individual stores, Seven-Eleven is able to determine early-on when a store is likely to be a failure and to close that store before much money is lost.

So the evaluation and control process at Southland Corporation relates as much to evaluating and modifying plans as it does to forcing activities to conform to existing plans. This two-pronged approach to evaluation and control is an important but sometimes overlooked aspect of strategic management.

In this chapter, we consider several attributes of the evaluation and control process. First, the purpose served by evaluation and control are described. This is followed by a very brief presentation of a simple model of the process. Then, we discuss standards— what they consist of, how they are established, and how standards for plans differ from those related to performance. Next, we describe the process of evaluating and controlling the strategy or the strategic plans. Then we turn our attention to strategic performance and review several formal techniques for evaluating and controlling how effectively the organization is carrying out established plans. Finally, we discuss the special challenges involved in evaluation and control in an international environment.

PURPOSES OF STRATEGIC EVALUATION AND CONTROL

In previous chapters we have discussed the process by which strategic plans are made and placed into effect. However, conditions change, obstacles and opportunities arise, and reconsideration of strategic questions brings forth better ways of doing things. Progress inevitably is above expectations in some areas, and below in others. For all these reasons, strategic evaluation and control are necessary. The purpose of strategic evaluation and control is to monitor and evaluate progress toward the organization's objectives (or the direction of progress if objectives are not established) and to guide or correct the process or change the strategic plan to better accord with current conditions and purposes.

Even though an organizational structure, including policies, procedures, and so forth, may effectively guide most activities, it does not guarantee conformity with needed standards of performance. Practically every subunit in the organization has a different view—not only of its own part in achieving organizational purposes, but also of what those purposes are. The evaluation and control process refines and makes more explicit strategic plans and purposes. No strategy is ever completely specified, and the imposition of controls provides a means of more complete specification. In fact, for most organizations it is only through the taking of corrective action that subunit managers discover the true directions they are to follow and the degree of top management commitment to those directions.

Gitlow and Hertz (1983, pp. 131, 140) argue that, in addition to having long-term top management commitment, in order to be successful a control system must (1) specify what the organization is supposed to produce, and (2) break down barriers between departments. All subunits are to some degree at cross-purposes, not only among themselves but also with the total organization. The sales department, for example, might prefer to have a diverse array of products and a large inventory of each item. The controller, however, might view this as an undesirable freezing of company funds because of the large investment in inventories it requires. Production may not worry too much about the total quantity of inventory but might oppose its diversity because of the difficulties involved in producing a wide array of items. Because of these cross-purposes, every subunit is continually tempted—and many yield—to test stated strategic plans, policies, and procedures. When the testing occurs, if control action is not forthcoming, the stated plan is modified through practice. ''The way we do things around here'' is a clearer reflection of actual strategic focus than ''the way things are supposed to be done around here.'' More often than not, when activities depart significantly from plans, or plans are out of kilter with current needs, it is because of the lack of an effective system of strategic evaluation and control.

THE STRATEGIC EVALUATION AND CONTROL MODEL

Figure 7-1 depicts strategic evaluation and control as a step-by-step process. After plans and standards are established, strategic performance ensues. Then, plans, standards, and performance are evaluated. Finally, strategic control occurs, with a dual focus on correcting or guiding performance and modifying plans and/or standards. This does not suggest, however, that managers actually evaluate and control strategy and performance in a precise sequence. Problems and opportunities do not arise according to time schedule. In fact, many strategic initiatives result when managers experience ''flashes of brilliance'' or entrepreneurial urges. Furthermore, plans and activities may be evaluated and controlled continuously or periodically while being activated or after substantial completion. Recognizing how inexactly this or any model represents real-world complexity, let us now look at the elements in the model as realistically as we can.

STANDARDS

We picture the evaluation and control process as an effort to bring performance into consonance with established plans and to modify plans where it is expeditious. *Any basis for comparison used in evaluating either plans or performance* is a ***standard***. Standards may be of two types: those related to plans and those related to performance.

FIGURE 7.1   The strategic evaluation and control process

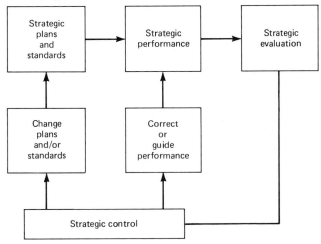

The standards against which strategies must be measured consist of the alternate plans or strategies which are available, including those followed by competitors, along with criteria established by managers. For example, in 1983 Beatrice Foods was a sprawling, decentralized giant with $9.19 billion in annual sales. For years the company had successfully followed a strategy of growth through acquisition. Beatrice generally used its own stock to pay for the companies it acquired, and then allowed them to operate more or less autonomously. A *Wall Street Journal* reporter (Shellenberger, 1983, p. 1) stated the need for change in 1983:

> But Beatrice's markets were changing. Its competitors, consolidated rather than decentralized, had become sophisticated marketers, building market share in Beatrice's product lines. Advertising and research-and-development spending by such giants as P&G had soared. General Mills, Inc., another adroit marketer, doubled its new-product development spending from 1975 to 1980 and tripled its ad spending to 5.1% of sales from 1.7%.
>
> Beatrice, on the other hand, continued to do things as it had. In 1980, it spent less than 2% of sales income on advertising. Its strengths were in low-profit businesses such as fluid milk and warehousing. Most of its few strong national brands, such as Samsonite luggage, had grown on their own, not because of anything the corporate parent had done. "Beatrice wasn't capitalizing on its strengths as a big company," says a former Beatrice executive.

Beatrice's chairman, James L. Dutt, developed what he thought was the best alternative strategy for the company. The plan was to centralize a number of major functions, including purchasing, reorganize the company into six operating groups, shed fifty subsidiaries, and consolidate the remaining ones into related business SBUs to increase marketing clout. Dutt proposed to decentralize R&D, placing responsibility for that function at the business unit level. Finally, he wanted to eliminate two layers of management and force about 700 employees and managers into early retirement. The new strategy became the standard against which the old strategy was measured. When the Beatrice board of directors compared the old strategy against the new standard, the old strategy was clearly seen to be deficient.

Standards for performance are usually less nebulous than the standards for the strategic plans themselves. However, performance standards can be quantitative or qualitative, precise or imprecise, and formally stated or only vaguely conceptualized by the strategist. The more concrete and specific a standard is, the easier it is to measure progress against it. For example, assume that Delta Airlines establishes strategies for improving customer relations. One of the standards for measuring the effectiveness of the strategies may be a level of customer complaints 10 percent below the current annual rate. It is a simple matter to compare the actual number of complaints with the standard. On the other hand, a plan to improve worker morale or to develop better managers through a management training program cannot be measured by such precise standards. When International Paper developed a management training program for young engineers some years ago, it was impossible to establish standards with any degree of preciseness. Yet, when complaints about the program exceeded the tolerance level of senior company officials, the program was modified significantly. The standards in that case were very nebulous ones, existing only in the minds of senior executives. But comparison with the standards did take place, deficiencies were noted, and corrective action ensued.

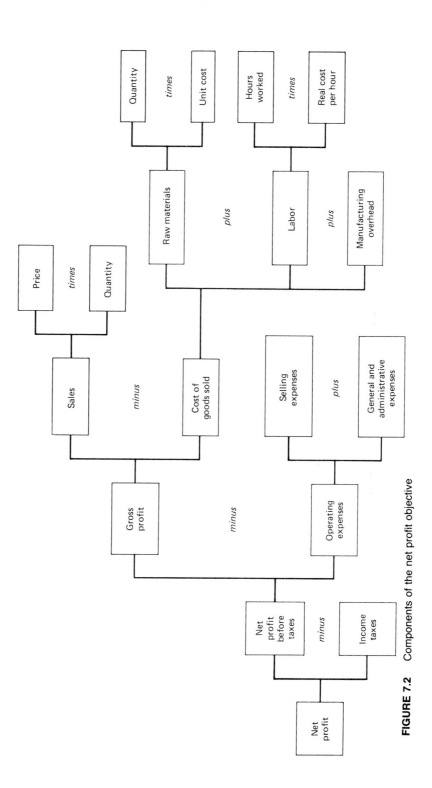

FIGURE 7.2 Components of the net profit objective

In a sense, control standards are objectives. But what are generally thought of as corporate objectives are typically too general to be useful as control standards. It is better to break such broad objectives down into separate elements for control purposes. For example, if a manufacturing firm has a certain goal for net profits before taxes for a given year, this might be broken down for control purposes as shown in Figure 7-2 Then strategic control standards can be set for each level of operation. The net profit goal might be the correct standard for the organization as a whole, although it will usually be thought of as an objective rather than a standard per se.

Further down in the organization, control standards may be set for raw material costs per unit of product, manufacturing overhead as a percentage of the cost of goods sold, selling price as a multiple of the cost of goods sold, or any other combination deemed to be of strategic importance at a particular point in time.

Perhaps the most successful control system of this general type was developed by the DuPont Chemical Company and is credited by many with the outstanding success of that company over more than eighty years. The DuPont system of financial control begins with ROI rather than net profit per se. Each division of DuPont is evaluated on the basis of whether they meet or exceed certain ROI standards. Within the product divisions, the ROI standard is computed as a multiple of asset turnover and earnings as a percentage of sales. This is illustrated in Figure 7-3. Under the DuPont system, as under the one discussed above, strategic control standards can be set for individual elements or for ratios among elements.

Of course, either of these approaches can be taken even further and applied to the individual worker. The typical factory worker is guided by control standards for size

FIGURE 7.3   The DuPont system of financial control (abbreviated)

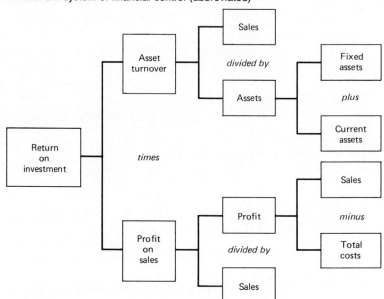

variations in units produced and amounts of time and material expended per unit, along with standards for wastage and a host of other variables. Such standards are discussed at length in production management texts and will not be given further attention here. It is important, however, to understand that the principles of control are the same at the higher levels of organizations, where standards are used to evaluate major elements of the organization, and at the very lowest levels, where standards might apply to the performance of one individual.

EVALUATING AND CONTROLLING THE STRATEGY

Evaluation of strategy should be a continuing process. Ideally it should not be encumbered by management egos. Managers should realize that, however sound the strategy is at the start, it can become outdated. An out-of-date strategy apparently was the problem at Beatrice Foods, discussed in the preceding section. In addition, new approaches to strategic planning are developed from time to time, and these often make it possible to improve strategic plans.

Even though practically every significant company engages in strategic planning, the process varies greatly from company to company (Gluck, Kaufman, and Walleck, 1980, p. 155). Most major firms engage in an annual strategy review process. Ram Charan (1982) has identified seven purposes of strategy review; these are shown in Table 7-1.

TABLE 7-1   THE PURPOSES OF STRATEGY REVIEW

---

1 To evaluate a business strategy for its validity and reality, testing it against the corporate goals, resource availability, and general strategic framework (assuming, of course, that top management has already developed its directions in these terms)

2 To ensure that the divisional general manager knows that the CEO knows that the general manager knows the business

3 To evaluate the trade-offs general managers make in a changing environment—their risk-taking attitudes, their emphasis on long-term versus short-term goals, and the realism of their perception of the changes in cost and competitive patterns, particularly in an inflationary environment

4 To forge a contract between top management and divisional management, whereby corporate management becomes committed to a certain resource allocation and the divisional general manager to delivering certain results; subsequent reviews, whether annual or quarterly, provide for monitoring and follow-up of this agreement

5 To negotiate and integrate strategic issues among interdependent divisions—especially critical in organizations which operate in some form of matrix structure

6 To broaden the scope of knowledge of all participants, including the chief executive; as one CEO put it: "The review forum could be the best device for education in realistic strategic thinking, business school seminars on the topic notwithstanding"

7 To provide a forum, sometimes hidden, but nonetheless real, where not only reviewers, but reviewees as well, can (and usually do) evaluate fellow executives' intellectual mettle, motivation, and attitudes

---

Source: Ram Charan, "How to Strengthen Your Strategy Review Process," *The Journal of Business Strategy* 2:3, Winter 1982, pp. 51–52.

All the tools which are useful in strategy formulation, including the experience curve and business portfolio matrices, are useful for strategy evaluation. Comparisons with strategies being successfully employed by competitors, or even by other companies which are not competitors, can often provide a basis for strategy evaluation. For example, Manville Corporation's successful use of bankruptcy reorganization in 1982 as a way of avoiding labor contracts, thwarting personal injury lawsuits, and perpetuating senior executives in office, undoubtedly impressed other companies. Within a few months a number of corporations followed the Chapter 11 strategy. Among them were Baldwin United, Continental Airlines, Altec Corporation, and a host of others, small and large.

Thompson and Strickland (1981, p. 26) have suggested six steps in strategy evaluation:

1 Review of why the present strategy was selected
2 Identification of what new external and internal factors may call for altering the strategy
3 Reappraisal of external opportunities and threats
4 Reassessment of internal strengths, weaknesses, and resource constraints
5 Consideration of risk-reward trade-offs and timing aspects
6 Judgment of how (if at all) to modify strategy in light of present and expected future conditions.

This approach is a good one, but it leaves unanswered the question: On what basis is strategy to be evaluated? A number of theorists have suggested criteria for evaluating strategy. The most popular and best known model is that developed by Seymour Tilles (1963) who suggests that the strategist ask the following questions:

1 Are the mission, objectives, and plans internally consistent?
2 Do the strategies fit the current environment?
3 Are the strategies consistent with the internal resources which are available?
4 Is the amount of risk appropriate?
5 Is the time horizon of the strategic plan an appropriate one?
6 Is the total integrated strategy workable?

Edmond P. Learned, et al. (1969) added to the Tilles model the following items, among others:

7 Does the strategy accord with the personal values and aspirations of organizational strategists?
8 Is it socially responsible?

J. Argenti (1974) endorses the Tilles model but suggests that strategists ask how effectively the strategy reduces weaknesses, avoids or diminishes threats, and exploits important opportunities. Milton Lauenstein (1981) has developed a set of criteria which can be used in evaluating corporate strategies. These are shown in Table 7-2.

In essence, the strategy evaluation process is simply a matter of comparing the existing strategy with the best alternative available and deciding whether and to what degree the strategy should be changed. The systematic procedure recommended by

TABLE 7-2   STANDARDS FOR EVALUATING STRATEGIES

● Are the financial policies with respect to investment (whether capitalized or expensed), dividends, and financing consistent with the opportunities likely to be available?

● Has the company defined the market segments in which it intends to operate sufficiently specifically with respect to both product lines and market segments? Has it clearly defined the key capabilities needed for success?

● Does the company have a viable plan for developing a significant and defensible superiority over competition with respect to these capabilities?

● Will the business segments in which the company operates provide adequate opportunities for achieving corporate objectives? Do they appear so attractive as to make it likely that an excessive amount of investment will be drawn to the market from other companies? Is adequate provision being made to develop attractive new investment opportunities?

● Are the management, financial, technical, and other resources of the company really adequate to justify an expectation of maintaining superiority over competition in the key areas of capability?

● Does the company have operations in which it is not reasonable to expect to be more capable than competition? If so, can the board expect them to generate adequate returns on invested capital? Is there any justification for investing further in such operations, even just to maintain them.

● Has the company selected business segments that can reinforce each other by contributing jointly to the development of key capabilities? Or are there competitors that have combinations of operations which provide them with an opportunity to gain superiority in the key resource areas? Can the company's scope of operations be revised so as to improve its position vis-á-vis competition?

● To the extent that operations are diversified, has the company recognized and provided for the special management and control systems required?

Source: Milton Lauenstein, "Keeping Your Corporate Strategy on Track," *The Journal of Business Strategy* 2:1, Summer 1981, p. 64.

Thompson and Strickland incorporating the criteria proposed by Tilles and others will help in determining what the best available strategy is.

EVALUATING AND CONTROLLING STRATEGIC PERFORMANCE

Performance Gap Analysis

Performance gap analysis is normally thought of as a corporate-level evaluation and control device (Hofer and Schendel, 1978), but the idea behind performance gap analysis is just as relevant at the business or division level. Of course, application of the concept may vary significantly depending upon the level in the organization. The term *performance gap* refers to *the difference between the actual performance of a given organizational unit and the planned performance of that unit.* For example, Southland Corporation reported a $3.6 billion sales level for the first six months of 1983. This represented an 11.6 percent increase over the same period in 1982. Even though this is a healthy increase, it is somewhat below the 15 percent annual growth rate Southland had anticipated. In addition, net earnings for the six-month period were actually down 6.7 percent from the year before. Based on a planned 15 percent growth in sales and earnings, a significant performance gap exists.

When this occurs for any company, it is worthwhile to analyze the reasons for the variation and to take action to bring performance back into consonance with the strategic plan. Hofer and Schendel (1978, pp. 98–100) have identified five approaches for doing this:

1 *Change business-level strategies.* This may involve the allocation of funds among functional departments or specific efforts aimed at building or enhancing the company's distinctive competence in a certain area. The overall focus here is to improve the competitive position of the business unit.

2 *Add new business units.* This can be done for the purpose of offsetting deficiencies in existing businesses through the purchase of excellent new businesses. More properly, though, the performance gap can be narrowed by seeking businesses which have significant synergy with the company's existing ones.

3 *Eliminate businesses from the corporate portfolio.* A business which performs poorly in comparison to plans, (i.e., has a large performance gap) is a likely candidate for divestiture. However, performance expectations for businesses are normally reflected in the potential selling price. Of course, if a poorly performing business has less synergy with other businesses in the corporate portfolio than it would have with other corporations, it would surely sell for more than its value to the current owner. If a business cannot be sold for as much as the present value of its expected contribution to corporate earnings, then it should not be sold. However, if the expected contribution of the business is unacceptable, its assets possibly should be liquidated.

4 *Use political action to decrease the performance gap.* This may involve seeking the cooperation of customers, unions, and even rival firms when this can be done without violating antitrust regulations. But it also includes obtaining special legislative relief, as Chrysler Corporation did several years ago. In essence, if an organizational unit is not able to perform acceptably within the rules of the game, political action might allow changes in those rules.

5 *Change objectives.* Very often objectives are set too optimistically, and the performance gap results more from that fact than from subpar performance of the unit involved. When Ennis Business Forms tried to compete in larger markets, the company was unsuccessful. Objectives were changed, and the company went back to the small-town areas it had historically served, obtaining a significant improvement in profitability (Mack, 1983). Also, conditions change, and objectives which seem reasonable when established may be far beyond organizational capability later on. However, if objectives are to be useful for guiding the organization, changing those objectives must be resisted. Every other approach to decreasing the performance gap should be attempted before objectives are changed.

In the Southland example discussed above, the diminished sales growth rate is partly explained by environmental changes. John Thompson, Southland chairman, says, "Sales growth was restrained by the current economic recession in Texas and other parts of the Southwest, as well as the unusually cool and rainy weather conditions which continued throughout much of the country.'' When external conditions change significantly, as in this case, it is often permissible and even beneficial to change performance objectives. When the conditions cause performance to improve, elevating the objectives somewhat may be justified. Of course, the reverse is also true.

Responsibility Centers

When a company has a decentralized organizational structure, as in the case of Beatrice Foods discussed earlier, autonomous units are usually treated as profit centers. A ***profit center*** is *any part of the organization for which profit is separately calculated as a part of the regular budgeting process.* Even if authority is centralized, as in the case of Seven-Eleven stores, subunits may be evaluated on the basis of profitability.

When the subunit concerned is not a separate business, or if the market value of inputs and outputs are not easily determined, it is often treated as an expense or cost center. An ***expense center*** is *any element of the organization for which costs are separately budgeted and controlled.* For example, the personnel department in most organizations has no way of calculating its contribution to the organization's revenues. But the personnel department is normally given a certain expense budget and expected to operate within it. In nonprofit and governmental organizations, practically every subunit is an expense center.

Revenue centers are *units which are evaluated on the basis of the revenues they produce.* Regional sales offices are usually revenue centers. Revenue centers are normally expense centers as well, but they are not profit centers. The revenue produced by a sales office, for example, produces profit for the total organization, including production, personnel, finance, and so forth. The sales office is simply given an expense budget. This expense budget normally represents a very small portion of the cost involved in producing and marketing goods and services.

A very common type of responsibility center is an investment, or ROI, center. The ***ROI center*** is *a special kind of profit center which is evaluated and given resources on the basis of the efficiency with which investment assets are employed as measured by ROI.* Standards for comparison and allocation of resources among investment centers is usually net profit divided by the book value of the assets employed. In some cases, before-tax profit or operating profit may be used as the numerator in the ROI formula. ROI is perhaps the single most common approach to allocating resources in large business organizations. It is treated more comprehensively below.

Return on Investment

Technically, ***return on investment*** is *net income divided by total assets.* For divisions of centralized corporations, however, it is often difficult to compute net income for the operating units. So operating profit or earnings before taxes divided by total assets may be used. In general, managers whose divisions earn high ROIs are promoted, and a division which has a high ROI will tend to receive additional resources, vis-á-vis those with lower ROIs. James Higgins (1983, p. 218) has identified a number of advantages and disadvantages of using ROI analysis to evaluate and control subunits. These are the advantages:

1 ROI is a single comprehensive figure influenced by everything that happens.

2 It measures how well the division manager uses the property of the company to generate profits. It is also a good way to check on the accuracy of capital investment proposals.

3 It is a common denominator which can be used to compare many entities.

4 It provides an incentive to use existing assets efficiently.

5 It provides an incentive to acquire new assets only when such acquisitions would increase the return.

These are the disadvantages:

1 ROI is very sensitive to depreciation policy. Depreciation write-off variances among divisions affect ROI performance. Accelerated depreciation techniques reduce ROI, conflicting with capital budgeting discounted cash flow analysis.

2 ROI is sensitive to book value. Older plants with more depreciated assets and lower initial costs have relatively lower investment bases than newer plants (note also the effect of inflation on rising costs of newer plants and on the distortion of replacement costs), thus causing ROI to be increased. Asset investment may be held down or assets disposed of in order to increase ROI performance.

3 In many firms that use ROI, one division sells to another. As a result, transfer pricing must occur. Expenses incurred affect profit. Since in theory the transfer price should be based on total impact on firm profit, some investment center managers are bound to suffer. Equitable transfer prices are difficult to determine.

4 If one division operates in an industry with favorable conditions and another in an industry with unfavorable conditions, one will automatically "look" better than the other.

5 The time span of concern is short range. The performance of division managers should be measured in the long run. This is top management's time span capacity—how long it takes for their performance to realize results.

6 The business cycle strongly affects ROI performance, often despite managerial performance.

As long as ROI is treated as a tool for evaluation and control to be used along with a number of other tools, the advantages typically outweigh the disadvantages. However, single-minded devotion to ROI can result in significant suboptimization. This is particularly true when divisions which operate old but efficient assets which have been depreciated substantially are compared with divisions which have similar new assets. The denominator in the ROI formula is typically the book value of assets, a number which may or may not represent the replacement value, liquidation value, or any other market-based measure. Alfred Rappaport (1983) has noted the deficiencies in ROI as a surrogate for shareholder wealth and proposed a more complex measure. Rappaport's "shareholder value contribution approach" is based strictly upon cash flow and therefore avoids the potential for meeting performance standards through "accounting gamesmanship."

Budgeting

Before there was an academic discipline and separate management field known as strategic management, there were budgets. Budgets are necessary to translate strategic plans into concrete activities. Peter Drucker once said that the test of a plan is not how good, well-stated, and potentially effective the plan is itself but ''whether management actually commits resources to action which will bring results in the future'' (Ewing, 1972, p. 5).

A **budget** is *a statement of planned receipts or expenditures from a specified source or for a specific purpose over a certain period of time*. Budgets may be of many kinds. They may relate to virtually anything managers wish to control. There are sales budgets, showing how much is expected to be sold by the sales department within certain territories and even by certain salespersons, and there are expense budgets, which specify expenditure levels for on-going expenses. Capital budgets state how much is to be spent on fixed assets and often precisely which fixed assets are to be purchased. Maintenance budgets describe expenditures for repairs and alterations, and human resource budgets state planned expenditures for recruiting, training, and compensating employees. Most budgets are expressed in monetary amounts, but some reflect physical activity levels. For example, a certain department might have a plan or a budget for producing a specific number of items.

As old-fashioned as budgeting may seem, it is a major mechanism whereby strategic plans are implemented. As a control device, the budget serves as a standard. Again in reference to Figure 7-2, it is usual to plan expenditures through the issuance of budgets. The budget for an individual department or division may be arrived at participatively, or it may be simply handed down from higher management. The budget typically states planned amounts for each of the components shown in Figure 7-2. Since this accords with the usual arrangement of the corporate income statement, except that the elements to the far right in Figure 7-2 are not commonly shown, budgets prepared according to this format are easily compared to the results shown in periodic financial statements. When expense centers are over the budget, control action is taken to reduce expenses or additional budget funds are obtained. When sales are under the budget, additional advertising or an intensified sales effort may be the appropriate control mechanism.

A budget normally assumes a sales level and provides for one level of expenditure or activity. In some cases, though, flexible budgets are used. **Flexible budgets** are *budgets which provide for several levels of budgeted expenditures or activity on the basis of varying sales levels or levels of output*. When output exceeds or does not meet expectations, the flexible budget does not have to be changed. Xerox Corporation has applied the idea of flexible budgets in the control of legal expenses which had been hard to control previously. Xerox lawyers are required to submit a budget for each case based upon stated assumptions. A special review is required if actual expenditures vary from estimates by as much as 10 percent. This program had a major part in trimming outside legal expenses from more than $12 million in 1976 to less than $3 million in 1982 (Banks, 1983). The benefits of flexible budgeting accrue mainly from the incentive it gives managers to state their financial needs responsibly rather than inflating funding requests ''just in case.''

RATIO ANALYSIS

Financial ratios are an important tool of the organizational strategist. Even if the strategist places little credibility in the strategic significance of the popular financial ratios, it is worthwhile to be familiar with them. Investment bankers, security analysts, and lenders of every sort find financial ratios a simple and widely understood method of evaluating corporate management. Certainly, ratios have their disadvantages. They are commonly based upon published financial data, which can be manipulated in many ways within the strictures imposed by "generally accepted accounting practices." When William Casey was chairman of the Securities and Exchange Commission he said, "The public has lost more money through the use of permissible variations in accounting to exaggerate earnings and growth than through the whole catalog of things which we have made impermissible" (Andrews, 1973).

While Casey may have a very good point, the strategist is normally in a particularly good position to evaluate and control strategic performance through the use of ratios. While outsiders may not understand the accounting practices followed by a given company, the strategist for that company typically does. So, as long as the accounting ratios are used intelligently, they are an effective tool of evaluation and control.

In a study of 221 firms, Pinches, Eubank, and Mingo (1975) identified seven ratios as having high predictive value:

1 Earnings before interest and taxes/total assets
2 Net income/total assets
3 Earnings before interest and taxes/sales
4 Net worth/sales
5 Sales/working capital
6 Debt/total capital
7 Debt/total assets

In addition to these ratios, the common liquidity ratios are frequently used by banks and others to evaluate company performance. The most popular liquidity ratios are the current ratio (current assets divided by current liabilities) and the quick, or acid test, ratio (current assets minus inventories divided by current liabilities).

Activity ratios are also useful to organizational strategists. The popular ones are asset turnover (sales divided by assets) and inventory turnover (net sales divided by average annual inventory or cost of goods sold divided by average annual inventory).

There are two usual standards for comparison in ratio analysis: (1) industry averages, and (2) past performance. Two popular sources of industry average ratios are Dun and Bradstreet (published monthly in *Dun's Review*) and Robert Morris Associates (published annually in *RMA Annual Statement Studies*). By comparing company ratios with the same ratios for past periods, trends can be identified, often in time to take corrective action. For example, if inventory turnover for the company as a whole is significantly below what it has been in the past (although it may be above industry norms), strategists should attempt to understand why. There are a number of possibilities: Accounting practices might have changed (from first-in-first-out to last-in-first-out inventory pricing, for example), consignment inventory may have been converted to owned inventory, anticipatory purchasing may have occurred, or inventory control practices might have become more slipshod. Also, inventory ratios may suggest a problem with total material control systems, factory operations, or even marketing or design engineering systems. In any case, continued attention to the inventory turnover ratio is a simple way to detect when things may be going wrong in inventory control.

While there are well-known standards for a number of the ratios, few put much stock in those standards. For example, many think that the quick ratio should be at least 1.0, yet many major department store chains operate with quick ratios well below 50 percent. The debt ratio is usually not far from 50 percent, but banks and savings and loan associations often have debt ratios above 90 percent. A typical approach to using such ratios for analysis, therefore, is to look for variations from past levels, or from industry standards. Then strategists should attempt to understand the variation and take corrective action as necessary. Ratio analysis is discussed in greater detail in Chapter 8.

EVALUATION AND CONTROL IN AN INTERNATIONAL ENVIRONMENT

Companies which engage in international business face special challenges in evaluating and controlling those businesses. This is true, of course, for companies which simply export to foreign countries or import from them. But it is more especially true for firms which have operating subsidiaries or divisions in other countries. There are differences in language, customs, laws, and many other areas. In addition, a great distance and in most cases an ocean separates the corporate headquarters from outlying divisions. Yet the trend toward international competition is a clear one (Hout, Porter and Rudden, 1983; Yoshino, 1966). International business not only offers major tax advantages for most competitors but also generally provides higher profits than domestic operations. For example, Holiday Inns has found its international division to be exceedingly profitable, as have a number of other hotel chains. David Jones, chairman of Humana, Inc., a leading operator of hospitals, says profit margins for R. H. Wellington Hospital in London are double those of its U.S. facilities. Compared to a 15 percent net profit in the United States, Humana makes 20 percent abroad (Hull, 1982). The trend toward internationalization of business is likely to accelerate if, as some predict, changes in oil, currency, and labor markets create a more favorable global environment for business in the 1980s (Gluck, 1983).

Establishing performance standards for foreign subsidiaries or divisions is difficult at best. Net profit may not be as accurate an indicator of success for a foreign subsidiary as it is for a domestic one. Companies have a wide range of options in treating the income from investment in foreign subsidiaries. The allocation of resources and other control activities may vary on the basis of certain tax ramifications or the need to shift resources from country to country without bringing them back into the United States, for example.

In evaluating foreign subsidiaries it is useful to use multiple performance criteria (Yoshino, 1966). A high level of profit in a country with a large risk of expropriation may not be as desirable as a lower profit level in Great Britain, for example. Sometimes the foreign subsidiary is involved in an international logistical network through which it contributes to the parent company's global operation but over which it has little control. In cases such as this, zero profit might be an acceptable condition.

The challenge is an immensely complex one, and though Yoshino, in 1966, attempted to move "toward a concept of managerial control for a world enterprise," no such concept has yet emerged. There are some ideas, however, which may prove helpful in this regard. First, in evaluating foreign subsidiaries and divisions it is important to develop criteria which are truly comparable. As previously suggested, this is a very difficult task. Pryor (1965, p. 134) recommended establishing "compensatory" financial goals by adding an amount to the profit or ROI goals of foreign subsidiaries to compensate for extra political and monetary risk as well as for the added costs of absentee management. Yoshino (1966) suggested grouping foreign subsidiaries and divisions into relatively homogeneous groups for which similar financial goals would be appropriate.

The type of information-gathering system to be used is a critical issue. Most international corporations use personal visits extensively. With the improving technology in international communications, however, it is becoming possible to use computer hookups, satellite communications, and other means similar to those used with domestic subunits. What is not adequate is a laissez-faire approach—allowing the foreign unit to run itself without intervention from the home office.

Hamel and Prahalad (1983) conclude that the degree of decentralization needed for a multinational corporation (MNC) depends primarily upon two factors: need for integration and need for national responsiveness. They suggest that MNCs evaluate their businesses according to each of these parameters, recognizing that the need for integration suggests centralization of authority and that the need for national responsiveness militates against centralization. Figure 7-4 is an adaptation of the Hamel and Prahalad analysis, with the hypothetical international divisions of two MNCs shown.

It is a happy coincidence if, as is the case for MNC 1, the company's international divisions are clustered near the axis of the diagram. In such cases, a high need for integration is facilitated by a low need for national responsiveness, and the company might opt for a highly centralized management system.

If a company's international divisions plot near the axes of the diagram but do not cluster, it is not feasible to have a corporationwide policy with regard to centralization versus decentralization of authority. This is the situation for MNC 2. This does not present an insurmountable obstacle because, with a high need for integration but a low need for national responsiveness, the West German division of MNC 2 may be highly centralized while the reverse is true for the Iranian division.

The most difficult problem in this regard arises when international divisions not only do not cluster on the diagram, thereby preventing a corporationwide policy regarding decentralization, but also fall far away from the axis, thereby creating conflict between the two needs. This is the situation for MNC 3. It will be necessary for corporate-level strategists in MNC 3 to recognize the conflict and to design strategies to minimize its negative impact. Because of the increased risk imposed by this kind of conflict, strategists should require higher levels of expected return to make investments such as those of MNC 3. The businesses of Dow Chemical Company provide an example of this conflict. Hamel and Prahalad (1983, pp. 345–346) say,

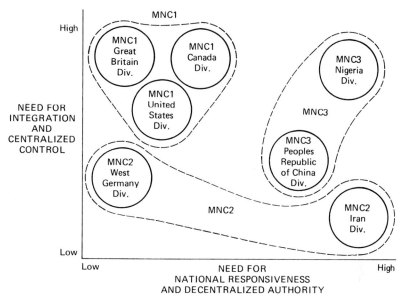

FIGURE 7.4   Centralization versus decentralization of control for multinational corporations (MNCs) [*Adapted from Gary Hamel and C. K. Prahalad, "Managing Strategic Responsibility in the MNC,"* Strategic Management Journal, *vol. 4, no. 4 (October–December 1983), p. 345.*]

"Although synergistic in scale, benefits require that basic chemical research be centralized. The need to adapt products to the peculiar process requirements of foreign industrial customers, and to provide on the spot technical service, requires a capacity for local product adaptation and technical support. . . . " This would seem to justify higher investment returns for Dow Chemical than for many other multinationals, especially for those divisions located in countries such as Iran and Brazil where the need for local adaptation is greatest.

Culture may impose extraordinary burdens on the manager who would control international business. Economic practices, language, and social customs must be respected. In some countries, laws require the use of host company managers and workers. In others, managerial talent from abroad is welcomed. Yoshino (1966, p. 589) says:

> The only permanently effective way to overcome these cultural gaps is to view managerial control as an educational process rather than a superior-subordinate authority relationship. Continuous educational effort is the only feasible way to provide management of foreign affiliates with the necessary background to understand the headquarters' points of view. With this background, local management could intelligently interpret policy directives from the home office as well as effectively participate in the formation of such policies. Such an educational approach would also minimize the sensitivity problem mentioned above.

While many of the attributes discussed above are not unique to international business, legal constraints on the ability to reclaim profits, to shift resources, and to maintain managerial control very nearly are. This makes it necessary for the MNC to extend the strategic domain of the enterprise to explicitly include the legal or political arena. The strategies which a MNC develops should be congruent with governmental policies in the field of international relations. Furthermore, by appropriate lobbying and the maintenance of close relationships with government, the firm, or other enterprise, can hedge its bets and minimize its potential losses from international operations by obtaining favorable legislation or discreet governmental intervention.

SUMMARY

Evaluation and control have played a large part in Southland Corporation's success. Strategic evaluation and control are necessary, because every company faces changing conditions. The purpose is to guide or correct the process or change the strategic plan to better accord with current conditions and purposes.

Even though an organization's structure may effectively guide most activities, it does not guarantee conformity with needed standards of performance. The evaluation and control process refines and makes more explicit strategic plans and purposes.

To be successful a control system must not only have top management commitment, but must also specify what the organization is supposed to produce and break down barriers between departments.

The evaluation and control process can be viewed as a step-by-step sequence, although it does not normally occur that way. Bases for comparison called standards must be established for plans and for performance. Standards of performance are usually less nebulous than those for plans, although either may be more-or-less precise and explicit. In a sense, objectives are standards, but strategic goals typically must be broken down into narrower elements to be really useful guides to performance, especially at lower organizational levels. Strategies or plans should be evaluated continuously. The process of strategy evaluation varies significantly from company to company. The tools for evaluation are the same as those for strategy formulation.

A six-step procedure for strategy evaluation has been proposed by Thompson and Strickland. Tilles, Learned, and Argenti have separately suggested that the strategist ask certain questions in order to evaluate strategy. And Launstein has developed a set of criteria for this purpose. But the strategy evaluation process is essentially a matter of comparing the existing strategy with the best alternative one.

In evaluating and controlling strategic performance, an important tool is performance gap analysis. When a performance gap exists, it is worthwhile to analyze the reasons for the variation and to take action to bring performance back into consonance with the plan. Hofer and Schendel provide five approaches for doing this.

Four kinds of responsibility centers are profit centers, expense centers, revenue centers, and ROI centers. ROI is perhaps the single most common approach to allocating resources in large business organizations. It has a number of advantages and disadvantages, but as long as ROI is used in conjunction with other tools of evaluation and control, the advantages typically outweigh the disadvantages.

Before there was an academic discipline and separate management field known as strategic management there were budgets. Budgets may be of many kinds. Most are expressed in monetary amounts, but some reflect physical activity levels. Budgeting is the principal mechanism whereby strategic plans are implemented. Most budgets are rigid, but flexible budgets provide for several levels of expenditure or activity based upon varying sales levels or levels of output.

Financial ratios are an important tool of the organizational strategist, partly because they are used by bankers, lenders, and other analysts. While ratios have many deficiencies from the viewpoint of those outside the organization, the internal strategist typically understands the organization's accounting practices and therefore is able to use ratios more effectively. Certain ratios have been shown to have a high predictive value. There are two usual standards for comparison in ratio analysis: (1) industry averages, and (2) the company's own past performance. There are also a number of rules of thumb. Few analysts put much stock in these rules of thumb, however.

Companies which engage in international business face special challenges in evaluating and controlling those businesses. Establishing standards of performance for foreign subsidiaries or divisions is difficult at best. A useful approach is to use multiple performance criteria. It is important to develop criteria which are truly comparable. Pryor recommended that "compensatory" financial goals be established, and Yoshino suggested that foreign subsidiaries and divisions be grouped into relatively homogeneous groups. The type of information-gathering system the international corporation uses is critical. Advances in international communications have made the matter simpler. The conflicting needs for integration and national responsiveness interact to determine the degree of management centralization which is appropriate. Culture may impose extraordinary burdens on the manager who must control an international business. Legal constraints, particularly, make it necessary for the multinational corporation to extend the strategic domain of the enterprise to explicitly include the legal/political arena.

IMPORTANT CONCEPTS

Standard	ROI center
Performance gap	Return on investment (ROI)
Profit center	Budget
Expense center	Flexible budgets
Revenue centers	

DISCUSSION QUESTIONS

1 Discuss how effective evaluation and control have contributed to Southland Corporation's success over the years.
2 Explain why strategic evaluation and control are necessary even though policies, procedures, and so forth, may effectively guide most activities.
3 Sketch and briefly discuss the strategic evaluation and control process model.
4 Explain how the alternate plans or strategies available may serve as standards for strategy evaluation.
5 Explain why standards should be as concrete and specific as possible.

6 Explain how the systematic strategy evaluation procedure proposed by Thompson and Strickland in conjunction with the criteria given by Tilles and others can help in determining what the best available strategy is.

7 Define *performance gap* and discuss several strategies for diminishing such a gap.

8 List and explain four kinds of responsibility centers.

9 Discuss the advantages and disadvantages of using ROI to evaluate and control organizational subunits.

10 Describe at least three kinds of budgets which may be used in a single company.

11 Explain how flexible budgets work.

12 Why should organizational strategists be familiar with common financial ratios even if those ratios are ascribed little credibility?

13 Why is the internal strategist better able to use financial ratios for analysis than the external analyst is?

14 Discuss the two usual standards for comparison in ratio analysis and explain where the necessary data may be obtained.

15 Explain, using company examples, why many companies participate in international business.

16 Why might net profit not be an accurate indicator of success for a foreign subsidiary? What other standards for comparison are potentially available?

17 Explain how the need for integration and the need for national responsiveness interact to suggest the degree of decentralization appropriate for multinational companies.

REFERENCES

Andrews, Frederick. "Abe Briloff Tees Off on Creativity in Accounting," *Wall Street Journal*, March 13, 1973.

Argenti, J. *Systematic Corporate Planning*. New York: John Wiley, 1974.

Banks, Robert S. "Companies Struggle to Control Legal Costs," *Harvard Business Review*, 61:2, March–April 1983, pp. 168–170.

Charan, Ram. "How to Strengthen Your Strategy Review Process," *Journal of Business Strategy*, 2:3, Winter 1982, pp. 50–60.

Ewing, David W. (ed.). *Long Range Planning for Management*. New York: Harper and Row, 1972.

Ewing, David W., and Millicent R. Kindle. "Monsanto's 'Early Warning' System," *Harvard Business Review*, November/December 1981, pp. 107–122.

Gitlow, Howard S., and Paul T. Hertz. "Product Defects and Productivity," *Harvard Business Review*, 61:5, September/October 1983, pp. 131–141.

Gluck, Frederick. "Global Competition in the 1980s," *The Journal of Business Strategy*, 3:4, Spring 1983, pp. 22–27.

Gluck, Frederick, Stephen Kaufman, and A. Steven Walleck. "The Four Phases of Strategic Management," *Journal of Business Strategy*, 2:3, Winter 1982, pp. 9–21.

Glueck, William F., and Neil H. Snyder. *Readings in Business Policy and Strategy from Business Week*. New York: McGraw-Hill, 1982.

Hahn, Dietger. "The Control Function in Major German Companies," *Long Range Planning*, 15:3, June 1982, pp. 21–50.

Hamel, Gary, and C. K. Prahalad. "Managing Strategic Responsibility in the MNC," *Strategic Management Journal*, 4:4, October–December 1983, pp. 341–351.

Higgins, James M. *Organizational Policy and Strategic Management: Text and Cases*. Hinsdale, Ill.: Dryden Press, 1983.

Hofer, Charles W., and Dan Schendel. *Strategic Formulation: Analytical Concepts*. St. Paul, Minn.: West Publishing, 1978.

Hout, Thomas M., Michael E. Porter, and Eileen Rudden. "How Global Companies Win Out," in Richard Hamermesh (ed.), *Strategic Management*. New York: John Wiley, 1983, pp. 170–185.

Hull, Jennifer Bingham, "Hospital Firms Are Expanding Foreign Work," *Wall Street Journal*, July 9, 1982, p. 19.

Lauenstein, Milton. "Keeping Your Corporate Strategy on Track," *Journal of Business Strategy* 2:1, Summer 1981, pp. 61–64.

Learned, Edmond P., et al. *Business Policy: Text and Cases*. Homewood, Ill.: Richard D. Irwin, 1969, pp. 22–25.

Mack, Toni. "Return of the Native," *Forbes*, May 23, 1983, pp. 56–58.

Petre, Peter D. "Meet the Lean, Mean New IBM," *Fortune*, June 13, 1983, pp. 68–71, 74, 78, 82.

Pinches, George E., Arthur A. Eubank, and Kent A. Mingo. "The Hierarchical Classification of Financial Ratios," *Journal of Business Research*, October 1975, pp. 78–83.

Pryor, Millard, Jr. "Planning in a World Business," *Harvard Business Review*, January/February 1965.

Rappaport, Alfred. "Corporate Performance Standards and Shareholder Value," *Journal of Business Strategy*, 3:4, Spring 1983, pp. 28–38.

Reddy, Jack, and Abe Berger. "Three Essentials of Product Quality," *Harvard Business Review*, 61:4, July–August 1983, pp. 153–159.

Shellenberger, Sue. "Beatrice Foods Moves to Centralize Business to Reverse Its Decline," *Wall Street Journal*, September 27, 1983, p. 1.

Steiner, George A., John B. Miner, and Edmund R. Gray. *Management Policy and Strategy: Text, Readings, and Cases*. New York: Macmillan, 1982.

Stobaugh, Robert, and Piero Telesio. "Match Manufacturing Policies and Product Strategy," *Harvard Business Review*, 61:2, March–April 1983, pp. 113–120.

Takeuchi, Hirotaka, and John A. Quelch. "Quality Is More than Making a Good Product," *Harvard Business Review*, 61:4, July–August 1983, pp. 139–145.

Thompson, Arthur A., Jr., and A. J. Strickland, III. *Strategy and Policy, Concepts and Cases*, rev. ed. Plano, Texas: Business Publications, 1981.

Tilles, Seymour. "How to Evaluate Corporate Strategy," *Harvard Business Review*, July–August 1963, pp. 111–121.

Yoshino, M. Y. "Toward a Concept of Managerial Control for a World Enterprise," *Michigan Business Review*, March 1966, pp. 12–27.

THE CASE METHOD

CASE ANALYSIS

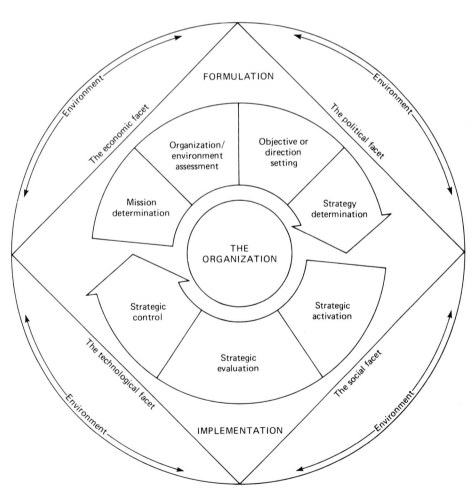

Michael Peterson, a senior management student at Northeast Louisiana University, had been looking forward to the first case discussion in the strategic management class, Business 409. The fall semester of 1983 was Mike's last term at NLU. Mike's teacher was Dr. Jerry L. Wall, NLU's director of business research. For the first five weeks of the seventeen-week semester Dr. Wall had presented lectures and guided class discussion on a wide range of strategic management topics. Mike had made a B on the first test, but he knew that class participation counted 40 percent of the course grade and he was hoping to bring his grade up to an A by doing a good job in the case discussions.

The company Dr. Wall had selected for the first case discussion was Solar Enterprise, Inc., (SEI), a small Colorado maker of solar energy equipment. In preparing for the case discussion Mike had first studied the case thoroughly. Then he had gone to the library to gather information on the solar energy industry. While at the library Mike ran across Mark Rainwater, who was also doing research on the case. The two young men studied together that day. Then, on the day before the scheduled class discussion, Mike got together with a group of four other students from the class to debate and discuss certain aspects of the case. Each member of the group had calculated certain financial ratios for SEI. Although several had attempted to find average ratios for the solar energy industry, no one had been successful. After about two hours of sharing information, Mike felt that he was ready for the case discussion. This is how Mike described what occurred when he came to class:

"The chairs had been arranged in a semicircle facing the teacher's podium. On each desk was a neat cardboard name sign mounted in a wooden holder which Dr.

Wall had made at home in his woodworking shop. Dr. Wall had apparently arrived early and had made a number of notes on the chalkboard. Before the bell rang I noticed several groups of students talking with one another, some apparently about the case, others about less imminent matters.

"As the class session began I was afraid that Dr. Wall would call on me to introduce the case. I thought I was ready but still was hoping that someone else would get the honor that first day. I was relieved when Dr. Wall called on Sylvia Prentice to tell the class some of the facts of the SEI case. Sylvia made a mess of it, though. As soon as Dr. Wall realized that she was inadequately prepared, I saw him look in my direction and knew that my feeling of relief had been premature. 'Mike, can you help Sylvia out?' he asked. 'Sure,' I replied, hoping that no one noticed the tremor in my voice, 'First, though, let me tell you what I've learned about the solar energy industry.' Dr. Wall moved to where he had written 'industry characteristics' on the chalkboard and made an abbreviated record as I related the very limited information I had on that topic.

"Dr. Wall called on another student to describe the company itself, and still another to list the qualifications and attitudes of SEI's management team. Then Dr. Wall asked the class if anyone would like to add anything to the notes he had made on the board.

"In an apparent attempt to redeem herself, Sylvia Prentice made what seemed to me to be a completely illogical remark about the company's mission. Dr. Wall then asked if someone would like to add to what Sylvia had said. That gave me a chance to tell the class what I thought was SEI's mission—to make as much money as possible for Roland Davis, the founder and main stockholder. I was surprised when several in the class disagreed with me. One student argued that Davis had been making more money as a consulting thermodynamics engineer than he could hope to make from SEI for several years. Besides, another said, the case gave Davis' net worth, not including his SEI stock, at $2.3 million, so he was probably more concerned with serving humanity or becoming famous than with maximizing profit.

"Before we had resolved that question, Dr. Wall led us into a discussion of the strengths, weaknesses, threats, and opportunities faced by SEI. One of the weaknesses I had identified before class time was excessive leveraging and illiquidity. The debt ratio, I pointed out, was 71 percent, and the current ratio was just over 1.0. Gloria Hawkins said that leverage was one of the company's primary strengths because, once the company's interest costs were covered, the high leverage would increase the return to the common shareholders. In addition, Gloria showed the class a cash-flow projection she had prepared showing increasing cash balances despite the low current ratio. I asked Dr. Wall to settle the leverage question, but he just wrote 'high financial leverage' under 'weaknesses' and under 'strengths' and asked me to explain to the class why I felt it was more a weakness than a strength. Three or four other students piped in—some favoring my side of the argument and some favoring Gloria's.

"We didn't really finish with that matter before moving on to a discussion of the strategies we felt SEI should follow in the future. Since we had not decided exactly what the company's mission was, there was a good deal of disagreement about the proper strategies. So Dr. Wall wrote two alternative mission statements on the chalkboard and asked the class for marketing, finance, production, and personnel strategies to accomplish each mission. Even then, few of us agreed on any important point and the argument got rather heated once or twice.

"It seemed to me that the discussion had been going for only about thirty minutes when Dr. Wall called on Brent Harper to summarize what we had learned about SEI. 'Not very much,' Brent said, 'I reckon it's always hard to evaluate company strategy unless we can agree on what the company's mission is. Even then, it seems to me that whether something is a strength or weakness, or a good or bad strategy, is just a matter of opinion.' To my surprise, there was only time for two other students to briefly tell what they had learned before the bell rang signaling the end of class.

"I thought surely that Dr. Wall would reschedule SEI for the next class period, since we had failed to finish it. But to my surprise, he said, 'Okay class, that's it for today. Remember to be ready for the Southland Corporation case next meeting'."

Mike Peterson's experience is a typical one. The story illustrates some of the frustrations as well as the benefits of case analysis as a method of learning about business topics. The SEI case did not contain all the needed industry information and, in fact, comparable ratios were not even available at the library. The facts presented were subject to a number of interpretations, and even when the facts, like Roland Davis' net worth, were clear, the implications were not. After extensive discussion the students continued to disagree about important matters, and the professor failed to resolve those disagreements. At the end of the session, Mike felt that much more could be learned from the SEI case. Yet the teacher signaled his intention just to move on to another case. Edge and Coleman (1981) identified eight possible sources of dissatisfaction with the case method, and they are presented in Table 8-1. Each of the complaints listed have some validity, and no attempt will be made to refute them. They should be viewed, however, as imperfections in a very useful pedagogical device rather than as crippling faults.

TABLE 8-1   REASONS FOR INITIAL DISSATISFACTION WITH CASE LEARNING

1 Cases have no unique answer.
2 Information is ambiguous and contradictory.
3 The issue is not stated.
4 Information is redundant and irrelevant.
5 Instructor does not solve case.
6 Case teaching is inefficient.
7 Note taking is difficult.
8 Instructor is not directive in discussions.

Source: Alfred G. Edge and Denis R. Coleman, *The Guide to Case Analysis and Reporting*, Honolulu: Systems Logistics, 1981, pp. 10–12.

Despite its acknowledged deficiencies, since the case discussion format became popular at Harvard University in the early decades of this century, it has been widely used by universities throughout the world, especially in teaching strategic management. In fact, the case method is the primary teaching mode followed in strategic management classes throughout the United States.

In this chapter we will explain what strategic management cases consist of and the purposes they serve. Then we will describe two tools of case study, WOTS-up analysis and ratio analysis. The final section of the chapter provides guidance to help the student prepare a case for classroom discussion and to prepare a written case analysis.

WHAT IS A CASE?

A *case* is *a written description of an organization covering a certain period of time*. Most cases contain information about the organization's history, its internal operations, and its environment. There is no standard order of presentation, but many cases include sections on industry and competitive conditions, products and markets, physical facilities, the skills and personalities of managers, and the organizational structure, together with financial statements and quantitative data relating to production, accounting, marketing, personnel, and so forth. Cases may relate to profit-seeking, governmental, or public service organizations.

A good case places students in a realistic situation where they can practice making decisions without the accountability for making mistakes which the real world imposes. Yet, there is no such thing as a truly complete case. Completeness would require more detail than can be presented in the few pages a student can be expected to read. Students frequently say that they have too little information. This is true, of course, but it is also representative of the real world—managers never have enough information.

The tendency of many students, and managers as well, is to delay making decisions until satisfied with both the quality and quantity of the information available. However, such a time never arrives. Yet, decisions must be made. A good manager—and a good strategic management student—will make the best decisions possible under the circumstances. Sometimes assumptions are made about the unknowns, and in other cases the unknowns are simply ignored. The student who feels unable to make valid decisions under such circumstances should realize that most management decisions are made with far less information than that presented in the typical strategic management case, and with far less opportunity for study and interaction with others. In addition, as Henry Rath (1981, pp. 107–108) has observed, a major benefit of using cases is derived from the process of evaluation, not necessarily from finding the one right answer.

OBJECTIVES OF THE CASE METHOD

Long ago, E. R. Schoen and P. A. Sprague (1954, pp. 78–79) stated four objectives of the case method. They are still current today:

1 Helping you to acquire the skills of putting textbook knowledge about management into practice.

2 Getting you out of the habit of being a receiver of facts, concepts, and techniques and into the habit of diagnosing problems, analyzing and evaluating alternatives, and formulating workable plans of action.

3 Training you to work out answers and solutions for yourself, as opposed to relying upon the authoritative crutch of the professor or a textbook.

4 Providing you with exposure to a range of firms and managerial situations (which might take a lifetime to experience personally), thus offering you a basis for comparison when you begin your own management career.

Charles I. Gragg (1954) has argued that "wisdom can't be told," contending that it is unlikely that accumulated managerial experience can be acquired through reading articles and listening to lectures alone. Certainly Gragg is right. Ready-made answers do not exist for most managerial problems. Each situation is different, requiring its own diagnosis and evaluation as a prelude to action. Case studies allow learning by doing to occur. They simulate the reality of the manager's job. During their college education few students have an opportunity to come into contact with the situations they will face later. Cases become laboratory materials and offer a reasonable substitute for actual experience by bringing a variety of management problems and opportunities into the classroom.

Just as importantly, the case method offers students an opportunity to convince their peers and their professor of the correctness of their viewpoints. This is analogous to the situation where a manager must persuade others in order to accomplish organizational purposes. Case analysis and discussion help the student develop the communication and interpersonal skills which are vital to success in management. Table 8-2 provides a checklist of management skills which are improved by case analysis.

ANALYTICAL TOOLS

There are a number of tools which have been shown to be effective in strategic decision making, both academically and professionally. Among the more prominent ones are (1) strengths, weaknesses, opportunities, and threats (WOTS-up) analysis, and (2) financial ratio, analysis. Webster (1983) also suggests the use of quantitative risk analysis, breakeven analysis, and the NPV method in evaluating strategies and performance. WOTS-up analysis and ratio analysis are discussed below.

WOTS-UP?

Through consideration of strengths, weaknesses, opportunities, and threats it is possible to sum up the very essence of strategic management. The job of the organizational strategist is to capitalize upon the organization's strengths while minimizing the effect of its weaknesses in order to take advantage of opportunities and avoid or overcome threats in the environment.

TABLE 8-2   ACTION SKILLS REINFORCED BY CASES

1 *Think clearly in complex ambiguous situations.* Successful experiences with cases give students the practice and confidence necessary for clear, intensive thinking in ambiguous situations where no one right answer exists. Since problems in management and administration are full of these situations, the skills are valuable to acquire.

2 *Devise reasonable, consistent, creative action plans.* Most cases require the student to detail a course of future action.

3 *Apply quantitative tools:* The management of modern organization demands the use of such quantitative tools and theory as net present value, ratio analysis, and decision tree analysis. Active employment of these techniques in actual situations requires more knowledge than one typically gains by introductory theory and problems. Cases give the student practice in using quantitative tools in these realistic situations.

4 *Recognize the significance of information.* Theories and observations of modern management have shown that managers sift through large masses of information, both formal reports and informal channels (the "grapevine"). The manager's task of defining problems and their solutions demands the ability to classify information.

5 *Determine vital missing information.* Successful decision makers must know where, and be able to determine when, to seek more information. Cases give the student practice in solving problems with the information at hand in the case, in researching standard industry sources, and in identifying the missing information that is vital to the formulation of an action plan.

6 *Communicate orally in groups.* Both the in-class discussions of cases and small group discussions preceding class are an integral part of learning by cases. The ability to listen carefully to others, to articulate one's views, and to rapidly incorporate the views of others into one's position are all important skills for managers.

7 *Write clear, forceful, convincing reports.* Managers and their staffs have to express themselves in writing. The best way to improve one's writing skills is to write; hence, the usefulness of the case report.

8 *Guide students' careers.* Many students would benefit from a greater awareness of the day-to-day tasks and responsibilities of managers. The wide variety of actual situations described in cases gives students valuable knowledge about the functions of many job positions.

9 *Apply personal values to organizational decisions.* Modern industrial society forces managers to make decisions which trade among business profits, government expenses, and the welfare of individuals and the public. This area of ethics and social responsibility is important and problematic in a professional education. The process of stating and defending positions in case discussions sharpens a student's awareness and maturity in the subjective area of value and moral judgments.

Source: Alfred G. Edge and Denis R. Coleman, *The Guide to Case Analysis and Reporting,* Honolulu: Systems Logistics, 1981, pp. 5–7.

Strengths are *special attributes or distinctive competences an organization possesses in comparison with other organizations, especially competitors, which give it an advantage over them.* Strengths are characteristics of the organization, not of its environment. For example, it is not a strength of Apple Computer Company that the home computer industry is growing rapidly. Apple's main strengths apparently lie in technological leadership and marketing expertise and perhaps in the entrepreneurial talent of its senior managers. As the above definition implies, strengths are relative rather than absolute. For example, a large asset base is not a strength of Jones and

Laughlin Steel Company because its competitors, U.S. Steel and Bethlehem, have larger asset bases. Marketing expertise is not a strength of the Adolf Coors brewing company because Miller Brewing, drawing on the marketing capabilities of its parent company, Philip Morris, is a far more competent marketer of beer. Strengths make an organization more competent in comparison to other similar organizations.

Weaknesses are *special attributes of organizations which tend to make them less effective in comparison with other similar organizations*. Like strengths, weaknesses are internal rather than external and relative rather than absolute. Being highly concentrated in a given industry, as Delta Airlines has always been, may be a weakness because it subjects the company to the vicissitudes of that industry. When the airline industry's fortunes turned downward in 1981–1983, Delta suffered extensively and in the first half of 1983 reported its first loss in thirty-seven years. During the same period, many diversified companies remained profitable, with income from thriving industry segments more than offsetting losses from declining segments.

But, concentration in a single industry may often produce significant strengths. Hewlett-Packard in computers, Lincoln Electric in arc-welding products, WalMart in discount merchandising, and Adolf Coors in beer brewing are among the lowest-cost producers in their respective businesses, partly because they have each concentrated upon doing one thing well. Failure to recognize this was the problem Mike Peterson experienced in the story at the beginning of this chapter. He viewed high financial leverage as a weakness because it exposed SEI to dangers in the marketplace. Gloria Hawkins, though, felt that it was a strength because it allowed SEI to earn higher profits on each common share when things went well. Both were right, as reflected by Dr. Wall's willingness to list high financial leverage as both a strength and a weakness. Because of such confusion it is best to state strengths and weaknesses as specifically as possible. For example, instead of listing high financial leverage as a weakness, Mike might have identified the decreased financing flexibility and increased cost of borrowed funds which result from high financial leverage. On the other hand, Gloria might have mentioned the potential magnification of earnings which financial leverage produces as a strength, while listing as a weakness the magnification of potential losses. If a company is concentrated in a given industry, it usually has the weakness of cyclical instability, along with the strength of being a more competent producer of goods and services than a diversified competitor.

Opportunities, as indicated, tend to be external to the organization. An **opportunity**, as used here, is *any chance to follow a new or revised strategy which would be of benefit to any legitimate constituency*. Opportunities seldom simply arise. They always exist and only need to be identified. For example, because BIC Corporation had such a great production and marketing capability for making small plastic items, the company had an exceptional opportunity to make and market disposable razors in the early 1980s. Because the American market was ready for a low-cost home computer, and because the founder of Apple Computer Company had the ingenuity and energy to make and market such an item, Apple had the opportunity to become the dominant home computer maker for several years.

So, opportunities represent potential new initiatives. They exist for every organization but are much easier to identify for some than for others. When Polaroid's patent on instant film expired, the opportunity this represented for Kodak was obvious. The same was true for Royal and Olivetti when IBM's patent on the ball-element typewriter expired.

Most opportunities have to be sought and in some cases even created. When R&D efforts allow the production of a good or service which could not be produced before, an opportunity to market that good or service is created. The main focus of strategic management must be upon identifying additional opportunities, selecting the ones that are the most promising, and capitalizing upon them.

Threats are *reasonably probable and more or less sudden events which can seriously hamper an organization's ability to serve one or more of its constituent groups.* For companies which recognize only the common shareholders as a constituency, a threat is any reasonably likely event which, if it occurs, will cause stock prices to decrease. For companies which recognize employees as constituents, a reasonably probable eventuality which will necessitate extensive layoffs is a threat.

Almost without regard to who an organization's constituents are, any probable event which would decrease the value of the organization's output constitutes a threat. The death of a dynamic chief executive becomes a threat when the executive becomes very old or suffers a minor heart attack. The loss of a position of market leadership becomes a threat when a competitor develops a superior product or service.

Like opportunities, threats always exist, but they become less severe when they are recognized and guarded against. When Hewlett-Packard's supremacy in the scientific computer market was threatened in 1982, the company made plans to enter the home computer market, thereby minimizing the possible impact of this threat. When the marketing of high-quality Japanese automobiles threatened U.S. auto companies, both Ford and Chrysler embarked upon extensive quality improvement programs and all the auto makers sought government limits on the number of Japanese cars which could be imported.

When a threat is recognized soon enough, it can often be converted to an opportunity. For example, when the owner of Newcomb's Truck Stop in Carlisle, Pennsylvania, learned that an interstate highway would soon bypass his location, he realized that such an eventuality would destroy his business. Rather than wait for his business to die, he bought property near an interchange on the proposed highway at a bargain price. By the time the highway opened he had built a much larger, more modern truck stop and sold his old one at a profit to another business which was not dependent upon truck traffic. When James Sharplin, owner of Sharpco Fabricators, Inc., in Monroe, Louisiana, anticipated the 1979–1983 economic recession, he realized that this would force him to lay off workers if it occurred. He decided to release a number of workers before the recession got under way, at a time when they were able to find other jobs. At the same time he raised prices on the items he sold in order to reduce the quantity demanded. The higher prices also helped pay for the increased overtime his employees had to work because of the layoffs. When the recession materialized, Sharpco was able to reduce prices and shorten working hours, thereby remaining profitable and avoiding layoffs during a time when workers would have found it difficult to get new jobs.

Strengths, weaknesses, threats, and opportunities analysis is a very complex process which can treat the whole organization at once. To simplify the process, students as well as organizational strategists might find it useful to develop a list of strengths, weaknesses, threats, and opportunities separately for the functional areas of production, marketing, finance, and personnel. The analyst should be aware, however, that much which is of strategic importance cannot be so neatly classified.

RATIO ANALYSIS

As stated earlier, however one chooses to view the business organization, it is primarily an economic entity. The use of financial ratio analysis allows us to take a purely economic view of the business. This is not to suggest that financial ratios should ever be considered in isolation. For one thing, there is much more to the firm than its economic nature—human and societal considerations are important. It is important to consider how the various financial ratios affect the functional areas of finance, production, marketing, and personnel. For example, whereas liquidity and leverage ratios have primary significance for the finance function, the profitability ratios have applications in the production area (efficiency) and perhaps the personnel function (wage policy). Inventory turnover has obvious implications for marketing and production, as do some of the other activity ratios. Still, financial ratio analysis is probably one of the most useful tools of strategic management. Table 8-3 shows some of the common financial ratios.

In discussing the topic we will presuppose a reasonably thorough knowledge of how to compute the ratios themselves and limit ourselves to a discussion of the various bases of comparison which may be used in financial ratio analysis. These are (1) rules of thumb, (2) historical data for the company being analyzed, and (3) historical data for similar companies.

Rules of Thumb

Almost every bank credit officer has certain generalized ideas about desirable levels for a number of the common financial ratios. For example, it is generally accepted that the quick ratio, or acid test ratio, should be 1.0 or higher. The current ratio, most believe, should be at least 2.0. Inventory turnover for high-margin businesses, so another popular rule of thumb goes, should be at least 4.0. And for dry goods and general merchandise retailers, the gross margin on sales in soft goods retailing should approach 40 percent. Despite the huge number of exceptions to these rules of thumb, and the belief of some that they are "dangerous," they are widely used by credit practitioners.

It is best to think of each ratio as a conceptual measure rather than a technical one before using it as a decision criterion. For example, the quick ratio measures the degree to which a company should be able to pay maturing liabilities from cash flows becoming available in the very short term. When a company buys and sells on similar terms, so that accounts receivable approximate accounts payable, the 1.0 rule of thumb for the quick ratio is probably appropriate. However, in the soft goods retailing industry, where companies typically sell for cash and buy on extended terms, quick ratios typically average in the range of 0.25. There are few receivables to flow in, but a

TABLE 8-3   COMMON FINANCIAL RATIOS

Liquidity ratios

$$\text{Quick, or acid test ratio} = \frac{\text{current assets} - \text{inventory}}{\text{current liabilities}}$$

$$\text{Current ratio} = \frac{\text{current assets}}{\text{current liabilities}}$$

Activity ratios

$$\text{Inventory turnover} = \frac{\text{net sales}}{\text{inventory}} \text{ or } \frac{\text{cost of goods sold}}{\text{average inventory}}$$

$$\text{Average collection period} = \frac{\text{average accounts receivable} \times 365}{\text{year's credit sales}}$$

$$\text{Accounts receivable turnover} = \frac{\text{year's credit sales}}{\text{average accounts receivable}}$$

$$\text{Fixed-assets turnover} = \frac{\text{sales}}{\text{fixed assets}}$$

$$\text{Total assets turnover} = \frac{\text{sales}}{\text{total assets}}$$

Leverage ratios

$$\text{Debt to total assets} = \frac{\text{total debt}}{\text{total assets}}$$

$$\text{Debt to net worth} = \frac{\text{total debt}}{\text{net worth}}$$

$$\text{Long-term debt to capitalization} = \frac{\text{long-term debt}}{\text{long-term debt} + \text{net worth}}$$

Profitability

$$\text{Profit margin on sales} = \frac{\text{net profit after taxes}}{\text{sales}}$$

$$\text{Return on assets or ROI} = \frac{\text{net profit after taxes}}{\text{total tangible taxes}}$$

$$\text{Return on net worth} = \frac{\text{net profit after taxes}}{\text{net worth}}$$

$$\text{Gross profit margin} = \frac{\text{sales} - \text{cost of goods sold}}{\text{sales}}$$

$$\text{Operating profit to assets} = \frac{\text{earnings before interest and taxes}}{\text{total tangible assets}}$$

Coverage ratios

$$\text{Interest coverage} = \frac{\text{earnings before interest and taxes}}{\text{interest}}$$

$$\text{Debt service coverage} = \frac{\text{earnings before interest and taxes}}{\text{interest} + \text{principal payments}}$$

$$\text{Fixed charge coverage} = \frac{\text{earnings before interest and taxes}}{\text{fixed charges}}$$

significant part of the inventory is converted to cash each month. This cash can be used to pay maturing debts, although it was not reflected in the previous month's quick ratio. A soft goods retailer who tries to maintain a 1.0 quick ratio would be significantly suboptimizing the use of investment funds. This is why Gloria's cash flow analysis in the story at the beginning of this chapter probably impressed Dr. Wall more than Mike's comment about financial ratios. The use of the quick and current ratios are simply short cuts to cash flow analysis and thus must be interpreted cautiously. Other financial ratios have similar shortcomings.

The Company's Own Historical Ratios

For the organizational strategist within a company, the company's own historical ratios provide a valid basis for comparison—perhaps a better basis than rules of thumb or industry ratios. However, for the student, who can easily be misled by changes in accounting practices, a comparison with past ratios may be less valid. In any case, a major change in a ratio should be a subject for investigation. The matter is a very complex one, and only a thorough understanding of accounting and financial analysis principles will allow one to make really valid judgments.

A few examples will illustrate how changes in financial ratios can reveal serious problems and how significant improvements in ratios can be explained away as essentially irrelevant. Assume that a dry goods retailer shows a decrease in inventory turnover compared to past patterns. This might result from a deterioration in inventory control practices or a decrease in sales per average inventory item brought on by less effective marketing, increased aggressiveness by competitors, or an economic downturn. But a decrease in inventory turnover might also result from the purchase of inventories which had previously been held on consignment, the increased stocking of items with a slower turnover but a higher margin, or a conscious effort on management's part to decrease stockouts and improve customer service. Finally, inventory turnover may decrease if the company buys additional inventory because of a manufacturer's incentive sales plan or in anticipation of a rapid economic upturn.

If a company's current ratio improves markedly, this may signal improved liquidity. But it may mean that the company has converted short-term debt to long-term debt by, for example, paying off a revolving loan with proceeds from a bond issue or installment note. Also, when the current ratio is above 1.0, it can be improved simply by using cash to pay off current liabilities or by failing to replace inventory as it is sold.

Asset turnover, ROI, or any other ratio with assets in the denominator can be increased by leasing fixed assets instead of buying them, or by failing to replace assets which are being depreciated on an accelerated basis. A decrease in net profit on sales may result from increased competition, worsening market conditions, or a conscious attempt by management to improve sales through price competition.

As one can readily see, financial ratios generally should not be used alone for decision-making purposes, but simply to identify areas which deserve further exploration. Reliance on financial ratios for even this limited purpose may be risky. In dealing with an unsophisticated business manager, the financial analyst may be able to sense worsening or improving conditions through the use of financial ratios. However, today's business managers are becoming more and more sophisticated. If a manager desires to do so, it is possible to maintain financial ratios within the expected ranges without violating accepted accounting practices while the condition of the firm steadily worsens. Still, of the three bases of comparison discussed in this section, the company's own past financial data are probably the most dependable.

Data from Similar Firms

No two companies are exactly alike, and it is often hard to find financial ratios which are precisely comparable to those of the firm being analyzed. The L. L. Bean Company of Freeport, Maine, for example, is a catalog merchandiser of outdoor clothing and equipment. The company manufactures 20 percent of the items it sells. In addition, about one-fourth of the sales are made through the company's 50,000-square-foot retail store. Finally, L. L. Bean's 1982 sales of $225 million were miniscule compared to those of J. C. Penney and Sears. When we were studying the L. L. Bean Company case in my graduate strategic management class, the students attempted to find ratios for comparison purposes. After a great deal of work, and much consideration, they gave up and relied on past data from L. L. Bean and, to a small extent, on rules of thumb. Still, it is possible to categorize most companies and to compare their ratios with those of companies of similar size and similar business areas.

To facilitate ratio comparison Robert Morris Associates, the national association of bank loan and credit officers, has published *RMA Annual Statements Studies* each year for more than half a century. These publications are available in most public libraries, as well as from Robert Morris Associates, Philadelphia National Bank Building, Philadelphia, PA 19107. Dun and Bradstreet maintains financial profiles on over 800,000 U.S. businesses. The company publishes financial data in several book formats as well as in a number of easy-to-use pamphlets. A very popular Dun and Bradstreet publication is *Selected Key Business Ratios in 125 Lines of Business*, which reports the median and the upper and lower quartiles for 14 ratios in each of the 125 business lines. Most university libraries carry one or more of the Dun and Bradstreet reports, which are also available from Dun and Bradstreet, Inc., 99 Church Street, New York, NY 10007.

Another handy source of financial ratios for comparison purposes is *Prentice-Hall's Almanac of Business and Industrial Financial Ratios*. This handy reference book is available from Prentice-Hall, Inc., Englewood Cliffs, NJ 07632, and in many business libraries.

The RMA *Annual Statement Studies*, Prentice-Hall's almanac, and some of the Dun and Bradstreet reports include common size balance sheet and income statement data, as well as ratios. This allows the student or financial analyst to create ratios for comparison purposes which are uniquely appropriate to a certain company.

All the cautions which relate to comparisons with a company's own past ratios also relate to comparisons with industry norms. What should mainly be kept in mind is that ratio analysis, as valuable as it is for revealing potential problems, should never be used alone. Ratio analysis is just one of the many tools the strategic management student or organizational strategist should use in evaluating corporate performance.

PREPARING A CASE FOR DISCUSSION

Figure 8-1 is a guide that students can use to make sure that they are fully ready for a case discussion. The environmental audit and the organizational audit were discussed in a previous chapter, and WOTS-up analysis was covered earlier in this chapter. In following the procedure specified in Figure 8-1, it is useful to refer to the basic strategic management process model (Figure 1-1). In evaluating past and present strategies the student should not only consider whether the strategies themselves were appropriate or inappropriate, but should also analyze the process of strategy formulation and implementation as it relates to the particular case under study.

It is very difficult to generalize about the expectations of other professors across the country regarding student preparation for a case discussion. However, much is generally agreed upon. First, students should be thoroughly aware of the facts of the case. Second, discussants should be able to relate each part of the case discussion, whether written or oral, back to the organizational mission. Third, case analysis should be carefully organized around some accepted model or models. Finally, case analysis should concentrate upon specific strategic issues. Let us consider these principles individually.

Know the Facts

A case is a technical paper. As such, it deserves careful reading. A good approach is to read the case three times: once rapidly, quickly scanning any exhibits; a second time thoroughly and slowly, paying careful attention to the exhibits; and a third time

FIGURE 8.1 A guide for case preparation

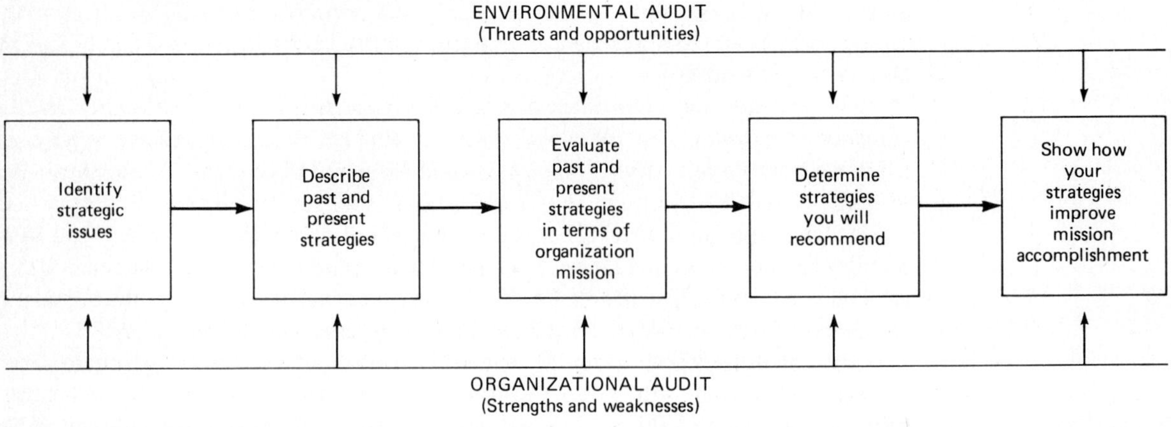

through rapidly to reinforce what has been learned. Robert Ronstadt (1980, pp. 12–14) suggests a two-step reading procedure which some may find appealing.

Most cases are two to five years old by the time they are discussed in the classroom. Many case teachers require that students bring cases up to date unless they are disguised cases. This often requires library research using Moody's industrial manuals, Standard and Poor's publications, and various business news periodicals such as *The Wall Street Journal, Fortune, Forbes,* and *Barron's.* If the company being discussed has a nearby facility, students are usually expected to obtain information about that facility. Many students choose to place phone calls to corporate managers in order to obtain up-to-date factual information about the company. It usually helps if students get together before class time, as the students did in the case described at the beginning of this chapter, and share information. For most publicly held companies annual reports, Securities and Exchange Commission Reports 10-K and 10-Q, and a wide variety of other sources of information are available.

In addition to learning about the organization under discussion, students are usually expected to obtain industry and environmental information. What are the characteristics of the industry? Who are the major competitors? What life-cycle stage is the industry in? What are the general economic conditions: interest rates, inflation rates, and so forth? The student should remember that all facts are not equally important and that a systematic approach to information gathering should be followed. More will be said about this later.

Consider the Organizational Mission

Each aspect of strategic management has its primary relevance, perhaps its only relevance, in its relation to the organizational mission. Remember that the mission is probably best stated in such a way as to answer the question: What is the company trying to do for whom? It is no longer adequate to think of a single corporate objective such as profit maximization or maximizing the wealth of the common shareholder. Students and other analysts should consider who the organization's stakeholders are and to which of them management is obligated. What are those obligations, in relatively specific terms?

It is important to consider the corporate mission from both a normative and a descriptive standpoint: what it is and what it should be. Students often ask whether a company should go public or not. The answer is: Only if the current shareholders—as well informed as they are or choose to be—collectively decide to do so. In the case of a closely held firm, an opinion can often be ventured as to whether the company would make more money as a publicly held firm and whether the stockholders would be economically wealthier. But the determination of what specific strategy the company should follow must await a statement of the organizational mission. Whether the objective of a student is to state, analyze, or evaluate organizational events and management actions, this should be done using the mission statement as a starting point.

The student should not shy away from taking a normative view and evaluating management actions from an ethical or moral standpoint. At the same time, however, students should neither confuse themselves nor others about whether their judgments are moral and emotional or rational and logical. In fact, as stated previously, every case discussant should be prepared to make both kinds of judgments.

Use Models

Even the simplest case is far too complex to understand in its totality at a point in time. So models (systematic abstractions from reality) are exceedingly useful. A very useful model is the strategic management process model in Figure 1-2. This model is useful as a descriptive device to express how strategies are being formulated and implemented, and as an evaluative device to compare this to what the process of strategic management should be like.

A second model, which is used in many classrooms, is the strengths, weaknesses, threats, and opportunities model discussed in a previous section of this chapter. The relationship among strengths, weaknesses, threats, and opportunities essentially sums up the process of strategic management. This is illustrated in Figure 8-2. In preparing to discuss a case in class, students should very carefully list the strengths, weaknesses, threats, and opportunities faced by the organization. An effort should be made to be objective wherever possible. For example, if "an effective management team" is listed as a strength, students should list the past experiences, educational levels, and accomplishments of managers upon which this generalization is based. If "a strong balance sheet" is listed as a strength, students should justify this by comparisons with the balance sheets of similar companies, competitors, and industry averages. If expansion into international markets is considered an opportunity, students should obtain information about what countries provide favorable marketing opportunities for the company's products and services and specifically how the company might profitably produce and distribute its products and services in those countries. Most teachers who use the case method respect the right of strategists such as Harvard's Mike Porter and Richard Hammermesh, Chrysler's Lee Iaccoca, and *The Wall Street Journal*'s Lindley Clark to generalize about strategic matters. However, they expect students to generalize only when their generalizations are supported by specifics. So it behooves the strategic management student to study extensively and rigorously.

FIGURE 8.2   WOTS-Up in strategic management

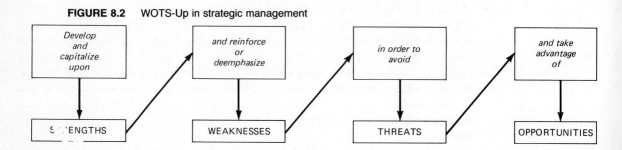

There are a number of other models which relate to the functional areas of marketing, personnel, finance, and production, which are useful for strategic analysis. The four P's of marketing, the DuPont system of financial control, the six functional areas of human resources management, and the management process model—planning, organizing, and controlling, are but a few. Some of these are static models. They don't describe a process—they simply consist of categories within which various strategic ideas can be placed systematically. They are models, nonetheless, and students will find these and many others useful for case analysis.

Consider Specific Strategic Issues

It is impossible to consider every aspect of company operations at once, so students will find it useful to key in upon certain strategic issues. Often the important issues are clear. When IBM unveiled its Peanut personal computer in 1983, this posed a serious threat to Apple Computer, long a leader in the personal computer field. How to meet that threat was a major concern of Apple's management and probably the most significant strategic issue the company faced that year. For the U.S. auto companies in 1983 and 1984, the most significant issue was probably how to diminish and meet Japanese competition. There are usually many important issues to be faced by corporate management, however, and they are often not quite so clear as in the above cases. So students should think carefully about the questions which are really important and deserve analysis.

SUMMARY

Michael Peterson's experience illustrates some of the frustrations as well as the benefits of the case method. Despite the acknowledged deficiencies cases have been widely used by universities throughout the world, especially for teaching strategic management.

A case is a written description of an organization covering a certain period of time. A good case places students in a realistic situation where they can practice making decisions. Yet no case is truly complete. The tendency of many students and managers is to delay making decisions while waiting for complete information. But decisions must be made, usually with less information than either would like to have.

Among the objectives of the case method are learning to put text knowledge into practice, learning to diagnose problems and formulate workable strategies, learning to *work out* solutions to problems, and learning about managerial situations through exposure to a range of firms. It is unlikely that accumulated managerial experience can be acquired through reading articles and listening to lectures alone. Cases become laboratory materials and offer a reasonable substitute for actual experience. Finally, the case method offers students an opportunity to persuade their peers and their professors, a situation analogous to that often encountered by managers.

There are a number of tools which have been shown to be effective in strategic decision making. Among them are WOTS-up analysis and ratio analysis. The job of the organizational strategist is to capitalize upon the organization's strengths while minimizing the effects of its weaknesses in order to take advantage of opportunities and avoid threats in the environment. Strengths and weaknesses are internal rather than external and relative rather than absolute.

Opportunities always exist for any firm, but must be identified. Opportunities represent potential new initiatives. Most opportunities have to be sought and in some cases even created.

Threats are events which might hamper an organization's ability to serve constituents. Any probable event which would decrease the value of the organization's output is usually a threat no matter who the organization's constituents are. Threats become less severe when they are recognized and guarded against. When a threat is recognized soon enough, it can often be converted to an opportunity.

The use of financial ratio analysis allows us to take a purely economic view of the business. This is probably one of the most useful tools of strategic management. There are three common bases for comparison in ratio analysis: (1) rules of thumb, (2) the company's own past data, and (3) historical data for similar companies. Almost every bank credit officer has certain generalized ideas about desirable levels for a number of common financial ratios. It is best to think of each ratio as a conceptual measure rather than a technical one before using it as a decision criterion.

Any major change in an important financial ratio for a given company should be a subject for investigation. But such changes should be interpreted cautiously. They may reveal serious problems, or they may be essentially irrelevant. Financial ratios should generally not be used alone for decision-making purposes.

No two companies are exactly alike, so it is hard to find financial ratios which are precisely comparable. It is possible to categorize most companies and to compare their ratios with those of companies of similar size and similar areas of business. Robert Morris Associates, Dun and Bradstreet, and Prentice-Hall, among others, provide summaries of popular ratios for this purpose.

There are four important guidelines which will help the student prepare a case for class discussion. First, the student should know the facts. A good approach to learning a case is to read it three times: once rapidly, a second time thoroughly and slowly, and a third time rapidly. Many case teachers require that students bring cases up to date. This often requires library research and sometimes telephone calls to corporate managers. Students also benefit from getting together for a discussion prior to class time. Second, students should consider the organizational mission. Each aspect of strategic management has its primary relevance in relation to that mission. The student should not only consider what the corporate mission is, but also what it should be. Third, case analysis should be developed around some accepted model or models. Finally, case analysis should be built up around certain strategic issues or questions which are important to the organization from a general management standpoint.

IMPORTANT CONCEPTS

Case	Opportunity
Strengths	Threats
Weaknesses	

DISCUSSION QUESTIONS

1 Explain how Michael Peterson's experience illustrates the frustrations and benefits of the case method.

2 What does a case consist of and how can the student adapt to its lack of completeness?

3 List four objectives of the case method and explain how case analysis accomplishes them.

4 Explain how a consideration of strengths, weaknesses, opportunities, and threats relates to the job of the organizational strategist.

5 Explain how a threat, recognized soon enough, may be converted to an opportunity.

6 What are the deficiencies in using rules of thumb for ratio analysis and how does thinking of ratios as conceptual measures help to overcome these deficiencies?

7 Explain how changes in financial ratios can reveal serious problems on the one hand or be essentially irrelevant on the other.

8 List three major sources of financial ratios for comparison purposes and explain how one might obtain these sources.

9 Using the four guidelines provided in the chapter explain how you would go about preparing a case for a classroom discussion.

REFERENCES

Edge, Alfred G., and Denis R. Coleman. *The Guide to Case Analysis and Reporting*. Honolulu: System Logistics, 1981.

Gragg, Charles I. "Because Wisdom Can't Be Told," in M. P. McNair (ed.), *The Case Method at the Harvard Business School*. New York: McGraw-Hill, 1954, p. 11.

RMA Annual Statement Studies. Philadelphia: Robert Morris Associates, 1983.

Rath, Henry J. "A Model for Business Case Analysis," *Journal of Business Education*, 57:3, December 1981, pp. 107–109.

Ronstadt, Robert. *The Art of Case Analysis*. Dover, Mass.: Lord Publishing, 1980.

Schoen, D. R., and Philip A. Sprague. "What Is the Case Method?" in M. P. McNair (ed.), *The Case Method at the Harvard Business School*. New York: McGraw-Hill, 1954, pp. 78–79.

Selected Key Business Ratios in 125 Lines of Business. New York: Dun and Bradstreet, 1981.

Sharplin, Arthur. "Teaching Policy the Hard Way." Working paper presented at the March 1982 meeting of Case Research Association.

Tedesco, Eleanor Hollis. "Effective Case Discussion," *Business Education Forum*, 37:5, February 1983, pp. 8–9, 12.

Troy, Leo. *Almanac of Business and Industrial Financial Ratios*. Englewood Cliffs, N.J.: Prentice-Hall, 1983.

Webster, Frederick A. *Guidelines for Preparing Comprehensive Strategic Business Plans for New Ventures*. Kawkawlin, Mich.: Webster and Associates, 1983.

CASES

MANVILLE CORPORATION (A)

Arthur Sharplin
Northeast Louisiana University

SELECTED STRATEGIC ISSUES

- Impact of socially responsible actions on stakeholder groups
- Social responsibilities of a new, hired-from-without chief executive in a socially irresponsible corporation
- Social responsibilities of a new, promoted-from-within chief executive in a socially irresponsible corporation
- Balancing personal interests of manager/directors against the interests of other stakeholders

Asbestos is an insidious poison. Microscopic fibers, as small as a human cell, cause progressive, irreversible, incurable disease. Asbestos causes scarring of the small airways and further scarring of the lung tissue itself, parenchymal asbestosis. Asbestos causes scarring, thickening and calcification of the lung linings, pleural asbestosis. Asbestos causes an always fatal cancer, mesothelioma, in the tissue surrounding the lungs. Asbestos causes lung cancer. Asbestosis causes an abnormally high level of lung infections which are unusually hard to treat.

For eight years in the boiler rooms of the USS Santa Fe, the USS Antietam and the USS Thomas F. Nickel, Ed Janssens used and repaired thermal insulation. He never knew he was planting a time-bomb deep within his lungs. Twenty years passed before he first felt its toxic effects. He was sick, but he didn't know why.

Ed Janssens has asbestosis. To be more specific, his asbestos exposure from 1943 through 1951 has caused thickening and calcification of the lining of his lungs, small airways disease, complication of his asthma, life threatening lung infections, and a progressive decrease in lung function. He will require close medical surveillance forever. If Ed Janssens, an

207

asbestotic, does not die soon of cancer, mesothelioma or massive lung infection, the inexorable march of asbestosis will eventually block his blood flow, swell his heart and cause death by coronary pulmonale.

In 1981, 30 years after his last exposure to its asbestos, Ed Janssens brought Johns-Manville to trial. For ten years, his asbestosis has been stealing his breath, complicating his asthma, retarding treatment for lung infections, keeping him out of work, making him lonely and reclusive, causing him depression and frustration, reducing the length of his natural life, and keeping him from sleeping in even the same bedroom with his wife, Patsy, the mother of his eight children. For years, he had to sit up in a chair to get any sleep; now, under more effective medical care, he can sleep lying down—sometimes.

It was 1978 when Ed Janssens, 35 years too late, first learned of the asbestos hazard. Who knew the death-dealing hazards of the asbestos fibers? Johns-Manville knew. Who knew in 1929, when Ed Janssens was just five years old? Johns-Manville did. Who exercised editorial prerogative over Dr. A. J. Lanza's 1935 United States Public Health Service report entitled "Effects of Inhalation of Asbestos Dust on the Lungs of Asbestos Workers"? Johns-Manville did. And who rushed on Christmas Eve 1934, to make sure "additions, omissions or changes . . . beneficial from the industry viewpoint" would be included in Dr. Lanza's official report? Johns-Manville did.

When an asbestos manufacturer's health credo was "our interests are best served by having asbestosis receive the minimum of publicity," it is no surprise to learn that no hazard warning besmirched [Manville's] asbestos bags and boxes until 30 years after Dr. Lanza acceded to his benefactor's demands; and, even then, only because Dr. Irving Selikoff had "held the smoking gun aloft"—publicly in 1964.

Wayne Hogan
Counsel for Asbestos Victims

The Janssens filed suit in 1979 and were eventually awarded $1,757,600 in compensatory and punitive damages. But Manville moved for a judgment, notwithstanding the verdict, then for a new trial, and then for a return of part of the adjudged damages (none of which had been paid). When all these motions were denied in December 1981, Manville initiated the formal appeal process. The appeal had not been heard—and Ed Janssens had not been paid—when the Manville board of directors met secretly on August 25, 1982, to decide whether to file for protection under Chapter 11 of the U.S. Bankruptcy Code.

Manville Corporation (Johns-Manville until 1981) is a diversified mining, timber, and manufacturing company. In 1982, the company employed about 30,000 people at more than 125 facilities (plants, mines, and sales offices), mostly in the United States. For many years, the company had been the world's largest producer of asbestos and asbestos-based products. In 1976, sales of asbestos fiber alone (mostly to manufacturers outside the United States) provided 52 percent of Manville's income from operations, although it constituted only about 11 percent of sales. In addition, asbestos was used by the company in making hundreds of products such as floor tile, textiles, filters, pipe, and roofing materials. Altogether, asbestos and asbestos products clearly accounted for more than one-half of Manville's sales and probably for three-fourths of its operating profit. The ruled insert on page 209 describes asbestos.

In 1957, the Industrial Health Foundation proposed a study on asbestos and cancer to be funded by the Asbestos Textile Institute (made up of asbestos manufacturers).

WHAT IS ASBESTOS?

This is taken from the *Encyclopedia Britannica*:

> *asbestos*, mineral fibre occurring in nature in fibrous form. It is obtained from certain types of asbestos rock, chiefly the chrysotile variety of the serpentine groups of minerals, by mining or quarrying. Valued since ancient times for its resistance to fire, asbestos fibre achieved commercial importance in the 19th century.
>   The fibre is freed by crushing the rock and is then separated from the surrounding material, usually by a blowing process.

This is from an article by Bruce Porter in *Sunday Review of the Society*:

> Perhaps no other mineral is so woven into the fabric of American life as is asbestos. Impervious to heat and fibrous—it is the only mineral that can be woven into cloth—asbestos is spun into fireproof clothing and theater curtains, as well as into such household items as noncombustible drapes, rugs, pot holders, and ironing-board covers. Mixed into slurry, asbestos is sprayed onto girders and walls to provide new buildings with fireproof insulation. It is used in floor tiles, roofing felts, and in most plasterboards and wallboards. Asbestos is also an ingredient of plaster and stucco and of many paints and putties. This "mineral of a thousand uses"—an obsolete nickname: the present count stands at around 3,000 uses—is probably present in some form or other in every home, school, office buildings, and factory in this country. Used in brake linings and clutch facings, in mufflers and gaskets, in sealants and caulking, and extensively used in ships, asbestos is also a component of every modern vehicle, including space ships.

The proposal was rejected by Manville and the other manufacturers at the March 1957 meeting of the institute. The minutes reported, "There is a feeling among certain members that such an investigation would stir up a hornets' nest and put the whole industry under suspicion."

In 1963, Dr. I. J. Selikoff of Mt. Sinai Medical Center in New York completed an extensive study of asbestos and health. The minutes of the Asbestos Textile Institute's Air Hygiene Committee meeting of June 6, 1963, noted Selikoff's forthcoming report:

> The committee was advised that a Dr. Selikoff will read at the next meeting of the AMA in about 30 days a paper on a study he has made of about 1,500 workers, largely in asbestos insulation application, showing a very large incidence of lung cancer over normal expectations.

Dr. Selikoff's report and the symposia and publications which followed revealed, for the first time to those outside the industry, the magnitude and character of the asbestos problem: Thousands had already died of asbestos-related diseases, and hundreds of thousands more would become disabled and die in the decades to follow. Breathing asbestos dust causes a progressive thickening and stiffening of lung tissue (asbestosis) and sometimes causes the always fatal asbestos cancer (mesothelioma); either of these diseases may disable the victim twenty to forty years after exposure.

The dangers of ingesting asbestos fibers began to be widely publicized in the 1960s and 1970s. Beginning in 1978, there were hundreds of newspaper stories, magazine articles, and television documentaries concerning the problem. Joseph Califano, Secretary of the Department of Health, Education and Welfare (HEW), estimated that between 8.5 and 11 million workers had been exposed to asbestos since World War II. In April 1978, HEW announced that it was warning present and former asbestos workers and their doctors about the hazards of asbestos, and the U.S. Surgeon General sent 400,000 warning letters to the nation's doctors. In June, the Environmental Protection Agency established limits for airborne asbestos resulting from building demolition. Then, in December, 1978, the Environmental Defense Fund claimed that millions of school children had been exposed to cancer-causing levels of asbestos because of use of the product in school construction.

MANVILLE'S LEGAL DEFENSES WEAKEN

The dozens of asbestos injury lawsuits against Manville in the twenties and thirties, scores during the forties and fifties, and hundreds in the sixties and early seventies became thousands in the late seventies. Although the asbestos litigation was not mentioned in Manville's 1977 annual report, it was described, as the law required, in the company's 1977 Form 10K, submitted to the Securities and Exchange Commission in April 1978. This form reported 623 asbestos lawsuits against Manville, some of them multiplaintiff cases involving many claimants. The claims for which amounts were given totaled $2.79 billion.

For nearly fifty years, Manville had been able to hide the fact that company executives knew the dangers of breathing asbestos dust from about 1930 onward and suppressed research and publicity concerning asbestos-related diseases. But, in April 1978, plaintiffs in a South Carolina asbestos tort case obtained the so-called Raybestos-Manhattan papers. These documents consist of asbestos industry correspondence and reports from the 1930s and 1940s. Coupled with the publications of Selikoff and other researchers, the Raybestos-Manhattan papers made a compelling case. The ruled insert on page 211 gives excerpts from a few of the papers.

In ordering a new trial, the South Carolina judge wrote:

> The Raybestos-Manhattan correspondence reveals written evidence that Raybestos-Manhattan and Johns-Manville exercised an editorial prerogative over the publication of the first study of the asbestos industry which they sponsored in 1935. It further reflects a conscious effort by the industry in the 1930s to downplay, or arguably suppress, the dissemination of information to employees and the public for fear of the promotion of lawsuits. . . .
>
> On two separate occasions, September 1977, pursuant to subpoena duces tecum, and December 1977, pursuant to a Request to Produce, plaintiff sought to discover the Raybestos correspondence in question. . . . it is uncontroverted that the same documents were produced in April 1977, in a New Jersey asbestos lawsuit. . . .
>
> It is also clear that the defendant, Johns-Manville, upon whom the December Request to Produce was also served, had in its possession since April 1977, the Raybestos correspondence, which also involved its corporate agents.

During the late seventies, asbestos plaintiff lawyers were able to obtain depositions from a number of retired Manville executives. Dr. Kenneth W. Smith (mentioned in

EXCERPTS FROM THE RAYBESTOS-MANHATTAN PAPERS

From a December 15, 1934, letter from George Hobart, Manville's chief counsel, to Vandiver Brown, Manville's corporate secretary and legal vice president:

> . . . it is only within a comparatively recent time that asbestosis has been recognized by the medical and scientific professions as a disease—in fact, one of our principal defenses in actions against the company on the common law theory of negligence has been that the scientific and medical knowledge has been insufficient until a very recent period to place on the owners of plants or factories the burden or duty of taking special precautions against the possible onset of the disease in their employees.

From a 1935 letter to Sumner Simpson, president of Raybestos-Manhattan Corporation, from Anne Rossiter, editor of *Asbestos*, an industry trade journal:

> You may recall that we have written you on several occasions concerning the publishing of information, or discussion of, asbestosis. . . . Always you have requested that for obvious reasons, we publish nothing, and, naturally your wishes have been respected.

From an October 3, 1935, letter from Vandiver Brown to Sumner Simpson, commenting on the Rossiter letter:

> I quite agree that our interests are best served by having asbestosis receive the minimum of publicity.

From a report by Dr. Kenneth Smith, Manville physician and medical director, on a 1949 study of 708 men who worked in a Manville asbestos mine (The report shows that only four of the 708 were free of lung damage and that those four had had less than four years' exposure to asbestos dust):

> Of the 708 men, seven had X-ray evidence of early asbestosis. . . . They have not been told of this diagnosis. For it is felt that as long as the man feels well, is happy at home and at work, and his physical condition remains good, nothing should be said. . . . The fibrosis of this disease is irreversible and permanent. . . .
>
> There are seven cases of asbestosis and 52 cases in a "preasbestosis group." These 59 cases are probable compensation claims . . . . There are 475 men with [fibrosis extending beyond the lung roots] all of whom will show progressive fibrosis if allowed to continue working in dusty areas.

the lined insert above) had been Manville's physician and medical director from 1945 to 1966 (except for one year). In a 1976 deposition, Dr. Smith testified that he became "knowledgeable of the relationship between the inhalation of asbestos fibers and the lung condition know as asbestosis" during his internship in 1941–1942, before he went to work for Manville. Following are other excerpts from Dr. Smith's testimony:

Q. Did you [tell other employees of Johns-Manville] of the relationship between the inhalation of asbestos fiber and the lung condition known as asbestosis?

A. Many people at Canadian Johns-Manville in supervisory positions already knew about the association of inhalation of asbestos fibers and disease. I just amplified that [and] made much more explicit the disease process.

Q. Did you or did you not have discussions with Mr. A. R. Fisher with respect to the relationship between the inhalation of asbestos fiber and the pulmonary lung condition known as asbestosis, both with respect to employees of Johns-Manville and what you defined as the civilian population? [Mr. Fisher had been involved in the asbestos litigation in the 1930s and was president in the 1950s and 1960s.]

A. Definitely, we discussed the whole subject many times, about dust and what it does to people, whether they are employed or not employed . . . . The good Lord gave us all the same breathing apparatus and if the asbestos fiber is present and the housewife, and the asbestos worker, and the fireman, and the jeweler, and doctor, and everybody else are all in the same room, they are all going to breath the same dust . . . . So wherever there is dust and people are breathing dust they are going to have a potential hazard.

Q. Did you at any point . . . make any recommendations to anyone at Johns-Manville in respect to the utilization of a caution label for the asbestos-containing products?

A. Hugh Jackson and I sat down with many people in other divisions suggesting that similar caution labels should be put on products which when used could create airborne dust that could be inhaled.

Q. When did you sit down with Hugh Jackson and come to that conclusion?

A. It would be late 1952 and early 1953.

Q. What was the reason . . . the asbestos-containing products were not labeled with a caution label back in 1952?

A. It was a business decision as far as I could understand. . . . application of a caution label identifying a product as hazardous would cut out sales. There would be serious financial implications.

Q. Did you at any time recognize the relationship between the inhalation of asbestos fibers and pulmonary malignancies, as you phrased it, or lung cancer, or pleural cancer?

A. Yes, I have recognized the alleged and sometimes factual association of malignancy with the inhalation of asbestos fibers.

Q. When would that have been, Doctor, for the first time?

A. The first time would be in the late 1940s.

Q. Had there not been studies in Britain and perhaps even in the United States prior to the beginning of the Saranac Lake Laboratories studies [1936] which had indicated [that fibrous asbestos dust caused lung disease]?

A. Very definitely. As I recall, Merriweather and his cohorts studied the effects of the asbestos textile dust many years prior to 1935 and their publications are well-documented and available world wide.

Dr. Smith died in 1977. In 1981, a Manville lawyer (appealing a $1.9 million damage award to asbestos victim Edward Janssens), argued that the Smith deposition should not have been admitted in court. The attorney said, "J-M made a conscious policy decision not to cross-examine Dr. Smith as fully as it otherwise would have. For example, Johns-Manville decided against examining Dr. Smith regarding the fact that he was an alcoholic and under psychiatric care."

Another Manville executive, Wilbur L. Ruff, who had worked for Manville from 1929 through 1972, much of the time as plant manager at a number of Manville plants, gave an extensive deposition in 1979. Excerpts follow:

Q. Do you know whether in fact, abnormal chest findings ever were discussed with any employee of the Johns-Manville plant?

A. I know of no specific cases.

Q. Was there a policy at that time not to talk to the employees about chest findings, findings that suggested asbestosis, pneumoconiosis, or mesothelioma [asbestos cancer]?

A. That was the policy.

Q. When did the policy change?

A. In the early 1970s.

Q. Have you on other occasions, Mr. Ruff, referred to this policy that we have been discussing as a hush-hush policy?

A. Yes.

Q. Were you aware that it was company policy back in the late forties that if a man had asbestosis or industrial lung diseases that nothing would be said to him until he actually became disabled?

A. That's the way it was done.

Q. You were aware that was the company policy?

A. Whether it was policy or not, it was somebody's decision.

In 1964, Manville placed the first caution labels on its asbestos products. The labels read:

> This product contains asbestos fiber.
> Inhalation of asbestos in excessive quantities over long periods of time may be harmful.
> If dust is created when the product is handled, avoid breathing the dust.
> If adequate ventilation control is not possible, wear respirators approved by the U.S. Bureau of Mines for pneumoconiosis producing dust.

In upholding a landmark 1972 district court decision against Manville and other asbestos defendants, the New Orleans U.S. Court of Appeals stated:

> Asbestosis has been recognized as a disease for well over fifty years. . . . By the mid-1930s the hazard of asbestos as a pneumoconiotic dust was universally accepted. Cases of asbestosis in insulation workers were reported in this country as early as 1934. . . . The evidence . . . tended to establish that none of the defendants ever tested its product to determine its effect on industrial insulation workers. . . . Indeed the evidence tended to establish that the defendants gave no instructions or warnings at all.

The court quoted Manville's caution label (above) and continued:

> It should be noted that none of these so called "cautions" intimated the gravity of the risk: the danger of a fatal illness caused by asbestosis and mesothelioma or other cancers. The mild suggestion that inhalation of asbestos in excessive quantities over a long period of time may be harmful conveys no idea of the extent of the danger.

NEW DIRECTIONS FOR THE 1970S

By the 1960s, several of Manville's older directors had died or retired. Among them were A. R. Fisher and E. M. Voorhees, senior Manville officials since before 1930. (Both Fisher and Voorhees were involved in the early asbestos lawsuits. Also, Fisher was chief executive in the fifties and early sixties.) Compared to the 1966 board of directors, the 1969 board contained a majority of new members. Departing from a tradition of promotion from within, in 1969 Manville brought in an outsider, psychologist Richard Goodwin, to fill a top management position. The next year, the board of directors voted to move long-time president C. B. Burnett to the position of chairman and to install Goodwin as president and chief executive officer. Goodwin led the company through at least twenty acquisitions and several divestitures, increasing the company's profit and sales but also increasing its long-term debt—from zero in 1970 to $196 million in 1975.

Goodwin arranged to purchase the 10,000-acre Ken-Caryl Ranch near Denver in 1971, moved the company there from New York, and made plans to build a luxurious world headquarters. The first phase of the project was to cost $182.2 million, 45 percent of Manville's net worth. The magazine *Industrial Development* called the Manville plan "a study in corporate environmental concern." *Fortune* magazine quotes Goodwin as saying, "A company's headquarters is its signature. I wanted a new signature for J-M that, frankly, would attract attention—that would tell everybody, including ourselves, that things were changing."

Things did change. When the asbestos problem grew out of control and the company lost the first of many asbestos lawsuits, Manville turned back to one of its own—its chief legal officer—for leadership. In what *Fortune* magazine called "the shoot-out at the J-M corral," the board of directors deposed Goodwin without explanation and installed J. A. McKinney as president in September 1976. McKinney charted the new course in his 1977 "president's review":

> We believe we can further improve the fundamental economics of a number of our operations and we will be working toward that end in the year to come. . . .
>
> Asbestos fiber, while contributing substantially to earnings, has assumed a less important position with the earnings growth of our other basic businesses. Although its profitability is expected to improve in the long term with reviving European economies, we do not expect asbestos fiber to dominate J-M earnings to the extent that it has in the past. . . .
>
> We have also consolidated and repositioned some businesses for more profitable growth and phased out others not important to the future direction of the company. . . .
>
> We have begun aggressively to seek out opportunities for growth. One example is the previously announced $200 million capital expansion program which will, by 1980, double U.S. fiber glass capacity over the 1976 levels. . . . We continue seeking still other growth possibilities that would markedly change the Johns-Manville profile, possibly through substantial acquisitions. . . .
>
> Our main thrust in 1978 will be to continue improving profitability by maintaining our expense control and pricing vigilance, by adding volume to below-capacity businesses, by better utilizing existing capacity and by adding capacity in sold-out businesses.

By that time, Manville had already begun to seek a large merger candidate—a "substantial acquisition"—employing the services of the Morgan Stanley investment banking firm to assist in the search. Manville quickly identified Olinkraft Corporation, a forest products manufacturer and timber company (owning 580,000 acres of timberland), as a likely prospect. After a brief bidding war, Olinkraft and Manville completed their merger agreement. The purchase price was $595 million. This was 2.24 times Olinkraft's June 1978 book value and over twice the average total market value of Olinkraft's stock in the first half of 1978.

Approximately half of the purchase price was paid in cash, and the other half with preferred stock. The preferred stock was described in the 1978 annual report:

> On January 19, 1979, the Company issued 4,598,327 shares of cumulative preferred stock, $5.40 series, to consummate the acquisition of Olinkraft. . . .

Under a mandatory sinking fund provision, the Company is required to redeem the $5.40 preferred series between 1987 and 2009 at $65 per share plus accrued dividends. The annual redemption requirements will consist of varying percentages applied to the number of outstanding shares on October 20, 1986, as follows: 5% annually from 1987 through 1996, 4% annually from 1997 through 2007, and 3% in 2008. All remaining outstanding shares are required to be redeemed in 2009.

While the Olinkraft merger was being negotiated, Manville common stock declined in market value to a low of $22.125, a total decrease of over $225 million. Olinkraft's stock rose, approximating the proposed acquisition price of $65 a share.

The merger was consummated on January 19, 1979. The purchase method of accounting was used. Essentially, the book values of Olinkraft's assets were adjusted upward by the amount by which the purchase price exceeded the net worth. The adjusted and unadjusted balance sheet values for Olinkraft are shown in the table below.

After the mergers and divestitures engineered by Goodwin and McKinney, Manville's mix of businesses (as described in the 1978 and 1979 annual reports) was as follows:

Fiberglass products: Residential insulations account for the largest portion of the product line, with commercial and industrial insulations and fiber glass making up the rest. . . . New home construction represented 55 percent of the total market while [insulation for existing homes] accounted for 45 percent. . . .

Non-fiber glass insulations: This business segment includes roof insulations, refractory fibers, calcium silicate insulation, and a broad range of other commercial and industrial insulating products. . . .

Pipe products and systems: Major products in this business segment are polyvinyl chloride (PVC) plastic pipe and asbestos cement (A-C) pipe. . . .

PURCHASE METHOD MERGER ACCOUNTING:
OLINKRAFT BALANCE SHEETS

	Adjusted	Unadjusted
Current assets	$ 137,557	$ 119,610
Investments in and advances to associated companies	6,886	6,078
Property, plant, and equipment	700,633	372,761
Deferred charges and other assets	799	3,513
	$ 845,857	$ 501,962
Current liabilities	$ 83,912	$ 67,793
Long-term debt	141,258	141,295
Other noncurrent liabilities	25,159	26,678
	$ 250,329	$ 235,766
Net worth	$ 596,546	$ 266,196

Source: December 31, 1978, Manville-Olinkraft joint proxy statement and Manville 1978 annual report.

Roofing products: The roofing products segment includes residential shingles and built-up roofing for commercial and industrial structures. New construction accounts for 40 percent of sales. Reroofing represents 60 percent. . . .

Asbestos fiber: Asbestos fiber is sold in markets throughout the world. A major portion of the fiber sold is used as a raw material in products where the fiber is locked in place by cement, rubber, plastics, resins, asphalts, and similar bindings. Products include asbestos cement products, brake linings, resilient flooring, roofing, and other products that require strength and fire protection, heat resistance, dimensional stability, and resistance to rust and rot. . . .

Industrial and specialty products and services: A diverse group of businesses that has as its principal areas: Holophane lighting systems, filtration and minerals [comprised of diatomite, perlite, and fiber glass filter products] and industrial specialties. . . . Perlite is . . . used by J-M in the manufacture of Fesco Board roof insulation. Other uses are in acoustical ceiling tile, horticultural applications, and in cryogenic insulations.

Forest products: Forest products include clay-coated unbleached Kraft and other paper-boards: corrugated containers; beverage carriers and folding cartons; Kraft bags; pine lumber, plywood, and particleboard; and hardwood veneer and flooring.

STRATEGIC MANAGEMENT IN THE 1980s

After Richard Goodwin was expulsed, top management continuity was maintained through the late seventies and eighties. The chairman of the board and chief executive officer, J. A. McKinney, the president and chief operating officer, Fred L. Pundsack, and all ten senior vice presidents listed in the 1981 annual report, were also listed in the 1977 annual report. In fact, the five most highly paid executives of Manville, as shown on the March 1982 proxy statement, had all been with the company for twenty-nine years or more. Only three of Manville's outside directors joined the board after the sixties. Except for John D. Mullins, former president of Olinkraft, who performed brief service, no new director was added after 1976. Then, in May 1982, the existing directors were renominated.

Manville's asbestos-related health costs were relatively insignificant (less than 0.5 percent of sales through 1981). But asbestos use, especially in the United States, declined sharply after 1978. The U.S. Department of the Interior reported a 36 percent drop from 1979 to 1980 alone. With a virtual U.S. monopoly of asbestos sales, Manville was hardest hit. The loss of asbestos profits was compounded by a deep recession in housing and other construction which began in mid-1978 and was to last through 1982.

Attempts to expand and diversify Manville had begun in 1970, when net sales totaled $578 million. The sixties had seen only a 1.5 percent real rate of growth, less than the rate of gross national product (GNP) growth. Because of the purchases of businesses by Goodwin and McKinney, the company had surpassed $1 billion sales in 1974 and $2 billion in 1978. However, on an inflation-corrected basis, sales declined from 1978 onward, despite the contribution of $500 million in annual sales by Olinkraft. Figure 1 illustrates Manville's sales and earnings patterns from 1977 through 1982. The corresponding financial statements and a record of Manville's common stock prices appear in the financial tables at the end of this case.

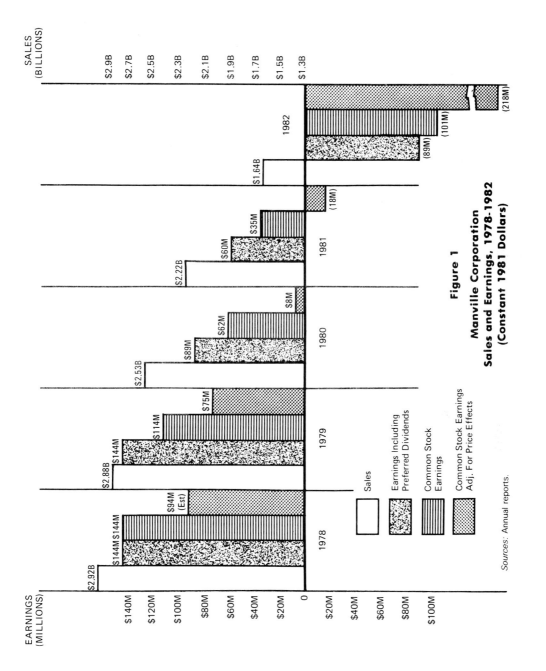

SALES
(BILLIONS)

$2.9B
$2.7B
$2.5B
$2.3B
$2.1B
$1.9B
$1.7B
$1.5B
$1.3B

EARNINGS
(MILLIONS)

$140M
$120M
$100M
$80M
$60M
$40M
$20M
0
$20M
$40M
$60M
$80M
$100M

1978   1979   1980   1981   1982

$2.92B
$144M $144M
$94M (Est)

$2.88B
$144M
$114M
$75M

$2.53B
$89M
$62M
$8M

$2.22B
$60M
$35M
$1.64B
(18M)

$89M
(101M)
(218M)

Sales

Earnings Including
Preferred Dividends

Common Stock
Earnings

Common Stock Earnings
Adj. For Price Effects

Figure 1

**Manville Corporation
Sales and Earnings, 1978-1982
(Constant 1981 Dollars)**

Sources: Annual reports.

Six pages of Manville's 1978 annual report and over half of J. A. McKinney's "chairman's message" were devoted to the personal injury lawsuits. Excerpts from these documents follow:

> During the past year a great deal of publicity has appeared in the media about asbestos health hazards—most of it attacking the corporation and nearly all of it needlessly inflammatory. Your corporation has acted honorably over the years and has led the asbestos industry, medical science and the federal government in identifying and seeking to eliminate asbestos health problems. . . .
>
> Individuals exposed to asbestos-containing insulation materials are particular victims of the incomplete knowledge of earlier years. . . . It was not until 1964 that the particular risk to this category of worker [insulation workers] was clearly identified by Dr. Irving J. Selikoff of Mt. Sinai Hospital in New York City. . . .
>
> Media representatives and some elected officials have consistently ignored J-M's intensive efforts to solve asbestos health problems and, in fact, have untruthfully portrayed those efforts. . . .
>
> Litigation is based upon a finding of fault, and with respect to asbestos-related disease, there simply is no fault on the part of J-M, a fact increasingly recognized by juries throughout the nation. Litigation is, of course, favored and fostered by lawyers in search of lucrative fees and by "media personalities" in search of sensational stories. . . .

Despite the worsening financial situation and though beseiged by thousands of asbestos victims seeking billions of dollars in damages, Manville was publicly optimistic. The 1979 annual report stated, "Johns-Manville has a strategy for the early 80's . . . and the commitment to succeed. . . . J-M's strategic plan embraces three major goals." The goals were described as follows:

> Goal 1: To rebuild our financial reserves. . . . As expected, the Olinkraft acquisition burdened our financial resources. . . . For this reason, our most immediate short-term goal is to improve and increase the financial strength of J-M's balance sheet. We will accomplish this by increasing productivity and using the better levels of cash flow that result to provide for most of our new capital needs.
>
> Goal 2: To improve productivity and cost efficiencies. . . . We will look for ways to increase the output of our manufacturing processes, concentrating first on those projects promising the shortest payback periods. . . .
>
> Goal 3: To reaffirm J-M's position as a technological leader in terms of product performance and cost of production. . . . to increase the effort and money spent on improving manufacturing methods, enhancing the competitive strengths of present product lines and developing new products.

In 1981 Manville accelerated efforts to avoid the asbestos claims. McKinney wrote to his shareholders, "You can be assured that we will continue to be aggressive in asserting our defenses." By spending millions on the defense efforts, Manville was able to avoid or delay payment of most tort judgments and to settle many for cents on the dollar. The company was reorganized into a parent corporation and a number of operating subsidiaries, with the asbestos businesses in one subsidiary.

THE DAY OF DECISION APPROACHES

It quickly became apparent that courts would see through the new corporate structure and treat the companies as one for asbestos liability purposes. Further, as the number and amounts of asbestos tort judgments skyrocketed, Manville's ability to avoid paying them grew increasingly questionable.

Manville's mid-year 1982 form 10Q (submitted to the Securities and Exchange Commission) described the worsening situation with regard to the asbestos injury claims:

> During the first half of 1982, J-M [Manville] received an average of approximately 425 new cases per month brought by an average of approximately 495 new plaintiffs per month. . . .
>
> J-M was, for the first time in 1981, found liable by juries for punitive damages in five separate asbestos-related actions. [Punitive damages are payments above the actual damages sustained—intended to punish defendants.] All of these cases are presently subject to post-trial motions or appeals filed by J-M. The average of the punitive damages awarded against J-M in these five cases (one of which involved eleven plaintiffs) and the five cases decided during the first half of 1982 and discussed below is approximately $616,000 per case. . . .
>
> *Hansen v. Johns-Manville.* $1,060,000 in compensatory damages and $1,000,000 in punitive damages were assessed against J-M. . . .
>
> *Bunch v. Johns-Manville Corp.* A jury verdict of $420,000 in compensatory damages and $220,000 in punitive damages. . . .
>
> *Dorell v. Johns-Manville Corp.* The jury awarded the plaintiff $100,000 in compensatory damages and $1,000,000 in punitive damages. . . .
>
> *Jackson v. Johns-Manville.* A jury verdict of $195,000 in compensatory damages and $500,000 in punitive damages. . . .
>
> *Cavett v. Johns-Manville Corp.* The jury awarded the plaintiff $800,000 in compensation damages and $1,500,000 in punitive damages.

Aside from actual and anticipated tort claims, Manville was in much worse condition in 1982 than the financial statements indicated. This was true for four reasons. First, $340 million of Manville's net worth resulted from purchase method accounting in the Olinkraft merger. Second, the $300 million in "preferred stock" shown on the balance sheet was essentially equivalent to a 16 percent long-term debt. Third, Manville had endured several years of negative cash flow requiring certain cash-producing strategies which tended to reduce asset values. For example, the 580,000 acres of timber farms obtained in the Olinkraft purchase were converted to a thirty-year planned life from a forty-year life. This rationalized immediate cutting of about one-fourth of the timber and continuing removal of one-thirtieth of that remaining each year instead of one-fortieth. Finally, the desire of Manville executives to show profits each year had resulted in "creative accounting" which tended to inflate reported earnings. The following are examples from the 1981 annual report: (1) a $9 million increase in "other revenues" which resulted largely from the sale of mineral exploration rights on 580,000 acres of timberland, (2) a $2.7 million increase in reported earnings due to the "reversal of a portion of the litigation reserves established at the time of the Olinkraft, Inc., acquisition," (3) a $9.8 million increase in reported earnings because of a new way of reporting foreign currency transactions, (4) an unspecified amount due to "the sale during 1981 of eight container plants [which] occurred as part of [the] asset management program,'' and (5) an $8.4 million increase in reported earnings brought about by ''changes in certain actuarial assumptions in computing pension expense.''

If Manville were to fail, not only would managers and directors lose their salaries, benefits, and perquisites, but they would also lose their corporate indemnification against personal liability for the asbestos injury claims. Undoubtedly each one would then be subject to hundreds, perhaps thousands, of tort lawsuits.

In December 1981, Manville formed a ten-member committee of inside and outside lawyers, the litigation analysis group (LAG), to study the firm's situation with regard to the asbestos injury liabilities. LAG employed a number of consultants to research various aspects of the issue and met each month to hear reports and discuss developments. The conclusion of LAG, arrived at in mid-1982, was that Manville would eventually have to pay about $2 billion to present and future asbestos injury victims.

In a subsequent lawsuit it was alleged that the $2 billion figure was contrived so as to be high enough to justify a filing for reorganization under Chapter 11 of the U.S. Bankruptcy Code but not high enough to appear to require liquidation of the company. At a meeting of the board of directors on August 4, 1982, J. A. McKinney (chairman of the board and chief executive officer) appointed four outside directors to a special committee to determine what Manville should do. Members of the special committee were briefed on Chapter 11 by company executives. A limited overview of the practical effects of a Chapter 11 reorganization is provided in the lined insert below.

A special meeting of the board of directors was called for August 25, 1982. The special committee was expected to present its recommendation at that meeting.

USUAL EFFECTS OF FILING FOR REORGANIZATION UNDER CHAPTER 11

All debts are stayed until a "plan of reorganization" is confirmed or special approval of the bankruptcy court is obtained.

The bankrupt corporation, with prefiling management, is declared to be the "debtor in possession" (DIP).

The DIP can carry out the "ordinary course of business," e.g., hiring and firing employees, incurring and repaying debts, making and executing contracts, selling and buying assets.

The DIP is allowed to enforce all claims against others, by filing lawsuits if necessary. Lawsuits against the DIP are stayed.

Unsecured creditors and common and preferred stockholders are represented by committees appointed by the bankruptcy judge.

The DIP is allowed to cancel contracts, including collective bargaining agreements and leases, to the extent that they have not been carried out.

The DIP is allowed 120 days to file a plan of reorganization and 60 days to seek the required approval of each creditor class (half in number holding two-thirds in amount) and equity class (holders of two-thirds in amount), either of which periods may be extended.

The plan of reorganization typically provides for:

1 Payment of postfiling debt, including costs of administering the case
2 Payment of secured prefiling debt up to the value of the liened property
3 Payment of some or all of unsecured debt over some period into the future, with or without interest
4 Discharge of all claims not provided for in the plan

MANVILLE CORPORATION INCOME STATEMENTS
(Amounts in Millions)*

	1982 6 mos.	1981	1980	1979	1978
Sales	$ 949	$2,186	$2,267	$2,276	$1,649
Cost of sales	784	1,731	1,771	1,747	1,190
Selling, gen., and admin. exp.	143	271	263	239	193
R&D and engineering exp.	16	34	35	31	33
operating income	6	151	197	259	232
Other income, net	1	35	26	21	28
Interest expense	35	73	65	62	22
Total income	(28)	112	157	218	238
Income taxes	2	53	77	103	116
Net income before extraordinary items	(25)	60	81	115	122
Div. on preferred stock	12	25	25	24	0
Extraordinary item	0	0	0	0	0
Net income available for common stock	$ (37)	$ 35	$ 55	$ 91	$ 122

Revenues and income from operations by business segment

	1981	1980	1979	1978	1977	1976
Revenues						
Fiberglass products	$ 625	$ 610	$ 573	$ 514	$ 407	$ 358
Forest products	555	508	497	0	0	0
Nonfiberglass insulation	258	279	268	231	195	159
Roofing products	209	250	273	254	204	171
Pipe products and systems	199	220	305	303	274	218
Asbestos fiber	138	159	168	157	161	155
Industrial and spec. prod.	320	341	309	291	301	309
Corporate revenues, net	12	9	11	20	12	(22)
Intersegment sales	(95)	(84)	(106)	(94)	(74)	(56)
Total	$2,221	$2,292	$2,297	$1,677	$1,480	$1291
Income from operations						
Fiberglass products	$ 90	$ 91	$ 96	$ 107	$ 82	$ 60
Forest products	39	37	50	0	0	0
Nonfiberglass insulation	20	27	27	35	28	18
Roofing products	(17)	9	14	23	14	8
Pipe products and systems	0	(5)	18	26	24	(3)
Asbestos fiber	37	35	56	55	60	60
Industrial and spec. prod.	50	55	43	36	25	19
Corporate expense, net	(23)	(38)	(23)	(23)	(24)	(49)
Eliminations and adjustments	3	11	(2)	1	3	2
Total	$ 198	$ 223	$ 280	$ 260	$ 212	$ 116

*Totals may not check due to rounding.
Source: Annual reports and June 30, 1982, Form 100.

MANVILLE CORPORATION BALANCE SHEETS
(Amounts in Millions)*

	June 30 1982	1981	1980	1979	1978
Assets					
Cash	$ 10	$ 14	$ 20	$ 19	$ 28
Marketable securities	17	12	12	10	38
Accounts and notes receivable	348	327	350	362	328
Inventories	182	211	217	229	219
Prepaid expenses	19	19	20	31	32
Total current assets	$ 576	$ 583	$ 619	$ 650	$ 645
Property, plant, and equipment					
Land and land improvements		119	118	114	99
Buildings		363	357	352	321
Machinery and equipment		1,202	1,204	1,161	1,043
		$1,685	$1,679	$1,627	$1,462
Less accum. depreciation and depletion		(525)	(484)	(430)	(374)
		$1,160	$1,195	$1,197	$1,088
Timber and timberland less cost of timber harvested		$ 406	$ 407	$ 368	$ 372
	$1,523	$1,566	$1,602	$1,565	$1,460
Invest. and adv. to assoc. cos.		0	0	0	0
Real est. sub. invest. and adv.		0	0	0	0
Other assets	148	149	117	110	113
Total assets	$2,247	$2,298	$2,338	$2.324	$2,217
Liabilities					
Short-term debt	$	$ 29	$ 22	$ 32	$ 23
Accounts payable	191	120	126	143	114
Comp. and employee benefits		77	80	54	45
Income taxes		30	22	51	84
Other liabilities	149	58	61	50	63
Total current liabilities	$ 340	$ 316	$ 310	$ 329	$ 329
Long-term debt	499	508	519	532	543
Other noncurrent liabilities	93	86	75	73	60
Deferred income taxes	186	185	211	195	150
Total liabilities	$1,116	$1,095	$1,116	$1,129	$1,083
Stockholders' equity					
Preferred ($1.00 par)	$ 301	$ 301	$ 301	$ 299	$ 299
Common ($2.50 par)	60	59	58	208	197
Capital in excess of par	178	174	164	0	0
Retained earnings	642	695	705	692	643
Cum. currency translation adj.	(47)	(22)	0	0	0
Less cost of treasury stock	$ (3)	$ (3)	$ (4)	$ (4)	$ (6)
Total stockholders' equity	$1,131	$1,203	$1,222	$1,196	$1,134
Total liab. and stockholders' equity	$2,247	$2,298	$2,338	$2,324	$2,217

*Totals may not check due to rounding.
Source: Annual reports and June 30, 1982 Form 10-Q.

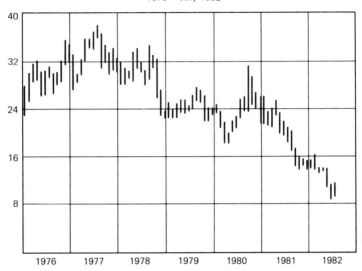

DISCUSSION QUESTIONS

1 List the benefits and detriments which might have accrued to each of Manville's major stakeholder groups if company executives had encouraged research and publicity about asbestos disease in the 1930s. Should they have done so? Explain.

2 When Richard Goodwin took over as chief executive officer of Manville, what do you believe were his major concerns? What should they have been? Why?

3 What should J. A. McKinney have done about (a) continued manufacture of asbestos products, (b) aggressive defense of the asbestos injury lawsuits, (c) acknowledging that Manville executives had known of the asbestos danger since the 1930s and had suppressed publicity about it, (d) placing stronger warning labels on asbestos products, and (e) the Olinkraft acquisition? How did McKinney's moral duty differ from Goodwin's? Why?

4 As an inside director of Manville Corporation, how would you vote on a motion to file a Chapter 11 petition? Defend your vote in terms of its impact on each constituent group you might identify.

THE COCA COLA COMPANY: BLACK ECONOMIC DEVELOPMENT

Robert D. Hay
University of Arkansas

SELECTED STRATEGIC ISSUES

- Equal opportunity versus affirmative action
- Free enterprise as the primary agent of response to human needs
- Minority activism and business social responsibility
- Validity of black demands for development assistance
- Relationship between corporate social responsibility and likelihood of additional demands by minorities

Here in hot Atlanta on August 10, 1981, at a press conference at Coca Cola's headquarters, the working press was reminded of the turbulent 1960s, when the civil rights movement came of age. There was Coretta Scott King, soft-spoken, refined, very strong, the widow of the slain leader and Nobel Peace Prize laureate Martin Luther King Jr. Over there was the Reverend Jesse L. Jackson, older certainly than in the days when he marched to Selma with the Reverend King, but, at 39, still brash, enigmatic, controversial, charismatic. He had grown to power through the Chicago-based activist organization People United to Save Humanity (PUSH) which he founded in the early 1970s, and had sought to extend black unity beyond the boundaries of the United States. Talking with him was the Reverend Joseph Lowery, another King protege, who was president of the Southern Christian Leadership Conference (SCLC), which was holding its annual convention in New Orleans this week. Present also was the Honorable Maynard Jackson, no longer simply an attorney, but the seasoned mayor of Atlanta, Georgia, which had a metropolitan area population of almost two million, who was retiring after two terms in office.

The dusty roads near Selma, the marble steps of the capitol, the streets of Birmingham were a far cry from the paneled conference room of a corporate giant where the group gathered today. Trying to get a word in and announce his company's expanded Minority Participation Program was Donald R. Keough, President and Chief Operating Officer of the Coca-Cola Company.

Coke and PUSH had invited the black leaders to the historic press conference called for August 10, 1981, at the multinational company's headquarters in Atlanta. Purpose of the conference was to announce expansion of the Company's entire minority participation program, a "moral covenant" which would channel $34 million from Coca Cola's general system into black economic development. President Keough addressed the press:

> Good morning. First, I want to acknowledge the presence today of so many of America's prominent Black leaders, especially the mayor of our city, the Honorable Maynard Jackson. I am happy to be part of this historic occasion for the Company, Reverend Jackson and the Black leadership assembled here. As an employee of The Coca-Cola Company I am proud for many reasons, not the least of which is the Company, through its decades under the guidance of Mr. Woodruff and other outstanding leaders, has always merited a place in the forefront of social justice.
>
> Over the years, the Coca-Cola Company has maintained a high level of involvement in the Black community through corporate gifts, scholarships, and executive time devoted to such organizations as United Negro College Fund, Atlanta University, Morris Brown, Spelman College and Morehouse Medical School. In addition, the Company has provided financial aid to the Martin Luther King Center and to many civil rights organizations, created career development films for Black youth, and has been involved in other endeavors too numerous to tick off here.
>
> As a result, when we were approached by Reverend Jackson and his associates in Operation PUSH last November, we had no reason to hesitate to enter into discussions with them to hear their views on minority participation in the Company's system.
>
> Over the months, we listened very carefully, and we matched their comments, suggestions and concerns with our own agenda for the Black community, which we recognize as a significant segment of our society in the decade of the '80s.
>
> From the beginning, however, we listened on a broader scope than just across the conference table or a telephone line. We had self-imposed tests to apply to the discussions—and the ideas arising out of them—to determine whether what we are now doing, and plan to do, is *what we ought to do.*
>
> Several months ago, the Chairman of The Coca-Cola Company, Roberto Goizueta, set forth his strategy for the Company for the decade of the '80s. This strategy statement has been shared with all our employees and stockholders. In it, Mr. Goizueta states, and I am quoting from the document: "All employees will have equal opportunities to grow, develop and advance within the Company. Their progress will depend only on their abilities, ambition and achievements." In addition, it is a focal point of Mr. Goizueta's strategy to nurture the sensitivity to adapt to change and to manage our enterprise in such a way that we will always be considered a welcomed and important part of the communities in which we operate.
>
> Those are not idle words, but the essence of what we fully intend to be. With nearly a century of operation behind us and our strategy for the '80s as a guideline, it was indeed easy for my associates to move forward in discussions with Reverend Jackson. In any human endeavor of this kind, there are inevitable periods of misconception which interrupt discus-

sions. However, throughout the process, our discussions have maintained the integrity of forthrightness, courtesy and respect.

Let me pause here to say that special words of gratitude are due to Mrs. Coretta Scott King, Rev. Joseph Lowery and his associates at the SCLC and others in this room whose counsel, advice and friendship were valuable to our discussions with Operation PUSH.

One point is critical to understanding the initiatives we are announcing here today. Since his election last November, President Reagan has been sending the business community a message which we at the Coca-Cola Company have heard very clearly. His philosophy on the subject we are discussing today was probably best presented in his June 29 speech to the NAACP.

In that speech, he noted the changing federal philosophy toward less interference by government in business and appealed to "business and industry to bring about an 'economic emancipation' of Blacks and the poor." Economic revitalization, the President said, is the "surest, most equitable way to ease the pressures on all the segments of our society."

Given this new direction and the new economic policy as recommended by President Reagan and as enacted by the Congress, the force of the free enterprise system is being unleashed. In direct response to this new direction, we are accelerating and enlarging our programs already in place. And the Black community, as an integral part of our system and society, will benefit with dignity and will receive a well deserved piece of the action.

We wholeheartedly endorse the potential of free enterprise. We believe that our understanding developed with Reverend Jackson is a clear indication on the part of a major American company that business can listen and respond to presidential and congressional actions for tax cut relief to business, and also to the message and the promise that the free enterprise system can do more to develop opportunity for all elements of society.

We are willing to put more than rhetoric behind this belief. We have defined our future plans and will aid Black entrepreneurs who seek to enter the beverage industry in the bottling and fountain wholesaling business. We have outlined programs in eight areas:

- Bottler franchises
- Fountain wholesaling and wine distributorships
- Minority business development opportunities
- Advertising
- Banking opportunities
- Management opportunities and employment
- Corporate contributions, and
- Professional service contracts and minority purchasing programs

Details about each of these areas are contained in the information handed out today.

In order to make sure we move expeditiously, we are engaging a research consulting firm who will help us select appropriate candidates.

In closing, I want to thank you, Reverend Jackson, and your associates for your patience and cooperation throughout our discussions. Personally, I am pleased to be the spokesman for a company that continues to demonstrate that it does *what it ought to do*.

THE COCA-COLA COMPANY

The foundation of the Coca-Cola Company was the soft drink Coca-Cola, which in 1980 accounted for 76% of the company's $5.9 billion in sales.

The company's origin dates to 1886 when an Atlanta, Georgia, pharmacist Dr. John Styth Pemberton, according to legend, cooked up the first syrup for Coca-Cola in a three-legged brass pot in his backyard. The first batch of the new soda fountain drink went on sale for 5¢ a glass on May 8, 1886, in an Atlanta pharmacy where, by design or accident, carbonated water was teamed with the new syrup to produce the drink. In 1888, rights to the product were purchased by Asa G. Candler, a businessman, who became the "sole proprietor of Coca-Cola," at a cost of $2,300. Sales grew, and in 1892 the company was formally incorporated as a Georgia corporation named the Coca-Cola Company, with a capital stock of $100,000.

In 1919, Candler sold out to Atlanta banker Ernest Woodruff and an investor group he had organized. The sale price was $25 million. Soon after that, the business was incorporated as a Delaware corporation and its common stock put on public sale for $40 a share. Its current financial position is shown in the financial statements (Exhibits 1 and 2).

Administrative Philosophy of Coca Cola

In March, 1981, Chief Executive Officer and Board Chairman Paul Austin was succeeded by Cuban-born Roberto C. Goizueta. Before his election in May 1980, Mr. Goizueta, the second highest paid officer of Coke (next to Mr. Austin) had not even made some of the lists of dark-horse candidates for the job. Immediately prior to his election, Mr. Goizueta was Executive Vice President responsible for administration, external relations, and legal and technical divisions.

Mr. Goizueta commented on the Company's business behavior in a formal statement adopted by the Board of Directors in March, 1981, and sent to the Company's 41,000 employees in 135 countries and its shareholders.

I have previously referred to the *courage and commitment* that will be indispensable as we move through the 1980s. To this I wish to add *integrity and fairness,* and insist that the combination of these four ethics be permeated from top to bottom throughout our organization so that our behavior will produce leaders, good managers, and—most importantly— opposed to being only reactive and that we *encourage intelligent individual risk-taking.*

Mr. Goizueta's philosophy and his objectives for the Company were contained in various speeches and interviews:

For the first time in years, the government is listening to business and trying new ideas. This state's (California's) favorite son has given American Business a window in time—one clear chance to prove that business *unfettered* will be business *unflagging* in the service to American society. For the first time in years, the overall psychological mood of the nation is becoming more favorable to business . . . We have, for all the years I can recall, asked government to get off our backs—to free us from punitive taxes, from burdensome regulations and costs, from mountains of red tape and forests of paper work. Today, we are beginning to get the opportunity that we have wanted for so long . . . the opportunity to prove that when private enterprise is relatively free, it can be the primary agent of response to human need.[1]

Thus I commend to all of us that the war on the economy is ours, that the war on inequality is ours, that the war on social injustice is ours.

---

[1] Roberto C. Goizueta, "Reflection on Corporate Citizenship in Today's Business Climate," speech presented at *Los Angeles Times* Dinner, September 28, 1981, p. 7.

EXHIBIT I THE COCA-COLA COMPANY AND SUBSIDIARIES
CONSOLIDATED BALANCE SHEETS
(In Thousands Except Per-Share Data)

	December 31	
Assets	**1980**	**1970**
Current		
Cash	$ 129,685	$ 106,886
Marketable securities, at cost (approximates market)	101,401	41,685
Trade accounts receivable, less allowance of $8,594 in 1980 and $8,113 in 1979	523,123	435,079
Inventories	810,235	669,614
Prepaid expenses	57,809	52,339
Total Current Assets	1,622,253	1,305,603
Investments and Other Assets	302,184	206,975
Property, Plant and Equipment		
Land and improvements	96,567	97,906
Buildings	537,235	518,517
Machinery and equipment	1,183,438	1,092,882
Containers	314,349	292,085
	2,131,589	2,001,390
Less allowance for depreciation	790,749	717,212
	1,340,840	1,284,178
Formulae, Trademarks, Goodwill and Contract Rights	140,681	141,285
	$3,405,958	$2,938,041
Liabilities and stockholders' equity	**1980**	**1979**
Current		
Notes payable	$ 87,587	$ 103,816
Current maturities of long-term debt	7,528	4,384
Accounts payable and accrued expenses	733,023	576,862
Accrued taxes—including income taxes	233,442	199,099
Total Current Liabilities	1,061,580	884,161
Long-Term Debt	133,221	30,989
Deferred Income Taxes	136,419	104,187
Stockholders' Equity		
Common stock, no par value—authorized 140,000,000 shares; issued 123,989,854 shares in 1980 and 123,960,295 in 1979	62,372	62,357
Capital surplus	113,172	112,333
Retained earnings	1,914,547	1,759,367
	1,090,091	1,934,057
Less 401,338 shares of stock held in treasury, at cost	15,353	15,353
	2,074,738	1,918,704
	$3,405,958	$2,938,041

EXHIBIT 2   THE COCA-COLA COMPANY AND SUBSIDIARIES
CONSOLIDATED STATEMENTS OF INCOME
(In Thousands Except Per-Share Data)

Year ended December 31	1980	1979	1978
Net sales	$5,912,595	$4,961,402	$4,337,917
Cost of goods sold	3,435,889	2,794,026	2,438,188
Gross Profit	2,486,706	2,167,376	1,899,729
Selling, administrative and general expenses	1,718,426	1,448,022	1,221,643
Operating Income	768,280	719,354	678,086
Interest income	40,774	37,048	34,718
Interest expense	(35,218)	10,676	7,762
Other income (deductions)—net	(9,537)	(3,534)	(13,646)
Income Before Income Taxes	764,299	742,192	691,396
Income taxes	342,191	322,072	316,704
Net Income	$ 422,108	$ 420,120	$ 374,692
Net income per share	$ 3.42	$ 3.40	$ 3.03

Consolidated statement of retained earnings

Year ended December 31	1980	1979	1978
Balance at January 1	$1,759,367	$1,581,406	$1,421,356
Dividends paid in cash:	266,928	242,159	214,344
The Coca-Cola Company (per share—1980, $2.16; 1979, $1.96; 1978, $1.74) Presto Products, Incorporated, prior to combination			298
Balance at December 31	$1,914,547	$1,759,367	$1,581,406

If we are realistic in our expectations . . . if we are willing, as a people, to live with the consequences of some difficult decisions now . . . then I am convinced that the underlying strength of this society will carry us through the full realization of what is known as the American dream.

I can only add that I want to join today's pioneers in the new corporate citizenship to reach heights of achievement for this country like this country has never seen before. The ball is surely on our side of the court.[2]

A Coca-Cola executive sent the following letter to the case researcher:

It is unfortunate that some accounts have portrayed our program a "cave-in" to the "withdrawal of enthusiasm" for our products announced by PUSH. That is not the case. The

[2] Thomas Oliver, "Coke-PUSH Pact No Danger to Firm's Finances, Analysts Declare," *Atlanta Constitution,* August 13, 1981, p. 8B.

PUSH activities had no adverse economic impact on the Company. And, it should be clearly understood that the plan announced does not channel any funds to the Reverend Jesse Jackson or PUSH.

However, special interest groups do offer insight that is sometimes useful in the refinement of our programs, and we are always willing to listen to their views, as well as those of any consumer.

The Coca-Cola Company has a proud tradition of bringing Blacks and other minorities into our business system through employment, advertising, educational opportunities and other means. The question in this instance was whether we are doing enough in light of the current message to the free-enterprise system from the Federal government.

Factoring in the views and perspectives of PUSH and many others, we decided that we were not and took steps to augment our minority participation programs. We believe that this is the right thing to do, both for the benefit of The Coca-Cola Company and society. As I am sure you realize, The Coca-Cola Company has long had a minority participation program. Under the new program, we will simply be accelerating and extending existing activities to bring more minorities into our business system.

Professor Hay, I hope this information is helpful and that it is responsive to your inquiry. We appreciate your continued interest.

Thank you for getting back in touch with me about Operation PUSH as it gives me the opportunity to share with you the philosophy and rationale behind our current program to bring more minorities into The Coca-Cola Company's business system. It also provides an opportunity to clear up some misconceptions about the action we have taken.

The point that is critical to understanding our program is that both President Reagan and the Congress, by their action regarding Federal budget cuts and lower individual and corporate taxes, have set a new economic policy designed to unleash the force of the free-enterprise system in this country. A portion of the corporate tax burden has been reduced. Some social welfare programs have been reduced as well. In these circumstances the free-enterprise system is being called on to utilize some of its resources, so that more segments of our society have not only an opportunity to purchase and consume, but an opportunity to become producers of our products.

Those of us in the business sector must do more than merely applaud the new direction from the Federal government. We must assume new responsibilities as a result of it. The Coca-Cola Company's program to enlist more minorities as business partners is aimed at meeting that responsibility.

It is unfortunate that some accounts have portrayed our program as a ''give-away'' activity. That clearly is not the case. The initiatives announced on August 10 are designed to bring more Blacks into our business system for the purpose of investing in, and contributing to, the production, marketing and distribution of our products. These businesses and investments would be subject to the usual risks of the free-enterprise system.

As mentioned in the fact sheet I sent to you, there are some 4,000 fountain wholesalers of Coca-Cola in the U.S., but only two are Black owned. Under our recently announced program, it is our hope that we will encourage more Black entrepreneurs to go into the fountain wholesaling business, thereby creating profit for themselves, for us, and creating jobs. There is no ''give away'' in this transaction. It's merely an opportunity to expand, concurrently, the business of The Coca-Cola Company and minority participation.

As another example, these initiatives include a minority purchasing program, which the Company established several years ago, but for which the current goal has been set at fourteen million dollars. This is not a ''give away,'' but a plan to purchase necessary goods and services from minority vendors.

COKE'S HISTORY OF SOCIAL RESPONSIBILITY

One example of Coke's exercise of its social responsibility was its response to migrant farm workers in its Minute Maid Corporation of Orlando, Florida, in 1968, its hiring and promotion of blacks, and its corporate financial contributions.

After it acquired Minute Maid, Coca-Cola, under the direction of former chairman Paul Austin, investigated living conditions of its inherited 1,200 agricultural workers. (Seventy percent of the workers were black, 20 percent were white, and 10 percent were Mexican.) Subsequently, Coke put workers on the payroll instead of paying a piece rate and sought to involve workers in seeking solutions to housing, educational, medical and other problems. At the time, the Company was criticized on national television as "the culprit" of the poor conditions, although other businesses were looking at Coke's program as a model of social responsibility.[3]

Mr. Austin was active in national associations of businesses to promote the hiring, training, and promoting of minorities. The Company had previously had black representation on its board of directors. A black served on the board from 1973 to 1977, when he resigned to accept a key position in the Federal government. When he left Washington in March, he chose to accept an executive position with the Company, and therefore did not return to the Board.

Even when the boycott was in effect, Mr. Woodruff, the former CEO, was honored by a predominantly black college. Morris Brown College bestowed upon Mr. Woodruff its "Centennial Man of the Year in Georgia" award, the *Atlanta Constitution* reported on August 2, 1981. Morris Brown President, Dr. Robert Threatt, called the Coca-Cola Company a "good friend," and said that Coke's leadership had meant a great deal to the college. Dr. Threatt cited financial gifts from the Woodruff family foundation of an endowment of Coca-Cola stock worth more than $500,000; a $100,000 donation for the recent renovation of Fountain Hall on the campus; and a $10 million donation to build the new Atlanta University Center library complex, which Morris Brown would use.

COKE'S PROGRAM FOR BLACK ECONOMIC DEVELOPMENT

In November of 1980 the Reverend Jackson, of Operation PUSH, approached Coca-Cola and suggested that they talk about Coke's minority participation program. Jackson took the initiative and Coke's executives listened.

Mr. Keough later said the decision to talk with Jackson was not a "huge decision" since it had been the philosophy of Coca-Cola "from time immemorial" to discuss its relationship with minorities.

Talks with Jackson were approved by himself, Keough said, and Roberto C. Goizueta, Chairman and Chief Executive Officer. He and Goizueta were kept informed of all talks with Jackson and PUSH, and the Board was routinely informed. Keough

---

[3] "Case 3-2: The Coca-Cola Company Foods Division and the Migrant Worker," prepared by Cecil G. Howard and Lynn E. Dellenbarger, Jr., and reprinted in *Business and Society: Cases and Text* by Robert D. Hay, Edmund R. Gray, and James E. Gates. Cincinnati: South-Western Publishing Co., 1976, pp. 224–235.

said the negotiations and final program did not require the formal approval of the Board, as the decisions were "in the purview of the Chief Executive Officer."[4]

During the next nine months the discussions between Jackson's PUSH executives and Coke's executives continued. Jackson's basic philosophy during those discussions became evident.

Reverend Jackson called his concept a development formula and stated:

> Black America, as an *underdeveloped nation,* must renegotiate the *relationship with corporate America* around three critical economic principles: 1) Reciprocity. No longer is generosity alone enough. Black America must demand its fair share in a mutually beneficial relationship. Jobs are not enough. Full employment with no pay is slavery, and employment without ownership is colonialism. The reinvestment of a rightful portion of Black consumer dollars in the development of our economic institutions and community is the new demand. 2) Development Plans and Formulae. Black America, as an underdeveloped nation, requires a development plan and formula. Development requires new rules—not just new rulers—that are designed for national development. All other such underdeveloped nations have development plans and formulae that must be complied with to do business in their community. Black America can settle for nothing less. 3) Supply-side Economics. There must be a concentrated focus on institutional economic development by Black America. Basic Black economic institutions—banks, savings & loans, insurance companies, newspapers, radio and television stations, advertising agencies and more—must be built. We must focus on the "supply side" as well as the "demand side" of the economic ledger. It is not enough to have affirmative action on the demand side—jobs and consumer protection. We must have affirmative action on the supply side—our share of ownership, wealth, and control.[5]

Other significant external events occurred during the nine-months which affected the discussions. For example, in January 1981, President Reagan was sworn into office. He started to loosen regulations on business and suggested that private business take on the obligations of governing its own affairs in social responsibilities. In fact, in June 1981, President Reagan addressed the NAACP and called for the private sectors of the economy to develop minority programs on their own without governmental prodding.

The new president of Coca-Cola, Roberto C. Goizueta, elected in March 1981, took over the reins from Paul Austin and became the CEO and Chairman of the Board. He agreed with President Reagan's assessment and was ready to push harder for minority programs with PUSH. In fact, by early July 1981, Coca-Cola's agreements with operation PUSH were 95% complete.

On July 7, 1981, the Reverend B. W. Smith delivered an address at the convention of Operation PUSH (Appendix 1). There was no mention of a boycott. Four days later the Reverend Jesse Jackson, however, called for Blacks to "withdraw their enthusiasm" from Coca-Cola products. He asked Black ministers to urge their congregations to boycott Coke.

[4] Thomas Oliver, "Coca-Cola Admits Its Mishandles PUSH Pact," *Atlanta Journal and Constitution,* September 3, 1981, p. 16a.

[5] Jesse L. Jackson, "Metropolitan Washington PUSH and Mid-Atlantic Coca-Cola Reach Agreement," PUSH News Release, August 25, 1981, p. 3.

Mr. Keough explained what happened: "Another misjudgement by Coca-Cola brought about the "withdrawal of enthusiasm." PUSH had invited Keough to Chicago prior to the group's annual convention in early July. Jackson and Keough were to put the finishing touches on the minority participation program, and Jackson would then have the agreement in hand when the convention convened. But Keough didn't go to Chicago; instead he sent William Allison, a Black who heads Coca-Cola's community affairs program.

Jackson interpreted the substitution of Allison, whom Jackson described as a "messenger with no authority," as a sign that Coca-Cola was "pulling back" in its commitment to the program. "We had to declare the withdrawal to get their attention," Jackson said.

But Keough said PUSH misunderstood Coca-Cola's intentions. He had not gone to Chicago, Keough said, because "the trip just didn't fit my calendar." Keough speculated that had he gone to Chicago, the boycott might have been avoided.[6]

Coca-Cola was caught unaware when Jackson called the boycott on July 11. The company was close to announcing a major expansion of its minority program which is updated annually as part of the firm's agreement with the Federal EEOC.

Keough went so far as to say that PUSH President Jesse Jackson called the boycott only because the final agreement could not be reached in time for Jackson to announce the agreement at PUSH's annual convention in early July.[7]

The Reverend Jesse Jackson, on the other hand, said: "When negotiations with Coke failed to get the company to beef up its economic support of Black businesses, the 'demonstration stage' began—the last stage before asking store owners to take Coke off their shelves. I asked Black ministers to preach on July 19 against drinking Coke."[8]

Syndicated columnist William Raspberry reported: "When the initial talks floundered," he said, "PUSH called its 50-city network into play, using ministers, politicians, and others to implement a 'withdrawal of enthusiasm' for Coke products. Shortly thereafter," he said, "Coca-Cola was taken off the shelves in four Black-owned Seven-Eleven franchises in Washington, D.C. alone, and was followed by similar action in White-owned stores. Gary's Mayor Richard Hatcher, Chairman of the Black Mayor's Conference, started a move to remove Coke machines from the 194 city halls under Black control. Coke came off the shelves in 100 Chicago stores."

THE COCA-COLA BOYCOTT

The rationale behind the campaign, the Reverend Jackson later said, was that blacks consumed a lot of Coke—more Coke than Coke's margin of profit, he claimed. In exchange for that, Coke was supposed to initiate some economic development in the

---

[6] Thomas Oliver, "Coke-PUSH Pact No Danger to Firm's Finances, Analysts Declare," *Atlanta Constitution,* August 13, 1981, p. 16A.

[7] Oliver, *op. cit.,* p. 8B.

[8] Emily F. Rubin, "Jackson An Activist Turned Economist in Battle with Coke," *Atlanta Constitution,* August 2, 1981, p. 4K.

black community. Coke was to contribute back to the black community what it had taken out.

PUSH's research showed that in the top 50 markets where blacks lived they spent $100 billion a year, and bought 25 percent of the Coke consumed in those markets, according to the Reverend Jackson.

A financial analyst interviewed by the *Atlanta Journal and Constitution,* said that Coca-Cola was targeted not so much because of a record of shortchanging minorities but because Coca-Cola was the "biggest name consumer product" in the world and was vulnerable to a boycott. One reason for Coke's vulnerability was the competitive nature of the beverage industry, which Coca-Cola once dominated with little thought of its rivals. Also, the company, under new leadership, had been launched on a new "entrepreneurial" course, which didn't allow for any diversion of management's time and energy.

Mr. Keough later told a reporter from the *Atlanta Constitution* that the boycott didn't receive "two minutes attention here because we just never considered it a real issue. We felt absolutely no impact from it and didn't think we would."[9]

Another spokesman said that because of the short duration of the PUSH boycott, Coke had been unable to estimate any impact the boycott had. Raspberry wrote, "Coke got the message, and Keough himself got involved in the renewed talks."[10]

For the next month the boycott was proceeding during which time negotiations were going forward. The Reverend Jackson credited the civil rights leaders Reverend Joseph Lowery, Coretta Scott King, and Hosea Williams; businessman Jesse Hill; Atlanta Chamber of Commerce President Herman Russell; and Atlanta City Council President Marvin Arrington as being instrumental in getting Coca-Cola and PUSH to the bargaining table.

In August, the newspapers reported: "We are still hammering out some critical details," the Reverend Jackson said in a telephone interview from his Chicago office to Thomas Oliver of the *Atlanta Constitution,* "but the negotiations are going well, and if completed on schedule we hope to be able to make a joint announcement Monday."[11]

Finally on August 10, 1981, the press conference was held. Upon finishing his remarks, Mr. Keough passed out the news release.

Reverend Jackson, acknowledging the program announced by The Coca-Cola Company, said,

This program will indeed become a model for American industry. President Reagan has put the ball squarely in the court of the private sector, and The Coca-Cola Company has responded. It is the intention of Operation PUSH to see that other leading companies in the private sector follow this initiative by The Coca-Cola Company.

The plan was designed to increase Black involvement in eight areas of the Company's business system:

[9] Thomas Oliver, "Coca-Cola Admits It Mishandled PUSH Pact," *op. cit.,* p. 1A.
[10] William Raspberry, "Jesse Jackson and The Coca-Cola Co." Syndicated column, late August.
[11] Thomas Oliver, "Coke and PUSH Accord Claimed," *Atlanta Constitution,* August 8, 1981, p. 1.

1 Bottler Franchises: Recognizing the need for Black Americans to share in owner-ship and wealth, the Company will identify bottling franchises which may become available and refer such opportunities to a pool of Black prospective investors.

2 Fountain Wholesalers/Wine Distributorships: The Company will appoint 32 Black-owned distributors across the country within the next 12 months and has committed to provide specialized training, lists of prospective customers and future advice and counsel as necessary to assist these businesses' success. The Company is also researching opportunities for Black participation in the distribution of its wine products. The estimated value of these programs is $1.3 million for over 100 new jobs, plus ownership.

3 Business Development: The Company will establish a venture capital fund of $1.8 million for the funding of Black participation in the areas associated with and serviced by the Company and the soft drink industry.

4 Advertising: The Company will double the amount of its advertising dollars in Black-owned newspapers and magazines and increase its advertising expenditures with Black-owned radio. The estimated value of this advertising is over $2 million. In addition, a Black-owned advertising agency will be given ''agency-of-record'' respon-sibility for a Company brand with an estimated budget of $8 million.

5 Banking: The Company will substantially increase its deposits and borrowing activities with Black-owned banks and increase the number of Black-owned financial institutions utilized by the Company. The total commitment in this area represents $2 million.

6 Management and Employment: The Company is actively searching for a Black to join its Board of Directors and expects to have selected that person within six months. The Company is also committed to continue its hiring and promotion of Blacks to management positions toward the goal of 12.5 percent of the management force. At least 100 of the blue collar openings during the next year will be filled by Blacks. The value of the jobs contained in these goals is approximately $5.2 million.

7 Corporate Contributions: The Company will continue to designate a significant portion of its corporate contributions to Black organizations and institutions. The initial annual value of these contributions is $250,000. In the area of education, additional scholarships and chairs will be endowed at Black colleges and universities.

8 Goods and Services: The Company will continue its active minority purchasing program and expand it in terms of numbers of minority vendors and dollars spent. This year, the level of this majority purchasing will increase to an estimated $14 million through over 800 suppliers.

Mr. Keough said that the Company viewed the ''withdrawal of enthusiasm'' as insignificant compared to the ''real barn-burners'' and ''honest-to-God boycotts'' it had experienced in Florida, Guatemala, and throughout the Arab world.

''We really kind of brushed it aside as a typical ploy. We flat didn't consider it to be a significant issue, so maybe from a public relations viewpoint, we made a misjudg-ment,'' he said.

''We were 95 percent completed without discussions (with Jackson) when the boycott issue was raised, but it obviously gave the people the mistaken belief we were bowing to pressure,'' he said.[12]

No substantive concessions were made because of the boycott, Coca-Cola officials said. In discussions with the Reverend Jackson during the boycott, these officials said, some timetables were added to the minority program and dollar values were assigned to a number of provisions. In a separate interview, the Reverend Jackson agreed with this assessment.

Operation PUSH studies indicated that black consumer sales with the Coca-Cola Company totaled more than $296 million. PUSH estimates of black sales with other companies were: $348 million, Proctor and Gamble; $317 million, General Foods; $476 million, Philip Morris; $306 million, McDonalds; $278 million, Pepsi Cola; $462 million, Sears and Roebuck; $117 million, Revlon; $200 million, Toyota. In addition, some PUSH estimates of the blacks' market share with companies were: 32% of Gillette's razor blade market, 11–12% of Nabisco sales, 15.2% of the Listerine mouthwash market, 11% of the total Pillsbury Hungry Jack biscuit market, 10% of the Pillsbury frosting mix and 7% of the Pillsbury cake mix market, 23% of the Johnny Walker Red market, 12% of the Chivas Regal market, 16% of the J & B market, 27.8% of the Old Forrester market, and 24.4% of the Old Taylor market. PUSH also said the leading products Jim Beam, Old Crow, Old Forrester, and Old Taylor have a total of more than 1½ million black customers and that blacks spent more than $6 billion on liquor in 1979 alone.

The Reverend B. W. Smith in an address entitled ''AWAKENING A SLEEPING GIANT: The Black Church—A Major Economic Force,'' delivered at the 10th annual convention of Operation PUSH at the Hyatt Regency in Chicago on July 7, 1981 (before the boycott), said, ''Coca-Cola has gross sales of $4.9 billion in 1979 and made a profit of $420.1 million. In addition to Coca-Cola this company markets Fresca, Sunkist, Dr. Pepper, Minute Maid Orange Juice, and Hi-C, and they are the fifth largest wine producer in the nation. Black consumer sales with this company total over $296 million.

''Coca-Cola is getting too much of our money, and there is not too much difference between the profit/loss margin and between Coke and Pepsi for us to let them off without being exactly where we think they ought to be,'' the Baptist minister exhorted.[13]

''The boycott was a problem they wanted to go away, and the cost to them was nothing,'' said the analyst. The $34 million agreement pales next to the $470 million in after-tax profits the company should earn this year,'' explained one analyst.

He pointed out that part of the $34 million is in the form of loans which must be paid back to Coke. Other parts of the settlement apparently require only a shifting of budgeted funds, not an increase in the overall budget of the company.[14]

Coke's Chief Financial Officer, Sam Ayoub, emphasized that the program was not a giveaway.

[12] *Ibid.*, p. 16A.
[13] See Exhibit 1.
[14] Thomas Oliver, ''Coke-PUSH Pact No Danger To Firm's Finances, Analysts Declare,'' *Atlanta Constitution*, August 13, 1981, p. 1B.

Another reason Operation PUSH targeted Coca-Cola, some say, was the Company's reputation for promoting minority participation, a record which made it open to further demands from civil rights organizations.

Reverend Jackson said, "Operation PUSH is now ending its national withdrawal of enthusiasm campaign and will take affirmative steps to promote and publicize the new relationships that has been established between Black America and The Coca-Cola Company."

APPENDIX 1:
Remarks by Reverend B. W. Smith before the Tenth Annual Convention of Operation PUSH, Hyatt Regency Chicago, Chicago, Illinois, July 7, 1981

"AWAKENING A SLEEPING GIANT:
THE BLACK CHURCH—A MAJOR ECONOMIC FORCE"

Exodus 4:2 And the Lord said unto him, what is that in thine hand? And he said a rod.

Exodus 14:15 And the Lord said unto Moses, wherefore criest you unto me? Speak unto the children of Israel that they go forward.

Somewhere in the scripture there, it says there arose a Pharoah in Egypt, and without recalling that entire story of how Joseph went there as a friend of the Pharoah and friended himself to the Pharoah, there were a series of incidents. Now, there was a spiral on the throne, and they put the children of Israel in bondage. As they grew old, their spirits waxed cold. And somewhere, it said that they refused to sing the song of Zion in a strange land. They lost their desire to think.

The blues grew out of our community because of us being down and feeling low—the song, "Don't Let the Sun Catch You Crying;" and the other song, "The Sun's Gon' Shine in My Back Door Someday." Well, they refused to sing; they lost their desire to sing. They were desolate, they were depressed. And in one place it says that they hung their hearts on the willows and wept by the waters as they remembered Zion. Crying is sometimes a release, expressing impotence, the inability to do anything about the situation you're in, and you weep because it sometimes typifies helplessness. And they wept. Many of us in the community are weeping because of the Reaganomics that is sweeping this country. Many of us now are refusing to sing because of Reaganomics.

But I want to tell you today, that the National Black Church Congress numbers better than 20 million persons. More than 11 million are Baptist. Twenty million consumers making up a major part of the $125 billion dollars spent by Black Americans each year. Many of us as church leaders have begun to look pessimistically at the future. We have accepted the fact that Reaganomics will destroy us all.

The Lord is speaking to us (ministers) like he did to Moses: *"Wherefore Criest Thou unto me? Speak unto the children that they go forward."* If Black Americans were a separate nation, we would be the ninth richest in the free world. We are not impotent; we are not helpless. All we need is to be sensitized to our resources. It was the Black church leaders that led the Montgomery bus boycott and brought an end to segregated bus service in Montgomery, Alabama. It was the Black church that formed the vanguard for the struggle in the South under the leadership of

Martin Luther King in the sixties. It was the Black church leaders that made Operation Breadbasket work under the leadership of our own Rev. Jesse Jackson. The Black church must come back and the Black church leader, the preacher/prophet, must once again take his rightful place in the leadership of this movement. Who better than the Black preacher is qualified to challenge the big insensitive corporations to do what is right. We will encourage our people to "withdraw their enthusiasm," as Mr. Daryl Grisham puts it.

Coca-Cola had gross sales of $4.9 billion in 1979 and made a profit of $420.1 million. In addition to Coca-Cola this company markets Fresca, Sprite, Sunkist, Dr. Pepper, Minute Maid orange juice, HI-C and they are the fifth largest wine producer in the nation. Black consumer sales with this company total over $296 million. Blacks consume 49 per cent of all the grape soda produced in the United States. *Why criest thou unto me?* is the question, *What is that that's in your hand?*

A $125 billion rod. Use it! Use what you have in your hand. Coke has had to change its mind. They have with us today their top Black executive, who is here with a mess of porridge to make a peace pact. We thought we were about ready to accept it, but we're looking at it again a little closer. I told them wait. Let their consumer patronage council look at that a little closer before we sign, or our good friend may have to go back to Atlanta with that and come back to us again. Coca-Cola is getting too much of our money, and there is not too much difference between the profit/loss margin and between Coke and Pepsi for us to let them off without being exactly where we think they ought to be.

Our Survival Plan

Since we (Black *people) are concentrated in mostly urban areas,* we've got to have a survival plan. Seventy-five per cent of us live in urban areas. And since four-fifths of our population attend some form of the Black church—the Black preacher/prophet becomes a real authentic leader, a 21-carat gold leader. The clergy speaks on a regular basis to more people than any person in our community. We cannot allow our people to continue to dissipate their resources like they are. Pastors must give their members direction. I'm a pastor. I refuse to pastor 3,000 members at St. John and let the politician tell them how to vote. I'm going to tell 'em how to vote! I refuse to pastor 3,000 folk and let the business people in the community tell them where to shop and what to buy. I'll tell them what to do about that. I refuse to turn my congregation over to the community leaders who know nothing about God or care less, for I lead a called-out people who have come ye out from among them and have decided to be also separated. So since they have come out from the world, then their instructions will come from me! "My sheep"— Lord I wish I could say—"They know my voice and a stranger they will not follow." My sheep will hear my voice and when politicians come calling, no sense in talkin'. They're going to say, "What does Reverend say?" I'll make sure that the politicians are accountable because before I give a member the right hand of fellowship, I register them to vote right in the lobby.

And every time a politician comes there, I say, "All of the registered voters stand up." And the whole house goes up. We see three or four people. And that says to them that this is a fella' we're going to have to deal with a little bit differently than is our usual technique, e.g. to bring Reverend a free ticket to Church's Chicken.

Operation PUSH is targeting these fifty cities in the United States for action based on their population. Some of these cities are Chicago, Boston, Buffalo, Newark, New York City, Philadelphia, Cincinnati, Cleveland, Kansas City, St. Louis, Detroit, Los Angeles, Baltimore, New Orleans, Memphis, Dallas, Houston, San Francisco, Oakland, Miami, Gary, Washington, D.C., and other cities. The fifty markets contain 65 per cent of the Black population and sustain 75 per cent of the income of Blacks or $98.7 billion. In each of these cities we need a council of clergy that are on the alert and have their congregations sensitized to the call for a selective buying campaign against any company that is unfair to the Black community in their hiring practices—advertising in Black media, investments in Black banks and savings and loans, contributions to Black colleges (UNCF—United Negro College Fund), scholarships to needy Blacks in the community, etc. We must insist upon our share of the franchises and the corporate positions.

We want a Black from the boiler room to the board room. We must get our share of the legal, advertising and public relations contracts, also in an amount commensurate to our spending power.

There are approximately *twenty five major companies* that we have zeroed in on for action, and others we are looking at closely. These are companies that get the largest portion of our consumer dollar. Some of them are Kelloggs, Church's Chicken, Pillsbury, R.J. Reynolds, General Mills, Scott Towels, Green Giant, Gallo Wines, National Distillers, K-Mart, Nissan Datsun, Toyota, Texaco, Oscar Mayer, Pizza Huts, Nehi, Royal Crown, Hilton Hotels, Marriott Hotels, Standard Oil, Carnation, Bob Evans Sausage, Cannon Towels, Del Monte, Colgate-Palmolive, Wrigley Chewing Gum, Mobil Oil (Montgomery Ward), General Foods, Holly Farms, Proctor and Gamble, Sky Chief, Campbells Soup, Honda, Winn-Dixie, Eastman-Kodak and Revlon. *"AND GOD SAID, WHAT IS THAT THAT'S IN YOUR HAND?"*

My response to you is IT IS *MONEY!* IT'S *LONG* AND IT'S *GREEN,* $125 billion. We cannot afford to spend that kind of money foolishly. The dollar changes hand in the white community 2 to 3 times, in the Chinese community, 10 to 12 times. That same dollar stays in the Black community about 6 to 7 hours. We must organize consumer clubs within our churches and in our community. These clubs will monitor the behavior of leading consumer companies, particularly the chain grocery or drug companies and the retail clothing industries.

A clergy representative from each of the target cities will form a national selective patronage council, of which I chair, and we will go over these companies' records. This council, with the aid of national staff, will contact companies targeted for review. Each company will receive an approach letter indicating our concern and identifying who we are. The letter will also call for a meeting wherein we can further detail our concerns and reasons for seeking an economic argument with that particular company. In that letter or one subsequent to it, a questionnaire covering the areas of concern will be submitted.

If the company is responsive, the negotiations will continue. We will present proposals based upon our research and the information they have submitted in the questionnaire and in the meetings. If the company chooses to evade negotiations to resist our objectives, we will report this to our local communities along with information about its sales and economic impact upon our community. At that time, we will prepare a selective patronage campaign (boycott) withdrawing our enthusiasm.

If the company chooses to return to the table (we call that reconciliation), the proposal will be restated and refined for further discussion and reflect the additional loss suffered by the Black community due to the company recalcitrance, while we were waiting on them to make up their mind. *We will up the ante, as you would say, in some areas.* The *minister,* the *preacher,* is the force that must make this happen. The moral authority of mankind has been entrusted to the preacher/prophet. We have the power and the authority to use it! We are the only ones who can tell corporate America that it is sinful—what you are doing to Black people.

WHAT IS THAT YOU HAVE IN YOUR HAND? YOU HAVE A ROD IN YOUR HAND, USE IT! You can build the Black business community, and you can tear down corrupt corporate entities. You can challenge schools, tear down corrupt corporate entities. You can challenge school teachers to teach and you can challenge young people to learn—*WHAT IS THAT THAT'S IN YOUR HAND?*

If you will speak unto the children and command them to go forward, the waters of the Corporate Red Sea will back up. If you speak, the winds of selective buying will blow and Black people can pass over on dry land. If you speak and command the people to march, the walls of injustice and discrimination in hiring will crumble. If you speak, cripple ghetto dwellers living below a decent level will rise up and walk to a job we have for them. If you speak, the blinded eyes of an insensitive media will open and see us in a different light and better understand our dissatisfaction.

If you speak, the jangling discords of our disunity will be transformed into a beautiful symphony. The multitudes that are basking in the economic valley of dry bones can be resurrected into a great army marching to independence and liberation. Therefore, I charge you to leave this place with a message to corporate America, that we demand respect commensurate to the $125 billion we spend. I charge you to meticulously examine the records of the target companies in the geographical area in which you live.

I charge you to mobilize your congregation, mobilize your community, the P.T.A.'s, the fraternal organizations, the civic clubs, the block clubs, yes, and even go into the streets and to the neighborhoods and knock on doors and ring door bells. We must let this country know we mean business.

Finally, my brethren, we must trust in God. When Moses trusted God, the Red Sea parted. When He said, "Why speak thou unto me?" Cry, "I speak to the children that they might go forward." When they stepped forward the Red Sea backed up. Moses trusted God. When Joshua trusted God, Jericho fell. When Abraham trusted God, Sarah bore a son. When Jacob trusted God, his cattle outnumbered Laban's. When Shadrack, Meshack and Abednego trusted God, Nebuchadnezer's fiery furnace could do them no harm. When Gideon trusted God, he defeated the Midianites with 300 men. When the widow at Zarephath trusted God and the man of God, her meal barrel ran over and her oil never failed. When Naaman trusted God and the man of God, when he dipped in Jordan seven times, he lost his leprosy.

Mr. Reagan can do what he likes. He can cut out food stamps. We made it without them. He can cut out C.E.T.A. We made it without it. He can cut out Medicare. We made it without it. He can cut our Social Security. We made it without it. But, let me tell you something. I know somebody that sits high and looks low. *HE PROMISED NEVER TO LEAVE ME, NEVER TO LEAVE ME ALONE!*

I've heard the lightning flashing. I've heard the thunder roar. I've felt sin breakers dashing, trying to conquer my soul. BUT I'VE HEARD THE VOICE OF JESUS TELLING ME STILL FIGHT ON. HE PROMISED (you don't hear me!) HE PROMISED, HE PROMISED NEVER, NEVER, NEVER TO LEAVE ME, NEVER TO LEAVE ME ALONE! The song writer says, "He walks with me, He talks with Me and tells me I am His own." Let me tell you, preachers, go back to your churches, go back to your congregations. Tell them if they rise up and walk, trust in God and follow your leadership, He'll bring things out alright. Ain't He alright? Ain't He alright? Have you tried Him? Ain't He alright? Won't he fix it if you trust Him? Ain't He alright? Ain't He alright? Ain't He alright? Ain't He alright?

DISCUSSION QUESTIONS

1 Contrast Mr. Goizueta's statement "All employees will have equal opportunities to grow, develop and advance within the company" with Mr. Keough's commitment to "aid black entrepreneurs who seek to enter the beverage industry."

2 Evaluate Mr. Goizueta's belief that "business *unfettered* will be business *unflagging* in the service to American society."

3 To what extent do you believe that the activism represented by Operation Push is responsible for Coca Cola's affirmative action efforts?

4 Evaluate the Reverend Jesse Jackson's ''development formula'' and his idea that ''Black America, as an *underdeveloped nation*, must renegotiate the *relationship with corporate America*.''

5 Explain why you believe Coca Cola was targeted by Operation Push. How might the company have avoided the boycott?

ALABAMA POWER COMPANY (B)

Arthur A. Thompson, Jr.
The University of Alabama

SELECTED STRATEGIC ISSUES

- The process of utility rate regulation
- Utility company strategies for dealing with an adverse regulatory agency
- Utility rate increase requests and the public's need for services
- Managerial constituencies for public utilities
- Appropriate criteria for approval of rate changes by public utilities

In fall 1982 Alabama Power Company (APC) was awaiting a decision from the Alabama Public Service Commission (PSC) on the company's petition for a record $454 million increase in its retail electrical rates, the tenth general retail rate increase filed by APC since 1968. Only the year before the PSC had, in a unanimous vote, issued a "zero order," denying Alabama Power any part of its $324.9 million rate increase request filed in March 1981, an action which prompted an APC official to remark, "It's hard to imagine any commission worse than the one we've got now." Exhibit 1 shows the history of APC's rate increase requests.

In APC's view, the Alabama PSC had failed to grant Alabama Power adequate and timely rate increases, causing the company to have to appeal a number of recent PSC decisions to the Alabama Supreme Court. Legal action was, in management's opinion, necessary to bolster Alabama Power's weakening financial condition. Several Wall Street analysts who watched the utility industry closely agreed. They rate the Alabama

This case was written by Professor Arthur A. Thompson, Jr., The University of Alabama. Copyright © 1983 by Arthur A. Thompson, Jr. Used with permission.

EXHIBIT 1   HISTORY OF ALABAMA POWER'S RATE INCREASE REQUESTS

	Revenue increase requested		Revenue increase granted	
Date of filing	Dollar amount (in millions)	Percent increase	Dollar amount (in millions)	As a % of request
A. *RETAIL RATES*				
February 1968	$ 7.4	4.7%	$ 6.9	94.6%
November 1970	19.9	8.5	16.9	84.9
June 1972	29.9	19.0	27.0	90.3
June 1974	64.5	16.5	54.2	84.0
November 1975	106.8	19.3	23.3	21.8
October 1976	205.3	33.0	91.1	44.4
December 1978	288.8	33.0	208.3	72.1
December 1979	122.3	10.3	80.0	65.4
March 1981	324.9	24.4	0.0[a]	0.0[a]
March 1982	454.0	16.9		
B. *WHOLESALE RATES*				
November 1971	$ 2.7	34.1%	$ 2.7	100.0%
June 1974	12.6	64.2	11.8[a]	93.7[a]
April 1976	14.5	27.0	9.6	66.2
December 1977	18.4	31.0	11.8	64.1
November 1980	23.4	33.6	18.7	79.9
January 1982	9.4			

[a] In February 1982, the Supreme Court of Alabama granted APC the right to collect $75 million in additional revenues, subject to refund pending a final appeal to the Court. The Court ordered the PSC to review the evidence presented again. In March 1982, APC filed a retail rate request seeking a $129 million annual rate increase over the $325.9 million increase requested in March 1981.

Source: Alabama Power Company.

PSC as among the "worst" in the United States in terms of allowing the utilities under its jurisdiction a "fair return."

From the general public's perspective, however, the Alabama PSC's recent rate decisions were seen as "consumer-oriented." The three members of the Alabama PSC were elected and the two commissioners whose terms expired in 1982 both won reelection in November to new four-year terms.

ALABAMA POWER'S RECENT PERFORMANCE

The past decade had been turbulent for Alabama Power. The company's customers had endured round after round of rate increases that more than tripled rates in ten years. Consumers had become increasingly price and use sensitive. Residential, commercial, and industrial customers tried to economize on electricity usage. APC's load growth was flattening as new generating plants, under construction since the early 1970s, were reaching completion (see Exhibit 2).

EXHIBIT 2
ALABAMA POWER COMPANY
DATA ON RATES AND CUSTOMER USAGE

Item	Actual							Projections*	
	1967	1972	1975	1978	1979	1980	1981	1982	1983
Number of customers (annual average):									
Residential	633,202	716,910	777,974	830,845	848,341	861,399	868,995	878,285	892,193
Commercial	92,886	99,801	106,269	114,253	115,639	115,452	116,295	117,621	119,321
Industrial	2,457	2,848	3,147	3,599	3,739	3,879	4,029	4,136	4,246
Average annual kwh usage per customer:									
Residential	6,279	9,285	9,954	10,939	10,231	11,041	10,621	10,497	10,507
Commercial	25,157	38,053	43,398	46,237	45,032	47,767	48,042	47,086	47,723
Industrial	3,121,838	3,493,603	3,319,631	3,834,133	3,912,699	3,737,916	3,636,389	3,733,801	3,747,292
Revenue per kwh (in cents):									
Residential	1.69¢	1.90¢	2.97¢	3.87¢	4.44¢	5.14¢	5.62¢	6.52¢	7.51¢
Commercial	1.83	1.97	3.05	4.03	4.66	5.32	5.82	6.80	7.68
Industrial	0.80	1.02	1.94	2.59	3.02	3.50	3.99	4.41	5.08
Overall average	1.17	1.41	2.46	3.23	3.71	4.21	4.68	n.a.	n.a.
Annual revenue per customer (in $):									
Residential	$ 106	$ 176	$ 296	$ 423	$ 454	$ 568	$ 597	$ 684	$ 789
Commercial	460	749	1,323	1,865	2,098	2,543	2,798	3,203	3,664
Industrial	25,045	35,495	64,298	99,386	118,273	130,906	144,956	164,751	190,508

* The projections for 1982 and 1983 were based on the full amount of the proposed $458 million rate increase being granted.
Source: Company records.

Electricity usage in APC's service area had dropped to the 1–3 percent range compared to 7–9 percent in the 1960s and early 1970s. Long-term load forecasts were for about 2–3 percent growth, nearly all of which was attributed to projected increases in the number of customers served rather than in average usage per customer. But it was arguable whether loads would grow even this fast. The nationwide economic recession had hit the Alabama economy especially hard. The state had the second highest unemployment rate among the fifty states in mid-1982 and thousands of Alabama workers in steel mills, tire plants, coal mines, auto parts plants, and construction were laid off. And for many years Alabama had ranked no higher than 47th in per capita income.

Prior to APC's first-ever general rate increase request in 1968, the company had been able to build new generating capacity, extend its transmission and distribution system, meet the growing electricity needs of customers, earn acceptable profits, maintain a strong financial condition, and set rates which resulted in a lower average price per kilowatt-hour every year between 1929 and 1968. But beginning in 1969 and accelerating during the 1975–1982 period, scale economies and technology-based cost savings ran out for Alabama Power, as they did for other electric utilities. Inflation hit the company very hard, pushing operating costs up an average of $100 million annually each year between 1970 and 1981 (after adjusting for sales growth).

The company's financial condition had been sharply weaker in 1981 than in 1970, or even in 1975. Profits in 1981 were $99.8 million, some 23 percent below the 1980 level of $129.7 million and almost 15 percent below the 1977 level of $117.3 million. Return on equity investment was only 8.2 percent in 1981 (compared to an industry average of 11.5 percent). In 3 of the past 6 years the company's dividend payments exceeded net income. (Exhibits 3 and 4 show recent financial statements.) To complicate matters further, the firm was a "cash hog," having issued over $2.1 billion in new long-term debt and preferred stock during the 1971–1981 period to finance the construction of additional generating, transmission, and distribution facilities. Internal cash flows were chronically stretched thin to handle operating expenses and dividends, much less provide funding for capital expansion. It was not certain that Alabama Power could continue to finance a $400–500 million annual construction program and, even if it could, it was not clear that investing so heavily in new capacity was warranted.

THE PHYSICAL SYSTEM

The company operated a generating, transmission, and distribution system that supplied electricity at retail to customers in over 850 communities, as well as in rural areas, and at wholesale to 15 municipally owned distribution systems and nine rural electric distributing cooperatives. The 1980 population in APC's service area was estimated at 3.1 million persons and average household size was 2.75 persons.

As of 1982, Alabama Power owned and operated 13 hydroelectric dams, 7 coal-fired generating plants, 1 nuclear plant, and 2 combustion turbine plants. It was part owner of two other coal-fired generating plants. Altogether the company had name-

EXHIBIT 3

ALABAMA POWER COMPANY:
STATEMENTS OF INCOME FOR THE YEARS ENDED DECEMBER 31, 1981, 1980 AND 1979

| | (in thousands) | | |
	1981	1980	1979
OPERATING REVENUES	$1,594,022	$1,421,997	$1,163,623
OPERATING EXPENSES:			
Operation—			
Fuel	504,930	439,488	365,628
Purchased and interchanged power, net	144,916	124,163	124,929
Other	192,502	153,552	129,430
Maintenance	135,727	99,040	80,660
Depreciation and amortization	147,581	127,840	123,075
Taxes other than income taxes	86,878	74,488	74,592
Federal and state income taxes	92,773	114,427	58,759
Total operating expenses	1,305,307	1,132,998	957,073
OPERATING INCOME	228,715	288,999	206,550
OTHER INCOME:			
Allowance for equity funds used during construction	39,471	32,189	28,554
Income from subsidiary	2,531	2,466	2,425
Other, net	4,925	8,060	9,796
Income before interest charges	335,642	331,714	247,325
INTEREST CHARGES:			
Interest on long-term debt	239,858	184,557	163,343
Amortization of debt discount, premium and expense, net	871	593	610
Other interest charges	5,882	65,686	51,909
Allowance for debt funds used during construction	(46,849)	(79,839)	(57,196)
Net interest charges	199,762	170,997	158,666
NET INCOME	135,880	160,717	88,659
DIVIDENDS ON PREFERRED STOCK	36,071	31,013	31,219
NET INCOME AFTER DIVIDENDS ON PREFERRED STOCK	$ 99,809	$ 129,704	$ 57,440

EXHIBIT 4   ALABAMA POWER COMPANY:
BALANCE SHEETS AT DECEMBER 31, 1981 AND 1980

| | 1981 | 1980 |
	(in thousands)	
Assets		
UTILITY PLANT		
Plant in service and held for future use, at original cost	$4,771,723	$3,854,627
Less—Accumulated provision for depreciation	1,063,897	934,606
	3,707,826	2,920,021
Nuclear fuel, at amortized cost	143,541	131,442
Construction work in progress—		
Nuclear	18,927	684,945
Other	564,109	462,705
	4,434,403	4,199,113
OTHER PROPERTY AND INVESTMENTS:		
Southern Electric Generating Company	16,400	16,400
Nonutility property, net	2,564	2,372
Miscellaneous	1,104	993
	20,068	19,765

EXHIBIT 4   *(Continued)*

	1981	1980
	(in thousands)	
Assets *(continued)*		
CURRENT ASSETS:		
Cash (Note 4)	4,400	13,429
Temporary cash investments, at cost	19,551	9,017
Receivables—		
Customer accounts receivable	94,515	90,745
Other accounts and notes receivable	10,632	7,132
Intercompany accounts	10,605	9,871
Accumulated provision for uncollectible accounts	(572)	(542)
Refundable federal income tax	25,000	20,000
Fossil fuel stock, at average cost	166,857	161,593
Materials and supplies, at average cost	24,087	21,734
Prepayments	28,952	24,871
	384,027	357,850
DEFERRED CHARGES:		
Cost of cancelled plant, being amortized	5,473	12,402
Debt expense, being amortized	7,343	6,878
Miscellaneous	29,176	21,935
	41,992	41,215
	$4,880,490	$4,617,943
Capitalization and Liabilities		
CAPITALIZATION		
Common stock equity	$1,231,061	$1,211,417
Preferred stock	374,400	334,400
Preferred stock subject to mandatory redemption	43,789	47,500
Long-term debt	2,394,674	2,159,793
	4,043,924	3,753,110
CURRENT LIABILITIES:		
Notes payable to banks	—	96,501
Long-term debt due within one year	52,687	47,424
Accounts payable—		
Intercompany accounts	33,367	38,922
Other	90,520	108,294
Revenues to be refunded	—	11,978
Customer deposits	22,362	19,891
Taxes accrued—		
Federal and state income	25,268	22,645
Other	10,236	10,462
Interest accrued	65,382	54,061
Miscellaneous	12,974	11,707
	312,796	421,885
DEFERRED CREDITS, ETC.:		
Accumulated deferred income taxes	436,594	370,439
Accumulated deferred investment tax credits	67,407	53,030
Miscellaneous	19,769	19,479
	523,770	442,948
COMMITMENTS AND CONTINGENT MATTERS		
	$4,880,490	$4,617,943

plate generating capacity of almost 8,500,000 kilowatts with 2,265,000 more under construction:

	In operation	
Type of generating unit	**Nameplate capacity**	**Percent of total**
Hydroelectric	1,342,225 kw	15.8%
Coal-fired	5,257,090 kw	61.9
Nuclear	1,720,000 kw	20.3
Combustion turbine	166,360 kw	2.0
	8,485,675 kw	100.0%

		Under construction		
Plant	**Capacity kilowatts (nameplate)**	**Type fuel**	**Planned commercial operation date**	**Estimated construction cost ($ millions)**
Miller Unit 2	660,000	Coal	1985	$ 457.7
Miller Unit 3	660,000	Coal	1989	686.3
Miller Unit 3	660,000	Coal	1991	730.9
Harris	135,000	Hydro	1983	188.1
Mitchell	150,000	Hydro	1985	168.3

The higher capital costs that Southern Company was incurring for nuclear facilities were offset to some extent by sharply lower costs for nuclear fuel per kilowatt-hour generated:

	Average cost of fuel per net kwh generated (in cents)				
Type of fuel	**1973**	**1976**	**1979**	**1980**	**1981**
Coal	0.45	1.06	1.55	1.70	1.91
Oil	1.36	2.93	3.92	5.36	7.09
Gas	0.40	1.54	2.29	3.11	4.08
Nuclear	—	0.21	0.46	0.55	0.63
Overall Average	0.49	1.13	1.52	1.61	1.81

In recent years, Alabama Power's generation mix had shifted to nuclear:

Source	Generation mix percentages			
	1979	1980	1981	1982 (est.)
Coal	74%	72%	73%	59%
Gas	3	*	*	*
Oil	*	*	*	*
Hydro	17	14	9	11
Nuclear	6	14	18	30
	6	14	18	30
	100%	100%	100%	100%

* Less than 0.5%.

Still, the company's average cost of fuel per net kilowatt generated had increased each of the previous years:

Type of fuel plant	Average fuel costs per net kwh		
	1979	1980	1981
Coal	1.61¢	1.80¢	2.08¢
Gas	2.55	**	**
Oil	**	**	**
Nuclear	0.51	0.60	0.77
Weighted Average	1.56¢	1.61¢	1.84¢

** Not meaningful because of minimal usage.

These fuel costs were sharply above the weighted average of 0.36¢ in 1971 and 1.07¢ in 1975, in line with the experience throughout the industry. Alabama Power paid an average of $49.31 per ton for coal in 1981, as compared to about $7 per ton in 1970 and $5.50 in 1960. APC owned substantial coal reserves and had contracted with an outside firm to mine coal from these reserves and supply part of the coal needs of its plants. APC also sold electric appliances through its own outlets—in addition to assisting other appliance dealers. The company's overall market share of the electric appliance business throughout its service territory was an estimated 5 percent.

OWNERSHIP AND CONTROL

Alabama Power was a wholly owned subsidiary of The Southern Company, the largest electric utility firm in the United States in terms of assets. The Southern Company was a regulated public utility holding company and was the parent firm of Alabama Power

Company, Georgia Power Company (serving almost all of Georgia), Gulf Power Company (serving the western part of the Florida Panhandle), and Mississippi Power Company (serving southeastern Mississippi). Each of the four operating affiliates had its own president and board of directors and operated more or less autonomously. Each operating company issued first mortgage bonds and preferred stock in its own name.

Southern Company issued common stock in its name (traded on the NYSE), but did not issue any long-term debt securities. Southern's common stock was the most widely held electric utility stock in the nation and was among the ten most widely held corporate stocks in America. The Southern Company system also included (1) Southern Systems, Inc., which provided engineering, financial, R&D, statistical, technical, and management services, at cost, to Southern's four operating affiliates; (2) Southern Electric International, Inc., a newly-formed subsidiary whose principal activity was international consulting but which could also function as a vehicle for other diversification efforts; and (3) Southern Electric Generating Company, which was owned in equal shares by Alabama Power and Georgia Power.

The Southern Company operated under a very decentralized management philosophy, with each operating company acting very independently. Southern Services functioned in a corporate staff role, but had no direct authority over the operating units. Cooperation and coordination was achieved mainly by consensus agreement. The long-time and widely-respected chairman of Southern Company, Alvin Bogtle, was scheduled to retire in 1983; speculation as to his successor was widespread throughout Southern Company, with the leading candidates thought to be the chief executive officers of Alabama Power, Georgia Power, Gulf Power, and Southern Services. The selection of one of these insiders was considered certain.

On the whole, Alabama Power's relationship with its sister companies in The Southern Company system was loose-knit; the chief cooperative benefits accrued from coordinated planning, diversity of loads, an ability to temper the impact of regulation on a single company, and mutual assistance in supplying power to each other. Specific economies arose from:

1 Staggered construction of generating plants so that each of the four operating companies could take advantage of building the optimal-size generating units

2 Locating their respective hydroelectric operations so as to capitalize upon the diversity among various watersheds in the Southeast

3 Combining and programming their energy loads in such a manner as to fully utilize hydro-resources at a time of high water flows

4 Coordination of maintenance operations, and

5 The opportunity of the companies to implement a computerized, coordinated dispatch of power from all generating plants based on the relative efficiencies of different generating units, the relative fuel costs at each plant, and the transmission line losses, all on an incremental (marginal cost) basis

In virtually all other areas, the managements of the four operating companies were free to pursue their own course, although numerous systemwide committees were set up to share information, discuss matters of mutual concern, and recommend policies and procedures to be applied throughout The Southern Company.

ELECTRIC SYSTEM OPERATIONS AT ALABAMA POWER

APC's generating and transmission facilities were operated on an integrated basis with those of Georgia Power, Gulf Power, and Mississippi Power so as to provide the most economical generation and dispatch of energy across the system, thus taking into account the transmission loss coefficients and the different costs and efficiencies of the various generating units. In addition, Alabama Power, either directly or through its sister companies, had transmission connections with Florida Power, Florida Power & Light, Duke Power, South Carolina Electric and Gas, Tennessee Valley Authority, Alabama Electric Cooperative, and Mississippi Power & Light.

In 1981, Alabama Power was a net purchaser of power from other companies (including its Southern Company affiliates), obtaining about 3 million kwh of its total sales of 36.3 billion kwh externally at a cost of $144.9 million. The company's generating reserve margin (the amount by which generating capacity exceeds annual peak demand) at the year-end 1981 was 31.6 percent, up from 11.3 percent in 1980. The jump was due to bringing a second 860,000 kw nuclear unit into operation at the company's Farley nuclear plant.

It was standard practice at Alabama Power to conduct tests of the efficiency of each generating unit at least once a year and to calculate average and marginal cost functions for each unit. The resulting cost equations were programmed into a computer so that average and marginal costs could instantaneously be calculated for each generating unit at whatever rate it was presently operating. Then, APC used computerized controls to generate and dispatch electric power over the system according to least cost criteria. During the course of a day as demand for electricity picked up, the Company's power control center monitored the marginal costs of generating more electricity at each on-line generating unit and sent impulses to raise the electricity output of the unit (or units) with the lowest marginal costs at that point in time. Similarly, when usage levels dropped, the units with the highest marginal costs were automatically signaled to operate at a reduced rate. The result was to supply customers' requirements for electricity at the minimum feasible fuel cost.

Since 1952 Alabama Power had been a summer peaking company due to growing use of air conditioning among residential and commercial customers. Company surveys showed in 1980 that over 75 percent of the residential customers had air conditioning whereas less than 20 percent utilized electric heat. It was thought that over 90 percent of commercial customers used air conditioning and that electric heating was used by less than 20 percent. It was this air conditioning—heating imbalance that accounted for why Alabama Power's summer peak tended to exceed its winter peak by 25 to 30 percent.

Typical load curves for summer weeks, winter weeks, and year-round are shown in Exhibits 5 and 6. Different customers had different load patterns. The company's large process-oriented industrial customers (such as chemical manufacturers, paper plants, and steel mills) which were geared to operate 24 hours a day on a year round basis had a relatively constant demand (and were termed "high load factor" customers because their average loads were 90 percent or higher of their peak load demand). Alabama Power's residential loads, on the other hand, were very temperature sensitive and

EXHIBIT 5

HOURLY LOAD PROFILE FOR ALABAMA POWER COMPANY
Week of July 26 — August 1, 1982

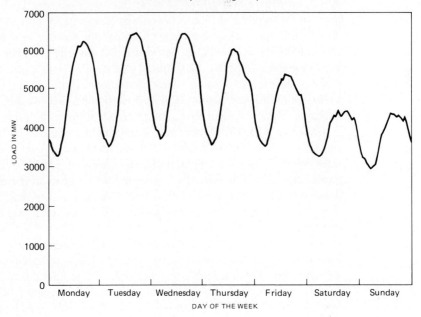

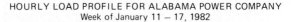

EXHIBIT 6

HOURLY LOAD PROFILE FOR ALABAMA POWER COMPANY
Week of January 11 — 17, 1982

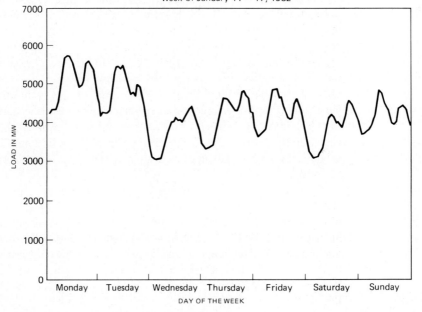

highly variable. Summer loads reached a broad daily peak usually extending from 12 noon to 8 p.m. and falling to a deep valley from 12 midnight to 6 a.m.; in winter months, the residential peak was bimodal with highest about 8 a.m. and 6 p.m. (see Exhibit 5). Street and highway lighting customers were off-peak users and exhibited their greatest usage during the nighttime valleys, imposing little or no demand on the system during the day. The loads of commercial customers were heaviest during business hours.

Overall, Alabama Power's daily load factor was usually in the 80–85 percent range, meaning that the average hourly load over a full 24-hour period was 80–85 percent of the peak hourly load experienced during the same period. Monthly load factors were in the 65–75 percent range (meaning that the average monthly usage was 65–75 percent of that month's peak load). Annual load factors were in the 57–61 percent range.

The nature of the company's system load pattern determined when maintenance could be performed on generating equipment. Alabama Power's maintenance program utilized the valley load periods in the spring and fall for major maintenance such as turbine overhauls and boiler retubing. The valley periods of nights and weekends were used for light maintenance—repair of coal pulverizer mills, feed water pumps, and other pieces of equipment which could be worked on while the generating unit operated at a reduced output. Company operating policy was to optimize its generation mix and its maintenance schedule in accord with the current load characteristics; changes in load patterns necessitated adjustments in both generation mix and maintenance activities.

By operating its 8,485,675 kw of nameplate capacity at 100 percent utilization year-round (assuming no maintenance, no breakdowns, and plenty of water in all of its hydro reservoirs), Alabama Power had theoretical generating capacity of almost 75 billion kwh annually (8,485,675 kw × 24 hours × 365 days). While this theoretical total was, of course, well in excess of what was feasible and practical owing to the need for maintenance, the lack of enough water in dam reservoirs to operate the hydroelectric facilities around-the-clock, unexpected "outages" of generating units, and the inherent up and down usage of customers, the company's actual kwh generation of 33.8 billion kwh in 1981 still represented just a 45 percent utilization of APC's nameplate capacity. Assuming an average annual 75 percent utilization of APC's 6,977,090 kw of nuclear and coal-fired capacity, 20 percent utilization of the 1,342,225 kw of hydroelectric capacity, and zero percent utilization of the combustion-turbine capacity (which was rarely used and then only for short summer peaking periods because of high fuel costs), APC had capacity to generate 48.2 billion kwh annually, an amount 43 percent higher than its 1981 kwh sales.

REGULATION

In 1920 the Alabama legislature passed a bill creating the Alabama Public Service Commission and giving it the authority to regulate Alabama Power Company with respect to the issuance of securities, the extensions of its electric plant, the rates and charges for the service it provides, and related matters concerning the exercise of its public utility responsibility. The law is similar to those in other states. According to

Alabama law, the Public Service Commission was responsible for seeing that every utility under its jurisdiction:

> shall maintain its plant, facilities and equipment in good operating condition and shall set up and maintain proper reserves for renewals, replacements and reasonable contingencies. Every utility shall render adequate service to the public and shall make such reasonable improvements, extensions and enlargements of its plants, facilities, and equipment as may be necessary to meet the growth and demand of the territory which it is under the duty to serve.

Alabama Power was precluded from constructing any plant, property, or facility for production, transmission, delivery, or furnishing of electricity except ordinary extensions of its existing system in the usual course of business without first obtaining approval from the Commission and being issued a certificate of convenience and necessity. A public hearing had to be held before the PSC could issue such a certificate. In addition, Alabama Power was prohibited from issuing securities (preferred stock and/or first mortgage bonds) without PSC approval.

Although the Public Service Commission was directly responsible for regulating APC's retail rates and charges for services, the law states that "the retail rates set by the Commission shall be reasonable and just to both the utility and the public." Further, the law stated that every utility:

> shall be entitled to such just and reasonable rates as will enable it at all times to fully perform its duties to the public and will, under honest, efficient, and economical management, earn a fair net return on the reasonable value of its property devoted to the public service.

The Federal Energy Regulatory Commission (FERC) had jurisdiction over Alabama Power's wholesale rates to municipal and rural electric cooperative systems and also over transactions involving the use of electric facilities interconnected with utilities located in other states. Section 201 of the Federal Power Act declared:

> that the business of transmitting and selling electric energy for ultimate distribution to the public is affected with a public interest, and that Federal regulation of matters relating to generation . . . and . . . the transmission of electric energy in interstate commerce and the sale of such energy at wholesale in interstate commerce is necessary in the public interest.

Section 202 conferred specific powers upon the FERC:

> for the purpose of assuring an abundant supply of electric energy throughout the United States with the greatest possible economy and with regard to the proper utilization and conservation of natural resources.

Alabama Power had to obtain licenses from the FERC to build and operate hydroelectric facilities. When such licenses expired, the federal government, by an act of Congress, could take over the project or the FERC could relicense the project either to the original licensee or to a new licensee. In the event of takeover or relicensing to another, Alabama Power was entitled to recover its net investment in the project (not in excess of the fair value of the property taken) plus reasonable damages to any other property directly associated with loss of the hydroelectric facilities.

As with other corporations engaged in interstate commerce, the Securities and Exchange Commission (SEC) maintained continuous surveillance over the financing activities of Alabama Power and The Southern Company. Both APC and Southern were required to register the sale of all securities with the SEC and were prohibited from issuing or selling any bonds, preferred stock, or common stock that did not comply with SEC policies and regulations.

Alabama Power had to comply with the regulations of the Nuclear Regulatory Commission (NRC) in constructing and operating nuclear plants. The NRC had dominion over matters concerning the public health, safety, and environmental impact of a proposed nuclear plant; the NRC was also empowered to investigate the benefits of nuclear plants relative to other means of power generation as a basis for deciding whether to issue construction permits. Issuance of operating licenses by the NRC was conditioned upon requiring changes in operating techniques or upon the installation of additional equipment to meet safety or environmental standards; moreover, opportunity was provided for interested parties to request a public hearing on health, safety, or environmental issue.

Alabama Power was also subject to regulation by the Corps of Engineers, the Alabama Water Improvement Commission, the Alabama Air Pollution Control Commission, and Alabama Public Health Department with respect to the construction and operation of plant facilities which could have an impact upon the environment.

RATE REGULATION BY THE PSC

When Alabama Power requested permission to increase its retail electric rates, it was customary for the Public Service Commission to postpone a final decision for six months during which time the request was studied. The company had to furnish whatever pertinent information was requested and, in particular, it had to present justification for its request in public hearings. This justification included an analysis of all costs incurred in its electric service operations during a particular time frame, usually referred to as a *test year*, and a determination of what level of revenue would have been required during the test year to cover the company's costs and also provide a fair return on the fair value of the company's property devoted to its electric service operations.

A company official explained the complicated procedure involved:

> Three main steps must be taken in applying the fair-return-on-fair-value rule of rate making. First, the rate base must be determined. The rate base represents the original cost of utility property and assets devoted to electric service less depreciation.
>
> Finally, the fair rate of return must be determined. This is the rate—in percentage form—which is applied to the rate base to give the dollar amount of return allowed to the utility as a profit on its operations to serve the public. One important factor in determining a fair rate of return is cost of capital, the cost to a utility of obtaining the capital it needs to go into business and stay in business. Cost of capital includes the interest expense associated with debt, dividends on preferred stock, and a return on common equity investment, for which dividends and appreciation of stock value are expected.
>
> A second test of a fair rate of return concerns stockholders. It is generally considered that a healthy business and one which is attractive to investors must have sufficient earnings to cover all expenses of operation and to provide a reasonable return to its common stockholders—the owners of the business.

A third important factor considered in determining a fair return is the ability of the company to attract capital. In fixing a fair rate of return, the commission considers what will be sufficient to enable the company to go into the money markets on a favorably competitive basis.

A fourth major factor which is beginning to be considered by some regulators in determining a fair rate of return is economic conditions. Since rates based on historical data are used in the future, it has been generally accepted that prevailing economics and discernible trends for the future are factors affecting the rate of return allowed. If a so-called prosperity period is accompanied by continuous and prolonged price increases, as in a period characterized by rapid inflation, public utilities are likely to be adversely affected by *regulatory lag*. Regulatory lag arises in Alabama Power's case because our PSC uses a 12-month historical test year and because the PSC delays any decision on the company's rate filing for at least 6 months. Though commissions throughout the country are not agreed on whether this lag should result in a somewhat higher or "catch-up" allowance, there has been some recognition of this problem in recent rate cases by a few commissions.

A simple numerical example shows how all this works. Suppose Alabama Power has property fairly valued and adjusted to indicate a rate base of $1 million. Assume that its test-year adjusted operating expenses are $250,000 a year, not including any construction loans. If the PSC finds that a five percent rate of return on the property value, or rate base, is fair and reasonable, this would mean a dollar return of $50,000 on the $1,000,000 rate base. It also means that the charges for service will have to produce revenue of $350,000 a year in order to cover the expenses ($250,000) plus about twice the amount of return allowed ($50,000). To achieve the return of $50,000 it is necessary to bill revenues of approximately $100,000 above expenses because of federal, state, and local taxes.

Once the revenues needed to produce a fair rate of return on investment have been determined, then the company files a schedule of rates which when applied to the test-year sales would generate this rate of return. After the new schedule of rates is approved, the commission orders the increase into effect on a certain date. On that specified date, the new rates are the only legal rates that the company may charge its customers.

In its last two rate cases, Alabama power had asked the PSC to approve rates that would yield an 18 percent return on common equity. Expert witnesses for the company testified that an 18 percent return on equity was needed to attract capital, provide an "A" rating on securities, and compensate stockholders for the business risk being incurred. Moreover, the company took special pains to emphasize that the rate of return that the Commission had granted was, in fact, not being earned because of regulatory lag effects. Exhibit 7 shows the widening gap between the rate of return the company had requested in previous rate cases, the rate of return allowed by the Commission, and the actual rate of return earned by the Company.

Alabama Power followed the practice of other electric utilities and had separate rate schedules for residential, commercial, and industrial users. APC's industrial users paid a lower price per kilowatt-hour because of their higher volume of use and because Alabama Power's cost of serving industrial users was lower (owing to lower investment requirements for distribution facilities and lower expenses in servicing industrial accounts). Exhibit 2 provided additional information on Alabama Power's rates and customer usage of electricity. In 1981 Alabama Power's retail rates were slightly below the national averages of the rates charged by some 240 other investor-owned electric utility companies.

EXHIBIT 7

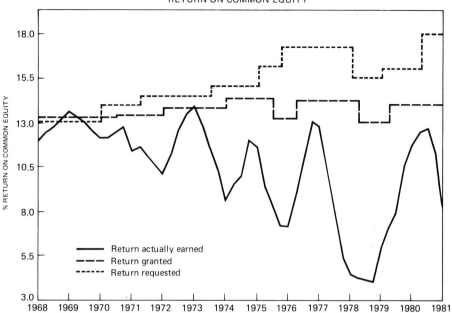

ALABAMA POWER COMPANY
RETURN ON COMMON EQUITY

ALABAMA POWER'S CONSTRUCTION PROGRAM

During the 1970–1981 period, Alabama Power spent $4.6 billion on construction of new facilities. The company had adjusted and revised its construction plans downwards on several occasions to reflect the declining growth rate projections for the next decade, but budgets still called for additional construction expenditures of $545.3 million in 1982, $556.8 million in 1983, and $588.2 million in 1984. During the 1982–1991 period, expenditures for new generating capacity alone were expected to total an additional $1.7 billion. The 1982 construction budget provided for expenditures of $270.3 million for generation facilities, $63.2 million for new business facilities, $27.6 million for transmission plant, $26.2 million for joint line and substation plant, $20.2 for distribution equipment, $63.5 million for general plant, and $74.5 million for nuclear fuel.

FINANCING CONSTRAINTS

A key factor affecting APC's ability to finance its construction program was the ratio of earnings to interest costs and to preferred stock dividends. These ratios were referred to in financial circles as "coverages." The mortgage indenture entered into by Alabama Power in 1942 (which the company had no authority to change without the consent of all bondholders) provided that the company's before-tax operating profit had to be great enough to cover pro forma annual interest charges on all first mortgage bonds outstanding by at least two times. Also, APC was prevented from issuing new first mortgage bonds if a new issue would cause its coverage to fall below two times earnings.

New preferred stock issues were forbidden if earnings were less than 1.5 times the total charges on indebtedness and on preferred stock dividend requirements. The coverage requirements for both bonds and preferred stock had to be met for a period of 12 consecutive months within the 15 calendar months immediately preceding any proposed new issue. The figures below show the company's year-end coverage ratios for recent years:

Year ended December 31	Earnings coverage on first mortgage bonds	Earnings coverage on preferred stock
1958	5.11	2.63
1964	4.70	2.58
1969	4.26	2.41
1970	3.31	2.03
1971	2.73	1.87
1972	2.23	1.61
1973	2.51	1.72
1974	1.66	1.36
1975	2.29	1.57
1976	1.61	1.37
1977	2.40	1.47
1978	1.51	1.14
1979	2.17	1.19
1980	2.59	1.51
1981	1.93	1.33

The deterioration in the company's coverages stemmed from higher interest rates on new securities issues, the large volume of new financing required to finance the company's construction program, and lagging earnings.

Rising interest rates posed a particular problem in meeting coverages. Whereas until the late 1960s the company was able to sell first mortgage bonds at interest rates in the 3–5 percent range, its most recently issued first mortgage bonds carried interest rates above 18 percent. Such increases, together with the fact that APC's long-term debt increased by $1.85 billion during the 1971–81 period, resulted in interest charges on long-term debt climbing from $33.2 million in 1971 to $199.8 million in 1981. Likewise, the combination of issuing $326 million in new preferred stock and paying dividends yields as high as 11.0 percent (versus 4 to 5 percent in the 1960s) caused dividend payments to jump from $4.8 million in 1971 to $36.1 million in 1981. Since each added dollar in bond interest and preferred stock dividends required an increase in operating earnings to maintain the company's coverage ratios, Alabama Power was caught again and again in a financial squeeze: inflationary forces kept driving up operating costs and cutting deeply into operating earnings at the same time that higher operating earnings were needed to keep financial coverages from falling. This squeeze prompted the company to file for higher rates in an effort to boost lagging operating earnings and falling coverages.

In February 1982, for the first time since December 1977, Alabama Power's earnings coverages on preferred stock were high enough to permit a new $40 million preferred stock issue. The company had three first mortgage bond issues in 1981: $100 million in January at an interest rate of 14.75 percent; a $75 million issue in April at an interest rate of $17.37 percent and $100 million in October at an interest rate of 18.25 percent. As of December 31, 1981 the average interest rate being paid on the company's $2.1 billion in outstanding first mortgage bonds was 10.04 percent, up from 8.3 percent in 1978.

CAPITAL STRUCTURE

Alabama Power's capital structure for selected years of the 1965–81 period was:

Year ended December 31	Long-term debt	Preferred stock	Common equity
1965	53.7%	10.6%	35.7%
1970	56.0	9.7	34.3
1975	55.9	10.9	33.2
1978	58.1	12.0	29.9
1981	59.2	10.4	30.4

Through 1981 The Southern Company had invested a total of $1.24 billion in the common equity capital of Alabama Power, of which $908 million had been invested since 1970.

A major concern of APC's management was the ratings on its first mortgage bonds and preferred stock. In 1975 and in early 1976, pending the decision by the Alabama PSC on the company's $106.8 million rate increase request, Moody's downgraded Alabama Power's preferred stock from A to Baa in December 1975. Standard & Poor's (S&P) rated both types of securities A−. However, following the PSC's denial of any part of the rate increase request (its first "zero order"), both agencies promptly downgraded their ratings on APC's first mortgage bonds: Moody's to Baa (lower medium grade) on both first mortgage bonds and on seven pollution-control issues, and S&P to BBB on both first mortgage bonds and preferred stock. The downgrading of the company's bonds from A (investment grade) to Baa not only meant lower interest rates on new bond issues but also the loss of a significant part of the market for the company's securities. A number of institutional investors (pension funds, insurance companies, savings banks) were precluded by law or by company policy from investing in securities below investment grade. In 1979 Moody's reduced Alabama Power's preferred stock rating to Ba, and S&P dropped its rating from BBB to BB. In 1982, the ratings were:

	Moody's	Standard & Poor's
First-Mortgage Bonds	Baa3	BBB−
Preferred Stock	Ba2	BB

The company's financial objectives included A ratings on both first mortgage bonds and preferred stock.

MARKETING AND ENERGY SERVICES

Even before the 1973 energy crisis, Alabama Power had stopped actively promoting greater usage of air conditioning because of the uneven load balance it created on the generating system between summer and winter months. During the 1960s and early 1970s, sharp increases in the use of air conditioning (both residential and commercial) caused the company to build new generating capacity to handle summer loads; however, this capacity went largely unused during the remaining months. To counter this, Alabama Power instituted several programs aimed at increasing off-peak loads so as to increase utilization of its facilities and to increase the revenues from its fixed investment. Programs were started to promote electric heating to increase the winter-time load factor and to promote dusk-to-dawn security lighting to increase the night-time load factor. The company's marketing goals of trying to balance the winter and summer peaks and to increase the overall load factor were undertaken because any resulting improvement in the utilization of existing facilities reduced average fixed costs per kilowatt hour.

Following the energy crisis in late 1973, Alabama Power's marketing efforts underwent significant change. Promoting greater use of electricity gave way to conservation themes. Advertising efforts were reduced and the whole marketing effort of the company was given lower priority. When the Alabama PSC turned down the company's entire rate increase request in June 1976, it also refused to consider advertising costs as an allowable expense in assessing APC's rate of return. The company responded by halting all media advertising, including ads which informed customers of ways to conserve electricity. The PSC's order on advertising was appealed to the Alabama Supreme Court and advertising was later resumed, although nearly all ads were conservation-oriented.

Alabama Power's marketing efforts between 1976 and 1982 centered on informing consumers of energy-saving practices; promoting the construction of energy-efficient "Good Cents" homes, apartments, and buildings; improving the handling of customer inquiries about rates, bills, and service; explaining to customers why the company was asking for higher rates; performing "energy audits" of customer facilities and recommending energy-conserving improvements; continuing to work closely with industrial and commercial customers; instituting load management programs; and conducting an active program of customer and market research. In 1978 the name of the Marketing Department was changed to "Energy Services." Similar name changes were made in the other sister companies of The Southern Company system. In late 1982, a decision was made to rename the Energy Services department at Alabama Power the "Marketing Department." The move to affix a "marketing label" once again to the activities of the Energy Services department was more than symbolic and similar actions were taken in the other sister companies of The Southern Company system.

In response to the requirements of the Public Utility Regulatory Policies Act passed by Congress in 1978, Alabama Power undertook a number of wide-ranging efforts in energy conservation and load management. With the exception of interruptible service agreements with several companies and a discount nighttime rate for industry, the company's efforts at load management were "passive" in the sense that they were based on the voluntary efforts of consumers to shift usage from peak to off-peak periods. "Active" load management and conservation efforts involved the aggressive use of price incentives to shift loads from on-peak to off-peak and the installation of remote-controlled devices on customer equipment which could be used by the electric utility to shut off power and reduce usage whenever peak loads strained system compatability.

Company surveys of residential customers confirmed widespread efforts to contain usage and hold down monthly bills—monthly residential electric bills averaged about $9 in 1967 versus $50 in 1981 and a projected $65 in 1983. A 1981 survey showed that 93 percent of the Company's residential customers had initiated efforts to conserve on electricity usage, up from 75 percent in 1977. Over 60 percent of the company's residential customers reported lowering their wintertime thermostat settings at night; some 47 percent had raised their summertime thermostat setting to 78°F or above; between 26 and 44 percent reported conservation efforts in using their electric range, water heaters, dishwashers, and dryers; and over 15 percent had upgraded their use of insulation and storm windows and doors.

Conservation and load management programs were, as of 1982, proving to be a mixed blessing to Alabama Power. On the positive side, many wasteful energy-use practices that had grown out of the cheap-energy era were on the wane and, to the extent that customers had instituted money-saving conservation measures, electric bills were lower than they might otherwise have been. The reductions in wasteful practices, price-induced conservation, and the introduction of more energy efficient products had all combined to slow down the growth in peak-loads, thereby allowing Alabama Power to trim its construction program and easing somewhat the severe financial strains that new construction costs posed during the years ahead.

But, on the negative side—at least from Alabama Power's standpoint, many conservation efforts had the effect of curtailing usage year-round rather than just at peak periods. The company's sharp rate increases had, within the last five years, begun to cut more and more into consumers' use of electricity during "shoulder" periods when adequate capacity was available. Growing numbers of Alabama Power's residential customers were using their air conditioners fewer hours per day and fewer days per year, as compared to past years when rates were much lower. When electricity was cheap it was common for household thermostats in Alabama to be set on 72°F year-round; this meant that in APC's service area air conditioning usage normally began in mid-April and continued until mid-to-late October. By 1982, however, more and more residential customers were switching to greater reliance on open windows, room fans, and attic fans during the late spring and early fall periods and, to some extent, even in mid-summer—at nights and on rainy or cloudy days when the heat and humidity subsided. During the winter months, electric heat customers were cutting back night-time thermostat settings to the 55°–65° range instead of leaving them at the waking hour setting. Many customers, both residential and commercial, had moved their summertime thermostat settings from 70°–72°F up to the 76°–80°F range and had shifted their wintertime settings down to the 65°–70°F range. Customer surveys in 1981 showed that 47 percent of residential customers with central air conditioning had set their thermostats at 78°F or above and over 45 percent of the electric heating customers had reduced their regular wintertime settings to 68°F or below. On the hottest summer days, however, virtually all air conditioners were in use and it was hard to see the impact of conservation during peak periods (although it was probable that daily peaks were lower than they might otherwise have been). The overall effect, though, was to produce loads which had narrower high-use periods and broader low-use periods.

Another problem Alabama Power was having from price-induced conservation concerned the slowdown in electric heat installations. In 1979 the company estimated that revenues from its residential and commercial electric heating users produced nearly $70 million in revenues over and above fuel costs, making a major contribution to operating income. The 20 percent of Alabama Power's residential customers with electric heating systems used almost 19,000 kwh annually compared to about 10,000 kwh for customers without electric heat. Yet, rate increases had hit electric heating users hard and had resulted, despite rising natural gas prices, in electric heating being generally perceived by the public as more costly than natural gas heating. Gas water heaters were also seen as more economical in APC's service area.

Generally speaking, the media coverage given to Alabama Power's rate increase requests and hearings at the PSC, as well as its appeals of PSC decisions to the Alabama Supreme Court, was substantially greater than for proposed increases in natural gas rates. This was thought to contribute to public perceptions about the relative cost of natural gas versus electricity and, also, about the size and frequency of future rate increases.

Marketing executives at Alabama Power were becoming concerned that the company was on the horns of a pricing dilemma. Future rate increases would be needed to cover the effects of inflation and to produce an adequate return on the company's investment in new plant and equipment. Yet, price-induced conservation measures were prompting a slowdown in kwh usage. At the same time, the PSC was pressing the company to adopt rate schedules which tended to make the average price per kwh more nearly equal across the three major classes of customers (residential, commercial, and industrial). Such approaches to pricing made it harder for the company to sell customers on using more electricity at off-peak periods when ample capacity was available.

There was considerable discussion both at the Company and at the PSC over how to price electricity across the three major customer classes. Alabama Power had presented cost of service studies to the Commission showing that its rates of return on sales to industrial and commercial customers were above its return on residential sales. There was sentiment within the company to set rates that would equalize the rate of return across the three classes. The PSC had not agreed to such equalization because it would mean further rate increases for APC's 869,000 residential customers. Industry representatives generally took the position that if rates had to be increased, then rates should be raised by the same percentage across all classes. Related to the question of industrial rates was the issue of whether and to what extent to keep Alabama Power's rates in line with those of surrounding states so as (1) not to competitively disadvantage firms located in Alabama and (2) to enhance Alabama's ability to attract new industry to locate in the state.

STRATEGIC PLANS

Alabama Power's current strategic plan contained the following statement regarding the marketing and energy services area:

> Current conditions require that emphasis be placed on policies for pricing of products and services to enable achievement of the financial goals for the Company, equity among customers, and the promotion of wise and efficient use of energy. However, since revenue requirements, as dictated by regulation are based on embedded costs which are significantly less than the incremental cost of providing service, pricing alone cannot be relied upon. Active marketing and customer service programs which provide customer education in regard to the wise and efficient use of electricity are crucial complements to pricing policy. Such programs can minimize long-range capital expenditures of the Company while fostering customer understanding and acceptance.
>
> Investigation of the Company's existing markets for new products and services, as well as unregulated business ventures, may also offer opportunities to improve the earnings position of the Company.

The company's strategic plan specified the following marketing area goals:

1 To maximize the contribution that all products and services make to the Company's earnings.
  a To explore continuously and take full advantage of each profitable opportunity to provide energy or energy-related products and services, including the formation of unregulated subsidiary organizations or other legal entities as means of conducting such business.
  b To identify, evaluate, and implement programs to "recapture" 800,000 kw of generating capacity by 1992 (Note: recapture programs involved ways to promote the installation of new equipment that used fewer kw of capacity while providing the same benefits—i.e., switching out an old central air conditioning unit or heat pump for a new high EER unit could result in the recapture of as much as 1.5 kw of generating capacity.)
  c To identify and assign priority to those energy uses which provide the potential to improve the Company's earnings.
  d To continue to identify and seek those industries which will provide maximum benefit to the State and the Company.
2 To price the products and services provided by the Company to enable the achievement of the financial goals of the Company, equity among customers, and the promotion of wise and efficient use of energy.
  a To develop and apply rate structures, policies, and procedures by 1990 which, to the maximum extent practicable, reflect cost and operational realities of the Company.

3 To maintain surveillance of or participation in technological developments which may impact on corporate activities and, as an outgrowth of such developments, to implement cost-effective applications within the Company on a timely basis.

Top management at Alabama Power was acutely aware of the challenges of the years ahead—the need to provide dependable electric service at a price producing a reasonable profit, the growing price and use sensitivity of customers, the ever-tightening web of regulation and restraints, and the importance of developing responses to emerging technological developments. The "acid rain" issue also loomed high on APC's management agenda. Since Alabama Power depended heavily on coal-fired generation, any new evidence that acid rain was a "real" environmental problem and that coal-fired power plants contributed heavily to acid rain pollution could mean important new environmental regulations. Alabama Power and Southern Company officials estimated that the added investment in pollution control equipment which might be needed to comply with the new regulations being studied and discussed relative to acid rain could run into the billions of dollars at the Southern Company and lead to as much as a 25 percent increase in electric rates (on top of other rate increases which the company foresaw might be needed). Executives viewed the company's future as being in energy. The recently adopted 1982 strategic plan stated that the company's mission was:

> To provide, at a price producing a reasonable profit, energy and energy-related products and services to all customers within areas we serve, at levels of service commensurate with fairness of price regulation.

The core of the Alabama Power's current strategy contained six elements:

1 Continue to file rate increase requests as necessary to cover the rising costs of providing electric service and pursue all reasonable legal procedures if adequate rate increases are not granted.

2 Seek the passage of legislation to promote fair and equitable treatment by the PSC.

3 Develop ways to improve the utilization of existing facilities.

4 Seek out temporary markets for capacity and energy sales beyond the Company's traditional territorial boundaries.

5 Research and analyze alternatives to existing and future energy sources and energy uses.

6 Focus marketing efforts on those products and services which have the best prospects of improving company profitability.

The company aspired to earn at least a 14.5 percent return on equity investment in 1983, with progressive increases to 18.0 percent by 1988. In the short run, the company's prospects for achieving its profit targets hinged on the size of the rate increases which it was granted. But management realized that depending on rate increases over the long-term posed major risks. When to begin the process of realigning short-term strategy to fit the emerging longer-term market and competitive realities and what form the long-range strategy should take was thus very much on the minds of Alabama Power's top management.

DISCUSSION QUESTIONS

1 Explain the process of utility rate regulation in Alabama as it relates to Alabama Power Company.
2 Evaluate the six elements of Alabama Power Company's current strategy. What changes would you recommend? Why?
3 Explain the relationship between the proposed rate increases for Alabama Power Company and the public's long term need for electrical power.
4 List the legitimate constituencies of Alabama Power Company management and explain the company's obligation to each.
5 As a member of the public service commission, upon what bases would you approve or disapprove Alabama Power's $324.9 million rate increase request filed in March 1981?

MILLER BREWING COMPANY

Lloyd L. Byars
Atlanta University

SELECTED STRATEGIC ISSUES

- Synergies between merger partners and their impact on postmerger success
- Product differentiation of a relatively homogeneous product to appeal to differing market segments
- Social justification for increased promotional expenditures
- Evaluation of a company's mix of businesses according to the Boston Consulting Group (BCG) business portfolio matrix
- Strategic management implications of industry life-cycle stages faced by strategic business units
- Social responsibilities of companies which sell potentially harmful products
- Relationship between elements of success and preferred future strategies

Miller Brewing Company was founded in 1855 by Frederic Miller, a 31-year-old former German brewmaster. Miller toured America for almost one year before selecting Milwaukee as the location to start his brewery. Miller purchased a small, idle brewery located west of Milwaukee. This small brewery was originally built in 1850 and was called the Plank Road Brewery. The brewing operation was discontinued in 1853 and the plant had been idle until Frederic Miller bought it in 1855 for $8,000. The

Research assistance on this case was provided by Barbara Jackson, Sheila Jordan, and Carole Riley. All are graduates of the Atlanta University, Graduate School of Business Administration.

266

plant had a capacity of 1200 barrels per year, but during its first year of operation Miller only produced 300 barrels of beer.

Frederic Miller's philosophy on brewing was to produce a product of uncompromising and unchanging quality. Miller also sought to expand the availability of Miller Beer into beer gardens and taverns throughout the Milwaukee area and also in eight surrounding states. Beer was dispensed on tap in these popular social centers, and thus Miller became a familiar fixture. Miller's strategy was to encourage people to "gather together to share the events of the day and savor the rich, good taste of Miller Beer."

Due to the popularity of his beer and the growing demand, Miller expanded his output capacity in 1870 by building a new brick brewery. By 1880, the plant was producing about 30,000 barrels a year. In 1883, Miller established his first bottling plant; within three years this plant was bottling 5000 of Miller's 80,000 barrels per year. Miller also constructed seven icehouses in the Chicago, Waukesha, and Milwaukee areas for the storage of his beer.

After Frederic Miller's death in 1888, his eldest son Ernest and a son-in-law, Carl A. Miller, took over the management of the company and effectively continued Frederic Miller's philosophy of business. The brewery continued to grow in size, capacity, product line, and sales volume.

In 1903, a contest was held to name Miller's premium beer, resulting in the name Miller High Life and the slogan "the champagne of bottled beer." The name remains today, but the slogan has since been phased out. Miller High Life's fame was also aided by the introduction of the girl-in-the-moon symbol for the beer. Much speculation surrounds the reason for the use of this symbol. However, the primary reason seems to be that it gave beer drinkers the impression that Miller High Life was the beer that was in keeping with the "high times" that existed at the turn of the century.

By the beginning of Prohibition in 1920, Miller was producing more than 0.5 million barrels a year. However, with the ratification of the Eighteenth Amendment, production of alcoholic beverages ceased and Miller faced a major crisis in its corporate life. The Miller family made the decision to keep the name of the company alive and began producing a line of products that included a cereal beverage, malt tonic, health drink, and carbonated soft drinks. All of these products carried the Miller label.

During the Prohibition era, Ernest Miller died and his younger brother, Frederick A. Miller, assumed the presidency of the company. With the aid of his sister and subsequent successor, Elsie Kay John, Frederick A. Miller reopened the brewery at the end of Prohibition. They immediately recognized that the end of Prohibition would open up new markets for beer and also realized that these new markets would require new marketing and production techniques. Under their leadership the company moved to adapt to the changed conditions, but it never sacrificed the quality of its products. In fact, management described its task to be positioning Miller High Life as one of "America's favorite pasttimes."

In 1947, Frederick C. Miller, the grandson of the founder, became president of the company. He succeeded Harry G. John, Jr., who followed his mother as president but only served for a short period of time. Under Frederick C. Miller's leadership, the company developed a major expansion program, including the construction of a brewhouse and three aging and fermenting cellars. He developed an aggressive merchandising and advertising campaign targeted primarily at the home consumption market. Miller was one of the first national brewers to concentrate on this market segment; as a result, the home consumption market was a significant factor in the growth of the company during the late forties and fifties. During this time, Miller also implemented policies that resulted in Miller Brewing Company becoming actively involved in community affairs projects. Miller High Life's sales increased dramatically, output nearly quadrupled, and the company moved from twentieth to ninth place nationwide. In December 1954, Frederick C. Miller and his son, Fred, Jr., died in an airplane crash.

Norman R. Klug succeeded Frederick C. Miller as president of the Miller Brewing Company. This was the first time in the history of the company that the president of the company was not directly related to the Miller family. Klug continued Miller Brewing Company's fundamental growth strategy by expanding the brewery's production facilities. This was accomplished largely through the acquisition of General Brewing Corporation's plant in Azusa, Calif. Despite this expansion program, production remained relatively constant and the company experienced very little real growth.

In September 1966, W. R. Grace & Company purchased controlling interest in the Miller Brewing Company, and following the death of Norman Klug, later that year Charles W. Miller (unrelated to the original family) was named president. Also during 1966, the company purchased Carling Brewing Company located in Fort Worth, Tex. Throughout the next three years, renovation and expansion of the newly acquired plant increased Miller's production capabilities to over 1 million barrels per year. In May 1969, J. Peter Grace, president of Grace, told the annual stockholders' meeting that W. R. Grace had decided to sell its Miller interest "because at the time of purchase, we expected to acquire the remaining 47 percent interest in Miller; however, in the intervening period, we have concluded that this holding will not be sold to us at any time. This situation, we feel, is undesirable as it handicaps the development of the full potential of this business." The remaining 47 percent of the shares of Miller Brewing was owned by the De Rance Foundation in Milwaukee.

Later that same month, PepsiCo offered W. R. Grace $120 million for its 53 percent interest in Miller. W. R. Grace initially accepted the offer, but in early June the company did an about-face and rejected the offer. On June 12, 1969, Philip Morris, Inc., purchased W. R. Grace's 53 percent ownership in Miller for $130 million. PepsiCo filed suit in the District Court for the Southern District of New York challenging the sale of Miller Brewing to Philip Morris. PepsiCo charged that Philip Morris and W. R. Grace had violated Securities and Exchange Commission (SEC) rules by failing to disclose material facts about their negotiations. PepsiCo asked that the sale be voided so that it could purchase Miller. W. R. Grace stated that the suit was "utterly without substance."

In January 1970, a federal judge dismissed the PepsiCo suit against W. R. Grace. In a statement, the judge said the PepsiCo had failed to prove its contention that the sale of the 53 percent interest in Miller to Philip Morris had violated the SEC laws. Later that same year, Philip Morris acquired the remaining 47 percent interest in Miller from the De Rance Foundation for $97 million, making Miller a wholly owned subsidiary of Philip Morris.

In late 1971, John A. Murphy became chief executive officer of Miller. Philip Morris also replaced the experienced beer managers at Miller with "homegrown cigarette marketers." The philosophy of these cigarette people was that beer and cigarettes have a great deal in common. Their philosophy on the beer and cigarette business was:

> Both are low-priced, pleasurable products made from agricultural commodities that are processed and packaged on high-speed machinery. Both are advertised the same way and are sold to many of the same end use customers through similar distribution channels. Your beer drinker and your cigarette smoker are often the same guy.

Since the purchase of Miller by Philip Morris, Miller's sales have grown from 5.2 million barrels to 35.8 million barrels and its market share has increased from 4.0 percent in 1972 to 20.8 percent in 1979.

In 1982, William K. Howell, president of Miller Brewing Company, characterized the growth and development that began in 1971 as follows:

> The change in the brewing industry began in October, 1971, when Philip Morris Inc., changed the management of Miller Brewing Company. But it took about two years for the change to show up as a real change in direction of the company and the industry. When the change was finally felt, beginning in 1973, it was explosive.
>
> Miller quickly shot up in sales and position, moving from seventh in the industry in 1972 to second place in 1977. Since 1972, we've increased shipments by 566 percent.

PRODUCT LINE (1972–1982)

During the seventies, the new management of Miller has followed a strategy of introducing several new brands. Its present product line includes the traditional Miller High Life, Lite Beer, Lowenbrau, Miller Special Reserve, and Magnum Malt Liquor.

Miller High Life is Miller's leading brand of beer and is currently the second-largest revenue-generating national premium brand in the industry. Initially marketed as the "champagne of bottled beers," Miller was targeted to occasional beer drinkers—the beer drinking elite. However, the new management at Miller changed the positioning strategy to include a new group of beer drinkers and not just the "country club set." The "champagne of bottled beer" slogan was changed to "time to relax" with the purpose of positioning the beer to sports oriented and blue collar types of drinkers: "an audience of the 30 percent of the consumers who drink 80 percent of the beer." High Life is presented to the new target market in TV advertising featuring "real people doing real jobs—and being rewarded at the end of their day with Miller Time: a time to relax and enjoy the best tasting beer you can find—If you've got the time, we've got the beer." In 1972, High Life was offered in the 7-oz. pony bottle. High Life is also offered in 12-oz. returnable and nonreturnable bottles, 12- and 16-oz. cans, 1-qt. bottles, and on draft.

Lite Beer from Miller has been acclaimed to be the most successful beer ever introduced in the history of the brewing industry. The Lite brand name was acquired in 1972 when Miller bought the trade name and distribution network of Meister Brau, Inc. of Chicago. Meister Brau Lite was one of the first low-calorie beers. Miller modified Meister Brau's formula, and according to the management of Miller, the big difference is that Lite actually tastes like beer.

Previous attempts to introduce low-calorie beers into the market place were characterized by appeals aimed at the diet-conscious consumer. Miller's sales pitch communicated its message through the use of "convincing beer drinking personalities" such as Mickey Spillane; baseball's Whitey Ford, Mickey Mantle, and Billy Martin; and football's Dick Butkus and Bubba Smith. "The typical beer drinker is not dietetically oriented, but when he sees a football player drinking this low-calorie beer, he figures he shouldn't be ashamed to drink it." The Lite Beer promotion (with "a third less calories than one regular beer") also suggests that the beer is not as filling as other beers; therefore, more Lite Beer can be consumed.

Since its introduction in 1973, Lite has become the third-best-selling brand of beer in the United States. Packaging for Lite includes 7-oz. nonreturnable bottles, 12-oz. returnable and nonreturnable bottles, 12- and 16-oz. cans., 1-qt. bottles, and on draft.

Lowenbrau Special and Dark Special are two other Miller products. The Lowenbrau brands were first brewed in Munich, Germany, in 1383 in the Lowenbrau Brewery, one of the most highly recognized names in the world. In April 1974, Miller Brewing Company entered into an agreement with the German brewery and acquired importation rights for Lowenbrau beer. In 1975, Miller was allowed to brew and market a domestic Lowenbrau in the United States. Lowenbrau was then introduced nationally in 1977.

As a super-premium beer, Lowenbrau is marketed as a beer "to be enjoyed on special occasions shared with special friends—Tonight, let it be Lowenbrau." Both the Special and Dark Special are packaged in foil-wrapped, 12-oz. nonreturnable bottles and on draft. In addition, the Special is distributed in 7-oz. bottles, called the *cub*.

Magnum Malt Liquor was Miller's first entry into the special market segment of malt liquor drinkers. In February 1981, Miller began testing the product in Atlanta and Savannah, Ga., Portland, Oreg., Birmingham, Ala., and Greensboro, N.C. The test results indicated that Magnum had the potential to capture a sizable portion of the malt liquor market and had strong acceptance by loyal malt liquor drinkers.

Magnum is primarily targeted at 18- to 25-year-old males. This audience accounts for nearly two-thirds of the total malt liquor drinkers. It's current sales theme suggests to malt liquor drinkers "to get on the M-train . . . it's your ticket to ride."

Miller's decision to go after the malt liquor market was based on their increased production capacity. President William Howell stated:

> It is not a new market for the company. We had Miller Malt out there in the early 1970s, but had to discontinue it during our rapid growth years to provide additional capacity for Miller High Life and Lite brands. In fact, the basic formula for Miller Malt proved very successful against current competition in our tests, and it was refined to produce Magnum. We are going back after that business because we now have the capacity to deliver Magnum at the highest consistent quality to this special market wherever it exists.

In 1981, Miller introduced another super-premium beer, Miller Special Reserve. At the launching of Miller Special Reserve, Miller Executive Vice-President Lauren Williams stated:

EXHIBIT 1   PRINCIPAL BRANDS OF MAJOR BREWERS

Company	Premium brands	Super-premium brands	Light brands	Imported brands
Anheuser-Busch	Budweiser	Michelob	Michelob Light Natural Light	Wurzburger Holbrau
Miller	Miller High Life	Lowenbrau	Lite	Munich Oktoberfest
Schlitz	Schlitz	Erlanger	Schlitz Light Old Milwaukee Light	—
Pabst	Pabst Blue Ribbon	Andeker	Pabst Extra Light	Fuerstenberg
Coors	Coors	Herman Joseph's 1868	Coors Light	Stella Artois
Heileman	Old Style Rainier	Special Export	Several entries	Beck's

Source: Company reports.

It was for those millions of beer drinkers who want the full, rich taste and extra quality of a super-premium brand on a regular basis. We feel that Miller Special Reserve will add a new dimension to our existing line of high-quality brands. Its entry into the market will enable us to cover the entire spectrum of the super-premium segment, one of the fastest growing segments in the beer industry.

Miller's advertising theme for Special Reserve is "Taste the Best in Life."

Between 1979 and 1981, Miller test marketed Munich Oktoberfest, an imported dark beer. This beer is brewed by Lowenbrau Brewery, which is the same company from which Miller had originally obtained Lowenbrau. Oktoberfest was test marketed in Boston and Washington, D.C. The test results were disappointing and, as of today, no decision seems to have been made on what to do with Oktoberfest. Exhibit 1 summarizes the principal brands of the major brewers by market segment.

PRODUCTION AND DISTRIBUTION

Miller has breweries located in Milwaukee, Wis.; Fort Worth, Tex.; Fulton, N.Y.; Eden, N.C.; Albany, Ga.; and Irwindale, Calif. A brewery was completed in Trenton, Ohio, in 1982. Canning facilities are located in Milwaukee, Wis., Fort Worth, Tex., Fulton, N.Y., Reidsville, N.C., and Moultrie, Ga. A bottling plant is located in Sennett, N.Y.

Description of Breweries

- *Milwaukee, Wis.* Oldest brewery and has a capacity of 9 million barrels annually
- *Fort Worth, Tex.* Purchased from Carling Brewing Company in 1966 and has a capacity of 8 million barrels annually
- *Fulton, N.Y.* Capacity of 10 million barrels annually
- *Eden, N.C.* Capacity of 10 million barrels annually

- *Albany, Ga.* Capacity of 10 million barrels annually
- *Trenton, Ohio* Capacity of 10 million barrels annually

Miller products are sold and delivered to retailers by a network of 800 independent distributors. Miller products can be purchased in all 50 states, Puerto Rico, St. Thomas, and 82 foreign countries. Miller also has its own company-owned distributorships in Milwaukee, Wis., New Orleans, La., Los Angeles, Calif., Salt Lake City, Utah, and Poughkeepsie, N.Y.

Distributors receive their beer shipments by truck and rail and use their own fleet of trucks to service retail accounts. To help its distributors, Miller has a sales force of 150 area managers operating from twelve regional headquarters. The sales force personnel help the distributors maintain proper inventories, work with retailers to obtain adequate shelf space for greatest product visibility, and conduct in-house training programs for the distributors' sales personnel.

One innovative technique developed by Miller marketing personnel is the Vertibrand system. The Vertibrand system is basically a method of arranging beer vertically by brand and horizontally by package. This provides an appealing arrangement for the customer, makes brand selection easier, and, more importantly, enables the retailers to utilize shelf space more effectively.

ADVERTISING

Before 1976, only certain brands such as Miller High Life and Anheuser-Busch's Michelob had very high per-barrel advertising expenditures. In 1976, however, the nature of advertising expenditures, particularly by the larger brewers, changed dramatically. Advertising on many major brands doubled, and with the introduction of large numbers of new brands, particularly in the light beer market, overall advertising expenditures increased dramatically. Miller's advertising for Miller High Life increased 230 percent to $29.7 million in 1976. High Life became the most heavily advertised brand in 1979. Miller Lite advertising increased between 1976 and 1978 by 58 percent, making Lite the third most heavily advertised beer. Advertising on Lowenbrau increased from $11.3 million in 1978 to $17 million in 1979. This is an almost unbelievable $16.97 per barrel.

In a listing of the ten most advertised beers, Miller has three brands in the top ten. No other brewer, with the exception of Anheuser-Busch, has more than one beer on the list. Miller's president, William Howell stated in 1981:

> We have built our success by doing our homework, finding out what beer consumers want and then delivering it. We have worked hard. We have been innovators in product, merchandising and advertising. Our most visible competitive act has been to advertise on television. Those commercials have been called some of the highest quality in American advertising history. We believe that just as American consumers deserve the highest quality beer, they ought to have those beers presented to them with the highest quality advertising. Our television commercials broke new ground in this industry because they were filmed with the same high quality film technique as a feature length film. No expense was spared.

FINANCES

Philip Morris, Miller's parent company, conducts business through six operating companies: Philip Morris, U.S.A.; Philip Morris International; Miller Brewing Company; The Seven-Up Company; Philip Morris Industrial; and Mission Viejo Company. Exhibit 2 gives a brief description of each of the subsidiaries and the operating revenues and income for each. Exhibit 3 gives a 15-year financial review for Philip Morris and its subsidiaries. Exhibit 4 provides the gross profit margin ratio for five years for each of the subsidiaries. The gross profit margin is calculated by subtracting the cost of goods sold from total sales and dividing this figure by total sales. Exhibit 5 gives the contribution to total revenue for each of the subsidiaries. Exhibit 6 gives the operating income as a percent of sales for several of the leading brewers.

Over the last ten years, Miller's operating revenues have increased at an average annual compound rate of 29 percent. During 1978, an increase in beer revenue resulted from both volume and price increases. Miller's income was reduced in 1980 due to the industry's competitive pricing environment and brewery start-up costs.

EXHIBIT 2

DESCRIPTION OF PHILIP MORRIS'S SUBSIDIARIES AND OPERATING REVENUES AND INCOME FOR EACH
(In Millions)

	Operating revenues	Operating income			Operating revenues	Operating income
Philip Morris U.S.A.[a]				**The Seven-Up Company**[d]		
1980	$3,272.1	$786.1		1980	$ 353.2	$ (7.1)
1979	2,767.0	701.3		1979	295.5	7.0
1978	2,437.5	568.1		1978	274.8	40.3
1977	2,160.4	474.4		1977	231.7	41.8
1976	1,963.1	401.4		1976	217.4	42.0
Philip Morris International[b]				**Philip Morris Industrial**[e]		
1980	$3,205.4	$328.5		1980	$ 276.5	$ 16.9
1979	2,581.3	260.6		1979	268.8	18.3
1978	1,810.9	188.6		1978	237.2	15.0
1977	1,349.3	153.8		1977	216.7	14.9
1976	1,084.0	130.1		1976	169.1	10.6
Miller Brewing Company[c]				**Mission Viejo Company**[f]		
1980	$2,542.3	$144.7		1980	$ 172.8	$ 30.6
1979	2,236.5	181.0		1979	153.8	22.4
1978	1,834.5	150.3		1978	125.9	19.8
1977	1,327.6	106.4		1977	148.0	33.2
1976	982.8	76.1		1976	94.8	16.3

[a] Markets Marlboro, Benson & Hedges, Parliament, Virginia Slims, and Merit cigarettes in the United States. Largest selling brand is Marlboro.
[b] Markets cigarette products of Philip Morris in more than 170 countries and territories.
[c] See case discussion for description of company.
[d] Markets 7UP and Diet 7UP in the soft drink industry.
[e] Markets specialty papers, packaging materials, tissues, and specialty chemical products in the United States and Europe.
[f] Plans and develops homes in southern California and Colorado.

EXHIBIT 3 15-YEAR FINANCIAL REVIEW OF PHILIP MORRIS AND ITS OPERATING SUBSIDIARIES
(In Millions, Except Per-Share Amounts)

	1980	1979	1978	1977	1976	1975
Summary of operations:						
Operating revenues	$ 9,822.3	8,302.9	6,632.5	5,202.0	4,293.8	3,642.4
Cost of sales						
Cost of products sold	4,567.3	3,778.7	3,072.1	2,401.7	1,966.9	1,656.8
Federal excise taxes	1,105.3	1,036.8	960.8	862.1	778.2	686.3
Foreign excise taxes	1,388.7	1,122.0	702.8	490.4	381.1	392.1
Operating income	1,299.7	1,190.6	968.1	782.7	634.5	492.8
Interest expense	215.0	205.5	149.8	101.6	102.8	99.0
Earnings before income taxes	969.8[a]	905.4	745.5	625.5	471.9	360.8
Pre-tax profit margins	9.9%	10.9%	11.2%	12.0%	11.0%	9.9%
Provision for income taxes	393.0	397.5	336.9	290.6	206.3	149.2
Net earnings	576.8[a]	507.9	408.6	334.9	265.7	211.6
Primary earnings per common share	4.63[a]	4.08	3.38	2.80	2.24	1.81
Fully diluted earnings per common share	4.63[a]	4.08	3.38	2.80	2.24	1.81
Dividends declared per common share	1.60	1.25	1.025	0.781	.575	0.463
Weighted average shares—primary	124.6	124.5	120.7	119.6	118.8	116.9
Weighted average shares—fully diluted	124.6	124.5	120.7	119.6	118.8	116.9
Capital expenditures	755.7	632.0	566.2	279.8	220.2	244.5
Annual depreciation	176.1	133.9	105.5	78.5	64.9	49.9
Property, plant and equipment (gross)	3,547.5	2,825.1	2,217.3	1,594.9	1,323.9	1,129.8
Property, plant and equipment (net)	2,813.9	2,229.5	1,737.6	1,202.4	993.9	851.1
Inventories	2,711.7	2,371.3	2,188.6	1,817.6	1,657.5	1,448.4
Current assets	3,410.1	3,028.3	2,756.8	2,221.0	2,005.7	1,788.1
Working capital	1,849.3	1,833.2	1,585.1	1,415.9	1,202.2	890.8
Total assets	7,366.4	6,378.9	5,608.2	4,048.0	3,582.2	3,134.3
Total debt	2,801.1	2,516.4	2,372.2	1,563.5	1,525.6	1,443.3
Stockholders' equity	2,853.0	2,471.0	2,114.7	1,690.1	1,430.0	1,227.8
Net earnings reinvested	377.9	352.3	283.8	253.7	197.2	157.1
Common dividends declared as percentage of net earnings	34.6%	30.6%	30.6%	27.9%	25.7%	25.7%
Book value per common share	22.87	19.84	17.00	14.08	12.00	10.32
Market price of common share high–low	$48\frac{1}{2}$–$29\frac{1}{8}$	$38\frac{5}{8}$–$31\frac{1}{8}$	$38\frac{3}{8}$–28	$32\frac{1}{2}$–$25\frac{3}{4}$	$31\frac{5}{8}$–$24\frac{7}{8}$	$29\frac{5}{8}$–$20\frac{1}{2}$
Closing price year-end	$43\frac{1}{4}$	36	$35\frac{1}{4}$	31	$30\frac{7}{8}$	$26\frac{1}{2}$
Price-earnings ratio year-end	9	8	10	11	13	14
Number of common shares—actual year-end	124.8	124.5	124.3	119.8	119.0	118.7

[a] During 1980 the Company adopted the last-in, first-out (LIFO) method of costing the leaf tobacco components of its inventories in the United States. Had this change in inventory costing not occurred, earnings before income taxes, net earnings, and earnings per share for the year 1980 would have been $1,091.5 million (+20.6%), $638.6 million (+25.7%) and $5.12 (+25.5%), respectively.

MARKET ANALYSIS

The coming decade is generally forecasted to be a different and more competitive one for the beer industry. Between 1980 and 1985, sales are expected to increase approximately 3½ to 4 percent per year. Between 1985 and 1990, an even slower growth of 3 percent per year is forecast. The major reason for this forecasted slowdown is the unfavorable shift in demographics that indicates the number of persons reaching the legal drinking age each year is expected to decline. Exhibit 7 shows the legal drinking

1974	1973	1972	1971	1970	1969	1968	1967	1966
3,011.0	2,602.5	2,131.2	1,852.5	1,509.5	1,142.4	1,019.8	904.8	772.0
1,290.3	1,060.8	832.9	700.0	577.1	454.7	409.9	363.1	311.8
619.5	558.9	494.8	441.1	372.1	319.1	295.9	271.1	235.0
349.4	334.5	228.2	201.4	147.1	54.2	41.8	39.7	30.1
403.6	329.5	287.5	241.1	203.2	153.2	126.2	101.8	81.9
82.7	51.0	37.9	35.5	35.4	28.6	15.9	10.2	8.1
297.5	255.6	229.6	189.8	150.0	115.6	100.1	81.3	65.1
9.9%	9.8%	10.8%	10.2%	9.9%	10.1%	9.8%	9.0%	8.4%
122.0	107.0	105.2	88.3	72.5	57.3	51.2	37.7	31.0
175.5	148.6	124.5	101.5	77.5	58.3	48.9	43.6	34.2
1.58	1.35	1.17	1.00	0.84	0.64	0.55	0.49	0.38
1.53	1.30	1.09	0.91	0.71	0.60	0.53	0.49	0.38
0.388	0.337	0.316	0.303	0.263	0.244	0.213	0.175	0.175
111.3	109.6	106.0	100.3	91.2	89.1	87.7	86.7	
114.7	114.6	114.5	113.1	113.2	99.1	90.1	88.0	
215.8	174.7	120.0	68.0	39.6	23.6	26.4	25.7	17.1
38.0	30.2	26.6	21.5	17.7	13.5	12.1	10.9	9.5
899.8	728.7	571.1	447.1	394.1	237.0	219.3	193.7	172.6
659.5	510.3	373.4	274.1	236.7	147.4	138.7	123.6	110.2
1,269.2	1,009.4	801.1	670.2	568.4	447.3	451.9	386.6	297.8
1,557.9	1,245.9	989.7	826.5	728.8	575.0	561.7	485.9	372.9
725.0	515.3	524.8	417.6	347.7	315.9	312.4	306.2	253.3
2,653.3	2,108.4	1,701.5	1,392.0	1,239.4	976.5	786.6	649.0	512.5
1,239.3	947.4	681.0	553.9	557.7	490.4	354.8	256.4	161.0
974.7	815.0	695.5	579.1	452.8	355.8	314.5	280.2	249.8
131.9	111.4	89.9	69.7	52.2	35.7	29.2	27.5	18.2
24.8%	25.0%	27.2%	30.6%	31.6%	37.4%	38.4%	34.9%	44.2%
8.48	7.33	6.28	5.36	4.47	3.70	3.28	2.94	2.62
$30\frac{3}{4}$-$17\frac{1}{8}$	$34\frac{1}{4}$-$24\frac{3}{8}$	$29\frac{5}{8}$-17	$17\frac{3}{4}$-$11\frac{3}{4}$	$12\frac{5}{8}$-7	$9\frac{1}{8}$-$6\frac{1}{4}$	$8\frac{3}{8}$-$5\frac{1}{2}$	$7\frac{1}{4}$-4	$4\frac{1}{4}$-$3\frac{1}{8}$
24	$28\frac{3}{4}$	$29\frac{3}{8}$	$17\frac{7}{8}$	$12\frac{3}{8}$	9	8	$5\frac{5}{8}$	$4\frac{1}{4}$
15	21	25	17	14	13	14	11	11
114.5	110.8	108.9	104.7	96.6	90.3	88.8	87.3	86.5

EXHIBIT 4   GROSS PROFIT MARGIN RATIO
(Percent)

Subsidiary	1976	1977	1978	1979	1980
Philip Morris U.S.A.	20.4	22.0	23.3	25.3	24.0
Philip Morris International	12.0	11.4	10.4	10.1	10.3
Miller Brewing Company	7.5	8.0	8.2	8.3	5.4
The Seven-Up Company	19.0	18.0	14.7	2.4	− 2.0
Philip Morris Industrial	6.0	6.9	6.3	6.8	6.1
Mission Viejo Company	17.2	22.4	15.7	14.6	17.7

EXHIBIT 5   CONTRIBUTION TO OPERATING REVENUE
(Percent)

Subsidiary	1976	1977	1978	1979	1980
Philip Morris U.S.A.	45.7	41.5	36.7	33.3	33.3
Philip Morris International	25.2	25.9	27.3	31.1	32.6
Miller Brewing Company	22.9	25.5	27.6	26.9	25.9
The Seven-Up Company			2.8	3.6	3.6
Philip Morris Industrial	3.9	4.2	3.6	3.2	2.8
Mission Viejo Company	2.2	2.8	1.9	1.9	1.8

EXHIBIT 6   OPERATING INCOME
(Percent of Sales)

Company	1976	1977	1978	1979
Anheuser-Busch	11.6	13.4	12.8	11.6
Coors	30.1	26.0	20.4	20.7
Miller	7.7	8.0	8.2	8.9
Pabst	12.6	10.5	7.0	7.6
Schlitz	14.5	10.9	9.0	4.1

age throughout the United States. Increasing consumption by older customers should compensate somewhat for the shrinkage in the younger customer base.

Of the six major beer market segments, four will grow in the next decade, one will decline sharply, and one will remain stable (see Exhibit 8). The popular beer market is undergoing a long-term decline caused principally by changes in the tastes of the consuming public. From its current 23 percent of the market, popular beers are forecasted to drop to a mere 5 percent of the market in 1990. Furthermore, barrelage will drop from 39 million in 1979 to just 13 million in 1990, a 66 percent loss in total volume.

Competition within the beer industry has been and will probably continue to be determined by Anheuser-Busch and Miller. Over the years the number of breweries has dropped from over 700 companies to just 45 companies in 1981. It is estimated Anheuser-Busch and Miller will probably control 59 percent of the market by 1985 and 63 percent thereafter. Anheuser-Busch and Miller are forecasted to increase their combined shipments by 88 percent, or 72 million barrels, by 1990. Beer consumption, however, will only grow by a total of 73 million barrels. Imports will increase by 17 million barrels, indicating a net deficit of 16 million barrels for the rest of the United States industry. Exhibit 9 gives the forecasted sales of the leading two, five, and ten brewers. Exhibit 10 gives the share of the United States market for the major brewers through 1980, Exhibit 11 gives the share of the market trends for the leading beer brands. Exhibit 12 gives the percentage of the light beer market for the leading light beer brands.

EXHIBIT 7   LEGAL DRINKING AGE

State	21	20	19	18	State	21	20	19	18
Alabama				A	Montana		A		
Alaska				A	Nebraska^d		A		
Arizona				A	Nevada	A			
Arkansas	A				New Hampshire				A
California	A				New Jersey				A
Colorado	A			B	New Mexico	A			
Connecticut				A	New York				A
Delaware		A			North Carolina	A			
District of Columbia	A			C	North Dakota	A			
Florida			A		Ohio	A			
Georgia^a			A		Oklahoma	A			
Hawaii				A	Oregon	A			
Idaho			A		Pennsylvania	A			
Illinois	A		E		Rhode Island		A		
Indiana	A				South Carolina	A			E
Iowa			A		South Dakota				B
Kansas	A			B	Tennessee				A
Kentucky	A				Texas				A
Louisiana				A	Utah	A			
Maine		A			Vermont				A
Maryland	A				Virginia	A			
Massachusetts				A	Washington	A			
Michigan^b	A				West Virginia				A
Minnesota^c			A		Wisconsin				A
Mississippi	A				Wyoming			A	
Missouri	A								

Key: A = all beverages; B = 3.2 beverages; C = wine not over 14% volume and beer; D = beer not over 4% weight; E = beer and wine.
^a Excluding military, which is 18.
^b 18 permitted to sell/serve legislation pending to 19.
^c 18 permitted to serve.
^d Those 19 before/on 7/18/80 legal age. Those 19 after 7/18/80 have to wait until they are 20 years old.
Source: Miller Brewing Company Legal Dept.

EXHIBIT 8   GROWTH IN BEER SALES BY SEGMENT: 1979–1990
(Millions of Barrels)

Type	1979	1985	Change Barrels	Change Percent	Annual rate (percent)	1990	Change Barrels	Change Percent	Annual rate (percent)
Popular	39	22	−17	−44	−9^a	13	−9	−41	−10
Premium	95	119	24	25	4^b	132	13	11	2
Super-premium	10	19	9	90	11	26	7	37	6
Light	19	37	18	95	12	50	13	35	6
Imports	4	10	6	150	15	20	10	100	15
Malt liquor	4	4	0	—	—	4	0	—	—
Total	172	211	40	22.7	3.5	34	16.1	3.0	

^a There will be an 18% decrease in 1980 as Pabst Blue Ribbon completes its repositioning, and 5% thereafter.
^b There will be a 10% increase in 1980 as Pabst Blue Ribbon completes its repositioning, and 3% thereafter.
Source: Beverage Industry, October 17, 1980.

EXHIBIT 9 SALES OF THE LEADING TWO, FIVE, AND TEN BREWERS, 1979–1990
(Millions of Barrels)

	1979		1985		1990	
	Barrels	**Share**	**Barrels**	**Share**	**Barrels**	**Share**
Anheuser-Busch and Miller	82	48%	124	59%	154	63%
Coors, Pabst, and						
Heileman	39	23	44	21	45	18
Total—five largest	121	70	168	80	199	81
Second five largest	40	23	28	13	23	9
Total—ten largest	161	94	196	93	222	91
Imports	4	2	10	5	21	9
Total beer consumption	172	100%	211	100%	245	100%

EXHIBIT 10 SHARE OF THE U.S. MARKET
(Percent)

Brewers	1980	1979	1978	1977
Anheuser-Busch	28.4	26.8	25.1	23.0
Miller	21.1	20.8	18.9	15.1
Pabst	8.5	8.8	9.3	10.0
Schlitz	8.5	9.8	11.8	13.9
Coors	7.8	7.5	7.6	8.1
All others	25.7	26.3	27.3	29.9

EXHIBIT 11 LEADING BEER BRANDS' SHARE OF MARKET TRENDS

	1970	1971	1972	1973	1974	1975	1976	1977	1978	1979
Budweiser	15.4%	16.3%	16.3%	17.7%	18.5%	17.8%	13.9%	15.9%	16.5%	17.5%
High Life	4.2	4.2	4.1	4.9	5.8	6.5	8.7	10.5	12.5	13.8
Pabst Blue										
Ribbon	8.4	9.4	9.5	9.6	9.9	10.4	11.1	9.8	8.6	7.9
Coors	5.9	6.8	7.4	8.1	8.6	8.1	9.1	8.0	7.3	6.6
Schlitz	9.4	10.3	11.2	12.4	12.5	11.9	11.4	9.8	7.8	6.5
Miller Lite	—	—	—	—	0.3	1.8	3.2	4.3	5.7	6.5
Michelob	0.9	1.2	1.5	1.9	2.4	3.1	3.4	4.0	4.5	4.8
Stroh	2.7	3.0	3.2	3.4	3.1	3.4	3.8	3.8	3.8	3.5
Olympia	2.8	2.5	2.5	2.7	3.0	3.8	4.0	3.4	3.2	2.8
Old Style	—	—	—	—	—	—	1.1	1.4	1.9	2.3
Old Milwaukee	2.0	2.2	2.3	2.4	2.5	3.0	2.9	2.5	2.2	2.0
Total	51.7%	55.9%	58.0%	63.1%	66.6%	69.8%	71.5%	72.0%	72.1%	72.2%

EXHIBIT 12 LEADING LIGHT BEER BRANDS' PERCENT OF LIGHT BEER MARKETS

	1974	1975	1976	1977	1978	1979
Miller Lite	100.0%	96.4%	73.8%	66.7%	61.8%	58.1%
Natural Light	—	—	6.2	14.7	15.8	13.6
Michelob Light	—	—	—	2.0	4.6	9.4
Coors	—	—	—	—	3.3	7.9
Schlitz Light	—	3.6	13.8	8.8	7.2	4.2
Olympia Gold	—	—	6.2	5.9	3.9	2.6
Pabst Extra						
Light	—	—	—	2.0	3.3	2.6
Total	100.0%	100.0%	100.0%	100.0%	100.0%	100.0%

MILLER—1981

John A. Murphy, group executive vice-president of Philip Morris and chairman and chief executive officer of Miller Brewing Company, summarized Miller's position in 1981 as follows:

The brewing industry produced and sold about 3 percent more beer in 1980 than in 1979. Per capita consumption also went up. Behind the leadership of its President, Bill Howell, Miller again outperformed the brewing industry and in the process earned an industry share of 21 percent.

Miller's total volume was up 4 percent to more than 37 million barrels, while retail sales were up 6 percent. The difference represents a reduction of field inventories which was good for our wholesalers in this inflation period and which was made possible by the commencement of production at our newly-completed breweries at Albany, Georgia, and Irwindale, California.

Because of this new capacity, our production has become more orderly and efficient. And with six breweries now in operation around the country, our trans-shipping costs are coming down. The picture will improve still further when our Trenton, Ohio brewery, now under construction, is completed.

Finally, in addition, the output of our sixth and newest container plant, opened early this year in Moultrie, Georgia, is already being put to good use. In making a substantial portion of our containers, we are realizing significant production cost savings.

Miller's policy continues to be one of combining traditional brewing methods with the most modern brewing equipment and technology, helping ensure the quality, freshness and uniformity of our products. And, being a part of Philip Morris, we are particularly proud that we continue to outspend the industry in quality control.

Because of the extremely high quality of Miller products, we believe they should be priced to ensure a return of all costs plus a good profit. Our experience shows that consumers will willingly pay that kind of price for that kind of beer.

Last year, despite the healthy consumer demand for beer, some in the industry decided to reach out for still more sales by not increasing their prices to cover what we know to be the increased costs of production. In some cases they reduced prices.

Miller resisted. We lost some sales. This, combined with the heavy start-up costs of the new breweries—which of course had been anticipated—led to a 20 percent decline in operating income.

We remain convinced that our traditional price policy is correct. The brewing industry has not been keeping up with the cost increases caused by inflation. Price promotions only make the situation worse by lowering profit margins. However, Miller is in a better position than most to make do in this environment.

The adverse impact of 1980's pricing environment was felt by our flagship brand, Miller High Life, the industry's second-largest seller. However, we expect these effects to be temporary. High Life is a strong brand and its "Miller Time" theme is as current today as it was when we introduced it.

In the meantime Lite, which has dominated the lower-calorie segment of the industry since its introduction in 1975, continued to grow strongly and last year became the industry's third-largest selling brand. Lite is clearly no longer a specialty item but has become a mainstream brand with a large and loyal following.

Our super-premium brand, domestically brewed Lowenbrau, is meeting sales objectives and doing well.

With these three brands Miller is well-positioned in the key segments of the industry for volume, profit, and potential.

Let me now touch briefly on some other matters.

We continue to oppose efforts to enact more forced-deposit laws. These are currently on the books in six states. They raise beverage prices to the consumer considerably without significantly reducing litter. Yet bottle bill proponents persist and have introduced legislation in both houses of the Congress again this year, as well as in some 30 states.

The beer business continues to be penalized by outdated and needless regulations, of which forced deposits constitute only one set. These regulations are imposed by the Federal Government as well as the 50 states, each with its own particular—I should say peculiar—set of restrictions. The cost of compliance is heavy on us and, indirectly, on all consumers of beer. And the cost of bureaucratic administration and enforcement is heavy on the states and thus on the taxpayer.

With economy in government at all levels now the order of the day, surely the time has come to abandon these wasteful anachronisms—to the benefit of both beer-drinkers and taxpayers, who are one and the same.

We also continue to be mindful of the potential dangers of alcohol abuse. Beer is an adult drink and a drink of moderation. Miller regularly supports the American Council on Alcoholism and other groups which work to check the spread of alcohol abuse through education and the encouragement of responsible use of all alcoholic beverages, beer included.

This is another aspect of Miller's commitment to quality—in this case quality of life for the society which permits us to be in business. It is an essential and permanent element in the Philip Morris way of doing things.

DISCUSSION QUESTIONS

1 Discuss the synergies which existed in 1969 between Philip Morris and Miller Brewing and explain how these synergies might have contributed to the success which Miller has experienced.

2 Describe the four main market segments recognized by the brewing industry and discuss how Miller differentiates its product for each of the market segments.

3 Why did advertising expenditures as a percentage of beer sales increase markedly in the

mid-70s? Were these increased advertising costs incorporated into product prices and, if so, how might they be justified from a societal standpoint?

4 Portray Philip Morris's six subsidiaries as separate businesses on the BCG business portfolio matrix and evaluate the company's mix of businesses according to cash-flow criteria. Do you consider this analysis to be valid from a strategic management standpoint? Why or why not?

5 Draw an industry life-cycle curve and place each of Philip Morris' major businesses on that curve. Discuss the strategic management implications of what your illustration shows.

6 In light of the acknowledged "potential dangers of alcohol abuse" how would you evaluate Miller's continued promotion and sale of its products, its support for the American Council on Alcoholism, and its announced commitment to "quality of life for the society which permits [it] to be in business?"

7 To what do you attribute Miller's overwhelming success over the last ten or so years? In light of your answer, what strategies do you think Miller should follow for the next several years?

THE GENERAL AVIATION INDUSTRY: AN INDUSTRY NOTE

Marilyn L. Taylor
University of Kansas

SELECTED STRATEGIC ISSUES

- Distinctive competences related to strategic foci of competitors
- Challenges and threats to an industry and their impact on industry health

Aerospace industry activities include research, development, and manufacture of aerospace systems, including manned and unmanned aircraft; missiles, space launch vehicles, and spacecraft; propulsion, guidance and control units for all of the foregoing; and a variety of airborne and ground based equipment essential to the test, operation, and maintenance of flight vehicles. Aerospace industry sales, of which general aviation is one component, reached $37.4 billion in 1978. In inflation-adjusted dollars, industry activity was at its highest level for the 1970s. International sales accounted for a $9 billion surplus. The aerospace industry led all other manufacturing industries in the United States in its trade balance contribution [1]. The future looked bright for the industry with substantial backlogs in aircraft orders, anticipated growth in non-aerospace products and service, and the NASA Space Shuttle Program.

The aerospace industry can be divided into five categories: (1) civil aircraft production (commercial transports, general aviation planes, and civil helicopter production); (2) military aircraft production (Army and Air Force); (3) missile programs (integral system of guidance rather than unguided rockets, which are used for automated

Written under the supervision of Marilyn L. Taylor, Assistant Professor, by a student team consisting of Teresa Wolfe, Brian Kaufman, Debbie Groce, Richard Hill, and Chad Kelly, all of the University of Kansas. The collaboration of V. K. Narayanan, Assistant Professor, University of Kansas, and Michael Neuburger, Senior Vice President of Beech Aircraft Company, is gratefully acknowledged.

weapons for warfare); (4) space programs (space vehicle systems); and (5) non-aerospace sales (residuals sales from the four categories, and all basic research done for and by the four categories). According to relative size and growth, the industry contained the following breakdown in sales dollars:

	1978	1977
Civil Aircraft Production:	$6.5 billion	$4.7 billion
Commercial Transports	$4.3 billion	$2.9 billion
General Aviation Planes	$1.8 billion	$1.6 billion
Helicopter Production	$ .33 billion	$ .25 billion
Missile Programs	$5.4 billion	$5.3 billion
Military Aircraft Production	$4.8 billion	$4.4 billion
Space Programs	$3.0 billion	$3.4 billion
Non-Aerospace Sales	$6.8 billion	$6.0 billion

The growth of these segments since 1968 can be seen in Exhibit I.

Excluding the missile and space programs, the industry is referred to as the aviation industry. The aviation industry can be segmented into six categories. The first category

EXHIBIT I   GROWTH OF AEROSPACE INDUSTRY SEGMENTS 1968 – 1978
Aerospace Industry Sales by Product (in billions)

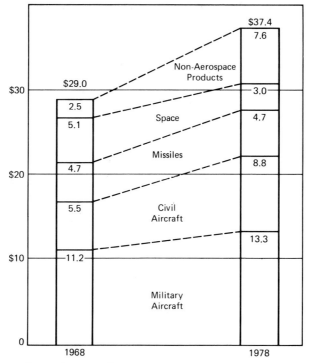

Source: Aerospace Facts and Figures 1979/1980.

consists of *military sales,* including companies such as Lockheed, McDonnell Douglas, and Boeing. McDonnell Douglas was the largest supplier for military contracts in 1978 with $2.574 billion of their sales attributed to this military segment. The second grouping consists of *commercial transport* planes, which includes such manufacturers as British Aerospace, Boeing, and McDonnell Douglas. The third segment, *engine suppliers,* contains such companies as Pratt & Whitney, Garrett, and Lycoming. The fourth grouping consists of *avionics* or *radar,* made by firms such as King, Sperry, and Collins. Other items such as *tires* and *propellers* and *general aviation* comprise the last two categories, respectively.

GENERAL AVIATION

General aviation includes all aviation other than commercial airlines and military. The general aviation industry was expected to have its first $2 billion year in 1979, only four years after its first $1 billion year in 1975. General aviation enjoyed its seventh year of record aircraft billings in 1978, with $1.78 billion in sales, up 19.2 percent from 1977 [2].

The general aviation industry usually breaks down its segments into types of aircraft rather than the use of the aircraft. But attempts to determine usage have found that approximately 75 percent of all general aviation flying is for business and commercial purposes. Areas within this section include corporate flying, air taxi, agricultural (aerial crop dusting and large range patrolling service), special purpose (pipeline patrol, power line inspection and patrol, highway traffic control, and policing activities), and instructional flying. Some flying is done for recreational purposes [3].

When the general aviation industry is broken down by types of aircraft in use, the growth or lack of growth and the reasons behind its standing can be examined. For instance, the continued growth of the single-engine market can be seen in Exhibit II, and is influenced by such factors as the continued introduction of new training aircraft, and new high-performance single-engine aircraft which offers pressurization and all-weather equipment. Conservative estimates for the multi-engine piston can be seen in Exhibit III. This estimate for 1979 is low considering the recent introduction of new models and the strong sales. The continued depressed state of the agricultural economy is examined in Exhibit IV, but this is off-set by the long-term worldwide food production demand potential. Officials and private businessmen in areas such as Africa will purchase aircraft for the developing nations. Exhibit V demonstrates the strong performance of the turboprop. Four new models have recently been introduced, and business and commuter sales are healthy. The turbojet is still in heavy demand, reflecting the steadily growing reliance of U.S. and overseas business firms on their fleets of high speed, over-the-weather jets for reliable, basic, economic company transportation. This segment, which includes the larger, faster, and higher-flying aircraft and has a strong backlog, is examined in Exhibit VI [4]. The rapid introduction of new models and products in these segments has been aided by research and development which has led to technological changes and advancements. Improvements have been seen recently in increased aircraft, engine, and component reliability; expanded fuel efficiency; increased cost effectiveness; and improved environmental

EXHIBIT II SINGLE-ENGINE MARKET GROWTH

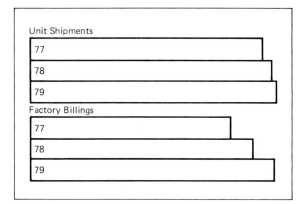

EXHIBIT III MULTI-ENGINE MARKET GROWTH

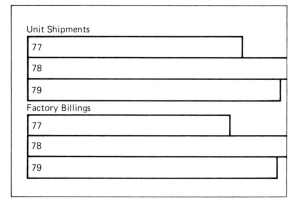

EXHIBIT IV AGRICULTURAL AIRCRAFT MARKET

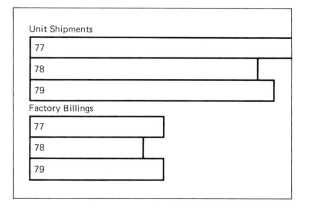

EXHIBIT V TURBOPROP MARKET GROWTH

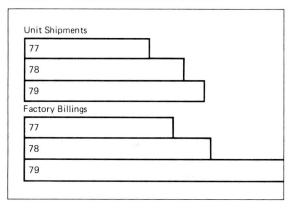

EXHIBIT VI JET MARKET GROWTH

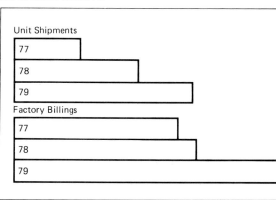

compatibility. These changes have increased due to competition within the industry. This competition has led to diversification of products along dimensions of speed, space, and distance.

TECHNOLOGICAL DEVELOPMENTS

Technological development has also taken place in the area of efficiency in fuel consumption by the aircraft. The general aviation industry has been affected by the price and availability of fuel, and it has responded by modifying their products, promotion, and research efforts. Aircraft can be compared on fuel efficiency, as well as speed, space, and distance. Among the technological advances which have led to better usage of fuel in the aviation industry include fuel management; fuel conservation; aerodynamic design in airframes, engines, and propellers; avionics systems; and design integration.

Fuel Management

The first development, fuel management, is needed to minimize the fuel consumption and maximize performance. Pilots are taught to learn the fuel mixture properly, to read and understand performance charts, and to perform weight and balance calculations. Pilots must consider the payload, the weather, and the reserve fuel carried.

Fuel Conservation

This second area, fuel conservation, has yielded structural changes in the aircraft and outlook modifications in pilots, and aims at developing lighter and more effective avionics, lighter aircraft bodies, lower-drag aircraft, and more efficient propellers, as well as teaching pilots to use favorable winds, to avoid weather obstructions, and use jet lanes. Design improvements from this conservation effort include retractable landing gear and turboprop aircraft.

The turbine engine used in turboprop airplanes has a rotating turbine which turns a propeller. Turboprop aircraft were first introduced in the late 1950s and the turboprop engines, as seen in Exhibit V, continue to be in heavy demand.

The turboprop product has led to further developments to improve payload and range. Turbofan engines have been adopted to meet pressure from customers for increased carrying weights and longer distance. The fan engine employs a "bypass ratio" which is a small increase in fan air flow compared to the gas generator air flow in a turboprop engine. Turbofans offer additional developmental advantages for the future.

Aerodynamics Design

The third major development has been in improvements in the aerodynamic design of components, materials, combustor technology, use of internal cooling air, and fan jet technology. Future developments in this area which look promising include hot-section materials; lightweight, high strength material; compressor aerodynamics with higher pressure ratio per stage; combustor technology resulting in better efficiencies at low pressures; "flexible" engine cycles; and expanded NASA support of small-engine technology in its research and technology base programs which, to date, have emphasized large commercial engines. The designs can be divided further into engine types such as the piston and turbine.

The *piston engines* have been employed for the past 50 years. The single-engine piston is purchased by smaller companies or an individual who uses it for both business and pleasure. This aircraft is extremely fuel-efficient and has improvements such as de-icing equipment and radar for all-weather flying. The multi-engine piston offers additional security and performance with the second engine. Although it uses more fuel and costs more than the single-engine model, it uses less fuel and costs less than a turboprop. However, the multi-engine piston is slower than the turboprop and requires more maintenance and has a lower residual value. There are two major suppliers of piston engines to worldwide airframe manufacturers—AVCO Lycoming and Teledyne Continental Motors. These companies produce engines that are the most reliable, durable, and fuel efficient ever made. Continental and Lycoming have worked toward energy conservation through in-house and government assisted programs. They have identified the following areas as future conservation possibilities:

1 Leaner-burning fuel metering systems (setting individual aircraft through "fine tuning" when finished)

2 Higher exhaust temperatures (at cruising speeds for maximum fuel economy)

3 Variable ignition timing (varying the spark timing to broaden the flammability limits of the fuel)

4 Low-drag air intakes (design changes to reduce the amount of air needed to cool the piston engine and reduce the cooling drag by transferring heat from the cylinder to the cooling fins around the cylinder)

Other potential advances include engines capable of burning more than one type of fuel, reduced fuel consumption, and minimal exhaust emission.

The second type of engine, the *turboprop*, represents the medium line. It is a low weight and high power engine, and is more fuel efficient than the turbojet and turbofan. The approximate cost for the turboprop is $1 million compared to the $1–7 million price for the turbojet/fan lines. The turbojets/fans are faster, and are more expensive than other types of general aviation aircraft. Turbojets and turbofans are usually sold to companies with sales over $50 million.

The *design of the propeller* is another important aerodynamic design improvement area. With the propeller, technology has led to improved efficiency. Computers are used to select the proper airfoil (surface or body, such as a wing or propeller blade, designed to obtain a reaction, as lift or thrust, from the air through which it moves) given a wide range of operating conditions. The use of high-strength, composite construction material will provide up to a 50 percent savings on propeller weight and give additional flexibility in tailoring the aerodynamic shape of the propeller.

Future Innovations

The general aviation industry is anticipating further technological developments which will aid in both fuel economy and their attractiveness in the marketplace. Future innovations could incorporate microprocessors and sensors which would enable automatic systems to control fuel mixture strength in piston engines on a continuous basis and over a full range of operating conditions. Benefits include a 5 to 10 percent savings in fuel, improved safety, reliability, and durability. There will also be increased efforts to reduce the amount of aerodynamic drag. Included in possible improvements are the use of flush-mounted antennas; improved wheel fairings (wheel coverings) in fixed-gear planes; elimination of protruding fasteners (now bonded with metal-to-metal adhesive), gaps and skin laps; and increased application of structural bonding and reinforced plastic structures.

Another future development is avionics equipment. Avionics (the electronic components in the aircraft such as the flight directors, autopilots, and gyros) will see an extended use of solid-state devices, microprocessors, and the application of Large Scale Integration resulting in reduction of size, weight, and electrical load requirements, while providing the pilot with a new variety of services and capabilities. For example, area navigation (RNAV) is now available for all aircraft, from single-engine planes to business jets, providing direct minimum-distance flight between airports. Vertical flight path guidance (VNAV) is being applied in high performance business aircraft, and is expected to penetrate other general aviation areas, providing fuel conservation through improved climb and descent profiles.

A number of cruise-control computers have been developed which provide the pilot with an instant indication of operation to maximize fuel economy. A growing line of on-board computers will assist the pilot with flight and mission planning for effective

EXHIBIT VII

Aviation activity	Number of aircraft	Fuel consumption
Aircraft & Engine Manufacturing (cert./testing)	—	.7%
General Aviation	183,000	7.5%
Military	19,000	23.0%
Airlines (air carriers)	2,500	68.8%

EXHIBIT VIII GENERAL AVIATION FUEL CONSUMPTION

Gasoline:
  11,079 barrels a year
  0.4% of all gasoline consumed (includes all uses of motor gasoline, including off-highway applications)

Jet Fuel:
  16,927 barrels a year
  4.5% of total jet fuel (both naphtha and kerosene type)

Source: Energy Data Reports, Energy Information Administration, U.S. Department of Energy, 1978.

use of the airspace with resultant time and fuel benefits. New lightweight color radars will provide the instrumental pilot with additional all-weather aids for better dispatch with increased safety [5].

To gain a perspective on the current status of general aviation's fuel consumption and number of planes, Exhibits VII and VIII break down the large segments.

ENVIRONMENT

Legislation

In addition to the technological advances, the general aviation industry has also been affected by other national and international events. Nationally, the Airline Deregulation Act of October 24, 1978, under President Carter [13], not only allowed airlines to set their own fares, but also permitted trunk carriers to abandon service to economically marginal markets. Airlines will tend to fly bigger planes between big cities and continue to reduce commercial airline service to smaller, regional airports on uneconomical routes [8]. As of May, 1978, the certified airlines serviced only 394 points in the continental United States, a 30 percent decline from the 567 served in 1960 [19]. On October 24, 1978, 385 points were served by domestic airlines, 219 of which received one carrier, 65 of which were cited as loss operations by airline companies, and 18 for which the airlines had filed for service stoppage [2]. This development led to a greater need for business and commuter aviation expansion to cover the cutbacks in service by the airlines.

The Airline Deregulation Act placed heavy emphasis on the development of commuter services. Direct subsidies were made available for the first time to commuter airlines, and government guaranteed equipment loans for the purchase of aircraft were available to commuter operators. In addition, the FAA issued new standards increasing both the safety and the seating (up to 55 passengers) and payload (up to 18,000 pounds) capacity of commuter aircraft. In 1978, commuter airlines carried 10.7 million passengers, up 18.4 percent from 1977, and cargo volume was up 48 percent to more than 200,000 tons. Commuter passenger miles increased from 946 million in 1977 to 1.1 billion in 1978. The number of commuter carriers increased from 242 to 258, and the total number of markets serviced from 2,258 to 2,393. Average trip distance remained at 111 miles according to the Civil Aeronautics Board report [6]. With this sudden expansion, the commuter airlines had problems with pilot training and the aircraft maintenance necessary for accident prevention.

On August 1, 1979, the rewritten Section 135 of the Federal Air Regulations went into effect. Section 135 called for more safety equipment on new commuter planes, additional pilot training and testing, and tougher maintenance standards for aircraft [7]. The required safety factors were important in general aviation's effort to promote its products.

Commuter and Business Markets

In spite of the negative affects on the industry of deregulation and safety concerns (to be discussed below), Exhibit IX depicts the favorable activity trends in the period 1970

EXHIBIT IX COMMUTER MARKET ACTIVITY

Commuter Air Carrier
Traffic Activity

Passengers
Average Annual Rate of Increase: 10.3%

Year	Passengers
1970	4,270,000
1971	4,698,000
1972	5,262,000
1973	5,688,000
1974	6,842,000
1975	6,666,000
1976	7,305,000
1977	8,505,000

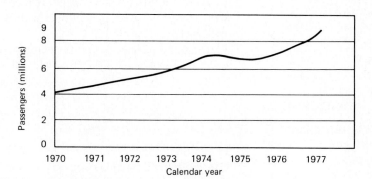

Cargo and Mail
Average Annual Cargo Increase: 30%

Year	Cargo (000 lbs.)	Mail (000 lbs.)
1970	43,527	73,479
1971	51,203	100,683
1972	74,573	126,177
1973	92,963	147,796
1974	138,279	156,293
1975	169,203	164,082
1976	216,811	108,507
1977	271,242	71,395

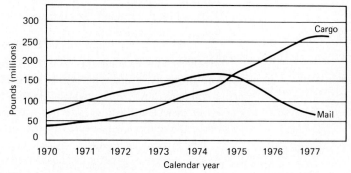

Source: "New Horizons," 1978 Annual Report of the Commuter Airline Association of America.

EXHIBIT X AVIATION ACTIVITY FORECASTS

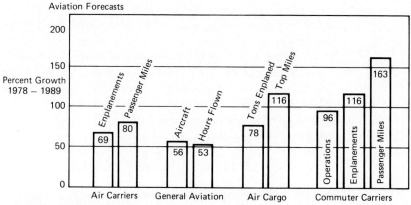

Source: Aerospace Facts.

to 1977. Furthermore, the aviation forecast from 1978 to 1989 in Exhibit X looked very favorable for the general aviation industry in general, and the commuter market in particular.

Another segment that the general aviation industry served was the business market. Until the 1971 recession, the business aircraft was merely a prestige toy. Mr. Slivinsky, President of the General Aviation Division, Rockwell International, speaking of that recession, said, "Finally we were all forced to become far more sophisticated marketers of our products, to expand our markets to reach the nonuser, and develop the aircraft more fully as a valuable tool; we *matured* as an industry." [8] By the late 70s, the business aircraft was looked upon as a vital and, sometimes, indispensable business tool.

More and more companies were using business aviation. Of the "Fortune 1000" companies, 514 operated fleets totalling 1,778 aircraft. There had been a 26.5 percent increase from 1969 to 1978 in the number of major firms that purchased their own aircraft. Exhibit XI shows that in terms of net sales, assets, net income, and stockholder equity, the corporations with aircraft perform significantly better than those without business aircraft [9]. This performance record creates a "chicken and egg" situation over whether planes help produce profit or if the company's profits permit the company to buy the planes. One authority settled the dispute by saying that business aircraft utility demonstrates progressive management—thus, the relationship between good management, plane ownership, and increased profits is established.

EXHIBIT XI   PERFORMANCE COMPARISON:
CORPORATE AIRCRAFT OPERATORS VS. NONOPERATORS

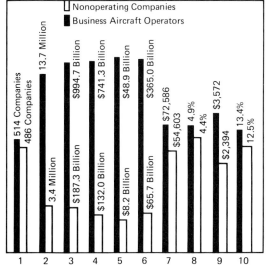

In 1978, 514 corporations of the top 1,000 operated 1,778 aircraft, an increase of 125 over 1977. These corporations performed significantly better than the remaining 486 nonoperators. (*Source:* Business and Commercial Aviation Study.)

Among the factors contributing to the increase in companies using their own planes was the trend toward decentralization. Companies were becoming more decentralized in their search for consistent labor pools, lower labor costs, more attractive surroundings for their employees, better tax situations, lower real estate and construction costs, and more state and local industrial development attractions. These companies were opening new facilities in small and medium-sized cities far removed from the major airports in Chicago, New York, and Los Angeles. Thus, a corporate fleet could increase a company's flexibility, mobility, and time utilization efficiency level [10]. Having their own planes gave a company numerous benefits. Among these were: (1) the fleets can serve destinations airlines do not serve; (2) they can fly at the company's convenience; (3) are two to six times faster than a car given the slower, legal highway speeds; (4) extend the personal reach and influence of top management; (5) improve multi-office operations and provide closer supervision and control; (6) accelerate customer service; (7) facilitate business expansion; (8) shorten reaction time to handle emergencies faster; (9) cut overhead costs; (10) reduce the need for additional personnel; and (11) help with employee morale.

Corporate fleets also provide security for key personnel [11]. Few aircraft carried company names or identifying markings. Some companies kept flight schedules secret even within the company to help prevent hijackings, terrorism, or kidnapping, especially abroad. Questions have come from Washington and the Internal Revenue Service about deductions from business expenses associated with the corporate planes on tax returns. Shareholders also demanded an accounting for such expenses.

International Market

Another market which offered both opportunities and obstacles was the international market. In 1978, exports accounted for $490 million, or 27.6 percent of U.S. general aviation industry revenues and 20.3 percent of U.S. general aviation production units. Export licenses were delayed due to human rights and other considerations. Zimbabwe (South Rhodesia) was the only country that officially had an embargo against it, but the State Department had held up the other countries' export licenses by its inaction. Federal law required that an export license be acted on within 90 days, unless the applicant was notified of the reasons for the delay. There was, however, a possibility for multilateral negotiations resulting in the worldwide free trade of civil aircraft in the future.

The major problem that U.S. companies faced in their struggle for foreign business was the government's attitude toward foreign trade. Other conditions which affected the foreign aviation business included double-digit inflation, an energy shortage, and battered money markets. Due to the lack of an aggressive national export policy, the continued trade deficits were weakening the dollar, fueling inflation, and eroding the nation's ability to structure an effective foreign policy [12].

Competition

Another major concern in the general aviation which each company faced was the domestic and international competition. Exhibit XII from *Aerospace Facts and Figures 1979/1980* gives manufacturers in the general aviation industry and the number of

EXHIBIT XII GENERAL AVIATION AIRCRAFT SHIPMENTS BY SELECTED MANUFACTURERS:
CALENDAR YEARS 1974 TO DATE

	1974	1975	1976	1977	1978
Number of Aircraft Shipped	14,166	14,072	15,450	16,910	17,817
Single-Engine	10,227	10,220	11,803	13,167	13,651
Multi-Engine, Piston	2,135	2,116	2,120	2,195	2,630
Agricultural	1,335	1,235	980	890	748
Turboprop	250	305	359	428	548
Turbojet	219	196	188	230	240
Value of Shipments[a] **(Millions of Dollars)**	$ 909	$1,033	$1,229	$1,551	$1,822
Single-Engine	209	257	364	435	486
Multi-Engine, Piston	257	286	343	389	492
Agricultural	42	41	37	39	33
Turboprop	130	174	223	295	393
Turbojet	271	275	262	393	418
Number of Aircraft by Selected Manufacturer					
Ayres	NA	NA	NA	NA	NA
Beech	1,303	1,212	1,220	1,203	1,367
Bellanca	636	444	315	252	370
Cessna	7,187	7,564	7,888	8,839	8,770
Gates Learjet	66	79	84	105	102
Gulfstream American	628	758	762	866	933
Lake	71	81	88	99	98
Lockheed Jetstar	1	-0-	3	16	9
Maule	114	114	96	108	88
Mooney	130	210	227	362	379
Piper	3,415	3,069	4,042	4,499	5,272
Rockwell International	545	434	595	432	244
Swearingen	24	26	30	28	51
Ted Smith Aerostar	46	81	100	101	NA

[a] Manufacturers' net billing price.
NA, not applicable.
Sources: Aerospace Industries Association and General Aviation Manufacturers' Association. Aviation Week and Space Technology, February 12, 1979.

planes and the dollar values for 1974 to 1978. Exhibit XIII also shows the domestic market and provides data for 1978.

Three companies dominated the general aviation industry: Beech, Cessna, and Piper. The group was appropriately termed the "Big Three" in general aviation.

The sales leader in the general aviation industry was Cessna Aircraft Company, founded by the late Clyde V. Cessna in 1911, and incorporated on September 7, 1927. For the years 1970 to 1977, Cessna's deliveries exceeded those of all other U.S. general aviation manufacturers combined. In 1978, Cessna was marketing a line of 56 types of commercial aircraft. These aircraft ranged from the Model 152, a small two-seater, to the Citation II, a ten- to twelve-seater twin-turbofan jet business aircraft used for executive transportation. The recent move into the Citation was planned to increase sales market share.

EXHIBIT XIII   BUSINESS AND UTILITY AIRCRAFT SHIPMENTS (DECEMBER, 1978)

Make and model	No. of units	Year to date	Factory billings	Make and model	No. of units	Year to date	Factory billings
Ayres				177 Cardinal	0	69	
600 Thrush	14	108		Cardinal RG	6	96	
800 Thrush	0	2		180 Skywagon	8	117	
Turbo Thrush	1	26		182 Skylane	44	596	
Ayres Totals	15	134	$1,073,600	F182 Skylane	0	34	
				F182 Skylane RG	4	18	
Beech				R182 Skylane RG	31	547	
19 Sport	0	31		T182 Skylane RG	47	113	
C23 Sundowner	6	115		185 Skywagon	13	226	
C24R Sierra	4	79		AgWagon	0	33	
F33A/C Bonanza	8	95		AgTruck	2	152	
V35B Bonanza	11	115		AgHusky	13	27	
A36 Bonanza	17	224		Stationair 6	26	351	
76 Duchess	19	120		Turbo Stationair 6	19	209	
B55 Baron	7	92		Stationair 7	4	44	
E55 Baron	1	28		Turbo Stationair 7	4	31	
58 Baron	9	101		210 Centurion	11	181	
58TC Baron	2	27		Turbo 210 Centurion	48	529	
58P Baron	9	52		P210	20	158	
B60 Duke	2	34		Skymaster	3	48	
C90 King Air	9	64		Turbo Skymaster	0	32	
E90 King Air	4	50		Press. Skymaster	1	25	
B100 King Air	2	23		310	13	127	
200 Super King Air	18	115		Turbo 310	6	72	
Beech Totals	128	1,367	$38,748,700	340	8	160	
				402	11	82	
Bellanca				404 Titan	4	76	
Super Viking	3	56		414A	8	129	
Turbo Super Viking	0	10		421 Golden Eagle	11	129	
Citabria	8	161		441 Conquest	6	69	
Scout	4	32		Citation 1	6	49	
Decathlon	9	111		Citation 2	4	38	
Bellanca Totals	24	370	$649,400	Cessna Totals	651	8,770	$54,980,400
Cessna				Gates Learjet			
152	104	1,852		25D	3	29	
152 Aerobat	3	66		35A	9	64	
F152	8	99		36A	1	7	
172 Skyhawk	137	1,810		Gates Learjet Totals	13	102	$26,710,000
F172	6	123					
B17 Hawk XP	11	213					
F172 Hawk XP	1	15					

Cessna Aircraft Company had four plants in Wichita engaged in production of commercial and military aircraft. Cessna's Fluid Power Division which manufactured fluid power systems was located in Hutchinson, Kansas. Other subsidiary companies owned by Cessna were Aircraft Radio and Control Division of Boonton, New Jersey; the McCauley Accessories Division of Dayton, Ohio; Cessna Fluid Power, Ltd., of Glenrogers, Fife, Scotland; Cessna Finance Corporation; and the International Finance Corporation in Wichita. It also had a 49 percent interest in Reims Aviation in France. The principle manufacturing and office facilities were located in approximately 5,000,000 square feet of space.

Cessna's Senior Vice President for Marketing, Robert L. Lair, said the marketplace was very strong in the higher-priced aircraft, but weak for the lower-priced aircraft.

EXHIBIT XIII   (*Continued*)

Make and model	No. of units	Year to date	Factory billings	Make and model	No. of units	Year to date	Factory billings
Gulfstream American				PA-34-200T Seneca	34	460	
AA-1C Lynx	1	96		PA-36-300 Brave	6	96	
AA-5A Cheetah	37	226		PA-36-375 Brave	0	70	
AA-5B Tiger	40	321		PA-38-112 Tomahawk	108	1,109	
GA-7 Cougar	42	101		PA-44-180 Seminole	35	183	
AgCat	11	172		Aerostar 600A	1	32	
Gulfstream 2	3	17		Aerostar 601B	2	8	
Gulfstream American Totals	134	933	$23,918,200	Aerostar 601P	8	68	
Lake 200 Buccaneer	7	98	$301,000	Piper Totals	406	5,272	$30,017,500
Lockheed Jetstar 2	0	8	N.A.	Rockwell International			
Maule M-5 235C	5	88	$145,000	112TC-A Commander	3	33	
Mooney				114 Commander	1	104	
201 M20J	4	351		500S Shrike Commander	1	14	
231 M20K	18	18		690B Turbo Commander	7	61	
Mooney Totals	22	379	N.A.	700 Commander	4	7	
Piper				60 Sabre	2	12	
Pa-18-150 Super Cub	10	178		75A Sabre	2	13	
PA-23-250 Aztec	11	127		Rockwell			
Pa-25-235 Pawnee	2	47		International Totals	20	244	$17,794,600
PA-28-161 Warrior	42	595		Swearingen			
PA-28-181 Archer 2	45	525		SA-236T Merlin 3A	4	13	
PA-8-201 Arrow 3	1	223		SA-226AT Merlin 4A	0	7	
PA-28RT-201T Arrow 4	6	6		SA-226TC Metro 2	5	31	
PA-28-235 Cherokee	1	1		Swearingen Totals	9	51	$9,810,000
PA-28-236 Dakota	15	65		Totals (December, 1978)	1,434		$204,148,400
PA-31-310 Navajo	5	55		Totals (December, 1977)	1,578		$161,391,000
PA-31-325 Navajo C/R	7	66		Totals (1978)	17,808		$1,777,785,100
PA-31-350 Chieftain	17	170		Totals (1977)	16,907		$1,491,117,000
PA-31T-820 Cheyenne	6	97		Exports (December, 1978)	268		$65,149,000
PA-31T1-500 Cheyenne	4	16		Exports (December, 1977)	331		$33,596,000
PA-32-300 Cherokee	16	174		Exports (1978)	3,613		$490,613,000
PA-32RT-300T Lance	11	305		Exports (1977)	3,611		$354,475,000
PA-32-RT300 Lance	13	328					

Source: *Aviation Week and Space Technology*, February 12, 1979, p. 63.

Lair, therefore, placed the top three priorities at Cessna on the recertification of the Conquest, producing the higher-priced aircraft it has scheduled, and emphasizing the flight training market. The turboprop Conquest, with its redesigned tail, was expected to receive its FAA recertification by the end of September, 1979 [14, 15, 18].

Piper Aircraft Corporation was second in sales behind Cessna. Piper was incorporated in Pennsylvania on November 10, 1937. On November 13, 1937, Piper acquired the total assets of Taylor Aircraft Company, a locally established firm. Piper was involved in manufacturing general aviation aircraft consisting of 16 models of small commercial planes. The aircraft ranged from the two-seater Super Cub Piper to the six to eleven-seat Cheyenne III.

The aircraft and accessories manufactured by Piper were sold to hundreds of independent dealers in the United States and approximately 34 distributors and 149 dealers internationally, who were responsible for marketing these products in their given areas. These dealers also operated aircraft repair and service centers which sold used aircraft. Piper operated flight centers which offered flight instruction and aircraft and the company had nine Corporate Aircraft Centers.

Piper unit market share in the general aviation industry has increased from 22 percent in 1973 to 29 percent in 1978. However, their market share in terms of sales dollars was 19.5 percent because the company concentrated on the lower end of the market [17]. In 1973, they held only 14.3 percent of sales dollars. The 1973-78 increase vaulted Piper to the second largest general aviation producer in terms of sales dollars, taking over the spot previously held by Beech. Sales for Piper were about $337 million in 1978. The management of Piper took an even more optimistic view of their future. They felt there are six reasons for their recent success and expected future growth. These reasons included: (1) strengthened management; (2) increased dealer professionalism; (3) improved aircraft financing plans; (4) increased advertising; (5) product refinement; and (6) new and improved aircraft models. In 1978, the company acquired Ted Smith Aerostar Corporation, which manufactured high performance twin-engine aircraft, a type not previously manufactured by Piper. The management felt that the broadened product line along with a 57 percent increase in advertising expenditures for 1979 would help considerably in attaining their goals.

In 1962, Piper formed Piper Aircraft International to handle sales distribution for Europe and North Africa. The Chief Executive Officer, J. Helms, noted that Piper's sales had been growing at about twice the rate of the U.S. general aviation industry average and that sales in Europe and North Africa, particularly in East Europe, were important factors in the company's plans for continuing this growth rate. Piper also sold assembly "kits" to government-controlled Brazilian, Argentinian, and Columbian companies. The kits consisted of all the components and parts necessary for assembly of an aircraft.

During 1969, Bangor Punta Corporation acquired approximately 51 percent interest in Piper Aircraft Corporation. Bangor subsequently acquired shares of Piper until on September 30, 1977, they owned approximately 95.7 percent of the Piper stock. Under Bangor's control, Piper Aircraft expanded its offices and plants in Lock Haven, Pennsylvania; Vero Beach, Florida; Lakeland, Florida; Piper, Pennsylvania; Santa Maria, California; and Renovo, Pennsylvania [14, 16].

In 1978, Beech ranked third in the general aviation industry in sales. Beech held 7.3 percent of the unit market share, but 16.8 percent of the sales dollar share. Behind Beech was Learjet which produced only corporate jets. Learjet held only .5 percent of the unit market share, but 13 percent of the sales dollar share because of the high unit price of jets [17].

Internationally, there were many competitors which could challenge these domestic companies' international picture. Attempts from Canada, Israel, France, Britain, and Japan were being felt in the worldwide general aviation market.

The Canadair Challenger, with its wide body, was a business jet with a Lycoming ALF502L-powered engine. Israel Aircraft Industry (IAI) had a turbofan called the Westwind I and plans for a Westwind II. The $2.4 million aircraft was among the lower priced in the mid-jet market and the company had been able to amortize development costs early. France's entry, manufactured by Dassault-Breguet, was the three-engine business jet, the Falcon 50. British Aerospace manufactured a twin-engine turbofan aircraft called HS. 125-1700. Further competition was expected from Mitsubishi International with their MU-2N, 22MU-2P, and Marquise. Mitsubishi MU-300s, which carried Pratt and Whitney engines, were just completing the testing stage of development.

Additional competition was expected from companies entering the aviation field, and others which were changing their product line to meet demand. Among this category was Learavia's Lear Fan, a twin-turbo shaft-powered aircraft. Also progressing was Foxjet International's Foxjet, a small twin jet. Foxjet had facilities near Minneapolis, Minnesota. Learavia and Foxjet planned to enter the market in 1980 or 1981 and had already begun to take orders for their planes [18].

Other Problems

Other problems in the industry included the aircraft noise issue, the economy, the availability of R & D money, personnel needs, safety, and airport needs. On the aircraft noise issue, there were cases in the courts on whether local airports should be allowed to arbitrarily ban any type of aircraft or if they should be allowed to establish reasonable noise criteria for all aircraft. The overall economy with its inflation, recession, and high cost of money affected aircraft sales and company investments. Government's trimming of the budget for money available for corporate research and development caused a great deal of concern among industry members who historically relied on this money for supporting technological advances. Within the industry, there was a need for more trained people, including engineers, technicians, airframe builders, mechanics, and pilots. A growing public concern in 1979 was the death rate of 2.79 passengers per 100 million miles flown reported by the commuter air industry in 1978. This represented 36 deaths, and was 400 times that of the .007 death rate of the commercial airlines. By the end of October 1979, over 50 people had died in commuter air accidents. To support airport needs, more general aviation runways are needed at hub airports and the facilities at existing reliever (or small airports around larger, more congested ones) airports needed to be upgraded [13, 6].

The U.S. general aviation industry faced a number of potential opportunities in the 1980s including technological advances, the growth of commuter and business markets, and expansion of its international operations. The industry and its members faced a number of important decisions which would affect their position not only domestically, but also internationally. The U.S. general aviation industry needed to assume an offensive as well as defensive strategy to remain competitive. In the midst of inflation, an energy crisis, volatile money markets, significant foreign competition, and domestic social legislation, the industry needed to continue efforts to improve current products and services and seek new ones to enhance its position.

REFERENCES

1 *Aerospace Facts and Figures 1979/80,* Karl G. Harr, Jr., Aerospace Industries Association of America, Washington, D.C., 1979.
2 General Aviation Manufacturers Association (GAMA) Data.
3 *Airports,* N. Ashfield and Paul Wright, John Wiley & Sons: New York, 1979.
4 GAMA Meeting; New York Security Analysts, New York City, January 12, 1979.
5 "General Aviation and Energy: A Status Report," GAMA.
6 *Aviation Week and Space Technology* (AWST), July 16, 1979, and April 23, 1979.
7 *Lawrence Daily Journal World,* October 24, 1979, Fred Bayles, Associated Press.
8 *Dun's Review,* January 1979.
9 "Business Aviation within the Fortune 1000," *Business and Commercial Aviation,* December 1978.
10 "Accelerating the Momentum of Success," Beech Aircraft Corporation.
11 "Corporate Flying; Changing the Way Companies Do Business," *Business Week,* February 6, 1978.
12 "Meeting Foreign Trade Competition," Allen H. Skaggs, National Meeting of the International Council, Aerospace Industries Association, New Orleans, Louisiana, October 3, 1979.
13 *New York Times,* Tuesday, August 14, 1979.
14 Moody's Industrial Manual, 1979.
15 Cessna Annual Report, 1978.
16 Bangor Punta (Piper) Annual Report, 1979.
17 Standard and Poor's Industry Survey.
18 *AWST,* February 12, 1979, and July 23, 1979.
19 "Corporate Fleets Fill the Skies," *Industry Week,* May 14, 1979.

DISCUSSION QUESTIONS

1 Describe the domestic and foreign competitors in the U.S. general aviation industry in terms of their distinctive competences and strategic foci.
2 Evaluate the overall health of the general aviation industry and describe the challenges and threats which the industry faces.

BEECH AIRCRAFT CORPORATION

Marilyn L. Taylor
University of Kansas

SELECTED STRATEGIC ISSUES

- Deciding whether to seek a merger
- Evaluation of merger candidates
- Strategic response to aging of an executive team
- Diversification into a high-technology area
- Impact of managerial stock ownership on success and financial conservation

As 1979 drew to a close, Mrs. Beech, the company's co-founder, knew she would be reporting record earnings for the seventh straight year. Olive Ann Beech and her nephew, Frank Hedrick, had directed the company since the death of her husband, Walter H. Beech, in 1950. Both Beech and Hedrick had participated in merger discussions for the past five years. To some, the question seemed to be not "Should Beech merge?" but, "With whom?" Accordingly, Beech had contracted with a New York investment banker to do a study of merger possibilities. More than a dozen potential partners were to be considered and the firm was to recommend the best candidate for merger with Beech. The name Beech had always stood for quality. How could the company plan a future which would maintain its identity as a producer of high-quality commercial and military aircraft, achieve a 15 percent sales growth every year, and continue the development of new aircraft and aerospace technologies?

This case received a "Best Case Award" at the 1981 Case Research Association meeting in Atlanta. The development of the case was supported in part by the University of Kansas Fund for Instructional Improvement and the School of Business. The case was prepared by Professor Marilyn L. Taylor of the University of Kansas. The collaboration of Michael Neuburger of Beech Aircraft Corporation and Carolyn Patterson, Brian Kaufman, and Teresa Wolfe is gratefully acknowledged.

299

COMPANY HISTORY

Walter Beech, who co-founded Beech Aircraft Corporation with his wife, was born on a farm near Pulaski, Tennessee, on January 30, 1891. Even as a child, Beech was mechanically inclined. Beech's interest in airplanes led to his first solo flight in an old Curtiss pusher biplane in 1914. In World War I, he served three years as an Army pilot, flight instructor, and engineer. With this experience, he became an exhibition pilot in 1920. He further increased his aeronautical knowledge, coming up with many ideas for improved aircraft design and construction. In 1923, Beech moved to Wichita to accept a job with Swallow Airplane Corporation. A year later, he formed his own aircraft company, Travel Air Manufacturing. By 1929, Travel Air was the world's largest commercial producer of both monoplanes and biplanes[1] which were known for their superior quality. As the depression deepened, sales in the aircraft industry fell. This led to a merger of Travel Air and Curtiss-Wright. Beech's responsibilities in the new company were mainly executive and he had little involvement in design and construction. Since his new duties were inconsistent with his personal goals, he resigned in 1931. In 1932, Walter and Olive Ann Beech co-founded Beech Aircraft in Wichita.

A long-time resident of Wichita commented on the Beeches' contributions to the company:

> Mrs. Beech was a source of strength and stability for the company. She put the organization together . . . [he was] the inventive genius; she was the organizational aspect of the company.

The Beeches formulated the company objective ''to design and build a five-place biplane having the interior luxury and passenger comfort of a fine sedan, a top speed of 200 mph or better, a landing speed no higher than 60 mph, a non-stop range close to 1,000 miles, and easy controllability and sound aerodynamic characteristics [7]. The first Beech biplane flew on November 4, 1932. Design improvements were added and by 1934, the Beechcraft B17L was ready for full-fledged production. Business was brisk and production doubled so that eighteen Model 17 planes were built during the year. Development work was initiated on a Model 18 plane, and it made its maiden flight in 1937.

In 1936, Beech Aircraft Company was succeeded by Beech Aircraft Corporation. The reorganization was purely a financial move increasing capitalization from $25,000 to more than $100,000 and creating a base for growth. Beech Aircraft Corporation prospered throughout the 1930s and Walter Beech realized one of his goals—sales exceeding $1 million. As the Axis powers gained strength, Beech went into the production of hospital transports and bombardiers and navigator trainers for the government. During World War II, except for priority orders, all commercial production was curtailed, as the company went into full support of the war effort. By the end of the war, the company had produced 7,400 airplanes for defense.

---

[1] A monoplane has one pair of wings. A biplane has wings at two different levels, usually one above and one below the fuselage.

In 1943, the company organized a subsidiary to dispose of surplus and obsolete materials resulting from war production. Although the subsidiary was dissolved when the surplus was depleted, this move was a unique idea in the industry and demonstrated the innovativeness of management. At the end of the war, Beech went back into commercial production. By the end of the 1940s, the Beechcraft line included an eight-place deluxe Model 18 and the start of the famous Bonanza line with Model 35. The Bonanza plane immediately had a 1,500-plane order backlog. In 1950, Mrs. Beech took control of the company when Walter died.

Operations were expanded to include leased plants at a former air base in Liberal, Kansas. The company added many models in the 1950s, including the world's first executive jet airplane, the MS760 ''Paris,'' the Beechcraft Twin-Bonanza and Beechcraft Travel Air. The first flight of a Beechcraft missile target was unsuccessfully completed in 1955.

In the 1960s, many milestones were passed. Beech expanded its product line in 1962 to include the Model 23 Musketeer, the Model 65 Queen Air, the Model 60 Duke and the 99 Airliner. The U.S. Navy accepted the Beechcraft supersonic missile target in 1963. In 1964, Beech introduced the turboprop engine into its corporate series by bringing the Model 90 King Air to the market.

The 1970s were prosperous years for Beechcraft. The first Beech Aero Club was initiated in 1974, and this idea spread widely. Beech won many defense contracts over competitors. In the closing years of the 1970s, Beech introduced the Executive Flight Plan to boost sales to companies. Beech also recorded its first sale to the Republic of China in over thirty years and international backlog was at an all time high. The company had been a subcontractor for the other major companies since 1944. Included in subcontracts in the late 1970s were parts for McDonnell Douglas's F-4 and F-15s and a $13 million subcontract for the space shuttle program for Rockwell.

The key to the company's growth was the breadth of its product line (Exhibit I). The Beech line included small single-engine planes like the Sierra and Sundowner; the larger, more widely known Bonanza line; the multi-engine Duke and Baron Series; and the larger Queen Air. The King Air line, consisting of turboprop aircraft, represented the top of Beech's line. These commercial sales plus military sales gave Beech a record sales level of $527 million in 1978, and a net income of $35 million (Exhibits II to V).

In 1979, Beech had one of the highest market shares in the general aviation industry. The company was second in terms of dollar volume and third in number of aircraft sold. Major competitors were Cessna and Piper. C. A. Rembleske, Vice President of Engineering echoed the company philosophy:

> We don't care about *most,* just better airplanes and customer service support. Beech has always prided itself in setting the pace.

COMPANY OPERATIONS

In 1978, Beech's facilities included the main plant and general offices in Wichita; a company-owned plant plus engineering and research and development facilities in

EXHIBIT I BEECH PRODUCT LINE

Price 1975	Model	Engine (single)	Recommended flight range	Maximum cruise speed
CESSNA				
Two-seaters:				
$ 17,995	152	110 hp Lycoming	403 miles	127 mph
19,000	152 Aerobat	110 hp Lycoming	662 miles	126 mph
Four-seaters:				
$ 23,495	Skyhawk	160 hp Lycoming	558 miles	174 mph
—	R172E	210 hp Continental	1010 miles	152 mph
31,595	R172HawkXP	195 hp Continental	662 miles	153 mph
49,975	Cardinal Classic	180 hp Lycoming	772 miles	160 mph
43,950	Cardinal RG	200 hp Lycoming	823 miles	180 mph
Agricultural:				
$ 43,950	AG Wagon (one-seater)	300 hp Continental	370 miles	151 mph
49,650	AG Truck (one-seater)	300 hp Continental	295 miles	121 mph
49,400	AG Carryall (2-6 seater)	300 hp Continental	565 miles	148 mph
Five- to Eight-seaters:				
$ 48,750	Stationair 6	300 hp Continental	702 miles	180 mph
54,750	Turbo Stationair 6	310 hp Turbo-chg. Con.	662 miles	192 mph
54,950	Stationair 7	300 hp Continental	449 miles	173 mph
61,500	Turbo Stationair 7	310 hp Turbo-chg. Con.	604 miles	196 mph
63,950	Centurion	310 hp Continental	1226 miles	202 mph
123,500	310	Two flat-six engines	1303 miles	238 mph
69,900	Skymaster	Two 210 hp Continen.	—	—
—	Skylane	—	—	—
34,950	Skywagon 180	One 230 hp Continen.	835 miles	192 mph
198,000	340A	Two 310 hp Continen.	1322 miles	281 mph
	402	Two 300 hp Continen.	1243 miles	264 mph
Eight- to Thirteen-seaters:				
$ 257,000	414A Chancellor	Two 310 hp Continen.	1316 miles	275 mph
316,000	421C	Two 375 hp Continen.	1440 miles	297 mph
280,000	Titan	Two 375 hp Continen.	1749 miles	267 mph
850,000	Conquest (turboprop)	Two Garrett-Aires.	1490 miles	340 mph
1,150,000	Citation I (turbofan)	Two Pratt & Whitney	1532 miles	403 mph
1,395,000	Citation II (turbofan)	Two Pratt & Whitney	1968 miles	420 mph
—	Citation III	Two Pratt & Whitney	2170 miles	540 mph

Boulder, Colorado; and two leased facilities in Liberal and Salina, Kansas. The Wichita site had complete manufacturing facilities (which included over 1,000 acres of land) and a flying field. All of the metal work along with most final assembly work was done at this plant because it was the only one with the necessary equipment. Portions of some models were shipped to Wichita from the other plants to be incorporated into Wichita-assembled aircraft, which were then thoroughly flight tested before being sold. All of the leased plants were former Air Force military bases. The Schilling Airbase in Salina, Kansas, a 582,000 square feet area which had been leased since

EXHIBIT I (*Continued*)

Price 1975	Model	Engine (single)	Recommended flight range	Maximum cruise speed
BEECHCRAFT				
Two- to Five-seaters:				
$ 31,750	Sundowner 180 C23	180 hp Lycoming	687 miles	123 kn.
26,300	Sport 150 B19	150 hp by Lycoming	747 miles	110 kn.
43,850	Sierra 200	200 hp Lycoming	790 miles	142 kn.
72,575	Bonanza	285 hp Continental	824 miles	182 kn.
91,850	Duchess 76	Two 180 hp Lycoming	818 miles	197 mph
115,500	Baron (up to $216,850)	Two 260 hp Continen.	1044 miles	231 mph
279,500	Duke B60	Two 380 hp Lycoming	1203 miles	283 mph
Six- to Twelve-seaters:				
$ 309,500	Queen Air	Two 380 hp Lycoming	1102 miles	248 mph
561,500	King Air (tubroprop)	Two 550 hp Pratt & W.	1295 miles	287 mph
Up to Seventeen-seaters:				
$ 937,000	B99 Airliner (turboprop)	Two 680 hp Pratt & W.	1456 miles	276 mph
825,000	King Air 100 (turboprop)	Two 680 hp Pratt & W.	1395 miles	270 mph
1,065,000	Super King Air 200 (turboprop)	Two 850 hp Pratt & W.	1370 miles	333 mph
PIPER				
Two-seaters:				
$ 21,750	Super Cub	150 hp Lycoming	460 miles	153 mph
15,840	Tomahawk	112 hp Lycoming	402 miles	109 kn.
Four- to Eight-seaters:				
$ 118,250	Aztec F Turbo	Two 250 hp Lycoming	1317 miles	253 mph
22,360	Warrior II	160 hp Lycoming	674 miles	176 mph
27,510	Archer II	180 hp Lycoming	679 miles	171 mph
40,650	Arrow III	200 hp Lycoming	1047 miles	214 mph
—	Dakota	235 hp Lycoming	801 miles	170 mph
43,860	Cherokee Six ($47,910)	260 hp Lycoming (300)	806 miles	180 mph
58,990	Lance II	260 hp Lycoming	900 miles	217 mph
193,000	Navajo (turbo-charged)	Two 310 hp Lycoming	1002 miles	261 mph
219,560	Chieftain (turbo-charged)	Two 350 hp Lycoming	869 miles	271 mph
519,500	Cheyenne I (turboprop)	Two 500 hp Pratt & W.	1133 miles	265 mph
532,300	Cheyenne II (turboprop)	Two 620 hp Pratt & W.	1589 miles	326 mph
91,000	Seneca II	Two 200 hp Continen.	902 miles	225 mph
—	Cheyenne III (11-seater)	Two 680 hp Pratt & W.	2452 miles	283 mph
Agricultural:				
$ 38,220	Pawnee D-235	235 hp Lycoming	290 miles	150 mph
54,760	Brave ($73,170)	300 hp Lycoming (375)	360 miles	149 mph
—	Tomahawk	552 hp Lycoming	552 miles	150 mph

EXHIBIT II   CONSOLIDATED BALANCE SHEETS

September 30:	1978	1977
Assets		
Current Assets		
Cash	$ 7,457,183	$ 2,883,889
Marketable securities—at cost (approximate market)	8,539,891	6,433,248
Trade notes and accounts receivable:		
Installment receivables, less allowances for losses and unearned finance charges	47,130,979	40,034,408
United States Government and prime contractors	11,742,846	6,503,490
Other, less allowances of $336,197 in 1978 and $329,848 in 1977	9,690,911	7,541,834
	$ 68,564,736	$ 54,079,732
Inventories	142,149,846	124,940,146
Prepaid expenses	1,202,940	715,556
TOTAL CURRENT ASSETS	$227,914,596	$189,052,571
Investments in Securities—at cost (approximate market)	$ 19,440,229	$ 17,269,666
Other Assets	494,102	393,206
Property, Plant, and Equipment		
Land	$ 1,700,000	$ 1,700,000
Buildings and improvements	18,846,625	18,392,506
Machinery and equipment	36,121,196	32,244,029
	$ 56,667,821	$ 52,336,535
Less allowances for depreciation	(37,888,849)	(34,897,728)
	$ 18,778,972	$ 17,438,807
	$266,627,899	$224,154,250

September 30:	1978	1977
Liabilities and Stockholders' Equity		
Current Liabilities		
Notes payable to banks	$ 4,766,560	$ 4,719,887
Trade accounts payable	37,654,035	31,046,598
Payroll and payroll deductions	12,411,763	8,899,833
Accrued expenses	7,076,851	5,408,840
Customer deposits	6,114,273	14,956,650
Federal and state income taxes (including deferred tax of $2,936,000 in 1978 and $1,849,000 in 1977)	17,107,770	10,051,601
Current portion of long-term debt	212,554	205,192
TOTAL CURRENT LIABILITIES	$ 85,343,806	$ 75,288,601
Long Term Debt	$ 24,096,940	$ 33,486,953
Deferred Income Taxes	2,200,000	
Reserves for Insurance Claims	8,919,246	6,059,388
Stockholders' Equity		
Common Stock, par value $1 a share:		
Authorized 15,000,000 shares; issued 1978—		
12,097,392 incl. 688,356 in treasury	$ 12,097,392	
1977—7,528,081 incl. 446,116 in treasury		$ 7,528,081
Additional paid-in capital	$ 30,122,432	$ 20,683,932
Retained earnings	107,892,250	85,027,416
Less cost of Common Stock in treasury	(4,044,167)	(3,920,121)
	$146,067,907	$109,319,308
Commitments and Contingent Liabilities	$266,627,899	$224,154,250

Source: 1978 Annual Report, Beech Aircraft Corporation.

EXHIBIT III   CONSOLIDATED STATEMENTS OF INCOME AND RETAINED EARNINGS

	Years ended September 30	
	1978	**1977**
Net Sales	$527,510,511	$417,419,646
Other Income	8,434,525	6,353,498
	$535,945,036	$423,773,144
Costs and Expenses		
Wages, materials, and other costs	$396,122,481	$317,909,910
Selling, general, & administrative expenses	48,184,146	40,435,377
Interest	3,264,442	3,455,903
Depreciation	3,751,244	3,354,028
Taxes, other than income taxes	11,693,847	8,847,425
	$463,016,160	$374,002,643
Income before income taxes	$ 72,928,876	$ 49,770,501
Federal and State Income Tax Provision	$ 37,408,000	$ 24,288,000
Net Income	$ 35,520,876	$ 25,482,501
Retained earnings at beginning of year	85,027,416	66,563,113
	$120,548,292	$ 92,045,614
Less:		
Cash dividends paid: 1978—$.76 a share	$ 8,383,192	
1977—$.65 a share		$ 7,018,198
Market value of Common stock issued as		
2% stock dividend	4,101,308	
Cash payment in lieu of fractional shares	171,542	
	$ 12,656,042	$ 7,018,198
Retained earnings at end of year	$107,892,250	$ 85,027,416
Earnings per share		
Primary	$3.14	$2.32
Fully diluted	$2.83	$2.08
Source:		
Primary	$3.14	$2.32
Fully diluted	$2.83	$2.08

Source: 1978 Annual Report, Beech Aircraft Corporation.

1966, produced the twin-engine pressurized Baron, the Duke, and wings for most Beech airplanes. The leased base in Liberal, Kansas, produced the smaller aircraft of the Beech line such as the Skipper, Sundowner, Sierra, and tail surfaces for other aircraft. This 113,000 square feet facility ran test flights and delivered the planes that it produced. In February 1979, Beech leased a base in Selma, Alabama, where the King Air 200 was modified into a surveillance aircraft. This site was also suited for the construction of commuter planes. Beech had also leased a plant in Newton, Kansas, in order to expand operations. Beech's other owned facility, in Boulder, Colorado, consisted of 111,000 square feet of plant and office space. Research and Development

EXHIBIT IV CONSOLIDATED STATEMENTS OF CHANGES IN FINANCIAL POSITION

	Years ended September 30	
	1978	**1977**
Source of Funds		
From operations:		
Net income for the year	$35,520,876	$25,482,501
Expenses not requiring use of working capital:		
Depreciation	3,751,244	3,354,028
Increase in reserves for insurance claims	2,859,858	565,251
Deferred income taxes	2,200,000	
Total from operations	$44,331,978	$29,401,780
Proceeds from long-term debt	—	2,930,000
Disposals of property, plant, and equipment	192,032	515,209
Issuance of Common Stock under stock option plans	812,740	1,358,688
Issuance of Common Stock for debenture		
conversions	9,093,763	168,383
	$54,430,513	$34,374,060
Application of Funds		
Increase in working capital	$28,806,820	$18,649,868
Additions to property, plant, and equipment	5,283,441	7,710,319
Increase in investments	2,170,563	220,076
Reductions of long-term debt	9,390,013	728,165
Cash dividends paid	8,383,192	7,018,198
Cash payments in lieu of fractional shares in		
connection with stock dividend	171,542	
Cost of Common Stock purchased for treasury	124,046	
Increase in other assets	100,896	47,434
	$54,430,513	$34,374,060
Changes in Components of Working Capital		
Increase (decrease) in current assets:		
Cash	$ 4,573,294	$(1,900,101)
Marketable securities	2,106,643	6,193,630
Trade notes and accounts receivable	14,485,004	11,287,510
Inventories	17,209,700	18,895,628
Prepaid expenses		
	487,384	20,529
	$38,862,025	$34,497,196
Decrease (increase) in current liabilities:		
Notes payable	$ (46,673)	$ 1,745,497
Trade accounts payable	(6,607,437)	(5,660,538)
Payroll and payroll deductions	(3,511,930)	228,698
Accrued expenses	(1,668,011)	(1,446,653)
Customer deposits	8,842,377	(7,310,767)
Federal and state income taxes	(7,056,169)	(3,382,459)
Current portion of long-term debt	(7,362)	(21,106)
	(10,055,205)	(15,847,328)
Increase in working capital	$28,806,820	$18,649,868

Source: 1978 Annual Report, Beech Aircraft Corporation.

EXHIBIT V FIVE YEARS IN REVIEW
(Dollars in Thousands—Except Per Share Data)

	Fiscal years ended September 30				
	1978	1977	1976	1975	1974
Summary of Operations					
Net sales	$527,511	$417,420	$346,926	$267,149	$241,603
Commerical	414,692	328,530	291,300	246,924	219,260
Defense/Aerospace	112,819	88,890	55,626	20,225	22,343
Wages, materials and other costs	396,122	317,910	264,309	198,114	186,488
Interest expense	3,264	3,456	4,135	4,818	4,257
Cash dividends paid	8,383	7,018	5,369	4,432	3,614
Cash dividends per share[1]	.76	.65	.50	.42	.33
Taxes on income	37,408	24,288	18,017	13,784	9,687
Net income	35,521	25,483	20,361	15,612	12,479
Net income as a percent of sales	6.7%	6.1%	5.9%	5.8%	5.2%
Earnings per share[2]					
Primary	3.14	2.32	1.88	1.46	1.15
Fully diluted	2.83	2.08	1.69	1.33	1.06
Financial Position					
Working capital	$142,571	$113,764	$ 95,114	$ 81,532	$ 66,376
Plant & equipment, net					
after depreciation	18,779	17,439	13,598	12,747	11,658
Stockholders' equity	146,068	109,319	89,328	73,786	62,864
Stockholders' equity per share[3]	13.13	10.09	8.34	6.93	5.82
Other Information					
Number of employees at					
September 30	10,395	9,076	8,216	7,747	7,580
Total salaries and wages	129,760	104,692	93,947	84,468	71,063
Expenditures for fixed assets	5,283	7,710	4,617	4,412	2,766
Depreciation	3,751	3,354	3,239	2,992	2,627
Taxes levied on company	49,102	33,135	26,014	21,124	15,992
Taxes levied on company per					
share[3]	4.41	3.06	2.43	1.98	1.48
Shares outstanding (less					
treasury stock) at year end					
(in thousands)	11,409	7,082	6,965	6,836	6,790

Source: 1978 Annual Report, Beech Aircraft Corporation.
[1] Based on rate paid and adjusted for the stock dividends and split.
[2] Primary and fully diluted earnings per share have been adjusted for the 3 for 2 stock split in 1978; one percent stock dividends in 1975, 1976; two percent stock dividend 1978 and the one percent stock dividend paid November 17, 1978.
[3] Based on average outstanding shares and adjusted for the stock dividends and split.

at the Boulder facility had accelerated with the use of the computer in designing products. The Boulder plant also manufactured aircraft-related products [10].

The manufacturing and assembling of airplanes had become increasingly automated. By the 1970s, shop orders were computerized and the parts were machine produced. A quality control inspector examined each lot to check for flaws. Beech used an expensive procedure, chemical milling, to reinforce stress points on the parts. The process included applying latex rubber cement to areas of the stress points. Chemical baths reduced the metal weight where the thickness was not needed. The process, though expensive, reduced excess metal weight unlike the design which most competitors used. The parts were then sent through an automatic electrostatic painting process, which accommodated 10,000 parts/hour. From here, the parts were ready for assembly. Nearly all parts for airplanes, except for engines, brakes, avionics and certain other components, are produced by Beech. Turbine engines for turboprop Beechcraft are manufactured by Pratt-Whitney and Garrett, while Continental and Lycoming produce engines for the piston-engine models.

Some of the satellite plants did sub-assemblies which were integrated into the final product in the assembly-line operation at Wichita. In the assembly process of a plane at Wichita, the bottom of the plane was structured first, and then the cabin and top added. The airplanes were physically moved from one work station to the next twice a day. The plant used three shifts: the first shift did most of the production and assembly; the second shift completed the work the first shift could not finish; and the third shift was mainly for security and maintenance.

The company had good employee relations. In fact, the only work stoppage in the entire history of the company occurred in 1969. Beech's employees—numbering over 10,000—were provided with benefits including a company-supported retirement income program, group insurance plans with life, medical, and dental benefits, a hospitalization program, a credit union, an employees' club offering hobby and recreational activities, a cafeteria and activity center, and a built-in cost of living pay increase in their contract. When the 1969 strike was settled, all employees returned to work. The company was not in a good financial position at the time and there was no backlog of work. One long-term employee recalled some executives urging Mrs. Beech not to recall the employees. He stated that Mrs. Beech would not hear of a layoff. She reportedly said, ''In spite of the strike, I won't have us laying off people just before Thanksgiving and Christmas.''

Beech stresses employee relations. Building quality airplanes requires high degrees of skill and experience. Good employee relations contribute to the low employee turnover required to develop an experienced workforce. In 1979 about 40 percent of Beech's employees had been with the company ten years or more and 25 percent for over 15 years [1]. ''Many families have more than one generation working here,'' said a long-time employee.

The labor market in the Wichita area in 1978 and 1979 was very tight, as was available space for plant expansion. The Wichita unemployment rate was about 2.5 percent compared to a national average of 7–9 percent. Beech had approached the capacity ceiling in Wichita and has thus been forced to expand company operations into other cities and states. The plant established in Selma, Alabama, was located there primarily because of the area's good labor market and enthusiastic community support. The quality control procedures that Beech employed ensured that all products from the Sundowner to the King Air were of high quality, regardless of where they were produced and assembled.

PRODUCTS

Beech products consisted mainly of airplanes for the general aviation industry. This industry consisted of four major market segments: business planes, commuter planes, personal planes, and defense aerospace aircraft. Of the four, Beech relied most heavily on the business market. Said Rembleske:

> The personal airplane is a business tool. The time loss is significant to executives. With air to ground telephones and such, executives can work while they're flying!

The business market was the largest segment of the general aviation market and accounted for about 55 percent of the mileage. The business market was also less cynical than the personal plane market [4]. Beech's prices in this market were higher than the industry average, but this factor had not affected sales because of Beech's reputation for quality and the planes' higher-than-average resale value.

Over 40 percent of Beech's total sales volume in 1978 was attributed to the King Air turboprop models. Beech held about 53 percent of the U.S. turboprop market. The King Air turboprop models, sold primarily for companies, all had pressurized cabins. Their seating capacity ranged from six to fifteen seats, and the maximum cruise speed ranged from 256 to 305 mph. The maximum flight range on a King Air was from 1,474 to 1,870 miles, and its price range was between $560,000 and $1,110,000.

Beech did not produce any pure jet aircraft for the business market. In 1975, it stopped marketing Britain's Hawker Siddeley after having sold 64 jets since the program's initiation in 1970. In 1979, Beech had no plans to develop a jet of its own because it saw greater opportunities in the turboprop—mostly because of greater fuel efficiency. Also, a jet was not compatible with the current design, building, and marketing of the turboprop. Regarding turboprop, Rembleske said,

> The turboprop airplane meets the travel requirements of most corporations in that it provides the speed, comfort, reliability, and economy demanded for the vast majority of business trips.

The personal or owner-flown market segment made up the other main component of Beech's general aviation commercial sales. This segment, which consisted entirely of piston-powered engines, could be divided into two subdivisions: the single-engine planes and the multi-engine. The single-engine planes were used almost solely for personal use with the exception of the Bonanzas which were used for some business flying. In 1977, these planes accounted for about 15 percent of the company's commercial sales dollars and held about 8.8 percent of the single-engine market share [4]. Sales of these planes were somewhat related to the state of the economy (Exhibit I).

The single-engine models were the Beechcraft Sport, Sundowner, Sierra, and Bonanza series. Their seating capacity ranged from two to six seats; the maximum cruise speed ranged from 127 to 209 mph; and the maximum flight range went from 687 to 790 miles. The price range fell between $35,000 and $100,000 [2]. A two-seater Skipper model was expected to be certified in January 1979, for delivery early in the spring. This model was intended to be competitive with Cessna's Model 152 and 152 Aerobat, and Piper's Super Cub and Tomahawk. The Skipper was intended to replace the Sport.

The multi-engine, piston-powered planes are used for personal and business flying. In 1977, these planes accounted for about 25 percent of Beech's commercial sales dollars and held about 17 percent of the multi-engine general aviation market [4]. Many buyers of these aircraft move up into more expensive Beech planes after owning these smaller Beech planes. The twin-engine models were the Duchess, Baron series, and Duke series. Their seating capacity ranged from four to six seats; the maximum cruise speed ranged from 191 to 275 mph; and the maximum flight range went from 898 to 1,517 miles. The price range fell between $90,000 and $315,000.

Beech saw good possibilities for expansion in the commuter market. In 1979, only 420 cities were served by the airlines and many companies were moving away from metropolitan areas. Beech first entered the commuter market in 1965 with the sale of the ten-place Queen Air to Chicago Commuter Air Lines. Sales to other commuter lines followed. In 1969, Beech made its first sale of the 15-place Model 99 to the commuter airline market. Beech planned in 1978 to divisionalize the company as part of the larger effort to pursue this market more vigorously. A separate division would market these commuter planes. Beech was designing a 19-passenger turboprop for the commuter market. Beech had been in the commuter market with a fifteen-seater 99 Airliner model. The 99 Airliner was refined and reintroduced to the market in 1981 as the Commuter 99.

The final Beech product class, defense-aerospace, accounted for about 22 percent of sales [4]. Major sales included the C-12 cargo transports for the Army, Navy, Air Force, and Marines; single- and multi-engine trainers for the Navy; and flight simulators for the Navy. Besides aircraft, Beech also made missile targets for the military and did major subcontract work for McDonnell Douglas and Bell Helicopter. In addition, the company had a $13 million production subcontract from Rockwell International and the space shuttle program. Defense aerospace contracts in 1978 totaled $122,430,000.

Included in commercial sales were international sales which reached $112,007,911 in fiscal 1978, a 61 percent increase over 1977. About half of these sales were military planes to foreign governments. Beech sold planes to over 130 countries, including the 1979 sale to the Republic of China. To avoid currency problems in the international market, Beech's policy required all payments to be made in U.S. dollars. In addition, planes to non-U.S. buyers were not delivered until full payment was received. Even with this strictly enforced foreign policy and Beech's higher prices, international sales continued to increase. Primary reasons for this consistent growth were Beech's reputation for quality aircraft and its emphasis on after-sale support. Beech had improved field service capability through company incentive programs and had increased the number of service technicians.

In 1978, Beech had fewer aircraft models available than Cessna and Piper, but production of the Skipper, twin-engine Duchess model, and introduction of additional King Air models decreased the gap.

MARKETING

Beech planes were manufactured to order for the end customer or distributor. The buyer had options on the plane's seating arrangement, its technical equipment, and its decor. "Give the customer what he wants" was Beech's key to developing versatile customer aircraft which could be adapted to the needs of many buyers.

Domestic Marketing

Domestic marketing was conducted through 21 corporate aviation centers, 17 of which were wholly owned. Twelve wholly-owned distributorships accounted for about 24 percent of domestic sales in 1977. The company's franchise organization consisted of three types. Corporate Aviation Centers handled the full line of aircraft, but concentrated on turboprop planes; Executive Aviation Centers concentrated on Bonanzas, Barons, and Dukes; Aero Centers were concerned with smaller aircraft, with most operating a Beech Aero Club. There were about 175 franchises in the United States and plans called for this number to increase to 500 [6].

In mid-1978, the marketing department developed an experimental, innovative Executive Flight Plan for some of the 60 Executive Aviation Centers [3]. This plan allowed businessmen to contract with Beech franchisees for blocks of flight time on an annual basis. Beech had three goals it hoped to achieve through implementation of this plan. First, it hoped to increase Executive Center cash flows and aircraft utilization. Franchisees could not afford to have aircraft sitting around idle, especially since inventory was so costly. Second, as the businessmen's companies grew, these customers would hopefully want to purchase their own airplane—a Beechcraft, of course. Beech's prospective customer list was made up of businesses not currently using business aircraft. Third, the program was used to train salespersons [3]. Beech expected to expand this program, if it continued to be as successful, as initial indications suggested.

Aero Centers had an established program similar to the experimental EFP. Members of the 120 Aero Clubs paid monthly dues and were able to take flying lessons or rent planes from Aero Centers [4]. The planes used for these Clubs were usually the smaller aircraft, such as Skippers and Sundowners, but also included Sierras, Duchesses, some Bonanzas, and Barons. The purpose of the program was to keep new pilots actively engaged in flying until such time as they could justify ownership of a Beechcraft. Almost all of the Aero Centers participated in this program.

Beech had integrated forward into establishing their own retail outlets for a number of reasons. The main reason was to create a strong position in the general aviation market, thereby increasing sales and profit potential. Other reasons for outlet ownership included enhancing the company's ability to learn about their products first-hand, and putting Beech's sales and marketing philosophies to work. The company had established dealerships where it found a potentially strong market and good physical facilities available. There had been increased marketing support from the factory, including retail outlet assistance in recruiting badly needed sales personnel. The company had also instituted a program where one of its representatives visited a sales outlet, instituted a program for job interviews, and then assisted the franchisee in employee selection, all at company expense. Beech was considering extending this program to help recruit service technicians who were in short supply.

In 1978, Beech's advertising expenditures grew 49 percent from the previous year to a high of $4.8 million. The reason for this increase was more advertising emphasis; more sales promotions; greater participation in co-op advertising; and inflation. Brewer, an advertising agency located in Kansas City, handled all of Beech's domestic advertising. The company's objective in advertising, according to Vice President Neuburger, was "advertising is addressed to the type of buyers the firm wants to attract." The advertising theme has consistently been "We are not the cheapest, but we are the best." Attempts were made to relate the Beech name with quality, speed, dependability, and comfort.

In planning the advertising programs, Brewer asked each distributor what models they would like to emphasize and in what magazines. Beech advertised in numerous aviation magazines such as *Aviation Weekly* and *Intervia,* and also placed ads in the *Wall Street Journal, Time,* and *Fortune.* Some advertisements included a coupon which could be returned to the company as a request for additional information. The follow-up on these coupons was estimated to have generated approximately $27 million in retail sales in the first eleven months of fiscal 1978. More importantly, 75 percent of these sales were to first-time buyers of aircraft. Beech had also run ads on the theme "America the Beautiful," which showed America's beautiful countryside being viewed from a Beechcraft plane. In addition, the company had spent some advertising dollars on civic causes, such as promoting free enterprise.

One factor of concern in Beech's marketing approach was that Beech had few smaller planes on the market. Marketing Vice President Roy McGregor stated that, "There's habit-buying in aircraft, just like anything else. If you get in a Beech when you buy your first airplane, chances are much better that we will get you in a King Air someday" [6]. However, in this segment, Beech would compete head on with the established lines of Cessna and Piper.

The commuter market presented a different challenge. Beech had a strong competitive position in the commuter market with both its twin-engine piston and twin-engine turboprop models. Beech's ability to compete effectively in the commuter market could, however, be challenged by introduction of new models or more aggressive marketing by Cessna, Piper, or other aircraft manufacturers.

International Marketing

As indicated in Exhibit VI, Beech had divided its international markets into seven regions. There were no company-owned distributorships outside the United States and, in fact, the foreign distributors entered into only one-year contracts with Beech. Despite this short contract length, however, many of the dealers had been associated with Beech for more than 15 years. The stability of these associations indicate the dealer loyalty which Beech had developed. Beech selected its dealers carefully. Each

EXHIBIT VI   BEECH AIRCRAFT CORPORATION REGIONS

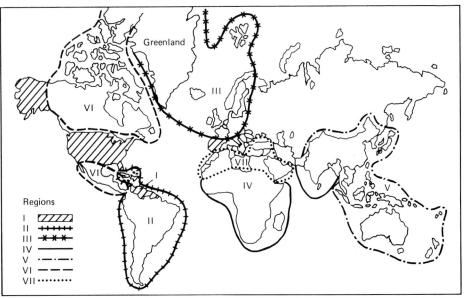

distributor was encouraged to carry the full product line and Beech supported its dealers through service arrangements and advertising.

One of Beech's goals domestically, as well as internationally, was to have complete service support for the Beechcraft owner. The company had established many service facilities around the world. To assist these field locations, Beech provided training and maintained a customer service organization staffed mainly by engineers who were multilingual and who could provide answers and assistance to inquiries involving the service and operation of their products.

The Beechcraft Product Improvement Committee published service instructions and publication changes, and kept in touch with desired product improvements through constant monitoring of customer feedback and field service records.

Advertising was also done overseas. Beech placed advertisements in many international publications. These ads carried the same basic quality theme that was used domestically. Michael Neuburger related a story illustrating this internationally known quality image. He said, "I was with a customer in Germany when his phone rang. A competitor was on the other end of the line and was offering to sell his company's plane at cost to the German businessman. My customer's reply was, 'No, thank you. I drive a Mercedes. I fly a Beech.' "

CRYOGENICS

One of the company's engineers remarked, "Technological advances are evolutionary, not revolutionary."

In the late 1970s, research and development efforts at Beech were geared to improvements in aircraft performance, subsonic and supersonic missile target systems and cryogenic systems for space use.[2] Beech was a pioneer in cryogenics and had conducted cryogenic research, development, and production since 1954. The cryogenic systems produced by Beech supplied hydrogen and oxygen for fuel cell power plants and breathing oxygen systems for NASA's manned Gemini, Apollo, and Skylab space missions. In 1979, Beech was under contract to design and produce the power reactant storage systems for the NASA Space Shuttle Orbiter.

Cryogenic technology includes the systems in which gases are cooled, liquified, and stored in specially built tanks which keep the liquified gas at -420° F until such time as the gas is used. In 1979, members of Beech management were excited over commercial application of the cryogenic technology. Beech had developed an automobile powered solely by liquid methane, a primary constituent of natural gas. Methane is a commonly occurring natural fuel that burns cleaner than gasoline. Methane can be produced in a number of ways, even from garbage or manure.

Beech estimated that converting the nation's 10 million fleet-operated motor vehicles to LNG would reduce gasoline consumption by the equivalent of 1.25 million barrels of oil per day. Mike Neuburger and R. G. Oestreicher envisioned a snowballing effect for cryogenics.

"The total technology system is what Beech has," said Oestreicher. He was referring to the process of LNG liquefaction, storage, transport, service stations, and automotive fuel systems.

Further experimentation in cryogenics, however, would require a substantial capital investment. One knowledgeable member of the engineering industry stated that an investment of $18 million would purchase only a minimal amount of the equipment required for experimentation.

FINANCE

Beech's strong financial position (Exhibits II, III, IV and V) made it an attractive merger candidate. Sales ($527 million in 1978) had more than doubled since 1974. During this same time, net income as a percentage of sales increased from 5.2 percent to 6.7 percent. As of September 30, 1978, the company had only $24 million in long-term debt, with about $200,000 of this amount maturing each year until 1993. Given this strong financial position, the Board of Directors voted to raise the annual cash dividend to $0.92 per share, up $0.12 from 1977. The increase was the eighth since 1973. Dividends were paid on a quarterly basis and the company had paid 122 consecutive dividends. The company held about $20 million in short-term investments and because of its overall position, Wey Kenny, Assistant Treasurer, asserted, "We could buy a company or have a stock exchange . . . and (we) could be the surviving company in a merger . . . Also, if needed we have enough credit in banks to borrow any needed funds." The firm's 1979 credit line was $23 million, but Kenny felt that it

---

[2] During the late 1940s, hydrogen and helium liquifiers were first commercially developed. This began a new era of cryogenics. (Data taken from *Cryogenic Fundamentals*, G. G. Haselden, Academic Press, 1971, p. 4.)

could easily be extended. The large cash flows that Beech's success had generated had made the treasury department an important administrative function. The treasury department's main responsibility was to manage the company's assets. Another important treasury responsibility was the management of Beech's cash flow. Whenever Beech finalized a contract, the treasury department in conjunction with the product manager, established a timetable. This was done to help the treasury department plan its cash flow picture. The department also kept track of the contract's progress. The system had been effective and the company had never experienced any major cash flow problems.

About 20 percent of Beech common stock was held by employees—mainly the management staff. The Beech family had about another 15 percent of the shares. The remaining 65 percent of the common stock was spread out over about 11,000 shareholders which were mostly comprised of institutions such as pension funds and mutual funds. Beech did not have to worry about a takeover by these institutions because any institution holding more than 10 percent of a company's stock must register with the Security Exchange Commission and state whether the ownership is for investment or takeover purposes. The 20 percent management ownership was a result of a stock option plan implemented in 1957. Beech felt that this program provided an incentive to various levels of management.

MANAGEMENT

In 1979, Beech was headed by President Frank Hedrick, age 69. Hedrick was a respected figure in the general aviation industry. He was well known for spearheading Beech's responsiveness to changing market demands, including the decisions to concentrate on turboprop technology, to pursue the business market aggressively and, more recently, to establish the company more firmly in the commuter market. The company's success could also be attributed to the management below Hedrick and to the influential Board of Directors, chaired by his aunt, Mrs. Beech. The Board of Directors consisted of Beech's top management plus several respected businessmen. Most members were involved in community affairs and/or served on committees affecting the aircraft industry. Involvement with the industry was essential in Beech's efforts to keep track of environmental changes. (See Exhibit VII for background on key executives.)

A concern had arisen, however, over Beech's future management. In the late 1970s, four of Beech's top executives were lost to the company because of death or illness. At least one of these employees was not replaced, but rather, managers who had reported to him began reporting directly to Hedrick.

Mrs. Beech's view on management manpower planning within the company was, ''We have very qualified people in lower management who could move up to top positions—otherwise they would not be working here.'' Mrs. Beech's statement about her employees' abilities to move up in the organization was based, in part, on the Management Manpower Reserve Chart system which began in the 1970s. These charts, prepared by officers, executive managers, and other management representatives who report to a member of the Executive Management Group, were used to

EXHIBIT VII KEY EXECUTIVES

Name	Age	Years with Beech (as officer)	Current positions	Education (college)
O. A. Beech	76	47	(35) Chm. of Board, Dir.	Wichita, KS—Business College
Frank E. Hedrick*	69	34	(15) President, Dir.	No college
E. C. Burns**	58	15	(8) Group VP, Dir.	Univ. of KS—Industrial Mgmt.
James N. Lew	63	26	Senior VP-Engr., Dir.	Curtiss-Wright School of Aeronautics (graduate)
M. G. Neuburger	64	23	(8) Senior VP-Intn'l., Dir.	Univ. of Munich (Ger.)—J. D. (Law)
Leddy L. Greever	66	23	VP & Corp. Dir., Dir.	No college
Seymour Colman	62	9	(4) Senior VP-Operations	Chicago-Kent College of Law-J.D.
Harold W. Deets	58	7	(1) VP-Material	Southwestern-Business-B.A.
Glenn Ehling	57	4	VP-Manufacturing	No college
George D. Rodgers	46	2	VP-Domestic Comm. Mkt.	Duke University, BA; Columbia University, MA
William G. Rutherford	59	1	VP-Gov't. Relations	San Bernardino Valley College, Kelsey Jenny Business College (attended)
E. C. Nikkel	61	7	VP-Aerospace Programs	Southwestern Inst. Tech.-Bus. Ad.
John A. Pike	48	4	VP-Research & Develop.	University of Colorado, BS and MS degrees—aeronautical engineering
C. A. Rembleske	59	4	VP-Engineering	Aeronautical University of Chicago—aeronautical engineering
Austin Rising	61	17	VP	New York University, BA
Stewart Ayton	62	2	VP	Beacom College—Acctg. & Fin.—B.A.

*Nephew of O. A. Beech.
**Nephew of Walter H. Beech.
(　)Active on indicated number of aviation-related committees.

identify and monitor executive talent in the organization. Information on the chart included name, age, and rating on the employee's promotability as well as a rating on his/her competence.

The Key Management Program was also developed to assist high-potential employees in preparing for future middle- and upper-management positions. Candidates for this program were selected on the basis of their performance within the company, their eligibility for promotion and their commitment to self development. Employees were recommended by their immediate superiors for the Key Management Program. Normally, Key Management employees had the prospect of at least ten years' future service at Beech. In addition to assessment by supervisory, executive, and personnel, the Key Management Program candidates were asked for their own personal assessment of their abilities and potential as well as input in the individualized plan of career development.

The attitude of management toward Beech employees was characterized by J. L. Sheldon, Manager of Personnel Placement, "At Beech, memos go from individual to individual, not title to title . . . . This whole organization is alive, it's dynamic!"

MERGER

Beech had held discussions with several companies about possible mergers. However, none of these talks progressed beyond the preliminary discussion stage. The qualities that Beech looked for in a merger prospect were the company's goods or products, the company's compatability with the general aviation industry, the company's technological base, the company's continuing research and development efforts, and the financial situation of the company. Basically, Beech wanted to find a company that would offer the possibility for an interchange of personnel, knowledge, and abilities. Beech did not want to merge with a company with products that would put Beech in competition with other aviation supplier companies. Potential merger possibilities in 1979 were General Dynamics Corporation, Raytheon Company, and Sperry Corporation.

General Dynamics Corporation, based in St. Louis, Missouri, mainly developed and produced military and commercial aircraft, space systems, and tactical missiles. The company was also engaged in shipbuilding and produced a variety of other products. In 1978, sales of military aircraft accounted for 31.1 percent of sales, tactical missiles 13.2 percent, marine 29.4 percent, telecommunications 5.7 percent, and the rest divided up in other areas. The F-16 jet fighter was an example of one product included in aircraft production. In 1978, General Dynamics had net sales of $3,205,205,000 and a net loss of $48,088,000 incurred because of a settlement with the Navy on a program which caused a total loss of $359 million. In previous years, however, net income had grown steadily from $2.5 million in 1969 to $103 million in 1977. Growth was primarily internal with a few acquisitions. In 1978, General Dynamics' debt totaled $82,534,000, and total assets were $1,778,723,000.

Raytheon Company, based in Lexington, Massachusetts, was a conglomerate with many products dealing with electronics. In 1978, electronics accounted for 56.6 percent of sales, energy sources 23.7 percent, major appliances 12.3 percent, and other 7.4 percent. U.S. government end-use business was 37 percent of sales. The company's subsidiaries included Amana Refrigeration, Inc.; Seismograph Service Corporation; Machlett Laboratories, Inc.; and United Engineers and Constructors, Inc. The company was known for its strong research and development work, particularly in electronics. Sales for 1978 were $3,239,302,000 with net income of $150,034,000. This net income figure has been growing steadily from the $35 million in 1969. Long-term debt was $76,060,000 and total assets stood at $2,060,945,000. Acquisitions and mergers accounted for much of the company's growth [5].

Sperry Corporation was a company with a worldwide business. In 1978, computer systems and equipment accounted for 49 percent of their sales; farm equipment, 20 percent; guidance and control equipment, 16 percent; fluid power equipment, 10 percent; and other, 4 percent. The guidance and control equipment consists of avionic and radar gear for airplanes ranging from those used in general aviation to gear used in large commercial airliners. Sperry was one of many avionic producers for the general aviation industry. Sperry's sales for 1978 were $3,649,487,000 and their net income was $176,619,000. Long-term debt totalled $496,112,000 and total assets were $3,286,610. Income had grown steadily from the 1970 level of $81 million. Sperry had experienced significant internal growth. The company's acquisitions, particularly in the computer field, provided additional growth [8, 11].

REFERENCES

1 *A Pocketful of Facts.* Prepared by the editorial staff of Beechcraft Corporation. Wichita, Kansas: McCormick Armstrong Company, 1978.
2 *A Tradition of Excellence.* Prepared by the editorial staff of Beechcraft Corporation. Wichita, Kansas: McCormick Armstrong Company, 1978.
3 *Aviation Week & Space Technology.* "Beech Planning Expansion in Wake of Record Sales." October 23, 1978, pp. 20–21.
4 *Barrons.* "Beech Aircraft—Its Earnings in Sharp Climb." Ed Steven S. Anreder. May 15, 1979, p. 39.
5 Bulban, E. J. "Beech Moves Toward Merger." *Aviation Week & Space Technology.* April 8, 1979, p. 78.
6 *Forbes.* "General Aviation: Beech's Choice." April 17, 1978, pp. 93–94.
7 McDaniel, William. *History of Beech.* 2nd ed. Wichita, Kansas: McCormick Armstrong Company, 1976, pp. 13–14.
8 *Moody's Industrial Manual.* New York, N.Y.: Moody's Investor's Services, Inc., 1979, p. 1412. (Annual.) An extensive listing of corporations listed on the NYSE and ASE listing their financial reports and current financial status.
9 *Public Relations.* Prepared by the editorial staff of Beechcraft Corporation. Wichita, Kansas: McCormick Armstrong Company, 1978.
10 Security Exchange Commission. *10-K:* Form. Washington, D. C.: U.S. Government Printing Office, 1978.
11 *Standard & Poor's Corporation Records.* New York, New York: Standard & Poor's Corporation, 1979, p. 1336. (Semiannual.)

DISCUSSION QUESTIONS

1 Should Beech Aircraft merge with or acquire another company? Why or why not?
2 What characteristics of a potential acquisition candidate would be most advantageous for Beech? Evaluate General Dynamics, Raytheon, and Sperry as possible merger candidates.
3 Explain the challenge posed by the aging executive group at Beech and discuss what you feel should be done about it.
4 Discuss the opportunity which Beech apparently sees in the cryogenics area. Should Beech make the necessary investment for success in this field?
5 To what degree do you believe Beech's success is attributable to the ownership of common stock by management? Does this have any connection with the distinctively conservative financial posture of Beech? Explain.

GERBER PRODUCTS COMPANY (A)

Edmund Gray
B. L. Kedia
Louisiana State University

D. E. Ezell
University of Baltimore

SELECTED STRATEGIC ISSUES

- Relating diversification strategy to corporate mission
- Financial ratios and the growth objective
- Strengths, weaknesses, threats, and opportunities and their relationship to strategy
- Marketing strategy in terms of the four P's of marketing

> Perhaps the single most important new fact of recent statistical vintage is that, in America, the Population Explosion has ended . . . And there is every indication that having ended, it will stay ended. The Baby Boom has been replaced by a Birth Dearth. Although the Dearth will not cure all the ills that were wrongly attributed to the Explosion, its effect will be quite salutary. In the years to come, it may well prove to be the single greatest agent of an ever-increasing, ever-wealthier middle class in America."[1]

The Gerber Products Company, the largest producer of baby foods in the world, found nothing salutary in Wattenberg's "birth dearth." To the contrary, starting in 1973 the decline in the baby population translated directly into lower sales and reduced profits for the company. In response to this adversity Gerber accelerated its diversifica-

This case was prepared with the assistance of, but not necessarily endorsement of Gerber Products Company. The statements made and the conclusions drawn are not necessarily those of the company except where direct quotations are indicated.

Distributed by the Case Research Association. All rights reserved to the authors and the Case Research Association. Permission to use the Case should be obtained from the Case Research Association.

[1] Ben S. Wattenberg, *The Real America*, Doubleday & Co., 1974.

319

tion efforts. The long downward trend in birth statistics came to a halt in 1976 and then drifted slightly upward, but the company continued to diversify. By 1980 the company's products included 140 varieties of baby food, various allied products such as baby clothing and baby furniture, insurance, child care centers, and a trucking operation.

BRIEF HISTORY

Gerber was founded in 1901 as the Fremont Canning Company in Fremont, Michigan. The fledgling company operated a canned food business that served the mid-western states. In 1928 it entered the commercial food business. Its name was changed to Gerber Products Company in 1941.

The corporate headquarters is still situated in Fremont, Michigan, and its food plants are located in Fremont; Oakland, California; Rochester, New York; Asheville, North Carolina; and Fort Smith, Arkansas. The company operates worldwide through exporters, licensees, and subsidiaries.

THE BABY FOOD INDUSTRY

In 1979, the baby food market was estimated to be a $524 million industry in the U.S. In recent years Gerber's share of the market has fluctuated between 60–70% of the total; the remainder being divided between Beech-Nut and Heinz. The East Coast is regarded as the strongest market for Beech-Nut while Heinz has its strength in the Midwest area. Gerber, on the other hand, has fairly uniform strength throughout the country and its foods are distributed in 95% of the major supermarkets in the United States. In recent years the consumption of baby food per baby has been relatively steady. However, the recent increase in the number of births has tended to offset this levelling effect. Furthermore, medical opinion appears to be shifting in favor of earlier introduction of solid foods depending upon a baby's weight, appetite, and growth rate, rather than upon age alone (4 to 6 months old rather than 6 months or older).

A very significant characteristic of the industry is the nature of its market. It loses its current customers after a year (babies outgrow baby food), and then must rely on the future population of babies for continued prosperity. Two other important characteristics of the industry involve competitive factors and demographic changes.

Competitive Factors

The third of the market which Gerber did not control was divided between Heinz and Beech-Nut. In the year 1976–77 Beech-Nut made significant gains in the market primarily through an advertising campaign which stressed that its baby foods contain "no added salt, preservatives, artificial flavors or colors." This "all natural" campaign propelled Beech-Nut into the number 2 position in the industry. Gerber and Heinz, interestingly, had also significantly reduced the salt and sugar content of their baby foods but did not emphasize this fact in their promotions. Hence, it appears Beech-Nut capitalized on something that had become common practice in the industry.

Even before Beech-Nut's "all natural" blitz, a movement was emerging where more and more mothers were forsaking the "little glass jars," for fresh foods they cook and strain themselves. This trend was in response to charges made by Ralph Nader, *Consumer Reports,* and others that the nutritional value in prepared baby foods was not all it should be. Although this "anti-processed" attitude gained acceptance across the country it was especially prevalent on the Pacific Coast. One survey showed an increase in the anti-processed attitude from 8% of baby food consumers in early 1970's to 15% in mid-1970's. It has also been suggested that some of the increased consumer resistance may have been due to the high prices as well. After the lifting of federal price controls in 1974, Gerber raised its prices 8% in May and boosted them another 10% in October.

Product price clearly is an important competitive factor in the industry. The first price war was initiated by Gerber's competitors in 1959. Although it was limited to California and Florida, it was a cause for concern because during this period Gerber's production costs were increasing and its profitability was declining. Fortunately for Gerber and the industry, the price war was short-lived and none of the producers of commercially prepared baby foods suffered great financial damage.

The next price war did not come for another ten years, but this time it lasted for three years. Again it was started by Gerber's competitors in reaction to the prediction of a continuing drop in both the birth rate and the total number of births in the United States. They felt they needed to get a larger share of the total dollars spent on babies. Gerber's Vice President of Marketing, Floyd N. Head, explained the action of his competitors as "a simple thing of economics." According to Head, you need so much volume and distribution in this business, and neither Heinz or Beech-Nut command a large market share, so they decided to cut prices in order to gain new customers. So long as the price differential was 1¢ per jar, Gerber was still able to compete effectively and hold its market share. However, when the spread opened up to 1½¢ to 2½¢ per jar, Gerber's market share started eroding, and when the spread hit 3¢ or 4¢ a jar, Gerber had to retaliate. For example, in Detroit, Gerber's local market share tumbled from 65% to 30%. In retaliation, Gerber lowered its prices and narrowed the margin to 1¢ to 1½¢ a jar. At this point in 1971, price controls were imposed and all three companies were trapped at their "bargain-basement" prices. To make matters worse the industry's costs increased significantly during the price war—meat costs alone nearly doubled during one twelve-month period.

Gerber was hurt by the price war, but its competitors were crippled. When the price controls were lifted in 1974 the price war was over and the wounded producers retreated to rebuild. At this time Swift and Company, which had held 3% to 4% of the market, withdrew from the industry. Heinz Baby Food profits suffered and Beech-Nut, a subsidiary of the Squibb Corporation, was sold to Baker Laboratories. Surprisingly enough, Gerber showed a profit during the period.

Birth Trends

Perhaps the most important environmental factors affecting the baby food industry are the rate of birth and the number of births per country. It can be said that the birth rate has a ripple effect on almost all industries, but when babies are your principal market, any change in this rate is critical. It is generally accepted that the baby boom of the 50's and 60's in the United States has slowed down. This is the result of such factors as improved birth control methods, abortions, and changing lifestyles. The fact that a large number of couples no longer feel the need to formalize their marriage has a depressing effect on the birth rate. Moreover, even among married couples there is a trend toward the wife working, resulting in smaller family units.

According to *Current Population Reports,* almost one-half (45 percent) of the women in the age group of 20 to 24 were unmarried in 1979. This level of marriage postponement was in sharp contrast to 28 percent in 1960. Furthermore, the number of unmarried women in the 25 to 29 category approximately doubled between 1970 (10.5 percent) and 1979 (19.6 percent) after showing no change during the 1960's. Divorce rates approximately doubled during the 1970–79 period, rising from 47 divorced persons per 1,000 married persons in 1970 to 92 in 1979. The number of divorces in 1979 (1,170,000) was approximately one-half the number of marriages (2,317,000); the corresponding numbers in 1970 were 708,000 and 2,159,000 respectively. The number of unmarried couples of opposite sex living together was more than twice as high in 1979 as compared to 1970 (1,346,000 versus 523,000).

The number of babies born in the U.S. in 1973 dropped to 3.1 million, the lowest level since World War II. The highest level of births occurred through 1956–62 averaging 4.2–4.3 million births per year, and was 3.7 million as recently as 1970. The number of babies born in the U.S. during the four year period 1973–1976 remained fairly constant, averaging 3.15 million births per year. The rate of births per 1,000 population, during this period, was also fairly constant averaging 14.8 births per 1,000 population. The birth rate increased in 1977 and 1978, when it was 15.3, and was still higher in 1979, when it reached 15.7 per 1,000 population. Table 1 shows population change for the United States during a ten-year period, from 1970 to 1980.

The fertility rate in 1979 was estimated to be 1,840 children per 1,000 women. The fertility rate has steadily declined from the 1955–59 period, when it was 3,690. It is believed that the declining rates of childbearing reflect changing attitudes about early marriage and childbearing as well as the pursuit of educational and career goals. There was, however, a slight increase in the fertility rate during the period 1977–1979. Table 2 shows the total fertility rate during the period 1920–1979. Figure 1 illustrates the total fertility rate as well as changes in numbers of live births in the 1970's.

The increase in births for the years 1977–79 in a proportion greater than the increase in the fertility rate is the result of a large number of women entering the main childbearing ages of 20 to 29. By 1985 there will be 21 million women in that age group, compared with 11 million in 1957. Even at the present low birth rate of 1.8 children per woman, the actual number of births should rise by 500,000 to 3.6 million in 1984. The normal childbearing ages are regarded to be between 15 to 44 years. Table 3 provides a perspective on the present and future age structures of the population. In 1978, the largest aggregation of females were those aged 15 to 24. This group and the category 25 to 29 years were the only age groups in which there were more females in 1978 than are projected for the year 2000. The size of these groups reflects

TABLE 1 ESTIMATES OF THE COMPONENTS OF POPULATION CHANGE FOR THE UNITED STATES: JANUARY 1, 1970, TO JANUARY 1, 1980
(Numbers in Thousands. Includes Armed Forces Overseas)

| Calendar year | Population at beginning of period | Components of change during year | | | | Net civilian immigration |
		Total increase[1]	Natural increase	Births	Deaths	
Number						
1980	221,719	—	—	—	—	—
1979	219,699	2,019	1,560	3,468	1,908	460
1978	217,874	1,825	1,403	3,328	1,925	427
1977	216,058	1,816	1,426	3,327	1,900	394
1976	214,446	1,611	1,258	3,168	1,910	353
1975	212,748	1,698	1,251	3,144	1,894	449
1974	211,207	1,541	1,225	3,160	1,935	316
1973	209,711	1,496	1,163	3,137	1,974	311
1972	208,088	1,623	1,293	3,258	1,965	325
1971	206,076	2,012	1,626	3,556	1,930	387
1970	203,849	2,227	1,812	3,739	1,927	438
Rate per 1,000 Midyear Population						
1979	(X)	9.2	7.1	15.7	8.7	2.1
1978	(X)	8.3	6.4	15.3	8.8	2.0
1977	(X)	8.4	6.6	15.3	8.8	1.8
1976	(X)	7.5	5.8	14.7	8.9	1.6
1975	(X)	8.0	5.9	14.7	8.9	2.1
1974	(X)	7.3	5.8	14.9	9.1	1.5
1973	(X)	7.1	5.5	14.9	9.4	1.6
1972	(X)	7.8	6.2	15.6	9.4	1.6
1971	(X)	9.7	7.9	17.2	9.3	1.9
1970	(X)	10.9	8.8	18.2	9.4	2.1

[1] Includes estimates of overseas admissions into and discharges from the Armed Forces and for 1970, includes error of closure between censuses.

Source: Data consistent with U.S. Bureau of Census, *Current Population*, Series P-25, No. 878. Estimates of births and deaths (with an allowance for deaths of Armed Forces overseas) are from the National Center for Health Statistics. Estimates of net civilian immigration are based partly on data from the Immigration and Naturalization Service.

the higher fertility rates of the post-World War II "baby boom," the effects of which can be seen carried through to the year 2000, when they will reach ages 35 to 54.

DIVERSIFICATION EFFORTS

With the declining birth rate it was felt that Gerber needed to diversify if it was to continue to grow and prosper. In keeping with the slogan that "Babies are our business," the company focused its diversification strategy around the concept of selling more items of merchandise per baby. To facilitate the diversification process, a Gerber venture group was established early in 1974. The group met every Monday

FIGURE 1   TOTAL FERTILITY RATE AND NUMBER OF LIVE BIRTHS: 1970 to 1979

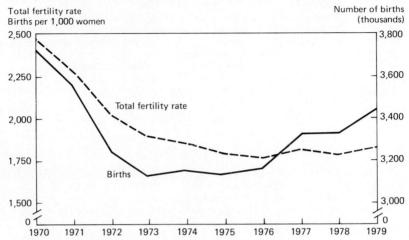

Source: U.S. National Center for Health Statistics, Monthly Vital Statistics Report (various issues) and unpublished Census Bureau estimates.

TABLE 2   TOTAL FERTILITY RATE: 1920 TO 1979

Year or period	Rate	Year or period	Rate	Year or period	Rate
1979	1,840	1971	2,275	1955–59	3,690
1978	1,800	1970	2,480	1950–54	3,337
1977	1,826	1969	2,465	1945–49	2,985
1976	1,768	1968	2,477	1940–44	2,523
1975	1,799	1967	2,573	1935–39	2,235
1974	1,857	1966	2,736	1930–34	2,376
1973	1,896	1965	2,928	1925–29	2,840
1972	2,022	1960–64	3,459	1920–24	3,248

The total fertility rate for a given year shows how many births a group of 1,000 women would have by the end of their childbearing period, if during their entire reproductive period they were to experience the age-specific birth rates for that given year. A fertility rate of 2,000 is necessary for long run replacement of the population in the absence of net migration.

Source: The rate for 1979 is estimated by the Bureau of Census; for 1940 to 1978, National Center for Health Statistics, Vital Statistics of the United States and Monthly Vital Statistics Report (various issues); for 1920–24 to 1935–39, U.S. Bureau of the Census, *Current Population* Reports, Series P-23, No. 36.

TABLE 3 ESTIMATES AND PROJECTIONS OF THE FEMALE POPULATION OF THE UNITED STATES, BY AGE: 1970 TO 2000
(Numbers in Thousands, as of July 1)

Sex, year, and series	All ages	Under 5 years	5 to 14 years	15 to 24 years	25 to 44 years	45 to 64 years	65 years and over	Median age
Women:								
1970	104,609	8,406	19,980	18,048	24,599	21,896	11,681	29.3
1975	109,346	7,765	18,497	19,898	27,238	22,711	13,236	30.0
1978	112,046	7,507	17,373	20,511	29,549	22,831	14,276	31.0
1985								
*Series I	122,437	11,161	16,965					31.9
**Series II	119,514	9,171	16,032	19,049	36,036	22,932	16,293	32.7
***Series III	117,564	7,919	15,333					33.2
2000								
Series I	144,746	11,517	24,270	20,972				34.1
Series II	133,790	8,699	19,087	18,018	38,409	30,473	19,105	36.8
Series III	126,714	6,899	15,786	16,042				38.5
Percent Distribution								
Women:								
1970	100.0	8.0	19.1	17.3	23.5	20.9	11.2	(X)
1975	100.0	7.1	16.9	18.2	24.9	20.8	12.1	(X)
1978	100.0	6.7	15.5	18.3	26.4	20.4	12.7	(X)
1985								
Series I	100.0	9.1	13.9	15.6	29.4	18.7	13.3	(X)
Series II	100.0	7.7	13.4	15.9	30.2	19.2	13.6	(X)
Series III	100.0	6.7	13.0	16.2	30.7	19.5	13.9	(X)
2000								
Series I	100.0	8.0	16.8	14.5	26.5	21.1	13.2	(X)
Series II	100.0	6.5	14.3	13.5	28.7	22.8	14.3	(X)
Series III	100.0	5.4	12.5	12.7	30.3	24.0	15.1	(X)

* Based on women who enter childbearing age and will average 2.7 births/woman.
** Based on women who enter childbearing age and will average 2.1 births/woman.
*** Based on women who enter childbearing age and will average 1.7 births/woman.
  Source: U.S. Department of Commerce, Bureau of the Census, Current Population Reports, series P-25, Nos. 800, 721, and 704.

morning for the purpose of screening new ideas and forwarding promising proposals to the company's planning committee. The concept of the venture group was abandoned within a year.

Categories below represent the major areas of Gerber's diversification.

Special Products

In keeping with the company's philosophy, Gerber has sought to grow through the sale of additional baby products and services (non-food items) primarily to families with infants and small children. There were approximately 400 different items in the special product line in 1979, which were sold through approximately 50,000 retail outlets (including a small number of company-owned outlet stores) in the United States. The success of special products is attributed to the confidence which parents have in products bearing the Gerber name. During the decade of the eighties, the company plans to become an increasing factor in the total baby needs market by adding new items to, and additional distribution of, special products.

Gerber first entered the infant clothing market in 1960 by acquiring a vinyl pants and bib company. During the year 1979–80, the company was the leader in the submarket of vinyl pants; however, a much larger market exists in disposable diapers. And disposable diapers eliminate the need for rubber pants. In addition to vinyl pants and bibs, the baby wear division produces shirts, training pants, and socks. Gerber has also expanded its clothing line to include children through their pre-school years. During 1978–79, new sneakers were introduced in six different patterns in sizes 2 to 8. The sneakers were a part of the Gerber "footwear line," which included shoes, socks, booties, and "funzie" slippers. A special line of screen-printed shirts in six different patterns was also added during the year.

In 1970, Gerber Products purchased an infant toiletries and accessories company operating under the name of Hankscraft. In 1979–80 Hankscraft was the leader in the sale of humidifiers and vaporizers. During this year, its line of carry-all bags, which serve as multipurpose bags as well as the familiar diaper bag, was expanded. In addition four new safety items were introduced—outlet covers, a cabinet lock, door knob covers, and outlet plugs. Hankscraft division also produced nursers and nurser accessories and a number of infant care products.

The Spartan Printing and Graphic Arts Company was acquired in 1971. This division now offers internal and external photographic, design, printing and advertising services. Additionally, Gerber Metal Products division was organized in the late 70's. This division consists of two units, a container manufacturing plant (acquired in 1971) and a metal lithographic operation (built in 1977) at which flat metal sheets are printed for later use in the manufacturing of containers. This division also serves both internal needs and outside customers.

In 1974–75, Gerber acquired the Walter W. Moyer Company, Inc., a manufacturer of children's underwear and knit apparel. At the time of the takeover, the Moyer Company, with plants in Pennsylvania and Arizona, had an annual sales between $16 and $17 million. It currently produces a broad line of knitwear garments for sale under the Gerber name as well as for private label distribution. The Health Care division, formed in 1978, distributes and sells an incontinent pant system and a variety of other products designed for use in medical and extended care facilities. In 1979, Gerber opened a subsidiary—G & M Finishing—for the purpose of bleaching and dyeing knit fabrics. In addition to supplying the needs of the Moyer plant, G & M Finishing has the capacity to provide bleaching and dyeing services to other knit users.

A line of plush stuffed toys are produced by the Atlanta Novelty division (acquired in 1973). The popular Gerber Baby doll is also produced and sold by this division. In the year 1980, Gerber purchased the Reliance Products Corporation of Wood-socket, Rhode Island. Reliance produces a broad line of products for infants, including the widely accepted NUK line of nurser bottle nipples and orthodontic exercisers for infants.

Life and Health Care Insurance

Gerber organized a life insurance subsidiary in 1968 to sell low-priced policies to young parents by mail. In 1970 a "child-care" policy, providing hospitalization insurance for children under legal age was introduced. The unique characteristic of this policy is that the child's parents need not be insured. Gerber considered this to be a natural extension of its business of helping young parents provide for their children. The company is licensed by most states to write and sell life and other types of personal insurance. While the company has used some licensed agents in its insurance business, direct response, including extensive newspaper and television advertising, remains the principal avenue of marketing insurance policies.

The life insurance division was a disappointment through 1975, having lost $858,000 in 1973 and $945,000 in 1974. However, Gerber tightened administrative control over the unit, and profits from the insurance operation amounted to $109,000 in 1976–1977, an increase of $49,000 from the previous period, 1975–1976. Life insurance has since continued to make contributions to the overall performance of the company and experienced the best year in 1980, at which time the company had about one-half billion dollars of insurance in force.

Day Care Centers

Gerber announced the formation of a Children's Centers Division in early 1971. The initial nursery schools were established in Villa Park, Illinois; Cleveland, Ohio; and Costa Mesa, California. In 1980, there were 32 such nursery school and day care centers in seven metropolitan areas of the United States. These centers have encountered some problems, mostly at the local administrative level. The company regards them as a test-marketing of the day care centers concept that will provide experience for determining whether or not to expand. Their performance, to date, has been only marginally profitable. In addition to expecting a major extension of child care activity in the decade of the eighties, the company is planning to operate a Gerber children's center for a private employer.

The Adult Market

Gerber faces a tough challenge in trying to crack the adult market. In hopes of appealing to this market, Gerber developed a "Rediscover Gerber" ad campaign, that promoted speciality fruits and desserts, waffle toppings, and "the 60-second parfait." One ad put it: "Next time you're looking for something to eat, baby yourself with the unexpected snack." A Gerber executive acknowledged the challenge of the adult market this way, "Let's face it, people think of baby food as pretty bland stuff." Currently, the firm is planning to re-introduce its "dessert line" and promote it as snack food for young people (particularly teenage girls).

Another attempt to penetrate the adult market was through single-serving adult foods under the "Singles" label introduced in 1974. At that time, about 11.2 million households, out of a total of 63.2 million households, were single-person households. In addition, the number of two-person households accounted for another 18.9 million.

Thus, the primary and secondary target markets for these products included nearly half of all households in the United States. This contrasts markedly with the 10% of U.S. households which have babies.

A number of problems have been encountered with the Singles line. In an interview reported in *Advertising Age,* John C. Suerth, then Chairman of Gerber, conceded that in spite of a different jar design and label, the Singles line still gave the appearance of baby food. He also conceded that the word "Singles" was misleading. When the company used the word "Singles" it was thinking in terms of single-serving and not in terms of food for singles. Because of these problems the Singles line did not gain consumer acceptance and was dropped, which resulted in a writedown of about $450,000.

Gerber also test marketed three other adult products—a peanut spread, a catsup, and a spaghetti sauce—during the 1974–77 period. These products would put Gerber in competition with such companies as Best Foods, makers of Skippy; Swift Derby Foods, makers of Peter Pan; Proctor and Gamble, makers of Jiff peanut spread; and Kraft Foods and Borden, which also recently entered the peanut butter market. In the catsup and spaghetti sauce market, Gerber would have to compete against companies such as Heinz, Hunt-Wesson, and Del Monte. The test market results led to the abandonment of these products.

C. W. Transport Acquisition

Gerber acquired C. W. Transport, Inc. in August 1979 through a stock transfer. The Wisconsin-based common carrier trucking firm serving eleven states in the Midwest and Southeast represents Gerber's largest acquisition to date. Company officials plan to integrate the new unit into internal shipping operations and also maintain it as a profit center in its own right.

MARKETING POLICIES

Distribution System

Traditionally, Gerber has marketed its baby food products through grocery stores and supermarkets across the U.S., as well as in 68 foreign countries. As noted earlier, however, grocery outlets are also asked to sell special products such as vinyl pants, baby and pre-school children's clothing, infant toiletries, vaporizers, and other infant accessories—the concept being to build a sort of baby center in the stores. The company has met some resistance in this effort, however. For example, Thriftmart, Inc., a southern California food chain, stocks many Gerber baby food items, but only one nonfood product: plastic pants. According to Thriftmart the traffic just did not warrant carrying other Gerber products.

In recent years in an attempt to increase market penetration, Gerber expanded its channels to include discount houses, drug chains, department stores and specialty shops for the growing line of nonfood baby products. Moreover in 1979 two divisions, grocery products and special products, were created. A principal reason for the reorganization was the divergent marketing channels utilized by the two product lines. The grocery products division concentrates on food stores while the special products division focuses on mass merchandising, drug outlets, and other segments of Gerber distribution.

A major strength of Gerber's distribution system is a new computerized market information system, covering 50,000 food stores, which account for about 85% to 90% of the country's total retail food sales. The system, called MARS (market auditing report service), provides instant information relative to various Gerber products in terms of store inventory, shelf space, mix, movement, and turnover compared with competition. The system enables the company to isolate almost any facet of its distribution.

Promotion

Gerber's promotional efforts have been largely directed toward two groups: mothers and pediatricians. The company tries to reach mothers through advertising in baby publications and by direct mail promotions. It also relies on the ''word-of-mouth'' advertising by mothers who have used Gerber products.

The direct mail campaign is perhaps Gerber's key promotional tool. The lists used in the campaign are derived from birth records. Three to six weeks after a birth, the new mother receives literature and coupons for Gerber baby foods that are redeemable at the local grocery stores. Afterwards, follow up coupons are sent. The redemption rate of these coupons is around 20%.

Promotion to pediatricians takes other forms. Gerber sponsors *Pediatric Basics,* a respected journal for pediatricians. The company also maintains a professional relations department whose staff calls upon hospitals and doctors to promote Gerber products. Information about new Gerber products and latest findings in infant nutrition are shared with the health professionals who serve new parents throughout the country.

In keeping with its attempts to diversify, in 1972 Gerber shortened its slogan from ''Babies are our business . . . our *only* business'' to ''Babies are our business.'' The slogan ''Gerber prepares foods for the most important person in the world . . . your baby'' is also used in various advertisements. The company considers its name a valuable asset. Former Chairman Suerth explained it this way, ''Everything we're doing is really based on our success in the baby food area. So you better keep the lead dog pretty healthy.''

FOREIGN OPERATIONS

Gerber was a late entrant in the overseas market. In 1965, it derived only 7% of its total sales from overseas operations. However, since 1974, international sales have ranged between 16 to 20 percent of the consolidated sales. In 1980, Gerber maintained subsidiaries in Canada, Mexico, Venezuela, and Costa Rica. It operated a joint venture in Brazil and had licensees in Australia, France, Italy, Japan, the Phillipines, and

South Africa. In addition, export shipments were made to about 80 countries around the world. Food items constituted most of the overseas sales, although some special products, particularly vinyl waterproof pants, nursers and nurser accessories, and vaporizers were also exported.

Sales and pre-tax earnings attributable to international operations (foreign subsidiaries, foreign licensees, and exports) as an approximate percentage of consolidated sales and consolidated pretax earnings for the years 1975–1980 were as follows:

	1975	1976	1977	1978	1979	1980
Sales	17.2%	19.6%	18.2%	16.2%	17.1%	16.9%
Pre-tax earnings	22.2%	16.9%	2.7%	2.8%	6.9%	7.2%

Increased sales were attained primarily in major Latin American markets despite political uncertainties in much of that part of the world. Subsidiaries in Mexico, Costa Rica, and Venezuela experienced growth in sales volume. However, contribution of international sales to earnings was severely limited due to increasing costs and stringent price controls in foreign markets. In Venezuela, for example, baby food selling prices have been frozen since limited price increases were permitted in the later part of fiscal year 1978.

In 1980, Gerber sold its 82% interest in the Venezuelan subsidiary. The Venezuelan company now produces and markets a broad line of Gerber baby foods under a licensing agreement.

Sales and pre-tax earnings of the Venezuelan company and the rest of the international operations for the years 1978 through 1980 were as follows (000's omitted):

	1978	1979	1980
International Sales:			
Venezuela	33,182	42,847	45,687
Other	38,628	42,717	56,305
International Pre-tax Earnings:			
Venezuela	951	2,990	1,100
Other	482	829	3,241

In spite of the pressures of rising costs, inflation, and price controls, Gerber expects continued growth in the international markets. Improvement in the economic and educational standards along with the knowledge of nutrition are regarded as the primary reasons for increasing demand of Gerber products.

FINANCE

After a steady growth in sales and profit, Gerber was faced with eroding sales and earnings during 1973, 1974 and 1975. "We got hit with so many things at one time: reduced births, price controls, rising costs, and severe price competition," said Suerth. The company has, however, recovered from the setback. With the exception of one

EXHIBIT 1
CONSOLIDATED INCOME ACCOUNT, YEARS ENDED MARCH 31

$000's	1969	1970	1971	1972	1973	1974	1975	1976	1977	1978	1979	1980
March 31												
Net Sales	202,180	217,171	261,851	282,601	278,473	285,437	328,140	372,418	404,598	443,078	499,016	543,922
Other Income	1,127	1,365	1,087	1,138	823	1,401	1,290	1,651	1,974	2,077	2,217	2,209
Equity Earnings									291	267	208	312
Transport Revenue												58,064
Total Income	203,307	218,536	262,938	283,739	279,296	286,838	329,430	374,069	406,863	445,422	501,441	604,507
Cost of Sales	116,381	126,306	156,466	170,793	176,742	189,818	214,164	236,409	263,569	291,870	336,457	368,790
Transport Expense												49,558
Selling Expense	55,669	59,665	69,303	73,570	71,369	73,556	79,658	90,358	95,507	104,895	110,740	126,130
Interest Expense	53		287	291	584	1,661	2,321	1,672	1,961	2,636	3,661	6,175
Eq. Affil. Earn.				cr 30	dr 964	dr 1,258	dr 645	dr 135				
Income Tax	16,620	16,880	18,170	18,699	13,980	9,100	16,070	22,281	22,611	22,033	22,798	24,254
Minority Interest	80	179	214	159	234	323	228	325	cr 251	cr 11	321	cr 116
Foreign Exch. Losses									1,060			
Net Profit	14,498	15,502	18,494	20,253	15,419	11,122	16,338	22,889	22,334	23,999	27,464	29,716
Prev. Retained Earn.	74,292	79,603	83,450	91,895	101,265	105,331	106,083	114,248	128,191	140,155	142,748	167,944
Com. Divs.	9,187	9,337	10,082	10,883	11,353	10,370	8,173	8,946	10,370	11,406	12,268	13,852
Pool Int. Adjustment			cr 32									
Retained Earning	79,603	85,768	91,895	101,265	105,331	106,083	114,248	128,191	140,155	152,748	167,944	183,808
Earn./Com. Share	$1.74	$1.87	$2.19	$2.40	$1.84	$1.35	$2.00	$2.81	$2.75	$2.95	$3.36	$3.45
No. of Com. Shrs.	8,304,629	8,295,230	8,447,214	8,440,130	8,250,800	8,214,680	8,132,803	8,133,201	8,134,014	8,164,278	8,192,264	8,901,151

EXHIBIT 2
CONSOLIDATED BALANCE SHEET, AS OF MARCH 31

$000's	1969	1970	1971	1972	1973	1974	1975	1976	1977	1978	1979	1980
Assets:												
Cash	3,591	3,579	3,877	1,408	2,861	2,722	4,357	3,045	1,558	2,366	3,254	7,105
Commercial Paper	12,079	8,190										
Market Security Cost	—	—	13,794	3,286	4,557	1,925	1,766	15,522	11,987	9,873	3,475	4,484
Receivables	14,761	16,672	21,686	23,244	25,128	28,939	28,192	30,233	35,815	42,914	53,662	65,733
Finish Products	34,933	39,880	29,640	47,975	44,886	45,542	47,571	43,984	49,320	49,713	59,475	62,940
Raw Mat. & Supplies	7,071	9,605	10,977	12,392	14,395	17,076	21,366	24,844	30,779	30,390	42,571	40,096
Total Current	72,435	77,926	89,974	88,305	91,827	96,204	103,252	117,628	129,459	135,256	162,437	180,367
Net Properties	35,800	37,890	43,184	53,250	58,844	62,834	68,523	70,823	80,700	89,820	100,978	129,060
Inv. Uncons. Sub.	5,089	5,509	56,527	8,772	9,311	9,462	10,000	10,572	11,778	12,813	13,455	24,912
Goodwill	1		1									
Misc. Receivables	1,596	1,990	3,442	2,327	1,921	3,645	3,636	4,729	4,759	6,555	7,376	10,308
Operating Rights												
Licenses, and Intangibles	701	854	1,083	867	767	1,413	1,171	406	431	324	238	8,149
Total	115,622	124,170	143,210	153,521	162,670	173,558	186,582	204,158	227,127	244,768	284,484	352,796
Liabilities:												
Accounts Payable	5,492	7,575	18,421	18,837	17,423	20,348	19,936	26,996	34,168	33,193	40,132	55,380
Notes Payable	259	83	1,420	1,701	10,986	18,562	14,015	1,802	8,317	12,321	24,173	40,262
Accruals	5,905	6,536										
Income Tax	3,395	3,849	4,383	3,934	2,360	2,388	2,566	6,875	4,860	3,368	4,139	5,492
Debt Due	414	—										
Total Current	15,465	18,043	24,224	24,472	30,769	41,298	36,517	35,673	47,345	48,882	68,444	101,134
Long Term Debt	75	—	1,904	1,808	2,835	3,420	13,244	17,360	15,728	18,112	21,994	19,990
Deferred Credit	550	825	1,816	1,963	3,250	4,239	4,654	4,666	5,836	6,535	6,855	8,505
Minority Interest	452	482	695	1,673	2,557	1,337	1,546	1,890	1,675	1,664	1,985	1,906
Pension Costs	680	583										
Common Stock (2.50)	21,234	21,234	21,234	21,234	21,234	21,235	21,234	21,235	21,235	21,235	21,235	22,980
Paid in Surplus	3,045	3,045	2,983	2,946	2,946	2,946	2,946	2,942	2,935	2,720	2,549	20,759
Retained Earnings	79,603	85,768	91,895	101,265	105,331	106,083	114,248	128,191	140,155	152,748	167,944	183,808
Stockhold Equity	103,883	110,047	116,113	125,446	129,511	130,263	138,428	152,368	164,325	176,703	191,728	227,547
Reacquired Stock	5,483	5,810	1,542	1,841	6,252	6,999	7,807	7,799	7,782	7,128	6,522	6,286
Net Stockholder Eq.	98,400	104,237	114,571	123,605	123,259	123,264	130,621	144,569	156,543	169,575	185,206	221,261
Total	115,622	124,170	143,210	153,521	162,670	173,558	186,582	204,158	227,127	244,768	284,484	352,796

year, profits have steadily increased since 1976. In the years 1979 and 1980, the profits were at an all time high. In 1980, Gerber had equity of nearly $228 million and long-term debt of only $20 million (see Exhibits 1 and 2).

Until the acquisition of CW Transport, Inc. in August 1979, the company's operations were divided into two industry segments: (1) sales of food and (2) sales of special products and services. In the year 1980, a third segment, namely, sales from transportation services, was added. The relative contribution of each segment to the consolidated sales for the last six years was as follows (000's omitted):

Year	Food	Special products and services	Transportation	Total
1975	283,512	44,627		328,139
1976	314,693	57,725		327,418
1977	335,412	69,186		404,498
1978	364,210	78,868		443,078
1979	404,203	94,812		499,016
1980	435,838	108,084	58,064	601,986

Net earnings from the new transportation services segment in 1980 were $2,328,000.

In the *Gerber's Annual Report to Stockholders* for the years 1979 to 1980, it was noted that the increases in sales of domestic food in the two preceding years of the report were primarily due to higher selling prices rather than increases in the sales volume. Furthermore, net earnings for special products and services declined in the last two fiscal years. This was especially true in petroleum-based products.

RESEARCH AND DEVELOPMENT

Gerber research activities are located at the corporate headquarters in Fremont, Michigan. Research efforts primarily concentrate on the development of new foods, product formulations, new processing methods, and improved material usage. In light of ever-increasing knowledge of infant nutrition and frequent feedback provided by practicing pediatricians, product formulas are continuously evaluated and retested. For example, the use of salt was completely discontinued in 1978 and sugar usage was significantly reduced. Studies in packaging and agricultural research are also carried out on a regular basis. Cornucopia Farms, headquartered at Barker, New York, which supplies the firm with fresh produce and apple juice, also serves as a natural laboratory for the company's agricultural research projects. Charles F. Whitten, Professor of Pediatrics, Wayne State University School of Medicine, and Dena C. Cederquist, Professor Emeritus, Department of Food Science and Human Nutrition, Michigan State University, are on the Gerber Board of Directors.

REFERENCES

"Anderson Clayton Withdraws Gerber Bid," *Financial Times,* (Sept. 20, 1977), p. 28.
"Baby Talk," *Forbes,* (August 1, 1975), pp. 40–41.

"But It's Cold Out There," *Forbes,* (Sept. 15, 1973), p. 40.

"Conversation with Gerber's John Suerth," *Advertising Age,* 46:29, (Feb. 3, 1975).

"Does Father Know Best?", *Forbes,* 121:31–2, (March 6, 1978).

Fifty Years of Caring, Gerber Products Co., internal brochure.

Gerber's Annual Report to Stockholders, Gerber Products Co. (1970–1980).

"Gerber Back on the Ad Track," *Advertising Age,* 49:1, (March 6, 1978).

"Gerber Finds There Is Still Plenty of Profit in Moppets," *Barrons,* 55L34–35, (March 3, 1975).

"Gerber Jumps on No-Salt Bandwagon," *Advertising Age,* (June 6, 1977), p. 4.

"Gerber Products Says Bid to Settle Walkout at Plant is Rejected," *The Wall Street Journal,* (April 4, 1977), p. 20.

"Gerber: Selling More to the Same Mothers Is Our Objective Now," *Business Week,* (October 16, 1978), pp. 192–195.

"Gerber: Where Have All the Babies Gone?", *Commercial and Financial Chronicle,* 221:3, (March 22, 1976).

"Growing Pains in the Baby Market," *Forbes,* (Dec. 15, 1959), p. 19.

"Lower Birthrate Crimps the Baby Food Market," *Business Week,* (July 13, 1974), pp. 44–48.

Moody's Industrial Manual, Gerber Products Inc., (1968–1978).

"Outlook on the Baby-Food Market," *Business Week,* (July 13, 1974), p. 45.

Standard and Poor's Industrial Manual, Gerber Products Inc., (1978).

Standard and Poor's Stock Report, Gerber Products Inc., (1978).

"The Bad News in Babyland," *Dun's* (December, 1972), p. 104.

"The Lost Generation Wasn't," *Forbes,* (October 1, 1965), pp. 51–2.

U.S. Bureau of Census, *Current Population Reports,* Series P-20, No. 350, May 1980.

"What Population Explosion?" *Forbes,* (March 1, 1967), pp. 60–61.

DISCUSSION QUESTIONS

1 Explain Gerber's corporate mission in terms of what is desired to be accomplished for whom and show how recent diversification efforts relate to that mission.

2 Calculate Gerber's major liquidity, activity, profitability, and leverage ratios and explain how each relates to the company's desire to achieve rapid growth.

3 List the significant strengths, weaknesses, threats, and opportunities faced by Gerber Products Company and explain how they determine the strategies you believe Gerber should follow during the next five years or so.

4 Explain Gerber's marketing strategy in terms of the four P's of marketing.

GERBER PRODUCTS COMPANY (B)

Edmund Gray
B. L. Kedia
Louisiana State University

D. E. Ezell
University of Baltimore

SELECTED STRATEGIC ISSUES

- Conflicting interests of management and stockholders
- Stock price manipulation before takeovers

Anderson, Clayton and Company, a Houston-based foods and oil-seeds group, offered on April 18, 1977 to buy all 8.1 million shares of Gerber at $40 a share. In 1976 Anderson, Clayton's profit was 11.5% on $759 million sales, while Gerber's was 16.6% on $372 million sales. According to President Guinee of Anderson, Clayton, the acquisition would boost his company's return on equity and increase its stake in the grocery products business. Gerber's stock has sold as low as 8½ in 1974, at 21 in November 1976, and around the mid-30's at the time of the offer. The purchase of 90,000 shares in the open market by Anderson, Clayton was instrumental in boosting the stock price.

Gerber executives defiantly resisted the takeover attempt and filed suits in state and federal courts charging: (1) Anderson, Clayton manipulated Gerber's stock price before making the offer, (2) the proposed offer would be in violation of antitrust laws because it would give Anderson, Clayton monopoly power in the baby food industry and reduce competition in the salad dressing market, which Gerber has been thinking about entering (Anderson, Clayton held 12% of the market with its Seven Seas brand), and (3) Anderson, Clayton had failed to disclose $2.1 million in illegal payments the company had made abroad during the preceding several years.

The situation resulted in legal entanglements and consequent delays. On September 19, Anderson, Clayton withdrew its offer, saying that because of the legal problems any takeover could not be completed until late 1978 or early 1979. "These delays aren't acceptable," said Mr. Barlow, the Anderson, Clayton Chairman.

During the takeover struggle, Gerber stock rose to a high of 39½. On September 19, the day Anderson, Clayton withdrew its offer, the price of the Gerber stock dropped from 34⅜ to 28¼. Those who bought a large number of shares anticipating a successful takeover lost heavily. In August and September 1977 four class action suits were filed by stockholders against Gerber alleging violation of the Securities and Exchange Act of 1934 because the company's opposition to the takeover was not in the best interest of the shareholders, but rather in the self-interest of the directors.

REFERENCES

"Bid by Anderson Clayton to Buy Gerber Dropped," *The Wall Street Journal* (Sept. 20, 1977), p. 38.

Koshetz, Herbert. "Gerber Charged with Damaging Its Shareholders," *New York Times* (August 10, 1977), p. Dl.

"Nothing Is Too Good for Our Stockholders," *Forbes,* 119:55, (May 15, 1977).

Serrin, William. "How Gerber Foiled a Takeover," *New York Times* (Sept. 2, 1977), p. F1-2.

DISCUSSION QUESTIONS

1 Explain how the interests of Gerber's management and those of its common shareholders may be in conflict during takeover attempts and oppose or support Gerber management's efforts to prevent the takeover by Anderson, Clayton and Company.

2 Explain how Anderson, Clayton may have been able to manipulate Gerber's stock price before making the takeover bid. Why would they do this and why might Gerber management legitimately oppose it?

WALL DRUG STORE 1983

James D. Taylor
Robert L. Johnson
Philip C. Fisher
University of South Dakota

SELECTED STRATEGIC ISSUES

- The elements for success for a unique small business
- The impact of government regulation on commercial efforts
- Relationship of mission to strategies
- Theme or atmosphere as a promotional tool
- Capital structure and riskiness
- Timing and mode of diversification for the family-owned business
- Development of personal area strategies

The Wall Drug Store is a complex of retail shops located on the main street of Wall, South Dakota, population 770, owned and managed by the Hustead family of Wall. It includes a drug store, a soda fountain, two jewelry stores, two clothing stores, a restaurant with four dining rooms, a western art gallery, a bookstore and shops selling rocks and fossils, camping and backpacking equipment, saddles and boots as well as several souvenir shops. Exhibit I indicates how the store has changed. In 1983, a major expansion was underway which would add five more shops and a chapel. "The decision, as when you first wrote the case in 1974,[1] is are we going ahead with our building program or not? That hasn't changed," announced Bill Hustead as he talked about his plans for Wall Drug. The tourist season was just beginning on June 1. The

---

This case was prepared by professors James D. Taylor, Robert L. Johnson, and Philip G. Fisher of the University of South Dakota as the basis of class discussion.

[1] Professors James D. Taylor and Robert L. Johnson are co-authors of "Wall Drug Store" a case written in 1974.

EXHIBIT I WALL DRUG IN THE 1940S AND IN 1983

Spring had been cool and wet, and sales for the year to June 1 were down considerably from the previous year. Bill continued,

> We are still going ahead with the building program. The building program is not necessarily to make more money, but mainly it is to enlarge and enhance the store, so that it makes more of an impression on the traveling public. The church, the art gallery, the apothecary shop— we naturally feel these things will pay their way and make money, but the good part is, when the signs go down, we will have a place that people just won't miss. The place is so crazy, so different—it's the largest drugstore in the world, it may get in the *Guinness Book of Records* as the only drugstore with a church in it. People and writers will have a lot to talk about. We will continue to seek publicity. We will advertise in crazy places, we will have packets for writers and we will try to seek national and international publicity.

WALL DRUG HISTORY

Ted Hustead graduated from the University of Nebraska with a degree in pharmacy in 1929 at the age of 27. In December of 1931, Ted and his wife Dorothy bought the drug store in Wall, South Dakota, for $2,500. Dorothy and Ted and their four-year-old son Bill moved into living quarters in the back twenty feet of the store. Business was not good (the first month's receipts were $350) and prospects in Wall did not seem bright. Wall, South Dakota, in 1931 is described in the following selection from a book about the Wall Drug Store.

> Wall, then: a huddle of poor wooden buildings, many unpainted, housing some 300 desperate souls; a 19th century depot and wooden water tank; dirt (or mud) streets; few trees; a stop on the railroad, it wasn't even that on the highway. U.S. 16 and 14 went right on by, as did the tourists speeding between the Badlands and the Black Hills. There was nothing in Wall to stop for.[2]

Neither the drugstore nor the town of Wall prospered until Dorothy Hustead conceived the idea of placing a sign promising free ice water to anyone who would stop at their store. The sign read "Get a soda/Get a beer/Turn next corner/Just as near/To Highway 16 and 14/Free ice water/Wall Drug." Ted put the sign up and cars were turning off the highway to go to the drugstore before he got back. This turning point in the history of Wall Drug took place on a blazing hot Sunday afternoon in the summer of 1936.

The value of the signs was apparent and Ted began putting them up all along the highways leading to Wall. One sign read "Slow down the old hack/Wall Drug Corner/Just across the railroad track." The attention-catching signs were a boon to the Wall Drug and the town of Wall prospered too. In an article in *Good Housekeeping* in 1951, the Husteads' signs were called "the most ingenious and irresistable system of signs ever devised."[3]

Just after World War II, a friend traveling across Europe for the Red Cross got the idea of putting up Wall Drug signs overseas. The idea caught on and soon South

---

[2] Jennings, Dana Close, *Free Ice Water: The Story of Wall Drug* (Aberdeen, South Dakota: North Plains Press, 1969) p. 26.

[3] Ibid, p. 42.

Dakota servicemen who were familiar with the signs back home began to carry small Wall Drug signs all over the world. Many wrote the store requesting signs. One sign appeared in Paris, proclaiming "Wall Drug Store 4,278 miles (6,951 kilometers)." Wall Drug signs have appeared in many places including the North and South Pole areas, the 38th parallel in Korea, and on Vietnam jungle trails. The Husteads sent more than 200 signs to servicemen requesting them from Vietnam. These signs led to new stories and publicity which further increased the reputation of the store.

By 1958, there were about 3,000 signs displayed along highways in all 50 states, and two men and a truck were permanently assigned to service signs. Volunteers continue to put up signs. The store gives away 14,000 6 by 8 inch signs and 3,000 8 by 22 inch signs a year to people who request them. On the walls of the dining rooms at Wall Drug are displayed pictures from people who have placed signs in unusual places and photographed them for the Husteads.

The signs attracted attention and shortly after World War II articles about Ted Hustead and Wall Drug began appearing in newspapers and magazines. In August, 1950, *Redbook Magazine* carried a story which was later condensed in October's *Reader's Digest*. Since then, the number of newspapers and magazines carrying feature stories or referring to Wall Drug has increased greatly. In June of 1983, Wall Drug Store files contained 543 clippings of stories about the store. The number by 10 year periods was as follows:[4]

1941–1950	19 articles
1951–1960	41
1961–1970	137
1971–1980	260
1981 through April 1983	59

The store and its sales have grown steadily since 1936. From 1931 until 1941 the store was in a rented building on the west side of Wall's Main Street. In 1941, the Husteads bought an old lodge hall in Wasta, S. D. (15 miles west of Wall) and moved it to a lot on the east side of the street in Wall. The building, which had been used as a gymnasium in Wasta, became the core around which the current store is built.

Tourist travel greatly increased after World War II and the signs brought so many people into Wall Drug that the Husteads claim they were embarrassed because the facilities were not large enough to service them. The store did not even have modern restrooms. Sales during this period grew to $200,000 annually.

In 1951, Bill Hustead, now a pharmacy graduate of South Dakota State University at Brookings joined his parents in the store.

In 1953, Wall Drug was expanded into a former storeroom to the south. This became the Western Clothing Room. In 1954, they built an outside store on the south of the Western Clothing Room. This was accompanied by a 30% increase in business. In 1956, a self-service cafe was added on the north side of the store. In the early 1950's

---

[4] Twenty-seven clippings were undated.

sales were in the $300,000 per year range and by the early 1960's had climbed to $500,000. (A map of the store with the dates of expansion are shown in Exhibit II.)

In the early 1960's, Ted and his son Bill began seriously thinking of moving Wall Drug to the highway. The original Highway 16 ran by the north side of Wall, about two blocks from the store. It was later moved to run by the south side of Wall, about two blocks also from the drugstore. In the late 1950's and early 1960's a new highway was built running by the south side of Wall paralleling the other highway. Ted and Bill Hustead were considering building an all-new Wall Drug along with a gasoline filling station alongside the new highway just where the interchange by Wall was located.

They decided to build the gasoline station first, and did so. It is called Wall Auto Livery. When the station was finished, they decided to hold up on the new store and then decided to continue expanding the old store in downtown Wall. This was a fortunate decision, since soon after that, the new interstate highway replaced the former new highway and the new interchange ran through the site of the proposed new Wall Drug.

EXHIBIT II · MAP OF WALL DRUG

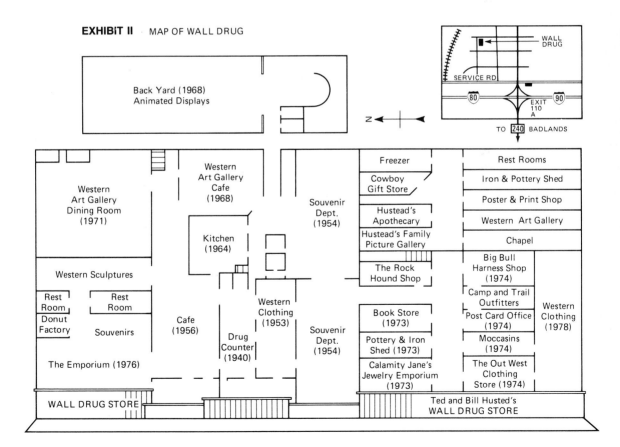

In 1963, a new fireproof construction coffee shop was added. In 1964, a new kitchen, again of fireproof construction, was added just behind the cafe and main store. In 1964 and 1965 offices and the new pharmacy were opened on the second floor over the kitchen.

In 1968, the back dining room and backyard across the alley were added. This was followed in 1971 with the Art Gallery Dining Room.

By the late 1960's and early 1970's, annual sales volume went to $1,000,000.

In 1971 the Husteads bought the theater that bordered their store on the south. They ran it as a theater through 1972. In early 1973 they began construction of a new addition in the old theater location. This is called the "Mall." By the summer of 1973 the north part of the Mall was open for business. The south side was not ready yet. That year the Wall Drug grossed $1,600,000, which was an increase of about 20% over 1972. Bill believes the increase was due to their new Mall addition.

The development of the Mall represents a distinct change in the development of Wall Drug. All previous development had been financed out of retained earnings or short-term loans. In effect, each addition was paid for as it was built or added.

THE MALL

The owners of Wall Drug broke with their previous method of expansion when they built the Mall by borrowing approximately $250,000 for 10 years to finance the Mall and part of 20 large new signs which stand 660 feet from the interstate highway.

During the last half of the 1960's and early 1970's Bill Hustead had thought about and planned the concept of the Mall. The Mall was designed as a town within a large room. The main strolling mall was designed as a main street with each store or shop designed as a two-story frontier Western building. The Mall is thus like a recreated Western town. Inside the stores various woods are used in building and paneling. Such woods as pine from Custer, South Dakota, American black walnut, gumwood, hackberry, cedar, maple, and oak are among the various woods used. The store fronts are recreations of building fronts found in old photos of Western towns in the 1880's. Many photos, paintings, and prints line the walls. These shops stock products that are more expensive than the souvenir merchandise found in most other parts of the store. The shops are more like Western boutiques.

The northern part of the Mall was open for business shortly after July 10, 1973. In the fall of 1973, Bill was uncertain as to whether or not to open the south side. The Husteads perceived a threat to the tourist business in the 1974 season. They agonized over whether to finish the Mall and order the normal amount of inventory, or to hold up the Mall and order conservatively. Among the conditions that seemed to threaten tourism were rising gasoline prices, periodic gasoline shortages in parts of the country, and trouble with the American Indian Movement (AIM) at Wounded Knee and on the Pine Ridge Reservation. The more long-term threat to the businesses that depend on tourists, especially Wall Drug, was the highway beautification laws of the 1960's that threatened the removal of roadside advertising signs.

Bill finally decided in the winter of 1973 to prepare for a full tourist season. Therefore, he had the Mall finished and ordered a full inventory for the 1974 season.

The decisions the Husteads confronted in the fall and winter of 1973 marked the first time they had seriously considered any retrenchment in their 27 years of growth.

In May and June, the opening of the 1974 tourist season, there were nine shops in the Mall. Bill estimated in the winter of 1974 that the year would be a record breaker of $2 million. June, July and August sales were up 15 to 20%. September business was up 20 to 30%, October was up 40%, and November was a record setter for that month.

Bill gave the following reasons for the 1974 season:

1 Many other businesses bought light, Wall Drug bought heavy. Therefore, while others ran short, Wall Drug had merchandise towards the end of the summer.

2 Expensive items sold well in spite of the recession scare of the late 1974 period. Bill indicated that articles in Eastern merchandising journals indicated luxury items were doing well all over. Wall Drug had to reorder even into the fall on hot items, such as books, jewelry, and Western clothes.

3 Wall Drug had more goods and space than it ever had before, and each person was buying more.

4 There were more hunters than ever before in the fall. Signs on the highway advertising free donuts and coffee for hunters brought many in and they bought heavy.

5 Although visitations to Mt. Rushmore were down in the summer of 1974, Wall Drug sales were up. Why? Bill speculates that more people from South Dakota and bordering states took shorter trips this year, and thus went to the Black Hills. These people had likely been in the Black Hills before and had seen Mt. Rushmore on their first trip. However, these people like to pay another visit to Wall Drug to eat, see what has been added and to shop.

In the fall of 1974, Wall Drug invested in more large signs to set 660 feet back from the interstate. By 1976, they had 29 of these signs. These were the only legal type signs that they could put up along the interstate, but by the spring of 1976, the language of the Highway Beautification Act was changed to put these signs outside the law also. Their signs (smaller ones) in neighboring states have been removed.

In 1975 and 1976, expansion continued with the addition of the Emporium, more dining area, and more restrooms at the north end of the store. (See Exhibit II, map of Wall Drug.)

In 1978, the location of the Wall post office at the south end of the store beyond the Mall, which had previously been purchased, furnished expansion for the western clothing stores and the boots and harness shop.

Currently, in 1983, there is further expansion under construction east of the Mall to the alley. The new area will feature a chapel modeled after a church built by Trappist Monks in Dubuque, Iowa in 1850. Also featured will be a replica of the original Wall Drug Store, which will be called Hustead's Apothecary and will serve as the Drug Store Museum. The store will sell Caswell-Massey products from the store of that name in New York which is the oldest drugstore in the U.S. Other shops will be a western art gallery, a poster shop and western gift shop, an iron and pottery shop, and Hustead's Family Picture Gallery. The shops will be modeled after famous old western establishments. There will also be a new set of restrooms. In effect, the new addition will be an extension of the Mall.

STORE OPERATION

Wall is a small town of 770 people as of 1980. The economic base of the town is primarily built around Wall Drug and is dependent on tourist business.

Wall is situated right on the edge of the Badlands and 52 miles east of Rapid City. For miles in either direction, people in autos have been teased and tantalized by Wall Drug signs. Many have heard of the place through stories in the press, or have heard their parents or friends speak of Wall Drug. In the summer of 1963, in a traffic count made on the highway going by Wall, 46% were eastbound and 54% were westbound. Of the eastbound traffic, 43% turned off at Wall. Of the westbound traffic, 44% turned off at Wall.

When people arrive at Wall (those westbound usually after driving 40 miles or more through the Badlands) they are greeted by the large Wall Drug sign on the interchange and an 80-foot-high, 50-ton statue of a dinosaur. The business district of Wall is two blocks long and is about three blocks to five blocks from the interchange. The town has eleven motels and a number of gasoline filling stations.

Cars from many states line the street in front of and several blocks on either side of the drugstore. Tabulations of state licenses from autos and campers parked in front of Wall Drug, June 1, 1983, at 12:00 noon are summarized as follows:

South Dakota (not local county)	20%
South Dakota (local county)	22%
Balance of states and Canada	58%

Wall Drug is more than a store. It is a place of amusement, family entertainment, a gallery of the West, a gallery of South Dakota history, and a place that reflects the heritage of the West. (See Exhibit III.) Nostalgia addicts find Wall Drug particularly interesting. Children delight in the animated life-size cowboys singing, tableau of an Indian camp, a stuffed bucking horse, a six-foot rabbit, a stuffed buffalo, old slot machines that pay out a souvenir coin for 25¢, statues of cowboys, dancehall girls and other characters of the old West, a coin-operated quick-draw game, and souvenirs by the roomful which make up part of the attractions.

The food is inexpensive and good, and although as many as 10,000 people might stream through on a typical day, the place is air conditioned and comfortable. The dining rooms are decorated with beautiful wood paneling, paintings of Western art are displayed, and Western music plays. One can dine on buffalo burgers, roast beef or steak, 5¢ coffee or select wine and beer from the rustic, but beautiful, American walnut bar.

About one-fourth of the sales in Wall Drug is food, plus about 5% to 10% for beverages and the soda fountain. (This varies with the weather.) About 10% to 15% is jewelry, 15% clothing and hats, 35% to 40% for souvenirs, and 5% to 10% for drugs, drug sundries and prescriptions.

The store is manned by a crew of 201 people, 76 of which are college girls and 25 are college boys who work there in the summer. Student help is housed in homes that

EXHIBIT III   FREE ATTRACTIONS AT WALL DRUG

The Orchestras

The Cowboy Orchestra and Chuckwagon Quartet (life-size and animated) sing and play in the store every half hour and sometimes more often from mid-May to October 1st.

In the back yard

We have a large replica of Mt. Rushmore, a bucking horse, a giant Jackalope replica, a six-foot rabbit (stuffed), a mounted buffalo, a covered wagon and the Ice Water Well . . . all for picture taking purposes during the busy season which is usually from May to the first of October. The 1908 Hupmobile, with a driver and his girl friend (life-size and animated), are also in the Back Yard.

Wall Drug Mall

Walk down the main street of Wall Drug's typical western town. These buildings are all constructed of native timber and old brick. The street is made from Cheyenne River Rock.

Western Art Gallery Cafe and Dining Room

Wall Drug has 179 original oil paintings, some in the dining room and the rest in other parts of the store. The Western Art Gallery Cafe is paneled in American Black walnut and has a life-sized carving of Butch Cassidy and the Sundance Kid, which is made from a 100 year-old cedar tree. Please note also the Silver Dollar Bar features a collection of Arikara Indian artifacts. In the West Art Gallery Dining Room is a collection of Tiffany-type lamp shades (bases of leaded glass) and 600 cattle brands, taken from the 1889 official South Dakota registered brand books. In a third dining room, called the Cowboy Art Dining Room, is a display of Tony Chytka's western sculptures, a Tiffany-type ceiling and brass bedstead booths.

Ice for Jugs . . . Free

CAFE   FREE ICE WATER!   COFFEE

FREE COFFEE and DONUTS—For Hunters, Skiers, Honeymooners,
Missile Crewmen and 18 Wheelers

---

have been bought and made into dormitory apartments. There is a modern swimming pool for their use, also. The clerks are trained to be courteous, informed and pleasant.

Orders for the following summer season begin being placed in the preceding fall. Orders begin arriving in December, but most arrive in January, February, March and April. Many large souvenir companies post-date their invoices until July and August. Each year brings new offerings from souvenir companies and other suppliers. Much of the purchasing is done by Bill, who admits he relies on trusted salespeople of their suppliers who advise him on purchasing. Many of these companies have supplied Wall Drug for 30 years or so. Wall Drug generally buys directly from the producers or importers including photo supplies and clothing.

Years ago, much of what Wall Drug bought and sold was imported or made in the eastern part of the country. In recent years, much of the merchandise is being made regionally and locally. Indian reservations now have small production firms and individuals who make much handicraft which is sold through Wall Drug. Examples of such firms are Sioux Pottery, Badlands Pottery, Sioux Moccasin, and Milk Camp Industries.

The Husteads rely a great deal on the department managers for buying assistance. The manager of the jewelry, for instance, will determine on the basis of last year's orders and her experience with customer reaction and demand, how much to order for the next season. All ordering is channeled through Bill.

HIGHWAY BEAUTIFICATION AND PROMOTION

In the year 1965, Congress passed the Highway Beautification Act, which was designed to reduce the number of roadside signs. Anticipating the removal of the many Wall Drug advertising signs, Bill Hustead invested in new signs that were allowed under that legislation. These signs were to be placed no closer than 660 feet away from the road. To be read, these signs must be larger than the older signs, and cost close to $9,000 each. Now even these large signs are included in the laws for regulation or removal.

There has been slow compliance with this legislation by many states, including South Dakota. Less populated states which have many tourist attractions find road signs the only practical way to advertise these attractions. Since the administration of President Reagan has been in office, there has been little enforcement of the sign legislation since there has been less money available for federal enforcement. There is new legislation being proposed by the Federal Highway Administration of the Department of Transportation as of 1983 that could have an impact on Wall Drug and other tourist dependent establishments.

Bill and Ted also decided that they must gain as much visibility and notoriety as possible, and to help achieve this, they began using advertising in unusual places. In the 1960's, Wall Drug began taking small ads in unlikely media such as the *International Herald Tribune*, and *The Village Voice*, in New York City's Greenwich Village, advertising 5¢ coffee and 49¢ breakfast as well as animal health remedies. This brought telephone calls and some letters of inquiry. It also brought an article in the *Voice* and probably attracted the attention of other media. In January 31, 1971, (Sunday) *The New York Times* carried an article about Wall Drug. This article may have led to Bill Hustead's appearance on Garry Moore's television program "To Tell the Truth." In the year 1979, there were 75 articles in newspapers and magazines about Wall Drug. In the August 31, 1981, edition of *Time*, a full page article in the American Scene featured the store and the Husteads. Also in 1981, Wall Drug was featured on NBC television's "Today Show" and Atlanta Cable's "Winners."

For a while, the Wall Drug was advertised in the London city buses and subways, in the Paris Metro (subway) in the English language, and on the dock in Amsterdam where people board sight seeing canal boats.

FINANCES

Tables 1 and 2 present summary income statements and balance sheets from 1973 through 1982. The Wall Auto Livery was consolidated into Wall Drug Store, Inc. in May 1975. Had this transition occurred prior to 1973, sales for 1973, 1974 and 1975 would have been about $192,000, $248,000 and $52,000 larger, and net profit would

TABLE 1 INCOME STATEMENTS WALL DRUG
(In 000's)

	1982	1981	1980	1979	1978	1977	1976	1975	1974	1973
Sales	4,733	4,821	3,970	3,552	4,125	3,777	3,464	2,679	1,991	1,607
Cost of sales	2,644	2,676	2,230	2,072	2,228	2,098	1,879	1,484	1,100	806
Gross profit	2,089	2,145	1,740	1,480	1,897	1,679	1,586	1,195	891	801
G + A exp.	1,802	1,857	1,473	1,433	1,578	1,453	1,312	1,000	754	691
Inc. from oper.	287	288	267	47	319	226	274	195	137	110
Other inc. exp.	36	81	43	–8	35	23	2	3	–8	–10
Inc. before tax	323	369	310	39	354	249	276	198	129	100
Tax	120	144	125	6	148	94	111	80	54	41
Net Income	203	224	185	33	206	155	165	118	75	59

TABLE 2 BALANCE SHEETS ON DEC. 31
(In 000's)

	1982	1981	1980	1979	1978	1977	1976	1975	1974	1973
Cash and short term invest.	$ 240	$ 282	$ 449	$ 11	$ 82	$ 65	$ 51	$ 93	$ 145	$ 74
Inventories	631	547	369	403	338	276	249	248	174	144
Other current assets	60	57	53	99	51	58	50	32	26	26
Total current assets	$ 931	$ 886	$ 871	$ 513	$ 471	$ 399	$ 350	$ 373	$ 345	$ 244
Property, equipment	2907	2591	2380	2297	2230	1960	1739	1484	1234	1130
Accumulated depreciation	–1355	–1254	–1147	–1030	–906	–790	–674	–576	–496	–428
Other assets	24	25	27	53	55	33	29	31	34	34
Total assets	$2507	$2248	$2131	$1833	$1850	$1602	$1444	$1312	$1117	$ 980
Current maturities of LTD	$ 43	$ 40	$ 46	$ 8	$ 11	$ 5	$ 8	$ 7	$ 21	$ 20
Notes payable	-0-	-0-	-0-	68	20	-0-	-0-	5	70	20
Accounts payable	56	58	63	47	43	64	36	42	31	23
Accruals + other current liab.	252	244	310	124	232	167	178	193	136	110
Total current liab.	$ 351	$ 342	$ 419	$ 247	$ 306	$ 236	$ 222	$ 247	$ 258	$ 173
Long-term debt	191	149	179	238	133	130	133	136	222	244
Deferred tax	7	1								
Stockholder's equity	1958	1756	1533	1348	1411	1236	1089	929	637	563
Total Liab. + equity	$2507	$2248	$2131	$1833	$1850	$1602	$1444	$1312	$1117	$ 980

have been about $19,000 larger in 1973, and $21,000 larger in 1974, with a negligible effect in 1975. The value of the acquired net assets was about $180,000.

The company's growth and expansion has been financed primarily by retained earnings, temporarily supplemented at times with short-term borrowings. A major exception was a $250,000, ten year installment loan in 1973 used to help finance the Mall and some large signs located 660 feet from the highway. In 1975, this loan was prepaid through 1980. At the end of 1982, only $34,500 remained to be paid on this loan. Other long-term debt at the end of 1982 includes installment contracts for the purchase of real estate and a stock redemption agreement (occurring in 1979) for the purchase by the company of some Class B, non-voting stock. As indicated on the December 31, 1982 balance sheet, current maturities of long-term debt were $43,436. Of this amount, $34,496 is the final payment on the 1973 loan due in 1983.

Both the growth and the volatility of the business should be apparent from the statements presented in Tables 1 and 2. Table 3 presents the income statements as a percentage of sales. Table 4 is an analysis of the rate of return on equity broken into the component parts on the basis of the following formula:

$$\frac{\text{Sales}}{\text{Assets}} \times \frac{\text{gross profit}}{\text{sales}} \times \frac{\text{operating income}}{\text{gross profit}} \times$$

$$\frac{\text{net income}}{\text{operating income}} \times \frac{\text{assets}}{\text{equity}} = \frac{\text{net income}}{\text{equity}}$$

Between 1973 and 1982, prices, as measured by the Consumer Price Index, increased by about 115%. Percentage increases in some balance sheet and income accounts for Wall Drug over this period are:

Sales	163%
Total G. + A. expense	145
Net income	159
Total assets	115
Equity	169

These percentages are based on combining Wall Auto Livery with Wall Drug in 1973 as if the merger occurring in 1975 has taken place.

Given below are percentage changes in some of the general and administrative expenses from 1976 through 1982:

Total G. + A.	37%
Utilities	137
Officers' salaries	2
Other salaries	42
Depreciation	5
Advertising	116
Profit sharing contribution	49

TABLE 3　PERCENT OF SALES STATEMENTS

	1982	1981	1980	1979	1978	1977	1976	1975	1974	1973
Sales	100.0	100.0	100.0	100.0	100.0	100.0	100.0	100.0	100.0	100.0
Cost of sales	55.9	55.5	56.2	58.3	54.0	55.6	54.2	55.4	55.2	50.2
Gross profit	44.1	44.5	43.8	41.7	46.0	44.4	45.8	44.6	44.8	49.8
G + A exp.	38.1	38.5	37.1	40.3	38.3	38.4	37.9	37.3	37.9	43.0
Inc. from oper.	6.0	6.0	6.7	1.3	7.7	6.0	7.9	7.3	6.9	6.8
Other inc. exp.	.8	1.7	1.1	− .2	.9	.6	.1	.1	− .4	− .6
Inc. before tax	6.8	7.7	7.8	1.1	8.6	6.6	8.0	7.4	6.5	6.2
Tax	2.5	3.0	3.1	.2	3.6	2.5	3.2	3.0	2.7	2.5
Net income	4.3	4.7	4.7	.9	5.0	4.1	4.8	4.4	3.8	3.7

TABLE 4　COMPONENTS OF RATE OF RETURN ON EQUITY

	1982	1981	1980	1979	1978	1977	1976	1975	1974	1973
Gross profit / Sales	.441	.445	.438	.417	.460	.444	.458	.446	.448	.498
Inc. fr. oper. / Gross profit	.137	.134	.153	.032	.168	.135	.163	.163	.154	.137
Sales / Assets	1.89	2.14	1.86	1.94	2.23	2.36	2.40	2.04	1.78	1.64
Inc. from oper. / Assets	.114	.128	.125	.026	.172	.141	.190	.148	.123	.112
Net income / Inc. from oper.	.707	.778	.698	.702	.646	.686	.602	.605	.547	.536
Assets / Equity	1.28	1.28	1.39	1.36	1.31	1.30	1.33	1.41	1.75	1.74
Net income / Equity	.103	.128	.121	.025	.146	.126	.152	.126	.118	.105

The items mentioned accounted for 77% of total general and administrative expenses in 1982 and 76% in 1976. These same items as percentages of sales were:

	1982	1976
Utilities	1.7%	1.0%
Officers' salaries	2.9	3.8
Other salaries	18.5	17.7
Depreciation	2.3	2.9
Advertising	2.1	1.3
Profit sharing contributions	2.0	1.8

Depreciation methods on various assets vary from straight line to 200% declining balance and over lives of from 15 to 40 years for buildings and improvements to 5 to 10 years for equipment, furnitures and fixtures. Although not evaluated or recognized on the financial statements, it is likely that some assets, such as the western art and the Silver Dollar Bar, have appreciated.

STORE MANAGEMENT

Recruiting and training the seasonal work force is a major task at Wall Drug. College students are recruited through college placement services. Training is of short duration but quite intense. Summer employees are tested on their knowledge of store operations and their ability to give information about the area to tourists.

Bill Hustead commented:

> I really think that there isn't anything more difficult than running a business with 20 to 30 employees in the winter and then moving into a business with 180 to 200 employees, and you have to house a hundred of them and you have to supervise them, and train them. This lasts through June, July and August, then the next year you start all over. It's kind of exciting and fun for the first 25 years but after 30 years you begin to think its a tough racket.

The store had a permanent nucleus of 20 to 30 employees. While the business could operate with fewer employees during the winter, the Hustead's believed that they needed the experienced employees to give stability to the operations in the summer. Permanent employees with seniority could get as much as six weeks paid vacation. Commenting on this policy Bill said:

> We probably go through the winter with more employees than we really need, but we give them time off in the winter because a seasonal business is so demanding. When the Fourth of July comes, you're working, when Memorial Day comes, you're working; when all those summer fun times come, you're working six days a week and it's quite a sacrifice. So, we try to be very generous with our paid vacations.

Dependence on seasonal tourists for the major portion of Wall Drug's business has inherent risks, and uncertainty over the future of the roadside signs, which have brought customers to the store for nearly 50 years, is a grave concern to the Husteads.

> We will try to have ideas to modify our outdoor advertising program to adapt to changes in the law which we are sure will be forthcoming. If they are drastic changes, they could put us out of business. If they nail it down so there isn't a sign on the interstate, that will do the job.

Asked about diversification as a hedge against this risk, Bill replied,

> We will try to diversify within our own community. By that I mean probably on our highway location in and around our Auto Livery. We have several hundred acres there (in sight of the interstate), and a motel and a modified drug store would be our last straw if we were wiped out in town.

The Husteads hoped to be able to create a fund to provide self-insurance for their dormitory houses. This fund would then also provide some measure of security from business risks as well.

Although over 80, Ted Hustead is still active in the management of the store, involved in everything from physical inspections of the premises to acting jointly with Bill in making policy decisions. Ted can frequently be seen on the grounds picking up litter. Dorothy, Ted's wife, comes to the store every day, summer and winter, helps with the banking, and spends from two to six hours each day on various chores. Bill's son Rick, 33, joined the store in 1980 and now shares in the management. Rick has a master's degree in guidance and counseling and spent four years as a guidance counselor and teacher in high school. Rick also spent two years in the real estate business and one year in the fast food business before returning to Wall. During his school years, Rick spent ten seasons working in Wall Drug. His wife, Kathy, is a pharmacist and also works in the store.

Bill Hustead expressed his continuous concern with the future of Wall Drug in light of future action concerning roadside sign advertising. Can the store expansion continue; should diversification be attempted in the community; should diversification be considered away from being effected by the tourist? Will Wall Drug be able to continue to gain publicity as they have in the past to keep people aware of their "attraction" characteristics? The costs of doing business are rising, such as the increase in utilities, which is sizeable. How can they plan for a bad year or two given the increasing uncertainty in tourist industry? With these thoughts in mind, the 1983 tourist season at Wall Drug was underway.

DISCUSSION QUESTIONS

1 To what do you attribute Wall Drug's success? Explain.
2 Evaluate the threat to Wall Drug which is posed by the prospect of new legislation and enforcement efforts relating to highway signs.
3 Explain the mission of Wall Drug as you see it and relate the strategies which Wall Drug has followed to that mission.
4 Explain the part which theme or atmosphere play in the customer appeal of Wall Drug.
5 Evaluate the capital structure of Wall Drug in relation to the degree of risk which the company faces.
6 Should Wall Drug or its owners attempt to diversify and, if so, what specific forms of diversification would you recommend? Explain your answer.
7 Explain your recommended strategy for Wall Drug in each of the four functional areas of production/operations, finance, marketing, and personnel.

HOLIDAY INNS, INC., 1984

Arthur Sharplin
Northeast Louisiana University

SELECTED STRATEGIC ISSUES

- Advantages and disadvantages of diversification into related product or service segments
- Market segmentation within a line of business
- Changing retail unit location policy with changing market conditions
- Market maturity and niche encroachment
- Book values versus market values for strategic decision making

Holiday Inns, Inc. (HI), headquartered in Memphis, Tennessee, is the world's largest hospitality company, with interests in hotels, casino gaming, and restaurants, having sold its Delta Steamships subsidiary in 1982. For the first half of 1983, 64.6 percent of operating income came from hotels, 32.9 percent from gaming, and 1 percent from restaurants. First-half net income and sales were at respective annual rates of $123 million and $1.5 billion. More detailed financial information is provided in the tables on pages 354 and 355.

The Holiday Inn hotel system includes 1744 hotels with 312,302 rooms in 53 countries on 5 continents and produces an estimated $4 billion in annual revenues. Licensed, or franchised, hotels account for 86 percent of total Holiday Inn hotels, 81 percent of total rooms, and 6 percent of HI sales. Franchisees pay $300 a room initially plus a royalty of 4 percent of gross room revenues and a fee for marketing and reservation services of 2 percent of gross room revenues. The company's reservation system is the largest in the hotel industry.

The research assistance of Connie Shum is gratefully acknowledged.

In 1982, less than 3 percent of Holiday Inn customers dropped in without room reservations, down from 95 percent in the fifties. In 1981, the company started to deemphasize highway locations. Virtually all new Holiday Inn hotels are placed near airports, industrial parks, and similar sites.

Business travelers account for about 60 percent of Holiday Inn room-nights occupied. The company is launching two new hotel chains aimed at the upscale business traveler. The first, Crowne Plaza hotels, offers fine dining, complimentary morning newspapers, continental breakfasts, twenty-four hour maid service, bellmen, and free HBO movies. Rates are $15 to $20 higher than the average rate of $44 at existing company owned Holiday Inns. Crowne Plaza hotels are now located in Rockville (Maryland), San Francisco, Miami, and Dallas. Four more will open in Stanford (Connecticut), Houston, and New Orleans by year end. The second new chain, Embassy Suite hotels, is targeted primarily at the business traveler near the upper end of the lodging market who stays three or four days, instead of the usual two, and will pay for specialized service. Each suite will offer a separate living room with a wet bar and the option of one or two bedrooms. The company plans to have six all-suite hotels in varying stages of development in 1984.

In December 1983, the company announced plans to develop a new budget hotel chain, called Hampton Inn hotels, to include 300 company-owned and franchised units within five years. The first will open in Memphis, Tennessee, in 1984. Room rates at these hotels will average about $30. They will feature rooms for smokers and non-smokers, free television and movies, local telephone calls, continental breakfasts, and arrangements for children under eighteen to stay free with their parents.

The Holiday Inn hotel group spent $60.1 million in 1982 to upgrade and renovate company-owned hotels. Old franchises were eliminated at the rate of about one a week, as minimum operating standards were raised. So drastic was the pruning that, even with 569 new hotels in the past eight years, there has been a net gain of only 45 in the number of Holiday Inns. At the end of 1982, there were 48 Holiday Inn hotels under construction worldwide. The Holiday Inn sign is being replaced with a new rectangular one bearing the chain's name topped with an orange and yellow starburst on a green background.

In March 1983, Roy E. Winegardner, chairman, and Michael D. Rose, president and chief executive officer, briefed stockholders on Holiday Inn's preparations for the future. Here are some excerpts from their comments:

> With the disposition of our steamship subsidiary, Holiday Inns, Inc., is now strategically focused on the hospitality industry. We also introduced a new sign and logo for our Holiday Inn hotel system, better reflecting the range of property types and level of product quality that will characterize the Holiday Inn hotel system in the decades ahead. Recognizing the increasing segmentation of the lodging market, we also began construction on two new hotel products. We also embarked on an aggressive expansion plan for our core Holiday Inn hotel brand. This represents the most aggressive company hotel development effort in recent years, and reflects our continuing belief in the long-term strength of the lodging market and of our Holiday Inn brand within the large moderate-priced segment of that market.
>
> Our company has prospered with the growth of Atlantic City, as our Harrah's Marina facility there has proven to be the most profitable hotel/casino in that market on a pre-tax,

HOLIDAY INNS, INC., AND CONSOLIDATED SUBSIDIARIES
STATEMENTS OF INCOME
(In Thousands, Except Per Share)

	Three quarters ended		Fiscal year ended	
	September 30, 1983	October 1, 1982	December 31, 1982	January 1, 1982
Revenues				Restated
Hotel	667,644	651,740	840,698	853,645
Gaming	449,239	360,608	472,792	388,148
Restaurant	71,016	70,865	100,584	96,366
Other	4,183	7,624	11,224	13,616
	1,192,082	1,090,837	1,425,298	1,351,775
Operating income				
Hotel	143,552	132,280	150,205	170,944
Gaming	98,576	63,647	74,595	56,291
Restaurant	3,486	2,714	5,029	6,547
Other	2,741	3,424	4,999	10,826
	248,355	202,065	234,828	244,608
Corporate expense	(22,058)	(17,860)	(24,487)	(25,736)
Interest, net of interest capitalized	(31,725)	(38,738)	(50,965)	(65,540)
Foreign currency translation gain (loss)	—	—	—	1,889
Income from continuing operations before income taxes	194,572	145,467	159,376	155,221
Provision for income taxes	85,612	58,187	62,157	56,515
Income from continuing operations	108,960	87,280	97,219	98,706
Discontinued operations				
Income from operations, net of income taxes	—	(22,100)	4,671	38,652
Loss on disposition, plus income taxes Payable of $5,505	—	—	(25,910)	—
Net income	108,960	65,180	75,980	137,358
Income (loss) per common and common equivalent share				
Continuing operations	2.86	2.23	2.50	2.68
Discontinued operations	—	(.58)	(.56)	.98
	2.86	1.65	1.94	3.66
Average common and common equivalent shares outstanding	38,055	38,305	38,216	39,449

pre-interest basis. We entered into a joint venture to build a new 600-room hotel and 60,000-square-foot casino on the Boardwalk. We believe this should contribute to Harrah's ability to achieve the same brand leadership position in Atlantic City that it now enjoys in Northern Nevada.

As a result of [a competitive] pricing strategy, operating margins suffered in our hotel business. However, this approach enabled us to maintain occupancy levels despite the fact that occupancies declined throughout the rest of the hotel industry. At Perkins Restaurants,

HOLIDAY INNS, INC., AND CONSOLIDATED SUBSIDIARIES
BALANCE SHEETS
(In Thousands, Except Share Amounts)

	December 31, 1982	January 1, 1982
Assets		Restated
Current assets		
Cash	49,945	39,655
Temporary cash investments, at cost	32,544	20,181
Receivables, including notes receivable of		
$12,618 and $31,927, less allowance for		
doubtful accounts of $18,925 and $15,080	73,008	91,782
Supplies, at lower of average cost or market	21,871	23,424
Deferred income tax benefits	13,510	11,190
Prepayments and other current assets	18,101	9,775
Total current assets	208,979	196,007
Investments in unconsolidated affiliates,		
at equity	108,480	46,535
Notes receivable due after one year and		
other investments	44,186	49,214
Property and equipment, at cost		
Land, buildings, improvements and equipment	1,635,310	1,496,491
Accumulated depreciation and amortization	(367,434)	(313,947)
	1,267,876	1,182,544
Excess of cost over net assets of business		
acquired, amortized evenly over 40 years	54,314	55,787
Deferred charges and other assets	24,172	31,275
Net assets of discontinued operations	—	111,297
	1,708,007	1,672,659
Liabilities and shareholders' equity		
Current liabilities		
Accounts payable	77,867	66,375
Long-term debt due within one year	31,267	30,478
Accrued expenses	123,283	133,256
Total current liabilities	232,417	230,109
Long-term debt due after one year	436,356	581,465
Deferred credits and other long-term liabilities	33,938	34,851
Deferred income taxes	62,334	53,857
Shareholders' equity		
Capital stock		
Special stock, authorized—5,000,000 shares;		
series A—$1.125 par value;		
issued—491,541 and 576,410 shares;		
convertible into 1.5 shares of common stock	553	648
Common stock, $1.50 per value;		
authorized—60,000,000 shares; issued—		
40,218,350 and 32,909,606 shares	60,327	49,364
Capital surplus	294,517	161,188
Retained earnings	671,609	626,310
Cumulative foreign currency translation		
adjustments	(3,804)	—
Capital stock in treasury, at cost;		
3,036,081 and 2,439,500 common shares		
and 72,192 series A shares	(78,660)	(63,170)
Restricted stock	(1,580)	(1,963)
Total shareholders' equity	942,962	772,377
	1,708,007	1,672,659

Inc., our restaurant subsidiary, this pricing strategy paid off, contributing to substantially higher customer count and improved unit profitability. We also made the decision to dispose of a number of restaurants and hotels which were not performing to our financial standards.

In addition to strengthening our market position, we also strengthened our balance sheet. The company's 9⅝-percent convertible subordinated debentures were called for redemption on March 2, 1982. The result was conversion to $143 million of additional equity, which provides the basis for significant new debt capacity to fund our future expansion. Consistent with our stated intention to reduce floating rate debt, we issued $75 million in fixed-rate, 10-year notes in August. In 1982 we commissioned an update of an independent study of the appreciated value of the company's tangible assets and certain contract rights. This study indicated that the net market value of these assets approximated $2.5 billion. [This] appraisal reflects the value of the company's franchise and management contract income streams as well as the appreciation of our real estate assets. [We have] also made substantial progress in improving the productivity of our most important resource, our people. We undertook a thorough review of staffing levels and programs to assure that we were bringing sufficient resources to bear on those things that matter the most, and not expending time or money on those efforts that yield more limited returns. As a result, we have eliminated significant overhead costs and focused our attention more clearly on those things that are most critical to our success in the future. We deliberately increased our expenditures on training and development. We believe that, in our businesses, people represent the greatest opportunity for competitive advantage.

As we look ahead, the economic picture remains clouded. We cannot accurately predict the impact of the unprecedented massive Federal budget deficits on our economy. We remain confident in our ability to manage our businesses effectively under both good and difficult economic conditions.

DISCUSSION QUESTIONS

1 Explain what you believe to be the diversification strategy and defend or oppose it.
2 Explain the hotel group's approach to market segmentation. Do you support it? Why?
3 Explain why Holiday Inn's hotel location policy has been successful in the past and justify or oppose the way that policy has changed.
4 Relate the life-cycle stage of the hotel industry to Holiday Inn's recent efforts to start new hotel chains.
5 Which is more valid for strategic decision-making purposes, the market value appraisals of assets and contract rights referred to in the case or the book values in the financial statements? Why?

MID PACIFIC AIR

Jim D. Barnes
Brenda J. Moscove
California State College, Bakersfield

Paula M. Alden
University of Honolulu

SELECTED STRATEGIC ISSUES

- Preoperation planning for an air carrier
- Impact on air travel market of a new entrant
- Appropriate goals and strategies for a new airline in a regional market

Mid Pacific Airlines, Inc., was organized in 1979 under the proposition that it would be a regularly scheduled commercial passenger airline service in the state of Hawaii between Honolulu on the island of Oahu and Lihue and Kahalui on the islands of Kauai and Maui. Target date for the first flight was anticipated as March 15, 1981.

Prior to a stock offering, Mid Pacific had conducted preoperating development activities and, not incidentally, developed some initial tactics among which were: an assessment of the interisland passenger market in the State of Hawaii; a plan for penetrating the market; and a determination of the availability of suitable aircraft. Lease or buy strategies were developed, initial fuel commitment was arranged and space at airports was secured for the required activities of the passenger service component of the business.

Federal regulations were complied with and CAB certifications were obtained while FAA certification was still being secured. Given all of the preoperation planning and analysis, the company anticipated that, unless it received operating revenues by May,

Jim D. Barnes was Chair and Professor of Marketing at the School of Business and Public Administration, California State College, Bakersfield. Paula M. Alden is an MBA graduate from Chaminade University of Honolulu.

1981, the proceeds of its stock offering would be depleted by the expenses of operating Mid Pacific Air.

Nine hundred thousand shares of common stock were issued by Mid Pacific Air through a prospectus and a commitment made by John Muir & Company as the underwriter. The shares were issued at $5, with realization of $4,500,000 for the offering and net proceeds of approximately $3,870,000.

The net proceeds from the stock offering constituted the foundation for the emergence of Mid Pacific into the commercial passenger airline service in Hawaii. Typical of the positive approach and success-minded enthusiasm characterizing Mid Pacific's management, the airline was the first in the country to go public before it had an airplane.

THE ENVIRONMENT

In 1980 the interisland air passenger market in the state of Hawaii was dominated by two major carriers, Hawaiian and Aloha. In addition, several small commuter airlines, like Royal Hawaiian, with a fleet of approximately fifteen eight-passenger Cessna 402s, carried passengers among the islands. Hawaiian Air operated DC 9-50s, owning at least ten aircraft, and was implementing plans to re-equip with DC 9-80s.[1] Both Hawaiian and Aloha utilized jet aircraft solely, and both airlines had sold or planned to sell or lease out aircraft.

The environment was characterized by increased fuel costs and declining passenger counts. In 1980, Hawaiian Air showed a decrease in revenue passengers carried of 15.3 percent and revenue passenger miles decreased 13.7 percent. However, fuel cost increased 41 percent.[2] Aloha showed a decrease in revenue passengers carried of 9 percent and a revenue passenger miles decrease of 10.1 percent. Fuel cost increases were 64 percent.[3] Third quarter and cumulative earnings through the third quarter of 1980 for Aloha Airlines are reported in Exhibit 1. Historically, the two major airlines had gone through periods of profit and loss and had operated mostly under a regulated environment.

Hawaiian and Aloha sought approximately nine fare increases over a fourteen month period. Although the fare increases were instituted over several months, the incremental approach to fare increases did have the net effect of elevating prices above the level considered economically feasible by local passengers. One-way fares for Aloha and Hawaiian between Honolulu/Kahului were approximately $51 and for Royal Hawaiian, $44.[4] Furthermore, Hawaii's visitor industry was suffering from the impact of increased costs and inflation in general, with a growing dependence on Asian travelers. Traditionally, the interisland carriers had generated patronage from Mainland U.S. visitors.

Of the four major islands, Hawaii was least visited by tourists. Direct Mainland/ Hilo service had dwindled to one flight per day, via United, from Los Angeles. Since

[1] Tichen, Kathy, "Fare War Hides Big Question: Is There Enough to Go Around?" *Honolulu Star Bulletin*, October 1, 1981, Section C, p. 1.

[2] *Hawaiian Air Annual Report*, 1980.

[3] *Aloha Airlines Annual Report*, 1980.

[4] Tichen, October 1, 1981, Section C, p. 1.

EXHIBIT 1 THIRD QUARTER AND CUMULATIVE EARNINGS,
ALOHA AIRLINES, 1980 AND 1981

Third quarter earnings		
	1980	**1981**
Profit/Loss	$ 1.41 million	− $847 thousand
Gain/Loss per Share	.66	− .40
Revenues	$21.41 million	$21.41 million

Cumulative earnings, first three quarters, 1980 and 1981		
	1980	**1981**
Total Earnings	$ 4.88 million*	$ 564 thousand**
Total Earnings per Share	2.28	.27
Total Revenues	$61.75 million	$65.73 million

*$3.3 million pretax gain from aircraft sale.
**$1 million pretax gain from aircraft sale.
Source: "Aloha Reports Earnings Loss," *Star-Bulletin Advertiser*, 1981.

the bulk of the state's visitors arrive and depart from Honolulu, visitor traffic to the island of Hawaii was declining. Furthermore, the focus of visitor traffic on Hawaii had shifted to Keahole (West Hawaii) from Hilo where the main airport is located.[5] However, Maui and Kauai showed percentage increases in their visitor counts over the past few years.

Increasing deregulation, an expected downturn in passenger count, and increased cost factors characterized the interisland carrier market. Occasional market entry attempts had been made by other carriers, but no carrier had succeeded as a challenger to the two dominant airlines.

The 1979 distribution of population and number of business firms among the state's four major islands are included in Exhibit 2. The population of the other islands in the state, to include Lanai, Molokai, and Niihau, is a very small portion of the total, with business activity reduced accordingly. The economy is heavily dependent on government expenditures (including the military), the visitor industry, and agriculture.

[5] Ibid.

EXHIBIT 2 SUMMARY OF POPULATION AND NUMBER OF BUSINESS FIRMS ON
FOUR MAJOR ISLANDS IN HAWAII

	Oahu	**Hawaii**	**Kauai**	**Maui**	**Total**
Population	779,300	88,400	41,500	66,000	975,200
% of Total	79.9	9.1	4.0	7.0	100
Number of					
Business Firms	14,282	1,887	792	1,619	18,580
% of Total	76.9	10.1	4.3	8.7	100

Source: *Data Book, 1979, A Statistical Abstract*, 1979.

THE EXECUTIVE TEAM

One of the fundamental requisites of sound business strategy, managerial expertise, was a recognized attribute of Mid Pacific Air. With the proceeds from the stock offering, the cumulative experience in the transportation industry of the management of Mid Pacific was brought into play. Furthermore, managerial experience in the industry on the part of key executives played a major role in the success of the stock offering itself.

Arthur D. Lewis is the Chairman of the Board of Directors and a Director of Mid Pacific. His background includes service in various capacities for airline, bus, and railroad transportation organizations. He was the President and Chief Executive Officer of the American Bus Association as well as Chairman of the Board and Chief Executive Officer of the United States Railway Association. Lewis also acted in several executive capacities with Eastern Airlines, Hawaiian Airlines, and American Airlines.

John J. Higgins is the President of Mid Pacific. He served as Executive Vice President, Chief Operating Officer, and Director of Hawaiian Airlines, Inc., a direct competitor in the regional market. He also served as Vice President for Finance for World Airways and as a consultant to Capitol International Airways.

Nolan J. Kramer is the Senior Vice President for Marketing and Customer Services of Mid Pacific. He was employed for thirty-eight years at Hawaiian Air, including the period 1971–79, when he was Vice President for Sales.

Edward S. Nielsen is the Vice President for Finance and Administration and Secretary/Treasurer of Mid Pacific. Previous service includes Controller of Hawaiian Airlines and Vice President and Controller of Bishop Trust Company.

The executive team is well-acquainted with the airline industry and the Hawaii market, with many years of experience in the industry and in the state. The individuals comprising the team were, of course, well known within the regional market. Furthermore, the management team utilized the services of Alliance III, an airline consulting group, and John Muir & Company to add to their expertise. In addition, Keith Haugen was appointed Manager for Public Relations and Advertising. Haugen is well acquainted with the Hawaiian business climate and has an established reputation for understanding and promoting Hawaiian culture.

THE COMPANY NAME

Several company names were considered by management. A name amenable to the Hawaiian market, but not limiting identity only to that market, was desired. Management finally selected Mid Pacific Air as a suitable name for the organization. Of course, many of the names initially considered were not available for use.

THE AIRCRAFT DECISIONS

Various types of lease-or-buy arrangements were investigated for the planes that Mid Pacific intended to put into service. It was decided to lease three jet-prop aircraft of the

YS-11 class. This is the same type of plane used by Piedmont Airlines, and the safety record of the plane at Piedmont Airlines was a key factor in the decision.

Of course, cost of operating the jet-prop airplane was one of the most significant considerations. The jet-prop was believed to be more economical to operate in the Hawaiian market than the competitors' more sophisticated jets. The resulting savings, in fuel costs for example, allowed for substantial ticket price reductions below competitors' fares while permitting Mid Pacific to realize profits. Furthermore, at the time the aircraft was selected, the executives ascertained the availability of fuel and aircraft and aircraft renovation costs. Regulations affecting the cost of flight operation related to type of aircraft were also evaluated as part of the selection process.

PERSONNEL PRACTICES

The attractions of "pioneering" with a new airline and of Hawaii itself as a place to live enabled Mid Pacific to select pilots from a pool of experienced applicants. Because safety was a prime concern of management and was a necessary component for establishing credibility for the new airline, experience was not sacrificed for cost in key positions. The Maintenance Manager with Mid Pacific was from Piedmont Airlines and brought with him a background of knowledge and experience in dealing with the aircraft. Also, the Manager of In-flight Services is a former flight attendant and instructor with Piedmont who possesses a wealth of experience. Other positions were filled with applicants mainly from Hawaii. An intensive training program preceded actual operation. Developing policies, hiring personnel, and training personnel adequately before the target date for operation were major endeavors. By utilizing non-unionized staff and having a ratio of part-time help far in excess of full-time help, Mid Pacific kept its payroll costs down compared to other airlines.

ROUTE SELECTION/SCHEDULING/FARE STRUCTURE

The two years of planning that went into the development of Mid Pacific were well spent. Initially, the advantages and disadvantages of mirroring the air routes already serviced by the two major local airlines, Hawaiian and Aloha, were analyzed. Among other things, analysis of industry data revealed that there were more than 2.24 million annual boardings between Honolulu and Lihue. These boardings were serviced primarily by only two scheduled carriers. By comparison to the New York to Washington, D.C., boardings of 2.25 million serviced by 6 or 7 scheduled carriers, Mid Pacific decided there was room for one more airline in the Hawaiian market. Furthermore, of the total number of passengers carried by Aloha and Hawaiian Air, 70 percent were visitor traffic and 30 percent were local traffic.

Mid Pacific managers determined that it was more advantageous to service two of the neighboring islands from Oahu than to just imitate the competitors' routes to all the major islands. Consequently, their efforts were devoted to developing the finest alternative service possible to the chosen destinations. Exhibit 3 includes proposed air routes at the beginning of service. Possible breakeven at the initial fares planned, 140,000 passengers, might be anticipated for July, after four months of actual opera-

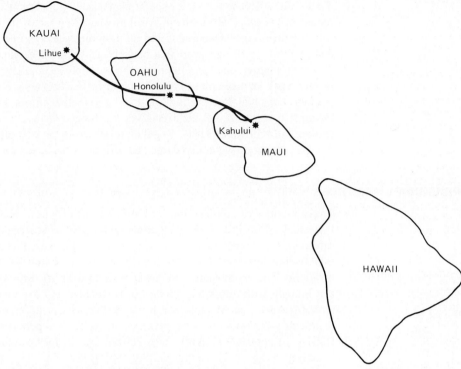

EXHIBIT 3   PROPOSED ROUTES AT BEGINNING OF SERVICE

tion. In fact, Mid Pacific could operate at 70 percent capacity with a fare of $22 and break even.

Flight service was to be phased in during the months of March and April. Exhibit 4 contains the timetable and initial projected fares, which were lower than Hawaiian and Aloha fares at that time. Basic one-way fares were $33 for Honolulu/Maui/Honolulu and Honolulu/Kauai/Honolulu. For Kauai/Maui/Kaui, one way fares were $44. A $99 triangle fare for Honolulu/Kauai/Maui was proposed. Certain discount fares were included as described in the timetable, such as the business or group plan including free tickets for multiple ticket purchases.

Terminal space was obtained for the airports to be serviced by Mid Pacific Air. However, space in the Interisland Terminal, housing Hawaiian Air and Aloha Airlines at the Honolulu airport, was not available. Therefore, Mid Pacific was the only interisland carrier located in the Main Terminal at Honolulu International Airport, resulting in a high degree of visibility for visitors and/or residents traveling on international or Mainland flights.

THE MARKETING PLAN AND IMPLEMENTATION

The prime target market for Mid Pacific was identified as residents of the state wishing to travel among the three islands serviced by the airlines for pleasure or for business purposes. The visitor market was also identified as viable.

EXHIBIT 4   TIME TABLE AND FARE SCHEDULE

To Maui			To Kauai			To Honolulu		
Leave	Arrive	Flight No.	Leave	Arrive	Flight No.	Leave	Arrive	Flight No.
From Honolulu			**From Honolulu**			**From Maui**		
6:40 am	7:11 am	2	6:25 am	6:56 am	21*	7:30 am	8:01 am	3
7:25 am	7:56 am	20*	6:50 am	7:21 am	11	8:15 am	8:56 am	23*
8:10 am	8:41 am	22*	8:25 am	8:56 am	3	9:00 am	9:31 am	25*
8:35 am	9:06 am	12	9:20 am	9:51 am	23*	9:25 am	9:56 am	13
10:10 am	10:41 am	4	9:55 am	10:26 am	25*	11:00 am	11:31 am	5
11:00 am	11:31 am	24*	10:20 am	10:51 am	13	11:50 am	12:21 pm	27*
11:40 am	12:11 pm	26*	11:55 am	12:26 pm	5+	12:30 pm	1:01 pm	29*
12:05 pm	12:36 pm	14	12:55 pm	1:26 pm	27*	12:55 pm	1:26 pm	15
1:50 pm	2:21 pm	6	1:35 pm	2:06 pm	29*	2:40 pm	3:11 pm	7
2:45 pm	3:16 pm	28*	2:05 pm	2:36 pm	15	3:40 pm	4:11 pm	31*
3:20 pm	3:51 pm	30*	3:35 pm	4:06 pm	7	4:10 pm	4:41 pm	33*
3:50 pm	4:21 pm	16	4:35 pm	5:06 pm	31*	4:40 pm	5:11 pm	17
5:05 pm	5:36 pm	32*	5:35 pm	6:06 pm	17	5:55 pm	6:26 pm	35*
5:25 pm	5:56 pm	8	7:10 pm	7:41 pm	9	6:15 pm	6:46 pm	9
6:20 pm	6:51 pm	34*	8:05 pm	8:36 pm	37*	7:10 pm	7:41 pm	37*
7:20 pm	7:51 pm	18				8:10 pm	8:41 pm	19
From Kauai			**From Maui**			**From Kauai**		
7:15 am	8:41 am	22* (1)	7:30 am	8:56 am	3 (1)	7:15 am	7:46 am	22*
7:40 am	9:06 am	12 (1)	8:15 am	9:51 am	23* (1)	7:40 am	8:11 am	12
9:15 am	10:41 am	4 (1)	9:00 am	10:26 am	25* (1)	9:15 am	9:46 am	4
10:10 am	11:31 am	24* (1)	9:25 am	10:51 am	13 (1)	10:10 am	10:41 am	24*
10:45 am	12:11 pm	26* (1)	11:00 am	12:26 pm	5+ (1)	10:45 am	11:26 am	26*
11:10 am	12:36 pm	14 (1)	11:50 am	1:26 pm	27* (1)	11:10 am	11:41 am	14
12:45 pm	2:21 pm	6+ (1)	12:30 pm	2:06 pm	29* (1)	12:45 pm	1:16 pm	6+
1:45 pm	3:16 pm	28* (1)	12:55 pm	2:36 pm	15 (1)	1:45 pm	2:16 pm	28*
2:25 pm	3:51 pm	30* (1)	2:40 pm	4:06 pm	7 (1)	2:25 pm	2:56 pm	30*
2:55 pm	4:21 pm	16 (1)	3:40 pm	5:06 pm	31* (1)	2:55 pm	3:26 pm	16
4:25 pm	5:56 pm	8 (1)	4:40 pm	6:06 pm	17 (1)	4:25 pm	4:56 pm	8
5:25 pm	6:51 pm	34* (1)	6:15 pm	7:41 pm	9 (1)	5:25 pm	5:56 pm	34*
6:25 pm	7:51 pm	18 (1)	7:10 pm	8:36 pm	37* (1)	6:25 pm	6:56 pm	18
						8:00 pm	8:31 pm	10
						8:55 pm	9:26 pm	36*

+ Effective: March 30, 1981
* Effective: April 15, 1981

Fares

Honolulu-Maui-Honolulu
Honolulu-Kauai-Honolulu
$33 Adults, each way
$21 Children 2 thru 11, each way
Adult discount fare—on flights
before 8 AM or after 2:59PM—$27

Kauai-Maui-Kauai
$44 Adults, each way
$26 Children 2 thru 11, each way

Triangle Fare
Honolulu-Kauai-Maui
$99 Adults
$66 Children 2 thru 11

Businessman or Groups
Buy a book of 20 tickets and get 3 tickets FREE.
Buy a book of 10 tickets and get 1 ticket FREE.
Tickets have no expiration date. No additional cost even
if rates increase.

The airline was to be "positioned" as the alternative to the two leading interisland aircarriers, Hawaiian Air and Aloha, to distinguish it clearly from the small commuter airlines. Flyers included the Mid Pacific theme that was particularly emphasized during the preoperative period, "Now There Are Three!" The intention was to elevate the newcomer to the ranks of the two familiar carriers so strongly identified with inter-island travel for many years.

A penetration strategy for pricing was followed, and the theme of making Hawaii's skies "affordable" again was stressed. Exhibit 4 illustrates the initial fare structure. One free ticket was offered with the purchase of a book of ten tickets, and three free tickets accompanied a purchase of twenty tickets. Advertising emphasized that the offer had no expiration date; therefore, no additional costs would be incurred at the time of ticket redemption even if fares increased. Revenues of 1.8 million dollars were derived from the discount book offerings.

Advertising and public relations, especially during the preoperative stage, indirectly addressed the risk factors inherent in the firm's operations. Virtually no business operates in a totally risk-free environment. However, Mid Pacific was in an environment characterized by risk of the highest order. In addition to the sheer economic impact of starting an airline, public consciousness of the safety factor as it impacts a new passenger airline operation was a major risk. It was a foregone conclusion that any accident occurring in the first few months of Mid Pacific's existence would literally spell the death knell of the fledgling airline. Aloha and Hawaiian Air had excellent safety records. Utility, economy and safety were keynotes in business decisions during the initial strategy sessions of the Mid Pacific founders. Pre-publicity and advertising emphasized "over 200 years experience in airline management" to overcome the safety factor.

Mid Pacific also promoted its Main Terminal location on Oahu, allowing for:

"Fast boarding and disembarking"
"Convenient adjacent covered parking"
"Fast computerized check-in, making pre-check obsolete"

Initially, Mid Pacific budgeted a quarter of a million dollars for advertising stressing the "affordable" and "Now There Are Three" approaches. Aided by an excellent advertising agency, an intense TV, print, and multimedia blitz carried the campaigns to the Hawaiian market prior to the airline's first flight in March. Advertising was supported by extensive public relations and promotion. Before a single aircraft was in operation, Mid Pacific engaged Aloha and Hawaiian Air in battle.

EVALUATING PREOPERATIVE STRATEGY AND ANTICIPATING OUTCOME

Based upon the highlights of the preoperative planning and strategies developed by Mid Pacific Air prior to launching its first flight in March, 1981, company managers evaluated the strengths/weaknesses of the preoperative stage. Also, anticipation of the impact of Mid Pacific's entry into the interisland air carrier market in Hawaii and actual study of the outcome were valuable in assessing the preoperative strategy. Such analyses also led to speculation about future strategies, if any, that could be developed by the airline.

BIBLIOGRAPHY

"Aloha Reports Earnings Loss." *Honolulu Star-Bulletin*. October, 1981.

Annual Report, 1980. Hawaii: Aloha Airlines. 1981.

Annual Report, 1980. Hawaii: Hawaiian Airlines. 1981.

Data Book, 1979, a Statistical Abstract. Hawaii: Department of Planning and Economic Development. 1979.

Hawaii Visitor Industry Reports, 1979–81. Hawaii: Hawaii Visitor Bureau. 1979, 1980, 1981.

Honolulu Star-Bulletin. Honolulu: Hawaii Newspaper Agency. 1981.

"Manulani, The Magazine of Mid Pacific Air." Hawaii: Mid Pacific Air. Vol. 1, No. 3. July, 1981.

Mid Pacific Air Timetable, Schedules 1 and 3. Hawaii: Mid Pacific Air. March/July, 1981.

Prospectus, Mid Pacific Airlines, Inc. John Muir & Co. September 16, 1980.

Tichen, Kathy. "Fare War Hides Big Question: Is There Enough to Go Around?" *Honolulu Star-Bulletin*. Hawaii: Hawaii Newspaper Agency. October 1, 1981. Section C, p. 1.

Weston, J. Fred and Eugene F. Brigham. *Essentials of Managerial Finance*. Illinois: The Dryden Press. 5th Edition, 1979.

DISCUSSION QUESTIONS

1 Evaluate the preoperation planning efforts of Mid Pacific Air with special emphasis on the organization's strengths and weaknesses.

2 Discuss the likely impact on Hawaii's air carrier market of Mid Pacific's entry.

3 State and justify the goals and strategies which you believe Mid Pacific should set.

SHARPCO, INC. (A)

Arthur Sharplin
Northeast Louisiana University

SELECTED STRATEGIC ISSUES

- Relating the organization mission to success for the small enterprise
- Valuing a one-owner business
- Organizational structure for a small business
- Social responsibilities of a sole owner
- Financing practices and financial structure for a small company
- The impact of ownership changes on small business strategies

I want to keep the company profitable, of course. There was a time when I wanted Sharpco to grow as big as it possibly could. Now, though, I place more importance on having some time for my family and myself and on my own health. I suppose I would like to see the company get to where it would furnish a good living for me and my family and only require half the time and energy it demands now. I would like for us to be a little more respected, too. Our competitors are pretty big boys—the Caterpillar dealer and the Fiat Allis dealer—and they have big fine buildings and nice machinery and a good deal of prestige. That doesn't bother me as much as it once did, but I would like to see us upgrade our public image a bit.

The speaker was James Sharplin. He had just assumed full responsibility for the company he had managed for nine years by buying out the interests of his brothers Art and Jerry. While he felt equal to the task, he knew the complexity of managing a small business and expected that the days ahead would be consumingly difficult. Neither of his brothers had worked full time in the firm for several years, but they had always been there when James needed them. Art had taken care of financial matters, making credit arrangements, establishing accounting controls, etc., and Jerry had provided technical expertise as well as sound business judgment. Like James, Jerry and Art had often pitched in as working supervisors on particularly difficult or urgent jobs. In the past, the three had made all major decisions as a team, with Art acting as catalyst and coordinator. Now, James would have final responsibility. James knew that he could still call on his brothers—they were not leaving the area—but all three felt that it would be best if he could be fairly independent.

COMPANY OPERATIONS

Sharpco is located on the outskirts of Monroe, Louisiana. The Sharpco plant is about 400 feet from Interstate Highway 20 and is clearly visible from that major east/west thoroughfare, but the nearest interchange is about three-fourths mile away. Sharpco, Inc., is engaged in four related businesses.

First, the company provides parts and service for crawler tractor undercarriages. The undercarriage for a crawler tractor consists of a heavy chainlike "track," which substitutes for the rubber tires on conventional tractors, along with the related sprockets and rollers which keep the track in alignment and in firm contact with the ground. Crawler tractors typically operate in sand, gravel, and dirt, and consequently wear away all portions of the undercarriage rather rapidly. A typical undercarriage will last for perhaps 1500 operating hours before it must be completely reconditioned. Usually, this involves building up the metal surfaces which are in contact with one another, replacement of the pins and bushings which hold the tracks together, and the repair of breaks and cracks which occur as a result of vibration and stress. A typical undercarriage reconditioning job may result in a customer billing of $2500 to $8000. In addition to performing repairs, Sharpco sells a wide array of undercarriage parts, sprockets, track chains (called "rails"), rollers, idlers, and sprockets to customers who do repair work themselves.

Second, Sharpco designs, fabricates, and sells tree-cutting blades for crawler tractors and digging buckets for backhoes and excavators. The company also makes a number of other specialized tools designed to be pushed or pulled by heavy tractors. This includes rice-field-leveling blades and land-clearing rakes, which are used to push timber into piles for burning once it has been cut. All these items are fabricated partly from extra-high-strength steel, using specialized welding materials and techniques.

Third, Sharpco provides custom welding services to commercial, agricultural, and industrial customers. This includes repair and fabrication of all kinds of steel items, both at Sharpco's plant and at customer locations.

Finally, Sharpco cuts and sells various steel plates and shapes, commonly called angles, rounds, channels, flats, and beams.

HISTORICAL SKETCH

In 1972, at the urging of his brothers Art and Jerry, James Sharplin left his job as a welding and undercarriage shop manager for a major Caterpillar dealership and accepted their offer to join them in their construction business. The Sharplins were engaged in industrial and plant maintenance contracting and, in addition, had completed a number of small concrete, steel, and mechanical projects for the U.S. Air Force. After just a few months, James, Jerry, and Art decided to build a shop at the present site of the Sharpco plant and to go into the steel fabrication business. Only $33,500 in initial investment was available, and much of this was in machinery and equipment contributed by the Sharplins. By personally signing the mortgage, along with their wives, the Sharplins were able to buy the necessary land and building materials. The initial 49 x 49 foot shop building consisted of a galvanized corrugated metal ("roofing tin") exterior over a frame made of used steel pipe and pine lumber. Art, Jerry, and James built the building themselves during breaks between construction jobs. A portable construction shack, purchased for $450, served as the shop office. Because of the shortage of funds, the only equipment available was welding machines, cutting torches, and hand tools previously owned by the three brothers.

Sharpco opened for business in early 1973. From the beginning, James managed the shop and Jerry and Art spent most of their time on other endeavors. Sales were slow at first, with the construction company giving Sharpco several small fabrication contracts and a few customers bringing welding jobs to the shop.

Being thinly capitalized, Sharpco could not have afforded a single unprofitable year. The first year saw profits in the range of $4000 to $5000. This was possible, James says, only because he took little salary and "used every method known to man to keep expenses down and sales up."

Because of his experience with the Caterpillar distributor, James was known in the northeastern Louisiana area as something of an expert in the design and construction of large tree-cutting blades for land-clearing tractors.

During 1974, drawing on his previous experience, James designed and built several of these blades for northern Louisiana land-clearing contractors. The blades ranged in weight from two to about eight tons and sold in the range of $4000 to $12000 each. This work turned out to be much more profitable than other types of fabrication. Sales and profits improved in 1974. In addition, a permanent office was added that year.

By the beginning of 1975, Sharpco had a work force of five men in addition to James. During 1975, Art worked about half time at Sharpco, managing the office and buying and selling steel, a sideline which he had gotten Sharpco into in late 1974. Jerry, the most expert of the three in the area of general fabrication, spent about one-third of his time at Sharpco. During this entire period, all three brothers did a great deal of physical work in the shop. Also during 1975, a 60 x 75 foot addition was made to the shop building.

The year 1976 was a banner year for Sharpco. Sales grew to $574,000, and profits, after reasonable salaries for the owners, were $40,510. Financial statements for 1976–1981 appear on pages 370 and 371.

During 1977, it became possible to take advantage of James' expertise and reputation in the area of crawler tractor undercarriage repair. Sharpco purchased several large machines which gave the company the capability of repairing undercarriages. From that point on, undercarriage work contributed a major part of Sharpco revenues and profits.

Art had completed his MBA degree in 1973 and moved away to Baton Rouge in 1976 for the purpose of completing his doctoral degree. While in Baton Rouge he commuted back and forth to Monroe every week or two to consult with James and to help in the management of the firm. James recalls that this was a particularly difficult period for him; but, because he knew Art had long dreamed of becoming a college professor, he didn't object. From 1977 onward, Jerry was totally involved in his construction activity and only infrequently consulted with James or worked at Sharpco.

In 1978, sales exceeded $1 million for the first time. Although steel fabrication revenue declined after 1977, the company prospered and the book value net worth exceeded $250,000 by the end of 1980. It was at this point that Art, having completed his doctoral degree and having accepted a full-time professorship at the university in Monroe, suggested to James that James become the sole owner of Sharpco. In the winter of 1981, James traded real estate holdings and a small amount of cash for the Sharpco stock held by his brothers.

ORGANIZATION

Figure 1 gives some idea of the organizational relationships which exist at Sharpco; however, like most small companies, Sharpco has no formal organization chart and all members of the organization routinely interact in ways not suggested by Figure 1. For example, Jerry Thompson often assigns work to Peggy Turnage, and James Sharplin often bypasses both of them and deals directly with workers. Peggy Turnage is a trusted employee and frequently accepts customer orders for work and assigns work directly to the welders, operators, and mechanics. Several of the workers are particularly knowledgeable about certain kinds of jobs and certain kinds of equipment.

FIGURE I   ORGANIZATION CHART

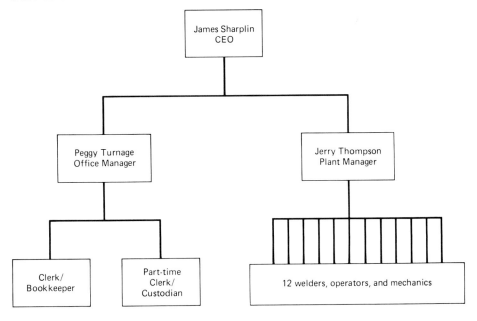

SHARPCO, INC., BALANCE SHEETS

	Calendar years				
	1976	**1977**	**1978**	**1979**	**1980**
Assets					
Current assets					
Cash	8,720	8,390	30,962	10,204	19,677
A/R—trade	83,420	98,994	88,405	82,688	54,394
Reserve for bad debts	0	(4,576)	(11,016)	(10,016)	(11,013)
A/R—other and N/R	2,359	3,688	85	1,650	10,689
Inventory	173,957	199,651	198,027	186,388	181,744
Total current assets	268,456	306,147	306,463	270,914	255,491
Fixed assets					
Improvements	12,307	17,225	16,495	16,495	16,495
Building	69,955	81,955	92,176	94,743	104,271
Machinery and equipment	57,817	108,793	128,518	142,641	133,712
Office furn. and equip.	2,090	7,749	9,524	18,149	16,113
Vehicles	23,129	38,475	36,183	30,084	36,223
Total	165,298	254,197	282,896	302,112	306,814
Less accu. depr.	(29,368)	(63,923)	(101,609)	(118,549)	(143,444)
Net depr. assets	135,930	190,274	181,287	183,563	163,370
Land	22,000	34,010	34,010	34,010	34,010
Total fixed assets	157,930	224,284	215,297	217,573	197,380
Other assets					
Deposit	0	500	500	500	500
Total assets	426,386	530,931	522,260	488,987	453,371
Liabilities and owners' equity					
Current liabilities					
A/P—trade	85,314	68,902	49,095	27,236	28,245
Accrued expenses	8,381	14,865	12,900	8,903	0
W/H and accrued taxes	3,901	4,907	3,539	5,909	3,071
Accrued payroll	0	14,082	0	0	0
Accrued income taxes	5,466	0	7,610	2,406	9,363
Notes payable	81,985	119,658	112,252	85,934	67,747
Total current liabilities	185,047	222,414	185,396	130,388	108,426
Long-term liabilities					
Notes payable	94,352	138,664	113,932	72,264	38,000
Stockholders' equity					
Common stock	33,582	33,582	33,582	33,582	33,582
Less treasury stock	0	0	0	0	(11,316)
Retained earnings	113,405	136,271	189,250	252,753	284,679
Total stockholders equity	146,987	169,853	222,832	286,335	306,945
Total liabilities and stockholders' equity	426,386	530,931	522,160	488,987	453,371

Without significant formality, they often take charge in their areas of expertise, acting as temporary working supervisors.

PERSONNEL

Sharpco employs seventeen persons (see Figure 1). Wages are partly based upon an infrequent survey of wages of similar workers in the Monroe area. There is a fairly standard medical care plan, and a one-week vacation is given after the first year. Only the assistant shop manager, Jerry Thompson, is allowed a two-week vacation. The workers average about forty-seven hours a week.

FINANCING

The initial equity investment in the firm was only $33,500. By 1981, this had been supplemented by about $250,000 in retained earnings. Machinery and equipment purchased over the years were financed through borrowing from a small country bank in Delhi, Louisiana. Vehicles and individual pieces of machinery were financed using individual installment notes. All notes were personally endorsed by the Sharplins. Recent financial statements are given on page 370 and below.

SHARPCO, INC., INCOME STATEMENTS

	Calendar years				
	1976	**1977**	**1978**	**1979**	**1980**
Revenue					
Shop	456,742	510,979	494,329	321,008	295,244
Undercarriage	0	184,497	420,348	431,110	354,564
Steel	115,139	155,224	197,354	194,789	92,048
Miscellaneous	2,261	9,572	8,949	3,112	4,366
Total revenue	574,142	860,272	1,120,980	950,019	746,222
Direct costs					
Materials	295,254	404,042	536,919	397,679	332,486
Shop labor	73,513	166,834	200,205	145,483	92,602
Subcontractors	3,276	1,374	2,300	2,894	4,440
Freight	1,107	6,525	5,062	6,812	4,631
Other direct costs	196	1,111	975	70	516
Total direct costs	373,346	579,886	745,461	552,938	434,675
Gross profit	200,796	280,386	365,519	397,081	311,547
Indirect costs	149,328	257,520	318,241	331,599	270,258
Profit before taxes	51,468	22,866	57,278	65,482	41,289
Income taxes	6,958	0	4,299	1,979	9,363
Net income	44,510	22,866	52,979	63,503	31,926

MARKETING

Sharpco's 1981 advertising expense is expected to be $21,000. This is being spent on a combination of direct mail (15 percent of total), newspaper (10 percent), and yellow-page (75 percent) advertising. James Sharplin and Jerry Thompson frequently make sales calls on customers within about fifty miles of Monroe. Primary reliance for advertising, though, is upon word of mouth. According to James Sharplin, "We make the best land-clearing equipment in the South. Our ability to do critical high-strength welding and fabrication is second to none. We also offer high quality undercarriage parts and service at a reasonable price. The word gets around." About one third of the steel items Sharpco manufactures are sold to equipment dealers who resell them. The remainder of Sharpco's sales are at the retail level.

INTERVIEW WITH JAMES SHARPLIN

The following interview was conducted at 5:30 a.m., October 16, 1981. The interview is not verbatim; some questions were omitted and the interviewee was allowed to read and edit his comments.

Q. James, I noticed that sales have been declining over the last several years. What do you think is the reason for this?

A. I think we are in a recession, to begin with, and construction activity is really depressed. Many of our sales are to contractors. Also, our dependence on the land-clearing business has created a problem for us. Not only is most of the land in this area cleared up now, but many of our major customers, like Chicago Mill and International Paper, are being prohibited from clearing some of their own land by the environmental authorities. Finally, we decided a couple of years ago to increase our prices at a rate well above the inflation rate. We expected that to cause sales to decrease. I think it has worked pretty well, too. In 1978, we had 28 employees and I was literally working myself to death. Although we made a good profit that year, I felt that things were just about out of control. I went to Houston to a trade show a few days ago and, besides that, I took two weeks off last year. I couldn't have done those things in 1978.

Q. Do you think the problem with the land-clearing business will continue?

A. Yes, absolutely! There just isn't much more land to clear in this area, and I think the government will continue to protect the hardwood bottomland. So a lot of the land-clearing contractors are hanging it up.

Q. How much of your business has been related to land clearing?

A. Our shop revenue last year was just under $300,000. Land-clearing equipment sales and repairs was well over half of that.

Q. Are you doing anything to make up for those lost sales?

A. Yes. We're changing directions somewhat. We're shifting to more emphasis on undercarriage work, although we'll continue to keep some welding and steel fabrication activity going. I negotiated an arrangement with a Florida company to furnish us a $200,000 inventory of undercarriage parts on consignment. We plan to increase the amount of undercarriage work that we're doing. Previously we have mainly sold the parts that we installed. Now, however, we are also advertising and selling the parts themselves.

Q. What kind of consignment deal do you have?

A. The best I have ever heard of. To begin with, the prices are about 5 percent better than those I have been able to get through outright purchases. At the end of each month I total up the sales of consignment items and then have to pay for them within thirty days. There are no interest charges.

Q. Don't consignment arrangements normally favor the supplier?

A. Yes, and that causes me to wonder. Art mentioned the other day that I might be helping to launder some money from the Florida drug trade. It's a good deal for me, though, and I don't know if I should check that out or not.

Q. What kind of wages does Sharpco pay?

A. Well, I pay the plant manager and the office manager pretty well. But I pay the others what I think I have to pay to keep them. If I make a mistake, I want it to be on the low side. It's easier to raise a worker's pay than to reduce it.

Q. I noticed that steel sales have declined a good bit, by 50 percent in one year. Why is that?

A. Well, the downturn in business activity affected it a good bit. But after Sol's Pipe and Steel started handling new steel and after O'Neal Steel Company bought out Monroe Pipe & Steel, the market just became too competitive. I also raised steel prices about 25 percent last year.

Q. How much of your inventory is steel?

A. About half of it—a little over a $100,000.

Q. You mentioned earlier that you have more time now than you did in the past. How many hours a week would you say you work now?

A. I am usually here at about 6:30 in the morning, although once every week or two I have to come in at 4:00 or 5:00 to get something for a customer, usually a land-clearing contractor. Those fellows have their tractors running at daybreak. I usually go home at 5:00 now, though, and sometimes even earlier. I don't have to work Saturdays, probably, but I usually do because Saturday afternoon is my best time to get caught up on paperwork.

Q. I noticed you are dressed in blue jeans and a work shirt. Do you still work in the shop?

A. Yes, particularly since I have cut the work force down. There is not a job in the shop that I can't do better than any worker out there.

Q. Do you do that because you enjoy it?

A. I do enjoy it, but I don't do it for that reason. I do it because every time I back away and try to stay uninvolved things get messed up. Just yesterday a tractor was started up without oil in the final drive. If I had not just happened by, it would have cost us $6000 or $7000.

Q. Do you consider Sharpco a success?

A. Oh, absolutely! I am just an ordinary guy. I would have been happy to have made service manager at Louisiana Machinery [the Caterpillar dealer] by this time. That pays $28,000 a year. Instead, I have my own company, pay myself $30,000 a year, drive a company car, and nobody tells me what to do. I expect the company to earn me $30,000–80,000 a year in addition to my salary. The company is worth a lot more than the $300,000 book value, too. Even though depreciation on the fixed assets has totaled nearly $150,000, altogether they would still sell for more than we paid for them. In fact, I would say that Sharpco has made me a millionaire.

DISCUSSION QUESTIONS

1 State the organizational mission at Sharpco? Is Sharpco a success? Defend your answer.

2 Has Sharpco really made James a millionaire? Explain.

3 Evaluate the real organizational structure at Sharpco. How would you improve it if you were in charge?

4 Discuss how well James is fulfilling his social responsibilities with regard to (a) the possible Florida drug connection and (b) compensating his employees?

5 Evaluate Sharpco's financing practices and financial structure.

6 How, if at all, should Sharpco's corporate strategies change now that Jerry and Art are not owners. Why?

THE REGENT OF HONG KONG

Steven M. Dawson
University of Hawaii

SELECTED STRATEGIC ISSUES

- Valuation of an international commercial investment opportunity
- The impact of potential overcapacity on an investment decision
- Impact of years-distant threats on current investment decisions

At last in September 1979 the update was finished. The hotel feasibility study was now ready to give to investors, thought Robert Burns, President of Regent International Hotels. Primarily a manager and marketer of hotels, rather than an owner, Regent already had hotels in Bangkok, Fiji, Kuala Lumpur, Manila, New York, and Puerto Rico. Once completed, the 605-room Regent of Hong Kong would be the finest addition to Hong Kong's luxury hotel market in 15 years, joining the tradition-rich Peninsula and Mandarin Hotels. The financials looked good: the projected cash flow forecast indicated it would be free of all external debt in five years and within seven years it would have generated sufficient funds to repay all initial equity capital. The return on initial equity capital of $16.7 million would rise steadily, reaching 58.5 percent by the tenth year. Burns now contemplated how to best present the project to investors.

Steven M. Dawson is Professor of Finance at the University of Hawaii.

Distributed by the Case Research Association. All rights reserved to the authors and the Case Research Association. Permission to use the case should be obtained from the Case Research Association.

REGENT INTERNATIONAL HOTELS LIMITED

Regent International was a hotel management and marketing company incorporated and based in Hong Kong. A private company, majority ownership was held by the executives who were responsible for its performance. Regent's role was to provide technical assistance to the owners of hotel properties during the development phase of the project and international management and marketing services when the hotel was operational. Regent's sole objective was to ensure a higher return on investment for the owner than could be achieved without its participation. In return Regent receives a base fee expressed as a percentage of revenues and an incentive fee calculated as a percentage of gross operating profit after deduction of the base fee, insurance of buildings, and capital renewals.

In the ongoing operation, as in the development phase, Regent reported to and worked for the owners. Annual plans, forecasts of financial results, budgets, and needs for capital appropriations were submitted to the owners. Results of operations were reported monthly in the form of full financial statements compared with approved budgets. Satisfied guests, especially those that returned, were the key to successful operations. Productive advertising, an effective sales force, and sound public relations would bring guests to the door. Thereafter Regent management emphasized first class accommodation, fine food, and excellent service.

In operating the hotel, Regent provided day-to-day supervision, control, and guidance in all operational aspects including housekeeping, food and beverage, reception, personnel, repairs and maintenance, and accounting. Manuals were compiled for every facet of the operation and continuous training programs were conducted.

Regent was presently managing and marketing the following hotels:

1. Thailand	The Regent of Bangok	400-room city hotel
2. Fiji	The Regent of Fiji	300-room beach hotel
3. Malaysia	The Regent of Kuala Lumpur	400-room city hotel
4. Philippines	The Regent of Manila	500-room city hotel
5. U.S.	The Mayfair Regent	300-room city hotel
6. Puerto Rico	Cerromar Beach Hotel	500-room beach resort
7. Puerto Rico	Dorado Beach Hotel	300-room beach resort

Expansion to approximately 20 hotels was planned with growth to be realized within certain strategic limits, the most important of which were: restriction to deluxe hotels; rate of expansion to retain the highest quality of management and marketing; and emphasis on the Asia and Pacific regions.

HONG KONG

Hong Kong became a British Colony in 1841. Its convenient location and ideal political climate made it the perfect crossroads for travel and trade in Asia. The Colony consisted of the islands of Hong Kong, the peninsula of Kowloon, the New Territories, and 235 islands. For the visitor Hong Kong could perhaps differ more for its 440 square miles than any other territory in the region. First, it had great natural beauty:

EXHIBIT 1

Year	Visitors	Annual % increase
1965	447,000	—
1971	907,000	12.5%
1972	1,082,000	19.3
1973	1,292,000	19.4
1974	1,295,000	0.3
1975	1,301,000	0.4
1976	1,600,000	23.0
1977	1,756,000	9.7
1978	2,055,000	17.0

Source: Hong Kong Tourist Association.

islands set in the South China Sea, secluded bays and beaches, and towering hillsides. There were also man-made reservoirs cradled in wooded valleys, spectacular winding hill roads with views of the harbor, and handsome skyscrapers rising 50 stories. Although Westernized on the surface in some areas, Hong Kong was essentially a Chinese city of over five million people. Beyond the wealthy central districts of Kowloon and Hong Kong Island were street upon street of Chinese shop fronts and living quarters, little different from those of any south or east China trading port of the 19th century. Rural China could be seen in the country side of the mainland New Territories and outlying islands, where farm and village life continued as it had for centuries.

The number of visitors arriving in Hong Kong had grown at a rapid rate. From 447,000 arrivals in 1965, the number grew to 2,055,000 in 1978, a compound annual growth of 13 percent (Exhibit 1). The worldwide recession during 1974–75 sparked by the fuel crisis led to a temporary halt which was followed by a major catchup growth in visitor arrivals in 1976. With reference to the purpose for coming to Hong Kong, approximately 68 percent of the visitors come to visit friends or relatives or for vacation purposes, 22 percent for business purposes, and 10 percent are short-term transit visitors. About half of the vacation visitors were members of tour groups.

Hong Kong had a range of hotel facilities catering to all segments of the market. There was no single hotel district as such but rather clusters of hotels, mainly in the Tsimshatsui area on Kowloon and on Hong Kong Island in the Central District and at Causeway Bay. The latest hotel room census showed 14,168 rooms distributed as follows:

Classification	Number of hotels	Rooms
Luxury class	2	947
First class	11	8,319
Second class	8	2,013
Third class	21	2,126
Hostels	7	763
	49	14,168

The total supply of rooms had grown 57 percent between 1971 and 1978 compared to a 127 percent increase in visitors. Occupancy rates were near 90 percent. About 90 percent of all visitors stayed in hotels and the average length of stay in 1978 was 3.9 nights.

THE REGENT OF HONG KONG

The proposed 605-room Regent of Hong Kong would be built on the harbor at Holt's Wharf in Tsimshatsui, generally considered to be the finest luxury hotel location in the city. Located on the Kowloon side between the Star Ferry and Salisbury Road, the site would be part of a major development, the New World Center, containing a major shopping complex, a 741-room economy hotel, luxury apartments, and an office building. Nearby was a large civic and cultural complex comprising a theatre and concert hall, planetarium, art gallery, museum, and city park. Within a quarter mile radius were five luxury or first class hotels which had created a major visitor destination area. Included were international standard restaurants, extensive shopping, easily used subway, train, bus and ferry transportation facilities, and all the various servicing agencies necessary for the successful handling of overseas visitors.

One of the most closely watched dates in Hong Kong was 1997, the year the 99-year lease on the New Territories expires. Kowloon, where the Regent Hotel would be located, and the Hong Kong Island are not involved. Although no decisions had yet been reached on what would happen to buildings and equipment in the New Territories, an increasing amount of new factories and residential highrise apartment buildings had been built there in recent years.

The target market for the Regent Hotel of Hong Kong was the very high tariff, frequent independent traveler. There were two hotels in Hong Kong that in the past ten years had captured the cream of this market—the Peninsula and the Mandarin. Both hotels enjoyed unprecedented success in attracting the international high tariff visitor and the very deluxe American and European tours. They currently represented only a very small part (10 percent) of the First Class and luxury hotel rooms in Hong Kong and their rates of occupancy and income per occupied room were a good deal higher than average for high tariff hotels. For the Regent the expectation was that 35 percent of the guests would be business visitors, 40 percent individual travelers, and 25 percent deluxe tours.

It was anticipated that the majority of employees would be male, under 30 and unskilled. They would be given extensive preopening training and careful ongoing supervision. Some middle management positions would be staffed by semi-skilled to skilled workers who had training in other restaurants or hotels. The labor market was plentiful and it was not anticipated that there would be any problem in attracting the highest calibre personnel to meet the needs of discriminating guests.

FINANCIAL PROJECTIONS AND ANALYSIS

The hotel site would be leased for an initial period of 20 years with the lessor being responsible for site preparation, foundation work, and hotel construction. A detailed

EXHIBIT 2   SUMMARY OF ESTIMATED PROJECT COST

	Per room	Total
Building-structure and equipment	$36,700	$22,220,000
Furniture, fittings and equipment	13,200	8,000,000
Finance and holding charges	3,300	2,000,000
Pre-opening expenses	830	500,000
Inventories	330	200,000
Working capital	826	500,000
	$55,186	$33,400,000

cost analysis placed the total outlay at $22.2 million or $36,700 per room.[1] Furniture would add $8 million or $13,200 per room for luxury accommodations. Finance and holding charges were principally construction interest and pre-opening expenses including staff recruitment and training, marketing, publicity, start-up costs, and the opening ceremony. Inventories and enough working capital to cover operating expenses until the hotel had developed an adequate cash flow brought the total funds needed to $33.4 million or $55,186 per room.

Proposed Funding

Factors to be considered in determining the financial structure included availability of financing, interest rates, earnings and return on gross capital invested, and amount of equity capital available. In establishing debt-equity ratios, financial gearing was used to obtain the maximum return on equity capital. Favorable leverage occurred with the return on gross capital invested exceeding the interest rate paid on debt.

Higher levels of debt financing were advantageous when a stable or rising stream of earnings was expected to be in effect over a long period of time. As earnings increased, the proportionate share of earnings accruing to ownership increased, as was the case with stable earnings after the debt was fully amortized. It was due to the excessive use of debt financing that many hotels had developed financial difficulty from which recovery was extremely arduous. The proper use of debt financing required sound cash flow planning, as well as sources of additional equity capital or short-term funds, especially during the intial operating period.

In the financial analysis for the Regent of Hong Kong, funding was based on a debt-equity ratio of 50 : 50 resulting in the following fund requirements:

Equity Capital	$16,700,000
Loan Funds	16,700,000
	$33,400,000

While the equity capital was shown as a full US$16,700,000, consideration was being

[1] In Hong Kong dollars the estimated project cost was HK$160 million and this had been translated into U.S. dollars using the September 1979 exchange rate of 5.1 HK dollars to $1 U.S. All subsequent costs in the study were also translated into U.S. dollars at the same exchange rate.

given to restricting the equity to approximately US$10 million with the balance provided by loans from shareholders.

Projected Operating Results

A detailed statement of annual operating results was prepared for the first five years of operation and then extended to 10 years in a less detailed projection. The forecast was based on the operating results of other Hong Kong hotels and on the experience of Regent properties generally. The forecasts assumed that the hotel would be in full operation from June 1, 1980, with 605 rooms and all food, beverage, and function facilities. Occupancy rates rose slowly from 68 percent in 1980 to 82 percent in 1984 which was considered conservative. Business-oriented hotels average 1.2 guests per room and resort hotels, 1.8. In view of the projected market mix for the Regent of Hong Kong, 1.45 guests per room per night had been estimated in the financial projections. The average revenue per room started at $72 per night in 1980 and increased at 10 percent annually, which was in line with the growth recently attained by similar hotels in Hong Kong

Based on the anticipated equity capital outlay, the percent return on equity totaled 286.7 percent over the next 10 years, starting at a loss during the opening year and reaching 58.5 percent by 1989. The annual results are shown in Exhibit 3.

Repayment of Loan

The proposed funding showed the debt needed as $16.7 million excluding any loans from shareholders. In the profit forecast the loan had an interest rate of 15 percent annually and the following repayment plan:

	Principal repaid ($000)
1980	$1,000
1981	2,000
1982	2,340
1983	3,340
1984	8,020
	$16,700

Cash Flow Forecast

The profit forecast was the main base for the ten-year cash flow forecast (Exhibit 4). In the pre-opening period the cash inflows were $16.7 million each of debt and equity, as indicated in the financing plan. The principal non-cash items were depreciation and the amortization of pre-opening expenses. In the cash outflow section the capital renewals were the estimated cost of normal ongoing renewal and replacement of capital items over the life of the hotel. The annual and progressive surpluses (deficits) were before the payment of dividends and showed that the project could be free of all external debt

EXHIBIT 3 THE REGENT OF HONG KONG
PROFIT AND LOSS FORECAST

Year	Net profit ($000)	% Return on $16.7 million equity
1980	$(3,323)	(19.9%)
1981	23	0.1
1982	2,036	12.2
1983	3,481	20.8
1984	4,937	29.6
1985	6,676	40.0
1986	7,144	42.8
1987	8,126	48.7
1988	8,998	53.9
1989	9,775	58.5
Total	47,873	286.7%

EXHIBIT 4 THE REGENT OF HONG KONG CASH FLOW FORECAST ($000)

	Pre-Opening	1980	1981	1982	1983	1984
Inflow						
Equity	$16,700	—	—	—	—	—
External Loan Funds	16,700	—	—	—	—	—
Gross Profit before Tax	—	$(3,323)	$ 23	$2,036	$4,099	$5,989
Non-Cash Items	—	2,100	2,100	2,126	2,157	2,188
	$33,400	$(1,213)	2,133	$4,162	$6,256	$8,177
Outflow						
Project Costs	$32,900	—	—	—	—	—
Profits Tax	—	—	—	—	—	$ 618
External Loan Repayments	—	$1,000	$2,000	$2,340	$3,340	8,020
Capital Renewals	—	—	—	208	208	208
	$32,900	$1,000	$2,000	$2,548	$3,548	$8,846
Annual Surplus	$500	$(2,213)	$133	$1,614	$2,708	$(669)
Progressive Surplus	$500	$(1,713)	$(1,580)	$ 34	$2,742	$2,073

	1985	1986	1987	1988	1989	TOTAL
Inflow						
Equity	—	—	—	—	—	16,700
External Loan Funds	—	—	—	—	—	$ 16,700
Gross Profit before Tax	$8,064	$8,628	$ 9,811	$10,862	$11,797	57,986
Non-Cash Items	2,127	2,174	2,229	2,291	2,335	21,847
	$10,191	$10,802	$12,040	$13,153	$14,132	$113,233
Outflow						
Project Costs	—	—	—	—	—	$32,900
Profits Tax	$ 1,052	$1,388	$1,484	$1,685	$1,864	8,091
External Loan Repayments	—	—	—	—	—	16,700
Capital Renewals	312	312	417	417	521	2,603
	$1,364	$1,700	$1,901	$2,102	$2,385	$60,294
Annual Surplus	$8,827	$9,102	$10,139	$11,051	$11,747	
Progressive Surplus	$10,900	$20,002	$20,141	$41,192	$52,939	$52,939

by 1984. The initial equity investment of $16.7 million could be repaid by 1986. In these cash projections no allowance was made for the cost of financing cash deficits or of interest income on cash surpluses.

DISCUSSION QUESTIONS

1 Should the Regent of Hong Kong be built? Explain your answer in terms of the returns which equity investors could expect on both the debt and equity portions of their investment and the riskiness of each part of the return.
2 Is construction of the Regent of Hong Kong likely to create an overcapacity condition among luxury class hotels in Hong Kong? Explain. What additional information would you require to give an authoritative answer?
3 If you assume that the 1997 lease expiration will result in the repossession by China of the New Territories with a consequent major reduction in business and tourist travel to Hong Kong, how might this affect the decision to build the Regent of Hong Kong?

WAR MEMORIAL STADIUM

Robert D. Hay
University of Arkansas

SELECTED STRATEGIC ISSUES

- Analysis of a public sector investment decision
- Strengths, weaknesses, and environmental factors in an expansion decision
- Cost-benefit analysis of an investment decision

Mr. Howard Pearce, General Manager of the War Memorial Stadium in Little Rock, Arkansas, sat back in his chair and surveyed the situation facing his stadium commissioners. Sellout crowds were commonplace for the 1977 University of Arkansas Razorback Football team which defeated the Sooners of the University of Oklahoma in the 1978 Orange Bowl game. The Razorbacks had traditionally played four games in Little Rock's War Memorial Stadium (and 3 games in Fayetteville, home of the Razorbacks) each year. Mr. Pearce wondered if War Memorial Stadium should expand its facilities since sellout crowds occurred in three of the four games played this past 1977 season.

War Memorial Stadium was built thirty years ago at an initial cost of $2 million. Since that time, an additional $2½ million had been spent on improvements. Rising

The research and written case information were presented at the Atlanta Case Workshop (October, 1979) and were evaluated by the Case Research Association's Editorial Board. This case was prepared by Dr. Robert D. Hay of the University of Arkansas, with the assistance of Tom Reed, Nancy Garner, Cindy Kane, and Wendell Fleming, as a basis for class discussion.

Distributed by the Case Research Association. All rights reserved to the author and the Case Research Association.

property values and other factors make the present structure worth approximately $15 million, according to Mr. Pearce.

The stadium, with a present seating capacity of 53,500, is one of approximately only five percent of the stadia in the United States that have no indebtedness. In fact, the stadium's borrowed capital was paid off three years early. Mr. Pearce took great pride in this.

Since the stadium is located in the center of the state, it draws football fans from nearly the whole state, which has a population of 2 million people. The stadium is somewhat unique in that it was created by an act of the state legislature to serve as a football stadium primarily for the Arkansas Razorbacks, whose home facility is located 200 miles to the Northwest, and other state institutions of higher learning.

Mr. Howard Pearce is the present general manager and has held this post for several years, having been appointed to this position by the state legislature. He reports to a commission of eight members, each of whom serves eight years and is appointed by the Governor and the legislature. Under Mr. Pearce's leadership, the stadium has been managed as a state business and has shown a profit in its operations.

The fact that the stadium is a profit center is unusual. War Memorial Stadium is run completely on its own, and no tax money is used for its operation.

The concessions at War Memorial generate yearly gross sales of $175,000. The present facility makes a 39% profit on these sales. The national average profit on concessions is around the 30% mark. Presently, there are 42 concessions in War Memorial Stadium.

At the present time, approximately 1,750 employees are needed to work the ballgame hours. These employees include parking attendants, police, ushers, concessionaires, gatekeepers, ticket sellers and takers as well as other miscellaneous employees. A source of supply of people has been available in the past years.

Clean-up crews are also available since many booster clubs or other organizations work on clean-up as money-making projects.

The stadium is 30 years old. The structure, while solid and architecturally sound, has increasing maintenance and repair problems. Obsolescence is definitely a problem.

Parking area around the stadium is not only very limited, but most of it is owned by the City of Little Rock and other state agencies. This is a problem because the stadium has no control over the parking area which consists of a limited space adjacent to the stadium. Some parking is allowed on the War Memorial Golf Course. The stadium management is responsible for much of the operation of the parking areas, but the City of Little Rock receives most of the revenues. Most stadia own their own parking areas, and thus have the added revenue.

Access to War Memorial, while not difficult, is not conducive to smooth traffic flow. Traffic tie-ups and congestion are common, before and after a game.

Seating in the present stadium now has 26 inches between the rows; new stadiums now have 30 inches between the seats for comfort and ease of crowd flow. Nothing more can be done to make the stadium more comfortable.

Capacity crowds are difficult to handle on existing ramps, elevators, and walkways, and little can be done to alleviate the situation.

Maintenance on the present facility is increasing tremendously. An example of increasing maintenance was the $60,000 cost of maintaining restrooms this year.

The location of the present facility is not in the best neighborhood in Little Rock. Although not in the highest crime area of Little Rock, the area does have problems. The stadium was broken into recently.

Land around the stadium is not available for much expansion. In addition, an estimated 3 parking spaces for each 8 people is needed, and parking space is very limited, as previously noted.

Mr. Pearce has stressed the idea that the University of Arkansas' athletic program and particularly its football team was created for enjoyment of the spectators as well as the participants. The team has produced enjoyment for many; it was scheduled to play three or four games regularly in Little Rock; and games were priced reasonably ($8.00 a ticket) so that as many people as possible could enjoy the benefits of the team. The stadium is indirectly involved in the marketing of the team, and it is a necessary facility for the team to provide the entertainment which fans desire.

The War Memorial Commission believes that to get additional use of the facility, it should try to stage other events in the stadium such as concerts, high school and professional football events, and other special events.

Mr. Pearce believes that the management of the stadium must be concerned with profitable operations. Although the Commission is a non-profit organization, revenue is used for bond retirement, maintenance, and renovation at times. Excessive profit is not desired, but some profitability is necessary.

Further, he believes that the stadium must involve itself in the enforcement and obedience of state, local, and federal laws.

Mr. Pearce wondered about the general economic forecast and its effect on his proposal to expand. He gathered the following information from *Fortune* magazine.

The economic outlook for the United States through 1978 and trends for the years beyond indicate an increasing and expanding economy. The Gross National Product is expected to reach approximately $1,890 billion in 1977 which is an increase of 10.7% over 1976, deflating to a real increase of 4.9%. In 1978, GNP is expected to have a real increase of 4.5% with further yearly increase through 1980 at 4%.

Government spending should increase in real terms over the next several years at approximately 5% per year. Much of this increase will be in defense, public works, and public jobs. The threat of Soviet superiority will override the desire for a balanced budget, while the increase in public jobs will be a response to the expanded work force. Disposable personal income is expected to rise to a rate of 5.6–6% through 1978, with per capita disposable income reaching $6,500 to $6,750. However, inflation should increase at 7% to 8% causing a real shrinking of disposable income or at best, break even.

The unemployment figures for 1977 are expected to be 6.5–7% at the end of the year. But an expanding workforce in 1978 and capital expenditures which are mainly replacement will cause unemployment to equal 7–7.5% next year.

In the financial markets, the economy will see further indications of an increasing inflation rate. The prime lending rate after reaching 7.25% in late 1977 should move upward to reflect the recent increases. The savings rate for 1978 should climb up to a historical average of 6.5%. It is currently at 5.3%. This rate will provide a stronger base for the construction industry with more funds available at savings institutions to finance increased construction activities.

Overall, the economy is in an upward growth pattern, but at a slower rate than has been experienced in the last few years. Most gains in critical areas will be in nominal terms only, as inflation will nullify them. In addition, the balance of trade should continue to be a problem with increasing demand for imported sources of energy. However, new construction should provide a bright spot in the economy with an increase of 10% a year providing a real benefit to the economy. Industries in Arkansas such as steel, aluminum, wood products, and other construction related business should show positive gains due to the increased construction.

College football attendance figures were kept by Mr. Pearce. They showed the following information:

Year	Collegiate football attendance of NCAA schools	Difference from year before
1968	27,025,846	596,207
1969	27,626,160	600,314
1970	29,465,604	1,839,444
1971	30,455,442	989,838
1972	30,828,802	373,360
1973	31,282,540	453,738
1974	31,234,855	(47,685)
1975	31,687,847	452,922
1976	32,012,008	324,161
1977	32,905,178	893,170

Unlike most other large universities, the University of Arkansas is in the unique position of having no direct competition. Although there are several other colleges in the state, most are small A.I.C. Division III teams, with the exception of ASU, a Division I team as directed by NCAA regulations for the 1978 season. The AIC schools draw fans from a very small area around each school. ASU, although a larger institution, is situated in the northeast corner of the state and draws little attendance from outside that area. Little Rock is located in the center of the state providing most fans with a relatively short drive from almost any point in the state. Most of the major highways in the state pass through Little Rock, providing easy access to the city. Razorback football has competition from the other colleges in the state, plus many other sporting events held in Arkansas. However, Arkansas football probably faces its biggest indirect competition from other games which are being televised nationally. Arkansas can even be competition to itself if home games are televised as some fans may prefer staying at home. Other events, meetings, and special activities that are taking place within the state also would provide competition to the games.

Football, like many other sporting events, is a recession-proof commodity. No matter what the economy is doing, football attendance has historically remained relatively strong.

Leisure activities have been growing at a rapid pace for the past twenty years, even in economic turndowns, providing a growing market. In addition, football fans' participation itself has also been growing both nationally and in Arkansas. Records of attendance at War Memorial since it was opened in 1948 show a general growth trend with some variations.

War Memorial Stadium, because of its construction, can be used for very few events other than football games. Concerts and special events such as the Billy Graham Crusade are among the few exceptions. This limits the use of the stadium and its revenue drawing power to a very seasonal basis from August through the first of December.

With the exception of the New Mexico State game, all Razorback games played at War Memorial this year were sold out. In fact, the actual attendance records for the other three games actually exceeded the seating capacity of 53,355. One game in particular, the Oklahoma State game, had an official attendance of 54,280, almost 600 more than the seats available. Because of the number of inquiries for tickets to these games, it was Mr. Pearce's opinion that an additional 8,000 tickets could have been sold easily, probably at higher prices than the $8.00 now charged.

Arkansas had been particularly fortunate this year to have been televised nationally three times. Mr. Pearce said, "Television coverage has also increased the awareness of football in general, raising it to the number one sport in the United States. Is has also served as an educational device, teaching the public the rules of the game and giving them a better understanding of how the game is played.

"Football has a good image both as a participation activity and as a recreational activity by individuals interested in watching the players. It is looked on as a sport that teaches discipline, self-confidence, and good sportsmanship."

The state population is increasing, providing a larger population from which to draw fans. As mentioned earlier, the Razorbacks are somewhat unique as they draw from the whole state. Therefore, any increase in the population of Arkansas gives War Memorial a bigger potential market.

War Memorial is a state-owned operation. Therefore, any funds for expansion must be voted on and approved by the state legislature. This is probably the only way to get the needed financing for any proposed structure.

Construction of the new addition must follow the building codes as set forth by the state and the city of Little Rock. One problem area would be insufficient bathroom facilities with the extra 8,000 seats. Present facilities include 8 bathrooms, each with 16 stalls. With the construction of the upper deck, at least 20 more stalls, 10 for each sex, must be constructed.

The new addition, as Mr. Pearce visualized, would be a cantilever style deck. This type of deck would have all of the superstructure on the outside of the stadium with the deck itself suspended over the lower level seats by a projected beam. There would be no column supports to obscure vision of the playing field. Ramps to the upper deck would be placed from a hill on the south side of the stadium. This would allow easy access to the upper level without inhibiting the flow of individuals entering or leaving the lower level. It would not affect the present parking facilities on the east side of the stadium.

Mr. Pearce provided the statistics shown at the top of page 388. In looking at the figures, he noted that the average per game attendance had not dropped below 42,000 at any time during the years shown. Of particular interest was the record of the

War Memorial Stadium attendance records

Year	Total attendance	No. games	Average per game	Razorback win-loss record	%
1966	135,000	3	45,017	8-2-0	80
1967	187,634	4	46,908	4-5-1	40
1968	148,221	3	49,407	10-1-0	91
1969	170,717	4	42,679	9-2-0	82
1970	194,000	4	48,500	9-2-0	82
1971	217,244	4	54,311	8-3-1	73
1972	209,102	4	52,227	6-5-0	54
1973	179,542	4	44,885	5-5-1	50
1974	200,309	4	50,077	6-4-1	54
1975	201,575	4	50,393	10-2-0	83
1976	192,463	4	48,115	5-5-1	45
1977	214,991	4	53,747	10-1-0	91

Stadium attendance information

1976	Utah State	50,536	
	Oklahoma State	53,103	
	Texas A & M	47,497	
	Texas Tech	41,327	(Win-loss at time
1977	New Mexico State	53,167	of game 5-3-1)
	Oklahoma State	54,280	
	Houston	53,924	
	Baylor	53,620	

attendance in 1976, when the Razorbacks' win-loss record was 5-5-1, one of the worst during Frank Broyles' tenure as head coach. Even at the Texas Tech game, attendance was 41,327 on a wet, rainy day in late November. The game time temperature was 22 degrees and there was a brisk wind blowing. In spite of the adverse weather conditions and the poor record at that point in the season, 5-3-1, the attendance still did not drop below 40,000.

Again in 1972, 1973, and 1974 the win-loss record was poor: 6-5-0, 5-5-1, and 6-4-1, respectively. However, average attendance for those years was 52,227; 44,885; and 50,077. Mr. Pearce believed that only stadium attendance over 40,000 was related to the win-loss record.

A trend-line analysis was made using the average per game attendance for the past five and the past ten years. The results were as follows:

**TREND-LINE ANALYSIS USING PAST
5 YEARS OF ATTENDANCE RECORDS**

Year	Expected attendance
1978	54,172
1979	55,749
1980	57,325
1981	58,901
1982	60,478
1983	62,054

Based on the growth pattern of the past five years, a 61,000-seat stadium would be filled by 1983.

When growth trends for the past twelve years were used, analysis showed that a 61,000-seat stadium would not be filled until 1997.

**TREND-LINE ANALYSIS USING PAST
12 YEARS OF ATTENDANCE RECORDS**

Year	Expected attendance
1978	51,989
1979	52,471
1980	52,953
1981	53,435
1982	53,917
1983	54,399
1984	54,881
1985	55,364
.	.
.	.
.	.
1996	60,667
1997	61,149

If additional seats were added, Mr. Pearce asked himself, "What effect will empty seats have on ticket sales until that time when the stadium can be sold out, whether it be 1983 or 1997?" Mr. Pearce expressed an opinion that it was better to have a situation where there was a shortage or potential shortage of tickets. As he put it,

> People want to want tickets. Psychologically, people seem to want something more if they feel there is going to be a shortage. In the case of football tickets, when people feel there is a shortage, the money for tickets will come in faster and there will be a bigger demand. Not only does the money come in at the first, but more and more people want tickets for later games, giving a bandwagon type effect. Therefore, there is something to be said for keeping the stadium at its present size.

Mr. Pearce considered the financial costs of adding 8,000 additional seats (this figure is the number that the Stadium Commission would like to consider). Two construction cost estimates were obtained from two established stadium contractors. One estimate was obtained from a Mr. Baxter, who had taken part in several stadium construction costs estimates and jobs, mainly in Memphis. Mr. Baxter had recently estimated that double decking the Liberty Bowl in Memphis would cost approximately $209 per seat.

Mr. Pearce, however, questioned the $209 per seat estimated. Recently, he had been a member of a committee of the International Association of Auditorium and Stadium Managers which had compiled some cost figures for various stadia built during the past 15 years. (See Exhibit 1.) Mr. Pearce estimated the cost per seat to be approximately $800–1000 per seat. If he used the $800 estimate, the total construction cost would be approximately $6,400,000 for adding 8,000 seats. This figure would include the cost of additional restrooms and concession stands on the second level.

EXHIBIT 1

Stadiums completed since 1970

1 King Dome—Seattle, Washington 1976
   64,275 $62,000,000   Per seat average: $946.61
2 Pontiac Silver Dome—Pontiac, Michigan 1975
   80,656 $51,700,000   Per seat average: $640.99
3 Philadelphia Veterans Stadium—Philadelphia, Pa. 1971
   69,000 $48,000,000   Per seat average: $695.65
4 Cincinnati Riverfront Stadium—Cincinnati, Ohio 1973
   58,000 $38,000,000   Per seat average: $665.77

Average since 1979–$741.60

Stadiums completed between 1960 and 1969 inclusive

1 Las Vegas Stadium—Las Vegas, Nevada 1968
   32,500 $ 3,500,000   Per seat average: $107.69
2 Atlanta Stadium—Atlanta, Georgia 1965
   60,000 $18,000,000   Per seat average: $300.00
3 Busch Stadium—St. Louis, Mo. 1966
   51,392 $28,000,000   Per seat average: $544.83
4 Anaheim Stadium—Anaheim, California 1966
   56,000 $16,000,000   Per seat average: $285.71
5 Busch Memorial Stadium—St. Louis, Mo. 1964
   50,000 $20,000,000   Per seat average: $400.00
6 Alameda County Coliseum—Oakland, California 1964
   54,500 $13,000,000   Per seat average: $238.53
7 Liberty Bowl—Memphis, Tennessee 1962
   50,180 $ 4,000,000   Per seat average: $ 79.71[a]
8 Falcon Stadium—Colorado Springs, Colorado 1962
   40,808 $ 3,500,000   Per seat average: $ 85.72
9 Mississippi Memorial Stadium—Jackson, Miss. 1961
   46,000 $ 1,800,000   Per seat average: $ 39.13[b]

Average for 1960–69 inclusive: $231.25

These figures are based on information obtained from questionnaires completed by stadium managers during the I.A.A.M. Convention in January 1978.
[a] Questionable construction cost.
[b] Open structure, end-zone type seating.

The stadium is presently rented to the University for 15% of ticket sales (gate receipts) for each game played in the stadium.

Another major source of revenue to the stadium is concessions, which amounts to approximately $175,000 gross per year. Additional sources of revenue to the stadium are rental receipts from high school football games, of which there are approximately 30 per year. The stadium receives $1500 per game or 15% of gate receipts, whichever is greater. The average attendance at each high school game is approximately 6,000. The stadium also received revenue from concession sales at these games. This averages approximately $600 gross per game.

The final source of revenue to the stadium is from parking, which averages less than $10,000 gross per year. The majority of the parking revenue goes to the City, approximately $27,000 net per year. An additional problem is that only a few parking spaces immediately around the stadium are owned by the stadium, the remainder by the City.

Mr. Pearce knew that there were no additional markets which the stadium could tap other than the ones which existed. There were no other professional teams in the area such as soccer, football, basketball, and so forth.

The stadium employs 10 people year round. However, during a University of Arkansas football game there are approximately 1750 people employed.

Additional income and expense information concerning present financial operations is shown in Exhibit 2.

"The Southeastern Conference is planning to raise ticket prices to $10.00 per ticket. If this happens as planned, then the Southwestern Conference will most likely follow suit. Therefore, an additional increase in income to the stadium will occur," Mr. Pearce commented.

"Considerable income has been lost each year from tickets being sold at less than full price. The following are examples:

1 In 1976, we lost $58,975 from selling 10,081 tickets at less than full price to the Utah State game.

2 In 1976, we lost $48,000 from selling 9,000 tickets at less than full price to the Oklahoma State game.

3 In 1976, we lost $63,000 from selling, 11,000 tickets at less than full price to the Texas A & M game.

Of course, War Memorial Stadium would have received 15% of that income. I feel that the stadium could be filled by selling all tickets at full price," Mr. Pearce continued.

"If the new seats were added and were completely sold out for each of the four games in Little Rock, the income would be as follows:

EXHIBIT 2 WAR MEMORIAL STADIUM COMMISSION:
INCOME, EXPENDITURES, DEPRECIATION, CASH BALANCES AS OF JUNE 30, 1969–1977

	1969	1970	1971	1972	1973	1974	1975	1976	1977
Income (Rental revenue, 10% ticket tax, interest earned) net	$143,644	$182,789	$172,070	$199,759	$205,625	$185,725	$220,762	$197,200	$244,665
Expenditures									
Operating	52,548	75,863	79,835	107,903	77,240	98,769	103,150	154,485	188,127
Interest on bonds	4,415	4,276	3,866	3,840	3,296	2,746	2,273	1,791	—
Interest on construction loan and Astro-Turf	—	—	22,477	19,737	16,897	11,504	6,225	—	—
Totals	$ 56,963	$ 80,139	$106,178	$131,444	$ 97,415	$113,019	$111,648	$156,276	$188,127
Depreciation	$ 24,632	$ 27,260	$ 82,375	$137,363	$138,156	$138,337	$137,413	$137,226	$137,128
Cash balances	$273,988	$295,655	$342,803	$386,316	$420,927	$452,031	$473,000	$258,673	$217,964

$$8,000 \text{ seats} \times \$8.00/\text{seat} = \$64,000 \text{ game} \times 4 \text{ games}$$
$$= \$256,000 \times .15/\text{War Memorial Share}$$
$$= \$38,000 \text{ Income to War Memorial}$$

This does not take into account concessions, which would be substantial. Also, parking income is not considered.

"I feel that with the addition of 8,000 seats in an upper deck, maintenance would probably not go up for a while as additional people would not have to be hired. In other words, the present employment could handle the maintenance work involved at no added costs."

Assuming that additional seating is needed and wanted by the U of A Athletic Department it is felt that a combination of the following organizations and individuals could present a strong appeal to the state legislature for financial support: U of A Board Trustees, War Memorial Stadium Commission, Frank Broyles and his staff, and Howard Pearce, stadium manager.

Presently, Mr. Pearce estimates the break-even point per game at approximately 40,000 people ($188,000 operating costs ÷ ($8.00 × 15% × 4 games). He has not calculated a break-even point if expansion were to take place.

Tickets were distributed through the Fayetteville ticket office (located in the new athletic facility on the University of Arkansas campus). The tickets not sold as season tickets or distributed to students are sent back to Little Rock and sold on a per game basis. Mr. Pearce said that the "leftover" tickets are advertised in the newspaper and over the radio.

When asked if any additional promotion efforts would be needed for the proposed addition, Mr. Pearce responded, "No, I would just announce extra tickets were available in a newspaper ad, and then get the hell out of the way to keep from being trampled."

It is possible, according to Mr. Pearce, that a new stadium may be built in the future

EXHIBIT 3   FIVE-YEAR TREND LINE ANALYSIS

	X	Y	XY	X²	Yc
1973	−2	44,855	− 89,770	4	46,293
1974	−1	50,077	− 50,077	1	47,868
1975	0	50,393	0	0	49,443
1976	1	48,115	48,115	1	51,018
1977	2	53,747	107,494	4	52,593
	0	247,217	15,749	10	

$$a = \frac{247,217}{5} = 49,443 \qquad b = \frac{15,749}{10} = 1575 \qquad Yc = 49,443 + 1575X$$

Projections

1978 = 54,168	1981 = 58,893
1979 = 55,743	1982 = 60,468
1980 = 57,318	1983 = 62,043
Average for 1978–1983 = 58,105	

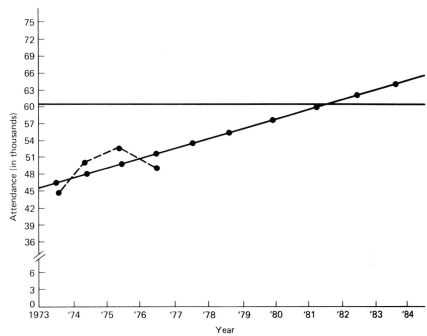

EXHIBIT 4   FIVE-YEAR TREND LINE ANALYSIS AND PROJECTIONS

EXHIBIT 5   TWELVE-YEAR TREND LINE ANALYSIS

	X	Y	XY	X²	Yc
1966	− 11	45,017	− 495,187	121	46,205
1967	− 9	46,908	− 422,172	81	46,687
1968	− 7	49,407	− 345,849	49	47,169
1969	− 5	42,679	− 213,395	25	47,651
1970	− 3	48,500	− 145,500	9	48,153
1971	− 1	54,311	54,311	1	48,615
1972	1	52,227	52,227	1	49,097
1973	3	44,885	134,655	9	49,579
1974	5	50,077	250,385	25	50,061
1975	7	50,393	352,751	49	50,543
1976	9	48,115	433,035	81	51,025
1977	11	53,747	591,217	121	51,507
	0	586,266	137,856	572	

$$a = \frac{586,266}{12} = 48,856 \qquad b = \frac{137,856}{572} = 241 \qquad Yc = 48,856 + 241X$$

Projections

1978 = 51,989	1982 = 53,917
1979 = 52,471	1990 = 57,773
1980 = 52,953	1995 = 60,183
1981 = 53,435	2000 = 62,593

EXHIBIT 6 TWELVE-YEAR TREND ANALYSIS

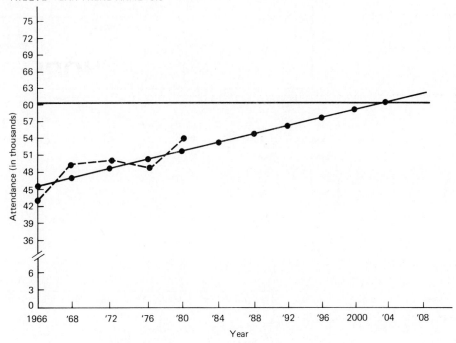

in the Little Rock area. An unnamed source might give to the State of Arkansas a tract of land for a new stadium and adequate parking. While not disclosing the donor, or the exact location of the proposed stadium, Mr. Pearce did say the management was hoping any new stadium would have interstate highway access, and be located near a large shopping mall so that the mall parking could also serve the stadium on ballgame days.

Senator Jim Caldwell, a state senator, felt the attitude of the state legislature would be much more favorable toward a new structure if land acquisition costs were exempted.

Mr. Pearce thought the state legislature could finance the $6,400,000 cost with a 5%, 30-year maturity bond issue. This would mean yearly payments of approximately $450,000. He was wondering if War Memorial Stadium should be expanded.

DISCUSSION QUESTIONS

1 Should the stadium be expanded? Explain.
2 State the strengths, weaknesses, and environmental factors in the case and relate them specifically to the expansion decision.
3 Evaluate the expected costs and benefits of expanding the stadium.

APPALOOSA HORSE CLUB (A)

Gary Whitney
University of San Diego

SELECTED STRATEGIC ISSUES

- Strategic attributes of individual career decisions
- Developing career alternatives in the context of managerial responsibilities
- Selection and implementation of career strategies

In September 1979, Bill Hostetler, Controller of the Appaloosa Horse Club was wondering whether there was any long run future for him at the Club. Bill was a full-time MBA student at Washington State University when he accepted the full-time position at the Club in September 1978. He continued his studies on a part-time basis.

During the 21 month period from January 1978 to September 1979 the Club was in a difficult transitional period. The once "dollar in a shoe box" organization had grown to an annual $2.6 million operation. The operational functions at the Club, however, had not kept pace with the growing membership. This contributed to heavy financial losses and serious membership dissatisfaction. Decisions by the Board of Directors and management to deal with these problems were concerning Bill as he pondered his future.

DESCRIPTION

The Appaloosa Horse Club (with national headquarters located in Moscow, Idaho) is a nonprofit organization that exists to (1) preserve, improve, and standardize the breed of horses known as "Appaloosa;" (2) establish, maintain, and publish a registry for recording pedigrees and transfers of ownership of Appaloosa horses; (3) promote the breeding, use, and exhibition of Appaloosa horses; and (4) collect and record data about the origin and development of Appaloosa horses. Since its inception in 1938, the Appaloosa Horse Club has become the third largest national horse breed registry, with more than 300,000 registered horses.

The Appaloosa horse first received national attention through an article published in *Western Horseman* in 1937. The demand for further articles inspired a small group of interested individuals to organize a club in support of the Appaloosa horse. Thus, in 1938 the Appaloosa Horse Club was incorporated at Moro, Oregon, with six charter members and Claude Thompson as its first President (a nonpaying position).

During World War II interest in the association was at a low ebb. However, in 1947 Mr. George Hatley was elected Executive Secretary (a nonpaying position until 1957) and the Club headquarters was relocated in Moscow, Idaho. The first Board of Directors (voluntary positions), consisting of seven members elected by the membership, served in an advisory capacity to the Executive Secretary. Mr. Hatley operated the Club from his home and came to be known as "Mr. Appaloosa." By 1961 (with membership in the Club approaching 3,000), the Club had outgrown the home location and was moved to an office in downtown Moscow.

Further growth (to nearly 11,000 members) prompted the Club to build and occupy the Appaloosa Horse Club building in Moscow, Idaho, in 1974. This building is located on the border between Moscow, Idaho, and Pullman, Washington, and is approximately 14,000 square feet in size.

With substantial continued growth (currently exceeding 18,000 active members), the Board of Directors expanded to fifteen elected members and the Club employed seven department managers and 85 supporting employees. There are now 216 affiliated regional Appaloosa horse clubs.

Concurrent with its membership growth, additional activities were embraced by the Club: first, the promotion of Appaloosa horse racing; second, the publishing of a monthly magazine—*The Appaloosa News*—which has 30,000 subscribers plus newsstand sales; third, the Youth Foundation of the Club sponsors seven annual $800 college scholarships for members of Appaloosa clubs (to promote the breed); fourth, the maintenance of an historical museum at the national headquarters; and fifth, the promotion of foreign markets for Appaloosa horses in cooperation with the United States Department of Agriculture.

The sustained rate of membership growth experienced by the Club has been accompanied by a corresponding increase in the workload. The additional activities undertaken have inflated the volume of work to be handled and the Club has suffered economic troubles in recent years, as shown by the audits of 1977 and 1978 (which showed losses of $69,000 and $179,000 respectively) (Exhibit 1). The losses prompted the Board of Directors to seek greater involvement in the operations of the club. Major changes in record keeping, management personnel, registration fees and procedures, and accounting are described.

The Board also authorized the selling of the Club's private plane and other vehicles to generate cash ($41,000 was realized). In addition, unlimited travel expenses for Directors were curtailed by placing authorization under direct supervision of the Executive Secretary.

EXHIBIT 1   INCOME STATEMENTS

For the year ended:	December 31, 1978		December 31, 1977	
Income				
Registrations	427,866.68		444,533.89	
Transfers to Permanent	12,164.50		17,635.00	
Transfers	230,152.00		214,805.70	
Miscellaneous Registry	12,953.22		12,296.12	
Member Dues	91,691.80		84,742.40	
Sale of Merchandise (Note 12)	14,050.71		15,494.72	
Services—Mailings	7,357.84		7,641.12	
Trail Ride	31,018.70		48,962.09	
Appaloosa News (Schedule 1)	904,807.62		747,918.27	
Shows (Schedule 2)	289,954.25		198,598.26	
Sales (Schedule 3)	345,166.50		191,396.50	
Racing (Schedule 4)	244,935.38		900.00	
Unclassified	37,995.32		8,092.36	
Total Income		2,650,114.52		1,990,016.43
Operating expenses				
Accounting	7,410.20		6,758.50	
Advertising	34,294.21		26,183.21	
Bad Debts	18,450.77		10,486.15	
Depreciation	41,057.83		37,648.62	
Donations	1,332.50		7,214.00	
Dues and Subscriptions	2,546.76		4,750.15	
Film Productions	19,398.06		19,737.50	
Heat and Light	9,934.75		9,195.12	
Inspections	6,210.19		3,651.91	
Insurance	19,241.43		8,415.36	
Legal Fees	49,811.73		6,514.82	
Maintenance and Repair	20,662.13		14,148.25	
Museum	4,244.72		1,832.80	
Office	133,249.51		101,483.33	
Printing	68,717.41		52,509.75	
Promotion	13,840.99		17,439.24	
Retirement Plan	18,884.46		19,543.29	
Salaries	301,985.82		232,459.10	
Taxes	35,637.36		30,522.01	
Telephone	27,377.40		19,303.82	
Travel—Staff	29,862.38		19,938.96	
Trail Ride	27,748.60		36,380.36	
Trophies and Awards	20,775.61		8,811.15	
Youth			4.03	
Directors Expenses	68,340.71		48,317.68	
Appaloosa News (Schedule 1)	892,039.53		832,764.82	
Shows (Schedule 2)	376,445.99		274,274.81	
Sales (Schedule 3)	323,662.51		185,143.32	
Racing (Schedule 4)	279,694.41		33,797.83	
Unclassified	9,334.68			
Total Operating Expenses		2,862,192.65		2,069,229.89
Non-operating items				
Interest Income	15,643.71		15,715.90	
Gain on Sale of Assets	23,930.16		11.89	
Interest Expense	(7,067.36)		(5,664.17)	
Currency Discount	(100.96)		(519.51)	
Total Non-Operating Items		32,405.55		9,544.11
Net Income (Loss)		$(179,672.58)		$ (69,669.35)

REGISTRATION

The registration of Appaloosa horses is the principal service provided by the Club and is the primary source of income. In response to the financial hardship of the Club, the Board significantly increased registration fees effective in January of 1979 (Exhibit 2). Fees charged by the Appaloosa Horse Club were much lower than those which other leading horse registries realized for comparable services (Exhibit 3). The Club has not increased fees since 1974. Notifications of the fee increases were mailed in December 1978, and resulted in an influx of registrations from members trying to avoid paying higher rates in January 1979 (over 125,000 Work Orders were received by the Club in 1978, whereas only 64,000 were received during the first nine months of 1979). Papers hurriedly sent to the Club without adequate identification pictures and containing many errors swamped the Registration Department.

The diverse composition of the membership and the subjective nature of decisions made in the registration of Appaloosa horses causes some dissatisfaction to occur. The Club's membership consists of a multitude of interests represented by the following types of people:

1 Horse owners, handlers, and ranchers
2 Show people and trainers
3 Racing enthusiasts and jockeys
4 Business people, track owners, motel owners, etc.
5 Hobbyists
6 Nonowners with other reasons for belonging

Paramount to the problems encountered in dealing with the diverse membership, however, is the complexity of categorizing Appaloosa horses. At present, the Ap-

EXHIBIT 2 APPALOOSA HORSE CLUB REGISTRATION FEE SCHEDULE

Year	Before 9/30 foaling year	Before 12/31 foaling year	Before 7/31 yearling year	Before 5/1 of 2-year-old year	After 5/1 of 2-year-old year	After 5/1 of 3-year-old year
1978	$15	$17.50	$20	$25	$45	$45
1979	$20	$25	$50	$75	$100	$250

EXHIBIT 3 1978 REGISTRATION FEES OF OTHER LEADING BREED REGISTRIES

Breed	Before 9/30 foaling year	Before 12/31 foaling year	Before 7/31 yearling year	Before 5/1 of 2-year-old year	After 5/1 of 2-year-old year	After 5/1 of 3-year-old year
Quarterhorse	$10	$15	$ 30	$100	$100	$500
Thoroughbred	$85	$85	$150	$350	$350	N/E*
Arabian	$35	$35	$100	N/E	N/E	N/E
Standard Bred	$15	$20	$100	N/E	N/E	N/E

* N/E = Not eligible for registration.

paloosa breed registry remains "open" allowing the registration of horses that do not necessarily have registered Appaloosa parents. A major goal of the Club, "to promote and improve the breed," permits the breeding of Appaloosas to other recognized breeds of horses. Paradoxically, Appaloosa coloration and/or characteristics may be obscured as a consequence of open breeding.

Appaloosa coloration (defined as an "easily recognizable coat pattern") and Appaloosa characteristics (such as "mottled" skin, white sclera around the eye, and/or striped hooves) provide the basis upon which horses are categorized. "Regular" papers are issued to horses which meet the coloration and characteristic requirements (as endorsed by the Board and subject to change). "Breeding Stock" papers are issued to horses of questionable coloration but which have Appaloosa characteristics. "Pedigree Certificates" are issued to horses with neither coloration nor characteristics.

The genetic possibilities of open breeding are virtually unlimited. For example: (1) two horses without coloration could produce a foal with or without coloration, (2) two horses with coloration could produce a foal with or without coloration, and (3) one horse with coloration and one horse without any coloration could produce a foal with or without coloration. The registration of an Appaloosa, therefore, must be based upon subjective determination.

To further complicate the registration process, Appaloosa coloration often changes with the horse's age. For example, a solid color Appaloosa foal may develop an "easily recognizable coat pattern" by four years of age. Whereas an Appaloosa with distinct coloration at birth may carry a "greying gene" which causes the coat pattern to fade (grey) as the horse matures. Thus, descriptive errors are indigenous to the registration process, and records must be continually updated. The failure of many horse owners to update the records of their horses has led to numerous complaints at Appaloosa horse shows and racing events because the horses do not match identification papers.

The arduous task of determining coloration and/or characteristics of Appaloosa horses has been compounded by the unresolved issue of "What is an Appaloosa?" The Board has attempted to deal with the recognition of coloration difficulties. Between January of 1978 and September of 1979 eight different motions were passed by the Board, which attempted to clarify the standards for an Appaloosa.

Judgmental errors have plagued the registration process. As of 1978, the Club was using over 200 inspectors as well as Board members to classify horses. Conflicting decisions by inspectors (who received no standardized training) resulted in frustrating the membership as well as a loss of credibility. In an effort to remedy the situation, the Board initiated the following steps:

1 In September 1978, the Board created the position of Registrar to oversee and review the registration decisions, thereby decreasing the probability of judgment errors.

2 In May 1979, the Board announced that any Appaloosa horses with regular papers must yield to inspection if a protest is filed. Mandatory horse inspection at all national shows was instituted in June of 1979 to correct any inaccurate coloration descriptions on registration papers (of 1400 horses inspected at a show in July 1979, 950 were found to be invalid due to descriptive errors).

3 The Club defended lawsuits filed by members when the Club would not register their horses. Legal fees ballooned from $6,500 in 1977 to $49,800 in 1978 to $57,000 for the first nine months of 1979.

4 In July of 1979, the Board passed Motion #60 requiring that "all horses be tatooed before showing at nationally sponsored events beginning with the 1980 National Show."

5 In September 1979, the Board abolished the system of using 200 untrained inspectors. A group of fifteen inspectors was handpicked and trained by the Club to promote standarization of judgment decisions and to minimize registration errors. However, the Board of Directors remained the final avenue of appeal should a registration decision be protested.

There are other sources of error that beset the registration department. The failure to utilize a means of positive identification of all horses thwarts efforts to control the accuracy of registrations (Appaloosa horses are not routinely required to be permanently marked for identification purposes). Further, the Club is continuing to register horses by means of photographs in lieu of a physical inspection. Falsification of records, therefore, remains a potential hazard. Likewise, the practice of issuing duplicate registration certificates (for lost papers) offers a potential for misuse. In addition, errors in recording may occur at the office.

ACCOUNTING

Bill Hostetler, when hired as Controller in September of 1978, noted that accounting procedures were extremely unorganized and lacked control procedures. His observations of shortcomings and actions that he instituted to correct some of them are listed.

1 A General Ledger had not been kept since the previous audit of December 31, 1977. The accounting firm hired by the Club to prepare the audit routinely made up the Ledger after the year ended in order to make their report.

2 The Checking Accounts had not been balanced since the 1977 audit. When more money was needed in a checking account, the Club would borrow money using their savings account as collateral.

3 Savings Accounts were kept without any central club record of the location of these accounts, the personnel authorized on accounts, or the amounts of money contained in the accounts. Personnel no longer working for the Club were still authorized to sign withdrawals. Passbooks were found in various locations. The Club received notification from a bank in Las Vegas that funds contained in an inactive account since 1969 were about to be surrendered to the state of Nevada. Another such notice was also received from an Idaho bank.

4 The Accounts Receivable had numerous problems. Incoming funds were lumped together as income rather than being dispersed into appropriate income accounts. Management could not tell how much money each area had generated, or which areas were having problems until completion of the audit (usually six months past the year end).

5 Opened envelopes with money attached were routinely kept in boxes on the floor until a Work Order could be typed (which could take several weeks). These boxes were not locked up at night because "everyone was honest" about the situation. Bill allowed only a few personnel to open envelopes and required that all cash be locked up.

6 If the money accompanying a registration was short by less than $20, the Work Order was processed. If a shortage was exceeded by $20, the work was placed in a "pending" file. This file contained over 4,500 registration applications dating back to 1973. Although the money accompanying these applications was deposited, it was not considered to be income until the work had been completed. This money was literally in limbo. Bill revised these procedures so that if a Work Order is short of funds, it is returned with the uncashed check to the member. When he initiated the dismantling of the "pending" file in July 1979, the registration applications, together with approximately $80,000 deposited as work-in-progress, were mailed back to members. However, it was discovered that copies of the Work Orders and amounts refunded were not kept for use by the Controller. The refunded money, therefore, was still on the books as work-in-progress, instead of being charged against income.

7 Records were not faithfully kept on checks returned for insufficient funds. In 1978 over $15,000 worth of NSF checks was owed the Club. Such checks were now placed on a suspension list if not paid within 30 days and this list is published in *The Appaloosa News*.

8 New Work Orders were accepted on delinquent accounts since the status of the accounts was not readily available for checking.

9 Delinquent Accounts Receivable for *The Appaloosa News* were not pursued so that in January 1979 $308,000 was delinquent. Bill established an interest penalty of 1.5% per month on accounts over 30 days delinquent, but no notice is sent until accounts are four months past due. Such accounts are then placed on a suspension list (and published in *The Appaloosa News*). As a result of these actions, receivables over 90 days old have been reduced to approximately $244,000.

10 The Accounts Payable records did not separate refunds by department. All refunds were deducted from one account, including those for *The Appaloosa News* (which is a profit-making area of the Club and therefore taxable).

11 Checks could be signed by several employees. This was changed so that only the Executive Secretary and the Treasurer may sign checks.

12 Personal loans were made to employees without interest. This was eliminated.

13 The Club did not have an operating budget. Such items as Director's expenses, supplies, and depreciation of machinery, for example, were not being budgeted.

14 Separate ledgers were not kept for events such as horse shows, horse racing, or biannual horse sales. The ledgers for these events had to be pieced together by the Controller at the end of the event. Income and expenses for horse shows, for example, were routinely handled by the Show Manager by opening a checking account at the location of the show. Income was deposited into the checking account, and checks were written for expenses. Following the show, the check stubs were turned in to the Club, but without record of what the money paid out was used for (there were no paid invoices). Bill set up procedures beginning in January 1980 for all show accounts to be handled at the Club, and for Sales and Racing to keep separate ledgers for each event.

COMPUTERIZATION

The computer consulting firm of Stephen S. Black of Pennsylvania requested and received permission to make a presentation to the Board concerning computerization of the Club's records. In November 1978, they recommended the Prime Computer, Model 400. The core memory of the Prime (512 million characters) exceeded that of competitive models, as did the number of allowable remote terminals (63 CRTs). The firm estimated that the records of the Club could be computerized within six months (although Black had not conducted an inspection of such records). The Prime computer was available for delivery by February 1979 at a cost of $300,000. Two negative factors existed: (1) the nearest repair outlet was located in Seattle (350 miles away), and (2) no personnel training programs were available.

Following this presentation, a committee consisting of the Executive Secretary (Mr. Nuber), the Controller (Bill Hostetler), and three Directors from the Board, was appointed by the Board to investigate the proposed computerization and alternative possibilities. The Board then authorized the expenditure of up to $300,000 for the purchase of a computer system for the Club.

The committee also investigated Digital Equipment Corporation computers and found they were not economically competitive. The Burroughs computer was found to have fewer capabilities than the Prime, and was eliminated partially because of the poor service record Burroughs had maintained with the Club on other equipment.

IBM representatives studied the requirements of the Club, and estimated that complete computerization could be accomplished within 18 months. They proposed a progressive approach. Two data collection centers (3742s) would be installed in February 1979, followed by a system 32 (to handle batch work) in April. A system 34 (with on-line capabilities) would be delivered in October, and a system 38 (with 512 million characters and 64 CRTs) would be available by October 1980, if needed. The system 34 would cost $200,000 and the 38 would cost $244,000.

The committee compared the IBM proposal with the Black proposal using the Prime computer and decided to accept IBM's proposal for the following reasons:

1 IBM had repair facilities 90 miles away in Spokane, versus 350 miles away in Seattle for Prime.

2 IBM offered a user training program with the computer. Prime did not.

3 IBM offered lease with option to buy. Prime offered purchase only.

4 The progressive approach required a smaller initial outlay and was therefore believed to be less risky for the Club.

5 IBM's estimate of 18 months to computerize the records appeared to be more realistic than Black's estimate of six months.

Among his other responsibilities, Bill Hostetler was asked to coordinate the computerization.

In January 1979 the first of the two data input centers (3742s) were received, and the entering of payroll records, member name and address files, and horse show data was begun. Also in January, the Board instituted a new Show Point program, requiring a custom program to process (there were no "canned" programs available). The Club therefore found it necessary to rent machine time on a system 34 in Lewiston, Idaho,

(35 miles away) to develop and test the Show Point program. It took eight weeks of calendar time to finalize this program at a cost of $10,000.

Because data was being entered at a faster rate than had been projected, the delivery date of the system 32 was moved forward by two months (installation occurred in February 1979). Although the payroll records had been entered, the printing of payroll checks was delayed, pending the delivery of continuous form checks (delivery time of computer supplies averaged 8–10 weeks). During a period of three months, 186 payroll checks per month had to be hand typed until the arrival of the necessary forms. Since changes were continually being made to improve the programs, only small quantities of computer supplies were ordered (thereby increasing the cost of such supplies). One shipment of Work Order forms came printed with serial numbers that had been used the preceding year and therefore had to be renumbered.

Accounts Receivable had been entered on the system 32 by April, and billing was accomplished by April 10th. The assignment of vendor numbers to the Accounts Payable was completed by April 20th, and the General Ledger was entered by April 27th without year ending account balances (which were unavailable at the time). Keying of the name and address files, including the assignment of numbers to non-members, was progressing (50,000 had been entered). There was a shortage of people to enter names and addresses because the Club was swamped with the influx of registration applications (because of the fee increases). At the same time, the correction of horse name and number inconsistencies had to be entered on the Show Point program. Also during this time, the computer department was receiving pressure from the management to demonstrate some results of the computerization. The Quarter Horse Association, which had given the Club valuable guidance in avoiding some of the trial-and-error that they had experienced, took ten years to successfully computerize.

To keep pace with incoming show data, a full-time night shift with additional computer personnel became necessary. The Club's Computer Specialist determined that the system 32 did not have adequate capacity to store data for the Show Point system. He estimated that it would take 13 million positions of disc to store records for one year, whereas the system 32 could accommodate only 9 million. The show data was transferred to the system 34 in Lewiston (forty shows had been entered by April 23rd). Employees did not like making the 70 mile round trip to Lewiston, and four experienced computer personnel quit during the week of May 20th.

The expense of renting the system 34 prompted the Club to order an additional system 32 (the system 34 was not yet available) to bring the Show Point program "in-house."

The second 3742 (data input center) arrived April 20th (two months late). The entering of expense and revenue transactions on the Accounts Payable and the General Ledger (also without year-ending account balances) were begun. On May 18th the Club's Computer Specialist warned management against haste, saying that "more time was needed to check data for accuracy" (hundreds of errors in data entry were being discovered).

On June 3rd the decision was made to duplicate completed Work Orders from the last two months of 1978 onto the IBM system 32, because serious errors had been discovered in the work done on the Burroughs accounting machine. During the week of June 15th the keying of 36,000 duplicated Work Orders held up the Accounts Payable and General Ledger. Meanwhile, data from 104 horse shows from the month of May had to be entered as well. Edits of March and April shows found that 80 percent of the show data contained errors (mostly horse name and number inconsistencies), necessitating multiple runs to clean up. The May shows averaged 2.5 edits per show.

Statements on the Accounts Payable and the General Ledger were run on June 29th, and coding of the revised Work Order system was begun. Because pertinent information contained in the membership files was not yet available, the program for processing the Work Orders had to be altered accordingly. Keying of the name and address files continued (155,000 as of June 22nd). Daily corrections of these files could not be accomplished without on-line capability (the information was recorded on floppy discs, which would have required hand sorting the files as well as valuable machine time to correct).

In July the additional system 32 was received. The Show Point program was converted from the system 34 in Lewiston and brought "in-house" August 10th. Printing of Accounts Payable checks also began on this date. Even with the second system 32, the Club needed more capabilities. The name and address files completed August 23rd (292,000) had to be taken to Lewiston for sorting by the system 34. These files were split into four groups and checked for duplicate customer numbers. After four days of running time, 20,000 duplicate numbers had been discovered. The hand correcting of these errors began in September, but was stopped (as well as other work-in-progress) in order to complete the processing of Show Points by the September 20th deadline. The failure of 20 shows to report their data forced the extension of this deadline to October 15th. This meant that the Club had to work overtime to process the year end results (including August and September show data and the 20 remaining shows). The full day crew from the computer department was assigned to the running of show data, and more computer personnel were hired for the night shift. In 1979 there were 617 shows and a total of 88,981 entries. Duplicate records were kept on all shows (for security) and a monthly print-out was made for *The Appaloosa News* to publish. The irony of the problems created by the new Show Point system was that the Board did not discard the old system used by the regional clubs (because the Board did not wish to antagonize the clubs). Thus, both systems were used to qualify horses for the World Horse Show during 1979.

In September the revised Work Order program was ready for implementation, but the duplicate keying of Work Orders from 1978 took priority over other work in order to complete the 1978 audit for the November 1979 Board meeting. The keying of horse record files, projected to begin in August 1979, was postponed until the first quarter of 1980.

The hand correction of the name and address files (scheduled for completion in mid-January 1980) had to be accomplished ahead of schedule in order for the Club to print ballots for the January 1980 election. The Board had ordered the printing to be done by computer instead of by the addressograph (which was still operable).

Throughout the process of computerization, work was being received at a record pace (due to the fee increases of January 1979). During the first nine months of 1979 the Club registered 21,500 horses, compared to 19,500 for the previous year. The ongoing task of training personnel (which had increased from 43 in 1978 to 91 in 1979) and the double workload (resulting from the duplication of Work Orders from 1978) were also a strain on the Club. It had also become apparent that a high rate of key punching errors had been made while entering data (due in part to insufficient supervision, and to a lack of integrity on the part of some operators in verifying their work before entering it onto the system). In a spot check of 500 accounts entered during 1979, errors totaling $37,000 were found (90 percent of these errors were from inaccurate key punching). Members who were expecting to receive better service because they were paying more money for registration became disillusioned. Registrations which had taken 4–6 weeks processing time in 1978 were taking 2–3 months to process in 1979.

MANAGEMENT AND ORGANIZATION

At the beginning of the period described, January 1978, the Club had a functional organization structure. The Executive Secretary, Mr. Hatley, was responsible to the Board of Directors. Reporting to Mr. Hatley were the Racing Secretary, Charles Nuber; the Editor, Don Pitts; the Office Manager; the Controller, Ray Rosch; and the Show Manager, Roy Young. (See Exhibits 4 to 7 for organization structure, as perceived by Bill Hostetler, at various points in time.)

In April 1978 the position of Assistant Executive Secretary was established and Mr. Charles Nuber was appointed to fill the position (in addition to his position as Racing Secretary) and receive a salary equal in amount to that received by the Executive

EXHIBIT 4   APPALOOSA HORSE CLUB ORGANIZATION CHART, January 1978

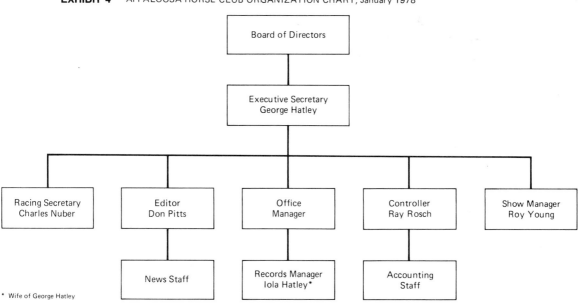

* Wife of George Hatley

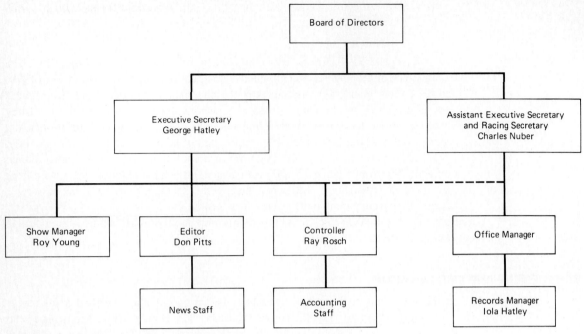

EXHIBIT 5 APPALOOSA HORSE CLUB ORGANIZATION CHART, June 1978

EXHIBIT 6 APPALOOSA HORSE CLUB ORGANIZATION CHART, February 1979

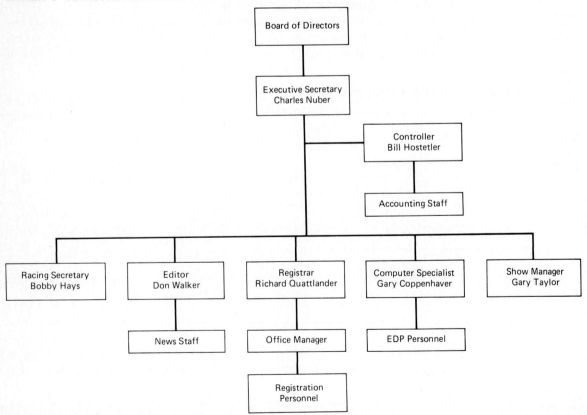

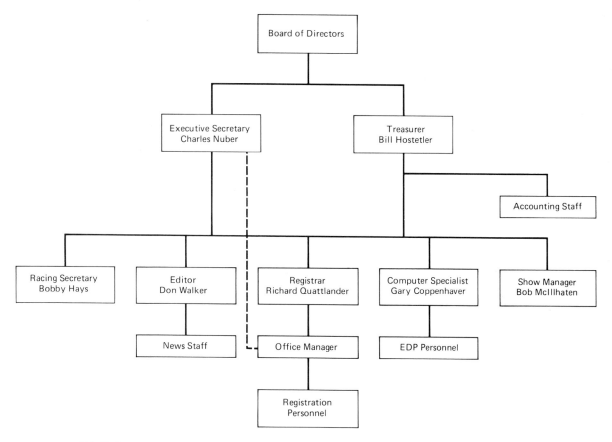

EXHIBIT 7 APPALOOSA HORSE CLUB ORGANIZATION CHART, September 1979

Secretary. In June 1978 the Board took the Personnel and Registry functions of the Club from the Executive Secretary, Mr. Hatley, and gave them to the Assistant Executive Secretary. His power of office had been significantly diminished by the removal of these two critical Club functions from his authority.

Mrs. Iola Hatley, "Mrs. Appaloosa," who had been supervising the record keeping operations of the Club for many years subsequently resigned, effective July 31, 1978. Ms. Debbie Lovell replaced Mrs. Hatley, but was relieved of her duties in November 1978 based on reported non-cooperation with the new management. At this time the head bookkeeper, Ms. Jane Hyko, and three other experienced office personnel resigned their positions (see Exhibit 8). Adequate training for new workers was not available, and many new employees resigned out of frustration (there were no job descriptions or guidelines to follow). For the year 1979 there were 157 different people on the payroll for 91 positions.

Mr. Hatley submitted his resignation as Executive Secretary in November 1978. It was unanimously accepted by the Board. At this time the Board authorized the title of Executive Secretary Emeritus for Mr. Hatley, and offered him a contract calling for the payment of $189,000 over a period of fifteen years. Mr. Hatley, finding portions of the

EXHIBIT 8   LETTER SENT TO CLUB MEMBERS BY MS. HYKO AFTER HER RESIGNATION

Moscow, Idaho
12 December 1978

To: Members of the Appaloosa Horse Club:

I first started working at the Appaloosa Horse Club in 1969. At this time George Hatley was the Executive Secretary and was actively engaged in managing the affairs of the Club. Under his direction, there was more than $300,000 in checking and savings accounts and savings certificates, plus a building fund for the new office building which was being planned.

Once the Club's yearly receipts exceeded the magic figure of one million dollars, the directors' ideas on how to spend money grew faster than the income. People with a yen for dollars and authority started making plans to "take over" the Appaloosa Horse Club. In 1974 Ben Johnson announced that the directors were going to manage the office, and from that time matters started to get out of hand. Richard Stranger was put in as president and began approving large expense accounts for the directors. Some of the directors seemed to think that there was an unlimited supply of money and that the Club should pay for their travel and telephone calls with no questions asked. In fact, they resented having to send in receipts to verify their expenses. It is necessary to have receipts on file for the I.R.S. and the annual audits.

New members elected to the board were "brain-washed" to think that the office was being mismanaged. However, none of the directors made an effort to come to the office, spend a few days and see how it was run. When the BOD decided that they should be actively involved in the day to day running of the office, they had no idea of the registration problems or other situations that the staff handled very efficiently.

When the BOD decided to hire and fire personnel the situation kept getting worse. The officials that the BOD hired were more interested in keeping on the good side of certain directors than they were in getting their work done. The Board asked for Don Walker's and Bob Blair's resignations. Before Mr. Walker left the ApHC he made the statement that several of the Board members were "after George Hatley." Then Bob Blair, Racing Secretary, was fired and the racing program started going downhill. Mr. Blair had always been a very dedicated employee who did his utmost to promote the Appaloosa racing program. He is also very loyal to George Hatley. Mr. Blair was fired by the Board so that they could put their hand-picked man in charge of the racing department. Mr. Charles Nuber, who was educated to be a Physical Education teacher and was handling the racing program at the University of Arizona—and who knows nothing about Appaloosas, was named Racing Secretary and Assistant Executive Secretary.

The next person was Iola Hatley. She had always had the Club and the members' best interests at heart. She was knowledgeable about all phases of registration and saved the girls in the office hours of research time by answering questions quickly on the phone. She also attempted to keep all expenses in line with the income of the Club. Some of the directors took it as a personal affront if she questioned their expense accounts.

At their last meeting, the Board named Mr. Nuber as Executive Secretary and Mr. Hatley was forced to retire. He was given the title of Secretary Emeritus.

---

contract unacceptable, refused to sign. The Board of Directors called a special meeting on December 17, 1978 and revoked their offer. Mr. Hatley was advised by telegram, and requested to return "all credit cards, keys, records, and other property of The Appaloosa Horse Club, Inc. to the Executive Secretary," and to "vacate his office no later than December 22, 1978."

As a result of this action by the Board, a public controversy developed. Dissatisfied members, former employees, and Board members wrote and mailed statements to the membership. Samples are included in Exhibits 8 and 9.

Newspaper stories containing rumors and unverified information, including the possible relocation of the Club headquarters to the state of Oklahoma, created addi-

EXHIBIT 8   *(Continued)*

In August, Mr. Nuber hired a "Registrar" for the office. He is Richard Quattlander—who also knows nothing about Appaloosas, but he had worked at the Jockey Club for about 1-1/2 years. A new show manager has been hired by the Board to take Roy Young's place. Mr. Nuber has hired a business manager for the Club, and also one for *The Appaloosa News* department. All of the new people are getting large salaries—not because of any job expertise, but because they are being bought by the current acting president, Dan Miller.

Some of the directors and their wives have made the statement that it was no trouble to learn any job in the office, and if everyone left, replacements could be quickly trained. I don't think this is feasible. There are some things a person knows instinctively that cannot be taught. Debbie Lovell, the office manager, was fired by Mr. Quattlander. Debby has worked with Appaloosas and other breeds of horses most of her life. She was a very capable manager. Shirley Stills, head of the addressograph department, resigned—several girls in the registration department have gone. I was bookkeeper and operated the Burroughs minicomputer. I resigned because of unreasonable firing of some of the staff. Most of the key personnel has either resigned or been fired. I hope that you members realize that there is no one left working in the registration department who really knows anything about Appaloosas—including the so called registrar.

Since the BOD decided that they should run the business of the Club, the financial status is going downhill fast. The new business manager has had to draw out the savings accounts in order to meet the payroll and other expenses. Cash flow is definitely a problem. With the new high fees going into effect the first of the year, some of the club members will find it a hardship to register their Appaloosas. If the registrations drop, there will be an adverse effect on the cash flow. All of the new programs being put into effect will have to be paid for by the club members—this includes the computerization of all registration records. The computers will cost at least $250,000 and that is only the beginning. In the minutes of the last meeting I noticed that the Board went into executive session to discuss finances. I hope this does not mean that the members will be kept in the dark about the Club's financial matters—after all, the members are the ones who pay the bills.

It is very sad to see an institution that was built up over a period of 31 years be ruined by Mr. Miller and a few other directors in such a short time. When Mr. Hatley was in charge of running the Club, it was in sound financial condition, with a back-up of savings accounts, savings certificates and checking accounts. At the end of November 1978 there was a deficit balance of over $52,000 in the regular checking accounts, and overdraft notices for other checking accounts. I realize that there are assets in equipment, the building and the land, but the cash flow is critical. The Club airplane has been sold, also the horse trailer and a car. How long will it be before they mortgage the building? Is Mr. Miller trying to bankrupt the Club so that he can buy it for a few cents on the dollar and convert it into a private business for himself? What are his motives in getting rid of the people who were loyal to Mr. Hatley, and then forcing Mr. Hatley to retire?? Why is he insisting that the Club be moved? This area is historically the right place for the ApHC. And don't forget, the Appaloosa has been officially named as the Idaho State Horse!!!

If you are not in agreement with all of these happenings, please take some positive action. You as members are the only ones who can. Since the new by-laws were not passed, it is still possible to recall the directors if you feel they are not acting in your best interests. Don't let the ApHC be ruined because of the selfish whims of a few directors.
Jane Hyko

tional unrest and confusion. Employees became concerned about their job security and the hiring of new personnel was adversely affected. Two employees were refused credit by local Moscow merchants who had read in the newspaper that the Club was going to move. The membership and the public, confused by the contradictory mailings and rumors, began to call the Horse Club in record numbers. As many as 300 calls per day flooded the switchboard, creating confusion and work slowdowns.

Board decisions concerning treatment of Mr. Hatley, as well as the large registration fee increase enacted with short notice, had repercussions at the June 1979 Board election. The five incumbent Board members running for reelection were replaced by vote of the membership.

At the time of Mr. Hatley's resignation, Mr. Nuber was appointed to the position of Executive Secretary (with a $5,500 increase in salary over the amount Mr. Hatley received) and given a three year contract.

The Controller was made directly responsible to the Executive Secretary in February of 1979. In September 1979, the position of Controller was subsequently changed (by amendments to the Bylaws) to Treasurer. This new position, which was to be appointed by the Board and directly responsible to the Board, gave the Treasurer more authority over the budget and provided the Club with a ''second'' in command.

Numerous other changes in key management positions also occurred during the 21 month period of this study.

• The Show Manager, Mr. Roy Young, was replaced for health reasons by Mr. Gary Taylor in August 1978.

• The new position of Registrar was created in September of 1978 and filled by Mr. Richard Quattlander.

• The Controller, Mr. Ray Rosch, was replaced by Mr. William Hostetler in September 1978.

EXHIBIT 9

APPALOOSA HORSE CLUB
CARTOON THAT APPEARED IN THE FACT SHEET

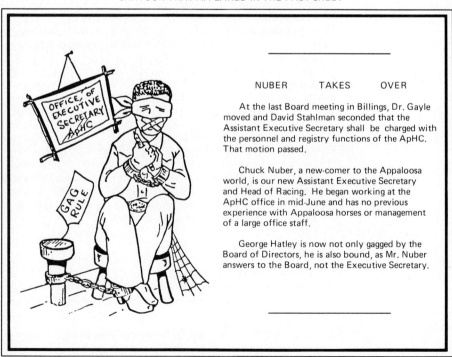

NUBER   TAKES   OVER

At the last Board meeting in Billings, Dr. Gayle moved and David Stahlman seconded that the Assistant Executive Secretary shall be charged with the personnel and registry functions of the ApHC. That motion passed.

Chuck Nuber, a new-comer to the Appaloosa world, is our new Assistant Executive Secretary and Head of Racing. He began working at the ApHC office in mid-June and has no previous experience with Appaloosa horses or management of a large office staff.

George Hatley is now not only gagged by the Board of Directors, he is also bound, as Mr. Nuber answers to the Board, not the Executive Secretary.

• The Editor of *The Appaloosa News,* Mr. Don Pitts, was replaced by Mr. Don Walker in December 1978.

• The new position of Computer Specialist was created in January 1979 and filled by Mr. Gary Coppenhaver.

• The Racing Secretary vacancy was filled by Mr. Bobby Hays in Feburary 1979 (following the promotion of Mr. Charles Nuber).

• The vacancy of Youth Director was filled by Mr. Gary Taylor (formerly the Show Manager) in August of 1979.

• The Show Manager vacancy was filled by Mr. Bob McIllhaten in August of 1979.

One or more changes of personnel occurred in every management level position at the Horse Club between January 1978 and September 1979.

Because the Club did not have a formally developed organizational structure, the changeover of management personnel was difficult. Employees accustomed to being supervised by the Executive Secretary, Mr. Hatley, were reluctant to accept direction from other management personnel. This remained a problem until the departuure of Mr. Hatley.

Several personnel policies and practices were improved to help reduce employee turnover among the office staff. A semi-annual salary review system was initiated, and personnel files were set up for all employees to accumulate pertinent information concerning employee performance. The minimum starting wage for clerical help offered by the Club was increased to be more competitive, but this increase was not matched with a corresponding raise in the salaries of existing Club employees performing comparable work. Thus, new employees were paid more than experienced employees. Traditionally, the office employees were single women and student wives. The waiting period to qualify for participation in the Club's retirement program was reduced to one year and six months of employment from three years and six months. Also, insurance benefits were updated.

During the transition, frequent changing of procedures were necessary. The lack of effective communication between the management and employees aggravated the difficulty of making changes. Procedures were often changed without making certain that everyone was aware of the change (word of mouth was the method used to inform employees). In early 1979, weekly meetings were instituted for department managers and other supervisory personnel. Although these measures have been helpful, the problem has not been entirely resolved.

DISCUSSION QUESTIONS

1 What threats and opportunities face Bill Hostetler in his current position.

2 What alternative career strategies are available to Bill and how do they relate to his responsibilities at the Appaloosa Horse Club?

3 Describe the career strategy which Bill should follow and explain how he might implement it.

APPALOOSA HORSE CLUB (B)

Gary Whitney
University of San Diego

SELECTED STRATEGIC ISSUES

- An ethical dilemma in career decision making
- Legal rights of executive to contest discharge
- How perceptions of mistreatment affect moral obligations

In late February of 1980 Bill Hostetler was called into Mr. Nuber's office. He said:

> Bill, I want you to submit to the Board of Directors your letter of resignation. If you do this, I guarantee that I will give the highest possible recommendation to any future employer. If you don't submit your resignation letter, I will ask the Board to terminate your employment.
>
> If you submit your letter of resignation, you may write your own letter of recommendation and I will sign it.

For the next few weeks Bill pondered whether to submit his resignation and accept the letter of recommendation or to fight what he believed to be an unjust request. In making this decision, some issues he considered salient were:

1 Age: early 30s
2 Family: wife and daughter
3 Experience: Manager of several Grant's discount stores until Grant's went bankrupt
4 Education: MBA expected in May 1980
5 Geographic: prefer not to move

DISCUSSION QUESTIONS

1 How should Bill respond to Mr. Nuber's ultimatum? Explain your answer.
2 What rights does Bill have regarding due process or justification for the resignation demand?
3 If Bill elects to resign, what should he put in the letter of recommendation for Mr. Nuber to sign? Defend your answer.

SOUTHERN FEDERAL SAVINGS AND LOAN ASSOCIATION (A)

William R. Boulton
James A. Verbrugge
University of Georgia

SELECTED STRATEGIC ISSUES

- The strategic impact of regulation and deregulation of the savings and loan industry
- Effects on earnings prospects of changes on the loan side and the saving side of thrifts
- Leverage and liquidity ratios of savings and loan companies versus those of other kinds of businesses
- The effect of inflation on potentially bad loans
- Advantages of mutual versus stock form of ownership
- The advantages of going public or merging for a savings and loan association

Southern Federal Savings and Loan Association grew from $15 million to over $160 million in assets between 1960 and 1980. In July, 1980, the association's officers were taking steps to introduce new services and activities allowed by the Depository Institutions Deregulation and Monetary Act of 1980. In commenting on South Federal's approach to these changes, Mr. Knight, the chief executive officer, explained:

This case was prepared by Drs. William R. Boulton and James A. Verbrugge of the University of Georgia's College of Business Administration. Permission was received from the authors and the Case Research Association.

Distributed by the Case Research Association. All rights reserved to the authors and the Case Research Association. Permission to use the case should be obtained from the Case Research Association.

Realizing that tremendous changes are going on in the banking world and the world of finance, we can't just sit here and say that we're going to be able to survive in the foreseeable future by operating just like we have in the past. I don't think we can do it. I've been telling our people for a year and a half that we're just not going to get the money in like we have— the game has changed. When they loosened up and went with CDs, that was the beginning of a great, great change in this business. Now with deregulation, though, it's a totally new ballgame!

THE IMPACT OF DEREGULATION

Savings and loan associations are not unfamiliar with changing regulations. Between 1968 and 1977, regulatory changes came with increasing regularity—everything from truth in lending to equal rights, as shown in Table 1.

New regulatory changes, however, open up competition between financial institutions. President Carter signed the 1980 Depository Institutions Deregulation and Monetary Control Act into law on March 31, 1980, after four years of efforts by bankers to equalize competition in, to update and to reform the financial industry. The new law included major provisions covering (1) expanded Federal Reserve Board management of the monetary system, (2) the phase-out of interest ceilings on deposits, (3) permanent authority for financial services of automatic transfers, remote service units and share drafts, and extension of NOW accounts nationwide, (4) expanded powers, especially in the areas of consumer credit and trusts for S&Ls and federal MSBs, (5) a federal override of state usury laws and (6) simplified disclosure requirements for Truth in Lending. Some key aspects of this deregulation include the following:

TABLE 1   FEDERAL LEGISLATION AFFECTING SAVINGS ASSOCIATION MORTGAGE LENDING

Item	Year
Truth-in-lending Act	1968
Fair Housing Act	1968
Fair Credit Reporting Act	1970
Flood Disaster Protection Act	1973
Real Estate Settlement Procedures Act	1973
Equal Credit Opportunity Act	1974
Amendments to the Truth-in-lending Act	1974
Fair Credit Billing Act	1974
Home Mortgage Disclosure Act	1975
Amendments to the Real Estate Settlement Procedures Act	1976
Amendments to the Equal Credit Opportunity Act	1976
Amendments to the Flood Disaster Protection Act	1976
Consumer Leasing Act	1976
Community Reinvestment Act	1977

Source: U.S. League of Savings Associations.

Regulation Q

Controls on interest rate ceilings will be phased out by March 31, 1986. The rate of the phase-out will be determined by a newly formed Deregulation Committee, composed of the Treasury, the Fed, FDIC, FHLBB, and FCUA, to reach market rates as soon as feasible. The new law suggests an annual ¼% phase-out through March 1983 and ½% annual phase-outs thereafter. Thrifts retain their ¼% rate differential during the phase-out.

Federal Reserve Controls

The Fed's control over the monetary system is expanded to all depository institutions for all transaction accounts and for all nonpersonal time deposits. Fed members will be phased into the new requirements by 1984 while nonmember and nonbank depository institutions will be brought under the requirements by 1988. The law will (1) reduce current reserve requirements for all Fed members, (2) require reserves for NOW accounts beginning December 31, 1980, (3) provide all depository institutions access to the Fed's discount window, and (4) require all nonmember and nonbank institutions to transmit required reserves to the Fed by March 31, 1988.

State Usury Laws

State usury laws for home mortgage loans, including mobile homes, are set aside as of April 1, 1980 unless reimposed by State action by April 1, 1983. All business and agricultural loans over $25,000 can also be made for up to 5% over the discount rate plus surcharge of the Fed's regional bank. All federally insured institutions are allowed to lend at up to 1% over the discount rate.

Truth in Lending

Financial regulators are allowed to order repayments to customers for Truth in Lending violations where the pattern finance charges on APRs since January 1, 1977, have been inaccurately disclosed beyond ¼% of the exact figure (within certain provisions and limited creditor civil liability).

Provisions for Thrifts and CUs

S&Ls and Federal mutual savings banks are allowed to add services and credit unions are freed from their 12% interest ceiling for loans. Federally insured S&Ls can (1) operate remote service units, (2) offer NOW accounts effective December 13, 1980, (3) offer lines of credit, consumer loans and credit cards, (4) offer mortgage loans of unlimited amounts, and (5) lend to customers without geographic restrictions. S&Ls can invest up to 20% of assets in consumer loans, commercial paper and corporate debt securities. Credit unions are allowed to offer share drafts and raise the interest limit on loans to 15%. Savings and loan associations were now allowed to broaden their services, thereby competing more directly with other financial institutions. With regard to these changes, Jack Pope, vice president of Southern Federal, commented:

> Since I've been with Southern Federal, we've never had so many significant changes at one time. With the suddenness in which the deregulation is coming, the advantage is shifting to the commercial banks because they already have the branches and have a head start. It will take S&Ls a long time to catch up.

HISTORY AND BACKGROUND OF SOUTHERN FEDERAL

Southern Federal Savings and Loan Association was incorporated in 1929 as the Mutual Building and Loan Association. The association didn't really get going until the 1930s when it became a federal association. In 1935, its name was changed to the Federal Savings and Loan Association, commonly known as Southern Federal.

Since Southern Federal's beginning, it has had four presidents serving the periods 1929–1931, 1931–1943, 1943–1964, and 1964 to the present. Long tenures had become the tradition, with Mr. Knight currently serving his sixteenth year as president and chief executive officer.

Between 1960 and 1970, Southern Federal more than doubled assets with growth from $15 to $39 million. By 1978, assets increased to over ten times the 1960 level reaching $160 million. As shown in Southern Federal's financial statements (Exhibits 1 and 2), the association more than doubled in size in the past five years. Exhibits 3 and 4 show comparative financial statements for all FSLIC-insured savings and loan associations in the industry. During this time, the nature of Southern Federal's business also continued to change. James Redding, Jr., Southern Federal's executive vice president, explained how different the loan side of the business had become:

> When I first came here, they had all their notes printed with 5½% like it was always going to be 5½% interest. We were probably paying four percent on savings back in the sixties. We continued that for a good while and did some FHA and VA loans. Our loans were primarily residential though we would make a church loan or rental property loan.
>
> As both the lending and savings aspects changed, they added the 90% loan so you could lend 90% of the value. Later on, residential loans went to 95% where you only needed 5% down. Then we got into land development loans—you know, financing subdivisions and lot development. Then they liberalized the amounts you could lend on apartment and commercial properties as a percent of total assets. They added student loans. I think property improvement loans came since I've been here. The wobbly boxes—mobile homes—we never have done much of that.
>
> At one point in time, they added nursing homes. You know, we had no need for nursing homes in 1960 because folks were kept at home, but the welfare state and mobility of people have changed. We financed the first one out here, this Heritage. They financed it for 6½%. We charged six percent on residential so we stuck them with another half of a percent.
>
> The condominium concept came and we made the first condominium loan in town, about nine years ago. There were 44 units and it took three years from the day they broke ground until they finished and sold them out.

EXHIBIT 1   SOUTHERN FEDERAL SAVINGS AND LOAN ASSOCIATION:
STATEMENT OF CONDITION FOR SOUTHERN FEDERAL (1973–1979) (Thousands of $)

Assets	1979	1978	1977	1976	1975	1974	1973
Mortgage Loans & Contracts*	$130,134	$119,327	$103,577	$ 84,035	$73,809	$63,480	$35,485
Guaranteed	2,631	2,581	2,374	1,912	1,762	1,383	1,229
FHA-HUD	302	437	259	111	270	191	199
Conventional	126,443	116,000	100,723	81,825	71,597	61,881	54,042
Other Loans*	5,067	3,727	3,078	2,060	1,070	926	743
Serviced by Savings							
Accounts	3,528	2,291	1,841	1,049	510	569	472
Unsecured Property							
Improvement	1,062	1,045	899	599	350	174	110
Mobile Home	0	0	0	0	0	0	0
Unsecured Education	302	249	222	201	194	162	155
Other	99	91	71	179	0	10	0
Cash & Investment Securities*	19,534	17,842	13,026	16,112	12,342	7,034	9,031
Cash & Demand Deposits							
Eligible for Liquidity	549	163	637	329	238	335	410
Investment Securities							
Eligible for Liquidity	17,195	14,923	13,807	14,154	11,496	6,159	8,098
FHLB Stock	1,002	923	734	630	554	467	400
Real Estate Owned*	0	34	0	0	0	0	0
Fixed Assets (Net)	1,708	1,315	1,424	1,223	1,207	1,086	713
Mtg. Backed Securities &							
Mortgage Participation							
Guaranteed by Fed. Agencies	3,536	3,869	2,737	3,129	1,471	1,022	0
TOTAL ASSETS*	$160,475	$146,607	$129,263	$106,848	$90,720	$73,358	$66,290

Liabilities	1979	1978	1977	1976	1975	1974	1973
Savings Accounts*	$145,773	$131,595	115,980	$ 97,132	$80,991	$65,804	$59,041
Earning in Excess of							
Regular Rate	119,951	101,484	85,981	68,969	54,936	42,589	35,459
Accounts Greater Than							
$100,000	4,474	719	388	616	N.C.	N.C.	N.C.
Accounts Less Than							
$100,000	115,477	100,765	83,393	68,352	N.C.	N.C.	N.C.
Earning At or Below Regular							
Rate	25,822	30,111	31,999	23,214	26,055	23,215	23,581
Borrowed Money*	1,215	2,522	1,945	730	730	730	0
FHLB Advances	1,215	730	730	730	730	730	0
Other	0	1,792	1,215	0	0	0	0
Debentures	0	0	0	0	0	0	0
Loans in Process	1,204	2,215	2,452	1,200	1,128	481	1,626
Specific Reserves	15	14	6	4	8	2	0
Deferred Credits	860	1,018	781	672	503	365	320
TOTAL LIABILITIES*	$150,649	$138,005	$121,684	$100,208	$84,762	$68,494	$61,521
Net Worth							
Permanent Stock & Paid-in							
Surplus	$ 0	$ 0	$ 0	$ 0	$ 0	$ 0	$ 0
General Reserves	4,916	4,916	4,190	3,334	3,545	3,304	2,954
Other Reserves	0	0	0	0	0	0	0
Surplus & Undivided Profits	4,910	3,686	3,389	3,086	2,505	2,061	1,814
TOTAL NET WORTH*	$9,825	$8,602	$7,579	$6,650	$5,959	$5,364	$4,768
TOTAL LIABILITIES AND NET							
WORTH*	$160,475	$146,607	$129,263	$106,848	$90,720	$73,358	$66,290

* Indicates Subtotal or Total.

EXHIBIT 2   SOUTHERN FEDERAL SAVINGS AND LOAN ASSOCIATION: INCOME AND EXPENSES FOR
SOUTHERN FEDERAL (1973–1979)
(Thousands of $)

	1979	1978	1977	1976	1975	1974	1973
Gross Operating Income							
Interest*	$13,296	$10,965	$9,081	$7,646	$6,230	$5,155	$4,339
On Mortgage Loans	11,080	9,139	7,427	6,303	5,378	4,527	3,689
On Investment Securities & Dep.	1,488	1,235	1,163	1,090	778	559	605
On Other Loans	417	342	242	158	74	69	45
On Mfg. Particip., Mtg. Bck. Sec.	311	249	249	95	—	—	—
Fee Income	392	482	613	328	318	253	257
Other	130	101	49	49	48	58	44
TOTAL*	$13,818	$11,548	$9,743	$8,023	$6,596	$5,466	$4,640
Operating Expense							
Compensation & Other Benefits	$ 854	$ 853	$ 708	$ 593	$ 496	$ 436	$ 337
Office Occupancy	299	283	250	221	188	139	153
Advertising	68	73	72	65	70	47	64
Other	351	353	304	257	196	168	153
TOTAL*	$ 1,572	$ 1,562	$1,334	$1,136	$ 950	$ 790	$ 707
Cost of Funds							
Interest on Savings Accts. Certificates	$ 8,605	$ 6,695	$5,396	$4,509	$3,500	$2,589	$1,913
Interest on Savings Accts. Passbooks	1,551	1,682	1,612	1,450	1,289	1,218	1,138
Interest on Borrowed Money	103	86	65	58	55	0	0
TOTAL*	$10,259	$ 8,463	$7,073	$6,017	$4,844	$3,807	$3,051
Non-Operating Income	$ 13	$ 1	$ 20	$ 84	$ 7	$ 4	$ 1
Non-Operating Expense	239	3	3	3	8	41	1
Income Taxes: Federal and State*	538	499	414	264	207	220	252
Net Income*	$ 1,223	$ 1,023	$ 939	$ 688	$ 595	$ 611	$ 631

   * Indicates Subtotal or Total

Exhibit 5 shows Southern Federal's mortgage loan composition from 1973 through
1979.

Redding also explained how the saving side of business changed:

Going back to the savings end, we now go for the jumbo accounts. We bid on university
money, state money, city money, county money, and individual's money of a hundred
thousand or more.

Of course, we've come up with various certificates. It used to be just a pass book. Now
you got the 90-day notice account pass book; the one-year CD and thirty month CD; and the
six-month, ten thousand dollar money market certificate. We still sell a four, a six and an
eight year if somebody wants it. We can go up to ten years with a 30 month CD—we go three
years on the stated rate and shave it off after three years. It's 9½% on the money market and
9¼% after three years for a ten year one, compounded daily. It used to be that we paid semi-
annually, then we started paying quarterly; compounding daily; and now we pay it monthly if
you have a sizeable account.

Exhibit 1 provides a detailed breakdown of Southern Federal's mix of savings and loan
business.

EXHIBIT 3 SOUTHERN FEDERAL SAVINGS AND LOAN ASSOCIATION ASSETS, LIABILITIES AND NET WORTH: ALL ASSOCIATIONS IN STATE, 1973–1979 (Thousands of $)

Assets	1979	1978	1977	1976	1975	1974	1973
Mortgage Loans and Contracts*	$ 8,699,063	$8,036,401	$7,179,452	$6,278,797	$5,493,408	$4,918,079	$4,366,741
VA Guaranteed	85,370	87,296	87,974	87,105	86,452	87,099	89,145
FHA-HUD	51,100	52,631	56,094	59,403	64,616	72,034	75,989
Conventional	8,527,492	7,864,218	7,002,309	6,106,816	5,331,931	4,754,501	4,398,996
Other Loans*	333,137	224,177	208,951	184,043	173,087	174,427	176,552
Secured by Savings Accounts	231,737	134,938	107,364	84,656	67,505	60,955	57,711
Unsecured Property Improvement	35,350	29,727	28,207	29,041	23,351	17,352	10,081
Mobile Home	31,572	33,753	50,234	56,203	68,714	34,707	97,545
Unsecured Education	18,435	14,146	12,113	11,673	11,254	10,410	9,697
Other	15,544	11,613	11,033	2,470	17,863	1,003	1,418
Cash and Investment Securities*	367,047	780,363	665,256	617,046	538,490	424,675	393,775
Cash & Demand Deposits Eligible for Liquidity	589,067	43,501	48,650	54,473	57,708	53,415	50,249
Investment Securities Eligible for Liquidity	659,612	626,210	533,631	494,384	417,366	303,353	285,282
FHLB Stock	76,213	67,509	58,628	53,593	51,102	50,954	45,183
All Other	72,255	43,143	22,346	14,596	12,314	16,953	13,059
Real Estate Owned*	19,034	27,395	43,922	53,893	38,784	8,976	1,925
Acquired by Foreclosure	18,541	26,955	43,557	52,722	38,174	8,755	1,477
Other	492	440	345	1,171	610	240	448
Fixed Assets (Net)	148,136	144,453	139,392	133,867	124,349	109,255	92,370
Mtg. Backed Securities & Mortgage Participation Guaranteed by Fed. Agencies	109,404	111,178	84,977	35,537	48,008	18,352	14,119
Other Assets	73,355	71,103	69,357	67,424	64,920	62,657	46,950
TOTAL ASSETS*	$10,233,312	$9,377,944	$8,372,119	$7,356,655	$6,470,620	$5,713,040	$5,291,948

Liabilities and net worth	1979	1978	1977	1976	1975	1974	1973
Savings Accounts	$ 8,594,248	$7,947,899	$7,168,534	$6,344,152	$5,444,236	$4,635,407	$4,277,753
Borrowed Money*	698,532	606,983	461,445	375,534	449,888	551,187	487,563
FHLB Advances	620,529	535,446	388,228	347,806	427,723	518,745	464,294
Other	62,004	55,537	57,218	11,728	6,165	16,442	7,270
Debentures	16,000	16,000	16,000	16,000	16,000	16,000	16,000
Loans in Process	157,904	146,834	138,883	93,381	74,954	51,979	83,388
Specific Reserves	1,687	2,020	3,701	3,915	4,863	2,174	1,308
Deferred Credits	86,726	81,167	89,150	80,924	74,161	68,976	68,311
Other Liabilities	98,022	63,037	44,789	37,159	32,644	31,110	29,498
TOTAL LIABILITIES*	$ 9,637,119	$8,347,939	$7,906,502	$6,934,066	$6,080,746	$5,340,832	$4,947,822
New Worth							
Permanent Stock and Paid-in Surplus	$ 0	$ 0	$ 0	$ 0	$ 0	$ 0	$ 0
General Reserves	383,419	345,338	300,580	259,258	239,569	216,196	199,141
Other Reserves	2,070	2,073	2,008	2,107	2,267	1,329	3,050
Surplus and Undivided Profits	212,704	182,593	162,976	149,907	148,037	153,384	141,936
TOTAL NET WORTH*	$ 598,194	$ 530,003	$ 465,363	$ 431,271	$ 389,375	$ 372,208	$ 344,127
TOTAL LIABILITIES AND NET WORTH*	$10,235,312	$9,377,944	$8,372,119	$7,356,655	$6,470,620	$5,713,040	$5,291,948

* Indicates Subtotal or Total.

EXHIBIT 4
SOUTHERN FEDERAL SAVINGS AND LOAN ASSOCIATION INCOME AND EXPENSE:
ALL ASSOCIATIONS IN STATE, 1973–1979
(Thousands of $)

	1979	1978	1977	1976	1975	1974	1973
Gross Operating Income							
Interest*	$813,770	$692,693	$589,169	$509,808	$444,546	$404,456	$353,722
On Mortgage Loans	711,757	623,474	537,436	462,036	399,388	359,159	318,179
On Investment Securities & Deposits	78,441	51,726	36,792	34,982	33,695	33,439	24,754
Other	23,572	17,494	14,941	12,791	11,463	11,857	10,788
Fees and Discounts on Loans	32,264	36,232	36,173	30,305	25,307	20,389	23,777
All Other	27,443	23,263	19,375	17,581	8,213	6,685	6,517
TOTAL*	878,477	752,188	644,717	556,695	478,065	431,530	384,016
Operating Expense							
Compensation and Other							
Benefits	61,514	54,814	49,129	43,565	39,742	37,032	31,786
Office Occupancy	12,970	11,646	11,142	10,335	9,151	7,868	6,863
Advertising	8,981	6,942	6,189	6,340	6,751	7,788	7,650
Other	44,594	39,484	37,244	34,774	26,205	22,138	18,679
TOTAL*	128,058	112,885	103,705	95,015	81,848	74,827	64,979
Cost of Funds							
Interest on Savings Accounts	598,089	503,829	444,433	383,828	323,782	273,710	228,231
Interest on Borrowed Money	58,853	42,775	27,026	30,027	35,623	40,928	27,577
TOTAL*	656,942	546,604	471,458	413,855	359,405	314,637	255,808
Non-Operating Income	6,043	4,653	5,946	5,145	4,271	4,746	4,169
Non-Operating Expense	5,162	5,809	8,263	8,935	11,446	6,610	4,094
Income Taxes*	25,699	26,479	18,681	12,100	8,594	10,864	16,027
Federal	25,645	26,441	18,618	12,019	8,514	10,864	15,990
State, Local and Other	54	38	63	81	81	0	37
Net Income*	$ 68,658	$ 65,064	$ 48,556	$ 32,933	$ 21,043	$ 29,338	$ 47,277

* Indicates Subtotal or Total.

Not only had Southern Federal's savings and loan activities changed, but their base of operations had also grown rapidly through the establishment of new branches as seen in Exhibit 6. Redding explained their approach to branching:

We've been out at Eastside Mall for about 10 years. It was a matter of feeling like that was a good area out there. The banks were branching so we followed the banks out there and that's turned out to be a good spot.

We went out and set up another branch on South Rim Road Mall and that's been a mediocre spot. We then started looking outside South County; looked at about six neighboring counties. I went to the county courthouses and looked at the mortgage loan records. To the south of here, about 90 percent of the mortgage activity was Farm-Home Administration. I noticed a good bit of activity in counties west of us and, after studying the population growth and a few other demographics, selected Lakeview in Lake County. It was a good spot as far as loan volume and sales. We went to the River County, just south of us, because we heard someone else was going out there. Its been sort of a stepchild—its out there and doing about four million. I don't think you can get profitable until you reach six or seven million.

We then started questioning whether we were going to put in a computer with all these new things coming up, changes and running out of space. This building (the main office) was designed for 50 million dollars in business and leisurely living—so we have to chop around

EXHIBIT 5
SOUTHERN FEDERAL SAVINGS AND LOAN ASSOCIATION:
SOUTHERN FEDERAL'S MORTGAGE LOAN COMPOSITION (1973–1979)
(Thousands of $)

	Total mortgage loans including mtg. participations*	Total insured loans (VA, FHA, HUD)	Total conventional loans	Mortgage participations, mortgage-backed securities	Total single-family loans	Total multi-family loans	Other RE, improved RE, land loans, other
1979	$133,670	$2,933	$126,443	$3,536	$100,607	$14,753	$14,016
1978	123,196	3,018	116,000	3,869	88,147	13,771	17,100
1977	106,334	2,633	100,723	2,757	79,861	11,719	11,776
1976	87,165	2,022	81,825	3,130	65,096	9,051	9,699
1975	75,280	2,032	71,597	1,471	56,160	8,275	9,193
1974	64,501	1,574	61,881	1,021	47,033	7,765	8,656
1973	55,483	1,428	54,042	0	40,405	7,497	7,568
Percentage							
1979	100.0	.022	.946	.026	.753	.110	.105
1978	100.0	.024	.942	.031	.716	.112	.139
1977	100.0	.025	.947	.026	.751	.110	.111
1976	100.0	.023	.939	.036	.747	.104	.111
1975	100.0	.027	.951	.020	.746	.110	.122
1974	100.0	.024	.959	.016	.729	.120	.134
1973	100.0	.022	.974	.000	.728	.135	.136

* Individual loan types will not add to total mortgage loans because some loans appear in several categories.

EXHIBIT 6   SOUTHERN FEDERAL SAVINGS AND LOAN ASSOCIATION:
SOUTHERN FEDERAL'S DEPOSITS BY BRANCH OFFICE (1971–1979)
(Thousands of $)

	Main Office	Eastside Mall	South Rim Mall	Lake County	River County	Total
1979	$94,028	$26,112	$9,471	$8,875	$3,335	$141,821
1978	90,437	22,149	7,322	6,656	2,160	128,724
1977	83,448	17,673	5,060	4,450	886	111,517
1976	75,653	13,193	2,765	3,828	—	95,437
1975	65,016	10,663	1,257	1,282	—	78,218
1974	57,568	6,408	—	—	—	65,976
1973	53,866	2,664	—	—	—	56,530
1972	47,251	—	—	—	—	47,251
1971	38,382	—	—	—	—	38,382

on it until it began looking choppy. We thought about adding on, or raising the roof, or going down stairs or into the parking lot. We decided we would go out on North Highway with an operations office; then we decided to put a branch in it while we were there. The branch then kind of became the tail that wagged the dog—and it's a real nice branch. We sent a lady out there that had a big following in savings and she's done real well so far—it's just amazing. I think the location is good on the by-pass. You can come around town now on the new by pass in just no time. It's given a lot of convenience to that spot. We have space out there with a big basement, if we ever put in a computer.

In addition to the development of its branches, Southern Federal had also completed a recent merger with the Building and Loan Association of North County. In discussing the merger's background, Redding explained:

> We decided we wanted to play the big game. We'd been talking to the president of North County B&L and dealing with his people for a good ten years. It started when two associations wanted to move into the neighboring county and we both objected. At that time, someone suggested that North County B&L wasn't going to survive and rubbed his feathers the wrong way.
>
> Since that time, we kept an eye on North County's operation. Two years ago, they decided they would merge with us. It took a year and a half to finally get it consummated. That was a lot of work. The Home Loan Bank was mighty slow and we finally got some outside help. In the meantime, we had to worry with the thing up there, trying to get the salaries the same as ours—that's a big problem with a merger. You either have it too low or too high—kind of like the farmers, either too wet or too dry. That was the last State chartered association and it was a 14 million dollar outfit.

THE SOUTHERN COUNTY FINANCIAL MARKET

South County, located 65 miles from a major Southern metropolitan center, is part of the rapidly growing sunbelt and continues to attract new families. Housing starts in the South now represented over 40 percent of all housing starts in the U.S. as shown in Table 2.

South County lies just below the foothills of a scenic mountain range and was the site of one of the state's major educational institutions. Its social and cultural attractions to families of wealth were evident by the fine federal style homes and grand mansions with massive columns and beautiful formal gardens.

While South County was one of the smallest in the state, it was in the top seven percent of counties in population with over 80,000 residents. The city dominated the county with 55,000 residents and was the major retail center, drawing over 300,000 residents into its trading area. Over 100 manufacturers and processors employ over

TABLE 2 PRIVATE HOUSING STARTS, BY REGIONS

Region	Number of units				Percentage distribution			
	1975	1976	1977	1978*	1975	1976	1977	1978*
Northeast	149,200	169,200	201,600	200,000	12.9%	11.0%	10.1%	9.9%
North Central	294,000	400,100	464,600	449,500	25.3	26.0	23.4	22.3
South	442,100	568,500	783,100	924,100	38.1	37.0	39.4	40.8
West	275,100	399,600	537,900	544,900	23.7	26.0	27.1	27.0
Entire U.S.	1,160,400	1,537,500	1,987,100	2,018,500	100.0%	100.0%	100.0%	100.0%

Note: Components may not add to totals due to rounding.
* Preliminary.
Source: Bureau of the Census.

10,000 persons while four industrial parks continue to attract new industry. The
university, with over 18,000 students, provided over 9,000 full- and part-time jobs.

Continued growth in South County can be seen by the deposit base growth in
Exhibit 7. For example, deposits grew from $261 million in 1975 to $380 million in
1979, a 46 percent increase over the period. The two savings and loan associations
accounted for nearly 50 percent of the total having grown 68 percent since 1975. The
four area banks increased by only 27 percent during this period.

Southern Federal Savings and Loan is the largest financial institution in the area,
with over $130 million in deposits in 1979—a 34 percent share of the deposit market.
The Republic Bank held a 23 percent market share ($87 million) followed by the First
National Bank with 19 percent ($74 million) and First Federal Savings and Loan with

EXHIBIT 7   SOUTHERN FEDERAL SAVINGS AND LOAN ASSOCIATION: SUMMARY OF DEPOSITS IN
COMMERCIAL BANKS AND S&L ASSOCIATIONS IN SOUTH COUNTY (1974–1979)
(Thousands of $)

	Deposits in commercial banks			
	Total bank time and savings deposits	Total bank deposits	Total S&L deposits	Total bank and S&L deposits
1979	$95,234	$192,386	$187,631	$380,517
1978	80,535	179,942	175,523	355,465
1977	76,329	160,390	156,011	316,401
1976	72,917	150,843	123,219	283,062
1975	77,128	150,159	111,000	261,159
1974	54,521	151,609	93,487	245,096

	Demand deposits	Public demand deposits	Savings deposits	Other time deposits	Public time and savings	All other
1979	$75,349	$17,360	$25,603	$55,047	$14,584	$4,945
1978	69,263	25,265	25,153	42,848	12,534	4,879
1977	61,908	17,405	23,443	38,053	14,833	4,748
1976	58,282	14,997	19,713	42,664	10,540	4,647
1975	56,307	10,156	16,667	37,097	23,364	6,568
1974	54,364	36,901	14,310	40,211	0	5,823

	Savings and Loan Associations		Commercial banks	
	Number of associations	Number of offices	Number of banks	Number of offices
1980	2	6	4	14
1979	2	5	4	13
1978	2	5	4	10
1977	2	5	4	10
1976	2	5	3	9
1975	2	5	3	9
1974	2	4	3	9

15 percent ($58 million). First American Bank held only 7 percent of the market ($26.6 million) followed by a new 1977 entry, South Bank and Trust, which held only one percent ($5.5 million) in deposits by 1979.

Exhibit 8 shows a breakdown of all the financial institutions in South County. By 1979, they had all branched beyond the downtown shopping area into the new shopping malls—Eastside Mall, South Rim Mall, and Westgate Plaza. New branches were recently opened by First American and South Bank on the major throughway passing Eastside Mall. In fact, major growth was expected to occur beyond the Eastside Mall area as a regional shopping mall was to be built just beyond South County.

First National Bank had long-established branches across from Eastside Mall, in Westgate Plaza and University Avenue; but all these branches appeared to be losing business and be marginal operations. Republic Bank, the South County branch of a multibillion dollar regional bank, had growing locations downtown (near the university), on the street leading from downtown into the North Highway, in the Eastside Mall, and in South Rim Mall. Southern Federal S&L had growing branches in Eastside Mall and South Rim Mall. First Federal S&L had one branch in Westgate Plaza. First American Bank had just opened its first branch across from South Bank and Trust on the main highway out of town, as mentioned above.

Southern Federal's growth in the financial community had not been accidental. "Personally, I like to play the offense rather than the defense," explained Knight. "I guess I'm lazy—I think its easier." Adding new services had been part of their offense. Redding explained:

> We haven't gone overboard though. We've been in on a conservative basis: land development, condos, commercials, lot loans. A fella can buy a lot and we'll finance it, pay it out in five years.

MANAGING THE INVESTMENT PORTFOLIO

The loan committee at Southern Federal includes Knight, Redding and Bob Thompson. In describing their processing of loan applications, Redding explained:

> Surprisingly, the branches are kind of like laundry pickup stations. You leave the laundry there and it's brought down to the main office and washed. Branches are primarily for savings. They seldom take loan applications, except for North County. Folks come down to the main office to make loan applications. I guess they know that's where the answer is going to come from anyway and that's the way we operate—we bring them all in here for the loan committee meeting once or twice a week.
>
> We don't have any schedule here, we look at the calendar and set every third Tuesday or fourth Wednesday. We're only meeting once a week now with the loan volume off. We don't set a fixed schedule, but maybe that's wrong and we'll have to do that as we get bigger. I think the lending operation is just a kind of bull session. We have Bob Thompson in charge of the mortgage loan department, and taking applications. Occasionally, I'll take an application, too.

When Redding was asked why Southern Federal had done so well with its loan portfolio in limiting bad loans, he replied:

EXHIBIT 8 SOUTHERN FEDERAL SAVINGS AND LOAN ASSOCIATION: SUMMARY OF DEPOSITS FOR COMMERCIAL BANKS AND S&L ASSOCIATIONS IN SOUTH COUNTY BY BRANCH (1974–1979) (Thousands of $)

	First National Bank				
	Downtown	Eastside Mall	Westgate Plaza	University Ave.	Total
1979	$64,685	$ 3,979	$ 2,798	$2,048	$73,510
1978	64,398	3,815	2,738	1,992	72,943
1977	51,172	4,599	3,300	2,400	61,471
1976	25,842	14,357	11,485	5,743	57,427
1975	38,012	5,231	12,747	4,300	60,340
1974	35,442	11,623	9,168	4,758	60,991

	Republic Bank				
	Downtown	North Highway	Eastside Mall	South Rim Mall	University Extn.	Total
1979	$54,819	$14,317	$14,317	$6,615	0	$87,158
1978	51,197	8,841	12,033	4,744	—	76,815
1977	49,455	7,947	11,135	3,990	—	72,526
1976	50,658	7,704	9,825	3,215	—	71,402
1975	49,989	6,953	9,761	3,263	—	69,966
1974	52,711	6,404	8,884	2,404	—	70,403

	First American Bank		
	Downtown	Metropolitan Highway	Total
1979	$26,628	$108	$26,636
1978	26,008	—	26,008
1977	24,055	—	24,055
1976	22,014	—	22,014
1975	19,853	—	19,853
1974	20,215	—	20,215

Well, I guess inflation has saved most of us. I'd hate to be thrust in the business of making loans with no inflation. I don't know if we could survive or not. But then I think South County has been protected from the economic ups and downs with the university and the technical school here. It's been pretty steady. We haven't been hit hard. Although, as we get more industrialized, things like that will affect us more.

We're lending on about 80% residential property. Everybody has to have a house; a house is just basic, and this has been growing.

But during the recent escalation of home mortgage rates, Southern Federal pulled out of the residential market. Knight explained:

It worries us if we have to pull out of the mortgage business. In the 16 years that I've been here, we've only pulled out of mortgage lending one time and that was in the recent time with

EXHIBIT 8   *(Continued)*

South Bank and Trust

	Main	Metropolitan Highway	Total
1979	$5,079	$403	$5,482
1978	4,176	—	4,176
1977	2,338	—	2,338
1976	—	—	—
1975	—	—	—
1974	—	—	—

Southern Federal Savings and Loan

	Main	Eastside Mall	South Rim Mall	Total
1979	$94,028	$26,112	$9,471	$129,611
1978	90,437	22,149	7,322	119,908
1977	83,488	17,673	5,060	106,181
1976	75,653	13,193	2,763	91,609
1975	65,016	10,663	1,257	76,936
1974	57,568	6,408	—	63,976

First Federal Savings and Loan

	Main	Westgate Mall	Total
1979	$52,600	$5,419	$58,019
1978	51,390	4,225	55,615
1977	44,953	4,877	59,830
1976	38,310	3,300	41,610
1975	32,785	1,279	34,064
1974	29,242	269	29,511

the escalation of interest rates. You would come in and make an application to us and we would quote you a fair rate, but before we could get your loan processed and closed, we would be paying more for the money than the rate we quoted you. Well, it didn't take me too long to realize that we were playing a losing game here. So we said, "Until the dust settles, so to speak, we are going to pull out of mortgage lending. We got the money; but, we don't know what to quote you unless we quote a rate that is going to insult you. So right now we're just not going to make any quotes." So we pulled out for about 8 weeks, because it didn't make any sense.

We were taking that money and matching up six month money markets we were paying 14 percent—we were probably getting 16 percent on like terms through channels we could invest in. Now we got through that and we got back in and there was a backlog of loans. So we've been just as active as we could be for about the last eight weeks.

Regarding Southern Federal's success in its commercial loan involvement, Knight further explained:

We're going to be aggressive and go after business; but, when it doesn't look like its good business, we're going to back off. James Redding, who at times acts kind of radical, is really a conservative when it comes down to money and the way it goes out of here. After appraising one project, he said "They don't have enough income producing units. There is no way this thing can go!" Since that was a friend of mine, we dodged it by saying, "At this time, we don't believe we can appraise it for enough money to generate what you are asking for it." We didn't do it.

On big loans, like the local Holiday Inn, we felt that for our size we should sell half that loan. We also participated in another Holiday Inn, because we could get a 90 percent guarantee from Farmer's Home Administration. I think that's being aggressive in getting out and getting loans but, at the same time, we feel fairly secure.

But we miss 'em. If you don't occasionally make a mistake you're probably not making enough loans. You're ultra-conservative I'd say. Now hopefully that mistake will be in the realm where it takes time on somebody's part to work it out and wouldn't be a loss to the association. For example, you can have some problems when you make loans that depend on one person. Those are the kind where I say, "Well, we're going into business with this one." You don't want to make too many of those.

Redding commented on some of the loans they had missed:

We were offered all the new motels that came into town. The only one we took was the Holiday Inn. About six motels and 550 beds were added after we made that loan. Several have already sold out under duress or been foreclosed.

We never could understand the big apartment complexes either. They would come in here with the MAI appraisals that look good, projected rents that weren't in the market, with a hundred percent financing, and about everyone of them went under. We make apartment loans, but we never could get the big ones because we couldn't bid low enough. Everyone was foreclosed or sold under duress.

We did the Cambridge development and they came over here with that Riverbend East— gonna build about 70 homes and had them priced more than the Cambridge and we'd been struggling with Cambridge for more than three years—it wasn't a struggle, but it was slow. They were projecting 3,500 more people and I was about to believe all that stuff. Riverbend East went under. We just got outbid.

We stuck to the smaller units and we try to stick with the one or two house builders. It's like the paint contractor who was in here this morning. He said, "If I do a million dollars in paint work, I make $120,000. If I do half a million in paint work, I make $135,000. I just lose control." These guys can handle two houses, but when they get more—they get six— they just can't handle it; stealing material and laying down on the job.

In addition to Southern Federal's success in making loans, the association had also maintained fairly high levels of liquidity. Redding commented:

Our liquidity's been as low as 10 or 12 percent and once got up to about 20 percent. Some folks are used to operating at 7 or 8 percent but we have just never got comfortable with that.

When asked about Southern Federal's current liquidity level, Knight commented:

It depends on whether you look at net or gross liquidity. Gross involves money we owe on escrow, taxes, etc. It was 16.6% as of last Friday and Saturday on gross. It was 15.96% on net. It's conservative in one sense and it's just been good business. It made us a lot of money when interest rates got up to 17 and 18 percent. That's one way we stayed in the black, so we're pretty close to it all the time. Now we'd like to get that money out except—if we could get it out on RRM's, I'd be ready to shove it on out.

It concerns me when I see people putting their money in 6 month CD's and I'm letting that money go out for 25 or 29 years. It concerns me. How do I know but what this government of ours, in all their wisdom, is not going to come out with something else? They're not going to do it with the full intent of doing it, but we might lose several million dollars to Merrill Lynch or whoever, and how do I cover that? What do I do? They'll say, "Well, if you're in bad enough shape, you can borrow from the Federal Home Loan Bank on our terms."

As part of Southern Federal's liquidity management strategy, Redding also used the Home Loan Bank. He explained:

We use advances—those innercity advances—those subsidized deals. We borrowed when money got scarce back during the last crunch. We borrowed from the Home Loan Bank. We owe two million right now in reverse repos which is another way of borrowing; but, instead of selling stuff to cover the withdrawal of those Jumbos, we just borrow on a reverse repo and handle it that way. It's easy and we get a little better rate. Just pick up the phone and call them and make the deal.

You know, if you go sell something, you're not going to get the deal because they have to find somebody else in there who will do it. They just work on a closer margin with the reverse repo. We only use it on a short term basis for dividend payments or when something unexpected comes up.

In explaining the current investment strategy, Redding continued:

It was a management decision to keep liquidity high in order to cover our money market certificate rates which were high. Now we've jumped out and bought a little over one million in participations. The fact is that I'm going up to Rocky Mountain on Monday to look over what they've got.

I tried standbys but found out long ago that they weren't very good. You see, for a million dollars, you could get a 10 thousand dollar commitment fee for a six month standby at 10½% on a Ginny Mae. It was an insurance hedge by people putting together packages of Ginny Maes. They would give the builder a commitment at 10% and if things didn't work out and rates went to 11%, everyone was happy and they would stick me with 10½% when rates were 11%. If it went to 10½% or lower, they wouldn't put it to me, and I would make my one percent or $10,000. Well that looked good and I did that a few times with half a million or so. But then I realized that you couldn't plan your liquidity management, not knowing if someone was going to call on you or not, to fund these things. So I quit.

Some S&L's and pension funds got to buying them. Twenty-five million at one percent is $250,000. Well $250,000 commitment fees for an association of 35 million dollars would be .7 percent. That's what most of them netted, if that, so the profit picture looked good with descending mortgage rates. Then the damn market turned over the last two years and the standbys were being put to them. They caught one or two in Georgia. One association of about $25 million committed $20 million. The pension fund in Houston got caught. All these hustlers were selling this stuff. I learned early that wasn't the way to go.

We bought Ginny Maes. I bought a package of Ginny Mae Mobile Homes the other day at 11½%, if it pays out on the average of six years—or whatever the life of them. But I just try to match up the liquidity.

When asked about the nature of Southern Federal's deposit structure, Redding explained:

We've been going after money market certificates, but, of course, this last month has turned around. The six month money market was about 38 percent of $66 million. Two and a half year money markets were seven percent and growing. The 7½% CD's is about 20 percent and decreasing. The regular passbook is about 14 percent and dropping.

We've been caught like everyone else, borrow short and lend long. But if the trend continues, we'll probably work out of it by the end of the year.

PLANNING FOR DEREGULATION

To continue its leading role in their financial community, Southern Federal planned to adjust to the changing environment, as Redding explained:

If it's going to be like it was in the old days, taking in savings and lending it out on houses, then you have to have the most attractive savings account in town or else they'll leave it somewhere where they can get other services and a checking account. So when they take off the differential, we're going to have to make ourselves just as attractive as the next place.

You have things like nice tellers, friendly people, pretty buildings, and good locations; but still you've got to have the services available. This is what we're just forced to do. It seems like looking at the future we just have no choice. We put in lock boxes at two branches; travelers checks for whatever good that was; money orders; we transfer money by phone for big accounts. What else can we offer? The NOW accounts, automobile loans, and consumer ''help momma get the icebox financed'' loans. But we'll be staying away from the commercial end of it.

But it's going to take a hell of a lot more people. I don't see how we'll be able to make money unless that consumer lending lets you really stick 'em. Had a quote this morning though. We quoted 17% APR, Republic was 14, the First National was, I think, 13. So we're out of the market. We thought we were entitled to that much on a smaller loan, but we're not, maybe we're making too much.

Hours of operation is another question. At North County we're closed on Wednesday afternoon and open Saturday morning. It's just five days a week, here. We close at four. Most of the banks are open on Saturday mornings. Whether we'll have to change to that for some branches in South County at some point in time is another question.

Southern Federal was also considering RRM's—rollover rate mortgages. Knight explained:

I'm just wondering if these 12 percent loans we're putting on the books today are good loans. We're getting top interest rates right now because loan activity is very good. We've done well in the last six or eight weeks. It's been hot. But is that a good loan for the association ten or 15 years down the road with almost universally expected 10 percent annual inflation for the decade of the 80's? If that's true, that's a poor loan to be putting on the books today.

But I don't think it will be easy to sell RRM's. People don't like to change—I want a fixed rate and know what it's going to be for the next 25 or 29 years, because you all might change something and I don't trust the government—I hear all these things. And from the standpoint of competition. First Investors is in the secondary mortgage business and that's what they do. I assume they will stay with fixed rates as long as they can sell them, so how do you combat that? We don't want to switch all our business over to First Investors. Republic will probably do about the same thing because they're strong in the secondary mortgage business. I don't think we'll be too concerned about First Federal.

LOOKING AT THE FUTURE

With continued deregulation and competition at the South County area, Southern Federal was concerned about its future actions. Redding explained:

Well, we worry about the competition with banks. That's the main thing once you take all the differential off. We're twice as big as the First National and the Republic—I think they run about half our size. I don't know what's going to happen when we get into the NOW account business. We'll soon be $200 million in assets. That ought to be something we can work with. We have a net worth of $10 or $11 million. With forts or branches around us, we can pretty much do anything; but, it's going to take a lot of people and a lot of scurrying about and a lot of expense.

We've talked about going into metropolitan areas, but getting it done is just too much right now. You just wonder about the logistics of it, or the ability to compete over there, or the cost of start-up in that high rent area. I don't know. One county has had a lot of racial problems and nobody is moving down there—we'd move up into the growth area.

I looked at the operating statements of some of the S&L's, wondering if any of them were getting tired and wanting to merge. I've toyed with the idea of just going it from a mortgage banking standpoint, opening something over there.

Expansion of Southern Federal's branch operations would probably not be necessary in the near future. Knight explained:

The North Highway branch turns out to be a great location. It has shifted our business from Eastside Mall and downtown and that is what we wanted. We had been having trouble waiting on the numbers of people we had in the manner in which we liked to wait on them. After looking at alternatives for two years, it was decided that, even though we didn't need another branch, another branch located in the right place would take pressure off this office and Eastside Mall. They had a constant stream of cars and would probably need another drive-in window. That's not necessary now.

A savings and loan association near Lakeview had just approached Southern Federal regarding possible merger. Knight explained:

The future of this association doesn't promise as much as it did in North County, because North County is more of a growth county than the Lake County area has been. I don't see how it is going to pick up all that much.

This association got anxious when they ran out of money. They haven't made a loan since last fall. But they had made a million dollars in loans in the previous year which had drained them. That's a problem.

It's a nice building; an old brick bank building that you feel good about. You won't have to go build an office. I think I'll let the board help decide this one. It's not one I'm going to jump up and down and crack my heels for.

I think that with NOW accounts and consumer loans, it could give us another office. That would give us a circle in the northeast part of the state.

Redding and Knight had also discussed the possibility of going public. With regards to taking Southern Federal public, Redding picked up a copy of a Savings and Loan magazine advertisement and explained:

We've discussed going public and I've cut out this ad: ''If an S&L goes public, it needs Schroders!'' Well, I thought I'd write that fat fellow there and see what he had to say. You know, it's pro and con. I talked to an outfit in the Orlando area—they're going public. He said the key people got a five year contract so, if somebody wanted to take them over they'd have to take them over with a five year contract. Whether he's speaking the truth or not, I don't know.

If you put a lot of effort in here, you feel like you ought to be able to take some of it with you. A mutual doesn't have that. You can go Federal, but it takes a year and a half or two years. I'm thinking of converting back to state when they get the state laws changed and it might be a heck of a lot easier to go stock with a state law.

Knight continued:

We're going to look at the stock form a little bit here. I think it has some promise. But it's not going to be me—somebody else is going to have to do that. It's going to be a lot of work to get into that. I think Redding is more or less fascinated by it. It has some dangers in it. If you get into that, you'll have a lot of people to deal with—they'll come in here and shake their finger at you and have the right to do it.

DISCUSSION QUESTIONS

1 Contrast the regulatory changes which began to affect the savings and loan industry in 1980 with those from 1968 through 1977 in terms of their strategic impact on the savings and loan industry.

2 Describe the changes which have occurred on the loan side and the saving side of Southern Federal's business from 1973 through 1979. In your view, how has this changed the earnings prospects for Southern Federal?

3 Calculate the major leverage ratios and liquidity ratios for Southern Federal for 1979 and explain why they might be allowed to differ so drastically from those of other kinds of businesses.

4 Explain how inflation has helped Southern Federal in limiting bad loans despite admittedly poor lending practices.

5 How serious is the maturity matching problem (borrowing short and lending long) and what should Southern Federal do to alleviate it.

6 Explain the advantages and disadvantages of Southern Federal remaining a mutual company.

7 Should Southern Federal seek a merger candidate? Attempt to "go public"? Explain your answers.

THE JAPANESE: A NEW MARKET FOR SADANA SHOES

Jim D. Barnes
Brenda J. Moscove
California State College, Bakersfield

Paula M. Alden
University of Honolulu

SELECTED STRATEGIC ISSUES

- Effect of traditions and policies on expansion
- Organization form and distribution channels for international business
- The impact of host company trade practices on foreign ventures
- Pricing strategy for entry into foreign markets
- Discovering and adapting to cultural differences
- Short- and long-term aspects of strategy making

Sometime in April of 1979, Mr. Nosaka visited the Sadana of California shoe factory, located in San Diego, California. Mr. Nosaka had noticed the popularity of Sadana's sandals in southern California and thought they would fit in with the merchandise he carried in his women's apparel shops in Tokyo. He bought from the available stock in the factory and took the shoes back to Japan with him. Evidently, he had made a wise purchase, because in May, he was calling the Sadana representative in Honolulu, Hawaii, from Tokyo, to inform him that he would be arriving in Honolulu on the fifteenth of June and would like to see what the representative had in available stock. The Hawaii sales rep for Sadana, Lloyd Suzuki, had heard about Mr. Nosaka's visit to the factory, but was still surprised to hear from him. Both had a little communication problem, which tended to be exaggerated due to a fuzzy long-distance connection. Mr.

Jim D. Barnes was Chair and Professor of Marketing at the School of Business Administration, California State College, Bakersfield. Brenda J. Moscove is currently Chair and Professor of Marketing, California State College, Bakersfield. Paula M. Alden is an MBA graduate from Chaminade University of Honolulu.

Nosaka was discussing in English, which is not his native tongue. Though he is quite articulate and though of Japanese ancestry, Mr. Suzuki does not speak Japanese.

Mr. Suzuki attended a sales meeting in Los Angeles during the first week of June and mentioned Mr. Nosaka's call to his boss, the president of Sadana, Mr. Thomas Sadana. They began discussing the possibility of Mr. Suzuki looking into the Japanese market in addition to his present territory. Geographically, it would be most appropriate to have the Hawaii representative, who also worked Guam, represent Sadana in Japan. Since neither man had dealt with Japan or any other foreign market before, there was a certain amount of apprehension involved, especially since there seemed to be so many cultural differences. Mr. Suzuki began investigating the Japanese market and developing a plan to export shoes to Japan for presentation to the company president at the September sales meeting.

THE COMPANY

Sadana of California came into being fifty-four years ago when Thomas Sadana's father, an immigrant, began making shoes at home. Sadana has since grown into one of the leaders in the junior and young women's fashion shoe market, especially on the West Coast. The family-owned company claimed net sales of $12 million for the first six months of 1979 and expected to double that figure by the end of the year. Sadana's factory in Southern California manufactures its entire line of shoes which is more the exception rather than the rule in the American shoe industry. This gives the company great versatility in keeping in step with the constantly changing fashions because its factory of 1,000 employees can make almost every style of shoe without depending on outside contracting or importing of materials and parts. While Sadana is doing very well in the young fashion market, partly because its merchandise is priced competitively or, in some cases, even less than the competition, the industry itself is highly competitive and every company in the industry is interested in developing new markets. Exhibit 1 summarizes the trends and characteristics of the company as perceived by the president.

THE JAPANESE MARKET

Japan has become the second largest consumer market in the world with a Gross National Product in 1977 of $696.2 billion. In that same year, Japan's total population stood at 114 million making it the sixth most populous nation in the world, with one of the world's highest population densities at 306 per square kilometer.[1] Japan is situated off the eastern coast of the Asian continent and consists of four major islands, as well as thousands of smaller islands.

In 1946, after World War II, the Japanese, with a new Constitution, adopted a democratic form of government. The Emperor became merely a symbol of the state, while the National Diet was established as the supreme organ of the government. For a

[1] *Japan, A Pocket Guide*. Tokyo: Foreign Press Center, 1979.

EXHIBIT 1   TRENDS AND CHARACTERISTICS OF SADANA

						Net sales (in thousands)							
	1970	1971	1972	1973	1974	1975	1976	1977	1978	1979	1980	1981	1982	1983
Actual Net Sales	9,000	8,000	7,000	6,000	4,000	6,000	8,000	12,000	16,000	12,000 (6 mos)				
Estimated Net Sales										24,000 (year)	36,000	46,000	60,000	75,000

Financial capabilities

1 Finance growth through earnings and
2 Finance growth through increased funds from EDA (Economic Development Administration)
3 Plan to triple sales volume in next 4 years

	Executive group		
Title	**Age**	**Title**	**Age**
President	62	Head Bookkeeper	50
Vice President:		Head Production	45
Sales & Design	31	Head Pattern Department	40
Sales & Purchasing	29	Head Credit	40
Financial	50	Foremen (8)	35–40 (mostly under 40)
Manufacturing	50	Salespersons (15)	35 or less (10 persons)
		36–67 (5 persons)	

Recruiting personnel
1 Develop most of own talent
2 Use employment companies in special cases

Labor force
1 1,000 employees
2 800 (80% on incentive basis)
3 Will provide training

Sales force
1 15 full-time salespersons
2 2 co-sales managers
3 Size has increased 300% in last 10 years

Research and development
1 10 full-time staff members
2 Size has increased 500% in last 10 years
3 Efforts emphasize "molding of bottoms" for product

Product mix
1 Junior and young women shoes styled for Sun Belt and Western states
2 Leaders in molded bottoms to enhance styling, comfort, and wear
3 Prices less or competitive with comparable shoes exported to U.S.A.

Market share
1 Market share heavier in West Coast than in Sun Belt
2 % of share not determined

Target market
1 Junior and young women
2 West Coast and Sun Belt states

Advertising
1 Trade periodicals
2 Newspaper ads placed by retailers

Complaints and returns
1 Normal amount of customer complaints and returns
2 Worn shoe returns less than 1%
3 Customers claim product well made, priced reasonably, sells well
4 Excellent goodwill with customers

Materials used
1 Leather for uppers, linings and sock linings from U.S., India, England, Argentina, Brazil
2 Other materials: soles, tapes, bindings, cements, thread, nails, screws, steel shanks, reinforcing material, cleaning solutions, solvents, shoe boxes, cartons, tissue

Production and equipment
1 Make own patterns, dies, last, molds for last, models for metal molds for injection molding machines
2 Mold own bottoms, heels, soles, and toplifts
3 Versatile in manufacturing

country that was ravaged by the war, Japan made a tremendous recovery regaining pre-war levels by the early 1950's and continuing its high development of economic growth through the 1960's. Japan registered its first negative growth since the war after the oil crisis in 1973. However, the economy again demonstrated its resilience; and, though the market has not completely pulled out of its slump, unemployment has been held at just over 2%. In 1978, the Japanese government announced that it planned to reach a growth target that year of 7%. However, the steep appreciation of the yen slowed down exports and increased imports, which in turn was expected to bring the GNP to about 6%. The momentum of economic recovery had been slowed by the great reduction of the U.S. dollar compared to the relative rise of the yen.[2] Exhibits 2 and 3 summarize national and comparative statistics for Japan.

THE JAPANESE CONSUMER

With a population of over 114 million and taste patterns continually becoming more Western, the Japanese are an interesting and attractive market. The market is basically middle class and tends to be young, with more than half the population under thirty years old, according to the statistics of the Ministry of Welfare. Eighty-four percent of the current population lives in urban areas and is concentrated in the cities of Tokyo, Osaka, Nagoya, and Kitakyushu. Japan's standard of living is comparable to that of most European countries, with the main difference existing in the lower levels of housing standards. With over thirty percent of the Gross National Product re-invested into industry, the area of housing had been severely neglected and housing loans very difficult to obtain until recently. Owning a home is a dream which may never be realized by many Japanese with the high cost of land and construction; therefore, a greater emphasis seems to be placed on making the crowded living conditions more pleasant.[3] While the average Japanese desires to acquire more luxury goods and further improve his/her standard of living, he/she is also a good saver, putting away about three times more than the average American, relative to personal income.

There is a great homogeneity in tastes and ways of thinking in Japan, with a strong feeling of group unity carrying over from the Tokugawa period when Japan was isolated from the rest of the world and the government imposed a restriction on movement about the countryside. The Confucian influences of the Tokugawa regime are retained today in the Japanese values of filial piety, working for the general good of the people, and a great respect for wisdom and education. This interest in education is shown in the very high literacy rate in Japan and an almost 100 percent attendance in the schools. The same religious attitudes are also shared by the general population with the two major religions being Buddhism and Shinto, which tend to overlap and be practiced alongside each other. Shinto, which developed as a national folk religion, conducts the rites that celebrate birth and marriage, while Buddhist ceremonies are performed at funerals and memorial services.

[2] Ibid. Tokyo: Foreign Press Center, 1979, pp. 37–8.
[3] *The Japanese Consumer*. Japan External Trade Organization, JETRO Marketing Series 6.

EXHIBIT 2 NATIONAL STATISTICS FOR JAPAN

Land Area: 372,313 sq km

General indicators	Unit base	1973	1974	1975	1976
Population (mid-year)	Mn	108.35	109.67	110.95	112.77
Growth rate	%	1.3	1.2	1.2	1.1
Labour force	000	53,660	53,100	53,230	53,780
Employed (ratio)	%	98.8	98.6	98.1	98
Unemployed (ratio)	%	1.2	1.4	1.9	2.0
Electricity production	Mn kWh	370,819	381,420	374,303	406,995
Public roads	000 km	1,049.7	1,059.1	1,066.0	—
Motor vehicles registered	000	24,630.0	26,319.3	28,900.0	—
Student enrollment:	Mn				
Up to secondary		20.92	21.33	21.78	—
Post-secondary		1.91	3.04	2.15	—
Hospital beds	000	1,125.6	1,147.0	—	—
Medical doctors registered		124,684	126,822	—	—
Telephone installed	000	34,021	38,698	41,905	43,300
Tourists arrivals		784,691	764,246	811,672	881,203
Housing construction starts	000 sq m	152,421	114,123	120,402	134,064
Economic performance indicators					
NATIONAL ACCOUNTS (CY)	Yen Bn				(3rd quarter)
GNP, market prices (mp)		111,061.0	132,472.8	144,865.2	164,419.6
GNP, 1970 mp		90,849.8	89,796.0	91,662.5	97,499.2
Gross domestic capital formation		44,285.9	50,673.7	46,598.8	—
INDEX OF PRODUCTION	1970 = 100				
Mining		82.2	77.3	72.8	73.1
Manufacturing		130.0	123.8	110.1	125.3
Composite		129.5	123.3	109.7	124.8
EXTERNAL TRADE (CY)	US$ Mn				
Trade balance		−1,384	−6,574	−2,110	2,426
Exports		36,930	55,536	55,755	67,225
Machinery and equipment		20,365	27,891	30,004	39,627
Metal and metal products		6,821	13,691	12,518	13,170
Iron and steel		5,304	10,758	10,176	10,485
Chemicals		2,147	4,059	3,889	3,747
Motor vehicles		3,612	5,227	6,190	8,903
Imports		38,314	62,110	57,863	64,799
Mineral fuels		8,327	24,895	25,641	28,287
Crude oil		6,000	18,898	19,644	21,185
Metal ore and scrap		4,033	5,328	4,417	4,579
Machinery and equipment		3,486	4,748	4,286	4,608
Coal		1,354	2,864	3,454	3,560

Source: Business Asia, p. 160.

EXHIBIT 3   COMPARATIVE KEY INDICATORS

Area and population

Country	Area (km²)	Mid-year population (in millions)					Average annual growth rate (%) 1973–77	Density mid-1977 (Persons/km²)
		1973	1974	1975	1976	1977*		
Hong Kong	1,046	4.21	4.32	4.40	4.44	4.51	1.7	4,315.5
Indonesia	1,904,345	124.60	127.60	130.60	133.70	136.91	2.4	71.9
Korea (R.O.K.)	98,758	34.10	34.69	35.28	35.86	36.44	1.7	369.0
Malaysia	329,749	11.31	11.81	11.92	12.24	12.56	2.7	38.1
Philippines	300,000	39.96	41.07	42.26	43.44	44.66	2.8	148.9
Singapore	602	2.19	2.22	2.25	2.28	2.31	1.3	3,837.2
Taiwan (R.O.C.)	35,981	15.43	15.71	16.00	16.29	16.66	1.9	463.0
Thailand	542,373	39.63	40.74	41.87	43.00	44.16	2.8	81.4
Japan	372,438	108.71	110.05	111.93	112.78	113.88	1.2	305.7

Note: * Provisional.

Per capita GNP and average annual growth rates (IBRD estimates)

Country	Per capita GNP at market prices (current US$)			Annual real growth rate of per capita GNP (%) 1970–75	Total GNP at market price	
	1974	1975	1976*		1975	1976*
					(current US$ mn)	
Hong Kong	1,610	1,760	2,110	4.2	7,700	9,410
Indonesia	200	220	240	3.5	29,120	32,440
Korea (R.O.K.)	480	560	670	8.2	19,850	24,050
Malaysia	720	760	860	5.3	9,340	10,900
Philippines	340	380	410	3.7	15,930	17,810
Singapore	2,170	2,450	2,700	7.3	5,500	6,150
Taiwan (R.O.C.)	850	930	1,070	5.7	14,890	17,500
Thailand	310	350	380	3.6	14,600	16,230
Japan	4,040	4,450	4,910	4.0	496,260	553,140

Note: * Provisional.

Growth rates of real products (percent)

Country	Base	1973	1974	1975	1976	1977
Hong Kong	GDP, 1966 mp	14.2	2.2	2.9	16.9	11.6
Indonesia	GDP, 1973 mp	11.3	7.6	5.0	7.0	7.5*
Korea (R.O.K.)	GDP, 1970 mp	17.1	8.8	8.8	15.0	9.8
Malaysia	GDP, 1970 fc	12.3	6.7	3.5	12.0	7.7
Philippines	GDP, 1972 mp	8.7	5.3	6.6	7.3	5.8
Singapore	GDP, 1968 mp	11.5	6.3	4.0	7.5	8.0
Taiwan (R.O.C.)	GDP, 1971 mp	12.0	0.6	3.1	11.8	8.0
Thailand	GDP, 1962 mp	10.3	4.6	7.7	8.2	6.2
Japan	GNP, 1970 mp	9.9	1.1	2.1	6.0	5.8

Note: * Provisional.

EXHIBIT 3   (*Continued*)

Country	General index of manufacturing production (1970 = 100)				
	1973	1974	1975	1976	1977
Hong Kong	—	—	—	—	—
Indonesia (1)	—	—	100.0	100.8	—
Korea (R.O.K.)	183.8	237.5	283.6	384.6	438.9
Malaysia	144.1	165.3	166.4	197.8	227.6
Philippines	154.1	138.3	134.3	140.0	145.6
Singapore (2)	96.0	100.0	98.0	108.2	116.4
Taiwan (R.O.C.)	185.3	180.3	188.4	236.9	262.2
Thailand	—	—	—	—	—
Japan	127.3	123.3	109.7	124.7	130.5

Notes: (1) 1975 = 100. (2) 1974 = 100.

Country	Electricity production (mn kwh)				
	1973	1974	1975	1976	1977
Hong Kong	6,809	6,722	7,374	8,342	9,451
Indonesia	2,932	3,246	3,345	—	—
Korea (R.O.K.)	14,826	16,835	19,837	23,118	26,587
Malaysia	4,481	4,971	5,408	6,025	—
Philippines	8,718	8,838	9,615	10,429	—
Singapore	3,719	3,864	4,176	4,605	5,115
Taiwan (R.O.C.)	19,805	20,536	22,894	26,877	29,724
Thailand	7,329	7,789	8,866	10,295	—
Japan	468,511	460,705	—	—	—

Source: Business Asia.

DOING BUSINESS IN JAPAN

Before embarking on any business venture in Japan, it would be wise to consult with auditors and lawyers, well versed in the language as well as the business practices, in regard to interpreting accurately and correctly the various Japanese regulations and procedures. Effective in 1976, Japanese regulations concerning capital investment were liberalized and a foreigner may now own 100% of an investment in Japan, with the only exceptions being certain primary and defense industries. Formal approval is required by the proper agency to establish a new enterprise in Japan or to purchase shares in an existing firm. Application for investment must be approved by the Bank of Japan, as well as screened by the ministry that has jurisdiction over the industry. This most recent liberalization of capital investments in Japan represents a very substantial change in Japan's policy towards the inflow of foreign capital, despite continuation of a small number of remaining restrictions.

There are various modes of entry into the Japanese business scene, the Kabushiki Kaisha, K.K. or Limited Stock Company, being the most common form, which is similar to the American corporation. Other modes of entry are: Yugen Kaisha, Gomei

Karsha, Goshi Karsha, Sole Proprietorship[4] and liaison office.[5] See Exhibit 4 for a description of each type of major organization.

Other methods of entering Japanese business also exist. The establishment of a branch or sales office for the purpose of taking orders and overseeing marketing operations in Japan has been free for quite some time; however, under the new set of regulations, the distinction between a sales office and manufacturing facility has been minimized. Setting up a sales office for the purpose of importing into Japan and marketing products currently comes under the heading of wholesaling and trading. When a sales office is set up for the purpose of importing or exporting goods, it is regarded as a trading enterprise and must be registered with the government. Because of a revenue flow, an office of this type must file a report with the tax authorities on an annual or semi-annual basis and pay taxes according to the prescribed computation formulas.

As was mentioned earlier, the foreign investor may directly invest in manufacturing facilities for all but a few industries. The foreign investor establishing manufacturing facilities in Japan, nevertheless, must comply with Japanese regulations regarding factory location, pollution control and the like. The proper reports must be filed with the tax authorities and the Ministry of Justice. If the manufactured goods are for the Japanese market, they are subject to the authority of the Japanese Fair Trade Commission; and corporate income taxes will be assessed at the national, prefectual and

[4] U.S. Department of Commerce. *Marketing in* Japan, prepared by T. A. Miyakawa. OBR 78-16. Washington: Government Printing Office, April, 1978.

[5] *Operating a Business in* Japan. Japan External Trade Organization, JETRO Business Information Series 1.

EXHIBIT 4   METHOD OF ENTRY INTO BUSINESS IN JAPAN

	Investment application screened by industry ministry and approved by the Bank of Japan					
Specifications	Kabushiki Kaisha (K.K.) or limited stock company	Yugen Kaisha (Y.K. or private limited company)	Gomei Kaisha (Unlimited liability partnership)	Goshi Kaisha (limited liability partnership)	Sole proprietorship	Liaison office
Requirements and Restrictions	7 or more promoters or incorporators (judicial entities or natural persons). Notary fees, registration tax (% of capital legal fees. 1 or more statutory auditors annual balance sheet)	Limitations on shareholding by foreigners	Partnership limited to natural persons. Partners have joint and unlimited liability	1 or more partners with liabilities limited to capital contributed and additional partners with unlimited liability. Limited partners cannot participate in management. Must specify liabilities of partners in incorporation forms. Trade name must include words "Goshi Kaisha"	1 individual engaging in business practice. High tax rate.	Temporary purpose of providing information about Japanese market or business contacts. No revenue in Japan. Salaries remitted from home office to Japan
Frequency of use among foreign investors	Most common form	Not used by foreign investors			Not usual for foreign investors	

municipal levels. Foreign investment in corporations in Japan regarded as domestic corporations is liable for taxes on its worldwide income.[6]

JAPANESE IMPORT REGULATIONS

Japan is continually attempting to further liberalize her foreign importing system; however, certain commodities remain on the Ministry of International Trade and Industry's (MITI) list of "non-liberalized items," which are subject to the Import Quota System (IQ). An importer must apply to MITI for an import quota allocation certificate to be able to import any of those items covered by the Import Quota system. All other items may be imported freely, but an importer must "declare" his/her intention to import a commodity to a foreign exchange bank.

Unfortunately for the foreign shoe exporter, hides and leather products are included in the list of "non-liberalized items." The Japanese feel that the items under the residual import restriction cannot be liberalized in this instance because the tanning and leather-product manufacturing industries are notably weak in their international competitiveness since Japan lags behind other nations in leather dressing techniques. Historically, those involved in these industries formed closed communities which are characteristically not modern in aspects such as information-gathering, material purchasing, equipment, merchandising, production, and pollution prevention. The major problem facing these industries is their inferior business management ability resulting in firms with extremely fragile business foundations.[7] See Exhibits 5 and 6 for charts on the Import Trade Control System and Customs Clearance Formalities.

IMPORT TARIFF SYSTEM

Japan's Customs Tariff is administered by the Ministry of Finance through its Customs Bureau. Under the Customs Tariff Law, the value for customs assessment is the price of the goods sold in ordinary wholesale quantity and in the ordinary course of trade in the exporting country at the time of exportation, plus freight, insurance, and other incidental costs incurred in connection with the shipment. The dutiable value for air shipments is usually determined on the basis of transportation other than air. Most duties are levied on an ad valorem basis, which is the price of the merchandise; consequently, the lower the prices on the imported goods, the lower the amount of the customs tariff levied. With the Japanese yen on the rise, the amount of tax imposed on imported goods has become lower today creating favorable conditions for the sale of imported items, especially those with prestigious brand names.

Ninety-two percent of all tariff items are charged on an ad valorem basis; however, for some commodities the import rate is a specific one.[8] For a few commodities, the tariff prescribes both an ad valorem and a specific rate giving the customs official the

---

[6] U.S. Department of Commerce. *U.S. Export Opportunities to Japan.* Washington: Government Printing Office, August, 1978.

[7] *Exporters' Guide.* Japan External Trade Organization, JETRO International Business Information Center, 1978, p. 3–4.

[8] Ibid, p. 37.

EXHIBIT 5   SCHEME FOR THE IMPORT TRADE CONTROL SYSTEM
                              (with Foreign Exchange)

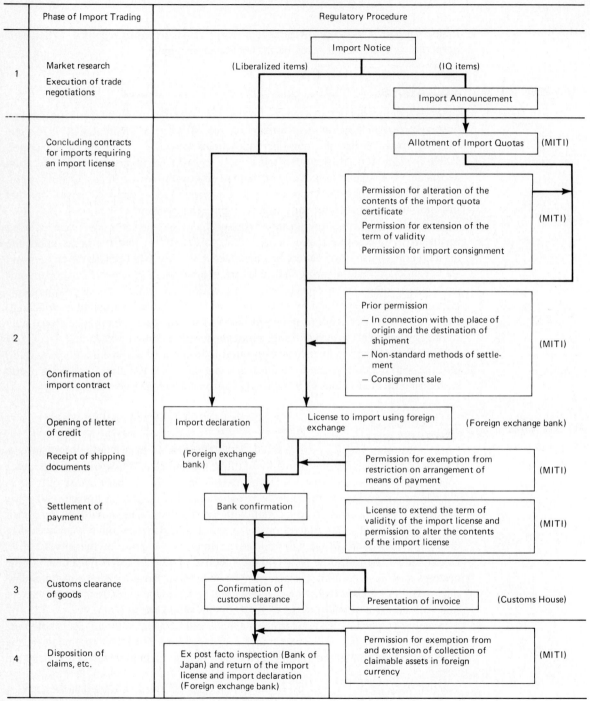

Phase of Import Trading	Regulatory Procedure

1 — Market research / Execution of trade negotiations

Import Notice
(Liberalized items)   (IQ items)
Import Announcement

2 — Concluding contracts for imports requiring an import license

Allotment of Import Quotas   (MITI)

Permission for alteration of the contents of the import quota certificate
Permission for extension of the term of validity
Permission for import consignment   (MITI)

Prior permission
— In connection with the place of origin and the destination of shipment
— Non-standard methods of settlement
— Consignment sale   (MITI)

Confirmation of import contract

Opening of letter of credit

Import declaration   License to import using foreign exchange   (Foreign exchange bank)

Receipt of shipping documents

(Foreign exchange bank)

Permission for exemption from restriction on arrangement of means of payment   (MITI)

Settlement of payment

Bank confirmation

License to extend the term of validity of the import license and permission to alter the contents of the import license   (MITI)

3 — Customs clearance of goods

Confirmation of customs clearance   Presentation of invoice   (Customs House)

4 — Disposition of claims, etc.

Ex post facto inspection (Bank of Japan) and return of the import license and import declaration (Foreign exchange bank)

Permission for exemption from and extension of collection of claimable assets in foreign currency   (MITI)

Notes: 1. Offices in parenthesis represent the authorities with which an application or declaration should be made.
        2. MITI stands for the Ministry of International Trade and Industry.

Source: Exporter's Guide, JETRO, p. 8.

EXHIBIT 6 CUSTOMS CLEARANCE FORMALITIES

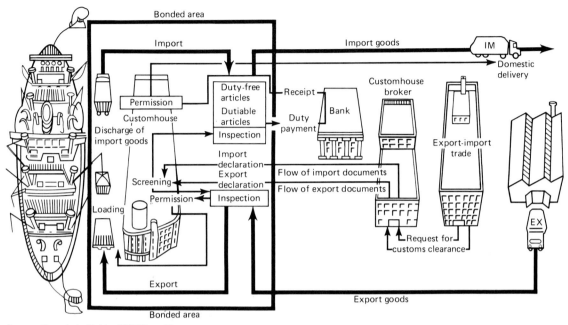

Source: Exporter's Guide, JETRO, p. 80.

option of assessing which ever duty yields the higher revenue. Duties are payable in the Japanese yen effective at whatever the official exchange rate may be. According to the most recent Table of Standard Import Quotas and Tariffs for Japan, leather products are assessed on an ad valorem basis of 30 percent of wholesale price plus freight.

THE DISTRIBUTION AND SALES CHANNELS

The distribution system in Japan is sometimes described overseas as a "nontariff barrier" and as an obstacle to the successful entry of overseas producers to the Japanese market. Despite these criticisms, a large number of companies have successfully established a market position in Japan by the use of distribution channels set up by import agents and trading companies, tie-ups with manufacturers of similar but noncompetitive products, and by establishing their own distribution channels.

A more apt description of Japan's distribution system would be a highly developed system which has evolved to satisfy the requirements of the fragmented retailing sector in Japan. Generally, the smaller the scale of the manufacturer and the smaller the size of the retail outlet, the larger the number of distribution intermediaries required which is also not uncommon in the U.S. Different modes of entry have been successful for different products. Considering all possible alternatives in detail and screening the potential import agents and tie-up partners with equal care is of key importance to the overseas manufacturer contemplating entry into the Japanese market.

Direct sales contacts between Japanese end-users and foreign producers are not common. In many cases, the average small Japanese manufacturer lacks the financial resources, the technical competence to import products, and/or the ability to communicate in a foreign language. Because of unfamiliarity with the Japanese language and market, most Americans have also been content to leave the importation and distribution of their products to trading companies. On occasion, an American firm may appoint a Japanese manufacturer of complementary equipment as its agent to take advantage of the natural compatibility of both firms' products and utilize the Japanese firm's distribution network. Direct sales operations at the wholesale and the retail levels through subsidiaries or branches may be quite feasible, assuming the U.S. seller is able to hire competent Japanese to assist in making the sales presentation and there are no governmental restrictions governing the industry.[9]

The Japanese government permits the establishment of wholly foreign-owned subsidiaries for the purpose of importing, warehousing, marketing, and servicing of one's own product provided that the products involved are not petroleum, leather and leather products, or primary products.

Distribution channels in Japan vary from industry to industry and from product to product, with the most common wholesaling setup consisting of three or more levels. Traditionally, the urban retail stores were either very small neighborhood outlets or department stores. The average big city department store carries approximately 500,000 items, all in very small supply, and makes 80 to 90 percent of its purchases from as many as 1,500 wholesalers, who commonly supply goods on consignment and must accept return of those items that do not sell. Even in multistore operations, centralized buying is the exception rather than the rule. Some stores are now establishing central purchasing offices to rationalize buying for all of their affiliate outlets. Exhibit 7 describes annual sales volume by industry for wholesalers and retailers in Japan.

A recent phenomenon in Japan is the growth of the self-service or superstores patterned after the American supermarket but, normally, much smaller. At present, self-service stores account for about 10 percent of total retail sales, compared to the department stores' 14 percent, and are presenting a significant challenge to the long-standing dominance of the department stores. The use of tertiary wholesalers has been almost totally eliminated by superstores and the role of secondary wholesalers has been reduced.

CULTURAL FORMALITIES OF DOING BUSINESS

Every culture has developed its own rules or customs in the area of business, and Japan is hardly the exception. The foreign businessperson should be knowledgeable of the basic differences which exist between his/her country and Japan if he/she is to be successful. The problems faced can be separated into two categories: (1) the appropri-

[9] Ibid., p. 3–34.

EXHIBIT 7   ANNUAL SALES BY INDUSTRY

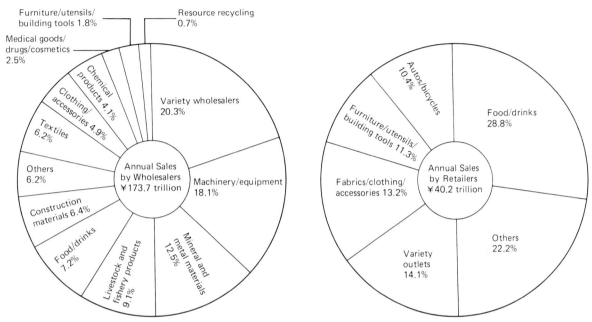

Source: MITI, p. 5

ate way to make an initial approach to a Japanese firm and (2) how to maintain and develop a business relationship. According to a JETRO publication some of the basic do's and don'ts when doing business in Japan are: (1) Take every opportunity for face-to-face contact rather than relying simply on written correspondence. (2) Use business cards on every occasion when a new business contact is made. (3) For matters of some importance, always have a major official in your company call on his/her counterpart in the Japanese organizations for a semi-social call, but do not try to accomplish matters of substance during the first meeting. (4) Whenever possible, obtain introductions from current acquaintances, embassy representatives, or others before visiting government officials or businessmen for the first time. (5) Observe standards of dress and behavior which are considered good form in your own country. (6) Use Japanese in negotiations only when you have become very experienced in the use of the language. (7) Be patient with the apparent slowness of negotiations which is usually due to the consensus decision making process; implementation may be very fast after a decision has finally been reached.

After the formalities in the initial business contacts have been overcome, the keynote is to take a strong personal interest in the problems of your customers and employees. For example, sales management techniques in Japan demand extensive care and interest in the problems of wholesalers and retailers; therefore, a special effort must be made to create the impression of understanding the problems of one's customers. To compete successfully for talent, non-Japanese firms must observe the Japanese labor practices or compensate for the lack of such things as permanent employment guarantee by higher wages and/or better fringe benefits.[10]

SADANA IN JAPAN?

Because Japan comprises the second largest consumer market in the world, and the Japanese are interested in spending their discretionary income on consumer goods, especially fashion items, the Sadana representative in Hawaii felt that Japan offered great possibilities as a new market. Of course, more detailed data were necessary on the shoe industry in Japan and on the channels of distribution, as well as the relative market share of imported shoes. A concern was whether it was necessary for the imported shoes to be high-fashion designer footwear, internationally recognized, or if a little-known foreign import could succeed in the Japanese market. Mr. Suzuki knew that Sandana could not compete with the well-known international shoemakers who advertised in the fashion magazines, etc. His products were promoted locally by the retailers in newspaper ads and in trade journals by the company. Yet, he felt he had a good product which the Japanese tourists were buying in Honolulu and Guam. No specific alterations were required to export the product, since the shoes fit the oriental population in Hawaii who had similar size feet as potential customers in Japan. Suzuki felt, if he could offer the Japanese woman a well-made imported shoe at a medium price, there would be a definite market for Sadanas in Japan.

Because of the weak position of the local shoe industry, and the fact that the Japanese consumer felt that Japanese-made shoes were inferior, Suzuki knew his shoes could do well even with the import quota on leather goods and the high tariff. Japan, like the U.S., has been experiencing a very high inflationary period which has made the Japanese consumer more discriminating in his/her purchases, looking for quality at a fair price. Suzuki was interested in the middle-price market, which is the position of Sadana shoes in the American market today.

More knowledge was needed on the distribution system in Japan before an accurate projection on price or feasibility could be assessed. In the U.S., Sadana shoes are distributed basically from the manufacturer directly to the retailer, with manufacturer's representatives taking the orders and servicing the accounts. Women's shoes are generally channeled in this manner, because they are considered "perishable" due to the ever-changing fashion market. Usually a period of three to six months is necessary from the time the order is taken until delivery. If the shoes could be distributed in a similar fashion in Japan with retailers purchasing directly from the foreign manufacturer, costs would be kept quite minimal even with the high duty on the shoes. However, every additional middleman would add to the price of the shoe and could also mean delays in getting the product to the retail outlets.

---

[10] *Doing Business in Japan.* Japan External Trade Organization, JETRO Marketing Series 8, Revised 1978, p. 2–3.

Initially, Suzuki proposed to handle the accounts in Japan as he does in Hawaii and Guam by checking on each business periodically and presenting his new samples as the lines are produced. The natural place to begin would be Tokyo, and he projected three to four trips a year to Japan. Since he has no business background in Japan and he is not familiar with the language, he would need to work with an interpreter, preferably one who had some experience with retailing if not specifically in the shoe business.

If the initial arrangements seem to work out satisfactorily, Suzuki then felt the market may warrant looking into the possibilities of seeking an agent in Japan to better service the accounts, take reorders, pursue new accounts, and keep him informed as to the changing trends in the marketplace. This might lead to a full-time sales representative in Japan should Sadana be successful in Tokyo. The new sales rep could further expand sales and develop new accounts in the other major Japanese cities, such as Osaka and Nagoya. The choice of a sales rep would be extremely important with one who was bilingual, understood the shoe industry in general, and was experienced in the Japanese women's shoe market, as well as possessed the necessary qualifications to make a good sales representative, being most desirable.

It is not clear at what volume of sales the establishment of a manufacturing facilitiy becomes a highly realistic and practical expansion. Further investigation into that aspect of Japanese business is needed. This becomes a real consideration, in light of the fact that leather product exporters to Japan are unable to set up wholly foreign-owned subsidiaries under the present government regulations. The factory could be foreign-owned or a joint venture whichever is more feasible in the long term.

Suzuki feels his strongest asset is the medium price that he would be able to offer the Japanese women, in addition to a quality shoe. It is impossible to calculate an accurate retail price with the limited information available; however, on the basis that the average Sadana shoe wholesales for about $20 and the air freight from the L.A. factory to Japan could not be more than $5 a pair, the duty would be around $7.50 a pair at thirty percent of the cost plus shipping. The wholesale and retail margins obtainable on items such as shoes were approximately 40% of the retail price, which would place Sadana's shoes in the $50–$60 range if they were sent directly to the retailer from customs.

Mr. Suzuki is generally optimistic about marketing Sadana shoes in Japan and would like to do further research on the Japanese market in the very near future due to the fact that there are not very many American manufacturers exporting to Japan yet and none that are directly competing with Sadana in the young fashion shoe market. While little information is available concerning the Japanese shoe market, he feels the market may be analogous to the imported apparel market. He is planning to enroll in a Japanese language class in addition to learning more about Japanese business practices. Competition in Japan will continue to grow keener; however, the market does offer a real opportunity for an aggressive, interested firm which does not look at Japan as a foreign dumping ground for its surplus production.

Mr. Suzuki wondered if he had adequately prepared for his presentation at the sales meeting. What factors, if any, had he overlooked in assessing the Japanese market potential? What questions are likely to be asked concerning the proposal at the sales meeting?

BIBLIOGRAPHY

Periodicals

Business Asia, Vol. XI, No. 24:185–87, June 15, 1979.

Business Asia, Vol, X, No. 18:137–60, May 5, 1978.

Pascale, Richard Tanner, "Zen and the Art of Management." *Harvard Business Review*, March-April, 1978, p. 153–62.

Redding, S. G. "National Traits." *Asia Business and Industry*, September 1977, p. 614.

Redding, S. G. "Samurai Spirit in the Boardroom." *Asia Business and Industry*, September 1978, p. 74–8.

Yang, Charles Y. "Management Styles: American vis-a-vis Japanese." *Columbia Journal of World Business*, Fall 1977, p. 23–31.

Jetro

A Case Study of Foreign Investment in Japan. Japan External Trade Organization, JETRO Business Information Series 3.

A Handy Guide for Businessmen. Japan External Trade Organization, JETRO Business Information Series 5.

A Handbook on Japanese Taxes. Japan External Trade Organization, JETRO Business Information Series 7.

Doing Business in Japan. Japan External Trade Organization, JETRO Marketing Series 8, Revised 1978.

Exporters' Guide. Japan External Trade Organization, JETRO International Business Information Center, 1978.

Japan as an Export Market. Japan External Trade Organization Business Information Series 4.

Now in Japan. Japan External Trade Organization, JETRO International Business Information Center, January 1977, No. 24.

Operating a Business in Japan. Japan External Trade Organization, JETRO Business Information Series 1.

Planning for Distribution in Japan. Japan External Trade Organization, JETRO Marketing Series 4, Revised 1978.

The Japanese Consumer. Japan External Trade Organization, JETRO Marketing Series 6.

The Japanese Market in Figures. Japan External Trade Organization, JETRO Marketing Series 10.

The Role of Trading Companies in International Commerce. Japan External Trade Organization, JETRO Marketing Series 2.

Books

Alexander, Ralph S. and others. "Appraisal of Company Strengths and Weaknesses," *Product Strategy and Management*, ed. Thomas L. Berg and Abe Shuchman. New York: Holt, Rinehart and Winston, Inc., 1962, p. 146–52.

Clark, Rodney. *The Japanese Company*, Ch. IV and VII. New Haven, Conn.: Yale University.

Keegan, Warren J. *Multinational Marketing Management*. Englewood Cliffs, N.J.: Prentice-Hall, Inc., 1980.

Terpstra, Vern. *The Cultural Environment of International Business*. Cincinnati: South-Western Publishing Co., 1978.

Pamphlets

Some Data about Japanese Economy by KEIDANREN (Japanese Federation of Economic Organizations) and Japan Institute for Social and Economic Affairs, 1979.

Facts and Figures of Japan, Foreign Press Center, Japan, 1978, Part 2.

Japan, A Pocket Guide, Foreign Press Center, Japan, 1979.

Government Publications

Bureau of Statistics, Office of the Prime Minister. *Statistical Handbook on Japan,* Japan, 1978.

Ministry of Foreign Affairs of Japan. *100 Questions and Answers on Japan's Economy and Japan—U.S. Trade,* October, 1978.

State of Hawaii, Department of Planning and Economic Development. *Hawaii's Foreign Trade,* 1972–73, published by Hawaii International Services Agency, Honolulu.

State of Hawaii, Department of Planning and Economic Development. *Hawaii's Trade with Japan, 1968–1977,* Trade Report No. 16, Hawaii International Services Agency, Honolulu, April, 1979.

U.S. Department of Commerce. *Marketing in Japan,* prepared by T. A. Miyakawa. OBR 78-16. Washington, D.C.: Government Printing Office, April 1978.

U.S. Department of Commerce. *U.S. Export Opportunities to Japan.* Washington, D.C.: Government Printing Office, August 1978.

DISCUSSION QUESTIONS

1 How is the proposed expansion to Japan affected by the history and policies of Sadana?

2 What type of organization and/or distribution channels are needed to operate successfully in Japan if the venture is pursued?

3 What trade practices exist for wholesaling and retailing in the Japanese market that are vital considerations for Sadana's proposed venture?

4 Will the price of Sadana shoes be competitive in the Japanese market and is it appropriate to market the shoes at the proposed price?

5 Has Suzuki correctly interpreted the desires of the Japanese consumer? What additional aspects of the market should be researched?

6 What are your short- and long-term recommendations for Sadana with regard to the Japanese venture.

SCHOTTHOEFER MOTOR SERVICE (A)

Fred L. Fry
Bradley University

James J. Chrisman
University of Georgia

SELECTED STRATEGIC ISSUES

- Impact of national economic trends on a small business
- Responding to intensified local price competition
- Strategies for growth

"How do we maintain or increase growth in a changing environment? Is expansion the answer? Should we diversify our product lines or should we concentrate on satisfying a specific segment of the market?" These were some of the questions facing Ron Noe as he considered the recent trends and events that seemed likely to affect his business. Although the company had performed well in the past, there was room for improvement. The major problem was developing a competitive strategy to cope with developments in the auto parts industry, particularly in the Peoria area.

BACKGROUND

Schotthoefer Motor Service began business in Peoria, Illinois, over sixty years ago as an auto machine shop. Like many machine shops of that era, it began stocking its own parts, and today, relies on parts sales for a significant portion of its business. Ron Noe began working for Schotthoefer in 1966. Before this time he was employed at another auto parts store. In 1974 Mr. Noe and partner James Rock purchased the business from the Schotthoefer family. Eager to grow, Mr. Noe later acquired two other parts stores in the nearby communities of Henry, Illinois, in 1976 and Chillicothe, Illinois, in 1980. The three stores were incorporated under the name Quality Machine and Engine

Parts, Inc., though each retained its original identity in order to maintain continuity with previous owners and customers.

THE AUTO PARTS INDUSTRY

The auto parts industry serves two distinct markets each requiring unique selling strategies. Retail customers, the ''do-it-yourselfers'' are generally most concerned with price while wholesale buyers such as service stations and car dealerships tend to weigh quality, delivery, and longstanding relationships more heavily in their purchasing decisions. Some stores cater almost exclusively to the retail customer while others primarily serve the wholesale market. Historically, Schotthoefer relied on wholesale customers for as much as 80% of their revenues but in recent years retail sales have increased in importance. Today the split is closer to 60/40 in favor of wholesale trade. However, the reason for this occurrence is not that the wholesale market has necessarily declined (see Table 1 below), but rather that the retail market has been growing at a faster rate.

Indeed, Table 2, presented below, clearly shows that the vast majority of automotive maintenance is still performed by service stations, repair shops, and dealers—or, in other words, wholesale parts customers.

TABLE 1   SALES OF AUTOMOTIVE PARTS AND SUPPLIES (WHOLESALE)

1974	$15,651,000
1975	$16,603,000
1976	$18,673,000
1977	$20,780,000
1978	$23,898,000
1979	$27,445,000
1980	$29,814,000

Source: "Autos-Auto Parts," *Standard & Poor's Industrial Surveys,* October 1, 1981.

TABLE 2   PLACES CONSUMER MAINTENANCE IS PERFORMED

41%	Service Stations
18%	New Car Dealers
10%	General Repair Shops
9%	Specialized Repair Shops
7%	Tire Shops
6%	Department Stores
5%	Auto Parts Stores
3%	Discount Stores
1%	Home and Auto Stores

Source: "Autos-Auto Parts," *Standard & Poor's Industrial Surveys,* October 1, 1981.

Auto parts stores stock two general types of products. The first type consists of small parts such as spark plugs, light bulbs, filters, various waxes, cleaners, and other products of this nature. For this type of product, competition is intense, the biggest threat coming from discount department stores. These products include nationally known brand items such as Champion spark plugs and Fram oil filters as well as generic items such as mirrors, floor mats, and windshield wiper solvent. In either case, price is the key competitive factor.

The second portion of the parts market involves bigger ticket items such as alternators, power steering units, brakes, carburetors, and engine parts. Due to the lower volume and the more technical nature of these products, discount stores do not carry many of them. Competition comes chiefly from other parts stores and auto dealerships. Buying motives are mixed for this segment of the parts market. Price is a major competitive factor, especially for retail trade, but quality and delivery are equally important to many customers.

Product quality is not readily apparent to the naked eye. Quality is determined by failure rates, number of defectives, or average life. Since some parts last as long as the car, the most important consideration is whether the part will function correctly once installed. Repair shops typically quote a single price to repair a car and allow customers little choice in regard to quality. Thus, garage owners usually demand the highest quality parts available to minimize rework and customer complaints. As a result, only high quality products are stocked by most reputable parts dealers who rely on wholesale trade for the majority of their business.

There is, of course, some overlap in parts sales in both directions. Some individuals do all their own repair work and therefore purchase big ticket items. Additionally, the smaller items account for a large portion of sales to service stations and garages. Because of this the auto parts market is partially price oriented, partially quality oriented and partially a mixture of the two. In either case, buyer-seller relationships and product availability cannot be overlooked by the parts suppliers.

PRICING

The prices charged for auto parts can vary depending on the type of customer and the type of store. Several terms are common within the industry and help explain the pricing mechanisms in use. Jobber price is the price the auto parts stores pay for the parts they buy. Selling prices can be set in any of the following ways:

- List Price is the suggested retail price. It is seldom the real retail price. This allows dealers to offer discounts from ''list.''
- Retail Price is the price charged to ''walk-in'' retail customers. Many parts stores set retail price at 20% off list, for example.
- Non-Stocking Dealer Price is charged to garages or other wholesale purchasers who buy limited amounts and do not carry their own parts stock. This price is usually 10–15% lower than retail.
- Stocking-Dealer Price is given to garages and other wholesale customers who buy substantial quantities of parts on a repeat basis. This price is usually about 7–10% lower than non-stocking dealer price.

Thus, a power steering pump listing for $80 might sell to retail walk-in customer for $64, a non-stocking dealer for $56, and to a stocking dealer for $52. Some parts stores favor retail customers and sell to everyone at non-stocking dealer price. Usually few wholesale buyers frequent these stores, the common complaints being longer waiting, lack of delivery, and the fact that they are not getting any better break than the retail buyer. Walk-in customers, on the other hand, feel they are getting a discount bargain.

RECENT NATIONAL TRENDS

The auto parts industry has undergone substantial changes in the past few years. Typically the parts industry has been viewed as countercyclical. When the economy moves into a recession, car owners tend to fix their old cars rather than trading them in on new ones. In fact, the average age of cars has been increasing as can be seen in Table 3, given below.

This trend suggests that auto parts sales should be increasing also. However, several other trends and events have occurred to disturb the auto parts market. Some of these are of a national or industry scope, while others are local.

The parts industry has changed significantly due to the energy crisis in the mid-seventies and the rapidly rising gasoline prices in the 1978–1980 time period. As a result, the American public began to demand smaller, more fuel efficient cars. Initially this meant shifting to foreign makes with Japanese manufacturers at one time holding as much as 25% of the new car market. American manufacturers in the 1980's have finally started producing smaller cars hoping to regain a portion of their lost market share.

These heavily promoted, fuel efficient cars made consumers rethink the tradition of fixing up the old clunker. Increasingly, families who previously kept the old station wagon for a second car, now purchase a fuel efficient small car for in-town use. The result of this small car buying trend was fewer people performing major repairs on their old cars. This could be an extremely important influence on parts sales because 93% of total repair dollars are spent on autos more than two years old. The energy crunch also resulted in the amount of miles driven to decrease markedly in 1979, as can be seen in Table 4. This trend continued in 1980. Thus, the countercyclical nature of the auto

TABLE 3   AVERAGE AGE OF VEHICLES (In Years)

1974	5.7
1975	6.0
1976	6.2
1977	6.2
1978	6.9
1979	6.9
1980	7.1

Source: "Autos-Auto Parts," *Standard & Poor's Industrial Surveys,* October 1, 1981.

TABLE 4   AVERAGE MILES TRAVELLED PER VEHICLE

1974	9,448
1975	9,634
1976	9,763
1977	9,839
1978	9,812
1979	9,485

Source: "Autos-Auto Parts," *Standard & Poor's Industrial Surveys,* October 1, 1981.

parts market was, at least partially, upset, though preliminary indications suggest there was a slight increase in number of miles travelled in 1981.

A second trend, related closely to the first, was a reduction in the number of service station repair shops and new car dealers. Because of the decline in sale of American cars, many car dealers were closing all across the country. Naturally this also meant the loss of their repair departments. Thus a key portion of the wholesale market diminished substantially. Further dampening the wholesale market was the move in many states toward self-service gas stations. In the past, most full-service gas stations also did repair work. A number of these businesses found that switching to a self-service operation was more profitable than maintaining repair capability. Although some of the auto repair business shifted to the remaining full service gas stations and garages, some sales were undoubtedly lost.

In the future, these trends are likely to result in substantial changes in the structure of the auto parts industry. The move toward fuel efficient cars could benefit parts suppliers because smaller cars typically operate at higher temperatures and RPM's, thus increasing the potential for breakdowns. Furthermore, to improve gas mileage, lighter components are being used which tend to wear out faster. This could result in a resurgence of the full service machine shops in order to handle engine re-works on these smaller, more fragile autos.

Additionally, rapid technological advancements in auto parts have taken place which could change the nature of parts production and supply. Auto manufacturers are now including microprocessors and other electronic devices in their product lines. By 1985 it is estimated that over $1.5 billion worth of electronic equipment will be in use in the automobiles found on American streets and highways. Technology has also resulted in widespread use of sub-system components, replacing many of the individual parts sold in the past. These sophisticated electronic devices and sub-systems will ultimately cause auto repairs to become more costly and complex. This event could alter the structure of the industry because the increasing complexity of auto parts and the auto parts business might influence suppliers to specialize their operations.

American parts suppliers can also expect increasing foreign competition. Toyota has been especially aggressive in their attempts to improve their parts business. Recently, the firm instituted a new jobber program called STAR, (Support To Aftermarket Repairs), in hopes of improving parts availability to independent garages and parts stores. Foreign parts suppliers are expected to capture as much as 10% of the total U.S. parts market by 1985 (foreign parts market share in 1980 was 5%).

LOCAL EVENTS

In addition to the problems that affected the industry as a whole, several events occurred in Peoria which further magnified the problems of local auto parts stores such as Schotthoefer. One was the arrival of Whitlock Discount Automotive Store.

Whitlock was an overnight success largely due to the age old strategy of selling at prices lower than the competition, coupled with substantial advertising of parts and accessories. Despite claims of lower quality and poor service, stores such as Whitlock are becoming increasingly popular. The supermarket atmosphere appeals to the economy minded consumer much the same as does the self service gas station. Besides Whitlock, other discount auto parts stores emerged throughout the area. Competition especially from the chain stores and franchises intensified. Currently, Ron Noe estimates that he has at least 30 competitors in Peoria. The approximate location of all Peoria auto parts suppliers, including Schotthoefer, are provided in Appendix A.

The prolonged economic downturn has done nothing to improve the situation. Peoria avoided the ill-effects of the recession for a while, but recently has experienced a sharp rise in unemployment and the cost of living. Layoffs and the lack of new jobs have forced many, especially factory and construction workers, to move to the more prosperous Southwest. Typically these individuals represent a major portion of walk-in customers.

Unlike many area businesses, Schotthoefer has not faired badly despite the recession and the other problems mentioned previously. This is due in part to the fact that Schotthoefer is a well established business. This is important in an industry where repeat customers can account for up to 90% of a store's sales. Another factor which has helped Schotthoefer was the relocation of their nearest competitor, a store geared primarily to the retail customer. Its departure from the area led to an increase in walk-in business for Schotthoefer.

STRATEGIC ALTERNATIVES

Despite his past successes, Ron Noe recognized the changes taking place in the auto parts industry and realized they required a reevaluation of the course his business should follow in the future. Schotthoefer has always catered to the wholesale buyer and built an image as a high quality supplier. Unfortunately, this strategy does little to attract the price conscious retail customers who account for an increasing proportion of Schotthoefer's sales. To attract the walk-in customer would require including a selection of lower quality parts as well as offering dealer discounts to everyone. This could adversely affect relations with long-standing wholesale customers. On the other hand, to try to satisfy the needs of both market segments at the same time could require extensive commitments to working capital mainly in the form of larger inventories. The potential cost of carrying this extra inventory could be quite expensive as well as risky.

Another alternative high on Noe's priority list was expansion. Though he favored locating near the affluent Lake of the Woods community just outside Peoria, preliminary inquiries gave no conclusive indication that this area could support a new store. However, Mr. Noe ruled out a definite decision until a more detailed analysis of this market could be conducted. In addition, Noe was considering adopting a single name for his three stores to save on advertising expenses and consolidate the image of his business in the marketplace. In the past, because Noe chose to retain each store's family name, separate advertisements were needed for all three.

PEORIA AREA MAP
AUTO PARTS STORES COMPETITOR LOCATION

△ Discounters	● Import parts stores	⊢———⊣ one mile
☐ Stores with machine shop	S Schotthoefer	
○ Traditional	🏛 Whitlock	

CONCLUSION

Schotthoefer Motor Service stands at the crossroads of a major decision. Several paths have been considered, but changing trends in the marketplace, local events and a stagnant economy make it difficult to determine the correct course to follow. Many questions remain unanswered. Should Schotthoefer maintain its high quality image or would more aggressive pursuit of the retail customer be more profitable? Will whole-sale buyers continue to demand high quality parts, when many consumers appear satisfied with cheaper products? Would a new store be feasible, and if so, is this the best way to grow? What the correct decisions should be and the effect a wrong decision could have remain to be seen. In either case some action must be taken if Schotthoefer is to achieve the growth and level of profits that Mr. Noe is determined to attain.

DISCUSSION QUESTIONS

1 How are recent U.S. economic trends likely to affect Schotthoefer Motor Service and how should the company adapt?

2 How should Schotthoefer respond to the emergence of discount auto parts stores in the Peoria area?

3 Should Schotthoefer seek rapid growth? If so, how should this be accomplished? Defend your position.

THE CRAFT COTTAGE

Wayne H. Decker
Thomas R. Miller
Memphis State University

SELECTED STRATEGIC ISSUES

- Expansion of a small business through purchase of competitors
- Information and control system design for a small business
- Marketing strategy for a small business
- Mission of a small business

Fred Randall was puzzled about what he should do. He had been considering the possibility of expanding his arts, crafts, prints, and picture framing business through purchase of the Frame Shoppe and/or Jefferson City Art and Frame, two local firms in the business districts of the city. If he acquired either of these firms, he knew he would need to secure management personnel to operate the new units for him. He anticipated continuing to manage his present store, the Craft Cottage, regardless of the decision to acquire the other firms. As he reflected, he thought the prospect of financing the acquisitions really bothered him less than the thought of managing these units. After all, he realized he had some problems to solve in just operating the Craft Cottage, as small as it was. The business had not generated a profit in its first four years and probably would not this year. And wouldn't the expansion of his business result in more headaches? But, on the other hand, maybe this was a unique opportunity that he should not forego. He struggled as to what he should do.

This case was prepared by Professors Wayne H. Decker and Thomas R. Miller, Fogelman College of Business and Economics, Memphis State University.

BACKGROUND

The Craft Cottage was a small store in one of the better residential areas of Jefferson City, a small southeastern city of about 30,000 population located about 35 miles from a major metropolitan center. The neighborhood was quite attractive with well-kept, modern, brick homes, built among mature trees. Four years earlier, Mr. and Mrs. Fred Randall established the Craft Cottage by converting their garage into a store and adding a wood-working shop to the back of their home. The store was located on a corner lot one block from a state highway and within one mile of Chancellor State University.

The Craft Cottage had opened in October, although inventory accumulation began during the preceding summer. Mr. Randall stated that he had started the business more for enjoyment than for money. Products initially offered were hand-made crafts, tole-painting[1] supplies, and tole-painting lessons. In fact, the business originally centered around his wife's skills in teaching tole painting. However, Fred Randall stated that he "did not want to have all his eggs in one basket." He felt he needed to diversify in case his wife's health were to prevent her from continuing in an active role in the business. Recently, increased emphasis had been placed on the sale of original prints[2] and picture framing. While the store had prints that were quite inexpensive, most of the prints stocked were in the $150 range. Tole painting was still a major part of the business, but handmade crafts were being de-emphasized.

OPERATIONS

The personnel of Craft Cottage include six employees: Mr. and Mrs. Randall and four part-time workers. Fred Randall, a retired military officer, also taught half time in the Industrial Studies Department of Chancellor State University and had turned down an offer of full-time employment at the university. He also had completed all work except the dissertation toward a doctoral degree in health, physical education, and recreation. Mrs. Randall had earlier received her doctorate in English Education from the university.

In discussing his employee situation, Fred Randall commented that "it is difficult to get good help." His part-time employees engaged in various activities, including bookkeeping, woodworking, matting and framing, cleaning, and yard work. The bookkeeper was a doctoral candidate in history who had no formal training in book-keeping. She worked no regular hours, but rather at her convenience. Two of the other employees were also university students.

From his observations of customers, Randall had identified his primary market as educators' wives and wives of other professionals, in particular, middle-class women in the 25–35 age range. Randall believed women who bought prints did so more for the appearance of the print than for its investment value. While not located in a business

[1] Decorative painting or lacquering of metalware popular in the 18th century and reproduced today for trays, lamps, etc.

[2] The Print Council of America considers a print original when the "artist alone" has created the image on the copper plate, stone, wood block, or other medium from which the print is produced and the finished product is approved by the artist. However, many dealers and curators do not feel the artist has to do the above entirely alone for the print to be considered original.

district, the Craft Cottage was close to many of its customers' residences or routes they travelled. The store had an appeal to customers because of its informal "non-commercial" atmosphere and environment. Randall viewed word-of-mouth and direct mail as his most effective forms of advertising. The latter consisted of a full-color newsletter published by a print distributor which carried the name of the Craft Cottage on each issue. It was distributed about every two months chiefly to people who had previously been in the shop. In addition to the daily newspapers and local radio, advertising had included high school and campus papers and the Yellow Pages telephone directory. In the Yellow Pages, the Craft Cottage was listed under "Picture Frames—Dealers," "Art Galleries and Dealers" and "Art Goods." Although several of its competitors used display ads, the Craft Cottage was listed in the smallest type. However, Randall planned to drop his listings next year, since he believed they were not effective and that people called and asked for "stupid things."

Those products not made in the shop at the Craft Cottage were generally purchased from distributors. However, Randall had also obtained some goods from vendors on a consignment basis. Prices at the Craft Cottage tended to be lower than those of the larger shops located in the Jefferson City business district. Randall set his prices according to his costs for an item and attributed his lower prices to lower overhead.

Randall stated that upon starting the business his goals were to generate sales of $1,000 per month within three years and to break even within five years. His current goal was to increase annual gross sales to $20,000 by the seventh year of operation. A balance sheet for all years of operations is presented in Exhibit 1 and an income statement appears in Exhibit 2. The figures for the first nine months of this year were not exact because depreciation had not been taken off, nor had the amount of inventory sold been deducted.

The bookkeeper did not have access to the file system, nor did she send out statements. She paid bills as they were given to her by Randall. Frequently, purchase discounts were missed because invoices were misplaced. Another aspect of the bookkeeper's job was to match sales tickets with the appropriate listings in the inventory book. Since the items in inventory were not numbered, it could take the bookkeeper 15–20 minutes to find a 50-cent item in the book. Descriptions and prices on sales tickets often did not match those in the inventory book and many items got into inventory without being listed in the book. The bookkeeper saw no record of items that were on consignment.

No sales-by-product or sales-by-month breakdowns were available. Although he had not done any monthly analysis, Mr. Randall was relatively certain that July and August were his slowest months. Sales on credit were given on a relatively informal basis and only to persons known well to the Randalls. There were no set policies on the amounts of down payments or monthly installments. However, a one percent per month finance charge was applied after three or four months.

Most of the recent inventory growth consisted of acquisitions of prints. Almost every room in the house contained stacks of prints. In fact, Mrs. Randall had expressed concern over the amount of money now invested in prints. According to Fred Randall, there had been "no conscious decisions" guiding inventory levels. Purchasing had been determined mainly by his feelings that there were shortages of particular kinds of prints (e.g., subjects or artists).

EXHIBIT 1   BALANCE SHEETS FOR YEARS OF OPERATION*

	9-Months current Year	Year-1	Year-2	Year-3	Year-4
Assets					
Current Assets					
Cash	98.10	572.39	221.49	89.62	484.26
Accounts Receivable	85.09	569.31	708.32 –	59.36	
Supplies, Selling	906.83	382.97	323.37	279.04	309.65
Supplies, Manufacturing	8,949.60	4,812.96	4,276.69	3,330.96	1,983.72
Merchandise	41,406.00	16,351.98	8,111.43	4,083.12	2,759.85
Total Current Assets	51,455.62	22,689.61	13,641.30	7,782.74	5,596.84
Fixed Assets					
Delivery Equipment	400.00	400.00	163.00	245.00	367.00
Store Equipment	1,803.22	1,487.81	977.64	802.73	795.04
Office Equipment	1,181.31	784.92	357.60	347.97	266.85
Manufacturing Equipment	9,053.70	7,595.40	5,591.33	2,999.74	2,334.44
Building	7,969.05	7,016.98	5,566.27	5,575.42	4,502.70
Total Fixed Assets	20,407.28	17,285.11	12,655.84	9,970.86	8,266.03
Total Assets	71,852.90	39,974.72	26,297.14	17,753.60	13,862.87
Liabilities and capital					
Current Liabilities					
Accounts Payable	93.55	399.85	1,048.61	757.51	680.11
Sales Tax Payable	60.24	137.94	79.68	46.04	35.81
Total Current Liabilities	153.79	537.79	1,128.29	803.55	715.92
Capital	71,699.11	39,436.93	25,168.85	16,948.05	13,146.95
Total Liabilities and Capital	71,852.90	39,974.72	26,297.14	17,751.60	13,862.87

* Year ends December 31; data as of September 30.

EXHIBIT 2   INCOME STATEMENT FOR YEARS OF OPERATION

	Year-1	Year-2	Year-3	Year-4
Revenues				
Sales	11,227,82	10,583.95	3,200.33	1,162.44
Miscellaneous Revenues	11.73	10.22	3.09	.37
Total	11,239.55	10,594.17	3,203.42	1,162.81
Cost of Goods Sold	7,622.93	5,937.69	1,488.58	46.36
Gross Profit	3,616.62	4,656.48	1,714.84	701.45
Operating Expenses				
Salaries	625.25	267.75	214.50	18.00
Supplies	2,029.68	1,110.27	1,048.92	331.71
Rent	628.14	628.08	628.08	33.38
Depreciation	1,909.48	1,274.57	930.79	797.34
Trips	854.55	424.67	1,085.98	699.65
Utilities/Taxes	594.36	541.05	402.34	200.98
Miscellaneous Expenses	3,706.97	3,189.29	2,603.13	1,663.44
Total	10,348.54	7,435.68	6,913.74	4,077.50
Net Income (Loss)	(6,731.92)	(2,779.20)	(5,198.90)	(3,376.05)

COMPETITION

Randall viewed his major competition to be the Frame Shoppe, the apparent leader in sales of prints in Jefferson City. The other major picture frame business in town was Jefferson City Art and Frame. Randall had stated that both of the above businesses would like for him to buy them out. He believed that these establishments would be more suitable outlets for print sales than the Craft Cottage.

The Frame Shoppe owner wanted about $125,000 for his business, $35,000–40,000 of which Randall estimates to be for goodwill. The owner of the Frame Shoppe estimated his annual gross sales as over $100,000 and his inventory turnover to be 2.0. The business was located in a leased building in downtown Jefferson City. Randall would be willing to lease the building for a year, but then he would want to buy another. He believed a proprietor should generally own his building unless located in a shopping center.

Randall estimated that Jefferson City Art and Frame could be purchased for $35,000–40,000. In addition the owners were asking $300,000 for their building, which was located at the edge of the city on a heavily traveled and commercialized state highway, and adjacent to a proposed loop around the city. Jefferson City Art and Frame's annual sales were reported to be about $80,000 with an inventory turnover of 2.5 to 3.0 times.

DISCUSSION QUESTIONS

1 Should Fred Randall consider purchasing one or both of the other businesses? Explain.
2 How could the information and control system at the Craft Cottage be improved?
3 Evaluate Fred Randall's approach to the promotional aspect of marketing.
4 State and discuss what you believe to be the mission of the Craft Cottage in terms of what is desired to be accomplished for whom.

SCHOTTHOEFER MOTOR SERVICE (B)

Fred L. Fry
James J. Chrisman
University of Georgia

SELECTED STRATEGIC ISSUES

- A retail outlet feasibility decision
- Competences required in retail versus wholesale operations
- The impact of future events on the correctness of present decisions

Ron Noe, owner and president of Schotthoefer Motor Service, stood at the crossroads of a major decision. Changing conditions both locally and nationally threatened to alter the competitive structure of the parts industry [see Schotthoefer Motor Service (A) for a more detailed description of the industry, the firm, and the economic climate]. Thus, Mr. Noe understood that despite past successes, the status-quo could not be maintained if the business was to continue to prosper and grow.

To meet these changing circumstances, Mr. Noe had evaluated several strategies. If growth was to be achieved there seemed to be four pursuable alternatives. First, the current wholesale business could be increased in the three existing Schotthoefer units. Second, retail sales could be increased in existing stores. Third, the purchase of a competing parts supplier had been considered. Of course, this option was limited to those willing to sell. The final possibility involved opening additional units to tap new markets. Mr. Noe was particularly interested in this fourth option. In the first place, the first two alternatives mentioned were really self-evident. Every business wants to increase their existing business activity. Expansion, however, is a different matter.

There are three basic questions or criteria to evaluate in any expansion decision: "Can the proposed acquisition or site be financed without exposing the firm to excessive risk or liquidity problems?", "Can the store make money?", and "How much business or market overlap will there be between the new store and existing outlets?'' Mr. Noe was confident that Schotthoefer's healthy financial state would allow expansion should an attractive opportunity develop. However, he was concerned with the possibility of taking business away from current units, especially the Peoria store. The obvious way to avoid this problem would be to obtain an entirely new outlet in an entirely new market area. One such market was the Lake of the Woods area.

LAKE OF THE WOODS

Lake of the Woods is a relatively self-contained sub-division located several miles north of the Peoria city limits. Essentially a ''bedroom community'' made up of affluent families, many middle-management personnel of Caterpillar Tractor Company (the dominant employer in the area) reside there, as do executives of many other locally based enterprises. The typical house in Lake of the Woods cost anywhere from $80,000 to $150,000 in 1980–81.

A small shopping center in Lake of the Woods Plaza meets most of the needs of residents and consists of a grocery store, a hardware store, a realtor, a pizza parlour, and a variety of other smaller shops. A self-service gas station is across the highway. No banking facilities are located in the shopping center except for automatic teller machines connected to Peoria banks. This is not a real inconvenience, since most of the residents work in Peoria anyway.

Approximately five miles west of Lake of the Woods is Dunlap, Illinois, an established community of approximately 700 residents. Dunlap is typical of the many mid-western farming communities, having a few locally owned stores, a bank, a school that serves the town and its surrounding area (including Lake of the Woods), a few churches, etc. Total population of the two relevant census tracts according to the 1980 census was 5,466 which includes the Lake of the Woods sub-division, other nearby sub-divisions, Dunlap, and surrounding rural areas. Assuming an average family size of 3.3, this amounts to approximately 1,650 households.

The Lake of the Woods Plaza is an area targeted by Ron Noe as a potential site for a new auto parts store. Currently no auto parts store exists in Lake of the Woods. The hardware store in the Plaza carries accessories such as spark plugs, and a Western Auto store in Dunlap carries a few parts along with its hardware line.

Residents of the Dunlap/Lake in the Woods area were surveyed concerning their auto parts needs. The following table summarizes the findings:

TABLE 1

Number of cars per household	2.1
Percent doing their own maintenance	66%
Percent doing their own repairs	36%
Average yearly dollars spent on maintenance	$90
Average yearly dollars spent on repairs	$170
Average yearly dollars spent on accessories	$25
Average miles driven to purchase auto parts*	9
Percent indicating a willingness to partronize a Lake of the Woods parts store	75%

* Some purchase parts near their work place.

TABLE 2   AVERAGE AGE OF CARS

Age	Target	National*
Less than 3	25%	25%
3-5	45%	25%
6-8	14%	25%
More than 8	15%	25%

* National data as of 1978.

Table 2 lists the age of cars in the target area compared to the national average.

Mr. Noe estimated that $250,000 gross sales per year would be necessary to make the store profitable. Of this, 90% would have to come from retail sales.

DISCUSSION QUESTIONS

1 Can the Lake of the Woods area support a Schotthoefer store?
2 Is Schotthoefer competent to operate a store which depends upon retail customers for 90 percent of its sales?
3 How might reasonably predictable national and/or local events affect the possible success of a Lake of the Woods store?

THE LINCOLN ELECTRIC COMPANY, 1984

Arthur Sharplin
Northeast Louisiana University

SELECTED STRATEGIC ISSUES

- Conservative financing policies and guaranteed employment
- Pronounced constituencies versus company practices
- Reasons for high productivity
- Evaluation of pro- or antiunion posture
- Theoretical capitalism and the four P's of marketing
- Transfer of a successful high productivity model to other companies
- Identifying threats and weaknesses for a successful company
- Relationship of corporate strategies to societal needs

The Lincoln Electric Company is the world's largest manufacturer of welding machines and electrodes. Lincoln employs 2400 workers in two U.S. factories near Cleveland and approximately 600 in three factories located in other countries. This does not include the field sales force of more than 200 persons. It has been estimated that Lincoln's market share (for arc-welding equipment and supplies) is more than 40 percent.

The Lincoln incentive management plan has been well known for many years. Many college management texts make reference to the Lincoln plan as a model for achieving high worker productivity. Certainly, Lincoln has been a successful company according to the usual measures of success.

James F. Lincoln died in 1965, and there was some concern, even among employees, that the Lincoln system would fall into disarray, that profits would decline, and that year-end bonuses might be discontinued. Quite the contrary, eighteen years after

Lincoln's death, the company appears stronger than ever. Each year, except the recession years 1982 and 1983, has seen higher profits and bonuses. Employee morale and productivity remain high. Employee turnover is almost nonexistent except for retirements. Lincoln's market share is stable. Consistently high dividends continue on Lincoln's stock.

A HISTORICAL SKETCH

In 1895, after being "frozen out" of the depression-ravaged Elliott-Lincoln Company, a maker of Lincoln-designed electric motors, John C. Lincoln took out his second patent and began to manufacture an improved motor. He opened a new business, unincorporated, with $200 he had earned redesigning a motor for young Herbert Henry Dow, who later founded the Dow Chemical Company.

Started during an economic depression and cursed by a major fire after only one year in business, Lincoln's company grew, but hardly prospered, through its first quarter-century. In 1906, John C. Lincoln incorporated his company and moved from his one-room fourth-floor factory to a new three-story building he erected in east Cleveland. In his new factory, he expanded his work force to thirty, and sales grew to over $50,000 a year. John Lincoln preferred being an engineer and inventor rather than a manager, though, and it was to be left to another Lincoln to manage the company through its years of success.

In 1907, after a bout with typhoid fever forced him from Ohio State University in his senior year, James F. Lincoln, John's younger brother, joined the fledgling company. In 1914, he became the active head of the firm, with the titles of general manager and vice president. John Lincoln, while he remained president of the company for some years, became more involved in other business ventures and in his work as an inventor.

One of James Lincoln's early actions as head of the firm was to ask the employees to elect representatives to a committee which would advise him on company operations. The advisory board has met with the chief executive officer twice monthly since that time. This was only the first of a series of innovative personnel policies which have, over the years, distinguished Lincoln Electric from its contemporaries.

The first year the advisory board was in existence, working hours were reduced from fifty-five per week, then standard, to fifty hours a week. In 1915, the company gave each employee a paid-up life insurance policy. A welding school, which continues today, was begun in 1917. In 1918, an employee bonus plan was attempted. It was not continued, but the idea was to resurface and become the backbone of the Lincoln management system.

The Lincoln Electric employees' association was formed in 1919 to provide health benefits and social activities. This organization continues today and has assumed several additional functions over the years. In 1923, a piecework pay system was in effect, employees got two-week paid vacations each year, and wages were adjusted for changes in the Consumer Price Index. Approximately 30 percent of Lincoln's stock was set aside for key employees in 1914, when James F. Lincoln became general manager, and a stock purchase plan for all employees was begun in 1925.

The board of directors voted to start a suggestion system in 1929. The program is still in effect, but cash awards, part of the early program, were discontinued several years ago. Now, suggestions are rewarded by additional "points," which affect year-end bonuses.

The legendary Lincoln bonus plan was proposed by the advisory board and accepted on a trial basis by James Lincoln in 1934. The first annual bonus amounted to about 25 percent of wages. There has been a bonus every year since then. The bonus plan has been a cornerstone of the Lincoln management system, and recent bonuses have approximated annual wages.

By 1944, Lincoln employees enjoyed a pension plan, a policy of promotion from within, and continuous employment. Base pay rates were determined by formal job evaluation and a merit rating system was in effect.

In the prologue of James F. Lincoln's last book, Charles G. Herbruck writes regarding the foregoing personnel innovations,

> They were not to buy good behavior. They were not efforts to increase profits. They were not antidotes to labor difficulties. They did not constitute a "do-gooder" program. They were an expression of mutual respect for each person's importance to the job to be done. All of them reflect the leadership of James Lincoln, under whom they were nurtured and propagated.

By the start of World War II, Lincoln Electric was the world's largest manufacturer of arc-welding products. Sales of about $4 million in 1934 had grown to $24 million by 1941. Productivity per employee more than doubled during the same period.

During the war, Lincoln Electric prospered as never before. Despite challenges to Lincoln's profitability made by the Navy's Price Review Board and to the tax deductibility of employee bonuses by the Internal Revenue Service, the company increased its profits and paid huge bonuses.

Certainly since 1935, and probably for several years before that, Lincoln productivity had been well above the average for similar companies. Lincoln claims levels of productivity more than twice those of other manufacturers from 1945 onward. Information available from outside sources tends to support these claims.

COMPANY PHILOSOPHY

James F. Lincoln was the son of a Congregational minister, and Christian principles were at the center of his business philosophy. The confidence that he had in the efficacy of Christ's teachings is illustrated by the following remark taken from one of his books:

> The Christian ethic should control our acts. If it did control our acts, the savings in cost of distribution would be tremendous. Advertising would be a contact of the expert consultant with the customer, in order to give the customer the best product available when all of the customer's needs are considered. Competition then would be in improving the quality of products and increasing efficiency in producing and distributing them; not in deception, as is now too customary. Pricing would reflect efficiency of production; it would not be a selling dodge that the customer may well be sorry he accepted. It would be proper for all concerned and rewarding for the ability used in producing the product.[1]

[1] James F. Lincoln, *A New Approach to Industrial Economics*, New York: The Devin Adair Co., 1961, p. 64.

There is no indication that Lincoln attempted to evangelize his employees or customers—or the general public for that matter. The current board chairman, William Irrgang, and the president, George E. Willis, do not even mention the Christian gospel in their recent speeches and interviews. The company motto, "The actual is limited, the possible is immense," is prominently displayed, but there is no display of religious slogans, and there is no company chapel.

Attitude toward the Customer

James Lincoln saw the customer's needs as the *raison d'etre* for every company. "When any company has achieved success so that it is attractive as an investment," he wrote, "all money usually needed for expansion is supplied by the customer in retained earnings. It is obvious that the customer's interests, not the stockholder's, should come first."[2] In 1947 he said, "Care should be taken . . . not to rivet attention on profit. Between 'How much do I get?' and 'How do I make this better, cheaper, more useful?' the difference is fundamental and decisive."[3] Mr. Willis still ranks the customer as Lincoln's most important constituency. This is reflected in Lincoln's policy to "at all times price on the basis of cost and at all times keep pressure on our cost. . . ."[4] Lincoln's goal, often stated, is "to build a better and better product at a lower and lower price."[5] "It is obvious," James Lincoln said, "that the customer's interests should be the first goal of industry."[6]

Attitude toward Stockholders

Stockholders are given last priority at Lincoln. This is a continuation of James Lincoln's philosophy: "The last group to be considered is the stockholders who own stock because they think it will be more profitable than investing money in any other way."[7] Concerning division of the largess produced by incentive management, Lincoln writes, "The absentee stockholder also will get his share, even if undeserved, out of the greatly increased profit that the efficiency produces."[8]

Attitude toward Unionism

There has never been a serious effort to organize Lincoln employees. While James Lincoln criticized the labor movement for "selfishly attempting to better its position at the expense of the people it must serve,"[9] he still had kind words for union members. He excused abuses of union power as "the natural reactions of human beings to the abuses to which management has subjected them."[10] Lincoln's idea of the correct

[2] Ibid., p. 119.
[3] "You Can't Tell What a Man Can Do—Until He Has the Chance," *Reader's Digest*, January 1947, p. 94.
[4] George E. Willis' letter to the author of September 7, 1978.
[5] Lincoln, 1961, p. 47.
[6] Ibid., p. 117.
[7] Ibid., p. 38.
[8] Ibid., p. 122.
[9] Ibid., p. 18.
[10] Ibid., p. 76.

relationship between workers and managers is shown by this comment: "Labor and management are properly not warring camps; they are parts of one organization in which they must and should cooperate fully and happily." [11]

Beliefs and Assumptions about Employees

If fulfilling customer needs is the desired goal of business, then employee performance and productivity are the means by which this goal can best be achieved. It is the Lincoln attitude toward employees, reflected in the following quotations, which is credited by many with creating the record of success the company has experienced:

> The greatest fear of the worker, which is the same as the greatest fear of the industrialist in operating a company, is the lack of income. . . . The industrial manager is very conscious of his company's need of uninterrupted income. He is completely oblivious, evidently, of the fact that the worker has the same need. [12]

> He is just as eager as any manager is to be part of a team that is properly organized and working for the advancement of our economy. . . . He has no desire to make profits for those who do not hold up their end in production, as is true of absentee stockholders and inactive people in the company. [13]

> If money is to be used as an incentive, the program must provide that what is paid to the worker is what he has earned. The earnings of each must be in accordance with accomplishment. [14]

> Status is of great importance in all human relationships. The greatest incentive that money has, usually, is that it is a symbol of success. . . . The resulting status is the real incentive. . . . Money alone can be an incentive to the miser only. [15]

> There must be complete honesty and understanding between the hourly worker and management if high efficiency is to be obtained. [16]

LINCOLN'S BUSINESS

Arc-welding has been the standard joining method in the shipbuilding industry for decades. It is the predominant way of joining steel in the construction industry. Most industrial plants have their own welding shops for maintenance and construction. Manufacturers of tractors and all kinds of heavy equipment use arc-welding extensively in the manufacturing process. Many hobbyists have their own welding machines and use them for making metal items such as patio furniture and barbeque pits. The popularity of welded sculpture as an art form is growing.

While advances in welding technology have been frequent, arc-welding products, in the main, have hardly changed except for Lincoln's Innershield process. This process,

[11] Ibid., p. 72.
[12] Ibid., p. 36.
[13] Ibid., p. 75.
[14] Ibid., p. 98.
[15] Ibid., p. 92.
[16] Ibid., p. 39.

utilizing a self-shielded, flux-cored electrode, has established new cost-saving opportunities for construction and equipment fabrication. The most popular Lincoln electrode, the Fleetweld 5P, has been virtually the same since the 1930s. The most popular engine-driven welder in the world, the Lincoln SA-200, has been a gray-colored assembly including a four-cylinder continental "Red Seal" engine and a 200-ampere direct-current generator with two current-control knobs for at least three decades. A 1980 model SA-200 even weighs almost the same as the 1950 model, and it certainly is little changed in appearance.

Lincoln and its competitors now market a wide range of general-purpose and specialty electrodes for welding mild steel, aluminum, cast iron, and stainless and special steels. Most of these electrodes are designed to meet the standards of the American Welding Society, a trade association. They are thus essentially the same in size and composition from one manufacturer to another. Every electrode manufacturer has a limited number of unique products, but these typically constitute only a small percentage of total sales.

Lincoln's R&D expenditures have recently been less than one and one-half percent of sales. There is evidence that others spend several times as much as a percentage of sales.

Lincoln's share of the arc-welding products market appears to have been about 40 percent for many years, and the welding products market has grown somewhat faster than the level of industry in general. The market is highly price-competitive, with variations in prices of standard products normally amounting to only 1 or 2 percent. Lincoln's products are sold directly by its engineering-oriented sales force and indirectly through its distributor organization. Advertising expenditures amount to less than one-fourth of 1 percent of sales, one-third as much as a major Lincoln competitor with whom the case writer checked.

The other major welding process, flame-welding, has not been competitive with arc-welding since the 1930s. However, plasma-arc-welding, a relatively new process which uses a conducting stream of superheated gas (plasma) to confine the welding current to a small area, has made some inroads, especially in metal tubing manufacturing, in recent years. Major advances in technology which will produce an alternative superior to arc-welding within the next decade or so appear unlikely. Also, it seems likely that changes in the machines and techniques used in arc-welding will be evolutionary rather than revolutionary.

Products

The company is primary engaged in the manufacture and sale of arc-welding products—electric welding machines and metal electrodes. Lincoln also produces electric motors ranging from $\frac{1}{2}$ to 200 horsepower. Motors constitute about 8 to 10 percent of total sales.

The electric welding machines, some consisting of a transformer or motor and generator arrangement powered by commercial electricity and others consisting of an internal combustion engine and generator, are designed to produce from 30 to 1000 amperes of electric power. This electric current is used to melt a consumable metal electrode, with the molten metal being transferred in a superhot spray to the metal joint being welded. Very high temperatures and hot sparks are produced, and operators usually must wear special eye and face protection and leather gloves, often along with leather aprons and sleeves.

Welding electrodes are of two basic types: (1) Coated "stick" electrodes, usually 14 inches long and smaller than a pencil in diameter, are held in a special insulated holder by the operator who must manipulate the electrode in order to maintain a proper arc width and pattern of deposition of the metal being transferred. Stick electrodes are packaged in 6- to 50-pound boxes. (2) Coiled wire, ranging in diameter from 0.035 to 0.219 inches, is designed to be fed continuously to the welding arc through a "gun" held by the operator or positioned by automatic positioning equipment. The wire is packaged in coils, reels, and drums weighing from 14 to 1000 pounds.

MANUFACTURING OPERATIONS

Plant Locations

The main plant is in Euclid, Ohio, a suburb east of Cleveland. The layout of this plant is shown in Figure 1. There are no warehouses. Materials flow from the half-mile-long dock on the north side of the plant through the production lines to a very limited storage and loading area on the south side. Materials used at each work station are stored as

FIGURE 1
LINCOLN ELECTRIC COMPANY
MAIN FACTORY LAYOUT

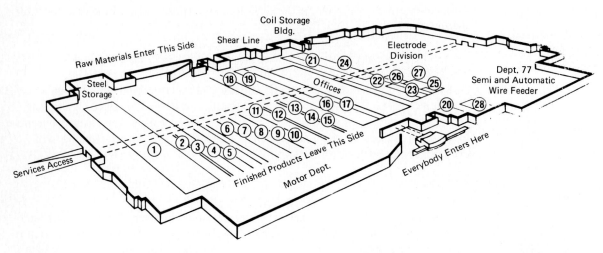

1. Winding Dept.
2. DC-600
3. R3R
4. Rotor Casting & Lamination Mfg.
5. AC-225-S
6. SP-200
7. AC-250
8. R3S
9. TIG/TM
10. SA-200 Line
11. SA-250 Line
12. Large Engine Line
13. PERKINS 300-400 Line
14. KOHLER Engine Line
15. ONAN Engine Line
16. Fabrication
17. Tool Room
18. Large Engine Accessory
19. Bracket Assembly
20. Welding School
21. Maintenance
22. Quantity Const.
23. Fork Lift Repair
24. Standard & Rebuild
25. Finish Area
26. Customer Service
27. Boom Assembly
28. Clean Room

close as possible to the work station. The administrative offices, near the center of the factory, are entirely functional. Not even the president's office is carpeted. A corridor below the main level provides access to the factory floor from the main entrance near the center of the plant. A new plant, just opened in Mentor, Ohio, houses some of the electrode production operations, which were moved from the main plant.

Manufacturing Processes

Electrode manufacturing is highly capital-intensive. Metal rods purchased from steel producers are drawn or extruded down to smaller diameters, cut to length, and coated with pressed-powder "flux" for stick electrodes or plated with copper (for conductivity) and spun into coils or spools for wire. Some of Lincoln's wire, called Innershield, is hollow and filled with a material similar to that used to coat stick electrodes. Lincoln is highly secretive about its electrode production processes, and the case writer was not given access to the details of those processes.

Welding machines and electric motors are made on a series of assembly lines. Gasoline and diesel engines are purchased partially assembled, but practically all other components are made from basic industrial products, e.g., steel bars and sheets and bar copper conductor wire, in the Lincoln factory.

Individual components, such as gasoline tanks for engine-driven welders and steel shafts for motors and generators, are made by numerous small "factories within a factory." The shaft for a certain generator, for example, is made from a raw steel bar by one operator who uses five large machines, all running continuously. A saw cuts the bar to length, a digital lathe machines different sections to varying diameters, a special milling machine cuts a slot for a keyway, and so forth, until a finished shaft is produced. The operator moves the shafts from machine to machine and makes necessary adjustments.

Another operator punches, shapes, and paints sheetmetal cowling parts. One assembles steel laminations onto a rotor shaft, and then winds, insulates, and tests the rotors. Finished components are moved by crane operators to the nearby assembly lines.

Worker Performance and Attitudes

Exceptional worker performance at Lincoln is a matter of record. The typical Lincoln employee earns about twice as much as other factory workers in the Cleveland area. Yet the labor cost per sales dollar at Lincoln, currently 23.5 cents, is well below industry averages.

Sales per Lincoln factory employee currently exceed $157,000. An observer at the factory quickly sees why this figure is so high. Each worker is proceeding busily and thoughtfully about his task. There is no idle chatter. Most workers take no coffee breaks. Many operate several machines and make a substantial component unaided. The supervisors, some with as many as 100 subordinates, are busy with planning and recordkeeping duties and hardly glance at the people they supervise. The manufacturing procedures appear efficient—no unnecessary steps, no wasted motions, no wasted materials. Finished components move smoothly to subsequent work stations.

Worker turnover at Lincoln is practically nonexistent, except for retirements and departures by new employees. The appendix includes summaries of interviews with Lincoln employees.

ORGANIZATION STRUCTURE

Lincoln has never had a formal organization chart.[17] The objective of this policy is to ensure maximum flexibility. An open-door policy is practiced throughout the company, and personnel are encouraged to take problems to the persons most capable of resolving them.

Perhaps because of the quality and enthusiasm of the Lincoln work force, routine supervision is almost nonexistent. A typical production foreman, for example, supervises as many as 100 workers, a span of control which does not allow more than infrequent worker-supervisor interaction. Position titles and traditional flows of authority do imply something of an organizational structure, however. For example, the vice president of sales and the vice president of the electrode division report to the president, as do various staff assistants such as the personnel director and the director of purchasing. With the use of such implied relationships, it has been determined that production workers have two or, at most, three levels of supervision between themselves and the president.

PERSONNEL POLICIES

Recruitment and Selection

Every job opening at Lincoln is advertised internally on company bulletin boards, and any employee can apply for any job so advertised. External hiring is done only for entry-level positions. Selection for these jobs is based on personal interviews—there is no aptitude or psychological testing. Not even a high-school diploma is required except for engineering and sales positions, which are filled by graduate engineers. A committee consisting of vice presidents and superintendents interviews candidates initially cleared by the personnel department. Final selection is made by the supervisor who has a job opening. Out of over 3500 applicants interviewed by the personnel department during a recent period, fewer than 300 were hired.

Job Security

In 1958 Lincoln formalized its lifetime employment policy, which had already been in effect for many years. There have been no layoffs at Lincoln since World War II. Since 1958, every Lincoln worker with over one year's employment has been guaranteed at least thirty hours per week, forty-nine weeks per year.

The policy had never been so severely tested as during the 1981–1983 recession. As a manufacturer of capital goods, Lincoln's business is highly cyclical. In previous

---

[17] Harvard Business School researchers once prepared an organization chart reflecting the below-mentioned implied relationships. The chart became available within the Lincoln organization, and the present Lincoln management feels that it had a disruptive effect. Therefore, the case writer was asked not to include any kind of organizational chart in this report.

recessions Lincoln had been able to avoid major sales declines. Sales for 1982, however, were about one-third below those of 1981. Few companies could withstand such a sales decline and remain profitable. Yet, Lincoln not only earned profits, no employee was laid off, the usual year-end incentive bonuses were paid (averaging $15,600 per worker for 1982), and common shareholders continued to receive about the normal dividend (around $8 per share).

Performance Evaluations

Each supervisor formally evaluates his subordinates twice a year using the cards shown in Figure 2. The employee performance criteria, "quality," "dependability," "ideas and cooperation," and "output," are considered to be independent of each other. Marks on the cards are converted to numerical scores which are forced to average 100 for each evaluating supervisor. Individual merit rating scores normally range from 80 to 110. Any score over 110 requires a special letter to top management. These scores (over 110) are not considered in computing the required 100-point average for each evaluating supervisor. Suggestions for improvements often result in recommendations for exceptionally high performance scores. Supervisors discuss individual performance marks with the employees concerned. Each warranty claim on a Lincoln product is traced to the individual employee whose work caused the defect. The employee's performance score may be reduced by 1 point, or the worker may be required to repay the cost of servicing the warranty claim by working without pay.

Compensation

Basic wage levels for jobs at Lincoln are determined by a wage survey of similar jobs in the Cleveland area. These rates are adjusted quarterly in accordance with changes in the Cleveland area Consumer Price Index. Insofar as possible, base wage rates are translated into piece rates. Practically all production workers and many others—for example, some forklift operators are paid by piece rate. Once established, piece rates are never changed unless a substantive change in the way a job is done results from a source other than the worker doing the job. In December of each year, a portion of the annual profits is distributed to employees as bonuses. Incentive bonuses since 1934 have averaged about the same as annual wages and somewhat more than after-tax profits. The average bonus for 1981 was about $21,000. Bonuses averaged $15,500 and $10,400, respectively, for the recession years 1982 and 1983. Individual bonuses are proportional to merit-rating scores. For example, assume incentive bonuses for the company total 110 percent of wages paid. A person whose performance score is 95 will receive a bonus of 1.045 (1.10 x 0.95) times annual wages.

Work Assignment

Management has authority to transfer workers and to switch between overtime and short time as required. Supervisors have undisputed authority to assign specific parts to individual employees, who may have their own preferences due to variations in piece rates.

FIGURE 2 MERIT RATING CARDS

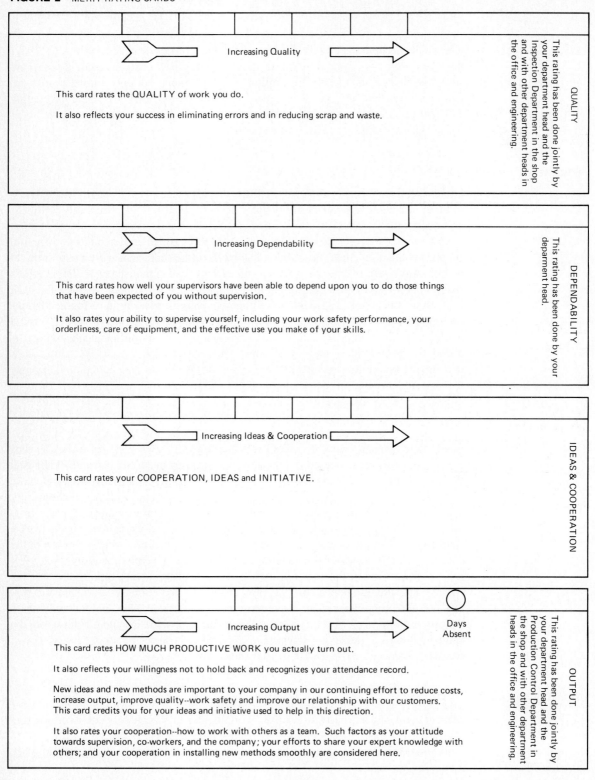

→ Increasing Quality ⟹

This card rates the QUALITY of work you do.

It also reflects your success in eliminating errors and in reducing scrap and waste.

QUALITY

This rating has been done jointly by your department head and the Inspection Department in the shop and with other department heads in the office and engineering.

→ Increasing Dependability ⟹

This card rates how well your supervisors have been able to depend upon you to do those things that have been expected of you without supervision.

It also rates your ability to supervise yourself, including your work safety performance, your orderliness, care of equipment, and the effective use you make of your skills.

DEPENDABILITY

This rating has been done by your deparment head.

→ Increasing Ideas & Cooperation ⟹

This card rates your COOPERATION, IDEAS and INITIATIVE.

IDEAS & COOPERATION

→ Increasing Output ⟹   Days Absent

This card rates HOW MUCH PRODUCTIVE WORK you actually turn out.

It also reflects your willingness not to hold back and recognizes your attendance record.

New ideas and new methods are important to your company in our continuing effort to reduce costs, increase output, improve quality--work safety and improve our relationship with our customers. This card credits you for your ideas and initiative used to help in this direction.

It also rates your cooperation--how to work with others as a team. Such factors as your attitude towards supervision, co-workers, and the company; your efforts to share your expert knowledge with others; and your cooperation in installing new methods smoothly are considered here.

OUTPUT

This rating has been done jointly by your department head and the Production Control Department in the shop and with other department heads in the office and engineering.

Employee Participation in Decision Making

When a manager speaks of participative management, he usually thinks of a relaxed, nonauthoritarian atmosphere. This is not the case at Lincoln. Formal authority is quite strong. "We're very authoritarian around here," says Willis. James F. Lincoln placed a good deal of stress on protecting management's authority. "Management in all successful departments of industry must have complete power," he said. "Management is the coach who must be obeyed. The men, however, are the players who alone can win the game."[18] Despite this attitude, there are several ways in which employees participate in management at Lincoln.

Richard Sabo, manager of public relations, relates job enlargement to participation. "The most important participative technique that we use is giving more responsibility to employees." Sabo says, "We give a high school graduate more responsibility than other companies give their foremen." Lincoln puts limits on the degree of participation which is allowed, however. In Sabo's words:

> When you use "participation," put quotes around it. Because we believe that each person should participate only in those decisions he is most knowledgeable about. I don't think production employees should control the decisions of Bill Irrgang. They don't know as much as he does about the decisions he is involved in.

The advisory board, elected by the workers, meets with the chairman and the president every two weeks to discuss ways of improving operations. This board has been in existence since 1914 and has contributed to many innovations. The incentive bonuses, for example, were first recommended by this committee. Every Lincoln employee has access to advisory board members, and answers to all advisory board suggestions are promised by the following meeting. Both Irrgang and Willis are quick to point out, though, that the advisory board only recommends actions. "They do not have direct authority," Irrgang says, "and when they bring up something that management thinks is not to the benefit of the company, it will be rejected."[19]

A suggestion program was instituted in 1929. At first, employees were awarded one-half of the first year's savings attributable to their suggestions. Now, however, the value of suggestions is reflected in performance evaluation scores, which determine individual incentive bonus amounts.

Training and Education

Production workers are given a short period of on-the-job training and then placed on a piecework pay system. Lincoln does not pay for off-site education. The idea behind this latter policy is that everyone cannot take advantage of such a program and that it is unfair to expend company funds for an advantage to which there is unequal access. Sales personnel are given on-the-job training in the plant followed by a period of work and training at one of the regional sales offices.

---

[18] Lincoln, *Incentive Management*, Cleveland, Ohio, The Lincoln Electric Company, 1951, p. 228.
[19] Incentive Management in Action, *Assembly Engineering*, March 1967, p. 18.

Fringe Benefits and Executive Perquisites

A medical plan and a company-paid retirement program have been in effect for many years. A plant cafeteria, operated on a breakeven basis, serves meals at about 60 percent of usual costs. An employee association, to which the company does not contribute, provides disability insurance and social and athletic activities. An employee stock ownership program, instituted in about 1925, and regular stock purchases have resulted in employee ownership of about 50 percent of Lincoln's stock.

As to executive perquisites, there are none. There are crowded, austere offices, no executive washrooms or lunchrooms, and no reserved parking spaces. Even the company president pays for his own meals and eats in the cafeteria.

FINANCIAL POLICIES

James F. Lincoln felt strongly that financing for company growth should come from within the company—through initial cash investment by the founders, through retention of earnings, and through stock purchases by those who work in the business. He saw the following advantages of this approach:[20]

1 Ownership of stock by employees strengthens team spirit. "If they are mutually anxious to make it succeed, the future of the company is bright."

2 Ownership of stock provides individual incentive because employees feel that they will benefit from company profitability.

3 "Ownership is educational." Owner-employees "will know how profits are made and lost; how success is won and lost . . . There are few socialists in the list of stockholders of the nation's industries."

4 "Capital available from within controls expansion." Unwarranted expansion would not occur, Lincoln believed, under his financing plan.

5 "The greatest advantage would be the development of the individual worker. Under the incentive of ownership, he would become a greater man."

6 "Stock ownership is one of the steps that can be taken that will make the worker feel that there is less of a gulf between him and the boss . . . Stock ownership will help the worker to recognize his responsibility in the game and the importance of victory."

Lincoln Electric Company uses a minimum of debt in its capital structure. There is no borrowing at all, with the debt being limited to current payables. Even the new $20 million plant in Mentor, Ohio, was financed totally from earnings.

The usual pricing policy at Lincoln is succinctly stated by President Willis: "At all times price on the basis of cost and at all times keep pressure on our cost." This policy resulted in Lincoln's price for the most popular welding electrode then in use going from 16 cents a pound in 1929 to 4.7 cents in 1938. More recently, the SA-200 welder, Lincoln's largest selling portable machine, decreased in price from 1958 through 1965. According to C. Jackson Grayson of the American Productivity Center in Houston, Texas, Lincoln's prices in general have increased only one-fifth as fast as the Con-

[20] Lincoln, 1961, pp. 220–228.

sumer Price Index from 1934 to about 1970. This has resulted in a welding products market in which Lincoln is the undisputed price leader for the products it manufactures. Not even the major Japanese manufacturers, such as Nippon Steel for welding electrodes and Asaka Transformer for welding machines, have been able to penetrate this market.

Huge cash balances are accumulated each year preparatory to paying the year-end bonuses. The bonuses totaled $55,718,000 for 1981 and about $41,000,000 for 1982. This money is invested in short-term U.S. government securities until needed. Financial statements are shown in Tables 1 and 2.

TABLE 1 BALANCE SHEETS: THE LINCOLN ELECTRIC COMPANY
(Dollar Amounts in Thousands)

	1980	1981	1982
Assets			
Cash	$ 1,307	$ 3,603	$ 1,318
Govt. securities and certificates of deposit	46,503	62,671	72,485
Notes and accounts receivable	42,424	41,521	26,239
Inventories (LIFO basis)	35,533	45,541	38,157
Deferred taxes and prepared expenses	2,749	3,658	4,635
	$128,516	$156,994	$142,834
Other intangible assets	$ 19,723	$ 21,424	$ 22,116
Investment in foreign subsidiaries	4,695	4,695	7,696
	$ 24,418	$ 26,119	$ 29,812
Property, plant, equipment, land	$ 913	$ 928	$ 925
Buildings*	22,982	24,696	23,330
Machinery, tools, and equipment*	25,339	27,104	26,949
	$ 49,234	$ 52,728	$ 51,204
Total assets	$202,168	$235,841	$223,850
Liabilities			
Accounts payable	$ 15,608	$ 14,868	$ 11,936
Accrued wages	1,504	4,940	3,633
Taxes, including income taxes	5,622	14,755	5,233
Dividends payable	5,800	7,070	6,957
	$ 28,534	$ 41,633	$ 27,759
Deferred taxes and other long-term liabilities	$ 3,807	$ 4,557	$ 5,870
Shareholders' equity			
Common capital stock, stated value	$ 276	$ 272	$ 268
Additional paid-in capital	2,641	501	1,862
Retained earnings	166,910	188,878	188,392
Equity adjustment from foreign currency translation			(301)
	$169,827	$189,651	$190,221
Total liabilities and shareholders' equity	$202,168	$235,841	$223,850

* After depreciation.

TABLE 2 INCOME STATEMENTS: THE LINCOLN ELECTRIC COMPANY
(Dollar Amounts in Thousands)

	1980	1981	1982
Income			
Net sales	$387,374	$450,387	$310,862
Other income	13,817	18,454	18,049
	$401,191	$468,841	$328,911
Costs and expenses			
Cost of products sold	$260,671	$293,332	$212,674
Selling, administrative, freight–			
out, and general expenses	37,753	42,656	37,128
Year-end incentive bonus	43,249	55,718	36,870
Payroll taxes related to bonus	1,251	1,544	1,847
Pension expense	6,810	6,874	5,888
	$349,734	$400,124	$294,407
Income before income taxes	$ 51,457	$ 68,717	$ 34,504
Provision for income taxes			
Federal	$ 20,300	$ 27,400	$ 13,227
State and local	3,072	3,885	2,497
	$ 23,372	$ 31,285	$ 15,724
Net income	$ 28,085	$ 37,432	$ 18,780
Employees (eligible for Bonus)	2,637	2,684	2,634

HOW WELL DOES LINCOLN SERVE ITS PUBLIC?

Lincoln Electric differs from most other companies in the importance it assigns to each of the groups it serves. Willis identifies these groups, in the order of priority Lincoln ascribes to them, as (1) customers, (2) employees, and (3) stockholders.

Certainly Lincoln customers have fared well over the years. Lincoln prices for welding machines and welding electrodes are acknowledged to be the lowest in the marketplace. Lincoln quality has consistently been so high that Lincoln Fleetweld electrodes and Lincoln SA-200 welders have been the standard in the pipeline and refinery construction industry, where price is hardly a criterion, for decades. The cost of field failures for Lincoln products was an amazing four one-hundreths of 1 percent in 1979. A Lincoln distributor in Monroe, Louisiana, says that he has sold several hundred of the popular AC-225 welders, and, though the machine is warranted for one year, he has never handled a warranty claim.

Perhaps best served of all Lincoln constituencies have been the employees. Not the least of their benefits, of course, are the year-end bonuses, which effectively double an already average compensation level. The foregoing description of the personnel program and the comments in the appendix further illustrate the desirability of a Lincoln job.

While stockholders were relegated to an inferior status by James F. Lincoln, they have done very well indeed. Recent dividends have exceeded $7 a share and earnings per share have exceeded $20. In January 1980, the price of restricted stock committed by Lincoln to employees was $117 a share. By February 4, 1983, the stated value, at which Lincoln would repurchase the stock if tendered, was $166. A check with the New York office of Merrill, Lynch, Pierce, Fenner, and Smith on February 4, 1983, revealed an estimated price for Lincoln stock of $240 a share, with none being offered for sale. Technically, this price applies only to the unrestricted stock owned by the Lincoln family, a few other major holders, and employees who have purchased it on the open market, but it gives some idea of the value of Lincoln stock in general. The risk associated with Lincoln stock, a major determinant of stock value, is minimal because of the absence of debt in Lincoln's capital structure, because of an extremely stable earnings record, and because of Lincoln's practice of purchasing the restricted stock whenever employees offer it for sale.

A CONCLUDING COMMENT

It is easy to believe that the reason for Lincoln's success is the excellent attitude of Lincoln employees and their willingness to work harder, faster, and more intelligently than other industrial workers. However, Richard Sabo, manager of publicity and educational services at Lincoln, suggests that appropriate credit be given to Lincoln executives, whom he credits with carrying out the following policies:

1 Management has limited research, development, and manufacturing to a standard product line designed to meet the major needs of the welding industry.

2 New products must be reviewed by manufacturing and all production costs verified before being approved by management.

3 Purchasing is challenged to not only procure materials at the lowest cost but also to work closely with engineering and manufacturing to ensure that the latest innovations are implemented.

4 Manufacturing supervision and all personnel are held accountable for reduction of scrap, energy conservation, and maintenance of product quality.

5 Production control, material handling, and methods engineering are closely supervised by top management.

6 Material and finished goods inventory control, accurate cost accounting, and attention to sales cost, credit, and other financial areas have constantly reduced overhead and led to excellent profitability.

7 Management has made cost reduction a way of life at Lincoln, and definite programs are established in many areas, including traffic and shipping, where tremendous savings can result.

8 Management has established a sales department that is technically trained to reduce customer welding costs. This sales technique and other real customer services have eliminated nonessential frills and resulted in long-term benefits to all concerned.

9 Management has encouraged education, technical publishing, and long-range programs that have resulted in industry growth, thereby ensuring market potential for the Lincoln Electric Company.

APPENDIX:
Employee Interviews

During the late summer of 1980, the author conducted numerous interviews with Lincoln employees. Typical questions and answers from those interviews are presented below. In order to maintain each employee's personal privacy, the names used for the interviewees are fictitious.

I

Interview with Betty Stewart, a fifty-two-year-old high school graduate who had been with Lincoln thirteen years and who was working as a cost accounting clerk at the time of the interview.

Q. What jobs have you held here besides the one you have now?
A. I worked in payroll for a while, and then this job came open and I took it.
Q. How much money did you make last year, including your bonus?
A. I would say roughly around $20,000, but I was off for back surgery for a while.
Q. You weren't paid while you were off for back surgery?
A. No.
Q. Did the employees association help out?
A. Yes. The company doesn't furnish that, though. We pay $6 a month into the employee association. I think my check from them was $105.00 a week.
Q. How was your performance rating last year?
A. It was around 100 points, but I lost some points for attendance with my back problem.
Q. How did you get your job at Lincoln?
A. I was bored silly where I was working, and I had heard that Lincoln kept their people busy. So I applied and got the job the next day.
Q. Do you think you make more money than similar workers in Cleveland?
A. I know I do.
Q. What have you done with your money?
A. We have purchased a better home. Also, my son is going to the University of Chicago, which costs $10,000 a year. I buy the Lincoln stock which is offered each year, and I have a little bit of gold.
Q. Have you ever visited with any of the senior executives, like Mr. Willis or Mr. Irrgang?
A. I have known Mr. Willis for a long time.
Q. Does he call you by name?
A. Yes. In fact he was very instrumental in my going to the doctor that I am going to with my back. He knows the director of the clinic.
Q. Do you know Mr. Irrgang?
A. I know him to speak to him, and he always speaks, always. But I have known Mr. Willis for a good many years. When I did Plant Two accounting I did not understand how the plant operated. Of course you are not allowed in Plant Two, because that's the Electrode Division. I told my boss about the problem one day, and the next thing I knew Mr. Willis came by and said, "Come on, Betty, we're going to Plant Two." He spent an hour and a half showing me the plant.
Q. Do you think Lincoln employees produce more than those in other companies?
A. I think with the incentive program the way that it is, if you want to work and achieve, then you will do it. If you don't want to work and achieve, you will not do it no matter where you are. Just because you are merit-rated and have a bonus, if you really don't

want to work hard, then you're not going to. You will accept your ninety points or ninety-two or eighty-five because, even with that, you make more money than people on the outside.

Q. Do you think Lincoln employees will ever join a union?

A. I don't know why they would.

Q. What is the most important advantage of working for Lincoln Electric?

A. You have an incentive, and you can push and get something for pushing. That's not true in a lot of companies.

Q. So you say that money is a very major advantage?

A. Money is a major advantage, but it's not just the money. It's the fact that, having the incentive, you do wish to work a little harder. I'm sure that there are a lot of men here who, if they worked some other place, would not work as hard as they do here. Not that they are overworked—I don't mean that—but I'm sure they wouldn't push.

Q. Is there anything that you would like to add?

A. I do like working here. I am better off being pushed mentally. In another company if you pushed too hard you would feel a little bit of pressure, and someone might say, "Hey, slow down; don't try so hard." But here you are encouraged, not discouraged.

II

Interview with Ed Sanderson, twenty-three-year-old high-school graduate who had been with Lincoln four years and who was a machine operator in the electrode division at the time of the interview.

Q. How did you happen to get this job?

A. My wife was pregnant, and I was making three bucks an hour and one day I came here and applied. That was it. I kept calling to let them know I was still interested.

Q. Roughly what were your earnings last year including your bonus?

A. $37,000.

Q. What have you done with your money since you have been here?

A. Well, we've lived pretty well, and we bought a condominium.

Q. Have you paid for the condominium?

A. No, but I could.

Q. Have you bought your Lincoln stock this year?

A. No, I haven't bought any Lincoln stock yet.

Q. Do you get the feeling that the executives here are pretty well thought of?

A. I think they are. To get where they are today, they had to really work.

Q. Wouldn't that be true anywhere?

A. I think more so here because seniority really doesn't mean anything. If you work with a guy who has twenty years here, and you have two months and you're doing a better job, you will get advanced before he will.

Q. Are you paid on a piece rate basis?

A. My gang is. There are nine of us who make the bare electrode, and the whole group gets paid based on how much electrode we make.

Q. Do you think you work harder than workers in other factories in the Cleveland area?

A. Yes, I would say I probably work harder.

Q. Do you think it hurts anybody?

A. No, a little hard work never hurts anybody.

Q. If you could choose, do you think you would be as happy earning a little less money and being able to slow down a little?

A. No, it doesn't bother me. If it bothered me, I wouldn't do it.

Q. What would you say is the biggest disadvantage of working at Lincoln, as opposed to working somewhere else?

A. Probably having to work shift work.

Q. Why do you think Lincoln employees produce more than workers in other plants?

A. That's the way the company is set up. The more you put out, the more you're going to make.

Q. Do you think it's the piece rate and bonus together?

A. I don't think people would work here if they didn't know that they would be rewarded at the end of the year.

Q. Do you think Lincoln employees will ever join a union?

A. No.

Q. What are the major advantages of working for Lincoln?

A. Money.

Q. Are there any other advantages?

A. Yes, we don't have a union shop. I don't think I could work in a union shop.

Q. Do you think you are a career man with Lincoln at this time?

A. Yes.

III

Interview with Roger Lewis, twenty-three-year-old Purdue graduate in mechanical engineering who had been in the Lincoln sales program for fifteen months and who was working in the Cleveland sales office at the time of the interview.

Q. How did you get your job at Lincoln?

A. I saw that Lincoln was interviewing on campus at Purdue, and I went by. I later came to Cleveland for a plant tour and was offered a job.

Q. Do you know any of the senior executives? Would they know you by name?

A. Yes, I know all of them—Mr. Irrgang, Mr. Willis, Mr. Manross.

Q. Do you think Lincoln salesmen work harder than those in other companies?

A. Yes. I don't think there are many salesmen for other companies who are putting in fifty- to sixty-hour weeks. Everybody here works harder. You can go out in the plant, or you can go upstairs, and there's nobody sitting around.

Q. Do you see any real disadvantage of working at Lincoln?

A. I don't know if it's a disadvantage but Lincoln is a spartan company, a very thrifty company. I like that. The sales offices are functional, not fancy.

Q. Why do you think Lincoln employees have such high productivity?

A. Piecework has a lot to do with it. Lincoln is smaller than many plants, too; you can stand in one place and see the materials come in one side and the product go out the other. You feel a part of the company. The chance to get ahead is important, too. They have a strict policy of promoting from within, so you know you have a chance. I think in a lot of other places you may not get as fair a shake as you do here. The sales offices are on a smaller scale, too. I like that. I tell someone that we have two people in the Baltimore office, and they say "You've got to be kidding." It's smaller and more personal. Pay is the most important thing. I have heard that this is the highest paying factory in the world.

IV

Interview with Jimmy Roberts, a forty-seven-year-old high-school graduate, who had been with Lincoln seventeen years and who was working as a multiple drill press operator at the time of the interview.

Q. What jobs have you had at Lincoln?

A. I started out cleaning the men's locker room in 1963. After about a year I got a job in the flux department, where we make the coating for welding rods. I worked there for seven or eight years and then got my present job.

Q. Do you make one particular part?

A. No, there are a variety of parts I make—at least twenty-five.

Q. Each one has a different piece rate attached to it?

A. Yes.

Q. Are some piece rates better than others?

A. Yes.

Q. How do you determine which ones you are going to do?

A. You don't. Your supervisor assigns them.

Q. How much money did you make last year?

A. $47,000.

Q. Have you ever received any kind of award or citation?

A. No.

Q. Was your rating ever over 110?

A. Yes. For the past five years, probably, I made over 110 points.

Q. Is there any attempt to let others know?

A. The kind of points I get? No.

Q. Do you know what they are making?

A. No. There are some who might not be too happy with their points, and they might make it known. The majority, though, do not make it a point of telling other employees.

Q. Would you be just as happy earning a little less money and working a little slower?

A. I don't think I would—not at this point. I have done piecework all these years, and the fast pace doesn't really bother me.

Q. Why do you think Lincoln productivity is so high?

A. The incentive thing—the bonus distribution. I think that would be the main reason. The pay check you get every two weeks is important too.

Q. Do you think Lincoln employees would ever join a union?

A. I don't think so. I have never heard anyone mention it.

Q. What is the most important advantage of working here?

A. The amount of money you make. I don't think I could make this type of money anywhere else, especially with only a high-school education.

Q. As a black person, do you feel that Lincoln discriminates in any way against blacks?

A. No. I don't think any more so than any other job. Naturally, there is a certain amount of discrimination, regardless of where you are.

V

Interview with Joe Trahan, fifty-eight-year-old high-school graduate who had been with Lincoln thirty-nine years and who was employed as a working supervisor in the tool room at the time of the interview.

Q. Roughly what was your pay last year?

A. Over $50,000—salary, bonus, stock dividends.

Q. How much was your bonus?

A. About $23,000.

Q. Have you ever gotten a special award of any kind?

A. Not really.

Q. What have you done with your money?

A. My house is paid for—and my two cars. I also have some bonds and the Lincoln stock.

Q. What do you think of the executives at Lincoln?

A. They're really top notch.

Q. What is the major disadvantage of working at Lincoln Electric?

A. I don't know of any disadvantage at all.

Q. Do you think you produce more than most people in similar jobs with other companies?

A. I do believe that.

Q. Why is that? Why do you believe that?

A. We are on the incentive system. Everything we do, we try to improve to make a better product with a minimum of outlay. We try to improve the bonus.

Q. Would you be just as happy making a little less money and not working quite so hard?

A. I don't think so.

Q. You know that Lincoln productivity is higher than that at most other plants. Why is that?

A. Money.

Q. Do you think Lincoln employees would ever join a union?

A. I don't think they would ever consider it.

Q. What is the most important advantage of working at Lincoln?

A. Compensation.

Q. Tell me something about Mr. James Lincoln, who died in 1965.

A. You are talking about Jimmy, Sr. He always strolled through the shop in his shirt-sleeves. Big fellow. Always looked distinguished. Gray hair. Friendly sort of guy. I was a member of the advisory board one year. He was there each time.

Q. Did he strike you as really caring?

A. I think he always cared for people.

Q. Did you get any sensation of a religious nature from him?

A. No, not really.

Q. And religion is not part of the program now?

A. No.

Q. Do you think Mr. Lincoln was a very intelligent man, or was he just a nice guy?

A. I would say he was pretty well educated. A great talker—always right off the top of his head. He knew what he was talking about all the time.

Q. When were bonuses for beneficial suggestions done away with?

A. About fifteen years ago.

Q. Did that hurt very much?

A. I don't think so, because suggestions are still rewarded through the merit-rating system.

Q. Is there anything you would like to add?

A. It's a good place to work. The union kind of ties other places down. At other places, electricians only do electrical work, carpenters only do carpenter work. At Lincoln Electric we all pitch in and do whatever needs to be done.

Q. So a major advantage is not having a union?

A. That's right.

DISCUSSION QUESTIONS

1 Relate Lincoln's conservative financing policies to the company's ability to offer guaranteed employment to its workers.
2 Who are Lincoln's constituencies in order of stated priority? Explain how company practices either do or do not appear to bear this out.
3 Why do Lincoln employees produce so much?
4 Is Lincoln Electric pro- or antiunion? Justify or oppose their position.
5 Relate Lincoln's marketing policy in terms of the four P's of marketing to the free-market ethic of theoretical (Adam Smith) capitalism.
6 Which aspects of the Lincoln system could be effectively applied elsewhere? Explain.
7 Discuss what you consider to be the major weakness of Lincoln Electric and explain how the company may or may not be subject to external threats.
8 Relate the overall Lincoln program to society's needs, particularly the needs for increased productivity, reduced inflation, and improved perception of trust in the business establishment.

LEVI STRAUSS AND COMPANY

Neil H. Snyder
Debie Alford
Karen Davis
Allison Gillum
Jim Tucker
Jeff Walker
University of Virginia

SELECTED STRATEGIC ISSUES

- Diversification as a strategic response to market maturity
- Repurchasing debt or equity with excess cash flow
- Appropriate percentages of women in sales and managerial positions
- Departmentation for U.S. versus international markets
- Source of value of a well-known brand name
- Strengths, weaknesses, threats, and opportunities as determinants of strategic focus

Levi Strauss, a Bavarian immigrant who was lured to the West during the gold rush in search of prosperity, did not strike it rich in gold, but he found his fortune in jeans. His first pair of jeans was sold in 1853 to a San Francisco gold digger who wanted a sturdy pair of pants which would hold up in the mines. In time, his jeans became so popular that young Strauss set up a shop in San Francisco. Today, the headquarters of Levi Strauss and Company (L.S. & CO.) stands near the same location as young Strauss's shop.

It was not until the 1930s that Levi's jeans reached the eastern market. Although attempts were made to promote jeans for resort wear, the basic clientele continued to be limited. World War II, however, created a sharp increase in demand, and they were sold only to individuals engaged in defense work. It also marked a turning point for Levi Strauss. L.S. & CO. had been largely a wholesale operation prior to WW II, but after the war, they began concentrating on manufacturing and direct sales. Before the war, L.S. & CO.'s annual sales were around $8 million, but by 1961 sales reached $51 million, mainly because of aggressive product diversification.

In 1981, L.S. & CO. was the largest manufacturer of jeans in the world, controlling about one-third of the jeans market. Additionally, they were the largest firm in the apparel industry with products in virtually every product line, and sales and profits by far the greatest in the apparel industry. According to L.S. & CO. Chairman of the Board, Peter E. Haas, "We'd like to outfit people from the cradle to the grave."

Levi's success has resulted in part from their skill in sensing an emerging new market and responding quickly and in part from their strong management and exceptional brand name acceptance. In addition, a focus on identifying market opportunities through segmentation in recent years has aided a diversification strategy. As a result, the company's growth and success has been strong despite the extreme competitiveness and cyclical nature of the apparel industry.

Top managers at L.S. & CO. are optimistic about the 1980s. Emphasis in the future will be on expanding womenswear and activewear and increasing the international market. A 1978 assessment by the *Wall Street Transcript* is valid today. It states, "There are few firms in any industry comparable to Levi Strauss from the standpoint of dynamic growth, above average return of equity, competitive strength and strong international consumer franchise."[1]

KEY EXECUTIVES[2]

Walter A. Haas, Jr. joined the Company in 1939 and served as its President from 1958 to 1970 and as its Chief Executive Officer from 1970 to 1976. He was named Chairman of the Board in December 1970 and Chairman of the Executive Committee in April 1976. He served in both of these positions until his retirement in 1981. He also served as a director since 1943. Mr. Haas controls 10.4% of the Company's stock. This figure includes shares owned by his wife, children, and estates and trusts for which he votes. He is the great grandnephew of Levi Strauss. He was 64 years old November 1981.

Peter E. Haas joined the Company in 1945 and became Executive Vice President in 1958. He became President of the Company in December 1970, and Chief Executive Officer in April 1976. In November 1981, he became Chairman of the Board. Mr. Haas controls 12% of the Company's stock. This figure includes stock owned by his family and stock owned by trusts and estates for which he has the voting power. He graduated from the University of California in 1940 and from Harvard University's

---

[1] *Wall Street Transcript*, January 23, 1978.

[2] The information included in this section was obtained from "Notice of Annual Meeting of Stockholders and Proxy Statement," Levi Strauss and Company, April 2, 1980, Page 1; *Standard and Poor's Register of Corporations, Directors, and Executives*, 1980, Directors and Executives, Vol. 2; and *Standard and Poor's Industry Surveys*, Vol. 1, Section 3, July 31, 1980, Page A95.

Graduate School of Business in 1943. He is the great grandnephew of Levi Strauss and was 61 years of age in 1981.

Robert T. Grohman joined the Company in April 1975 as President of Levi Strauss International and was elected a Vice President of the Company in May 1974. In 1975 he was appointed International Group President and Senior Vice President. He has been Executive Vice President since April 1976 and was President of the Operating Groups for fiscal years 1977–1980. He was named chief member of the office of the President in June 1978. In November 1981 he became President and Chief Executive Officer. He has served as a director since 1974. He was 56 in 1981.

Francis J. Brann joined the Company in 1965 and was elected Vice President in November 1972. He assumed the position of Levi Strauss International Division Area Manager Central Europe in June 1974 and the position of President of the Canada and Latin America Divisions in January 1976. In July 1976, he was elected Senior Vice President and assumed the position of Senior Vice President, Corporate Planning and Policy in December 1976. He was named Executive Vice President of the U.S. Sportswear Group in June 1978 and was promoted to President of Levi Strauss U.S.A. in January 1980. He joined the Board of Directors in July 1979. Mr. Brann graduated from the University of San Francisco in 1961 and from City College of New York, Graduate Business School in 1965. In 1981 he was 43.

Thomas W. Tusher joined the Company in 1969. He was named President of Levi Strauss International in January 1980, having served as Executive Vice President of the International Group since December 1976. During most of 1976, he held the position of President of the European Division. Prior to 1976, he functioned as general manager for various international divisions and areas. He was elected Vice President of the Company in April 1976, and Senior Vice President in December 1977. He joined the Board of Directors in July 1979. Mr. Tusher graduated from the University of California in 1963 and from Stanford University Graduate Business School in 1965. In 1981 he was 39 years old.

Robert D. Haas joined the Company in January 1973 as Project Analyst in Inventory Management and became Jeanswear Product Manager in August 1973. He then joined the Levi Strauss International group as Marketing Services Manager in October 1975. He became Director of Marketing in May 1976, and Assistant General Manager–Far East Division in December 1976. In November 1977, he was elected Vice President of the Company and was appointed Director of Corporate Marketing Development. He was elected Senior Vice President–Corporate Planning and Policy in June 1978, and was appointed President of the New Business Group in January 1980, when he joined the Board of Directors. On December 1980, he became President of the Operating Groups. In 1981 he was 38.

Exhibit 1 contains the names, positions and ages of the key executives of Levi Strauss.

THE APPAREL INDUSTRY

If one were forced to select one word which describes the nature of competition in the apparel industry, it would have to be fierce. In the United States alone, there are more than 15,000 manufacturers in the apparel industry. However, the industry is experienc-

EXHIBIT 1   KEY EXECUTIVES

Name	Position and office	Age
J. P. Berghold	Vice President and Treasurer	42
Thomas C. Borrelli	Vice President and President of the Jeanswear Division	60
Francis J. Brann	Senior Vice President and President of Levi Strauss USA, Director	42
Jams W. Cameron	Vice President—Human Resources	49
Harry H. Cohn	Vice President and Executive Vice President of Group III—Levi Strauss USA, Director	50
Robert T. Grohman	President, Chief Executive Officer, Director	56
Peter E. Haas	Chairman of the Board, Director	61
Robert D. Haas	Senior Vice President and President of the Operating Groups, Director	38
Walter A. Haas, Jr.	Retired November 1981, Director	64
Thomas E. Harris	Vice President—Community Affairs	
Roy C. Johns, Jr.	Vice President—Corporate Communications	51
Peter T. Jones	Senior Vice President and General Counsel, Director	50
David A. Kaled	Vice President—Corporate Planning and Policy	37
Robert B. Kern	Vice President, Corporate Secretary, Director	60
James A. McDermott	Vice President and Executive Vice President of Group II—Levi Strauss USA	44
Robert F. McRae	Vice President and President of the Canada Division	48
Richard D. Murphy	Vice President—Controller	37
Gerald E. O'Shea	Vice President and Assistant to the Chief Operating Officer	58
Alfred V. Sanguinetti	Senior Vice President and President of Group I —Levi Strauss USA, Director	52
Karl F. Slacik	Senior Vice President—Finance and Chief Financial Officer	51
Peter T. Thigpen	Vice President and Executive Vice President of Group I—Levi Strauss International	41
Thomas W. Tusher	Senior Vice President and President of Levi Strauss International, Director	39
William K. Warnock	Vice President, Executive Vice President of Diversified Apparel Enterprises and President of Koret of North America	59

Sources: 10-K Report for the fiscal year ended November 25, 1980, Standard and Poor's Corporation, New York.

ing a trend toward consolidation (large firms diversifying by buying smaller firms). This fact is evidenced by a 16 percent reduction in the number of domestic producers over the past 5 years. For the larger firms in the industry, consolidation via acquisition has led to rapid diversification of product lines and to an increased ability to cope with fluctuations in market demand. At the same time, it has resulted in market concentration. Currently, 5 percent of the firms in the apparel industry generate over 70 percent of industry sales.

Blue Bell, Inc. (manufacturer of Wrangler jeans), V.F. Corporation (producer of Lee Jeans), and L.S. & CO. are the major competitors in the apparel industry in terms of sales. In 1979, Blue Bell had sales of $1.029 billion and V.F. Corporation had sales of $544 million. Sales growth in these two companies has been steady, but slow. From 1974 to 1979, Blue Bell and V.F. experienced a 17.7% and a 8.8% average annual sales growth, respectively. In comparison, L.S. & CO. had sales of $2.1 billion in 1979, and their sales have more than doubled since 1975.

Market Saturation

According to Standard and Poor's, the United States apparel market has been saturated by both foreign and domestic producers. While imports of apparel have been growing gradually since the 1950s, in recent years imports have captured a considerable portion of the domestic market. Imports have continued to increase, albeit at a decreasing rate. Import volume doubled in the 1975 to 1978 period. Thus, domestic producers have found that it is becoming increasingly difficult to pass along to their customers the increased costs of raw materials, labor, energy, etc. In response to this trend, domestic manufacturers are turning toward mechanization, adoption of a global view of the business, diversification toward products that are more import-resistant, and a reliance on brand-name marketing and product exclusivity to counteract pressure on price.

Automation, particularly in design and cutting, is being used to increase productivity and thereby reduce average unit costs. In general, significant automation initiatives have been limited almost exclusively to larger firms who can afford the increased investment in plant and equipment. Thus, automation has resulted in a weakening of the competitive position of smaller firms. One consolation for smaller producers, however, is that the largest production cost component in the apparel industry is the cost of fabric. Except for better fabric utilization, automation affects directly only a small portion of total production costs, and service centers which offer automated pattern marking and cutting on a pay-as-you-go basis to smaller firms have been established. Furthermore, many smaller firms have focused on market niches to avoid severe price competition.

Designer Jeans

For a short time, designer jeans such as Gloria Vanderbilt, Calvin Klein, and Jordache were perceived as threats to the major producers of jeans. However, by 1981 the designer jean fad seemed to have peaked, and consumers began returning to the basic styles. Furthermore, designer jeans never accounted for more than an estimated 3 percent of the jean market.

Counterfeiting of Jeans

Jean counterfeiting is an emerging threat to the manufacturers of popular name brand jeans. Counterfeiting is a profitable undertaking since counterfeiters need not invest heavily to establish demand for their products (jean manufacturers have already done this), and they have no regard for product quality (jean manufacturers will bear the cost of dissatisfied customers).

For the most part, consumers who buy counterfeit jeans are unaware that they are not the real thing. These jeans are sold for a lower price than the "true brand," and they are often of inferior and/or inconsistent quality. Counterfeiters use lighter weight fabric; the seams in counterfeit jeans often come apart after one washing; and the zippers and rivets in counterfeit jeans are of low quality. Additionally, many counterfeiters purchase phony labels from label-makers in New York and attach the labels to jean seconds and irregulars purchased from other jeans manufacturers. Counterfeiting is a major concern of apparel manufacturers. They perceive counterfeits as a threat to their franchise and to overall sales.

In 1980 alone, L.S. & CO. uncovered a U.S. counterfeiting operation that produced approximately 50,000 fake pairs of Levi jeans per month. Moreover, L.S. & CO. recently won a $500,000 settlement in London from the operators of an international counterfeiting operation selling fake Levi jeans in Europe. This underscores the tremendous value of Levi's trademark.

OUTLOOK FOR THE DOMESTIC APPAREL MARKET

The future of the domestic apparel industry looks extremely good for various product lines such as activewear, sportswear, womenswear, jeans, and western styles. As the baby boom population moves into a higher age bracket, emphasis on leisure remains high; the proportion of women in the work force is increasing; and the population is shifting to the Sunbelt. Thus, these segments should continue to grow.

Many firms who are surviving the effects of increased competition are doing so primarily because of diversification into various segments of the apparel market. By broadening their scope and focusing on different markets, firms find it easier to avoid the potentially serious negative effects resulting from rapid style changes which characterize the industry.

Activewear is becoming an important factor in the apparel industry, and it is expected to remain popular through the 1980s. The success of activewear is due largely to the popularity of sports and physical fitness in the United States. Additionally, activewear has both functional and fashionable qualities which make it versatile enough for use as everyday wear. Since "casual is the wave of the future"[3] and the refreshed, relaxed and youthful appearance is also in vogue, the outlook for activewear is very good. Furthermore, the popularity of activewear is inducing strong growth in related sportswear apparel. L.S. & CO. is the only major apparel producer offering a full line of activewear.

Industry experts believe that womenswear has an exceptionally promising future, since more women are entering the labor market. There is evidence of a strong trend toward dressier fashions, sportswear, activewear, and separates for women. This trend looks promising to the executives at L.S. & CO. since their recent acquisition of Koracorp Industries made them a leader in the production of women's sportswear.

The future of western styles looks bright also. Their popularity is expected to continue because of the trend in the United States and foreign countries toward wearing

[3] *U.S. Industrial Outlook,* 1980, Page 367.

rugged American styles. From the perspective of the apparel producer, western styles are appealing for a number of reasons. First, most western-style clothes are made from cotton materials which are readily available and easy to work with. Second, they are durable, versatile, and comfortable. Thus, demand for these products is expected to remain strong for many years. Finally, corduroy products, which add color and variety to western styles, are experiencing increased demand. L.S. & CO. is encouraged by this trend since they are the leading producer of western styles in the world.

THE OUTLOOK FOR THE INTERNATIONAL MARKET

As the United States apparel market has become more saturated, growth-oriented apparel producers in the U.S. have directed their attention toward the market potential overseas. Between 1974 and 1979, the value of U.S. apparel exports increased from $332.7 million to $819 million. Furthermore, industry analysts believe that by 1985, 4 percent of total U.S. apparel production will be exported. Large U.S. apparel firms have relied on their financial, marketing, and research and development capabilities to compete successfully with foreign producers. Additionally, the popularity of American styles overseas has resulted in increased demand for name brand U.S. products.

Countries in Western Europe, such as Italy, Belgium, Austria, Switzerland, and West Germany, offer the most promising possibilities for future export growth. Growth prospects in these countries look good for several reasons. First, they have high standards of living. Second, they are experiencing declining domestic production. Finally, apparel imports in these countries are increasing rapidly.[4]

THE STRUCTURE AND PRODUCTS OF LEVI STRAUSS & CO.

Levi Strauss designs, manufactures, and markets casual wear for just about every taste. Their product line includes everything from jeans, skirts, and suits to shoes. The majority of their products are manufactured and sold under the Levis® trademark. In 1980, Levi Strauss and Company consolidated its three operating divisions into two units, Levi Strauss U.S.A. and Levi Strauss International. It also has miscellaneous other divisions and a corporate staff. Each unit contains several divisions which facilitate production and marketing in various segments of the casual wear market. (See Exhibit 2.)

Levi Strauss U.S.A.

Levi Strauss U.S.A. consists of 3 groups which are divided into operating divisions: Jeanswear, Youthwear, Resistol Hats, Womenswear, Koret of North America, Menswear, Activewear, Accessories, Employee Purchase Plan, and Retail Stores. L.S. & CO.'s Jeanswear division is the largest jeans manufacturer in the United States, and the largest division in the company. Additionally, it is responsible for producing all styles

---

[4] *U.S. Industrial Outlook*, 1980; p. 367.

EXHIBIT 2   OPERATING STRUCTURE OF LEVI STRAUSS & COMPANY

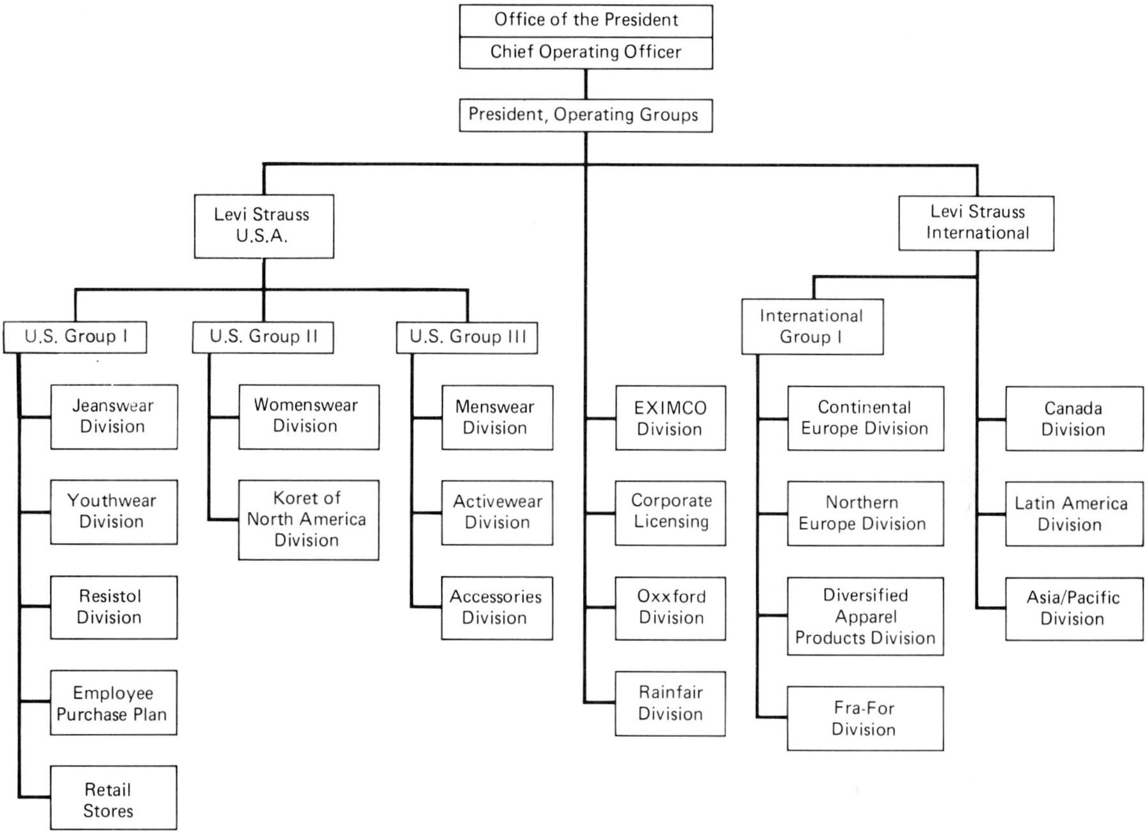

Source: 1980 Annual Report of Levi Strauss & Company.

of jeans (i.e., straightleg, bell bottom, pre-washed). However, this group also produces various styles of shirts, jackets, vests, shorts, and western wear for men.

The Youthwear division is the second major product division in the U.S.A. unit. It produces apparel for children from toddlers to teens, but it focuses primarily on the 7 to 14 year old market. Like the Jeanswear division, its products range from jeans, jackets, shirts and overalls to T-shirts. Sportswear for youngsters is a new product recently added to the Youthwear division.

Resistol Hats is the world's largest producer of brand-name western and dress hats. This division was formally part of Koracorp Industries which was a large and successful manufacturer in its own right.

Womenswear is another important product division in the U.S.A. unit. Products included in this division are pants, shirts, sweaters, and shorts. A recent introduction to the Womenswear line, "Bend-Over"® pants, which are made from a stretch material, is the hottest selling product in the group.

In Levi Strauss' 1979 Annual Report, the following statement was made concerning the Womenswear group:

> Womenswear, the company's most rapidly growing division, nearly doubled its sales last year. . . . This sharp growth indicates the division's potential in the vast womenswear market, which exceeds the menswear in size.

Koret of North America Division was formerly Koret of California®. They produce high brand-loyalty apparel products.

The Menswear Division manufactures stretch pants called Levi's Action Slacks which are becoming popular. Among the other products in the Menswear Division are men's shirts, vests, sweaters, and jackets.

Activewear is the newest product division in the U.S.A. unit. This division manufactures such products as warm-up suits, shorts, skiwear, and other sports apparel for both men and women. According to L.S. & CO.'s 1979 Annual Report, "The division's entry into the marketplace followed a three-year comprehensive study of the activewear market. . . . The activewear market was found to be large and highly fragmented, with no major American brands offering a full range of products." L.S. & CO.'s top managers indicate they will place substantial emphasis on activewear in the future as they attempt to carve out a niche for themselves in the market.

The Accessories Division produces a wide range of products such as belts, hats, and wallets. The Accessories Division produces the smallest sales volume of any product line in Levi Strauss & Co.

Exhibit 3 shows sales figures for Levi Strauss U.S.A. from 1976 to 1980.

EXHIBIT 3   DIVISION'S PERCENT OF TOTAL SALES
(Dollar Amounts in Millions)

	1979 Sales	% Sales	1978 Sales	% Sales	1977 Sales	% Sales	1976 Sales	% Sales
Levi Strauss USA								
Division								
Jeanswear	743.1	57	658.7	61	695.5	65	569.1	66
Youthwear	217.8	17	184.2	17	171.6	16	126.8	15
Sportswear and Activewear	120.7	9	120.6	11	108.8	10	94.1	11
Womenswear	197.4	15	99.2	9	62.8	6	47.4	5
Accessories	15.6	1	14.3	1	33.6	3	26.5	3
Total	1294.6		1077.0		1072.3		863.9	
Levi Strauss International								
Europe	389.7	53	305.7	52	237.4	49	146.1	41
Canada	139.6	19	114.8	20	122.7	25	111.4	31
Latin America	134.7	18	103.5	18	79.3	16	51.7	15
Asia/Pacific	74.1	10	61.0	10	47.6	10	46.7	13
Total	738.1		585.0		487.0		355.0	

Source: 1976–1979 Annual Reports for Levi Strauss & Co.

Levi Strauss International

Levi Strauss International is the second component in the company's structure. The international unit is divided into 4 groups (Europe, Canada, Latin America, and Asia/Pacific Divisions) of which the Europe Group is the largest. The Europe Group is further divided into operating divisions. L.S. & CO.'s primary export product is jeans, but sportswear, youthwear, and womenswear have proven to be successful export items as well.

Exhibit 3 shows sales figures for the International Division from 1976 to 1980.

Other Operating Units

Four operating divisions have been separated from the two main operating units (Levi Strauss USA and Levi Strauss International) due to their unique nature.

The EXIMCO Division was set up to develop special markets for L.S. & CO. and to manage sales in Eastern Europe, China, Switzerland, and Hong Kong. It provides Levi Strauss with the ability to take advantage of new opportunities in international markets.

The Oxxford Division produces top quality men's suits in the U.S., and the Rainfair Division produces industrial clothing and coated compounded products for industry. Both of these divisions produce products formerly produced by Koracorp Industries.

PRODUCTION FACILITIES

Levi Strauss & Company has numerous plants and distribution centers located in North America and throughout Asia, Latin America and Europe. Exhibit 4 presents a list of facilities L.S. & CO. owns or leases. According to *Fortune* magazine, "During the next 5 years, the company plans to spend some $400 million to build no fewer than 40 new factories and enlarge several existing ones; more than $250 million will go into production facilities for sweaters, blazers, and a variety of other garments that were not in the company's product line a few years ago."[5]

MARKETING

The marketing orientation of Levi Strauss has undergone significant change since the company's inception in the 1850s. Originally, Levi's jeans were worn almost exclusively by gold miners who considered them to be essential equipment because they were both rugged and durable. However, in the 1950s jeans became a teenage fad, and later they became a trend. Thus, L.S. & CO. adjusted their marketing orientation to take advantage of this trend. Currently, Levi's products are oriented toward the more fashion conscious 20 to 39 year old age group. There are 71.1 million people in this age group in the United States today, and there will be 77.6 million people in this age group by 1985.

[5] *Fortune,* November 19, 1979; p. 86.

EXHIBIT 4 FACILITIES OWNED AND LEASED

Location	Number of facilities	Square feet	Purpose	Term expires
Facilities owned				
Arkansas	1	295,000	Distribution center	
	3	156,000	Manufacturing	
California	3	282,000	Manufacturing	
	2	323,400	Distribution center	
Georgia	2	197,900	Manufacturing	
Illinois	1	111,000	Manufacturing	
Kentucky	1	324,200	Distribution center	
Nevada	1	315,800	Distribution center	
New Jersey	1	50,000	Manufacturing	
New Mexico	2	189,700	Manufacturing	
North Carolina	2	262,400	Manufacturing	
Pennsylvania	1	126,700	Manufacturing	
South Carolina	1	54,600	Manufacturing	
Tennessee	9	898,900	Manufacturing	
Texas	16	1,559,900	Manufacturing	
	1	123,000	Curing	
	2	1,399,000	Distribution center	
Virginia	2	99,700	Manufacturing	
Wisconsin	2	283,000	Manufacturing	
Argentina	2	72,700	Manufacturing	
Australia	1	103,600	Manufacturing	
	1	37,000	Distribution center	
Belgium	4	213,500	Manufacturing	
Brazil	1	38,300	Manufacturing	
	1	250,000	Manufacturing and distribution center	
Canada	4	236,200	Manufacturing	
	1	96,000	Manufacturing and warehousing	
	1	183,000	Distribution center	
France	6	317,400	Manufacturing	
	1	77,200	Manufacturing and warehousing	
	1	116,600	Manufacturing and distribution center	
Mexico	1	253,800	Manufacturing and distribution center	
	1	104,000	Manufacturing	
Puerto Rico	1	54,000	Manufacturing	
	1	20,000	Distribution center	
Sweden	1	18,800	Distribution center	
United Kingdom	3	178,000	Manufacturing	
	1	96,000	Distribution center	
Total	85	9,518,300		

Brand Awareness

L.S. & CO. is the leading producer in the apparel industry. Much of their success can be attributed to the marketing strength they developed over many years of producing and selling jeans. The most important competitive advantage L.S. & CO. has, and their most important marketing strength as well, is wide consumer acceptance of the

EXHIBIT 4   *(Continued)*

Location	Number of facilities	Square feet	Purpose	Term expires
Facilities leased				
Arkansas	5	238,400	Manufacturing	1981–1989
	2	45,000	Warehousing	1982–1989
California	1	18,000	Manufacturing	1985
	1	155,000	Distribution center	2013
	2	85,000	Warehousing	1986–2001
Georgia	2	145,900	Manufacturing	1984–1996
New Mexico	2	116,000	Manufacturing	1992–1994
	1	50,300	Manufacturing and warehousing	1989
North Carolina	1	25,000	Warehousing	1984
Ohio	1	105,000	Manufacturing	2006
South Carolina	1	92,000	Manufacturing	1991
Tennessee	3	142,900	Manufacturing	1983–1998
	3	75,500	Warehousing	1982–1986
Texas	9	377,700	Manufacturing	1981–1997
	1	200,000	Manufacturing and warehousing	2009
	1	15,900	Warehousing	1983
	1	310,000	Distribution center	1998
Utah	1	29,000	Manufacturing	1993
Argentina	1	51,000	Distribution center	1982
Australia	1	83,600	Manufacturing and warehousing	1983
Belgium	1	88,300	Distribution center	1986
	1	65,000	Warehousing	1981
Canada	1	105,900	Distribution center	2002
	8	429,300	Manufacturing	1981–2002
	2	31,200	Warehousing	1981–1986
France	1	32,300	Manufacturing and warehousing	1981
	1	37,000	Distribution center	1986
Germany	1	171,800	Distribution center	1987
Hong Kong	1	93,200	Manufacturing	1982
	1	50,700	Warehousing and distribution center	1981
Italy	1	43,100	Distribution center	1983
Japan	2	26,800	Distribution center	1985
Netherlands	1	17,900	Distribution center	1985
Norway	1	11,300	Distribution center	1981
Philippines	1	38,800	Manufacturing	1984
	1	32,500	Distribution center	1984
Switzerland	1	16,800	Distribution center	1981
United Kingdom	2	116,000	Manufacturing	1999–2000
	1	144,000	Distribution center and warehousing	2000
	1	20,000	Distribution center	1981
Total	70	3,933,100		

Source: 10-K Report for fiscal year end November 25, 1980.

Levi's brand. L.S. & CO. sells high quality products at reasonable prices, and this fact is recognized throughout the world.

Distribution

L.S. & CO. sells most of their products through department stores and specialty outlets. In addition, they promote many accessories (i.e., belts, hats, and totebags) inside retail establishments by using attractive point-of-sale racks which complement the products on display. Pants specialty stores began to play a more dominant role in L.S. & CO.'s distribution system in the early 1970's. These stores and the more broadly oriented "Levi's Only" stores represent welcomed alternatives to distributing almost exclusively through department stores where sales have been sluggish recently. Approximately 90% of the products sold in "Levi's Only" stores are manufactured by Levi.

Advertising

L.S. & CO. employs both national and local advertising, and they utilize all advertising media (i.e., T.V., radio, magazines, and newspapers). L.S. & CO.'s promotions emphasize quality and style as the two most important attributes of their products. The slogan "quality never goes out of style" appears whenever the Levi's brand name is advertised.

L.S. & CO. maintains flexibility in their advertising programs so they can shift their emphasis to high volume markets quickly. They focus on anticipating consumer demand and gearing their advertising accordingly, rather than attempting to dictate consumer preferences. Furthermore, they employ advertising programs which parallel and complement their special selling support.

Other Marketing Strengths

Diversification   Levi's extensive diversification is a major strength. They offer a wide variety of products to consumers throughout the United States and the world. This diversity makes L.S. & CO. less vulnerable to dramatic shifts in consumer preferences for any particular product or in any particular place.

Dependable Delivery   L.S. & CO. employs an advanced computer system to define fashion trends and anticipate changes in consumer demand for apparel. This system enables L.S. & CO. to manufacture and inventory products which are selling well or are expected to sell well. Thus L.S. & CO. has achieved a reputation for dependable delivery.

Market Research   When Levi Strauss develops a new product, they utilize test marketing to determine the most effective approach for advertising it. They concentrate on understanding the nature of demand for the product by identifying trends which might affect that demand and determining if that demand can be served. First, they segment the markets they serve according to consumers preferences and the types of retail outlets which serve them. Then, they identify locations where the Levi's brand has achieved acceptance. Thus, L.S. & CO. adjusts its advertising to meet the needs of specific products in specific markets.

Marketing Weaknesses

Despite their numerous marketing strengths and their number one position in the apparel industry, L.S. & CO. has marketing weaknesses as well. First, their pricing policy is subject to Federal Trade Commission (FTC) regulations. Specifically, the FTC does not permit forced price maintenance by manufacturers at the retail level. In recent years, this has cost L.S. & CO. millions of dollars for out-of-court settlements of cases in which they were accused of price maintenance. As a result, L.S. & CO. is susceptible to price wars. Retailers will drastically cut the price of Levi products to attract customers to their stores from their competitors. This may pose a possible threat to the quality image of a branded product.

PERSONNEL

The apparel industry employs approximately 1,134,000 production workers, and employment in the industry has been stable for 5 years. Heavy concentrations of jobs in the apparel industry are found in New York, Pennsylvania, California, North Carolina, and Texas, but most production is done in the South due to the low cost of labor.

Apparel production is highly labor intensive, and apparel industry wages are among the lowest of all manufacturing industries. This is because the production process used by apparel firms is suited to employing unskilled and semi-skilled workers. Two major unions represent apparel workers (International Ladies Garment Workers Union and Amalgamated Clothing and Textile Workers Union), and 81 percent of workers in the apparel industry are women.

L.S. & CO. employed over 44,700 individuals in 1979. Seventy-five percent (75%) of them were production workers, and over 60 percent of L.S. & CO. production workers were union members. Relations between L.S. & CO. and the production workers are satisfactory. As evidence of this fact, there has never been a major interruption in production due to labor disputes.

At L.S. & CO., in 1979, 11 percent of officials and managers were minority persons; 15 percent of officials and managers and 4 percent of sales personnel were women; and the Board of Directors includes both minority persons and women. Further, L.S. & CO. supports minority economic development, and management's community concern is evidenced by its objective of allocating at least 3 percent of after-tax profits to social responsibility efforts. All L.S. & CO. plants have strong community relations programs, and L.S. & CO. encourages all employees to be socially concerned and socially active.

EXHIBIT 5 TEN-YEAR FINANCIAL SUMMARY
(In Millions Except Per Share Amount)

	1980	1979	1978	1977
Net sales	$ 2,840.8	$ 2,103.1	$ 1,682.0	$ 1,559.3
Gross profit	$ 1,040.2	$ 793.8	$ 623.6	$ 562.6
Interest expense	25.0	12.4	11.2	20.0
Income before taxes	401.9	345.6	280.4	270.0
Provision for taxes on income	178.2	154.1	135.4	140.2
Net income	$ 223.7	$ 191.5	$ 145.0	$ 129.8
Earnings retained in the business	$ 170.2	$ 151.1	$ 110.0	$ 108.0
Cash flow retained in the business	213.3	176.9	125.5	128.7
Income before taxes as % of sales	14.1	16.4	16.7	17.3
Net income as % of sales	7.9	9.1	8.6	8.3
Net income as % of beginning stockholders' equity	32.8	33.3	31.3	35.8
Current assets	$ 1,122.5	$ 1,047.1	$ 824.2	$ 694.2
Current liabilities	452.4	489.7	302.4	263.5
Working capital	670.1	557.4	521.8	430.7
Ratio of current assets to current liabilities	2.5/1	2.1/1	2.7/1	2.6/1
Total assets	1,455.5	1,291.1	973.9	824.2
Long term debt—less current maturities	$ 138.8	$ 99.1	$ 83.3	$ 80.6
Stockholders'—equity	831.6	681.2	575.3	463.9
Capital expenditures	$ 119.8	$ 51.3	$ 42.9	$ 31.4
Depreciation	25.4	18.2	16.1	13.7
Property, plant & equipment—net	280.8	188.5	141.3	119.3
Number of employees	48,000	44,700	35,100	37,200
Per share data:				
Net income	$ 5.36	$ 4.58	$ 3.28	$ 2.93
Cash dividends declared	1.30	1.00	.80	.50
Book value (on shares outstanding at year end)	20.34	16.50	13.14	10.66
Market price range	44–30	$34\frac{1}{2}$/17	$19\frac{3}{8}$–$13\frac{3}{8}$	$15\frac{7}{8}$–$12\frac{1}{8}$
Average common and common equivalent shares outstanding	41,763,108	41,784,058	44,229,872	44,257,346

Source: 1980 Annual Report for Levi Strauss & Company.

RESEARCH AND DEVELOPMENT

Research is considered one of L.S. & CO.'s most important competitive advantages. Their Product Research and Development Department is responsible for the company's progress in new fabrics and garments, and their goal is to improve functional performance. Additionally, an Equipment Research and Development Center is maintained by L.S. & CO. so that it can remain a leader in automated and semi-automated production equipment. Further, Corporate Marketing Research has an on-line computerized data bank to monitor major fashion directions, general apparel pricing, retail point-of-sale

1976	1975	1974	1973	1972	1971
$ 1,219.7	$ 1,015.2	$ 897.7	$ 653.0	$ 504.4	$ 432.0
$ 439.9	$ 347.4	$ 275.5	$ 184.4	$ 160.3	$ 129.6
12.2	13.1	13.7	10.1	4.3	4.4
206.8	136.7	72.7	33.8	48.1	35.7
102.1	71.9	37.9	22.0	23.0	16.0
$ 104.7	$ 64.7	$ 34.9	$ 11.9	$ 25.0	$ 19.7
$ 94.8	$ 58.6	$ 29.6	$ 6.6	$ 20.9	$ 16.3
110.6	71.7	45.7	17.7	28.6	22.5
17.0	13.5	8.1	5.2	9.5	8.3
8.6	6.4	3.9	1.8	5.0	4.6
39.5	31.4	19.8	7.0	16.8	23.2
$ 570.1	$ 407.6	$ 383.5	$ 305.5	$ 252.4	$ 202.8
226.6	155.4	188.1	155.7	98.2	67.9
343.5	252.2	195.3	149.8	154.2	134.9
2.5/1	2.6/1	2.0/1	2.0/1	2.6/1	3.0/1
678.0	496.3	470.4	382.7	307.1	247.9
$ 79.2	$ 68.7	$ 72.8	$ 48.1	$ 37.6	$ 28.4
362.4	265.2	206.0	176.4	169.7	148.8
$ 19.5	$ 10.4	$ 24.3	$ 28.8	$ 17.6	$ 15.6
11.6	9.3	9.7	8.3	6.4	5.1
102.4	82.1	82.3	68.0	48.0	39.6
32,500	29,700	30,100	29,100	25,100	21,400
$ 2.35	$ 1.47	$ .80	$ .27	$ .57	$ .47
.23	.14	.12	.12	.10	.08
8.25	6.08	4.73	4.05	3.90	3.42
$13\frac{3}{8}$-9	$10\frac{3}{4}$-$3\frac{1}{8}$	$5\frac{5}{8}$-$3\frac{1}{8}$	$12\frac{1}{2}$-$4\frac{1}{4}$	15-$10\frac{1}{8}$	$16\frac{1}{8}$-$8\frac{3}{8}$
44,476,748	43,899,028	43,520,320	43,520,320	42,344,000	

trends, the company's image, and consumer attitudes toward products currently offered. Research also pretests the effectiveness of proposed advertisements and receptivity of the marketplace to new products.

FINANCIAL MATTERS AT LEVI STRAUSS

Exhibits 5, 6, 7, and 8 present L.S. & CO.'s ten year financial summary, consolidated income statement, consolidated balance sheets, and consolidated statement of changes in financial position, respectively.

EXHIBIT 6 LEVI STRAUSS & CO. AND SUBSIDIARIES: CONSOLIDATED STATEMENT OF INCOME[a]

	Year ended		
	November 30, 1980 (53 weeks)	November 25, 1979 (52 weeks)	November 26, 1978 (52 weeks)
Net sales	$ 2,840,844	$ 2,103,109	$ 1,682,019
Cost of goods sold	1,800,665	$ 1,309,263	$ 1,058,439
Gross profit	1,040,179	793,846	623,580
Marketing, general and administrative expenses	635,870	464,086	344,536
Operating income	404,309	329,760	279,044
Interest expense	25,018	12,449	11,178
Interest and other income, net	(22,606)	(28,238)	(12,503)
Income before taxes	401,897	345,549	280,369
Provision for taxes on income	178,208	154,095	135,400
Net income	$ 223,689	$ 191,454	$ 144,969
Net income per share	$ 5.36	$ 4.58	$ 3.28
Average common and common equivalent shares outstanding	41,763,108	41,784,058	44,229,872

[a] Dollars in thousands except per share amounts.
Source: 1980 Annual Report for Levi Strauss & Co.

FUTURE

At L.S. & CO. the word future means diversifiction. In November of 1977 L.S. & CO. began a coordinated corporate strategy of diversification which it intends to continue into the future "at full speed". Four facts suggest this course of action:

1 "In all probability the jeans business in the U.S. is slowly maturing."[6]
2 L.S. & CO. is generating more cash than it needs to finance its 20 percent annual growth in jeans.
3 Market research shows better returns could be made by putting the Levi's® Trademark on other products.
4 In all likelihood antitrust laws would block an attempt by L.S. & CO. to acquire another jeans-maker.

Peter Haas, Chairman of the Board, states "diversification has become the most prudent course we can follow."

Fortune magazine foresees two dangers in L.S. & CO.'s diversification plans. "One danger inherent in these ambitious plans is that keeping track of all the ever-changing fashions and maintaining the huge assortment of sizes and styles in all the new fields could tax the company's managerial capabilities beyond their limits." Also L.S. & CO. is "vulnerable to the same profit-eroding markdowns the minute inventories get out of hand."[7]

[6] *Business Week,* May 19, 1979.
[7] *Fortune,* November 19, 1979.

EXHIBIT 7   LEVI STRAUSS & CO. AND SUBSIDIARIES: CONSOLIDATED BALANCE SHEETS[a]

	November 30, 1980	November 25, 1979
Assets		
Current assets		
Cash	$ 36,192	$ 27,454
Temporary investments of cash	51,693	195,297
Trade receivables (less allowance for doubtful accounts:		
1980–$9,368; 1979–$8,340)	446,461	340,131
Inventories		
Raw materials and work-in-process	252,538	216,820
Finished goods	275,017	225,001
Other current assets	60,606	42,411
Total current assets	1,122,507	1,047,114
Property, plant and equipment (less accumulated depreciation:		
1980–$113,301; 1979—$101,989)	280,783	188,495
Other assets	52,070	55,510
	$1,455,360	$1,291,119
Liabilities and stockholders' equity		
Current liabilities		
Current maturities of long-term debt	$ 14,963	$ 15,832
Short-term borrowings	48,642	53,535
Accounts payable	135,006	154,929
Accrued liabilities	93,875	83,802
Compensation and payroll taxes	55,313	57,636
Pension and profit sharing	20,982	27,545
Taxes based on income	68,309	85,069
Dividend payable	15,335	11,357
Total current liabilities	452,425	489,705
Long-term debt—less current maturities	138,754	99,126
Deferred liabilities	32,552	21,098
Stockholders' equity		
Common stock—$1.00 par value:		
authorized 100,000,000 shares: shares issued—		
1980—43,998,808, 1979—21,999,404	43,999	21,999
Additional paid-in capital	59,837	82,424
Retained earnings	806,257	636,010
	910,093	740,433
Less treasury stock, at cost: 1980—3,105,482 shares:		
1979—1,354,949 shares	78,464	59,243
Total stockholders' equity	831,629	681,190
	$1,455,360	$1,291,119

[a] Dollars in thousands.

Robert T. Grohman, President and Chief Executive Officer, says, "In order to maintain something close to the rate of growth we have experienced in the last five years, we are looking at much more rapid expansion in other segments." He adds, "We are not a fringe house and we are not high-fashion innovators, but we are looking at product lines that have a long-term appeal to the mainstream consumer." Furthermore, Grohman says, "Our size and diversification give us tremendous flexibility."

EXHIBIT 8 LEVI STRAUSS AND SUBSIDIARIES:
CONSOLIDATED STATEMENT OF CHANGES IN FINANCIAL POSITION[a]

	Year ended		
	November 30, 1980 (53 weeks)	November 25, 1979 (52 weeks)	November 26, 1978 (52 weeks)
Working capital provided by:			
Operations:			
Net income	$ 223,689	$191,454	$144,969
Add items not currently involving working capital:			
Depreciation and amortization	30,004	20,430	17,606
Other, net	13,066	5,380	(2,140)
Working capital provided by operations	266,759	217,264	160,435
Common stock issued in acquisition of Koracorp Industries Inc.	—	37,261	—
Proceeds from long-term debt	54,586	8,400	14,411
Common stock issued to employees	6,322	4,999	5,077
Working capital provided	327,667	267,924	179,923
Working capital used for:			
Additions to property, plant and equipment	119,824	51,254	42,863
Cash dividends declared	53,442	40,391	34,972
Acquisition of Koracorp Industries Inc. (less working capital of $34,961):			
Property, plant and equipment	—	17,702	—
Other assets	—	4,885	—
Goodwill	—	39,341	—
Long-term liabilities assumed	—	(26,054)	—
Purchases of treasury stock	26,130	87,451	3,611
Reductions in long-term debt	14,958	15,505	11,766
Other, net	640	1,862	(4,379)
Working capital used	214,994	232,337	88,833
Increase in working capital	$ 112,673	$ 35,587	$ 91,090
Increase (decrease) in working capital, represented by change in:			
Cash and temporary investments of cash	$(134,866)	$(32,070)	$ 93,880
Trade receivables, net	106,330	99,006	37,886
Inventories	85,734	143,327	4,391
Other current assets	18,195	12,624	(6,188)
Current maturities of long-term debt and short-term borrowings	5,762	(48,003)	20,290
Accounts payable and accrued liabilities	9,850	(83,667)	(51,983)
Other current liabilities	21,668	(55,630)	(7,186)
Increase in working capital	$ 112,673	$ 35,587	$ 91,090

[a] Dollars in thousands.
Source: 1980 Annual Report for Levi Strauss & Co.

Brenda Gall of Merrill Lynch, Pierce, Fenner & Smith says of L.S. & CO., ''They have instant name recognition, strong ties with retailers and the marketing talent to identify and go after basic, profitable product lines. They have many opportunities ahead of them, and their growth rate over the last five years is not unsustainable.''

DISCUSSION QUESTIONS

1 Evaluate Levi Strauss and Company's diversification strategy in light of the maturation of the apparel industry. Would you recommend a different strategy? Why?

2 What are the advantages and disadvantages of clearing off long-term debt and/or repurchasing common stock with the excess cash flow which Levi Strauss is producing? Do you think this would be a reasonable strategy? Explain.

3 What should Levi Strauss do about the small percent of managers and sales personnel who are female in light of the well-known fact that most apparel workers are women? Why do you suppose women constitute such a small percentage of the sales force?

4 Why might Levi Strauss' international division be departmentalized geographically while, in the United States, departmentation is by product line?

5 What accounts for the value ascribed to the Levi name brand as signified by the prevalence of counterfeiting of Levi apparel? How might Levi Strauss enhance that value and keep it proprietary?

6 Discuss the major internal strengths and weaknesses Levi Strauss has and the significant external threats and opportunities the company faces. From this analysis, develop what you believe to be an appropriate strategic focus for Levi Strauss for the next five years or so.

NISSAN U.S.A.

Walter E. Greene
Middle Tennessee State University

Gary D. Walls
Phillips University

SELECTED STRATEGIC ISSUES

- The effect of unionization on cost and quality
- Japanese versus American views of labor-management relations
- Japanese versus American management style
- U.S. legal problems of foreign manufacturers
- Strategic problems created by cultural differences

HISTORY

Nissan Motor Co. Ltd. was incorporated in Japan in 1933 and in 1980 acquired a 37% stake in Motor Iberica S.A. of Barcelona. Nissan manufactures and sells Datsun automobiles, rockets, textile machinery, boats, other machines and appliances, and their respective parts as well as other operations incidental to these activities. Their distributors are located in 130 foreign countries. Their properties include 13 plants in Japan and 24 knock down plants abroad with production capacity of 210,000 units per month. Nissan also owns a fleet of 16 auto carrier ships (see Exhibit I).

Nissan Co. has a total of 56,285 stockholders as of 1980 and employs 56,702. Their head office is located in Tokyo with Nissan Motor Corp. In the U.S.A. the head office is in California.

Walter Greene is Area Coordinator for Business Administration and Associate Professor, Middle Tennessee State University, and Gary D. Walls is Assistant Professor of Marketing, Phillips University, Enid, Oklahoma.

EXHIBIT I

PARTS-SELLING ORGANIZATION

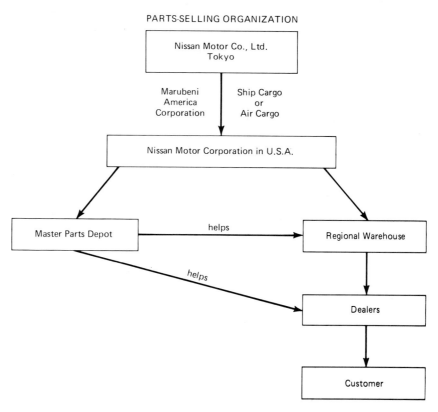

When Nissan Motor Corporation U.S.A. reached its twenty-second year, it was a vigorous, successful organization. It was securely established as the second-largest seller of import cars in the U.S., close enough to the leader, Toyota, so that reaching first place could be seen as a reasonably attainable goal. Sales continued to be strong; in fact, the impetus given to purchases of small cars in 1979 carried on as fuel prices kept escalating, so that each successive month saw new records in Datsun sales. The half-million target set for 1980 five years before had already been reached and passed; the 1980 sales figures would top 600,000. Behind NMC-USA stood Nissan Motor Co., Ltd., now the world's fourth-largest manufacturer of motor vehicles, following General Motors, Ford, and Toyota in that order.

As the year began, NMC-USA was an organization with a capitalization of $6 million, and 1582 employers. The largest number, 680, were at the National Headquarters complex in Carson, California; the others were in the regional offices; Boston, 77; Chicago, 83; Columbus, 43; New York, 86; Jacksonville, 88; Dallas, 78; Memphis, 42; Norfolk, 84; Denver, 68; Los Angeles, 109; Portland, 47; San Francisco, 41; Sacramento (Parts Warehouse opened in 1978 replacing San Francisco and Portland depots), 56. There were 1083 dealers, with a total of 30,215 employees (see Exhibit II).

EXHIBIT II

DISTRIBUTION OF VEHICLES
FROM PLANNING STAGE THROUGH RETAIL SELLING

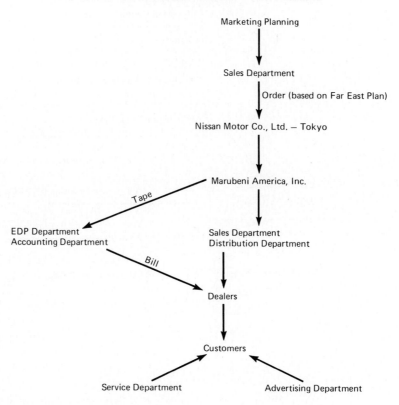

INTRODUCTION

The truck plant that Nissan Motor Corporation U.S.A. is currently building in Smyrna, Tennessee will be an example of the latest Japanese management techniques and technology for producing vehicles. The Nissan truck manufacturing plant will be a $500 million dollar complex. Production is scheduled to begin in August 1983, and 219 robots will be operating in the body assembly, stamping and painting areas. This will make Nissan one of the most robotized factories in the world. Automation will also be installed in the plant for operations where a robot's flexibility is not needed. Unfortunately, robots do eliminate workers, but many skilled people are needed to keep them working. In Japan those workers whose jobs are taken by robots are retrained to do new jobs within the company.

Tennessee's Department of Employment Security is screening applicants and sending suitable applicants to Nissan. Applicants are expected to complete, on their own time, a pre-employment training program which is conducted by the state's Department of Economic and Community Development's industrial training division. The training programs vary in length according to the previous training and experiences of the individual and the type of job applied for. Nissan selects their employees out of the applicants that successfully complete the state's training program.

Many of Nissan's top management have come out of retirement and are between 50 and 65 years old. For example, the president of Nissan, Marvin Runyon, was the former vice-president at Ford Motor Company for 37 years. Nissan hired John Bryan as Human Relations manager because he is a native Tennessean and familiar with the state's work force. Key positions and first-line production supervisors are being filled by workers from Tennessee through an agreement with the state. The state agreed that if Nissan would hire Tennesseans for these jobs, then the state would pay for the training programs. Several hundred employees of Nissan will receive specialized training in Japan. The length of this training will vary from 2 to 4 months.

Marvin Runyon said, "Nissan will have participative management, employee meetings every morning, multi-skilled tradesmen, almost continuous education programs and probably no unions." Runyon believes that many of the Japanese management techniques are American methods the U.S. abandoned. Nissan plans to establish a work-motivating environment to help improve efficiency. The aim is for bottom-up management as opposed to the U.S. method, where managers hand out work directives. Nissan will encourage all workers to offer their input. For example, at the start of each shift, foremen will hold meetings with their staff to discuss the day's objectives and safety measures.

Suppliers will have to bow to the Japanese ways because Nissan plans on keeping stocks as low as possible. The production process of each supplier will be certified in detail by Nissan's quality control staff. Another feature of Nissan's system is maintenance. Nissan will have a team of maintenance engineers; however, the operators will be responsible for minor jobs.

EMPLOYEES AND THE UNION

Runyon aims to import the Japanese technique of using temporary or subcontract workers for a percentage of the jobs in the Smyrna plant. That means, for example, that janitors will not earn the same pay as assembly line workers, and many temporary factory workers will not be eligible for fringe benefits. As a result, the UAW is fighting hard to organize the Nissan plant.

Failing to organize the newcomer could mean trouble for the UAW. If the Japanese can operate at lower costs and without a union, then the UAW's bargaining strength with GM and Ford could be weakened.

Jim Turner, who is in charge of UAW unionizing effort here in Tennessee said, "This is nothing new. We expect it because every Japanese plant that has been built in this country has attempted to defeat the unions. We have made no secret of wanting to unionize the Japanese plants here in the US and we have no doubt that the employees, freely given their choice, without discrimination, will join the union."

Nissan will be employing 2,200 employees at the Smyrna plant. Nissan has seen the day when employees and management did not see eye to eye. This is the problem the U.S. is facing today, which is somewhat similar to those the Japanese faced almost three decades ago.

Mr. Shioji, president of the Confederation of Japanese Automobile Workers' Union, in 1954 as a young auto worker for Nissan proposed the first wage reduction in order to secure jobs. It was a time period when Nissan had decided to lay off employees because of sagging profits. However, the union voted to take a reduction in order to save jobs. From then on the Japanese management has had a different outlook concerning their employees.

Mr. Shioji remarked, "The consultation system is to increase the pie, the fruit of the company. Collective bargaining is for cutting up the pie for the good of the union members."

The Japanese Auto Workers Union has offered to send a team of its workers to Nissan U.S.A. to urge unionization of the plant. The UAW feels this is a positive move because the Japanese team would encourage employees to join the UAW. Unlike American unions, in Japan there is a harmonious relationship between management and labor. In Japan each company has its own union which works with management.

Runyon said he does not expect word from Nissan Ltd. on the proposal, "It's between the UAW and the Japanese Auto Workers." The question of whether or not the Smyrna plant will have a union is between the American union and Nissan, USA. Douglas Fraser appeared on NBC television's "Meet the Press" and said, "The UAW will organize the Smyrna plant because the American work force will demand it." Local union sources will make an all-out effort to unionize Nissan workers prior to August, 1983. Fraser said, "We have the support of the AFL-CIO." AFL-CIO leader, Lane Kirkland says,"The nation needs a program of re-industrialization that will mobilize the available capital and channel it into reviving the capacity and modernizing our industrial facility. The Japanese economy is the worst advertisement for so-called free trade that could possibly exist."

MANAGEMENT STYLES

Japanese

When Nissan Motor Corporation, U.S.A. began production in August 1, 1983, American employees will be working under Japanese management styles. The Japanese management style is strongly supported by Runyon, who plans on using the Japanese style at the Nissan plant in Smyrna. Runyon said, "Management attitudes and policies that encourage quality are part of the reasons Japanese workers output now equals that of France, Britain, Switzerland combined or a little less than 40% of the national output of the U.S." The Hudson Institute predicts that by the year 2000, Japanese will be the richest people on earth.

Runyon outlined, for the author, five differences between U.S. and Japanese styles of management. These differences are:

1 Most Japanese work for the same company for their entire life, unlike Americans who are prone to job-hopping. In Japan seniority is more important than merit. Because of the low turnover rate, Japanese businesses are willing to invest more money in training programs for employees, which improves both the confidence of workers and the quality of their products.

2 The relationships between management and labor are harmonious and stable. While labor negotiations are intense and strikes do take place, basically the overall attitude is friendly.

3 Top priority is given to employee satisfaction and welfare. Japanese treat their employees as resources, which when properly trained will reap great benefits for the company. The result of Japanese regard is that employees are very loyal to the company and most Japanese regard the future of the company as their own. Japanese businesses' long-term view is also a major reason for its steadily increasing productivity.

4 Japanese have a strong sense of teamwork. This feeling of teamwork is due to the concept of quality control circles. Quality control circles encourage employees to make suggestions on how to improve efficiency and at the same time encourage communication between higher management and workers.

5 Decisions are made through consensus. Employees have a say in the decision-making process throughout, from the planning and engineering to the production and sales. Suggestions are encouraged from employees at every level and taken into consideration and often put into effect. Open communication between the workers and management creates a form of collective participation and the result is more and better ideas, many of which can mean savings to the company.

Another Nissan executive, Shuichi Yoshida, Vice-President of Quality Assurance, plans on using Japanese management practices. Yoshida plans are to maximize the human resources of Nissan-USA. Nissan will make use of continued training programs within the company. Job enlargement and job enrichment programs will be used to help workers develop all their skills. Management will use an interdisciplinary approach and will also encourage workers to go beyond the boundaries of their particular job. In a personal interview with the authors, Yoshida declared, ''the biggest problem between the Japanese company in Smyrna and Nissan itself is the language barrier.''

The success of Japanese companies is based on their utilization of human resources. The success comes from three interrelated strategies (see Exhibit III).

1 An internal labor market is created to secure a labor force of the desired quality and to induce the employees to remain in the firm.

2 A company philosophy is stated that expresses concern for employee needs and emphasizes cooperation and teamwork.

3 Close attention is given both to hiring people who will fit well with the values of the particular company and to integrating employees into the company at all stages of their working life.

American

Most American auto workers feel the need for a union. This decision will have to be considered in August 1983, when Nissan begins production. The executives at the

EXHIBIT III

A MODEL OF JAPANESE MANAGEMENT

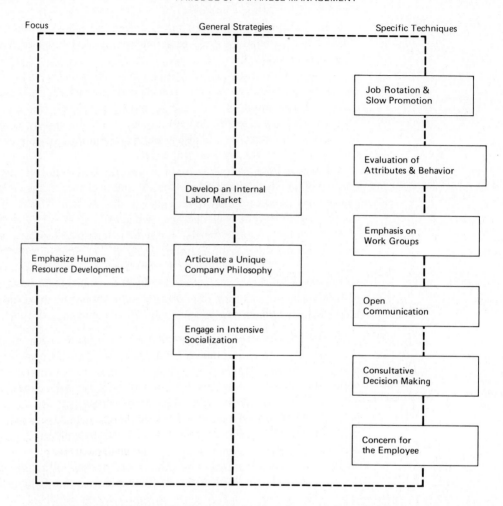

Smyrna plant are against the union, but the UAW strongly wants to unionize Nissan employees. Runyon believes a union shop will cheapen the quality of the Nissan trucks. It is believed that the adversary relationship between the United Auto Workers and the American automobile managers is not good for the employees or the company. It seems that the UAW and management have different objectives. In Japan employees and management are both interested in creating a good quality product that will be competitive in the market place. Runyon says, "Nissan is proemployee. We want a participating management and we think the only way to do that is to be union free. The union methods are fine as long as there is no competition. However, unions in America are not ready to face up to the fact that when they work against management, they are threatening their own future."

LEGAL

Foreign Trade Zone

As an enticement for Nissan to locate in Smyrna, foreign trade zones were established. Foreign trade zones, which are monitored by federal customs officials, allow industries such as Nissan, which imports parts and raw materials, to delay paying import taxes on the goods until they are assembled in the finished product and ready to ship to other areas. This can result in tax savings for the industry because taxes on the finished product are often less than the cumulative tax on the individual parts. The Smyrna City Council, with all members present, voted unanimously in favor of establishing a foreign trade sub-zone at the Nissan plant.

Import Quota

U.S. Trade Ambassador Bill Brock said, ''The restrictions on Japanese auto imports which I negotiated will not affect the Nissan plant.'' Brock came back from Japan where he negotiated an agreement where Japan would limit its exports to the United States to no more than 1.4 million next year.

The agreement kept Congress from acting on legislation that would have restricted Japanese auto imports. Brock said, ''We've avoided protectionist legislation, the Japanese have been very reasonable and we have made a good approach to the thing.'' The aim is for a two-way street between America and Japan. Legislation is being discussed to insure that American workers can sell their products in Japan just as readily as Japanese workers can sell their products in America.

Domestic Content Law

Recently the Fair Practices in Automotive Products Act or the Domestic Content Bill has received much attention. The D.C.B. would force Nissan to purchase 90% of the parts for its trucks on the domestic market, which will take away much of the benefit of the foreign trade zone. Under terms of the legislation being considered by the House Energy and Commerce Committee, the trucks would be required to contain at least 90% domestic parts by the year 1985. Runyon stated, ''Nissan will not be able to meet the content requirement demanded by the legislation.'' Under present production schedules, Nissan plans to begin production in mid-1983 for model year 1984 and they expect to use only 38% domestic parts.

Nissan plans to increase that percentage gradually after production begins. They believe that at present their production volume of 156,000 vehicles is too small to justify the manufacture of engines and drive trains at the Smyrna facility. Runyon said, ''At present Nissan will have to continue to import these major parts.''

Views from Nissan

The D.C.B. will seriously threaten all manufacturers who export to the U.S. says the president of Nissan Motor Co. Ltd., Takashi Ishihara. Ishihara said, ''The bill is a serious threat not only to manufacturers, but also to those who work in industries related to exported automobiles. I do not think it is the American intention that this legislation should pass. I feel an amended version of the legislation also would not be acceptable.''

In the original form, the D.C.B. would require companies that sell automobiles in the U.S. to use 90% domestic parts by 1985. A proposed amendment would use the amount of a company's total U.S. sales the preceding year to determine the required domestic content. That would lower the required domestic content for Nissan to 71% based on 1980 sales. Ishihara stressed that there are no industrialized countries in the world where such legislation is imposed. Currently, there are about 30 countries that have domestic content laws, but most are developing countries such as Kenya.

CONCLUSION

Nissan Motor Co. Ltd., being the third largest automotive industry in the world, has finally made the giant step of building a plant in the U.S. The different cultures and management techniques will either become a hindrance to the new Nissan plant located in Smyrna, Tennessee or maybe it will become a plant of the future for U.S. firms to follow. Whether Nissan USA is a success or not only the future will tell.

DISCUSSION QUESTIONS

1 How is unionization likely to affect production quality and costs? Why?
2 Compare and contrast the Japanese and American views of labor management relations.
3 Which management style would work best at the Smyrna plant, Japanese or American? Defend your position.
4 What kinds of legal problems might a foreign manufacturing company encounter when establishing operations in the United States?
5 Do you believe the cultural differences between Japan and the United States will pose serious problems for Nissan? Explain.

FLINT SPECIALTY DIE, INC.

Robert P. Crowner
Eastern Michigan University

SELECTED STRATEGIC ISSUES

- Problem of dependence on one industry for sales
- Solving working-capital problems
- Strategic importance of financial ratio information
- Making the information and control system meet company needs

As Bill Brewer thought about the continuing cash flow and negative net working capital problems facing the company, he reminded himself that these problems had existed from the beginning. Bill's father, Fred, who was President of Flint Specialty Die, Inc., began his association with the company in 1960 as a manufacturing representative. He also represented fifteen other accounts. In March 1967, one of the two partners who owned Flint died and Fred bought his half of the company from the estate. The balance sheet at the final closing of the sale unexpectedly showed working capital had been depleted, and thus the problem began.

In 1971 Flint Specialty Die, Inc. bought out the other original partner's half so that Fred Brewer owned all of the 6,250 outstanding shares. In 1980 Bill Brewer, who was the Vice President, bought 375 shares from his father. It was planned that he would buy or inherit the balance of the outstanding stock over the next several years. Thus, in the long run, Flint's problems as well as its many strengths would be Bill Brewer's concern alone.

THE PRODUCT

Flint Specialty Die, Inc. was a tool and die shop located in Flint, Michigan, which specialized in machining carbide dies used primarily in cold forming metal parts. Cold forming is forging done cold with a power hammer in a progressive manner in a series of dies. The company tried to specialize in areas other shops did not like to do or could not do. The dies for the transaxle for front wheel drive cars was an example of this policy.

Flint purchased most of its unfinished carbide dies from General Carbide Corporation located in Greensburg, Pennsylvania. Carbides have several unique properties. Wear resistance to abrasion is very high, outlasting steel alloys by 3 to 1. Carbides have a modulus of elasticity or resistance to bending under load which is two to three times that of steel. Carbides have a torsional (twisting) strength about twice that of high speed steel. Compressive strength is extremely high with carbides being used in pressing applications of over one million pounds per square inch (PSI). Corrosion resistance is also high. The main disadvantage to carbides, other than their high cost, is their brittleness in tension. This limits interference fits to .0005 inch.

Flint provided the customer's finished drawing to General Carbide who then designed its part oversize so that adequate material would be available to provide for Flint's machining operations. Flint checked the incoming parts from General Carbide to determine how much tolerance was available. This check was made by the operator

EXHIBIT I

ORGANIZATION CHART
FLINT SPECIALTY DIE, INC.

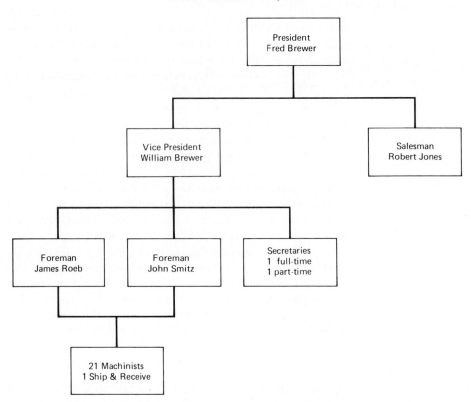

doing the machining. If allowances beyond common practice were found, an adjustment in the price to Flint was made since carbides were very expensive to remake.

MANUFACTURING

A chart which indicates how the company functioned as an organization is shown in Exhibit I. Bill Brewer, who was 33 years old in 1982, assumed the Vice President position in 1971 and was responsible for all plant operations and in addition spent about 10% of his time selling jobs and 10% estimating jobs. He went through his apprentice training at Flint Specialty Die and he also had taken several management courses at Flint Community College. He characterized his management style as participatory. He did all of the fixturing planning for the company.

Direct supervision of the machinists was carried out jointly by the two foremen, Jim Roeb and John Smitz. Each man had been with Flint for about fourteen years. Jim Roeb was strong in the area of advanced technology and setup, while John Smitz was stronger in dealing with people. The foremen were responsible for hiring, firing and supervising employees, scheduling and doing the processing for machining each job. They also did some direct labor work. Typically 400 jobs from 25 different customers might be in the shop at any one time. A typical job took 1½ months to complete from the time the material was ordered and consisted of less than ten pieces.

Flint rented 6,200 square feet in an industrial park in Flint, Michigan. About 2,000 square feet were used for storage of tool steel, carbide and tools, and the balance for manufacturing. The manufacturing space was tightly filled with universal type machines as listed below. The company also had much special purpose tooling, gaging and quality control apparatus. All heat treating of tool steel parts that hold the carbide die inserts was performed by outside contract.

Number	Description
1	Extrusion Hone
7	ID/OD Combination Grinder
2	OD Universal Grinder
1	ID Universal Grinder
1	Reciprocating Hone
2	Rotary Surface Grinder
5	Plane Surface Grinder
3	High Speed Polishing Lathe
3	19″ Engine Lathe
2	Electric Discharge Machine (EDM)
3	Vertical Mill
2	Vertical Drill Press
1	Shaper
1	Cut-off Saw
1	350 Ton Hydraulic Assembly Press
1	650 Ton Hydraulic Assembly Press (due in 9/82)

Employees did not belong to a union and a union had never attempted to organize the company. Employees had been with the company from 1 to 14 years. No one had ever quit voluntarily although five or six had been fired for various reasons. The company's policy was to pay above the average wage in the area based on word-of-mouth reports from employees and business associates. Wages ranged from $6 to $13.75 depending upon skill and experience with an average of about $10.25 per hour. Fringe benefits included life, hospitalization, emergency accident, major medical and dental insurance, paid vacations, and paid holidays. Tuition was reimbursed if the subject was related to the employee's work. Interest free loans, up to the equivalent of one week's pay, were made for tool purchases made by employees.

Pay raises were given as often as quarterly based upon merit if the company was doing well. A blanket raise was given once a year if the company was doing well. Seniority was only used to determine when an employee could take his vacation since only 20% could be gone at any one time. Layoffs were governed by the skills needed to do the work in the shop at that time.

Cost control was maintained annually. A 5″ by 8″ card was used for each tool number. The secretaries filled in the data by summarizing the daily job cards made out by each employee. Subsequent orders for the same tool were shown on the same card.

An estimate form, as shown in Exhibit II, was developed for each job as it was estimated by either of the Brewers. The back of the form carried the detailed labor usage by individual employee. The labor groups shown on the form consisted of the following:

Group 1—Lathes, mills
Group 2—OD, ID, form grinders
Group 3—Top & bottom, surface grinders
Group 4—EDM, finish polish

The completed form provided a comparison between the actual costs and the price quoted for the job. Labor was priced at $13.00 per hour for estimating purposes and 100% of the labor figure was used to cover all overhead. Material and outside services such as heat treat were priced at cost. To the sum of all of these costs was added a percentage figure for profit based on what the traffic would bear. Sometimes the company "farmed out" an entire job to a small carbide shop, if not much precision was needed, and added 10% to cover Flint's profit and overhead.

A manually prepared shipping report was made out monthly showing the job number, customer, price, material, subcontracts, labor plus 100% and estimated profit. A summary of 1981 shipments by month is shown in Exhibit III. A final yearly summary report showing sales and profit by month was made for 1981.

Labor performance versus the original estimate is evaluated on a subjective basis. Bill Brewer has in mind development standards of some kind to aid in this evaluation.

MARKETING

Fred Brewer, the President, who was 70 years old in 1982, was in charge of marketing. He was assisted by a salesman, Robert Jones, who was hired in April 1981. From

EXHIBIT II

JOB ESTIMATE FORM
FLINT SPECIALTY DIE, INC.

CUSTOMER_____   P.O.#_____   JOB#_____

PART#_____   QUANTITY_____   DATE DUE_____

                                                          DATE OF SHIPMENT:

       UNIT PRICE_____   LOT PRICE_____

ESTIMATOR_____   PROJECT MANAGER_____

COST SUMMARY

	HOURS				COSTS			
LABOR	UNIT	TOTAL	ACTUAL	VAR.	UNIT	TOTAL	ACTUAL	VAR.
GROUP 1								
GROUP 2								
GROUP 3								
GROUP 4								
TOTAL								

REVIEW COMMENTS:

MATERIAL				
O.S.				
TOTAL PRIME				
% O.H.				
B.E.				
% PROFIT				
BID				

DATE	PURCHASE-ITEMS (Vendor)	COST
		Total

DATE	OUTSIDE SERVICES (Vendor)	COST
		Total

EXHIBIT III SUMMARY OF MONTHLY SHIPMENTS—1981: FLINT SPECIALTY DIE, INC.

Month	Completed orders	Material	Outside services	2 × Labor	Profit
January	$ 146,044	$ 60,841	$ 3,396	$ 52,975	$ 28,832
February	175,450	72,811	6,953	62,214	33,472
March	229,153	81,558	9,648	95,951	41,996
April	216,383	73,465	11,816	80,923	50,179
May	166,313	64,546	5,516	62,335	33,916
June	225,653	86,675	13,796	81,770	43,412
July	113,165	35,648	9,249	48,954	19,314
August	212,758	85,534	7,705	64,343	55,176
September	245,055	90,656	12,805	94,656	46,938
October	235,064	86,293	17,909	85,614	45,248
November	170,848	56,965	8,303	69,286	36,294
December	185,239	52,728	2,311	67,178	63,022
Total—1,053 jobs	$2,321,125	$847,720	$109,407	$866,199	$497,799

January 1981 through June 1982 the company was represented by a manufacturer's representative in Ohio but this firm was dropped because of unsatisfactory results. Fred did most of the estimating for jobs, although Bill did some.

Selling was done through direct sales calls. Bob Jones spent all of his time calling on customers. Fred Brewer did more of the long distance and preliminary calls, often combining these with vacation trips. Leads for new customers were obtained by word of mouth and noticing where industry was locating, i.e., Texas. New industry ideas were followed up by using the Thomas Register to pinpoint the location of specific potential customers.

The company's advertising was limited to the Thomas Register, the Harris Book, and the Society of Carbide Engineers' quarterly magazine. A color brochure describing the company's facilities and capabilities was used to promote sales. These brochures were usually handed out on personal sales calls.

The company had about eighty active customers who were primarily in the auto-motive field. Exhibit IV shows the company's major customers in 1981 which illus-trates Pareto's Law at work. Bill believed "price is the #1 consideration for the customer" although the company brochure says "Our difference is service." The company's favorable sales growth during the severe recession in the automotive industry was due to "higher penetration." Bill said "competition is dropping the ball by not servicing their customers and their quality is down." Flint's three major competitors were located in Romulus, Harbor Beach, and Melvindale, Michigan. Flint tried to eliminate smaller jobs which seemed less profitable and avoided small "header shops." This policy resulted in no bad debts in 1981.

Although pricing was currently very tight because of the recession, Bill believed Flint "could get more business even if the recession continued or got worse." Flint was currently seeking new customers in Ohio, particularly in the Dayton area, because the Brewers thought this was the coming technical/industrial area. They were also actively seeking jobs in Texas—one new customer was Walker Manufacturing who

EXHIBIT IV CUSTOMER LIST—1981: FLINT SPECIALTY DIE, INC.

Customer	Sales	Profit	%
1. General Motors			
Plant A	$ 339,620	$ 53,660	15.8
Plant C	161,153	26,371	16.3
Plant E	144,688	99,799	69.0
Plant T	112,934	18,781	16.6
Plant Q	88,776	24,509	27.6
Plant M	76,230	12,800	16.8
Plant H	46,840	7,285	15.6
Plant Y	41,766	5,716	13.7
Plant Z	22,180	9,071	40.9
Plant F	14,754	2,290	15.5
Plant O	10,718	1,919	17.9
Plant J	7,863	1,418	17.9
Overseas	7,070	1,166	16.5
Plant R	613	(188)	(30.8)
Total GM	$1,075,205	$264,597	24.6
2. 1093	319,469	N.A.	
3. 1100	176,746	76,728	43.4
4. Ford Motor	174,104	6,209	3.6
5. 1246	147,191	34,536	23.4
6. 1231	97,966	12,113	12.4
7. 1052	96,128	9,895	10.3
8. 1074	90,961	18,533	20.3
9. 1150	87,995	24,093	27.3
10. 1123	86,740	15,740	18.1
11. Chrysler	61,326	6,400	10.4
12. 1254	32,651	2,791	8.5
13. 1182	21,813	2,731	12.5
14. 1088	14,570	3,328	22.8
15. 1205	14,378	4,390	30.5
16. 1012	11,785	3,959	33.6
17. 1034	11,654	(921)	(7.9)
18. 1121	11,331	3,698	32.6
	$2,532,013	$488,820	22.1
Other Customers (37)	111,311	(3,489)	(3.1)
	$2,643,324	$485,331	20.9

made mufflers for automobiles and trucks. General Magnetic, a producer of ferrite magnets which were formed from powdered metal, was another relatively new customer. In 1981 Flint made 1,280 quotes for approximately $12 million and received $2 million in orders, which illustrates the state of competition. The company did do rework jobs and was now marketing a polishing bit for die maintenance.

Cold formed parts made with carbide dies could replace parts made on screw machines if sufficient volume was available. The tooling cost for a certain die was about $150,000 but the customer's labor costs using the die were only one-tenth of that used for screw machines. So volume alone determined whether the part should be made with a carbide die or on a screw machine. This part was used in automotive steering gear in large volume.

FINANCIAL CONDITION

Flint retained a local firm of certified public accountants to prepare quarterly income statements, balance sheets and analyses of manufacturing overhead and selling, and general and administrative expenses. Exhibits V, VI, VII and VIII show these statements for 1978 through the first half of 1982. Accounts receivable were pledged as collateral for the bank loan. Trade accounts payable represented approximately eight months interest free credit extension by General Carbide, Flint's major supplier of material.

Bill Brewer was currently stressing keeping cash in the company. After delivery of the new assembly press in September 1982, which cost $67,000, he said no more machine purchases would be made until cash flow improved. Expansion of the business was actively being considered as a way to increase sales and profits. Another 1,000 square feet of shop space and 1,000 square feet of office space for a design area was needed, but there was no room on the present site. Presently the customers did all design work, but, if the design space were available, a designer/sales engineer and two draftsmen would be needed to provide this new service. Also, more management people might be needed to achieve higher productivity or higher volume. Bill thought a

EXHIBIT V INCOME STATEMENT: FLINT SPECIALTY DIE, INC.

	1978	1979	1980	1981	1982 (6 months)
Net Sales	$1,413,379	$2,035,178	$1,988,865	$2,546,963	$1,568,769
Cost of Sales:					
Materials	515,675	834,198	709,455	867,793	515,440
Subcontractors	66,725	124,680	145,203	187,940	136,293
Freight	2,871	4,546	5,293	8,561	5,582
Direct Labor	339,520	463,015	510,445	578,929	352,482
Manufacturing Overhead	280,573	357,870	356,665	374,350	257,851
Total	$1,205,364	$1,784,309	$1,727,061	$2,017,573	$1,267,648
Gross Profit on Sales	208,015	250,869	261,804	529,390	301,121
Selling, Administrative & General Expenses	184,500	218,449	232,520	368,198	243,213
Operating Income	23,515	32,420	29,284	161,192	57,908
Other Charges (Income):					
Interest	20,848	24,223	35,224	43,338	24,791
Gain on Sales of Fixed Assets	—	(1,250)	(35,000)	(6,250)	—
Total	20,848	22,973	224	37,088	24,788
Income before Taxes	2,667	9,447	29,060	124,104	33,117
Income Taxes—Less Investment Credit	—	—	—	—	—
Net Income	$ 2,667	$ 9,447	$ 29,060	$ 124,104	$ 33,117

EXHIBIT VI   BALANCE SHEET: FLINT SPECIALTY DIE, INC.

	1978	1979	1980	1981	1982 (6 months)
Current Assets:					
Cash	$ 226	$ 1,164	$ 6,765	$ 16,075	$ 10,049
Accounts Receivable:					
Trade	87,103	172,426	250,599	221,781	257,963
Other	—	654	606	—	—
Inventories	175,925	244,955	139,366	368,154	256,114
Prepaid Expenses	—	—	5,980	—	2,514
Total	263,294	419,199	403,316	606,010	526,640
Property and Equipment, at cost:					
Machinery	494,145	588,651	590,170	688,944	798,535
Automotive Equipment	22,081	28,201	28,201	49,829	49,829
Office Equipment	5,679	5,679	8,718	12,120	12,936
	521,905	622,531	627,089	750,893	861,300
Less Depreciation	325,898	346,278	346,309	372,638	398,503
	196,007	276,253	280,780	378,255	462,797
Leasehold Improvements		3,106	4,650	4,650	4,650
Less Amortization		1,397	2,271	3,146	3,776
	821	1,709	2,379	1,504	874
Net Property and Equipment	196,828	277,962	283,159	379,759	463,671
Other:					
Deposits	5,250	5,250	5,250	7,750	7,750
Organization Expense	369	369	369	369	369
Cash surrender value of $200,000 officers' life insurance less loan of $26,550 in 1981	15,625	19,475	20,825	562	1,238
Total	21,244	25,094	26,444	8,681	9,357
Total Assets	$481,366	$722,255	$712,919	$994,450	$999,668
Current Liabilities:					
Notes payable to bank (collateralized by accounts receivable)	72,347	146,502	102,643	200,212	69,400
Loan Payable—officers	6,250	13,750	13,750	16,250	16,250
Accounts payable—trade	223,055	374,305	392,416	421,970	532,466
Accruals:					
Interest	—	—	2,000	2,940	6,190
Salaries and Wages	11,646	9,123	15,978	30,663	27,376
Taxes	3,222	7,605	6,543	4,836	1,903
Insurance	—	—	—	5,821	—
Income Taxes	3,653	7,556	9,006	20,625	9,123
Current Maturities of long-term debt	23,750	22,536	22,536	44,651	34,792
Total	343,923	581,377	564,872	747,968	697,500
Long-term Debt	59,287	53,275	31,384	5,715	28,280
Total Liabilities	403,210	634,652	596,256	753,683	725,780
Stockholders' Equity					
Common Stock—$10 par value, 12,500 shares	125,000	125,000	125,000	125,000	125,000
Retained Earnings	53,156	62,603	91,663	215,767	248,884
	178,156	187,603	216,663	340,767	373,884
Treasury Stock, at cost, 6250 shares	100,000	100,000	100,000	100,000	100,000
Stockholders' Equity	78,156	87,603	116,663	240,767	273,884
Totals	$481,366	$722,255	$712,919	$994,450	$999,668

EXHIBIT VII   ANALYSIS OF MANUFACTURING OVERHEAD: FLINT SPECIALTY DIE, INC.

	1978	1979	1980	1981	1982 (6 months)
Plant supervision	51,449	91,405	56,283	51,618	30,966
Supplies	59,393	73,225	60,992	91,334	47,823
Repairs and maintenance	14,579	22,391	15,439	12,015	6,272
Payroll taxes	30,984	40,604	39,039	46,149	41,868
Employees insurance benefits	28,549	34,235	35,189	44,862	36,336
Bonuses	3,487	2,688	94	—	—
General taxes	4,480	4,064	6,829	7,254	5,250
Janitor and delivery labor	15,581	18,883	17,840	21,782	11,916
Shop travel	1,550	1,895	2,425	2,455	246
Insurance	23,479	23,104	37,520	36,102	17,563
Laundry	1,951	1,697	2,056	2,318	1,440
Engineering and development	8,539	4,250	94	8,375	—
Depreciation and amortization	11,616	23,538	27,356	36,079	22,054
Rent	21,375	22,500	22,500	22,500	11,250
Utilities	10,225	10,941	12,569	12,873	9,908
Decrease (increase) in inventory	(5,664)	(17,550)	20,440	(21,366)	9,168
Indirect labor	—	—	—	—	5,794
Total	$280,573	$357,870	$356,665	$374,350	$257,851

EXHIBIT VIII   ANALYSIS OF SELLING, ADMINISTRATIVE, AND GENERAL EXPENSES: FLINT SPECIALTY DIE, INC.

	1978	1979	1980	1981	1982 (6 months)
Salaries:					
Officers	76,375	80,750	83,831	117,680	73,596
Office	14,880	14,729	15,004	11,865	6,024
Sales	—	—	—	19,430	13,675
Auto and travel	14,041	18,569	22,033	27,916	21,701
Promotion and advertising	22,585	42,346	46,601	55,304	25,458
Payroll taxes	3,750	3,750	4,000	5,250	7,500
Commissions	12,969	10,945	2,854	30,573	15,725
Employee benefits	5,309	4,866	8,050	23,631	—
Retirement payments	—	—	3,375	6,500	3,250
Depreciation	4,513	4,474	7,985	9,094	4,440
Supplies	3,662	5,861	5,415	6,371	4,891
Dues and subscriptions	3,640	4,076	4,569	6,615	3,786
Officers' life insurance	3,295	3,388	5,887	(5,687)	3,076
Telephone	7,345	7,549	8,866	11,414	6,856
Professional services	4,031	11,496	8,124	14,976	43,360
Donations	446	431	625	1,150	419
State taxes	5,625	5,000	5,000	25,000	8,750
Miscellaneous	2,034	219	301	1,116	706
Total	$184,500	$218,449	$232,520	$368,198	$243,213

small computer would be useful in maintaining financial data and particularly useful in estimating jobs and following their progress. Still another longer range proposal was the establishment of another shop, 6–9,000 square feet of floor space, in the Dayton area which was estimated to cost $170,000. The company presently does 42% of its business in the Dayton area.

As Bill thought of these longer term moves, he pragmatically came back to the current cash flow situation and mused "first things first." The first half of 1982 had brought some higher expenses. The increase in professional services had been due to legal fees over an employee discrimination suit alleging the employee handbook had not been followed in laying him off. He sued for $10,000 and Flint finally settled for $1,000 just before the trial because of the tremendous costs expended that far. Bill thought that, "since the company was right, it was a matter of principle" but "standing up for principle can be costly."

DISCUSSION QUESTIONS

1 To what extent is Flint Specialty Die's dependence on the automobile industry as its major customer a problem and what approach do you think that the company should take to solving the problem?

2 Describe the nature of the working capital situation which exists at Flint Specialty Die and explain what Bill should do about it when he takes control. Defend your answer.

3 Calculate the key financial ratios for Flint Specialty Die for 1978 through 1981. Evaluate the situation existing as of 1978 and identify any trends which you see. Discuss the strategic importance of what you have discovered.

4 Evaluate the information and control system at Flint Specialty Die and describe any changes you would make if you were Bill Brewer.

RIVERVIEW
MEDICAL CENTER
HOSPITAL (A)

Michael Swartz
Boston University

Linda J. Edwards
James Whitcomb Riley Hospital for Children

SELECTED STRATEGIC ISSUES

- Types of information needed to make and sell an investment decision in a nonprofit institution
- Problems encountered by an outsider who attempts to gather strategic information

Steve Elliott, a second year student in a noted health care administration master's degree program, was delighted when he received a call from Jennifer Abrahms, Director of Planning at Riverview Medical Center Hospital, asking if he were willing to work on a project part-time during the forthcoming semester. From Ms. Abrahms' brief description of the project on the telephone, Mr. Elliott anticipated that the time the project would require would fit in well with his course schedule. The topic, determining the impact of additional beds in the medical intensive care unit and the cardiac care unit, was one that interested him from a number of perspectives.[1]

[1] The intensive care unit (or ICU), which permits electrocardiographic monitoring of acute coronary-artery disease, became a popular treatment of cardiac arrhythmias in the early 1960's. At first reserved for patients with known or suspected myocardial infarction, it was soon expanded to include patients with serious arrhythmias or heart failure, as well as patients with pulmonary insufficiency, coma, sepsis, gastrointestinal bleeding, acute renal failure, and many other kinds of urgent problems. (*Source:* Editorial, April 24, 1980, *New England Journal of Medicine,* vol. 302, No. 17, p. 965).

BACKGROUND: THE HOSPITAL

Riverview Medical Center Hospital, with 447 beds, was one of four major medical center hospitals in the metropolitan area and the primary teaching hospital for one of the two medical schools in the city. Affiliated with the State University's School of Medicine, it sat at the edge of a 16-acre campus that included the Schools of Dentistry and Veterinary Medicine. Riverview, a center for patient care, teaching and research, had an international reputation in the fields of cardiology, cancer, endocrinology, and kidney disease.

The hospital admitted 14,000 patients annually. Outpatient visits had increased from 151,162 to 257,264 in the preceding five years. Many of its ambulatory clinics were speciality clinics, reflecting the center's role in research and teaching. Almost 13% of the patients came to Riverview from surrounding states in the Midwest and another 5% from more distant areas. Riverview, located in an aging area of the city, also considered itself the primary provider of health care services for many of the area's local residents. Two of the state's major highway arteries intersected only blocks from the entrance to Riverview's emergency room.

MEETING WITH MS. ABRAHMS

Because Abrahms and Elliott knew one another quite well, Abrahms came right to the point of the project:

This is the project, Steve. I believe we may need additional beds in our medical intensive care unit (MICU) and our cardiac care unit (CCU). Currently we have 6 MICU beds and 4 CCU beds, as well as 17 SICU (surgical intensive care unit) beds.

I am concerned with how often we seem to be at full capacity. Last year, monthly utilization in the MICU and CCU averaged almost 90%. There have been complaints that patients have been moved from the unit prematurely to make room for new patients coming in. Also, we have a hospital policy that on any shift when both the medical intensive care and cardiac care units are full, we contact the dispatch service of the local city-county ambulance and emergency services department and request that they reroute ambulances away from Riverview for the remainder of that shift. Recently the city-county Health Commissioners' Office has been complaining about how frequently ambulances have been rerouted from Riverview. In response to this, the planning committee has requested that the issue of the adequacy of the current number of intensive care beds be examined.

The frequent rerouting and high monthly utilization suggest that we need more beds, though I do not know how many more. If we conclude we should add beds, we will have to be able to make a strong case to the area health planners. Converting or adding beds requires a Certificate of Need.[2] This requirement places certain demands on us. As you are probably aware, the new Governor is committed to revitalizing the CON process in an attempt to limit health care costs. Mr. Detter, the staff analyst at the CON office with whom we have had preliminary discussion, has not been encouraging about the prospects for approval of any

---

[2] The Certificate of Need (CON) program was established as a means of containing health care costs. Proposals for new or expanded capacity must be approved by State Health Coordinating Councils. One of the important criteria in deciding whether to approve a CON application is that the expansion serves the public needs.

additional ICU beds. However, I feel he fails to understand our unique situation. If a solid analysis demonstrates the need for more beds, I am confident we will be able to obtain a CON.

We have developed some preliminary estimates of the cost of adding ICU beds. Conversion of existing space at the hospital to ICU beds will cost about $35,000 per bed. In addition, fixed and movable equipment will require an additional $30,000 per bed. A consultant hired by us last year conducted an assessment of Riverview's debt capacity. His report concluded that the Medical Center has sufficient debt capacity for several small to moderate size projects like adding ICU beds, plus a major building or renovation project, if needed. Hence, financing of additional beds, if we can justify their need, is not a problem.

What I need now is for you to gather and analyze data to determine the need for more beds in the MICU and CCU. I need the analysis presented to me in such a way that it will make sense when I then present it to the planning committee. I want the members to be able to visualize the current problems—what we are currently doing—and I want them to see the effect of adding this number of beds or that number, in terms of improvements in service. Since we are under some pressure to change our policy of ambulance diversion, I need to be able to see the effects of a change in policy. If a case can be made for adding beds, I would hope your analysis is sufficiently complete, or you can tell me what other work has to be done, so that it can be used to persuade Mr. Detter to support our CON application.

I will contact the appropriate people here in the medical center, letting them know what you are doing. Before I do that I need from you a short memo that outlines the kind of information you will need. While I have some ideas, I would like your suggestions on how to go about the analysis.

THE NEXT STEP

Elliott knew, from working on committees with Abrahms, that she liked succinct memos and that she was busy and would not have time to meet with him often. At the same time, he had noted that she relied extensively on staff work such as this in meetings with others both in the hospital and in the community. Also, it seemed she planned to rely heavily on his analysis in preparing a CON, should a decision be made to add beds. Consequently, as well as estimating the impact of adding beds, she would want his analysis to address issues such as: what information was not included, what assumptions have been made, what pitfalls might there to be using a particular approach, what might be done as a next step.

His internship experience, with the Dean of the Medical School affiliated with the medical center, had led him to expect that if he were willing to do the "legwork," he would have little difficulty in obtaining whatever hospital information was available for the project. He could, in theory, list every possible kind of data to examine. If he did propose a "laundry list," however, he could expect to receive the memo back with some cryptic comment to the effect, "You don't really expect to gather all *that* and get any school work done, do you?"

DISCUSSION QUESTIONS

1 What kinds of information should Elliott propose to gather? Explain the relevance and suggested use of each type.
2 What kinds of problems is Elliott likely to encounter in gathering information? Explain how he might avoid or minimize them.

RIVERVIEW MEDICAL CENTER HOSPITAL (B)

Michael Swartz
Boston University

Linda J. Edwards
James Whitcomb Riley Hospital for Children

SELECTED STRATEGIC ISSUES

- Required assumptions for use of a queuing model in strategic decision making
- Use of queuing theory in practical decision making
- Cost-benefit considerations in information gathering

In response to a request from Ms. Jennifer Abrahms, the Director of Planning, Steve Elliott had just completed a relatively extensive compilation of data concerning the medical intensive care unit (MICU) and the cardiac care unit (CCU) at Riverview Medical Center Hospital.

DATA COLLECTION

Occupancy

He had begun with basics: occupancy rates over the last two years for the two units. (Exhibit 1.) For the year prior to his study, the average occupancy for the hospital's 265 general medical/surgical beds had been 90.3%. The average occupancy for the 17 surgical intensive care unit (SICU) beds had been 81.9% for the entire year, but had ranged between 87.9% and 93.1% for the last three months.

EXHIBIT 1   OCCUPANCY OF MICU AND CCU 1977 AND 1978

| | % Occupancy | | | |
| | MICU | | CCU | |
Month	1977	1978	1977	1978
January	90.5%	85.1%	92.9%	86.6%
February	95.2	95.2	92.0	95.5
March	92.4	93.8	77.9	89.3
April	70.2	95.2	72.3	91.1
May	88.1	92.3	87.5	80.4
June	94.8	90.5	85.7	85.0
July	92.3	81.6	85.7	86.6
August	87.5	85.3	94.6	81.0
September	82.9	81.9	77.9	78.6
October	72.6	88.7	88.4	92.0
November	73.2	88.1	70.5	91.1
December	85.2	93.5	79.3	94.3

Note: MICU has 6 beds. CCU has 4 beds.
Source: Riverview Medical Center Hospital Inpatient Statistical Reports.

Number of Admissions

Using admissions log books for the two units, he had compiled information on the number of daily admissions. He was able to find daily records for the period from November 1, 1978 to May 1, 1979 for each unit. To assist the planning committee who would review the data and to make the information easier to visualize, he prepared a table of the data by day of the week. The table (Exhibit 2) showed days on which both the MICU and CCU were full on the same shift and days on which one or the other unit was full, but both units were not full on the same shift.

Ambulance Diversions

Elliott had learned initially that it was the hospital's policy to close its emergency room to city-county ambulances whenever no MICU or CCU beds were available, that is, when both units were filled on the same shift. In this case, the hospital called the central city-county dispatching services for emergency vehicles and requested that ambulances be rerouted to other hospital emergency departments in the area (most notably the city-county hospital). The admissions log books noted the days on which emergency vehicles had been diverted during at least one eight-hour shift that day. (Exhibit 3.)

Elliott had also examined more detailed records of the calls to the city-county ambulance dispatcher in order to determine diversions of the ambulances by day of the week and by shift. (Exhibit 3.) On the average, whenever both units were filled at the same time and thus ambulances diverted from the emergency room, the diversions lasted for two shifts.

EXHIBIT 2

NUMBER OF MICU AND CCU ADMISSIONS BY DAY OF THE WEEK: NOVEMBER 1, 1978 THROUGH MAY 1, 1979

Dates	Monday MICU	Monday CCU	Monday *	Tuesday MICU	Tuesday CCU	Tuesday *	Wednesday MICU	Wednesday CCU	Wednesday *	Thursday MICU	Thursday CCU	Thursday *	Friday MICU	Friday CCU	Friday *	Saturday MICU	Saturday CCU	Saturday *	Sunday MICU	Sunday CCU	Sunday *
11/1–11/5							0	0		1	4	X	1	1		2	1	X	0	0	X
11/6–11/12	1	1	X	1	1	X	2	1	X	2	2		0	0	X	0	0	X	0	0	
11/13–11/19	0	2		4	1		3	1	X	2	1	X	2	3	X	3	0		4	0	
11/20–11/26	0	0		3	2		2	1		0	1		1	0		0	0		1	1	
11/27–12/3	4	1		1	0		3	2		0	0		0	1		2	0		2	1	
12/4–12/10	3	3	X	2	0		2	1	X	2	2	X	1	1	X	1	1	X	2	1	X
12/11–12/17	0	1	X	1	1	X	2	1	X	1	2	X	0	1	X	0	0	X	0	0	
12/18–12/24	2	0		2	2	X	0	1		0	0		3	0		1	1		2	0	
12/25–12/31	1	2		1	1		1	0		0	2		3	3		3	0		1	0	
1/1–1/7	1	0	X	1	2		0	1	X	0	2	X	0	1	X	3	0	X	0	3	
1/8–1/14	1	2	X	2	2	X	0	1	X	0	1	X	3	1	X	1	1	X	2	2	
1/15–1/21	2	1	X	2	1	X	2	1	X	1	2	X	0	0	X	1	2	X	0	1	X
1/22–1/28	3y	1y	X	1	1	X	4	2	X	2	1	X	1	1	X	1	1		1	1y	
1/29–2/4	0	0		3y	0y	X	1y	0y	X	3y	0y	X	2y	1		2y	1		1	1	X
2/5–2/11	0	2y		2	1	X	0	1	X	4y	2		1y	1	X	1y	1	X	1	2	
2/12–2/18	2y	2		3	0		3y	2y	X	2y	1y	X	0y	3y	X	0	1y		2y	0	
2/19–2/25	1	3		1	2		1	0		2	1		2	0y	X	1	0y		1	0	
2/26–3/4	3	4y		2	0		0y	3y		2	1	X	0y	1y		2	2y		1	0	
3/5–3/11	1	1y		4y	3	X	1	1y	X	5y	3y	X	2y	0y	X	1y	1		1y	0	
3/12–3/18	2	2		1	0		4y	1		1y	3y		1	1y		0	1		2	1	
3/19–3/25	0	0		3y	1		1y	2		4y	1y		2y	0		1	2y		1	0	
3/26–4/1	2	2y		3	1		3y	2		1	1		1	0		0	0		0	0	
4/2–4/8	3y	3y		2	0y		1	0		1	3y		3	2		3y	1y		2	3y	
4/9–4/15	2y	1y		1y	0y		1	0y		1	1		2y	3y		1	2y		2y	1y	
4/16–4/22	1	1		1y	2y		2y	0y		1y	1y		2y	0		0	0		1	2	
4/23–4/29	1	2y		1	1		1	3		2	0		3	1		2	0		1	1	
4/30–5/1	1			5y	2y																

*: X: Days on which ambulances were rerouted during at least one shift, (i.e. both units were filled on the same shift).

y: Days on which the indicated unit was filled on at least one shift (however, if each unit has a y, both units were not filled on the same shift and hence the ambulance was not rerouted).

EXHIBIT 3
DISTRIBUTION OF AMBULANCE DIVERSIONS

By Day of Week: 11/01/78 through 10/31/79

Day	Total shifts	Shifts diverted	% of total
Monday	156	31	20%
Tuesday	156	55	34
Wednesday	156	55	35
Thursday	156	64	41
Friday	156	53	34
Saturday	156	24	15
Sunday	156	18	12
TOTAL	1095	309	28%

By Shift: 11/01/78 through 10/31/79

Shift	Total shifts	Shifts diverted	% of total
7 AM–3 PM	365	107	29%
3 PM–11 PM	365	102	28
11 PM–7 AM	365	100	27
TOTAL	1095	309	28%

EXHIBIT 4
LENGTH OF STAY DISTRIBUTION IN ICU'S: NOVEMBER 1978 THROUGH APRIL 1979

Length of stay (days)	Number of cases in: MICU	CCU
1	97	64
2	61	43
3	27	28
4	29	21
5	9	7
6	5	5
7	7	8
8	4	4
9	4	2
10	6	2
11	3	3
12	1	1
13	1	1
14		1
15		
16		
17	1	
18	1	
19	2	
36		1
Total	258	191

Lengths of Stay, Initial Diagnosis, Patient Origin and Disposition

From the admissions log book, Elliott created a frequency distribution, which indicated the number of patients with different lengths of stay. (Exhibit 4.) As a basis for consideration of the appropriateness of placement in the ICU, Elliott was able to gather information on the initial diagnosis of ICU patients. (Exhibit 5.) He had also found both the origin and disposition of patients recorded in the log books. (Exhibits 6 and 7.)

Policies and Procedures for Admission and Discharge

Elliott reported to Abrahms that the necessary policies and procedures regarding admission and discharge criteria for both units were in order at the time of the last semi-annual review of the units. The medical director for each unit was responsible, overall, for decisions about who should be admitted to and discharged from the units. In practice, when there was a question about discharging someone from a unit—typically to make room for someone coming onto an already full unit—the MICU or CCU head nurse on the shift and the chief resident weighed the severity of illness of the incoming patient against what they knew about the least severe case already in the unit. Sometimes a person would be "inappropriately" placed while waiting for a bed in

EXHIBIT 5   INITIAL DIAGNOSIS AT MICU AND CCU: MARCH 1978 THROUGH FEBRUARY 1979

	MICU			CCU	
Initial diagnosis	# Cases	% Total	Initial diagnosis	# Cases	% Total
R/O MI	89	27.5%	R/O MI	186	45.3%
GI Bleed	37	11.5	Acute MI, MI	47	11.4
Miscellaneous[1]	31	9.6	Unstable, crescenda angina	38	9.3
Renal failure	30	9.3	A/V fibrillation	28	6.8
Respiratory failure ARDS	28	8.7	Miscellaneous[1]	22	5.4
Drug toxicity or OD	21	6.5	Congestive heart failure	16	3.9
Pulmonary edema	18	5.6	Stenosis, COPD, pulmonary		
Acute MI, MI	12	3.7	embolism	13	3.2
Congestive heart failure	12	3.7	Pulmonary edema	12	2.9
Hyper/hypotension	10	3.2	Drug toxicity or OD	10	2.4
Pneumonia	9	2.8	Hyper/hypotension	8	2.0
Stenosis, COPD, pulmonary			Cardiogenic shock	6	1.5
embolism	8	2.5	Respiratory failure, ARDS	5	1.2
Unstable, crescendo angina	7	2.2	GI bleed	5	1.2
A/V fibrillation	5	1.6	Pneumonia	5	1.2
Cardiogenic shock	3	.9	Pacemaker dysfunction	5	1.2
S/P surgery	2	.6	S/P surgery	3	.7
Pacemaker dysfunction	—	—	Renal faiure	2	.5
TOTAL[2]	322	100.0%		411	100.0%

1. Category includes diabetes and other endocrine problems, MS, syncope, UTI, asthma, cirrhosis, moninitus, seizures, ectopy, myeloma, and various cancers.
2. Actual MICU admissions totalled 453; however, no diagnosis was marked for 131 patients.
Sources: Log books for MICU, CCU.

EXHIBIT 6   ORIGIN OF MICU AND CCU PATIENTS: MARCH 1978 THROUGH FEBRUARY 1979

	MICU		CCU	
Patient origin	# Patients	% Total	# Patients	% Total
Emergency Room	230	50.8	211	51.3
Transfer from other hospital	21	4.6	116	10.5
Transfer from Riverview				
general medical/sugical	157	34.7	116	28.2
MICU	n/a	n/a	13	3.2
CCU	8	1.8	n/a	n/a
Surgical ICU	27	5.9	14	
Clinics (renal,				
pulmonary, medical)	10	2.2	14	3.4
TOTAL	453	100.0%	411	100.0%

either the CCU or MICU to become available. The head nurse for the day shift in CCU felt that about one-half the time the unit was full, she had the name of a patient to be moved in as soon as a bed became available. The head nurse in the MICU agreed this seemed true for her unit also. Neither nurse could remember ever having a case where more than one patient was waiting for an ICU bed.

EXHIBIT 7 DISPOSITIONS OF PATIENTS DISCHARGED FROM MICU AND CCU: MARCH 1978 THROUGH FEBRUARY 1979

Disposition of patient	MICU		CCU	
	# Patients	% Total	# Patients	% Total
Inpatient bed	359	79.3	338	82.2
Deceased	44	9.7	39	9.5
Discharged	12	2.6	4	1.0
Transferred	5	1.1	2	.5
To SICU	20	4.4	14	3.4
To MICU	n/a	n/a	8	1.9
To CCU	13	2.9	n/a	n/a
To Operating Room	—	—	6	1.5
TOTAL	453	100.0%	411	100.0%

Overall, about 50% of the patients admitted to each unit were arrivals through the emergency room. However, a special study undertaken last year had found that during periods in which the ambulance was not rerouted, about 60% of both MICU and CCU patients were arrivals through the emergency room.

Conversations with Physicians and Nurses

Ms. Abrahms had been able to arrange for Elliott to meet with Dr. Shwaman, the Medical Center Director; Dr. Platt, the Chief of Cardiology; several staff physicians in the Department of Internal Medicine; and Ms. Godell, the Director of Nursing.

Dr. Shwaman, an elderly, thoughtful man, had said it was his personal feeling that perhaps some of the patients in the MICU and CCU could and should be treated in the general medical units. He felt many physicians were not sufficiently aware of the effect of their decisions on overall health care costs. Specifically, they were not sensitive to the costs that resulted from keeping a patient in an ICU longer than medically necessary. Despite his interest in using health care resources efficiently, Dr. Shwaman had shared with Elliott his own frustrations in not being able to affect the treatment patterns of many of his colleagues.

Dr. Jones, one of the physicians in internal medicine, told the story of a recent patient of his who, because he could not obtain an ICU bed when needed, almost died. When Elliott asked how often was Dr. Jones not able to obtain a bed for one of his patients, Dr. Jones replied, "If you were the patient who didn't get an ICU bed and died, would you care how many other times that happened?" Dr. Jones strongly criticized the mentality of health care regulators far removed from daily encounters with illness and death who attempted to limit resources that could help suffering individuals. Dr. Marcotti agreed. He told of a patient of his who, with some misgivings, he had moved from the CCU to free up a bed for a recent heart attack victim. As a result of situations like this, Dr. Marcotti cautioned Elliott that the length of stay information he had collected might underestimate what length of stay should be if there were sufficient ICU beds for patients who needed them.

Elliott had been particularly interested in talking to Dr. Platt about the possibility of combining the MICU and CCU, something he knew had been done at many hospitals. He had been surprised by the vehemence of Dr. Platt's response. Aside from the fact that each unit has specialized nurses and equipment, combining the units would totally disrupt the cardiology training programs. Dr. Platt said it would be unworkable, infeasible and uneconomical, and if any attempt were made to combine the units, he would go directly to the Board of Trustees to fight it.

Ms. Godell emphasized the important role that nurses played in the ICU. They were very highly trained and had many specialized skills. Being in such intimate contact with patients over the course of their time in the ICU, Ms. Godell felt the ICU nurses were often able to make helpful evaluations of the need for patients to remain in the ICU. She said that many of the ICU nurses felt there was a problem of patients being misplaced in the ICU's. Also, some nurses had expressed the belief that the higher ancillary charges for intensive care patients were in part the result of physicians ordering the same wide array of tests and procedures for all their patients on the unit despite individual differences and needs.

Operational Costs and Reimbursement

Though Ms. Abrahms had been clear that the focus of Elliott's study was to be on the need for ICU beds, and that there was sufficient debt capacity to support conversion of space to beds if the need existed, she had suggested that Elliott talk to Joyce Walen in the Finance Office about the operational costs of ICU beds and reimbursement for costs, mainly to provide background for Elliott and increase his understanding of hospital operations and incentives.

Ms. Walen was most cooperative. Elliot learned that the per diem charge for an intensive care bed was $430 per day, while the charge for a comparable private room on a routine unit was $152 per day. Most of the difference in cost was due to the additional nursing staff (often 2 to 3 times higher than on routine units) and the depreciation costs associated with the additional equipment. Ancillary costs (that is, the cost for laboratory, pharmacy, respiratory therapy, etc.) were also higher than for patients on routine units. Riverview's overall average charge for ancillary services was $242 per day. But a special study Walen had done estimated the average daily charge for ancillary services for ICU patients was almost twice as high as for patients on routine units. To some extent this was not surprising, since the most critically ill patients were in the ICU.

For most hospital services provided at Riverview, the hospital was not reimbursed directly by the patient, but rather by a "third party" (Blue Cross, other commercial insurers, or government programs such as Medicaid and Medicare). This had a predictable effect—the costs associated with construction, equipment and direct nursing services would be reimbursed. In addition, the charge structure of the medical center's major ancillary services allowed them to average a "contribution" of 8.5% of charges for these services.

EXHIBIT 8   ADULT MEDICAL/SURGICAL BEDS, INTENSIVE CARE BEDS, AND AVERAGE ICU OCCUPANCY IN OTHER HOSPITALS IN 1978

	City/county hospital	Private university affiliated	Downstate #1	Downstate #2
Medical/surgical beds	856	305	265	370
ICU beds*	65	28	32	21
ICU average occupancy	80.3	89.6	87.9	72.7

* Where separate MICU's and SICU's exist, the number of beds have been added. Figures also include CCU and specialty intensive care units.

Local Comparisons

Anticipating that Abrahms would encounter questions from the planning group about how the proportion of ICU beds and ICU occupancy rates at Riverview compared with other medical centers in the area, Elliott collected some background information on intensive care units in the other hospitals. He selected two hospitals in the city and two other hospitals downstate that were considered "comparable," e.g., considered themselves tertiary care (research and teaching) centers, but also hospitals serving local populations. (Exhibit 8.) The proportion of ICU beds (including SICU beds) to general adult medical surgical beds ranged from 5.7% to 12.1%. Occupancy varied widely from 72% to almost 90%. Unlike Riverview, two of the hospitals, the hospital affiliated with the local private medical school and one of the two downstate hospitals, had combined surgical and medical intensive care units.

DISCUSSION QUESTIONS

1 Analyze the data provided to determine if the assumptions for a queuing model (which can be solved analytically) are met (consider only the first three months of arrival data).
2 Analyze the system assuming a limited queue of size one can build up; also perform the analysis assuming an unlimited queue. Why would you do this analysis?
3 Evaluate the validity of your results and explain whether you would collect additional information in terms of the costs and benefits of such information.

RIVERVIEW MEDICAL CENTER HOSPITAL (C)

Michael Swartz
Boston University

Linda J. Edwards
James Whitcomb Riley Hospital for Children

SELECTED STRATEGIC ISSUES

- Decision making by a hospital oversight agency
- The tendency of utilization to fill available capacity in nonprofit institutions

Steve Elliott was working on a project in which he was analyzing the need for additional medical intensive care (MICU) and coronary care (CCU) beds at Riverview Medical Center Hospital, for Jennifer Abrahms, Director of Planning.

During the bed need project, he was continuing his graduate studies in health administration. As part of a health planning and policy course, he selected the topic of determining need for beds in intensive care units for a short exploratory project.

He contacted the local health systems agency (HSA) to see how they approached the question of determining the appropriate number of intensive care beds. He was pleased to discover that an alumnus of the health administration program, Kirk McKenzie, was responsible for acute care planning. He had in fact drafted the original ICU guidelines.

Informally over coffee, Kirk discussed the issue of intensive care beds candidly with Steve.

Elliott: How were the guidelines used by the HSA developed? They set a ratio between total intensive care beds and total patient days for adult medical surgical services as the basis for determining the appropriate number of ICU beds. Where did the appropriate ratio come from?

McKenzie: The guidelines we use—and for that matter, since many places have pretty much taken our approach, the guidelines that are used in several other parts of the Midwest—are really a stopgap measure, *ad hoc.* That does not mean they are not justified, just that one person, me, developed them. There has not yet been other completed systematic review and input. We are doing more extensive work now and with time we and the entire health planning field will have better bases for our decisions.

Elliott: But, how did you decide on the appropriate ratio?

McKenzie: The ratio decided upon was the existing ratio of intensive care beds to total patient days in the area. Our primary intent is to limit expansion in intensive care beds. By using total adult patient days, rather than total adult beds, as for example they did in Massachusetts, we avoid penalizing a hospital that has fewer beds but higher occupancy when compared with the hospital down the road. For any given hospital, the ratio appears to have been relatively stable for quite a long time.

We didn't and don't have any way of knowing exactly how many intensive care beds there should be and who should be in them. We do know from several recent studies that it is not clear that everyone currently in intensive care units needs to be there. Being in intensive care doesn't necessarily mean someone is more likely to be better off in the long run than if he or she had been in a typical general medical/surgical bed.

Elliot: Is the area's historic ratio justifiable?

McKenzie: We compared our ratio of ICU beds to patient days with ratios in other areas, both nearby and around the country. The range of ratios was fairly wide. Our ratio was very close to the middle and also close to the mode. Let's say it isn't unjustifiable.

Elliott: What about the argument that tertiary care hospitals, involved in research and serving extremely ill patients, require proportionately more intensive care beds?

McKenzie: The guidelines allow a higher ratio of intensive care beds to patient days for tertiary care hospitals. Throughout the planning process remember, however, we have not totally resolved the issue of what constitutes a tertiary care hospital. This is a state with relatively few medical schools but excellent standards of care and many referrals to some large, relatively geographically isolated hospitals.

Elliott: Why is there a lower limit on the number of beds in a unit?

McKenzie: For economies of scale. There are high fixed costs for staff and equipment in intensive care units. In addition, when the lower limit on size is combined with the required ratio of beds to patient days it means that small county hospitals won't have intensive care units.

Elliott: Why is it necessary to have any specific limit on intensive care beds?

McKenzie: From my view, it is essential to control the amount and the intensity of services provided by hospitals in order to control costs. It is evident to me that over the past 20 years the primary source of the increase in health care costs is the increase in the intensity of services rendered. True, the unit costs of labor, supplies, etc., have gone up. And the number of patient care episodes, total and per capita, has increased.

But a good case can be made that costs are higher primarily because each episode is on average using more services, more tests, more nursing care, more, more, more.

I believe that in this area, especially, with two medical schools, the system needs to be protected from the explosion in sophisticated technology. It generates added costs—both capital costs and operating costs—without comparable, demonstrable benefits.

If a hospital wants to increase its number of intensive care beds it is allowed to do so, but it must demonstrate that there will be a net incremental benefit. We need to compare the marginal costs, both pecuniary and non-pecuniary costs of course, and the marginal benefits. Look at the next best alternative. Hospitals always have the alternative of moving the least sick patient in the ICU to the next lower level of intensity of care. Furthermore, to some extent utilization of intensive care, especially for postoperative surgical intensive care patients, can be scheduled, controlled.

Remember Roemer's Law: if a bed is available it will be used, especially an intensive care bed for which hospitals are reimbursed more. The hospital has a financial incentive to fill ICU beds. And while collectively at budget time governments and businesses might be concerned about health care costs, individual people, patients and physicians view intensive care as better care. Adding beds in intensive care does not ensure that one will be available when a critically ill patient needs it.

At that point, the conversation moved to more general issues.

DISCUSSION QUESTIONS

1 Compare and contrast the analysis done by Elliott to the type of justification which will sell the health systems agency on the need for additional beds.
2 Explain the validity of ''Roemer's Law'' and its relevance to the proposed decision.

SOUTHERN FEDERAL SAVINGS AND LOAN ASSOCIATION (B)

William R. Boulton
James A. Verbrugge
University of Georgia

SELECTED STRATEGIC ISSUES

- Appropriate organizational structure for a savings and loan association
- The desirability of a financial institution taking a leadership role in the community
- The desirability and nature of formal goals and objectives for a savings and loan association
- Useful strategic changes as consumer lending increases compared to real estate lending for a savings and loan association

Southern Federal Savings and Loan Association's officers were gearing up to offer consumer loans, NOW accounts and renegotiable rate mortgages (RRMs) which were now allowed by the Depository Institutions Deregulation and Monetary Control Act of 1980. By July of 1980, steps to introduce these new products were well underway. Mr. Knight, the chief executive officer, explained:

> We'll get into consumer loans as early as September 1st or 15th—whenever we can gear up and get in. We're trying hard to get in just as soon as possible because we know it will affect all our branch offices—all branch managers and at least one other person have got to be trained and familiar with them. That's a big job. But we need to get on with it just as quickly as possible because NOW accounts are coming January 1st, and we don't want two things of this magnitude slapping us at the same time. If we can get into consumer lending in September then we'll have a little bit of time to get feeling comfortable with that before starting to feel uncomfortable when NOW accounts go.

542

SOUTHERN FEDERAL'S MANAGEMENT

Mr. Knight was in his sixteenth year as president of Southern Federal. He had not grown up in this business, but had become president of Southern Federal after selling his poultry business. In describing how he became involved, Knight explained:

> I sold out my interests in the poultry business on February 1, 1962, became mayor of the city on January 1, 1964, and came over here in December, 1964. My predecessor had reached retirement age but they didn't give him until the first of January as was customary. There was some internal conflict. I replaced him on the eleventh of December. That didn't set well with him, but I didn't have anything to do with it. I wasn't an applicant for the job.
>
> I didn't seek the job and didn't particularly want it, but one of the directors came by and asked me if I'd consider filling in for an interim time. I assumed he was talking from January on. I said, "Well, I hadn't thought about it, but I might be interested," because the position as mayor was supposed to be a part-time job. After that, four directors fell in behind me—they said, "We'd just like to have you fill in." So I've been filling in since 1964; but, my filling in time is about up, because I turned 65 on June 17. I don't know what my relationship will be after January 1.

James Redding, Southern Federal's second in command, also came from the outside in 1960. Prior to joining Southern Federal, he had been in the real estate and insurance business, and had been helping the association part-time. He explained:

> I was helping them out part-time with problems they were having in the appraising and construction end of the business, and decided to try it full time. I did the appraising and developed inspection sheets for builders to use in drawing money for construction loans. I worked on that end of it and later just sort of became general flunky around here.

A copy of Southern Federal's current organization structure was not readily available to Jack Pope, vice president and the one to develop such charts. He explained:

> I've done some sketches of the organization chart, but passed them on to Redding and didn't keep a copy. We've talked about it. We know how it works, or at least the department heads know.

Exhibit 1 shows the organization chart which Pope drafted for the writer. Knight commented on the development of their organization.

> There was no organization 16 years ago. We were small by comparison. But we are a whole lot larger, so we have had to departmentalize. We had to gear up for that. We had to employ people. Besides Redding and Billings, assistant in mortgage loans, I've employed everyone in front line management. They are more or less the type of people that I like on my side.

In discussing the actual structure of Southern Federal, Knight continued:

> The direct line is myself, Redding and Jack Pope. After that you break down into various departments. Bob Thompson is mortgage loan officer. Jim Heart is controller.
>
> I'm the managing officer and the president and the chairman of the board; but, after January 1, if I stay I'd probably like to take a little different role—back off just a little bit—and let James and Jack and those folks really run the association and I act more in policy and advisory capacity. If the board is willing to do that, I'd like to do it, because I'm not a retirement type person.

EXHIBIT I

SOUTHERN FEDERAL SAVINGS AND LOAN ASSOCIATION
ORGANIZATION CHART, August 4, 1980

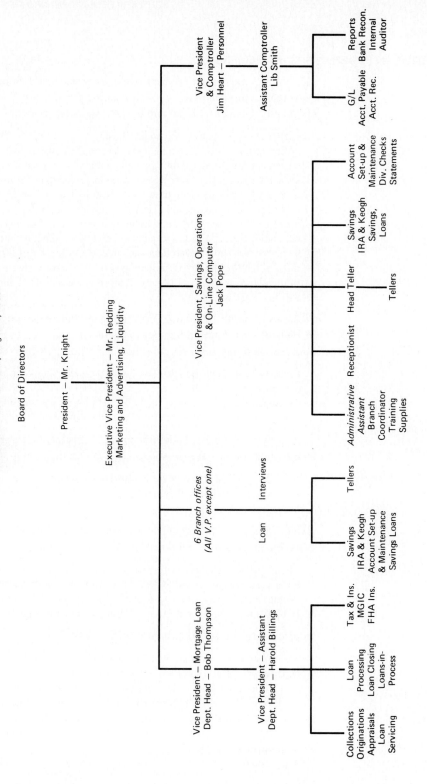

With regards to the key positions at Southern Federal, Jack Pope explained the concept:

I took an ideal S&L organization chart and tried to compare it to what we once had. I think that may have assisted in the decision to reorganize our loan department and put someone in control. The loan department had been split up between Thompson, Billings and Heart into loan organizations, loan processing and taxes and insurance so that no one person was in charge. Now Bob Thompson is department head. Harold Billings is responsible for closings, and handling loans-in-process.

Jim Heart was put in charge of accounting. Elizabeth Smith had reported to me in accounting. Jim didn't have any training as controller, but it was felt he could do the job and he has. I didn't think Elizabeth was particularly pleased at first, but it has worked out well. Jim is also responsible for personnel—interviews new employees, keeps EEOC and affirmative action records in order. He has little to do with daily personnel operations except in his own department.

My duties are in operations. I have responsibility for tellers and savings counselors. I have a branch coordinator working for me now. I'm responsible for the on-line computer service, so I write the procedures or make any changes when we change the system. Supplies and purchases also come under my jurisdiction. Someone else is responsible for custodial services.

The new branch coordinator position has responsibility for branch communication and training. Knight explained the branch coordinator's role:

We just promoted one of the girls who has a lot of talent and ability to branch coordinator. From that respect she has no supervisory jurisdiction over a branch manager, but she is really coordinating personnel. If someone doesn't show and the manager doesn't think he can operate, he calls her; and we get somebody on the road to help out. The same for supplies. When you get six branches, you just can't do it from your hip pocket. You have to have some plan of handling things.

THE BOARD OF DIRECTORS

Southern Federal's board of directors significantly changed since Knight joined the association. He explained the early structure:

When I came over here, the average age of the board was about 70. We had one that was 90. Another that was 80. Several in the 70's—they were the young guys. I was just a babe in the woods. That had to be changed. You may think that's no trouble, but it is.

We set limits of 70. When I reach 70, I'm off the board and that's the way it ought to be. We finally agreed that if they served three years, from the time we made that agreement, that was fair and they would become emeritus members and leave the board. It just takes time to do those things.

In describing the current membership of the board, Knight continued:

We have the director of campus planning, who has been here a long time. The university football coach also represents another area of thinking as a director. We also have the owner of a downtown retail men's store, and a fine doctor and surgeon who has a good financial mind. We have the controller for a local textile plant, and an ex-government official that now heads up the university research lab. We then have myself, Redding, the president of North County B&L, and one of our retired executives that know the business.

Southern Federal's board of directors held meetings on the second Tuesday of every month. Knight explained the role of his board members:

We have an agenda which includes basic items that are required, then gets into new business and things that need to be brought to the board's attention.

Two of the members, Redding and myself, serve as members of the loan committee. We provide a written report from the loan committee and the board acts on that. The director of campus planning is a good board member who takes the time to read the information we send him. So I usually ask if he has any comments on the loan committee meeting's minutes. If he sees one he doesn't understand, he'll ask a question. We may give our reasons for that particular loan and the interest rate charged, or whatever attracted his attention.

The controller over at the textile mill has a real good financial mind. I usually ask him for comments on the financial statement that's prepared by Jim Heart. He's sharp enough that if he sees an unusual figure, it flags him and he'll put a circle around it. So we get into things that he doesn't understand or needs clarification. Sometimes he'll understand it, but he'll do it for the benefit of the other board members. That kind of takes care of the nuts and bolts.

Redding commented further on their board's involvement:

Our board is made up of a pretty knowledgeable group of folks here in town. They set the policy and the tone of what we're going to do. For what services we offer, I think they take most of the recommendations that management makes.

They turned us down on a logo one time. We've got to get us a logo. I was talking to our advertising man the other day about getting me up a logo. We have about three logos and they turned them all down. You have to get some uniformity in advertising as you get bigger. We're working on that, sorta hit and miss.

They were quite active in the designing, planning and style ideas for the North Highway branch. Quite active. But they're not like down at South Bank and Trust—they're down there all the time. Of course South Bank and Trust almost lost all the money they had down there, too.

They weren't active in the North County merger, but of course, participated in some group meetings and gave the green light to see if we could go ahead and affect it. That was a chore and we don't have all the strings tied together, yet.

They had a discussion of consumer loans last meeting. Bob Thompson was also at the last meeting talking about the rollover rate mortgage, explaining that. We had one meeting on NOW accounts, talking about that—they said go ahead on those two things.

SOUTHERN FEDERAL'S MANAGEMENT PHILOSOPHY

Southern Federal had become a leading institution in the community. This had not always been the case, as Knight explained:

When I came here we had several problems that I perceived. One was that we were really an organization that survived or prospered or declined based on its participation in the community. If you don't participate in the community, I don't now how the community is going to participate with you. The way that they participate with us is to put their savings here and put their loans here. But the association was really just withdrawn, it wasn't out-going. It took no real part, for instance, in the United Way or in supporting those things that make a good community. It did not actually suggest that the officers of the association join the civic clubs and take part. These are things that I believe you've got to do if you're going to be successful in your operation and have the name and image out there all the time.

We gave just a little token to financial drives. Today we are the largest financial institution in South County, given the fact that Republic is a branch and the chain could swallow us up many times; but, one on one we're larger. We try to give a leading gift. I think we have to.

Besides attempting to have a meaningful leadership role in the community, Southern Federal also attempted to maintain a good working environment for its employees, as Jack Pope explained:

We have a good working environment—somewhat relaxed. We don't push people. We assign a job and expect it to be completed in a reasonable period of time. Most people like that.

This atmosphere did not mean that employees lived a ''life of ease,'' as Knight pointed out:

One thing that Jack Pope places a lot of emphasis on is encouraging employees to take advantage of the courses that we pay for which are furnished by the U.S. League's financial education section. They are constantly involved in courses.

This is part of our merit program—to be qualified for a position, you must have passed satisfactorily those courses to make you qualified for that position. Now if it comes down to two people going for the same position, the one who had qualified his or herself in the best manner—and, if it came down to a fine line, had the best grades—would probably be the one to get that position, everything else being equal. Most of these people will make A's and A+'s. When these girls go after something they usually work at it and do a good job.

Southern Federal also had been able to attract and keep good people. With regard to their low employee turnover, Knight explained:

Generally speaking we don't have much turnover. We have always had a great esprit de corps. We have tried to encourage that with fringe benefits, uniforms, family get-togethers, etc. So far we've screened our employees pretty darn good. We've been darn lucky. We've had some misfits, but I think they realized they were and eventually worked on out.

Now First National Bank works on a different concept. They employ an awful lot of students and have an awful lot of turnover. They kind of accept that turnover and I think it costs them too. We'd rather have continuity and have you see the same person when you come in here—if it's possible.

In commenting on the loss of several employees earlier in the year, Knight explained:

Gosh, we took a siege here about three months ago and we lost them bam, bam, bam, just like that. And we're losing another next Tuesday. You just can't help it—she used to work for this dentist. That joker is now going to also have an office here and he remembered and made an offer she couldn't turn down. He offered her $2,500 more than we are paying here. She's a good employee and, dog-gone-it, we hate to lose her, but there is no way we can keep her without destroying the whole scale. You lose some like that reluctantly.

Redding also expressed his feelings about the recent turnover:

> We had the quitting bug come through here about a year ago, and everyone got to quitting. And then we'll have the baby bug come by here, and it'll bite a bunch of 'em. And then we'll have the hysterectomy bug—that's broken out here now—but it seems to come like that.

James Redding had primary responsibility for managing short-term investments. In commenting on the process, Redding explained:

> I handle the investments, but go through the executive committee, which meets once a month, to get approval. It takes two signatures—Knight is generally the one to sign and approve the transaction.

As Redding turned and pointed to the large calendar scheduling board on the wall behind his desk, he explained:

> Right now you see a lot of yellow stuff—that's short term to match up with the six month stuff that's been feasting on us. I made an error because I didn't move quickly enough to go out long. Then we have a lot of Jumbo CD's and we have to keep up with that too. We have six or seven million of those, I guess. It will vary from four million to eight million. We got into bidding on the university and got them more money. They were kind of getting low balled a little bit. We got the first one we bid on.

EMPLOYEE COMPENSATION AND INCENTIVES

Along with having a good work environment, Southern Federal had also attempted to provide competitive salary and benefits for its employees. Pope explained:

> We try to be competitive on salary with the banks around here and benefits are on top of that. We have not had a great deal of turnover except for earlier this year. Usually the bank people come to us for jobs because they hear good things about us.

All employees with over six months employment in the association participate in Southern Federal's profit sharing. Knight explained the system:

> We have profit sharing—I guess you would call it that. There is no setting aside and waiting ten years. We have a little formula, and Redding works it up, that for the last two years has, generally speaking, amounted to between 10 and 14 percent of salary. How long you have been here and how much you are making is all tied into it. If you've been here less than six months you're gonna get a ham. If you've been here over six months, you're gonna get your prorata.
>
> We take a fixed percentage of income which we're adding to net worth. It's about a 50 percent deal. I believe it behooves us to treat the employees well and try to have people who are willing and ready to wait on people when they come through our doors and make the person want to come back. Most of our people go out of their way.

The association also provided employee uniforms and other benefits as Redding explained:

> Many years ago we put in a dress code. We give the ladies dresses. They got to squabbling about the thing here the other day so we put it to a vote and they voted 34 to 4 to keep the dresses.

We also furnish meals here. We have a dining room downstairs. The branch personnel get $1.75 a day to buy their cokes and soup. Here it's free cokes, free coffee, free doughnuts, free lunch, free uniforms. Whether we should put that in a paycheck and forget about it, I don't know; but I like it this way.

We provide hospital insurance, retirement, all of that—not for the dependents; but, we have life insurance tied in with their retirement and hospitalization.

SOUTHERN FEDERAL'S MANAGEMENT CONTROL AND INFORMATION SYSTEMS

Southern Federal did not set formal goals and objectives for the association. Knight explained about the absence of objectives:

We just haven't set any objectives over here that we're trying to reach. I'll tell you, we would have missed them so far. I told the board at the first of the year that we would be lucky if we were in the black for the year. Well, we made so much money in the first four months on penalties that they said, "What are you talking about?" I said, "Just wait. It's coming." It came, but now, again, we're turning it back the other way. Our projections don't look all that bad for the rest of the year, if we can hold it. It's very upsetting. There is no real way to keep up with it.

There just doesn't seem to be any real way to cope with some of the things we encounter. Suppose that last January we had set up some goals and objectives. We would have missed them for various reasons. We would have missed it on income for four months. We had the best income we've ever had because we were collecting penalties. I wasn't smart enough to look ahead and say we were going to collect penalties, because I didn't even know we were going to be levying penalties. It's not from lack of thought or desire to do it that way; it just seems beyond our control. Everybody else seems to be controlling what you can do. The only thing we can do is operate as best we can with what they give us to operate with, and try to better our performance. This is what we tell our employees, "We have to do better than we did last year," and we try to tell them various ways to do it.

No, we don't set goals, except that we try to do better each year than we did the year before. It's a relative thing. We're working against ourselves to do better. I don't know how you can set goals with the Federal Home Loan Board and with policies, now, of the DIDC committee. You could set some goals, but you don't have the ability to meet them. They're changing things so fast. Now, if they ever settle down, it may be different.

Redding commented further:

We don't have any formal goals. We don't belong to the Rotary Club. I guess subconsciously we'd like to be the biggest one in the state, try to build up our deposits, get savings. We look at it and, if it looks like the loan volume is off and we got money and feel the economy is better, we'll have our advertising man go after the loans, start working with the real estate people, try to be competitive with rates, and scheme best we can. We would like to get one percent net, but we haven't done it. We're on profit sharing here and everyone participates— its not going to be as good a year as it has been.

Southern Federal's savings operations had been installed on NCR's time sharing system which allowed management to trace savings throughout the day. Jack Pope explained:

When we first started using the NCR system, Redding used to come in every hour to find out how savings and withdrawals were coming. We found that you couldn't tell how you were doing until late afternoon because it fluctuates so much from hour to hour.

Besides tracking their savings operations, management also tracks the association's overall performance. Knight, as he picked up a summary of branch profit performance, explained:

I can show you expenses and income from each branch. Of course, some of it's hard to come by exactly, but we can come within sight of it and that's all you really need to know. The total accounting picture is accurate. River County, for instance, has a little branch out there. It's not a profitable situation. It's slowly growing.

We keep strict accounting on each branch. We separate them so I can look at my records and tell you how each one of them is doing. I can look at my daily record and tell you what each one of them is doing in savings. It is good to know how much you're receiving. You certainly don't want to put more money into an area than you're taking in. It varies. This month, Lakeview's having a real good month on savings.

North Highway is the leading branch on savings and has been ever since Mary Defoe went out there. That's the way I knew it would happen, because she really has a good rapport with people that save with us.

Redding further explained:

We have an annual budget—keep up with it and track variances monthly. It's done by hand. We have a Wang upstairs, but don't use it. The damn thing takes a chauffeur and we don't have one.

Jack Pope commented on the reason Southern Federal had the Wang computer:

We bought the Wang because we were going to put our loan processing records on the computer. We bought that system because we thought it would be easy to adapt the software—but then we got our lawyers involved and we couldn't decide what format was legal, etc. It's been a year and a half and we still don't use it.

Management had also planned to have a more extensive computer facility in the future. Knight explained:

I was ready to buy a computer about two years ago, but Jack Pope, the operations officer, and Jim Heart, the controller, both felt like it would be money that could be better spent somewhere else. They felt we could stay on NCR until we reached about $250 million. Well, with NOW accounts coming in, I think that time table is going to be changed.

The North Highway office was designed—the floor, wiring, and everything is ready to go—to set the computer in there and everything that goes with it. That will go into the basement out there—it's a good place because the temperature won't change as much and it's easy to keep it cool, which is better for the computer.

Pope also commented on their planning system:

We have looked at several models, but haven't decided on one yet. We do some hand calculations, or what ifs, of existing figures. But it isn't done with much depth.

With regard to keeping in touch with the critical operations of the association, Redding looked at the papers covering his desk and responded:

Gosh, I don't know. You see how tidy my desk is! I guess Knight and I talk and we talk with the other people in the departments, listen to all sorts of rumors, talk to other people in the business—other associations. We watch our profit picture—it looks gloomy right now though. The money market rates being what they are, it'll be October before we really get rid of the bad stuff.

I think we've done a pretty good job in spite of the fact that we're not organized. We're not highly structured. I'm just now getting around, after 20 years, to getting some little plan for the janitor. This has become a problem, now, on how to keep the darn branches cleaned up. The thing out on North Highway has weeds everywhere. We have about three acres out there. We ought to have better sense. We had to paint the Eastside Mall Branch because it wasn't quite so clean—you see we throw a little competition in there. Get them competing with each other. South Rim and Lakeview, they're about the same size—I pick on them and ask them why they're not doing so well.

With Southern Federal's first priority being entrance into the consumer loan business, there was a need to recruit a new manager. James Redding, executive vice president, was concerned about the kind of person they were going to need. He explained:

Now facing us is the consumer loan which we'll be getting into by September. That will entail adding someone who is knowledgeable of consumer lending which will include automobile loans, signature loans, 90-day loans, or anything oriented to family financing. We want someone who will charge enough. We might get someone from one of these short loan places. I used to be in the short loan business. I'm the secretary and treasurer for Equitable Loan Company. We took it over. We had a manager and I supervised it from afar. Our motto was, "Consolidate all your little bills into one huge staggering debt." That's from the lending end.

With the rapid introduction of consumer lending activities, Southern Federal also had to prepare employees to handle them. Redding continued:

That's a problem in going into consumer lending. You're going to have to do it in the branches, and what do they know about consumer lending? Nothing! So you're gonna have to get them trained. Whether they do one automobile a day or a week or an hour, we're going to have to give them responsibility and work from there. Jack Pope is reviewing that.

Of course, with consumer lending you're going to have to be able to give customers answers in ten minutes or an hour—so we're also going to have to change our approval process.

DISCUSSION QUESTIONS

1 Evaluate the organizational structure at Southern Federal. What changes, if any, would you make? Explain.

2 Explain the pros and cons of Southern Federal's age limits on directors, the diversity of the current group of directors, and the effect of age and diversity on the performance of boards of directors. It is important that Southern Federal take a "meaningful leadership role in the community?" Why?

3 Should Southern Federal set goals and objectives? If so, what should they be? Explain.

4 Discuss the strategic changes which will be useful as Southern Federal expands its consumer lending business.

NORTH LOUISIANA SUPPLY COMPANY

Arthur Sharplin
Northeast Louisiana University

SELECTED STRATEGIC ISSUES

- Valuation of a going concern
- Collusion among competitors in a local market
- Justifications for managerial secrecy
- Relationship of technological knowledge to marketing success
- Determining the number of common shares to issue
- Advantages and disadvantages of arbitration in settling business disagreements

North Louisiana Supply Company is a welding products distributor that sells to welding shops and industrial users of welding products and compressed gases in the vicinity of Monroe, Louisiana, an area of about 120,000 people. There are three other such distributors in Monroe, all much larger. The welding products market served from Monroe is estimated at $8 to $10 million a year and, in most cities, is oligopolistic. This means that a few competitors sell a relatively homogeneous group of products. About half the sales of a typical distributor consist of compressed gases, principally oxygen, nitrogen, and acetylene, which generally are supplied in heavy steel cylinders or vacuum-insulated liquid tanks leased to the customer. Customers typically buy most of their welding products from the company that sells them compressed gases. As these do not differ significantly from manufacturer to manufacturer, customers are prone to buy from whomever offers the best combination of price and service. However, once a selection is made, most customers find it difficult to change suppliers because of the complexities in switching one supplier's leased gas cylinder for another's. Further, in

EXHIBIT 1   WELDING PRODUCTS DISTRIBUTION CHANNEL

Channel members	Path of products through channel (by percentage of retail sales value)								
	Gases X			Machines and electrodes X			Accessory items X		
Manufacturers and manufacturer/merchants	60%	15%	25%	60%	20%	20%	10%	70%	20%
Specialized regional wholesalers		X			X			X	
Retail welding products distributors	X	X		X	X		X	X	
End users	X	X	X	X	X	X	X	X	X

many cities price collusion among distributors minimizes the customer's incentive to switch. While this practice is illegal, it is nevertheless encouraged by the danger of local price wars. As a result, individual customers with similar usage rates pay very different prices for gas products. The distribution channel for welding products is illustrated in Exhibit 1.

COMPANY HISTORY

In the spring of 1978, Art and Jerry Sharplin negotiated a supply agreement with Lincoln Electric Company, a Cleveland, Ohio, manufacturer of welding machines and electrodes, and Big Three, Inc., a Houston-based distributor of compressed gases, and opened their welding products distributorship adjacent to Interstate Highway 20 at the eastern edge of Monroe. With $100,000 initial capitalization and extensive experience in the welding industry, the brothers expected rapid success. The average gross margin of welding supply distributors exceeded 37%, and they attributed this partly to the illegal price collusion among distributors. Art Sharplin, who had known the other distributors for years, visited each and made the following presentation:

> We are in the welding supply business in Monroe. Our customers will come from two sources: (1) those who now buy welding products and gases from you, and (2) future new users of welding products and gases. As the growth in the Monroe market will not be great enough to support our distributorship for some years, it is inevitable that we will attempt to take away some of your customers. I know that the practice has been that you tell one another the gas prices you charge to individual customers upon request. I will not participate in any way in this illegal practice. At the same time, you are our friends and we will cooperate with you in every way that we can within the bounds of legality and certain ethical principles which we hold dear.

At this and subsequent meetings, Art was pressured by one of the distributors to "join the club" and, in addition to price collusion, to follow certain other rules, particularly that no welding distributor should discuss employment of someone then working for another distributor. Both Art and Jerry refused and proceeded to solicit customers on any basis they considered effective, particularly price.

Sales did not come easily, and North Louisiana Supply did not have its first profitable quarter until the spring of 1980. During the preceding two years, the Sharplin brothers had hired and trained a competent staff, including an assistant store manager, a bookkeeper/clerk, a route driver, a warehouseman, and an outside salesman.

Jerry Sharplin was to manage the business over the long term, with Art pursuing other interests and serving in an advisory role. In the spring of 1980, however, Jerry became ill and was unable to continue active management of the business. Unwilling to forsake other commitments and plans, Art placed the assistant store manager, Roy Dews, in charge and proceeded to visit the store only about once a week.

Sales during the first half of 1980 approached a $750,000 annual rate, and continued profitability seemed ensured. However, during the second half sales plum-

EXHIBIT 2 EARNINGS STATEMENT—NORTH LOUISIANA SUPPLY COMPANY, MONROE, LOUISIANA

	5.3 Months ended 11-10-80	First quarter 8-31-80	Year ended 5-31-80	Year ended 5-31-79
Income:				
Sales and rentals	$248,550	$146,660	$739,805	$501,630
Interest and other	945	408	3,296	2,381
Total income	$249,495	$147,068	$743,101	$499,249
Cost of sales	154,571	83,666	460,001	398,116
Gross profit	$ 94,924	$ 63,402	$283,100	$101,133
Operating expenses				
Advertising	7,502	2,629	13,377	10,738
Depreciation	12,300	5,211	22,851	17,614
Gas and oil	2,262	1,044	12,743	8,923
Insurance	1,273	1,071	19,711	14,201
Interest	10,147	10,598	35,575	20,006
Loss on sale of assets	—	—	6,344	—
Management expense	—	—	—	—
Office and miscellaneous	448	392	3,075	2,424
Professional fees	—	1,801	25,443	18,650
Repairs and maintenance	1,172	184	7,122	9,230
Supplies	2,120	1,859	1,939	1,496
Payroll taxes	2,138	1,255	6,805	5,413
Other taxes	448	547	4,470	961
Telephone	3,044	1,895	9,469	6,646
Travel and entertainment	—	2,229	5,633	4,315
Utilities	1,327	746	1,595	1,111
Wages and commissions	29,871	16,835	77,587	61,391
Bad debts	—	—	4,010	7,690
Total operating expenses	74,052	48,296	257,749	190,809
Income before tax	$ 20,872	$ 15,106	$ 25,351	($89,676)
Income tax	5,000	—	—	—
Net profit	$ 15,872	$ 15,106	$ 25,351	($89,676)

meted, possibly due to a nationwide recession that seemed particularly intense in the Monroe area. Another distributor revealed a similar, but less severe, decline in sales. At this time, Art and Jerry decided to sell the business to someone who could manage it more effectively. Even outright liquidation was considered but it was estimated to provide a net revenue of only about $100,000. Based on analysis of company financial statements (Exhibits 2 and 3), Art and Jerry decided to market the company as a "going concern."

A few days later, a friend and business acquaintance, Jerry Phillips, offered to buy the company. Art was surprised because no one had been told of their plan to sell. After a review of recent financial statements and some discussion, Art and Jerry priced the company at $250,000. Jerry Phillips accepted that price with two stipulations: first, that the inventory figure reflected in the May 31, 1980, financial statement be guaranteed not to have diminished; second, that he would only pay $100,000 down, with the remainder to be represented by a 15-year, 15.5% installment note secured by a first mortgage on the building and land and all gas cylinders owned by North Louisiana Supply. Art and Jerry Sharplin accepted both conditions with a further requirement that, if the inventory taken on the date of their agreement (December 10, 1980) was higher than the May 31 amount, the difference would be added to the selling price. The

EXHIBIT 3   BALANCE SHEET—NORTH LOUISIANA SUPPLY COMPANY, MONROE, LOUISIANA

Assets	11-10-80
Cash	$ 5,777
Accounts receivable	56,942
Inventory	164,722
Deposits receivable	1,199
Total current assets	$228,640
Fixed assets	364,057
less accumulated depreciation	(45,571)
Total fixed assets	$318,486
Total assets	$547,126
Liabilities	
Accounts payable	$ 51,207
Accrued expenses	3,073
Income tax payable	6,401
Other tax	3,394
Notes payable—current portion	38,513
Total current liabilities	$102,588
Notes payable—long term	261,400
Total liabilities	$363,988
Shareholders' equity	
Common stock	$100,000
Additional paid in capital	168,309
Deficit	(85,171)
Total shareholders' equity	$183,138
Total liabilities and shareholders' equity	$547,126

deal was struck and the agreement signed to sell the North Louisiana Supply stock. On signing this agreement, Jerry Phillips paid the Sharplin brothers $10,000 in "earnest money." The agreement required that the remaining $90,000 be paid not later than January 19, 1981. Jerry and Art Sharplin had signed continuing guarantee agreements with the company banker, and Jerry Phillips agreed to renegotiate the company debt to free the Sharplin brothers from any liability should the company default.

On January 5, 1981, Jerry Phillips advised Art that he could not fulfill the agreement as written because he had been unable to obtain the necessary financing without pledging the company real estate. Therefore, he asked that Jerry and Art accept a lien on the inventory and other chattels in lieu of the promised real estate mortgage. Art and Jerry refused.

About two years earlier, North Louisiana Supply had canceled its gas supply agreement with Big Three Industries and negotiated a more favorable arrangement with Liquid Air Corporation, a U.S. subsidiary of the French company Air Liquide, a worldwide manufacturer and distributor of welding products and gases. The Sharplins were aware that Liquid Air had been aggressively expanding its sales organization in three ways: (1) by franchising distributors such as North Louisiana Supply; (2) by opening company-owned stores in various cities across the country; and (3) by purchasing existing welding distributors with an established market share (the approach currently preferred by Liquid Air).

Based on this, Art contacted Liquid Air headquarters in San Francisco and spoke to operations manager Kent Taylor, who was responsible for corporate acquisitions. Taylor immediately expressed an interest in North Louisiana Supply and referred Art to Jack King, the company's financial analyst. At Jack's request, Art provided him with the following documents: (1) May 31 and December 10, 1980, financial statements; (2) a title opinion on the company real estate; (3) a list of gas cylinders and liquid containers, by serial numbers, owned by North Louisiana Supply; (4) copies of all notes payable and lease agreements; (5) a copy of the December 7 inventory; (6) a list of all company bank accounts; and (7) a schedule of employee names and salaries.

Jerry and Art had decided not to tell the employees of their plan to sell until they were sure of a firm deal unless an employee became suspicious.

In a telephone conversation with Jim Sheridan, president of Liquid Air Corporation, Art offered to sell all North Louisiana Supply stock for $270,000 (Exhibit 4). The prospective store manager, Karl Bird, then came to Monroe to view the facility, tour the market area, and discuss various aspects of the business. To avoid exposing the deal to the employees, Art and Karl visited the store at night. Karl was satisfied with the business and recommended that Liquid Air go ahead with the purchase.

On January 12, 1981, Art and Jerry flew to San Francisco to negotiate the final agreement. On January 13, they met with Jim Sheridan, Kent Taylor, Karl Bird, and Jack King to settle the final details. Jim Sheridan suggested that the $270,000 purchase price be paid in three equal installments—one on signing the agreement, one at the end of six months, and one at the end of the year—with no interest to be paid on outstanding balances. Jerry suggested two equal payments—one on signing and one at the end of three months. In a discussion of the income taxes that might be due from North Louisiana Supply, Jim Sheridan stated that these were the responsibility of Art and Jerry but acknowledged that there was no way to compute them accurately.

EXHIBIT 4   VALUATION WORKSHEET

	Asset valuation method		
	Book value	Liquidation value	Replacement value
Assets			
Cash	$ 5,777	$ 5,777	$ 5,777
Accounts receivable	56,942	54,664	54,664
Inventory	164,722	131,778	164,722
D/R	1,199	1,199	1,199
Fixed assets	318,486	268,864	325,610
Liabilities	(363,988)	(363,988)	(363,988)
Net value	$183,138	$ 98,294	$187,984

Capitalization of earnings method

Earnings history: 1979, $89,676 loss; 1980, $25,351; 1981 projection, $35,936.60.
Earnings to be capitalized: $35,000/py (in real dollars)
Discount rate: 13% [short-term interest rate (19.5%) plus risk premium (4%) minus inflation expectation (10.5%)]
Computation: PV = $35,000 ÷ 0.13 = $269,231

Finally, Art suggested the following plan: Liquid Air would pay one-half the purchase price on signing of the agreement, one-fourth at the end of 90 days, and one-fourth at the end of 180 days. Interest would be due on outstanding balances at the average prime rate charged by the Chase Manhattan Bank. The purchase price would be adjusted downward by $5000 to allow for any income taxes due. Jim Sheridan and the others agreed. The agreement was signed on January 30, 1981. Excerpts are included in Exhibit 5, page 558.

DISCUSSION QUESTIONS

1 What do you think would have been an appropriate price to pay for North Louisiana Supply Company? State the pros and cons of the two valuation methods Art used.
2 Should Art and Jerry have "joined the club?" Explain how the "minicartel" might have acted to keep its members in line or punish new entrants into the marketplace who would not abide by the cartel rules.
3 What do you think about Art and Jerry's decision not to tell the employees about the sale until it was finalized and of the clandestine visit to the company by Art Sharplin and Karl Bird?
4 How important do you believe it was to their success that the Sharplin brothers had extensive experience in the welding industry?
5 Why might there have been only one share of common stock?
6 Why would the parties have agreed to the arbitration provision in the agreement? In what ways is arbitration superior to filing suit to settle disagreements? Inferior?

EXHIBIT 5   EXCERPTS FROM SALES AGREEMENT, NORTH LOUISIANA SUPPLY COMPANY

1 Sale of Capital Stock

Subject to terms and conditions hereinafter set forth, upon the closing and in the manner herein provided, the Seller shall sell and deliver to LAI all of the issued and outstanding shares of North Louisiana Supply, consisting of one share of common stock, no par value, which is presently owned of record and beneficially by Sellers.

2 Purchase Price

a On the terms and conditions of this Agreement, LAI agrees to purchase from the Seller and the Seller agrees to sell LAI at the date of closing all outstanding capital stock of North Louisiana Supply for a total aggregate purchase price of two hundred sixty-five thousand dollars ($265,000).

3 Adjustment of the Purchase Price

The abovementioned purchase price shall be adjusted on or before the post closing as follows:

a The purchase price will be decreased to the extent that the sum of the cash balances, bank balances and all other cash accounts of the company as of the tenth day of November, 1980, is less than five thousand seven hundred and seventy-seven dollars ($5,777).

b The purchase price will be decreased to the extent that the sum of all liabilities of the company as of the tenth day of November, 1980, is more than three hundred sixty-three thousand nine hundred and eighty-eight dollars ($363,988).

c The purchase price will be decreased to the extent that the sum of the accounts receivable balances of the company as of the tenth day of November, 1980, shall not include any portion of the November 10, 1980 accounts receivable for which the company has not received payment on or before the date of post closing, which unpaid portion of said accounts shall be assigned by LAI to the Seller at the post closing.

12 Competition

Jerry L. Sharplin and Arthur D. Sharplin, each for himself and not for the other, agrees that for a period of five (5) years after the Closing he will not act as a stockholder, officer, director, employee, agent, sole proprietor, partner or consultant of, or otherwise particpate in, any enterprise or organization that is or becomes, within such period, competitive with the business of North Louisiana Supply or any of its affiliated firms or corporations within a radius of two hundred (200) miles of Monroe, Louisiana.

17 Arbitration

Any disputes arising out of, or in connection with, the Agreement shall be submitted by the parties hereto for resolution to a panel of three arbitrators (one chosen by each party hereto, and one chosen by the arbitrators selected by the parties), whose decision as to the disputed matter or matters so submitted:

(i) shall be made in accordance with the rules and regulations of the American Arbitration Association, (ii) shall be deemed by the parties to be final and conclusive with respect to the matter or matters so submitted. Judgment on any such matter may be enforced in any court of competent jurisdiction.

KITCHEN MADE PIES

James J. Chrisman
University of Georgia

Fred L. Fry
Bradley University

SELECTED STRATEGIC ISSUES

- Product line expansion or contraction
- Analysis of financial trends and condition
- Functional area strategies and their relationship to organizational mission

In late 1981, Paul Dubicki, owner and president of Kitchen Made Pies, was faced with a difficult problem. Company sales had been stagnant, and the firm was about to suffer its fourth straight year of losses. Further compounding the problem were unfavorable economic and industry conditions, both nationally and locally, as well as difficulties with certain customers and creditors. In addition, the firm's financial condition had deteriorated, which served to limit the range of feasible alternatives available to turn the situation around. In spite of these concerns, Mr. Dubicki was determined to return the business to profitability; and, in fact, was confident that this task could be accomplished if he could only get away from day-to-day decision making.

When commenting on the current situation at Kitchen Made, Mr. Dubicki emphasized volume as the key to success. ''We must increase our customer base and we must somehow encourage our present distributors to provide the promotional support retailers need to sell our products. One well-publicized special can sell more pies in one day than can be sold in a normal week without one. That's what I'd like to concentrate on, but every day something else comes up around here.''

Prepared by James J. Chrisman, the University of Georgia, and Fred L. Fry, Bradley University, 1982.

COMPANY HISTORY

Kitchen Made Pies is a regional producer of a wide variety of pies, as well as other bakery products. Located in Peoria, Illinois, the firm traces its history back 30 years. The firm was founded by Frank Dubicki, the father of the current owner, and was run like most family businesses. Paul Dubicki grew up in the bakery business, but was not really very interested in the firm in his earlier years. After leaving the business for a while to pursue other activities, Paul returned in 1968 to work and later become, along with David Dubicki, a minority stockholder. During this time, he was dissatisfied because he never could get away from the operational aspects of the business. Later, however, Paul was running the business. In early 1981, the elder Dubicki was persuaded to sell out, though he did retain ownership of the company's land and facilities. This sale was actually a redemption of Frank Dubicki's stock by the corporation in a transaction that also eliminated his debt to the corporation. During the same period, David exited from the business leaving Paul as the sole owner. Upon assuming control, Paul immediately set about changing and updating the firm's operations (i.e., revised inventory stocking measures) and for the first time, established a commitment to strategic planning. Unfortunately, at the same time, problems building up over a long period of time began to surface.

PRODUCT LINE

Kitchen Made Pies, as the name implies, is primarily engaged in pie baking. The company makes a full line of pies, some on a regular basis, some seasonally. Table 1

TABLE 1   PIE CATEGORIES

4 inch	8 inch	9 inch	Other
Apple	Apple	Apple	Shortcake
Pineapple	Applecrumb	Applecrumb	10″ Cakes
Cherry	Peach	Peach	
Blackberry	Pineapple	Pineapple	8″ Cakes
Lemon	Lemon	Blackberry	Sheet Cakes
Coconut	Coconut	Black Raspberry	
Chocolate	Chocolate	Walnut	
Peach	Black Raspberry	Cherry	
	Pumpkin	Lemon Meringue	
	Cherry	Coconut Meringue	
	High-top Meringues	Chocolate Meringue	
	Regular Meringues	Banana Meringue	
		Pumpkin	
		Chocolate Boston	
		Boston	
		Lemon Whip	
		Coconut Whip	
		Chocolate Whip	
		Banana Whip	
		Pumpkin Whip	

lists all major sizes and flavors of pies currently produced by Kitchen Made, as well as other bakery products the firm makes.

Kitchen Made sells both fresh and frozen pies, though the former is preferred due to better turnover and more predictable ordering on the part of the customers. Another problem restricting frozen pie sales is limited freezer space. Kitchen Made can currently freeze only 3,500 pies at one time. Since this represents the maximum amount of pies per day it can freeze, frozen pie sales are limited.

Kitchen Made has long been proud of the fact tht they use only the highest quality ingredients in their products. Many would agree that Kitchen Made pies taste better than competitors' products. Of course, this also means that Kitchen Made pies are usually more expensive. Mr. Dubicki views this quality as a major strength, especially to maintain repeat business. Still, he concedes that many times customers are more concerned with price; but in the end, Mr. Dubicki believes quality will win out.

MARKETS/CUSTOMERS

The majority of Kitchen Made's sales are to food/bakery distributors who basically supply two major markets. The first is the institutional market which consists of restaurants, as well as university, hospital, corporate, and government cafeterias. The second is the retail market which includes grocery stores and convenience outlets. The institutional market accounts for the majority of cake and 9″ pie sales, while the retail market buys mainly 4″ and 8″ pies. Most distributors concentrate on one market or the other, thus determining the type of products they buy. Buying motives for both markets vary depending upon the customer and market area involved. Some customers are very conscious of price, especially in institutional markets, while others—most notably restaurants and grocers—can be more interested in quality or promotional support.

Most of Kitchen Made's products are sold in the Peoria and St. Louis areas, but the firm also serves customers in other parts of Missouri and Illinois, as well as in Iowa and Wisconsin. Major distributors of Kitchen Made products, as well as their served markets, are included in Table 2, presented below.

Besides the differences in buying motives and the type of products purchased by the two end markets, there are several other distinguishing features which differentiate them from each other. Institutional markets frequently prefer frozen pies because of buying habits (institutional customers often buy to satisfy monthly needs) which prevent extensive use of fresh varieties. On the other hand, in the grocery business,

TABLE 2 CUSTOMERS

Dean's Distributing	40% (institutional)
McCormick Distributing	10% (institutional)
Lowenberg	11% (retail)
Eisner's	8% (retail)
Master Snack & New Process	13% (retail)
Edward's	4% (retail)
Other (including Schnuck's)	16% (retail)

turnover is a way of life; therefore, customers usually prefer to make weekly or bi-weekly purchases. Retail customers like fresh pies better because they can be put directly on the shelf, which eliminates storage, thawing, and the extra work involved in moving and stocking products twice. However, fresh pies in the grocery stores sell best through the in-store bakeries since the connotation of ''freshness'' lies in this area.

Unlike institutional markets, retailers depend heavily upon promotional assistance for sales. One reason Dean's Distributing has become a less important customer for Kitchen Made is that they refuse to offer grocers this type of support. As a result, Dean's, and therefore Kitchen Made, has lost much of their retail grocer business in recent years, especially in the Peoria area. Today, most of Dean's pie distribution business done in the Peoria vicinity, as well as in other markets, is institutional.

Distributors use two basic methods to sell products to grocers. Some distributors sell on a guaranteed basis with unsold products returned to the dealer at no charge. Others sell products unguaranteed, or in other words, grocers take full responsibility for all products they buy. Naturally, profit margins for the methods differ. Grocers usually make about 23 to 25% on guaranteed sales, while unguaranteed sales yield margins of approximately 35 to 40%. However, because of the inherent risks involved in unguaranteed purchases, most grocers prefer the lower-but-safer profit margins of guaranteed arrangements when dealing with ''door-to-store'' distributors such as Dean's. Non-guaranteed sales work well through efficient drop shipment techniques that may be used by bread bakers.

There is a basic difference between the two distribution methods. Door-to-store distributors accumulate individual orders on a daily basis and deliver merchandise direct from the pie baker to the grocer. On the other hand, drop shipments involve larger orders which are taken first to warehouses for later delivery to individual stores. For example, drop ship distributors, such as Eisner's, sell direct to their own or an affiliated grocery chain, and thus, enjoy profits on both the delivery and retail end. This can be an important competitive advantage since 40–50% of the product cost is in distribution. Thus, Mr. Dubicki has expressed a desire to focus on these direct distributors because of the reduced price for retailers, and hence consumers. This, he feels, could help circumvent the higher prices charged for Kitchen Made products on the wholesale end. Furthermore, since drop shippers order large quantities, longer production runs and, therefore, lower costs are possible.

In addition to sales to bakery wholesalers, Kitchen Made also operates their own delivery truck which is used primarily to deliver specialty or rush orders. No plans have been made to expand this portion of the operation.

THE BAKING INDUSTRY

Though the outlook for the baking industry has been helped by softening of flour and sugar prices, overall prospects have been unfavorable and should continue to be so as long as economic conditions remain depressed. The baking industry, and particularly the pie and cake segment, is more susceptible to cyclical economic variabilities than other foodstuffs due to the discretionary nature of purchases. Pies and cakes are more or less luxury foods; thus, sales are dependent upon the disposable incomes of consumers. When times are rough it is these discretionary items that consumers cut-back on first. Further dampening the outlook for the industry is the national swing toward nutrition. Sweets and sugar intake have decreased because too much is considered unhealthy, besides, of course, being very fattening. Additionally, because of demographic changes, the average age of the population is higher. Historically, younger individuals account for a large portion of the consumption of pies, cakes, and other desserts.

The frozen segment of the bakery industry is doing even worse. Consumers view frozen foods as being more expensive, and sales have therefore suffered. No relief appears in sight here, at least in the near future.

In addition to the conditions previously cited, other developments are occurring in the industry. Between 1972 and 1977 the number of firms included under SIC code 2051 dropped from 3,323 to 3,062; but at the same time, the number of establishments employing less than 20 workers increased. This, of course, has widened the gap between the large and the small bakeries. A major contributor to this trend was the energy shortage which made transportation costs, already high due to the perishable nature of bakery products, even higher, thus providing cost advantages to the huge firms with internal delivery capabilities and the smaller firms who emphasize local business. Medium-sized firms who were unable to maintain their own delivery function and who depended on a more diffuse range of customers were hurt most by this event.

Other factors which could affect the performance of the industry in the future are recent trends toward ''eating out'' and the emerging popularity of pre-prepared foods. In today's fast-paced world, people no longer have as much time to cook their own meals. The increasing participation of women in the work force has also been a contributor to this turn of events. It should be noted that those fast food chains that are gaining popularity usually use desserts on a nationwide basis and do not like to buy from local dessert manufacturers.

Overall, the bakery industry is very mature. There has been little real growth in sales over the past few years. However, prices and costs have risen substantially, reflecting inflationary conditions and shortages of certain ingredients. Since ingredient costs represent a major expense (approximately 50% of total costs), recent price declines (e.g., sugar prices fell from $.55 per pound in November 1980 to $.26 per pound in October, 1981) have given bakers the opportunity to improve profit margins. Changes in several food and bakery prices, both wholesale and retail, as well as the Consumer Price Index, for the past six years are provided in Table 3.

THE LOCAL ECONOMY

Changes in the retail market, prompted by changing demographics and a fluctuating economy may have a dramatic effect on Kitchen Made. The retail segment of Kitchen Made's market is susceptible to changes in the economy, as is the institutional side. However, some segments of the institutional market, such as hospital cafeterias, do not always reflect economic variables.

The Peoria area, like most mid-western cities, has shown little or no growth in the past decade, as the U.S. population shifts to the Southwest. Peoria itself showed a population decline according to the 1980 census, although the number of households

TABLE 3 FOOD PRICE CHANGES

	1975	1976	1977	1978	1979	1980
Retail						
Cereal and bakery products	+11.3%	−2.2%	+1.6%	+8.9%	+10.1%	+11.9%
All foods	+8.5%	+3.1%	+6.3%	+10.0%	+10.9%	+8.6%
Consumer price index	+9.1%	+5.8%	+6.5%	+7.7%	+11.3%	+13.5%
Wholesale						
Cereal and bakery products	+4.0%	−3.3%	+0.1%	+9.8%	+10.5%	+12.2%
All foods	+6.7%	+3.8%	+4.4%	+10.5%	+9.6%	+8.2%

Source: Department of Labor.

increased. The economy in Peoria has traditionally been solid due to the dominant impact of Caterpillar Tractor Co., a Pabst Brewing plant, a Hiram-Walker distillery, a number of other medium-sized manufacturing facilities, and a host of small plants—many of which are suppliers of Caterpillar. As a result, Peoria wage rates have consistently ranked in the top twenty cities in the nation. Many have stated that ''Peoria doesn't have recessions.''

That appears to have changed in the last few years. Caterpillar endured a twelve-week strike in the fall of 1979 that idled many of the 30,000 Peoria area Caterpillar workers that depended either directly or indirectly on the firm. In addition, the Hiram-Walker plant closed in 1981; the Pabst plant is scheduled to close in March of 1982; and Caterpillar, for the first time in twenty years, laid off substantial numbers of workers in 1981 and 1982. These events could have a significant impact on the sale of pies and other desserts in the Peoria area. For instance, Caterpillar uses less than half as many pies today as it did ten years ago. Similar problems are expected in other markets.

COMPETITION

Kitchen Made competes against a variety of firms who do business both nationally and locally. Some rivals make a full line of pies. Additionally, some firms are also diversified into breads and other bakery products. Others have been successful concentrating on specific sizes or types of pies which allows longer production runs, lower

TABLE 4 COMPETITORS

Company	Location	Markets	Product lines
Lloyd Harris	Chicago	East of Rockies	Fresh 9″ pies,
(Div. of Fasano)		(in & re)	8″ and 10″ frozen
Chef Pierre		Nationwide (in)	8″ & 10″ frozen
Mrs. Smith		Nationwide (in)	8″ & 10″ frozen
Bluebird Baking	Dayton	Midwest (re)	4 ″ & 8″ fresh
Shenandoah Pie	St. Louis	St. Louis (re & in)	Full line fresh

Notes: (re) = retail customers, (in) = institutional customers and in-store bakeries; 10″ pies compete with Kitchen Made's 9″ variety.

inventories, and thus, lower costs, in some cases. Mr. Dubicki feels, however, that Kitchen Made's full line of pies gives the firm an advantage over competitors in attracting new customers, and protects sales from changes in customer taste.

Kitchen Made has no direct competition in the Peoria area although they do compete against a variety of regional rivals. In some cases, the firm must compete against their own customers who possess in-house baking capabilities. Table 4 provides a list of some of Kitchen Made's major competitors, as well as available information concerning product lines, major customer segments, and market areas.

PRODUCTION

Baking and production techniques at Kitchen Made are relatively uncomplex, though not without their own special problems. In most instances, pie crusts and fillings are made via the assembly-line method. One person operates the dough machine which flattens the dough and rolls enough out to make one crust. The dough is passed to a second person who places it into a pie pan. The machine then presses the dough into the pan. Afterward, the crust passes under a filling machine which is set according to the size of pie being made. After the crust is filled with the desired ingredients, the pie passes under another station where the top crust is molded onto the sides of the pie pan and the excess dough removed. This excess is transported by conveyor back to the dough machine. Once the pies are assembled, they are placed on racks and wheeled over to the ovens for baking. (All fresh pies are baked. However, frozen pies may or may not be, depending on customer preference.) It should be mentioned that a more efficient pie machine is available but would be expensive ($150,000) and would require long production runs to be efficient.

A major problem associated with production is the frequent conversions required each time the size or the flavor is changed. It takes approximately 15–20 minutes to change over pie size, and 4–5 minutes to change the type of ingredient. Size changes usually occur twice a day (from 4″ to 8″ to 9″), but ingredients must be changed from 20–25 times per day depending upon the production schedule.

All fruit pies are put together by the method described above, but currently cream pies are filled by hand. Mr. Dubicki intends to make all of Kitchen Made's pie products on the assembly line in the near future.

One way to greatly reduce production costs would, of course, be to limit the numbers of different types of pies made. However, Mr. Dubicki is concerned that this move could hurt the firm because many retail and institutional buyers prefer to buy full lines of products from the same supplier. Despite this perceived concern, substantial savings are available by limiting pie varieties. For example, with full crews, Kitchen Made currently bakes about $30,000 worth of pies and cakes per week. In some instances, when the firm receives a special order, a half crew will be brought in on an unscheduled shift. On these days, production has reached as high $10,000. In other words, if sales potential were exploited on a limited number of varieties, the change-over time savings would generate cost savings.

Recently, the first production manager, not a member of the Dubicki family, was appointed. Despite opening up this new position, Mr. Dubicki has continued to spend a significant portion of his time in the shop. The production manager has helped, and Mr. Dubicki expresses confidence in her ability, but sometimes fails to delegate. Another problem is that all of the aspects of the operation have not been completely worked out and some are in the midst of changes.

One positive development has been the ability of Mr. Dubicki to reduce inventory. Though done as much out of necessity as out of design, the move has, nonetheless, helped in many respects. In the past, ingredients were often bought in six-month quantities. Today, the firm tries to buy only what it needs for one or two weeks, except in special cases when supplies are hard to find or favorable price breaks can be obtained.

FINANCIAL INFORMATION

Given Kitchen Made's current product mix, sales of approximately $35,000 per week ($1,820,000 per year) are needed to break even, according to Mr. Dubicki. Variable expenses are estimated to be about 15% of sales revenue. Exhibit 1 provides a breakdown of sales and operating profits by product line in percentages and dollar amounts. The 4″ pies and the cakes appear to be the biggest money-makers, with margins on the 8″ and 9″ varieties substantially lower.

Prices have not changed much at Kitchen Made in recent months and, in fact, are the same as they were the year before. Table 5 shows the relative prices for the various types of pies made by Kitchen Made.

Management is particularly pleased with their high top meringue pie. Because of its superior looks and acceptance by consumers, the price is much higher than the regular meringue, but costs are almost identical. Thus, profit margins are signficantly higher.

Because of weak sales over the past several years, the financial condition of Kitchen

EXHIBIT 1   SALES/OPERATING PROFITS BY PRODUCT LINES

	Sales		Operating profits		Profit margin %
	%	($ in 000's)	%	(in 000's)	
Four inch	33.5	(536)	61.5	(147.6)	27.5
Eight inch	18.5	(296)	10.3	(24.7)	8.3
Nine inch	44.0	(704)	21.0	(50.4)	7.2
Other	4.0	(64)	7.2	(17.3)	27.0
Total	100.0	(1600)	100.0	(240.0)	15.0

TABLE 5   WHOLESALE PIE PRICES

4″ pies	$.25	8″ regular meringue	$.90	9″ fruit pies	$1.30
		8″ high top meringue	$1.40	9″ whips	$1.30
		8″ fruit pies	$1.00	9″ meringue	$1.25
				9″ specialty	$1.60
				9″ walnut	$2.00
				9″ cherry	$2.25

Made has deteriorated. Exhibit 2 provides the operating results for the years 1971 through 1981. Exhibit 3 shows the balance sheet for 1981. Exhibit 4 presents the computable financial ratios for Kitchen Made as compared to industry averages for SIC code 2051 businesses (i.e., bread, cake, and related products) with sales of under $50 million.

Besides the apparent financial problems implied by these statements, several other events have served to increase their seriousness. The most immediate problem relates to the bank note which had currently come due. Kitchen Made has an agreement with a

EXHIBIT 2 OPERATING RESULTS 1971–1980

| | ($ amounts in 000's) | | (Costs %) | | | | |
	Sales	Profits	Materials	Labor	Selling	Admin.	Production
1971	844	14 (1.7%)	51.2%	30.0%	2.9%	9.9%	7.8%
1972	955	8 (.8%)	50.5%	29.3%	2.8%	9.5%	7.1%
1973	1246	24 (1.9%)	52.7%	24.6%	2.8%	9.2%	8.9%
1974	1453	18 (1.2%)	57.0%	22.3%	2.5%	7.7%	9.3%
1975	1604	110 (6.9%)	53.9%	20.7%	2.2%	6.9%	9.4%
1976	1580	109 (6.9%)	48.8%	23.0%	2.6%	7.4%	11.3%
1977	1642	7 (.4%)	48.9%	26.0%	2.7%	8.5%	13.5%
1978	1608	−24	50.9%	26.3%	2.2%	9.4%	12.7%
1979	1601	−58	50.6%	27.0%	2.8%	10.0%	13.1%
1980	1506	−91	51.3%	28.3%	3.3%	10.3%	12.8%
1981	1635	−178	54.3%	27.7%	4.1%	11.2%	13.5%

Note: All cost figures are not comparable due to changes in allocation procedures.

EXHIBIT 3 BALANCE SHEET 1981

Assets (in 000's of $)		Liabilities & Equity	
Current:		*Current Liabilities:*	
Cash	$ 2	Accounts payable	$291
Accounts Receivable	163	Unsecured Bank Note	70
Inventory	137	Accrued Payroll & Taxes	25
Prepaid Expenses	17	Note—F. Dubicki	8
Total Current Assets	$319	Total Current Liabilities	$394
Fixed Assets:		*Long Term Liabilities:*	
(After Depreciation)			
Leasehold			
Improvements	$ 1	Note on truck	$ 15
Machinery & Equipment	48	Note on equipment	12
Autos & Trucks	28		
Total Fixed Assets	77	Total Long Term	$ 27
TOTAL ASSETS	$396	TOTAL LIABILITIES	$421
		EQUITY (Deficit)	$(25)
		TOTAL LIABILITIES & EQUITY	$396

EXHIBIT 4 COMPANY & INDUSTRY FINANCIAL RATIOS: 1981

	Industry SIC code 2051	Kitchen Made pies
Current Ratio (X's)	.76	.81 (without Dean's .66)
Net Profit/Sales (%)	3.8	Negative
Net Profit/Total Assets (%)	6.5	Negative
Net Profit/Equity (%)	19.5	Negative
Sales/Equity (X's)	7.6	Negative
Sales/Total Assets (X's)	2.5	4.1
Collection Period (days)	14	36 (without Deans 23)
Sales/Working Capital (X's)	8.8	Negative
Sales/Inventory (X's)	53.3	11.9
Fixed Assets/Equity (%)	131.6	Negative
Total Debt/Equity (%)	201.7	Negative

Source: Key Business Ratios 1980, Dun & Bradstreet.

local financial institution which allowed them to borrow $70,000 on a program resembling revolving credit. Kitchen Made paid only interest on this loan, with the principal due in a lump sum at the end of the borrowing period. Mr. Dubicki had hoped to refinance the loan, but the attitude of the bank caused him great concern and dissatisfaction. One major complaint was that despite keeping 20–30 thousand dollars in cash in their bank account, they received no interest relief. Furthermore, when discussing the possibility of refinancing the loan, Mr. Dubicki was informed that in the future he would be required to sign a second mortgage on his house to secure the note. Without renewal, the firm would be faced with a considerable liquidity problem. However, Mr. Dubicki was hopeful that other institutions would welcome their business if his present bank does not choose to continue their current relationship. It must be understood that this note is not secured in any way, and arrangements to place the bank in a secured position with options for renewal may be possible.

Another problem causing concern was slow payments by some customers. Most firms paid on time, however. Lowenberg and Eisner's consistently takes advantage of discounts for early payment (usual terms are 2%/10 days, net/30 days) for example. The major delinquent was Dean's Distributing. Dean's currently owes over six months back payments amounting to $60,000. Mr.Dubicki feels most of this account is uncollectible, but has not, as of yet, written this amount off the company's books. Mr. Dubicki has expressed a desire to eliminate or substantially cut back on the business done with this customer, but despite their unfavorable relations and payment record, Dean's still accounts for a large portion of sales. Thus, Kitchen Made must continue to rely upon this customer to maintain sales levels. However, all dealings are conducted strictly on a cash basis with this firm today.

In spite of these financial difficulties, Kitchen Made has been able to keep current on most of their current payables and pay small amounts on older accounts. Thus, while the situation is far from ideal and the firm is very vulnerable to unforeseen events, liquidity is probably not a life-or-death concern at the moment. However, Mr. Dubicki realizes that any further decline in this condition could be extremely hazardous and potentially fatal.

PERSONNEL

Most of the managerial activities at Kitchen Made Pies are handled directly by Mr. Dubicki. Besides the production manager, Ms. Barbara Britt, the only other management personnel are Ms. Charolette Watson, office manager, and Mr. Lonnie Beard, the sales promotion manager. Mr. Beard is responsible for making sure products are stocked and advertised properly at the individual stores, which he visits periodically. Mr. Dubicki, besides being president and owner, also acts as general manager, sales and distribution manager, as well as a variety of other functions. Mr. Dubicki prepares projected cash flow statements, searches for new accounts, and, of course, handles many other day-to-day activities. He also is the only person involved in strategic planning and really is the only person who completely understands all aspects of the business. About the only activity he is not directly involved with is the actual assembly of the pies.

Kitchen Made currently employs about thirty production workers as well as a half-dozen office workers. The shop is unionized and pays wages comparable to other like-sized area firms. In addition to production and office personnel, Kitchen Made also employs several maintenance workers and a truck driver.

CONCLUSIONS

Though the current situation at Kitchen Made Pies is far from ideal, there are several indications that the situation is not hopeless. Mr. Dubicki is committed to the planning process and has made some long needed improvements in operations. Furthermore, the owner has developed good employee relations which should facilitate some of the changes being considered. Naturally, there are many questions yet to be answered such as, "Would lengthening production runs really reduce costs?" "How important is a full product line?" "Would more equipment decrease costs or increase production, and if so, what equipment should be acquired?" "How do customers actually perceive quality/price differences in their buying habits?" and "What type of product mix will maximize sales and more importantly profits?" The answers to questions such as these will determine the company's fate in the future.

Again, despite all of the problems, Mr. Dubicki remains confident. "I'm optimistic about our future, but then again, isn't that the only way I can feel?" Whether this confidence can be turned into results remains to be seen. However, if hard work and dedication are enough, the future should begin to show some improvements.

DISCUSSION QUESTIONS

1 Should Kitchen Made shorten its product line? Defend your answer.
2 Evaluate Kitchen Made's financial trends and condition and explain how the financial condition might be improved.
3 What specific strategies should Kitchen Made follow in production, marketing, finance, and personnel? Explain how these strategies can be integrated into one coherent plan to accomplish the organizational mission.

THE UNDERCROFT MONTESSORI SCHOOL*

C. Richard Roberts
James W. Cagley
University of Tulsa

SELECTED STRATEGIC ISSUES

- Conservatism versus growth for a private school
- Organizational crisis as a unifying force
- Organizational structure and goal accomplishment
- Specification and solution of a financial crisis

The Undercroft Montessori School was a small private school located in Tulsa, Oklahoma. The school had been in operation continuously since 1964. The school had been managed by a Board of Trustees consisting of parent volunteers. Administative decisions had been made by an Executive Committee within the Board. Salaried staff included a professional School Administrator, three Montessori directresses, an art teacher, a music teacher, three teaching assistants and an office secretary.

The school offered a somewhat unique educational program for children of pre-school age. Demand for the school's services had increased on trend for the past five years and enrollment in the preschool program had been at near capacity. The prevailing attitude of the Board has recently shifted from generally conservative to a position of greater commitment in terms of growth. The school had also suffered a major crisis leading to significant changes in policy.

THE CRISIS

At the close of the previous Fall term in late December, the school's head directress resigned for personal reasons after nine years of employment, returning to her previous home in Sri Lanka. Her resignation was a complete surprise and necessitated an emergency meeting of parents and trustees to discuss the loss and prospects for continuing with the spring term scheduled to open in January.

The school had previously operated with two directresses, but a more or less continuous turnover of the second position had restrained overall effectiveness. The possibility of opening the school for the spring term with only one directress with limited teaching experience created considerable anxiety among the parents at the meeting. Some expressed grave doubts about the school's future since the head directress had been considered irreplaceable.

The crisis was resolved when a parent, Betty Kaylor, acting as chairperson of an emergency search committee, located a capable substitute barely one week before the scheduled opening date.

Although the transition period was not without problems, the integrity of the program was sustained and the spring term unfolded without further incident. By the end of the spring term most parents were optimistic that the academic quality level previously enjoyed would eventually be regained and little reluctance to preenroll their children for the next fall term was apparent.

THE REORGANIZATION

An organizational chart is shown in Exhibit 1. Executive authority related to the school's policies, programs and resource commitments rested with the Executive Committee consisting of the President, Vice President, Secretary and Treasurer. The Treasurer, Phil Wilson, was primarily responsible for preparation of the school's operating budget, collections and disbursements. The Secretary, Pauline Rielly, had primary responsibilities for preparation of the minutes of board meetings and routine correspondence such as requests for information from prospective parents, schedules and announcements. The nominal functions of the office of the Vice President, held by Lois Bradford, were personnel acquisition and development, and second level counseling on issues involving relations between parents, children and the teaching staff.

Christine Johnson was the current President of the school and had served in that office for one year. Christine had been a parent volunteer serving first on the Hospitality and Arrangements Committee, and then Vice President before being elected to her present office. The job description of the President stated that the person occupying the office had authority to determine an appropriate schedule and agenda for board meetings necessary to conduct the business affairs of the school, and represented the institution in affairs involving constituents and the public at large. As a practical matter, Christine viewed her job as one of coordinating all classroom, board and parent activities where school policy issues were involved, or leadership was indicated. The office required an extraordinary level of involvement and dedication by the occupant and the school had experienced a progression of exceptional individuals in the past who had contributed a great deal to the previous success of the program.

EXHIBIT 1

ORGANIZATIONAL CHART
THE UNDERCROFT MONTESSORI SCHOOL

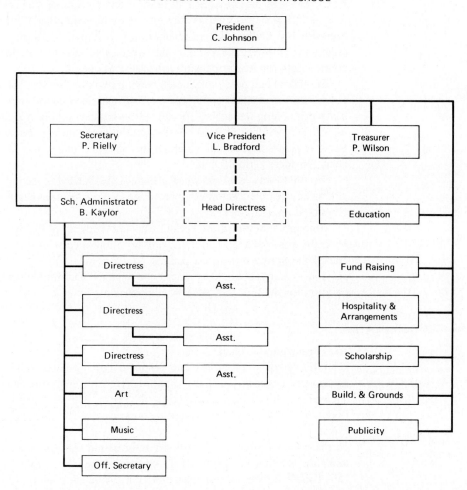

In reassessing the history of the events leading to the untimely resignation of the head directress, the Executive Committee resolved to reduce the vulnerability of the school to such events in the future. There was substantial support at that time for dissolution of the organizational role of head directress who functionally served as an intermediary between the Board, directress, and to an appreciable extent, parents, (dotted line on Exhibit 1). It was decided that the title of head directress would be abolished in favor of a full-time, non-teaching, salaried school administrator.

Although her children had previously graduated from the school, Betty Kaylor enjoyed considerable esteem of parents and members of the Board that developed through a number of years of service to the school as chairperson of the Education Committee. This experience and a relevant background in special education made her an obvious choice of the Board for the new position.

The role of School Administrator is generally defined in terms of parent, teacher and Board liaison. Although the Administrator did not possess voting authority, the person occupying the position controlled a good deal of sensitive information and assisted the Board in problem solving and planning. The Administrator performed routine day-to-day administrative functions of the school previously performed with varying degrees of consistency by other members of the Board. Example functions performed by the Administrator included: 1) reviewing the evaluating applications for teaching and teaching assistant positions; 2) preparation of the annual school calendar; 3) parent counseling and routine communications; 4) supervising maintenance of school enrollment policies; 5) organizing and conducting teacher meetings; and 6) general maintenance of Montessorian education philosophy in academic situations requiring interpretation.

As shown in Exhibit 1, the School Administrator nominally reported to the President, but in reality the function had greatest impact upon the position of Vice President. Although the Vice President retained authority to recommend and vote for employment or termination of teaching personnel and serves at an advanced level in the counseling process, the duties were now largely perfunctory.

With the exception, perhaps, of an uncommon degree of personal motivation, members of the Board of Trustees were representative of the ''typical'' Montessori parent in terms of demographic, social and economic characteristics. They tended to be white Protestants of middle to upper-middle class status with one child currently enrolled and an infant on the waiting list for future enrollment. Parents were typically employed in either professional, teaching or managerial work situations and typically possessed college training.

THE DECISION TO EXPAND

The organizational crisis, having been successfully managed, proved unifying. Board and parent meetings were never attended in any previous year with more enthusiastic individuals than those parents attending in the spring. Cooperation, contribution and patience became the foundations of a new spirit of confidence. The culmination occurred in April when a decision was made to expand the program by adding new classroom space and generally renovating the old facilities. After consultation with an architect, a budget limit of $65,000 was established for the project which was to be funded out of cash reserves and parent donations.

After her election in June, Christine Johnson's first official act was to authorize the purchase of two pre-fabricated classrooms from the Tulsa School Board. These collectively, would double previous space, providing two additional classrooms, a gymnasium, and a separate music room. Given that a third directress could be located, the total capacity in the preschool program would increase from 80 to 110 children in the 3–6 year-old age group.

THE ELEMENTARY PROGRAM

At the following monthly Board meeting in July, a serious debate arose between several board members about the benefits and costs of a possible vertical expansion of the program to include elementary school education for the 6–9 year-old age group. It was conceded by opponents to the plan that the option would be appealing to a substantial number of parents, but the added costs and administrative problems were expected to be significant. An elementary educational program would require a substantially greater investment in terms of teacher salary and classroom materials than addition of capacity to the more comfortable preschool program. Given the recent increase in school indebtedness, others questioned the wisdom of pursuing an inherently risky venture. The issue finally turned after much discussion on the curious, and at first seemingly unrelated, point of fund raising. The school had been unsuccessful in the past in raising funds among Undercroft alumni and community institutions. It was reasoned that the three year preschool experience was insufficient to develop lasting loyalties and preschools were of lesser importance to many parents than six year elementary programs.

The final vote was not unanimous, but an amended motion to expand in both directions carried. Installation and remodeling were accomplished by the end of the summer without appreciable difficulties. The budget, however, overran by nearly 20%, causing a severe depression in the school's capital reserves. To the relief of the Board, the school opened in September, but two weeks behind schedule and out of cash.

REFLECTIONS OF THE PRESIDENT
UPON THE FIRST YEAR OF OPERATIONS

Having just completed the first year of operations in their new facility, Christine Johnson was preparing an agenda for the July meeting. The statements and reports spread before her were complex and subject to differing interpretations. She felt that it had been an exciting but often exhausting year. On balance she was satisfied with the progress that had been made, but privately she admitted some disappointment too.

A full-time Administrator had relieved the Board of much time-consuming detail which in the past had eroded the enthusiasm of parent volunteers. The position was, nonetheless, controversial and a number of parents were raising the issue of divided authority between the Administrator and the Board of Trustees. A decision to eliminate the long-standing graduation ceremony and reduce the all-day preschool program by 10 children angered a number of parents. Although the teaching staff supported termination of these programs on the grounds that they were not Montessorian, many parents were unimpressed and several tried unsuccessfully to recall Betty Kaylor. Christine was particularly disturbed by this action because Betty had given so much of her time and personal resources negotiating and coordinating the construction project the previous summer. She had also acted decisively to hire a qualified Montessori elementary teacher for the 6—9 year-old program. This task proved unexpectedly formidable, requiring a diligent search that took nearly nine months to complete including training schools, national and international directories, and personal contacts. A candidate with outstanding qualifications was finally located and Christine attributed the successful outcome to Betty's uncommon determination.

Promotion of an elementary program had been largely through word-of-mouth and a recent June 9 letter to the parents (Exhibit 2). Tuition was set to cover operating

EXHIBIT 2 _____

June 9, 1982

Dear Parents,

We are pleased and proud to announce the opening of a Montessori elementary* class at Undercroft beginning this fall with the 1982–83 school year. This class will serve children between the ages of six and nine, or the equivalent of first through third grades. In keeping with Montessori principles, the elementary class will be ungraded and completely oriented to the individual needs of each child. The child who works below grade level will be permitted to do so without the stigma of remedial labeling or the humiliation of repeating a grade. The child who works above grade level will be permitted to do so without the discomfort of "skipping" a grade. Children in an age-blended and individualized program are spared the damaging feelings of either inferiority or conceit.

Enrollment in the elementary class will be limited to 21 children, with admission preference granted to those with prior Montessori experience. Children without such experience will be admitted after individual evaluation. Tuition for the elementary class will be $1995 with an advance deposit of $175. There will be no surcharges for materials or field trips. Tuition will be payable either by semester or (by application) on a monthly basis.

The directress for our elementary class will be Mrs. Jane Lawson of Hamilton, Ohio. Mrs. Lawson holds a B.S. degree in Elementary Education from Miami University in Oxford, Ohio, and a Master's degree in Montessori Elementary Education from Xavier University in Cincinnati. She originated and taught a Montessori elementary class at St. Mary School in Hamilton from 1974 until 1981. During this time she also served as the school's assistant principal. Mrs. Lawson's supervisor during her training period was Nancy McCormick Rambusch, an internationally famous Montessorian. Mrs. Rambusch has given Mrs. Lawson her unqualified endorsement. We are most fortunate to secure the services of such a well-trained, well-recommended and highly experienced professional.

If you wish to enroll your child in our exciting new elementary class, please request an application from the school office as soon as possible.

Sincerely yours,

The Staff and The Board of Trustees
Undercroft Montessori School

_____

* Also known in Montessori language as a primary class, a junior class, a transitional class, or 6–9.

_____

expenses, educational materials, and the cost of one classroom. Planned enrollment was 21 (Exhibit 3). Although enrollment was initially less than expected, Christine believed that demand would improve in the future and eventually a waiting list similar to that in the preschool program would be commonplace. In any case, part of the cost of the elementary program was being subsidized by a parent who had given Christine assurances that he would underwrite marginal costs not covered by tuitions for an unspecified but reasonable length of time. This generous offer would enable the program to begin in the fall.

But, the subject of school finances was not a particularly pleasant issue for Christine to deal with and she was the first to admit that her knowledge of accounting principles was mostly intuitive. A set of projected financial statements had been recently produced by the Treasurer and there were indications that the financial situation had

EXHIBIT 3   ENROLLMENT AT UNDERCROFT MONTESSORI SCHOOL 1978–82

	1982*	1981	1980	1979	1978
Preschool Program					
Morning session	50	31	36	35	34
Afternoon session	42	25	35	33	30
All day session	15	24	24	23	26
Elementary School Program					
6–9 year olds	10	—	—	—	—
Total Enrollment					
All categories	117	80	95	91	90

* Projected fall enrollment at time of compilation, June 30, 1982.

changed considerably after the reorganization (Exhibits 4–7). Promised economies of scale presumed associated with expansion had not occurred. In addition to the expected start-up subsidies to the elementary program, an extraordinary loan had been arranged with a parent the previous fall to meet payroll expenses. The terms of the loan were quite generous, but the fact that cash needs of that magnitude were not anticipated bothered Christine. "In retrospect," she thought, "the decision to not increase tuitions last year and help some parents meet their personal financial problems was in error. A budget probably should have been prepared before we became so heavily involved in the new program. Next time, I'll insist that a budget be prepared and officially approved before we do anything."

Deposits were required to hold classroom positions for children admitted to the school for future enrollment and also for those children who were currently enrolled. The balance of the tuition was due in full on or before the first day of class each semester. Although the general tuition policy did not anticipate exceptions, the Treasurer was given authority to review extraordinary cases and permit some parents to pay tuitions on an installment basis. In previous years the number of families permitted to enroll under this arrangement rarely exceeded 10. However, the list of parents paying tuition on a monthly installment basis rather than a lump sum had jumped to 30 during the past year, the highest level in the history of the school. Late payments were causing

EXHIBIT 4   PROGRAM TUITION SCHEDULE: FALL TERM 1982

	Annual tuition	Classroom limit	Enrollment at June 30
Preschool Program			
3–6	$995		
	(First Child)		
Half Day	$930		
	(Second Child)	95	92
5–6 Year Olds All Day	$1795	15	15
Elementary School Program			
6–9 Year Olds All Day	$1995	21	10

EXHIBIT 5
UNDERCROFT MONTESSORI SCHOOL, INC.
PROJECTED CASH DISBURSEMENTS
IN EXCESS OF CASH RECEIPTS:
PERIOD FROM 7/1/82 THRU 6/30/83

Receipts	
Tuition	$120,728
Interview Fees	885
Interest Income	1,732
Donations	17,950
Sales	7,421
Sign Rental	300
Loans	10,000
Miscellaneous	844
Total Receipts Projected	$159,860
Disbursements	
Teachers	$ 81,068
Office	11,198
Classroom	9,442
Building	86,754
Grounds	2,515
Misc. Disbursements	5,154
Total Disbursements Projected	$196,131
Total Projected Cash Disbursements in Excess of Cash Receipts	($36,271)

EXHIBIT 6
UNDERCROFT MONTESSORI SCHOOL, INC.
PROJECTED INCOME STATEMENT:
FISCAL YEAR 1981–1982

Revenue	
Tuition	$121,864
Interview Fees	885
Interest Income	1,732
Sales	7,421
Sign Rental	300
Miscellaneous Receipts	884
Total Revenues Projected	$133,046
Expenses	
Teachers	$ 81,068
Office	11,198
Classroom	9,442
Building	10,118
Grounds	2,515
Miscellaneous Expenses	5,154
Total Expenses Projected	$119,495
Total Projected Income Before Depreciation	$ 13,551

EXHIBIT 7 UNDERCROFT MONTESSORI SCHOOL, INC.
PROJECTED BALANCE SHEET: MAY 30, 1982

Assets			Liabilities & Net Worth Liabilities	
Current Assets			Tuition Deposits Received	
Cash	$ 27,099		but not Earned	$ 11,305
Tuitions Receivable	-0-		Land Mortgage	19,955
Total Current Assets	$ 27,099		Building Mortgage	1,421
			Loan	10,000
			Total Liabilities	$ 42,681
Other Assets				
Original Building and			*Net Worth*	
Equipment	$ 39,683			
Less Accumulated			Net Worth at 6/30/81	$ 52,134
Depreciation	24,234		Projected Income from	
	$ 15,449		6/30/81 thru 7/1/82	
			Before Depreciation	13,551
New Classroom and			Receipts from donations	17,950
Equipment	$ 84,636		Less Accumulated	
Less Accumulated			Depreciation 6/30/81	
Depreciation	10,156		thru 6/30/82	14,125
	$ 74,480		Total Net Worth	$ 97,760
Land	$ 22,653			
Total Other Assets	$112,582		*Total Liab. & Net Worth*	$139,681
TOTAL ASSETS	$139,681			

some problems and there was a growing feeling among some Board members that the extended-payments program should be funded some way to cover probable costs.

Parent disinterest was another bothersome issue to Christine. At a time when school enrollment was at an all-time high, only five applications for new Board positions opening in the fall had been received. Christine could not determine whether the relatively few applications were indicative of parent apathy, or contentment with the way things were progressing. "In looking back," thought Christine, "those suspenseful months in the spring last year, when the school's future hung in the balance, served to unify the parents as no other issue had done before. Probably what is needed now is a challenge, or a significant goal to pursue." Christine then recalled some interesting data that another parent had recently mailed to the office about enrollment demographics (Exhibits 8—10). The thought occurred to her that a complementary 9–12 year-old elementary program might present such a challenge. Although she

EXHIBIT 8   POPULATION BY AGE GROUP IN TULSA SMSA. APRIL 1980

Age group	Total population
Under 1 to 2 Yrs.	32791
3–5 Yrs.	31439
6–9 Yrs.	42936
10–13 Yrs.	43823
TOTAL	150,989

Source: Metropolitan Tulsa Chamber of Commerce, Report Dated April 1981.

EXHIBIT 9   TULSA AREA SCHOOL ENROLLMENT ESTIMATES AND PROJECTIONS: 1975–1985

Year	Nursery	Kindergarten	Elementary	Total
1985	1900	8600	77400	142200
1980	2500	7300	71300	136800
1975	2500	7700	76500	140500

Source: Office of Manpower Planning, City of Tulsa. Report Dated October 1981.

EXHIBIT 10   TABULATION OF PRIVATE NON-SECTARIAN, PAROCHIAL AND PUBLIC SCHOOLS WITH ACADEMIC OFFERINGS IN TULSA AREA, 1982

	Private		Public	Total School
	Non-Sectarian	Parochial		
Pre-School and Kindergarten	25	22	3	50
Elementary K–6	8	24	85	117
Total Schools	33	46	88	167

Source: Tulsa Telephone Directory, January 1982.

expected the topic to be controversial, she decided to include it for discussion on her meeting agenda. She was wondering what else should be included on the agenda when the telephone rang. It was one of the five parents who had previously submitted an application for a Board position. She had recently taken employment with an investment company and didn't feel that she would have enough time to serve.

DISCUSSION QUESTIONS

1 Evaluate the Board's shift in ''prevailing attitude'' from ''generally conservative to a position of greater commitment in terms of growth.''
2 Explain the part which the apparent crisis played in unifying board members, parents, and employees. Can such a unifying force be re-created purposefully?
3 Explain and assess the organizational structure at the school in terms of its contribution to goal accomplishment, and if it should be changed describe how and why.
4 Explain, in both quantitative and qualitative terms, the financial situation at the school and describe how any problems you identify might best be solved.

INDEX

INDEX